MW00577030

Grace in
Galatia

Grace in Galatia

*A Commentary on
St Paul's Letter to
the Galatians*

Ben Witherington III

WILLIAM B. EERDMANS PUBLISHING COMPANY
GRAND RAPIDS, MICHIGAN

Copyright © T&T Clark Ltd, 1998

Published in Great Britain by T&T Clark Ltd,
59 George Street, Edinburgh EH2 2LQ, Scotland

This edition published under license from T&T Clark Ltd by
Wm. B. Eerdmans Publishing Co.,
255 Jefferson Ave., S.E.,
Grand Rapids,
Michigan 49503

All rights reserved. No part of this publication may be reproduced,
stored in a retrieval system, or transmitted, in any form or by any means,
electronic, mechanical, photocopying, recording or otherwise,
without the prior permission of T&T Clark Ltd.

First published 1998

ISBN 0 8028 4433 2

Typeset by Waverley Typesetters, Galashiels
Printed and bound in Great Britain by Biddles Ltd, Guildford

That this Epistle breathes an indignant spirit is obvious to everyone even on the first perusal . . . Since Paul then saw the whole Galatian people in a state of excitement, a flame kindled against their church, and the edifice shaken and tottering to its fall, filled with the mixed feelings of just anger and despondency . . . he writes the Epistle.

— John Chrysostom

The Epistle to the Galatians is my Epistle; I have bethrothed myself to it; it is my wife.

— Martin Luther

I set out for London, and read over in the way that celebrated book, Martin Luther's Comment on the Epistle to the Galatians. I was utterly ashamed. How have I esteemed this book, only because I heard it so commended by others; or at best because I have read some excellent sentences occasionally quoted from it! But what shall I say, now I judge for myself? Now I see with my own eyes? Why, not only that the author makes nothing out, clears up not one considerable difficulty; that he is quite shallow in his remarks on many passages, and muddy and confused almost on all; but that he is deeply tinctured with mysticism throughout and hence often dangerously wrong.

— John Wesley, 15 June 1741

Luther speaks as Paul would have spoken had he lived at the time when Luther gave his lectures.

— Hans Dieter Betz[1]

1. Betz, *Galatians*, p. xv. The other quotations are easily found in the beginning of Chrysostom's Commentary on Galatians, in Luther's comments on Galatians and in Wesley's Journal.

Contents

Preface

For a Protestant such as myself, it is self-evident how important Paul's Galatians is on many fronts. Not only is this the document that caused a Copernican revolution in Luther's thinking, but it was also the document, along with Romans, that helped precipitate a similar transformation in the life of my spiritual forebear, John Wesley. It may be said that there would be no Methodists at all today if Wesley had not reacted as he did to hearing and reading from Luther's commentaries on Galatians and Romans during the crucial and formative period in his life of 1737–38. My interests in Galatians, which has been described as theological dynamite, are not, however, limited to its influential role in the history of Protestantism.

This document is also important to me because it raises crucial questions about the nature of the truth of the Gospel and what sort of pattern of life Christians ought to embrace in light of that Gospel. It raises important questions about how Christians should view the OT in general and the Mosaic covenant and Law in particular. It raises questions about the basis of unity in Christ, and how issues of diversity ought to be handled. How much diversity is too much diversity? For the church at the end of the twentieth century it also raises major questions about what the relationship ought to be between Jews and Christians, as well as between modern day Jewish and Gentile Christians. Equally importantly, this document has much to teach us all about conflict resolution.

Since H. D. Betz's landmark commentary on Galatians in 1979, this document more than any other NT document has been subject to rhetorical analyses of various sorts and with varying degrees of success. This is not surprising when one considers that this document can be said to be more like an ancient speech than any other in the NT, having only the briefest lineaments of epistolary form at the beginning and endings of the document, and leaving out various familiar epistolary features such as the thanksgiving section, travelogues, and greetings to and from various persons. It is a document that could easily be a transcript meant to be delivered orally by one of Paul's co-workers, and by delivered I mean presented in a rhetorically effective manner. In short it is a document that is in many ways a perfect subject for a socio-rhetorical study. Herein I intend to engage in such a study in much the same fashion and form as in my earlier work *Conflict and Community in Corinth* (Eerdmans, 1994). I believe that such a study sheds fresh light on the unity of this document, on Paul's powers of persuasion, on the character and history of early Christianity, on the basis of human freedom and on a host of other subjects. The reader must judge whether I am right about these matters.

Christmas 1996

Abbreviations

ABD	Anchor Bible Dictionary	Celsus	
Aeschines		Med.	Meditationes
Tim.	Timarchus	Cicero	
AnglTR	Anglican Theological	Brut.	Brutus
	Review	De Inven.	De Inventione Rhetorica
ANRW	Aufstieg und Niedergang	CII	Corpus Inscriptionum
	der römischen Welt		Iudaicarum (Rome,
Apoc.Ab.	Apocalypse of Abraham		1936–)
Aristides		CIL	Corpus Inscriptionum
Or.	Orationes		Latinarum (Berlin,
Aristotle			1863–)
Nic. Eth.	Nicomachean Ethics	Clem.	Clement
Pol.	Politica	ConcJourn	Concordia Journal
Rhet.	Rhetoric	CurrTheoMiss	Currents in Theology
Assump. Mos	Assumption of Moses		& Mission
BAR	Biblical Archaeology	DanskTeolTids	Dansk Theologisk
	Review		Tidsskrift
Bar.	Baruch	Demosthenes	
BDF	Blass-Debrunner Funk,	Or.	Orationes
	A Greek Grammar of	Did.	Didache
	the New Testament	Dio Chrysostom	
	(1961)	Or.	Orationes
BGU	Berlin: Griechen	Diogenes Laertius	
	Urkunden I-VIII	Vit. Phil.	Vitae Philosophoi
BiblSac	Bibliotheca Sacra	DSS	Dead Sea Scrolls
BibRes	Biblical Research	En	Enoch
BT	Babylonian Talmud	Epictetus	
BZ	Biblische Zeitschrift	Diss.	Dissertiones
CBQ	Catholic Biblical	Epiphanius	
	Quarterly	Haer.	Refutation of All
CalvTheoJourn	Calvin Theological		Heresies
	Journal	EQ	Evangelical Quarterly

ET	Expository Times	Jub.	Jubilees
Ezr.	Ezra	Justin	
FilolNT	Filologia	Dial.	Dialogue with Trypho
	Neotestamentaria	Juvenal	
FoiVie	Foi et Vie	Sat.	Satires
FreibZ	Freiburger Zeitschrift für	Lactantius	
	Philosophie und	Div. Inst.	Divine Institutions
	Theologie	Libanius	
GraceTJ	Grace Theological	Or.	Orationes
	Journal	LouvStud	Louvain Studies
Horace		Lucian	
Sat.	Satirae	Vit. Auct.	Vitarum Auctio
HTR	Harvard Theological	Macc.	Maccabees
	Review	Menander	
HUCA	Hebrew Union College	Fgr.	Fragmenti
	Annual	MichQR	Michigan Quarterly
IG	Inscriptiones Graecae		Review
	(1873–)	NovT	Novum Testamentum
Ignatius		NTS	New Testament
Magn.	Letter to the Magnesians		Studies
Phil.	Letter to the Philippians	NT	New Testament
Rom.	Letter to the Romans	OG	Ostraka Griechische
ILS	H. Dessau, Inscriptiones		vol. 1
	Latinae Selectae (1892–	OT	Old Testament
	1916)	Philo	
Int	Interpretation	Abr.	De Abrahamo
IrTQ	Irish Theological	Cher.	De Cherubim
	Quarterly	Cong.	De Congressu
Isocrates		Fuga	De Fuga et Inventione
Ep.	Epistulae	Deus	Quod Deus Immutabilis
Or.	Orationes		Sit
JBL	Journal of Biblical	Leg. Alleg.	De Legum Allegoriae
	Literature	Migra.	De Migratione
JETS	Journal of the		Abrahami
	Evangelical Theological	Op. Mundi	De Opificio Mundi
	Society	Post. Cain	De Posteritate Caini
JLawRel	Journal of Law &	Praem.	De Praemiis et Poenis
	Religion	Quaest. Ex.	Quaestiones et
Josephus			Solutiones in Exodo
Ant.	Jewish Antiquities	Sacrif.	De Sacrificiis Abelis et
Apion	Against Apion		Cain
Life	Life of Flavius Josephus	Spec. Leg.	De Specialibus Legibus
War	Jewish War	Virt.	De Virtutibus
JSNT	Journal for the Study of	Vit. Mos.	De Vita Mosis
	the New Testament	Philostratus	
JSOT	Journal for the Study of	Vita Apoll.	Vita Apollonii
	the Old Testament	Plato	
JT	Jerusalem Targum	Rep.	Republic

Plautus
  Bacc.   *Bacchides*
Plutarch
  De lib. educ.   *De liberis educandis*
  De tranq.
    animi   *De tranquillitate animi*
  De virt. mor.   *De virtute morali*
  Peri Phil.   *Peri Philopoemen*
  Quaest. Rom.   *Quaestiones Romanae*
P.Oxy   *The Oxyrhynchus Papyri,* ed. B. P. Grenfell, et al. (1898–1972)
Ps. Sol.   Psalms of Solomon
Pseudo-Aristotle
  Rhet. ad Alex.   *Rhetoric to Alexander*
Pseudo-Clement
  Hom.   *Homilies*
  Hom. Ep. Peter   *Homilies, Epistle to Peter*
  Recogn.   *Recognitions*
Pseudo-Lucian
  Amor.   *Amores*
Pseudo-Phocy.   Pseudo-Phocylides
Quintilian
  Inst. Or.   *Institutio Oratoria*
RevExp   *Review & Expositor*
Rhet. ad Her.   *Rhetorica ad Herennium*
SBL   Society of Biblical Literature
Seneca
  Ep. Mor.   *Epistolae Moralia*
Sib.   Sibyline Oracles
SJT   *Scottish Journal of Theology*
SNTS   Society for New Testament Studies
SR   *Studies in Religion*
Stobaeus
  Ecl.   *Eclogues*

SvEx   *Svenak Exegetisk Arsbok*
SWJournTheol   *Southwestern Journal of Theology*
Tertullian
  Adv. Marc.   *Adversus Marcionem*
  De Cor.   *De Corona Militum*
Test. Ash.   Testament of Asher
Test. Ben.   Testament of Benjamin
Test. Iss.   Testament of Issachar
Test. Jos.   Testament of Joseph
Test. Levi   Testament of Levi
Test. Reub.   Testament of Reuben
TheolEduc   *Theological Education*
Tob.   Tobit
TRE   *Theologische Revue*
TrinJ   *Trinity Journal*
TuTQ   *Texte und Untersuchungen Theologische Quartalschrift*
TynBull   *Tyndale Bulletin*
TZBas   *Theologische Zeitschrift* (Basel)
USQR   *Union Seminary Quarterly Review*
VT   *Vetus Testamentum Wdienst*
WestTJ   *Westminster Theological Journal*
Wis.   Wisdom of Solomon
WUNT   *Wissenschaftliche Untersuchungen zum Neuen Testament*
Xenophon
  Anab.   *Anabasis*
  Cyr.   *Cyropaedia*
  Mem.   *Memorabilia*
ZNW   *Zeitschrift für die neutestamentliche Wissenschaft*

Black Sea

CE

BITHYNIA

GALATIA

PONTUS

Byzantium

Ancyra

MYSIA

Troas
Assos
Adramyttium

ASIA

GALATIA

ce

tylene

Thyatira

PHRYGIA

CAESAREA

ios

LYCAONIA

CAPPADOCIA

EPHESUS
Samos

Iconium

Miletus

PISIDIA

Lystra
Derbe

Cos

PAMPHYLIA

Perge

TARSUS

Cnidus

LYCIA

Attalia

CILICIA

Antioch

Patara

Myra

Seleucia

Rhodes

SYRIA

lmone

Salamis

ens

Paphos

Cyprus

e r r a n e a n

DAMASCUS

Sidon

Tyre

Ptolemais

GALILEE

CAESAREA

Sharon

Samaria

Joppa

Lydda

JERUSALEM

JUDAEA

Gaza

ALEXANDRIA

ARABIA

EGYPT

Introduction

On a superficial inspection of Galatians, it would seem possible to conclude that this is not one of the more difficult NT documents to comprehend. After all, there is no, or almost no, dispute by anyone, scholar or lay person, that Paul wrote this letter. Furthermore, with only very rare exceptions,[1] no one disputes that this document as we have it (bearing in mind the occasional textual problems) is a unity.[2] The problems one faces with 2 Corinthians in regard to the unity of the document, or the later Paulines in regard to authorship, are quite absent in the case of Galatians. Furthermore, there are few serious textual problems in Galatians.[3]

This impression of lack of problems unfortunately is largely incorrect, for almost everything else about this document, including most of the other questions of introduction about the audience, date, structure, character of this document, and its relationship to data in Acts are in dispute. For instance, it is

---

1. See J. C. O'Neill, *The Recovery of Paul's Letter to the Galatians* (London: SPCK, 1972), but few if any scholars have really been persuaded by his arguments that various glosses have been added to the text after Paul wrote it, but before the earliest copies we have of the manuscript, such as p46.

2. The one manuscript that raises some interesting questions about the original text of Galatians at various points is p46. This manuscript has recently been dated to the late first century A.D. (see Y. K. Kim, "Paleographical Dating of p46 to the Late First Century," *Biblica* 69 (1988), pp. 248-57), but the arguments of Kim are weak as B. W. Griffin has urged in his Nov. 1996 SBL lecture "The Paleographical Dating of p46", and probably the earliest possible date for this manuscript is the mid-second century A.D.

3. This is not to say that there are not some interesting and theologically motivated textual variants, but they are relatively few, and few of them have much of a chance of being original readings. But see the discussion of p46 by H. Eshbaugh, "Textual Variants and Theology: a Study of the Galatians Text of Papyrus 46," *JSNT* 3 (1979), pp. 60-72.

not even agreed as to whom Paul is referring when he speaks of the 'Galatians'. It behooves us then to take some time to address some of the thorny introductory issues before embarking on the commentary proper.

Who were the Galatians?

The term Γαλάται was used interchangeably with Κέλται or Κέλτοι by Greek writers, as were the terms Galatae, Galli, and Celtae by Latin writers. These terms were used to refer to a group of people originating in central Europe in the Danube river basin but who migrated into Switzerland, southern Germany, northern Italy, France (hence the Roman name Gaul for this region), Britain (the Celts) and then finally into the Balkans, and Asia Minor. The region which these peoples inhabited and took control of in Asia Minor came to be called Galatia or even Gallogrecia (the land of Greek-speaking Gauls).

It was in about 278 B.C. that this migratory people made their way into Asia Minor, originally on the invitation of Nicomedes the king of Bithynia who sought to use them as mercenaries. Basically these people settled around Ancyra, and after a series of battles with their neighbors were confined to an area in north central Asia Minor bordered by Phrygia to the west, Cappadocia and Lycaonia to the south, Pontus to.the east, and Bithynia and Paphlagonia to the north. By 189 B.C. Galatia had suffered the same fate as the rest of Asia Minor by coming under the control of Rome.

It is fair to say that the Galatian people, who had originally migrated to Asia Minor, and their descendants, retained a great deal of their original culture well beyond the NT era. They spoke a Celtic dialect which continued to survive into the fourth century A.D., at least in rural areas of ethnic Galatia. They had a distinctive form of Celtic religious and political organization and were widely revered and feared as great warriors and mercenaries. They were considered barbarians due to their strange dialect, considerable physical stature, and wild appearance, though by Paul's time most of them seem to have been capable of speaking Greek.[4]

At first, Galatia was a dependent kingdom under Rome's rule, but in 64 B.C. it became, because of its friendship with Pompey, a favored client kingdom. In about 40 B.C. Marc Antony elevated a one time king's secretary, Amyntas, to the status of king of portions of Phrygia and Pisidia. He is important because when Kastor the king of Galatia died in 36 B.C. Galatia was turned over to Amyntas, who continued to retain his Phrygian and Pisidian territory, and as a

---

4. See S. Mitchell, "Galatia," *ABD* II, pp. 870–72.

bonus also received a part of Pamphylia. He was also later given at least a part of Lycaonia, and after the battle of Actium Octavian gave him a portion of Cilicia Tracheia as well.

In 25 B.C. Amyntas was killed in a battle with tribes from the region of northern Taurus and at this point the entire Galatian kingdom controlled by Amyntas, except for parts of Pamphylia and Cilicia which were placed in other regions, was reorganized as a Roman province which was governed by a praetorian legate.

The province of Galatia continued to have territory added to it by the Roman authorities up to and beyond the time when Paul visited and wrote to people in this region.[5] For example, in 5 B.C. portions of Paphlagonia in the north was added to Galatia, and then perhaps about A.D. 4 a part of Pontus was added to the region (this portion being called Pontus Galaticus). Sometime just before or during the reign of the Emperor Claudius (A.D. 41–54) a part of the northern Taurus region was added to the province of Galatia as well. In short, in Paul's day the province of Galatia was an enormous province, usually governed by a legate rather than a consul from the Senate, until at least the time of Nero. This is what made it a praetorian province.[6] It bordered on the Black Sea in the north and the Mediterranean Sea in the south, and in theory when Paul addressed persons as Galatians, if he used Roman provincial designations, he could be addressing people anywhere in this region. Strabo in his discussion of Galatia confirms that the province included old Galatia, Pisidia, Lycaonia, parts of Pamphylia, and Cilicia Trachea (12.5.1). At least thirteen Roman colonies were established in the province of Galatia, mainly in its southern portion, either by founding cities or reconstituting cities. Among these were Pisidian Antioch, Iconium, and Lystra.[7]

Despite the enormous size of this province there does not seem to have been any regular presence of legions in Galatia during Paul's time there, though there were of course retired soldiers in various of the colony cities. One reaches this conclusion because after years of quiet the Parthian tribes did arise in rebellion in about A.D. 55 in Armenia and Nero put the Galatian legate Cn. Domitius Corbulo in command of the eastern forces to check the

---

5. It was standard procedure for the Romans to add areas to already existing provinces rather than create many separate provinces. See R. K. Sherk, *The Legates of Galatia from Augustus to Diocletian* (Baltimore: John Hopkins Press, 1951), p. 16.

6. See the discussion by Sherk, *The Legates*, pp. 18–19.

7. There is extensive discussion of Antioch and Lystra in B. M. Levick, *Roman Colonies in Southern Asia Minor* (Oxford: Oxford University Press, 1967). Also helpful on the creation and development of the Galatian province is D. Magie, *Roman Rule in Asia Minor to the End of the Third Century. Vol. I: Text* (Princeton: Princeton University Press, 1950), pp. 453–66.

advance of the Parthians. However, as Corbulo hastened east he had to requisition two legions from the governor of Syria in order to have troops for the task. Furthermore, it took him two years of training to get them ready to fight the Parthians and he had to conduct levies throughout Galatia and Cappadocia as well.[8] Sherk goes so far as to say that during the period from Augustus until Nero there were no legions stationed in the Galatian province.[9] This reminds us that it is a mistake to over-estimate the Roman military presence in most of the regions Paul evangelized.

In part, what made the province, especially its southern portion, governable was the building of a great Roman road, the Via Sebaste, sometime around or just before 6 B.C. This road linked most of the major colonies of the southern part of the province including Pisidian Antioch, Iconium and Lystra. It is important to bear in mind that Roman roads in the northern part of the province were only constructed for the first time in the 70s and 80s A.D. which led to great growth in Roman military presence in that part of the region thereafter. The existence of Roman roads in the south but not in the northern part of the province in Paul's day must be factored into the discussion of the audience Paul is addressing in Galatians.

What must also be borne in mind is that since the Roman province of Galatia included many different tribes and peoples and not just the descendents of the Celts or Gauls, the only term which could be predicated of all of them in Paul's day would be Galatians. He could not for instance call them Phrygians or Lycaonians if he had evangelized a cross section of the residents of this Roman province. In fact, there is clear evidence from the inscriptions of the period that the entire region was regularly called Galatia in the NT era (cf. *ILS* 9499; IG Rom. 3.263, Eutropius 7.10), and not just the Celtic or Gallic part.

There is no evidence of major social upheavals in the form of wars in the Galatian province during the period we are interested in, but some-time[10] after A.D. 54 Nero did install another consular governor (the first since Quirinius in about A.D. 6), Cn. Domitius Corbulo, which suggests that there was some significant unrest in the 50s for the first time since Augustus set up the province in A.D. 25. Just before this, however, during the period between about A.D. 49 and A.D. 54 the legate in Galatia had been one M. Annius Afrinus, and his time of rule seems to have been a quiet one. We shall have more to say on the social history of the province and the place of Jews in it below.

8. See the discussion in Sherk, *The Legates*, pp. 18–19, 32–35.
9. This is the deciding factor for Sherk, p. 19 proving that Galatia was a praetorian rather than consular province since the latter had standing legions within their borders.
10. See B. M. Levick, "The Augustan Restoration" in *The Cambridge Ancient History Vol. X* (Cambridge: Cambridge University Press, 2nd ed. 1996), pp. 650–51.

The further history of this province is of some relevance to our discussion because the earliest Christian discussions of Paul's Galatians were undertaken with a knowledge only of subsequent developments in the province. By this I mean that we need to be aware that Vespasian detached almost all of Pisidia from Galatia in A.D. 74 and about A.D. 137 Lycaonia Galatica was removed and added to an enlarged province of Cilicia. In A.D. 297 southern Galatia was united with surrounding regions to form a new province of Pisidia with Antioch as its capital, and this in turn meant that the province of Galatia at this point reverted back to its original ethnological dimensions. It was this later truncated form of Galatia that was known as the province of Galatia to Christian commentators who discussed Paul's Galatians between the fourth and nineteenth centuries of this era. It is not surprising under these circumstances that these commentators assumed that by 'Galatians' Paul was referring to the residence of ethnic or old kingdom of Galatia which coincided with the Roman province of Galatia after A.D. 297. The older commentators were all or almost all north Galatianists in regard to where they located Paul's audience. It was only with the rise of the age of archaeology that this assumption about the locale of Paul's Galatian converts began to be challenged by W. M. Ramsay and others, starting at the end of the nineteenth century.[11]

There is no internal evidence in Paul's letter to the Galatians to settle who Paul particularly has in mind when he speaks to and of the Galatians, and so the debate has centered on several passages in Acts, in particular Acts 16.6 and Acts 18.23. Several factors must be taken into consideration when evaluating these texts. Firstly, while Paul does normally use Roman provincial designations (cf., e.g., 1 Cor. 16.15 and 19), Luke seems to use mainly the local and ethnic terminology. Secondly, if one gives at least some credence to the itineraries of Paul's journeys in Acts, in this case the itineraries for the second and third missionary journeys, it is in order to point out that there is no clear evidence even in Acts that Paul ever evangelized the cities of the northern part of Galatia. At most there might be a reference to his passing through the region and strengthening existing converts in the area, but even this conclusion is doubtful.

Acts 16 relates that after going through Derbe and Lystra, cities Paul had visited on his first missionary journey, he then proceeded on to Mysia and Ephesus. It is not really feasible to argue that Paul detoured some 200 kilometers north and east out of his way in order to pass through old ethnic Galatia on his way between Lystra and Ephesus, especially knowing what we know about the lack of Roman roads in north Galatia in the 40s and 50s A.D.

11. See W. M. Ramsay, *A Historical Commentary on St. Paul's Epistle to the Galatians* (London: Hodder & Stoughton, 2nd ed. 1900).

(see above), and knowing about the Via Sebaste which led on to Pisidian Antioch and beyond.[12]

Thirdly, there is now very clear evidence for the adjectival use of the word Phrygian in Greek.[13] This means that the phrase found in Acts 16.6 can indeed refer to one region, not two, the Phrygian part of Galatia (Phrygia Galatica would have been the Roman term, like the term Pontus Galatica). In other words Luke means that Paul passed through the territory already covered (including presumably the city of Pisidian Antioch) and then presumably on into uncharted Phrygian territory on the way to Ephesus. The grammatical construction here in Acts 16.6 is the same as in Lk. 3.1 where one region is also referred to, not two.

As for Acts 18.23 there is room for more dispute.[14] The reference to strengthening the disciples here favors the conclusion that Luke is talking about Paul retracing his steps through an area already evangelized. Here, however, the Greek reads a little differently from that in Acts 16 – Γαλατικὴν χώραν καὶ Φρυγίαν. It may well mean the same thing as Acts 16.6, but there is a chance more is meant here because Phrygia is used as a substantive here rather than as an adjective, and the term region is only coupled with Galatia. Furthermore, the term καθεξῆς would seem to point to the visiting of two regions, for the term means in order, assuming a sequence of at least two members. Thus I agree with Hemer[15] that it is likely that here Luke uses the term Galatia to refer to the southern Galatian cities previously visited, or the province as a whole which included these cities, and the term Phrygia is used with the awareness that Phrygia extended beyond the Galatian province into the province of Asia and that Paul went through both Phrygian Galatia and Phrygian Asia on his way to Ephesus. This may mean Paul went through and evangelized in cities such as Apamea Cibotus or Eumenea on the way to Ephesus, but we cannot be sure. There is in any case no reason to think that Luke assumed that Paul took a major detour after Lystra, going far to the north to the region of Ancyra before coming to Ephesus. In short, there is no reason either in Galatians or in Acts to assume that Paul evangelized north Galatia.

12. See the strongly worded conclusion of Mitchell, p. 871 that the work of Ramsay should have put the matter beyond dispute that Paul in Galatians is referring to the cities of Pisidian Antioch, Iconium, and Lystra which he visited on his first missionary journey. In this period they certainly could be called Galatian cities. It is telling that archaeologists, indeed all the archaeologists I know of who know something about the history and excavation of this region and have commented on the matter, appear to be south Galatianists.

13. See the extended discussion in C. Hemer, *The Book of Acts in the Setting of Hellenistic History* (Winona Lake: Eisebrauns, 1990), pp. 283ff.

14. See my discussion in *The Acts of the Apostles. A Socio-Rhetorical Commentary* (Grand Rapids: Eerdmans, 1997), ad loc.

15. Hemer, *Acts*, p. 120.

Recently, J. M. Scott has made the interesting suggestion that Paul's image of the world, which he learned while a Jew, be taken into consideration. Specifically he suggests that Paul shared the same view as Josephus and other Jews that the table of nations in Gen. 10 determined how a Jew would view the pagan nations. Josephus identifies Gomer, the first son of Japheth with the Galatians "who are understood as occupying the whole Roman province of Galatia, including south Galatia (*Ant*. 1.123, 126)".[16] Paul may have thought in similar fashion as Josephus, but Paul's use of provincial terminology elsewhere in his epistles, and the fact that he is addressing mainly Gentiles who are unlikely to have been familiar with the traditions Josephus cites, makes it more probable that Paul is simply using provincial terminology in Galatians.

In closing this part of the discussion it is important to note that everything in Galatians suggests that the majority, perhaps the vast majority, of Paul's Galatian converts are Gentiles not Jews, otherwise all these arguments about not submitting to circumcision would not be on target. Then too, these arguments also suggest that these Galatian Christians were attracted indeed even bewitched by the Judaizing suggestions[17] or demands of the agitators and this makes it natural to suppose that the Galatian Christians had already had some exposure to Judaism before becoming Christians. Perhaps they had even had a positive and close exposure by spending time with Jews in the synagogue in at least some cases. One must also make sense of the fact that Paul feels he can use an elaborate Jewish allegory in Gal. 4 and arguments about covenants and Abraham and the development of salvation history to convince them not to listen to or follow the teaching of the agitators. In short, Paul is using Jewish arguments to convince Gentiles not to become more Jewish! This too suggests an audience conversant with Judaism and perhaps the basic lineaments of the Hebrew Scriptures as well. All of this is understandable if Acts 13–14 is right that Paul's standard operating procedure

16. J. M. Scott, *Paul and the Nations* (Tübingen: Mohr, 1995), p. 218.

17. I use the term 'Judaize' advisedly though with some caution. Notice how Paul contrasts his former life in Judaism in 1.13 with his present Christian life. The Greek word ἰουδαΐζειν can of course mean to live like a Jew (cf., e.g., Josephus *War* 2.454) but if one looks carefully at Esther 7.17 LXX ('many of the Gentiles were circumcised and judaized for fear of the Jews') it will be seen that this transition in the Gentile's life took place because someone else urged them and circumcised them and inducted them into Judaism. In other words, while it is true that Jews may not have been very evangelistic in the first century, it is nonetheless also true that they were prepared to and indeed sought to 'Judaize' various Gentiles who expressed some interest in Judaism, attended synagogue, or became regular God-fearers or God-worshippers. In Galatians, however, the issue is between conservative Jewish Christian missionaries in Galatia whom we may choose to call the agitators, and Paul. In other words, the issue is *not* between non-Christian Jews and Christians but between one Jewish Christian (Paul) and another group of Jewish Christians in between whom are the largely Gentile Galatians who find themselves in the midst of a game of tug of war.

when he was in the province of Galatia was to preach in the synagogue first until he was thrust out, and that his converts, both Jewish and Gentile came out of that Jewish matrix (cf. Acts 13.43, 48; 14.1). In other words, Galatians would be a word on target if his audience already knew a good deal about Judaism and the Hebrew Scriptures, it would be a word on target if he is in the main addressing God-fearers. It would be less apt if the Gentiles he is worried about had had no association with or knowledge of Judaism prior to Paul's arrival in Galatia.

When was Galatians written?

The reader interested in dating Galatians may be excused for being baffled when turning to recent commentaries on Galatians. Some scholars who advocate a northern Galatia destination of the letter have opted for a relatively early date for this document while others have dated it closer to the time when Romans was composed. On the other hand, some who have advocated a southern Galatian destination for the document have managed to date it relatively late while other South Galatianists have dated it early, and some have even suggested it is the earliest of all of Paul's extant letters. It is obvious that while there may be some correlation in scholars' minds between the destination and the date of this document, it is not clear what that correlation may be.[18]

There are a number of factors which must be taken into consideration not the least of which is the relationship between the historical information offered in Galatians and that offered in Acts, and the degree to which one thinks Acts can be trusted to give reliable data about Paul's life and ministry. Unlike the case with the issue of destination, there appear to be some internal clues in Galatians to the date of the document though they are not absolutely decisive in determining the issue.

The first point of note is that quite obviously this letter was written considerably after the time of Paul's conversion. Gal. 1–2 suggest that this letter could not have been written less than fourteen years after Paul's conversion and it may have been written as much as seventeen years or more after the encounter on Damascus Road, depending on whether Paul is referring to calendar years or whole years in his time references in 1.18 and 2.1.[19] Whatever else one makes of these data, it certainly indicates that Galatians is not the

---

18. See now the useful discussion in M. Silva, *Explorations in Exegetical Method. Galatians as a Test Case* (Grand Rapids: Baker, 1996), pp. 129–39.
19. See the discussion in the commentary on the relevant material in Gal. 1 and 2.

product of a neophyte in the Christian faith, or from the 'early' years of Paul's Christian life. This document is not an example of the polemics of an angry young man. I have explained elsewhere my reasons for dating the conversion of Paul in about A.D. 33 or 34,[20] and as we will explain more fully in the commentary it appears likely that Paul made his second trip up to Jerusalem a little more than fourteen years after his conversion, or in about A.D. 48. It follows that Galatians could not have been written earlier than some time in A.D. 48.

There is, however, an incident mentioned after the second visit to Jerusalem, namely the incident at Antioch between Peter and Paul in 2.11ff., and more likely than not we are meant to think of this event transpiring *after* Paul had returned from his second visit to Jerusalem, because Paul's visits with Peter in Jerusalem prior to the Antioch incident reflect only a positive relationship and understanding of each other's ministry. Paul says in 2.11ff. that Peter had acted with 'hypocrisy' in withdrawing from table fellowship in Antioch. In other words, he had implicitly violated the understanding he and the other pillar apostles and Paul had, as well as acted against his own prior pattern of living.[21] This surely suggests a prior understanding between Paul and the pillars, which Paul thinks Peter has now gone back on.

It must also be taken into account that this letter itself must be written some time after the Antioch incident because at the time of the composition of Galatians the inception of the trouble that plagued Antioch is apparently now some distance in the past and the problem is now said to be bewitching the Galatians. It is hard to doubt that the problem hit Antioch before it did the Galatian churches not least because the difficulty has something to do with Judaizing, Jerusalem, and men who came from James to Antioch. They would not naturally visit Galatia before Antioch, especially if Antioch was the first major ἐκκλησία with more Gentiles than Jews as participants, or at least a large number of Gentiles. Taking these considerations together this would likely mean that Galatians cannot have been composed *before* A.D. 49.

The real internal chronological issue of importance is how soon after Paul's visit to the Galatian province he had written this letter. I have argued in my Acts commentary that Paul's first missionary journey took place no earlier than about A.D. 48.[22] There must have been time after this journey to return to Antioch, go up to Jerusalem, go back to Antioch, have the disagreement with Peter, and have the Galatian churches be troubled by agitators, because all

20. See my *The Acts of the Apostles*, pp. 69ff. on Pauline chronology and its relationship to Acts chronology.

21. See pp. 15ff. below and the interesting discussion in P. F. Esler, "Making and Breaking an Agreement Mediterranean Style: A New Reading of Galatians 2.1–14," *Biblical Interpretation* 3.3 (1995), pp. 285–314.

22. See my *The Acts of the Apostles*, pp. 69ff.

these events are mentioned in Galatians. This again would seem to point to no earlier than A.D. 49 for the date of this letter.

Some weight must be given to the following considerations in dating Galatians. In Gal. 1.6 Paul expresses surprise and dismay that the Galatians are 'so quickly' (ταχέως) deserting the true Gospel for a false one. For those who insist on a northern Galatian provenance for the Galatian church this might mean shortly after the second or third missionary journeys, but we have already seen that the northern Galatian theory is considerably less likely than the southern Galatian hypothesis. This means that the letter was probably composed only a fairly short time after the Galatians had first heard Paul's Gospel during his first missionary journey. This short time might be a year or two, but it is unlikely to have been much more than that.

A second and often overlooked clue to the date of Galatians is the lack of evidence of social networks and leadership structures in this letter. Paul sends no greetings to individual Christians in Galatia. He appeals to no leaders to rectify the problems in the Galatian churches. It is clear enough that Galatians is a problem-solving letter not a progress-oriented letter and in such letters Paul normally appeals to the local leadership to help solve the problems (cf. 1 Cor. 16.15–16; Phil. 4.2–3; 1 Thess. 5.12–13). In view of how severe Paul seems to think the problems are in Galatia it is hard to doubt that he would have appealed to the local leaders if a leadership structure or a social network of co-workers was already in place in Galatia. That there is no such appeal or in fact any clear allusion to local leadership bespeaks an early stage in the development of the Galatian church.

A third factor of some weight is the people and places that *are* spoken of in Galatians, namely Peter, James, John, Titus, and Barnabas and the cities of Jerusalem and Antioch. In an often overlooked but important article, T. H. Campbell has pointed out by detailed comparison the similarities between Paul's letters, if aligned in a certain order, and the progression of events in Acts. That order entails placing Galatians as first among Paul's letters followed by 1 Thessalonians. As Campbell argues, Paul's letters are topical and they tend to refer to events of the recent past.[23] It is only really in conjunction with the period before, during, and immediately after Paul's first missionary journey that Barnabas and Paul are mentioned together as being in the same place at the same time. It is also only in Galatians that we get any sort of detailed discussion of Paul's pre-Christian years and conversion and the events that immediately followed that conversion. Furthermore, it is only in Galatians that we learn that Paul spent time in Damascus on more than one occasion, in Antioch, and in his native region of Cilicia. All other

---

23. T. H. Campbell, "Paul's 'Missionary Journeys' as Reflected in his Letter," *JBL* 74 (1955), pp. 80–87.

things being equal, this points to a date early in Paul's missionary career for this letter.

A bit more must be said about the Barnabas factor. As R. Bauckham has argued in some detail the relative silence in Galatians about Barnabas is telling, and yet clearly Paul assumes his converts in Galatia know precisely who Barnabas is.[24] He is right, I think, to argue that there is no serious reason to doubt the basic historical accuracy of the references to Barnabas in Acts, which means he was involved in the evangelizing of the Galatians, and yet he is not co-authoring this letter to the Galatians. Paul must do it alone for he had fallen out with Barnabas in Antioch over table fellowship. The 'even Barnabas' reference in Gal. 2.13 shows Paul's shock and dismay over this development. If Paul could have cited Barnabas' current agreement with Paul's views, surely he would have done so, as this would strengthen his case presented to the Galatians. Yet it should be observed from Acts 15.22–35 that immediately after the Jerusalem Council Paul and Barnabas once again work and teach for some time together in Antioch before another falling out transpires having to do with John Mark. This is clearly seen by Luke as subsequent to the Judaizing visit to Antioch (Acts 15.1) which caused dissension there and helped precipitate the Apostolic Council and also subsequent to the council. Yet when Galatians is written the episode in Antioch is fresh in Paul's mind and there is as yet no indication of détente between Paul and Barnabas. No date for the epistle better fits these data than one after the Antioch incident but before the resolving of the Antioch crisis in the Jerusalem meeting and before the reunion of Paul and Barnabas, which again brings us back to A.D. 49.

A fifth factor is the reference to the Galatian congregation in 1 Cor. 16.1. Here Paul informs his Corinthian converts that they should do what he told the Galatians to do about the Collection. Now it will be noted that nothing whatsoever is said in Paul's letter to the Galatians about gathering a Collection for the Jerusalem church. There is probably an allusion to the impetus behind and first request for such a Collection in Gal. 2.10, but no appeal is made to the Galatians about this matter. F. Watson has put the matter succinctly:

> Galatians must have been written *before* 1 Corinthians. Paul refers in Gal. 2.10 to his eagerness to fulfil the request of the 'pillars' for a collection from the gentile churches, but nowhere in Galatians does he indicate that such a collection is or has been in progress in Galatia. Since so much of the letter is concerned to prove his independence of the church of Jerusalem, he would have had to refer to the collection if he had already initiated it in Galatia, in order to explain why the collection did not imply any subordination to Jerusalem or any compromise with its desire to 'compel the Gentiles to Judaize' (2.14).[25]

24. R. Bauckham, "Barnabas in Galatians," *JSNT* 2 (1979), pp. 61–71.
25. F. Watson, *Paul, Judaism, and the Gentiles* (Cambridge: Cambridge University Press, 1986), p. 59.

Since Paul does mention in 1 Cor. 16.1 that he has spoken to the Galatians about what they must do about the Collection, we must assume that this communication whether oral or written transpired after Paul wrote Galatians and before he wrote 1 Corinthians. Since 1 Corinthians was in all likelihood written in A.D. 53–54 then we must date Galatians before that time.[26]

Thus far we have been able to place the date of Galatians no earlier than about A.D. 49 and no later than about A.D. 53–54. If we are to identify the date more precisely we must consider first what to make of Gal. 4.13 and the use of τὸ πρότερον there, and secondly we must give more extended treatment to a comparison of Acts and Galatians.

It is often urged that Gal. 4.13 indicates that Paul is writing to the Galatians after he has already visited them on more than one occasion. This is sometimes seen as the decisive argument that proves that the letter could not have been written immediately after the first missionary journey and immediately before the Jerusalem council recorded in Acts 15. But is it so? It is quite true that the adjective πρότερος can function as a comparative (the former of two) in distinction from πρῶτος (the first of a series), but in Hellenistic or Koine Greek the two terms often were equivalent.[27] In their detailed analysis of the papyri and comparison of them with the New Testament, J. H. Moulton and G. Milligan pointed out that πρότερον in all its NT uses has the more general sense of 'previously' or 'originally', not the comparative sense (on the former of two occasions). They provide clear examples of this regular use of the key term from the papyri. For example in Ptebt. II.302 from about A.D. 71 we find 'which previously belonged to the aforementioned Gods' where 'previously' is the proper translation for τὸ πρότερον (cf. also BGU IV. 1096 and P. Lond. 1221).[28] Other grammarians of the Greek NT are in agreement that it is unlikely that we have a comparative use of the neuter substantive here.[29]

Even if we take the less likely option, however, that the term is used comparatively, it can be made sense of by either the north or south Galatian theories. On the former view Paul is referring back to the first missionary journey through Galatia and there has now been at least one other. On the latter view Paul could be referring to the fact that Acts 13–14 mentions that

26. On the date of 1 Corinthians see my *Conflict and Community in Corinth*, pp. 71ff.

27. See the discussion in Longenecker, *Galatians*, pp. 190–91.

28. See J. H. Moulton and G. Milligan, *The Vocabulary of the Greek Testament* (Grand Rapids: Eerdmans, 1930), p. 554.

29. See BDF #62 p. 34: "πρότερος has surrendered the meaning 'the first of two' to πρῶτος and now means only earlier." Cf. Moule, *Idiom Book*, p. 98, and N. Turner, *Grammatical Insights into the New Testament* (Edinburgh: T. & T. Clark, 1965), pp. 90–91, perhaps an elative superlative. It is right to compare 1 Tim. 1.13 at this point where the meaning is surely 'formerly' with no comparison with another previous event.

Paul visited Pisidian Antioch, Iconium and Lystra *twice* on the very first missionary journey, once when he was heading west, and then again on the return journey east. I for my part tend to think that Longenecker is right that τò πρότερον is being contrasted with the νῦν of vs. 16 so that "the contrast throughout vv. 13–16 . . . [is] . . . between the Galatians reception of Paul when he *first* proclaimed the gospel to them and their response to him *now* after the Judaizer's intrusion."[30] In other words, it is unlikely that Gal. 4.13 implies that Paul had already made two missionary trips to Galatia.

Acts and Galatians compared

Much ink has been spilt over the relationship between the meeting described in Galatians 2.1–10 and the one Luke describes in Acts 15. Probably the majority of scholars think these are two different accounts of the same meeting. It then becomes very difficult to explain why it is that Paul nowhere in Galatians mentions the decision of the Jerusalem Council in support of his rejection of the suggestion by the agitators that his Galatian converts be circumcised, nor for that matter does he mention citing the Decree when he opposed Peter to his face over the matter of table fellowship between Jews and Gentiles. Some silences are rather quiet silences, but these omissions shout out for an explanation if in fact Galatians was written after the Apostolic Council. Even ascribing a bare minimum of historical authenticity to the account in Acts 15, the bottom line is that this account suggests that circumcision and probably also the full Kosher food rules would *not* be imposed on Gentile converts to Christianity. Had Paul known of and had the Jerusalem Church agreed to such a compromise before Galatians was written it is very difficult to explain why Paul did not refer to it in this letter to support his arguments. As it is, he only is able to say rather weakly that Titus was not *compelled* to be circumcised and that Peter had previously been living like a Gentile before he withdrew from table fellowship in Antioch under pressure.

This difficulty of course has led various scholars to the conclusion that Acts cannot be trusted in this matter, but this is a council of despair for it means rejecting the only possibly independent account we have of the meetings between Paul and the authorities in Jerusalem. It also means that one must reject the possibility outright that Acts was written by a sometime companion of Paul, something I have argued for at some length elsewhere.[31] If some other explanation of the data could be provided that did not require

---

30. Longenecker, p. 190.
31. See my *The Acts of the Apostles*, pp. 39ff.

such radical conclusions about the trustworthiness of Acts as a historical source and about the mysterious silences and elliptical statements in Gal. 1–2, it would surely be preferable. That explanation involves seeing Galatians as written shortly prior to the Council recorded in Acts 15.

Before we compare Acts and Galatians in regard to the Jerusalem meetings in which Paul participated, it is in order first to address the tendency in Pauline scholarship to treat Galatians as a clear primary source for what happened between Paul and the Jerusalem church and Acts as a decidedly secondary source on these matters. Paul, it is reasoned, was an actual participant in these events. This is true enough but it does not take into account at least three crucial factors:

(1)   The rhetorical and tendentious character of Paul's letters (on which see below) including especially Galatians;

(2)   Paul's comments on these crucial matters are highly selective and on various subjects only offered in passing while at least in Acts we have a direct narrative account by someone who does not seem to have a personal stake in how these particular events are narrated;

(3)   The author of Acts intends to be writing good Hellenistic history with some measure of objectivity and claims to have consulted sources including some eyewitnesses (cf. Lk. 1.1–4).

These observations lead to the conclusion that while a slight preference should probably be given to the account in Galatians over what we find in Acts, it would be best to scrutinize critically both sources and see them as of about equal weight in assessing what happened at the Jerusalem Council.

We must at this time assess the usual arguments for the most popular scholarly equation about the Jerusalem meetings, namely that Gal. 2.1–10 = Acts 15. The reasons for this equation can be summed up as follows:

(1)   Both texts refer to an important event that happened in Jerusalem;

(2)   Both texts have the same major players involved (Paul, Barnabas, Peter, James and Judaizing Christians);

(3)   Both texts seem on the surface to be dealing with the same subject, namely the basis of acceptance of Gentiles as full participating members in the Christian fellowship;

(4)   Both texts mention that circumcision was not required of Gentiles;

(5)   Both texts agree that the discussion was about 'in house' problems, not about the relationship between non-Christian Jews and Christians.

These parallels at first appear to be rather impressive until one looks a little more closely at the texts in question and notices:

(1) There remains the problem that Paul only mentions two visits up to Jerusalem, whereas by Acts 15 Luke has already mentioned three, a problem which is only compounded if Luke was at any point a companion of Paul or if he knew Galatians;

(2) In Acts Paul is sent up to Jerusalem as a representative of the Antioch church while in Galatians Paul says he went up by revelation;

(3) In Galatians the matter seems to be raised after Paul arrives in Jerusalem, while in Acts it is clear that the issue and its discussion is going on before then;

(4) Paul says he met privately with the three pillar apostles whereas the Council in Acts 15 appears to be a larger and more general meeting of the Jerusalem church leadership;

(5) Paul calls the troublemakers false brothers while Luke simply refers to Pharisaic Jewish Christians who insisted that Gentiles must be circumcised to be allowed to be full participants in Christian fellowship;

(6) Paul does not mention the decree of James at all in Galatians which surely he would have done had he known it, in order to stop the Galatians from even considering what the agitators were suggesting they must do, namely circumcise themselves and observe various days of the Jewish calendar (see Gal. 4.10).

(7) In Galatians 2 Paul plays an important even central role in the discussions, but in Acts 15 he is clearly overshadowed by Peter and James. Indeed, Luke gives Paul, who might be dubbed Luke's hero to judge by his presentation in Acts, a scant one verse in Acts 15! This is passing strange if Luke knew he played a more important role.

Not all of this list of seven items is of equal weight but I would place especial stress on numbers 3–7. It is understandable how conservative Jewish Christians might claim James' support and claim that Paul's Gospel was inadequate for Gentile acceptance prior to the Jerusalem Council and the Decree but it is much more difficult to imagine this happening after such an event. Also Paul's polemical approach in Galatians and Peter's and Barnabas' vacillations are all more easily understood before rather than after the Acts 15 council.

The above data leads one to reconsider the proposition that the meeting mentioned more fully in Gal. 2 is the same as that referred to briefly in

Acts 11.30 and 12.25, even though this proposition is not entirely problem free. The problem of course is that Luke only mentions this meeting during the second visit to Jerusalem very briefly, but then if as Paul says he only had a private meeting with the pillars then perhaps Luke's brevity is understandable.

In both the meetings in Acts 11 and 15, Barnabas and Paul are major figures and so the mention of them in Gal. 2 gives no greater support to one or the other of the proposed equations (i.e., that Acts 15 = Gal. 2 or that Acts 11 = Gal. 2). The same can be said for the locale of the meetings – Jerusalem. The mention of a meeting in Jerusalem in Galatians favors neither view or it favors both proposed equations.

Perhaps more telling is the reference to going up in response to revelation. It will be noted that Paul does not say in Gal. 2.2 that he went up to Jerusalem in response to revelation that he himself was given directly from God. This leaves the door open for the suggestion that what Paul is referring to is mentioned more fully in Acts 11.27–29 which says that the prophet Agabus came to Antioch and revealed that there would be a severe famine and hence the need for famine relief in Jerusalem. Notice that Gal. 2.10 clearly mentions that Paul and Barnabas were asked to remember the poor. This is understandable if the famine was ongoing and what Paul and Barnabas had brought (cf. Acts 11.30) was only a start to solving the problem. Notice that Gal. 2.10 says literally that 'this very thing I *had been eager* to do'. The aorist verb ἐσπούδασα clearly suggests that Paul had *already* been concerned about this matter before this request came, which comports nicely with the report in Acts 11.30 that Paul brought famine relief with him to this second meeting in Jerusalem. Furthermore, the verb μνημονεύωμεν is in the subjunctive and means 'we were to continue to bear in mind the poor' also implying an ongoing activity.[32]

The discussion in Gal. 2.1–14 is about events that transpired in Antioch and in places visited on Paul's first missionary journey which were then further discussed in Jerusalem – events involving Peter, Barnabas, Paul, and the Judaizers. For what it is worth, the main discussion in Acts of the Antioch church comes in Acts 11 not in Acts 15, and Peter is a prominent player in Acts 10–12, while Acts 13–14 records the first missionary journey which also transpires before the Acts 15 council. Then too, Peter is not portrayed as a major figure *after* Acts 15. The Judaizers appear in Acts 15.1 and 5. The point I am making is that the configuration of prominent figures and events mentioned in both Gal. 2 and Acts, all occur in portions of Acts that *precede* the decree in Acts 15, indeed all occur in the material that immediately precedes the Jerusalem Conference.

32. On this see H. D. Betz, *Galatians* (Philadelphia: Fortress, 1979), ad loc.

Another possible indication of the earliness of Galatians is found in Gal. 2.1–21. As J. D. G. Dunn points out, the Antioch incident is the last rehearsed in the *narratio* and it appears to be fresh in Paul's mind. It is possible, since Paul does not tell us how the confrontation with Peter turned out, that Paul lost that battle and now he re-expresses his essential arguments used there to the Galatians (especially in 2.15–21) only with more force. "This suggests that the Antioch incident was still vividly alive in Paul's memory, and indeed that his failure there was something still deeply and sharply felt by Paul."[33] Paul apparently was determined not to lose the same sort of battle twice in a row over the same issue.

Another crucial point in evaluating this matter is that the incident in Antioch, according to Paul in Gal. 2, is in fact over table fellowship, *not* circumcision. This comports with the earlier discussions recorded in Acts 10–11, but less well with the later discussions in Acts 15 where the circumcision issue is settled and a different kind of food and fellowship is discussed, namely food and fellowship in pagan temples.[34]

Paul in Galatians is clearly on the defensive, not merely because of the Judaizers but also because of the behavior of Peter, Barnabas, and perhaps even James. He contemplates the possibility of people preaching other Gospels (Gal. 1), and his position seems more vulnerable here than in any of his other letters. Notice that in 1 Corinthians Paul is able to speak of Peter in more positive tones as a fellow apostle whose behavior could be emulated by Paul if he chose to do so (1 Cor. 9.5 and 3.22).[35] This sense of alienation, even from his fellow apostles that Galatians seems to exude, is much more understandable if this letter reflects a period before some sort of agreement had been hammered out at a conference in Jerusalem on these matters.

33. J. D. G. Dunn, *The Theology of Paul's Letter to the Galatians* (Cambridge: Cambridge University Press, 1993), p. 15.
34. Cf. the discussion below pp. 19–20 on Acts 15 and on εἰδωλόθυτον see my article "Not so idle thoughts about *eidolothuton*," *TynBull* 44.2 (1993), pp. 237–54. As C. Hill, *Hebrews and Hellenists* (Minnesota: Fortress, 1992), p. 109 says "But the incident at Antioch did not have to do with the conditions surrounding Gentile admission; it had instead to do with the conditions surrounding mixed fellowship which is to say, laws governing food or purity. In other words the issue in Antioch, unlike that at the Jerusalem Conference, was not Gentile but *Jewish* obedience." *Notice* that Paul in Gal. 2 does not tell us the outcome after he rebuked Peter. I would suggest this is because the issue was not settled then and there, but later at the Jerusalem conference, after Galatians was written.
35. Note that there is no evidence that the opponents dealt with in 2 Cor. 10–13 have anything to do with Peter, James or the Jerusalem church leadership. In fact there is not even clear evidence that they are Judaizers, since circumcision is not an issue in these chapters, or even earlier in 2 Corinthians. On these matters see now my *Conflict and Community in Corinth* (Grand Rapids: Eerdmans, 1995), ad loc.

It is understandable how agitators might be able to come to Antioch and then go on to the churches of Galatia presenting themselves as representatives of the Jerusalem church and of its views, before a public resolution of the circumcision matter had happened. This sort of influence with any sort of Jerusalem backing is much less understandable after the Jerusalem council. Taken cumulatively these various points favor the suggestion that Acts 11–12 = Gal. 2 not that Acts 15 = Gal. 2.

Why then has Luke not told us in Acts 11–12 that the second trip up to Jerusalem involved Paul in significant discussions with the pillar apostles? As I have already said, Paul says that his meeting with James and the pillars was a private one. Apparently the Galatians will not have heard of it before this Pauline letter was written. Luke by and large is recording the significant events of early Christianity that were of a broader and more public character. Furthermore, whatever may have been privately agreed upon on the occasion of Paul's second visit to Jerusalem, it is clear that it did not settle the crucial issues about food and circumcision for the church as a whole, nor did the church as a whole know that Paul's Gentile mission had been basically approved by the pillars. In short this private meeting may have settled things for Paul and in his mind, but it settled nothing for the church as a whole. A further public conclave was required.

I must conclude that there are no views that are without problems, but the one which creates the most problems is the suggestion that Luke's account has little or no historical value and involves major distortion. The other two views, outlined above one of which involves equating Acts 15 with Gal. 2 and the other of which involves equating Acts 11 with Gal. 2, both have their pluses and minuses but on the whole the view which creates the least difficulties and solves the most problems is the view that the visit mentioned in Gal. 2 is equivalent to the one mentioned briefly in Acts 11 and 12.

It is not at all improbable that while Paul had privately received endorsement for his mission to the Gentiles from the pillar apostles on his second visit, there were many who opposed such a mission if it was pursued on the basis of a law-free Gospel preached to the Gentiles. Until there was a public pronouncement, the Judaizing controversy could and would go on, and could claim implicit endorsement from the Jerusalem church and perhaps even from James.

Notice that in Acts 11.2 Peter is criticized by the circumcised believers because of the Cornelius episode. I suspect that it is this occasion and the later one when the same sort of Christians came and criticized Peter in Antioch for the very same thing (cf. 'Why did you go to uncircumcised men and eat with them?' Acts 11.3 to Gal. 2.12), combined with the visit from 'the men who came from James' that cumulatively caused Peter to withdraw from fellowshipping with Gentiles in Antioch.

I also suspect that we are meant to think that it is representatives of this same group of very conservative Jewish Christians who are referred to again in Acts 15.1, 5 as having gone to Antioch and argued that circumcision was necessary for salvation. This comports well with what we read in Gal. 2.4, 12 where they are clearly called the circumcision faction.

The Galatians material suggests that before the council mentioned in Acts 15, James may have been sympathetic to the cause of the circumcision faction and their concerns, and actually may have sent some of them to investigate what was happening in Antioch. Perhaps he had not yet decided what to do about the matter, especially since the Cornelius episode could be viewed as an isolated exception, but a Gentile mission with many Gentile converts could not be viewed in such a light. What we know about James from other sources, including especially Josephus, strongly suggests that James was especially careful to maintain his Jewish piety after he became a follower of Jesus, and it is understandable why he would be sympathetic to the circumcision party's concerns and views.

Luke, of course, ever the apologete and diplomat, does not convey the magnitude of trouble and tension created between the Judaizers and people like Paul in the early church, much less the tensions between Peter and Paul, or Paul and James. Nor does he suggest, as Gal. 2.12 may (but see below), that James may have at least initially been in broad agreement with the circumcision party's views. Yet as Paul says, by the second visit (in 48), it is clear that James is not vocal about imposing circumcision on the likes of a Titus. Thus I think we must suppose that if the 'men who came from James' are the same as the 'false brothers' they came authorized to investigate by James, but went beyond their writ when they came and urged circumcision. The alternative is to suppose that the group mentioned in Gal. 2.4 are the agitators, while those mentioned in 2.12 are those who came from James to do damage control and manage the problem, by means of suggesting a withdrawal from eating with Gentiles by Peter and Barnabas. If there are indeed two groups, as I am inclined to believe, Paul opposes both the one (whom he calls false brothers) and the other whom he sees as appeasers who compromise the basic principles of a Law-free Gospel to the Gentiles.

Luke in Acts writes retrospectively knowing that these issues were eventually resolved, in part by the fact of who came to adhere to the Gospel message in large numbers in the middle decades of the first century. But to his credit, Luke makes clear in Acts 15.1 and 5 that there *was* a circumcision party in the Judean church, while at the same time carefully avoiding identifying this group with James or the whole Jerusalem church. In Luke's presentation, the Judaizers are a faction and an important factor within the Jerusalem church, but they don't speak for that church as James does. If James had at some earlier point identified with the Judaizers, the

Decree in Acts 15 suggests he distinguishes himself from them in important ways.

What James decided was to be required of Gentiles was avoiding pagan idolatry and immorality, in particular by avoiding pagan temple banquets. This is what is meant by avoiding 'the pollution of idols' (Acts 15.20). Avoiding idolatry and immorality was the heart of the Mosaic law, as the Ten Commandments make clear, and surely it was the Ten Commandments along with the Shema that one could most regularly expect to hear read in synagogues within range of the listening ears of Gentile proselytes and synagogue adherents (Acts 15.21). James is most concerned with Gentile Christians alienating Jews from being or becoming followers of Christ by continuing to behave like Gentiles in regard to matters of idolatry and immorality. This is also what Paul is concerned about in 1 Cor. 8–10, and in that text, in one of the first letters we have from Paul's hand written *after* the Jerusalem conference, we see how Paul attempted to implement the ruling of James about the behavior of Gentile Christians.[36]

In the end Luke was right *not* to portray James and Peter and Paul as always at odds with one another. Though there was much initial tension and many ongoing problems, at least at the level of early Christian apostolic leadership, as a result of the Jerusalem Conference there was, by and large, a meeting of the minds about what would and would not be required of Gentiles as they became followers of Jesus. The old Baur hypothesis, as Hill has shown, should be laid to rest once and for all.[37] Paul sums up well the essence of the matter in 1 Thessalonians, the very first letter he wrote after the Jerusalem council (about A.D. 51), when he boasts that in the whole region people know how the Thessalonians 'turned to God from idols, to serve a living and true God' (1 Thess. 1.9). This is what Moses demanded, James required, Paul preached, and the Thessalonians came to practice. It was also what Paul in good faith tried to make the Corinthians practice as a way of honoring the Decree. Luke has not deceived us about the meetings mentioned in Acts 11 and Acts 15 and their impact. The former set the Collection in motion, the latter provided the official basis of a Law-free Gospel, that paradoxically was true to the heart of what Moses and God required of all believers. The implications of all this for our determination of the date of Galatians is that no date better explains all the factors and details discussed above than A.D. 49 or just before Paul went off to the Jerusalem council recorded in Acts 15.

---

36. I have argued at length for these conclusions in several places. See my *The Acts of the Apostles*, pp. 425ff.; and *Conflict and Community in Corinth*, pp. 224–32.

37. See especially Hill, *Hellenists and Hebrews*, pp. 103–47.

The Agitators

Scholarship of late has been more wary than it used to be about the practice of mirror-reading Paul's letters.[38] By mirror-reading I am referring to the practice of reading statements or assertions in Paul's letters and *assuming* that Paul's adversaries were arguing just the opposite. A classic example of this comes in the very first verse of Galatians where Paul tells us who did and did not commission him to be an apostle. It is assumed, without proof, that since this opening is different in what it denies from other openings to Paul's letters, and since Paul mentions troublemakers in this Galatian letter, that someone must have been contesting Paul's apostolic status. This assumption may or may not be warranted (see below), but it makes evident that the practice of mirror-reading is usually used in the service of constructing a picture of Paul's opponents and what they proclaimed or taught. It will be worthwhile then to make some cautionary remarks about mirror-reading and identifying Paul's opponents, especially in view of the rhetorical character of Paul's letters.

In an important study, J. L. Sumney has pointed out at length the difficulties in identifying Paul's opponents, and the even greater difficulty in assuming that there was some sort of united front of opponents that appears in a variety of Paul's letters, such that we can read about the troublemakers in Corinth and assume these are the same persons with the same views causing difficulties in Galatia.[39] This sort of synthetic approach is often done on the basis of the flimsiest verbal parallels between Pauline letters, but of course Paul was perfectly capable of using the same invective language to cover a variety of troublemakers. Sumney makes various valuable suggestions in dealing with the issue of opponents to which I have added several more:

(1) Reconstructions should be used only *after* it has been made clear that opponents are *actually mentioned* in the text. It is wrong to allow the identity of the opponents to be determined by a reconstruction of the historical situation or of the text or by a composite picture of opponents based on other Pauline letters.

(2) The identification of the opponents cannot be based on the assumption that we know the historical situation Paul is addressing better than Paul himself. We should assume Paul's assessment is accurate unless there are strong reasons to think otherwise.

38. For cautions in regard to this practice as applied to Galatians in particular see most recently J. M. G. Barclay, "Mirror-Reading a Polemical Letter: Galatians as a Test Case," *JSNT* 31 (1987), pp. 73–93.

39. J. L. Sumney, *Identifying Paul's Opponents: The Question of Method in 2 Corinthians* (Sheffield: JSOT Press, 1990).

(3) Context is crucial to the meaning of words, and thus mere verbal similarities between passages in two Pauline letters are not a sufficient basis for transferring ideas about opponents from one letter to another. There must be a *shared conceptual framework*, which can only be determined by a full interpretation of the relevant passages in their respective contexts.

(4) Certainty of reference and reliability of reference should be two primary criteria applied to any statement to evaluate whether and what a text tells us about Paul's opponents.

(5) Explicit statements, allusions and affirmations provide a descending order of reliability.

(6) Statements in thanksgiving periods or didactic contexts are likely to be more reliable or straightforward than material in polemical or even apologetic contexts.[40]

(7) Mirror-reading of allusions in polemical texts, assuming what Paul claims is the opposite of what the opponents were saying, is not a very reliable way to proceed and should only be used with great caution as a support for explicit statements.

(8) One should begin with easier and more explicit statements and work one's way to more difficult ones.

(9) If the same kind of idea about opponents can be found in at least two different kinds of texts, for example in a didactic and also in a polemical text, it probably reflects something about the opponents.

(10) Obviously, one's view on the dating of a particular Pauline epistle may come into play in assessing the issue of opponents, and one must take into account one's own views on such matters. For example, in my view if one wishes to avoid possible anachronism in assessing Paul's opponents it would be well to be very cautious about reading what is said in Galatians on the basis of what is said for instance in the Corinthian correspondence.[41] This is also so because Corinthians says nothing about opponents insisting on circumcision whereas in Galatians this is clearly the main bone of contention.

(11) The way one assesses remarks in Paul's letters about opponents must in part take into account the sort of rhetoric Paul is using. There is a considerable difference between remarks made in the heat of a piece of forensic rhetoric and remarks made in a piece of deliberative rhetoric, although deliberative rhetoric can involve polemics as

40. Note that this means we are likely to have difficulties with Galatians because there is no thanksgiving section to this letter and references to agitators in Galatians are always in polemical contexts.

41. I am assuming here, what I have argued above, that Galatians is the earliest extant letter we have from Paul's hand.

we shall see. Remarks about opponents serve different sorts of functions in different kinds of rhetoric.

The matter of Paul's opponents must be discussed more fully in the commentary itself but at this juncture we must make certain preliminary remarks. Firstly, it is not at all clear that we should simply identify the 'men who came from James' in Gal. 2.12 with the false believers referred to in Gal. 2.4 (see above). At issue here is whether James was behind the Judaizing or whether those that he sent to Antioch were not hardliners but rather appeasers intended to come and resolve a crisis created by Peter and others eating and living like a Gentile which had scandalized the more conservative Jewish Christians in Jerusalem and Judea.

Secondly, it is even less clear that the men who came from James are also those who are bewitching the Galatians, though the false believers mentioned in Gal. 2.4 might well be the agitators.[42] The point is that these assumptions must be subject to close scrutiny. I will argue that when we consider the function of Paul's remarks in Gal. 2 it appears clear that Paul is drawing an analogy between the situations he faced in Jerusalem and Antioch and that which now faces the Galatian Christians in regard to their interaction with agitators there. Analogies are not identity statements. The point Paul is making is that as he opposed Peter and the false believers on issues of principle involving Judaizing, so also they must oppose the agitators with similar agendas in their own churches. In other words his arguments serve a deliberative function meant to guide the future behavior of the Galatians, not merely provide interesting autobiographical data.

Another point of importance is that close scrutiny of Galatians suggests that Paul does not know precisely who it is that is troubling the Galatians. We must take very seriously the question in 3.1 – 'Who has bewitched you?' As well as the further question in 5.7 – 'who prevented you from obeying the truth?' Consider also the remark in 5.10 – 'Whoever it is that is confusing you will pay the price'. We may suspect that Paul has an idea who these agitators are, but it seems clear from the remarks just cited that he is not certain of their identity. If he is not certain, it is hardly likely that we can be more certain about who they were. There is, however, perhaps one important clue which helps us to rule out the suggestion that the agitators were in fact members of the Galatian churches. As J. D. G. Dunn points out "Paul always refers to the troublemakers in the third person, while addressing his converts in the second person".[43] It perhaps does not need to be added that since the arguments in the letter are directed to better inform Paul's converts that they must reject the

---

42. What is relatively more clear is that Paul sees analogies between the opposition in Jerusalem, in Antioch, and in Galatia.
43. J. D. G. Dunn, *The Theology of Paul's Letter to the Galatians*, p. 8.

advise of those who Paul says offer an alternative Gospel that included circumcision and Jewish feast days, it is highly likely that the agitators were both Jews and also Christians.

Furthermore, a lot of the composite drawings of Paul's opponents in Galatia are based on the assumption that Paul knew in detail the exact vocabulary and arguments being used by the agitators and is turning them on their heads or rebutting them. This is a precarious assumption. Paul surely had some kind of report of the effect of the agitators on the Galatians and he may have heard about their essential line of argumentation (cf., e.g., Gal. 4), but more than this he does not seem to know.[44]

It cannot be emphasized too much that Paul is not directly addressing the agitators in Galatians, rather he is trying to persuade his converts to take a certain course of action. Furthermore, Paul does not, so far as we can tell, cite the arguments of his opponents before rebutting them. He talks about the agitators' effect on the Galatians but he is talking to the Galatians and assumes they know very well what the agitators had been saying and doing. As J. Barclay suggests, the Galatians were probably not ignorant but naive, having not worked out the implications of what the agitators were suggesting.[45] Paul's address to the Galatians then is attempting to make some mid-course corrections in the thinking of the converts by making clear the implications of what being circumcised and keeping the Law would mean and imply, especially what it would mean about the cross, about the Holy Spirit, about faith, about justification, about the Christian community and the like.

Though we cannot give a definitive answer to the 'who' question in regard to the opponents, we do have a few rather clear clues in Galatians as to what they advocated. In Paul's view it amounts to 'another Gospel' (1.8), one contrary to the one Paul had first preached among the Galatians. Paul defines for us in this document's *propositio* in 2.15–21 the portion of the essence of his own Gospel that is germane to the Galatian problem. It becomes clear that what he is standing for is a Gospel based on the redeeming and justifying grace available through the death of Christ on the cross and what he is opposing is the Galatians practising 'works of the law' by which is meant the Mosaic Law. In particular someone has advocated that the Gentile Galatians needed to be circumcised (5.2), and apparently also to observe special days and seasons and years in the Jewish calendar (4.10). Paul seeks to prevent such actions. In his view this would be a step backward in salvation history not a step forward into the eschatological future. It would be turning to what Paul used to be and gave up when he encountered Christ.

44. See rightly Barclay, pp. 82–83.
45. Barclay, p. 75.

To sum up, it seems reasonable and probable that the agitators in Galatia were Jewish Christians who wanted the Galatians to be circumcised and follow at least some of the Law, in particular its ritual aspects. This brought the adequacy of Paul's Gospel into direct question. It seems probable, due to the prominence of the mention of Jerusalem at various points, that these agitators had connections with the Jerusalem church, and it is also very believable that the agitators had used certain Scriptural arguments having to do with Abraham among other subjects to persuade the Galatians.

I see no evidence that these agitators were commissioned by James or the Jerusalem church to undertake these tasks, though they seem to have connections with the Jerusalem church (cf. Acts 15.1).[46] Paul distinguishes between the pillar apostles, some of whom may have been guilty of errors of judgment but whom Paul is not prepared to call false brothers or spies. It also seems probable that we must distinguish between the agitators in Galatia and the 'men who came from James' although one could argue that the latter came to Antioch and exceeded the limits of what James sent them to do.

I also see no clear evidence that the agitators were complaining that Paul was a subordinant of the Jerusalem church and so not an independent apostle. They were more likely to complain that he was independent of the Jerusalem church and a maverick than the other way around! It is not Paul's apostolic status but his Gospel that is at issue in Galatians, or if we wish to nuance this a bit, Paul's apostolic status is only called into question very indirectly because Paul perceives that his Gospel is being challenged and/or supplemented by the agitators. I see no evidence that the agitators openly questioned Paul's apostolic status or his commission to preach to the Gentiles, nor more importantly do I see any evidence that the Galatians doubted Paul's apostolic office or commission. It was the adequacy of his message to guide the Galatians in how they should live which was in doubt, as the paraenetic thrust of this entire discourse called Galatians makes clear.[47]

The rhetoric of Galatians

It is hard to over-estimate the degree to which the world Paul and his converts lived in was saturated with rhetoric. It was the staple of Greco-Roman education and listening to and evaluating rhetors was one of the great spectator sports of the first century A.D. D. Litfin puts the matter succinctly:

46. See rightly Barclay, p. 89.
47. Dunn, *Theology*, p. 104 n. 6 has helpfully pointed out that the issue is neither getting in nor staying in, but 'going on' and how the Christians in Galatia were supposed to live out their faith. I quite agree, but it is also true that Paul points the Galatians back to their conversion experience to remind them how they 'got in' in the first place, and this in Paul's view has implications for how they should go on.

Rhetoric played both a powerful and pervasive role in first century Greco-Roman society. It was a commodity of which the vast majority of the population was either producers, or much more likely consumers, and not seldom avid consumers . . . [O]ratory became more prevalent than ever. In both the Roman and Greek setting the frequency with which speakers rose to address audiences, for whatever reasons, seemed to be on the rise during the first century. The quality of oratory may have declined but the quantity had not.[48]

But what was rhetoric? Basically it was the learned art of persuasion, though in the hands of some first-century sophists it degenerated into little more than the art of speaking well. There were numerous specific guidelines for how to structure and deliver a speech so that it would successfully persuade its target audience, and Paul's letters reflect that he was well aware of how to use the art of rhetoric to achieve his aims in proclaiming the Gospel of Jesus Christ. I have undertaken elsewhere to discuss at some length the basic character of Greco-Roman rhetoric, but here it will be in order to focus on some more particular questions.[49]

Paul's letters were surrogates for his own oral proclamation since he could not be present to deliver his message in person. Furthermore, there is good reason to believe that Paul intended for his letters to be read aloud to his congregations (cf., e.g., 2 Cor 13.11; Col. 3.16). They were documents meant primarily for the ears not the eyes of his congregations and this raises the likelihood that Paul took into account the aural dimensions of his text, so that it could be properly and effectively 'delivered' in the full sense of that term. He would have one of his trusted associates carry and perform the letter with attention to its rhetorical character so that it might be a persuasive exercise in communication.

It is fair to say that Galatians is one of the most rhetorical of all of Paul's communiqués included in the NT. It includes some epistolary elements in 1.1–5 and parts of 6.11–18, but for the most part it is pure speech material. There is no thanksgiving section, no greetings to particular persons, no health wish, no mention of present or future travel plans, unlike what we find in most of Paul's other letters. Gal. 1.6–6.10 in the eyes and hands of any good rhetor would be seen as and could be made to be a very effective speech full of arguments and rhetorical devices.[50] But what sort of rhetoric is it?

---

48. D. Litfin, *St. Paul's Theology of Proclamation. 1 Corinthians 1–4 and Greco-Roman Rhetoric* (Cambridge: Cambridge University Press, 1994), p. 132. In my judgment, Litfin provides the finest short survey of the history and development of rhetoric from the time of Aristotle until the second century A.D. in pp. 1–134 of this monograph. It helps to make quite clear the atmosphere or ethos in which Paul did his preaching.

49. See the discussion in my *Conflict and Community in Corinth*, pp. 39–48 and the bibliography that follows it.

50. On Galatians as letter see pp. 36–41 below.

Since H. D. Betz's landmark commentary on Galatians in 1979,[51] there has been an enormous amount of discussion of this topic and among those who agree that Galatians should be read in light of Greco-Roman rhetoric scholars have been basically divided into two camps. Some have followed Betz and have seen Galatians as basically apologetic and therefore forensic in character, while others, following the lead of G. Kennedy, have concluded that the document is largely an example of deliberative rhetoric. J. D. Hester seems to be a rarity in his attempt to argue that we have epideictic rhetoric in Galatians.[52] I must confess that I am in the deliberative camp, though before I had occasion to examine Galatians closely, it appeared to me on the surface to be an apologetic document, at least in its first two chapters.[53]

I, like various others, had mistaken polemics and emotive rhetoric for apologetics and forensic speech when in fact the two can and must be distinguished. There is a difference between the emotional *tone* of a document and its argumentative substance. On closer inspection, all the arguments in Galatians are intending to convince the Galatians not to submit to circumcision and the Mosaic Law and instead to continue to walk in the way of freedom in the Spirit which Paul had taught them when he first delivered the Gospel to them. In other words Galatians is an example of deliberative rhetoric intending to convince the audience by various means to take a particular course of action in the near future, and it argues on the basis of what will be the possible, expedient, useful, and honorable course for them to follow. As Kennedy puts it "The letter looks to the immediate future, not to judgment of the past, and the question to be decided by the Galatians was not whether Paul had been right in what he had said or done, but what they themselves were going to believe and to do."[54] As has been often noted, the best way to determine the sort of rhetoric one finds in a particular speech is to ask what sort of judgment or decision Paul's argument is attempting to get his audience

51. Actually Betz was already arguing in this fashion as early as the SNTS meeting in 1974, and in some articles that he wrote at and shortly after that time, but it was the commentary that had the largest impact. See his earlier articles "The Literary Composition and Function of Paul's Letter to the Galatians," *NTS* 21 (1975), pp. 353–79 which is a form of his SNTS lecture and also "In Defense of the Spirit: Paul's Letter to the Galatians as a Document of Early Christian Apologetics," in *Aspects of Religious Propaganda in Judaism and Early Christianity* (ed. E. Schüssler Fiorenza; Notre Dame: University of Notre Dame Press, 1976), pp. 99–114.

52. See J. D. Hester, "The Rhetorical Structure of Galatians 1.11–14," *JBL* 103 (1984), pp. 223–33 and his "Placing the Blame: The Presence of Epideictic in Galatians 1 and 2," in *Persuasive Artistry*, ed. D. F. Watson (Sheffield: JSOT Press, 1991), pp. 184–208.

53. See for example Longenecker's analysis in his *Galatians*, pp. c–cxix.

54. Kennedy, *New Testament Interpretation through Rhetorical Criticism* (Chapel Hill: University of North Carolina Press, 1984), p. 146.

to make.[55] In the case of Galatians the judgment is not about Paul's past but about the Galatians' future. Paul's past comes up in order to present a negative (pre-conversion) and positive (post-conversion) example for his converts to heed.

There are various reasons why a forensic analysis of Galatians does not work. There is firstly the important matter of the material found in Gal. 5.1–6.10 which Betz continues to call the *exhortatio*.[56] Whether we call it 'exhortation' or paraenesis or ethics or something else, it is quite clear that this sort of material does not fit into a piece of forensic rhetoric the function of which is to defend or attack some past event or course of action, not give advice about present and future behavior.[57]

Even a cursory glance at the basic ancient handbooks of rhetoric show that exhortations belong to the deliberative form of rhetoric which seeks to persuade or dissuade about a future course of action, not to the forensic genre which is concerned with attacking or defending some aspect of the past. Consider what is said in the *Rhetorica ad Alexandrum*: ". . . one delivering an exhortation must prove that the courses to which he exhorts are just, lawful, expedient, honorable, pleasant and easily practicable . . . One dissuading must apply hinderance by the opposite means: he must show that the action proposed is not just, not lawful, not expedient . . ." (1421b 23ff.). The author of this important early treatise also makes quite clear that proposals concerning religious ritual and whether they should be changed or maintained is properly within the scope of deliberative rhetoric (1423a 30ff.).[58]

A second problem for Betz's analysis is the material in Gal. 3–4 which argues in essence that the Galatians are foolish to listen to the instructions of the agitators and will be harming themselves and losing the advantages they have in Christ if they submit to circumcision and the Mosaic Law. These are precisely the sort of arguments one would expect in a deliberative speech, not a forensic one. Furthermore, a careful analysis of the central *logoi* or arguments in this document shows their paraenetic thrust and essential unity. The theme announced in the rhetorical question at 3.3 'Having begun in the Spirit, are you now ending with the flesh?' is picked up again at 5.16 'But I say walk by the Spirit and do not gratify the desires of the flesh' and again at 6.8 and 6.12–15. As J. Fairweather says, the entire argument in this letter has a paraenetic aim

---

55. See Lyons, *Pauline Autobiography*, p. 117.

56. See his article "Galatians, Epistle to the," *ABD* II, pp. 872–75 which appeared in 1992.

57. See J. Smit, "The Letter of Paul to the Galatians: A Deliberative Speech," *NTS* 35 (1989), pp. 1–26, here pp. 4–5 and also R. G. Hall, "The Rhetorical Outline for Galatians: A Reconsideration," *JBL* 106 (1987), pp. 277–87.

58. See the discussion in J. Fairweather, "The Epistle to the Galatians and Classical Rhetoric: Part 3", *Tynbull* 45.2 (1994), pp. 213–43, here pp. 222–23.

and she is able to sum up the deliberative arguments offered between Gal. 2 and 6 as follows: (1) No to Gentile circumcision; Yes to the Spirit; (2) No to the Law; Yes to faith; (3) No to slavery: Yes to Sonship; (4) Yes to freedom; No to the flesh.[59]

Thirdly, there is the matter that Paul calls for his audience to imitate his own behavior and become as he is (4.12), an appeal suitable to deliberative rhetoric but not to forensic rhetoric. But what exactly about Paul's life does he want his audience to emulate? The answer in part comes at the very beginning of Galatians in the narrative material in Gal. 1–2. I will argue in the commentary that the *function* of the narrative material we find in Gal. 1–2 is to provide examples to the audience of what sort of behavior to adopt or shun (shun – Paul's pre-Christian behavior, the behavior of Peter and Barnabas at Antioch, and the behavior of the false brothers; adopt – Paul's post-conversion life style and behavior and the behavior of the pillars when Paul met with them in Jerusalem and did not compel Titus' circumcision and endorsed Paul's mission to the uncircumcised Gentiles). In other words, Paul is providing *exempli* in his *narratio*, both positive and negative and by means of a συγκρίσις or comparison he intends to show his audience what sort of behavior to emulate and what sort to avoid.[60]

There is then a substantial *narratio* in Gal. 1–2 which was not absolutely required in a piece of deliberative rhetoric, but was also not inappropriate. Aristotle reminds us that if there is a *narratio* in a deliberative speech that it will speak of things past 'in order that being reminded of them, the hearers may take better counsel about the future' (*Rhetoric* 3.16.11). As we have said, this is precisely the function of the discussion of Paul's past in Gal. 1–2 just as it is the function of the discussion of the Galatians' own past experiences in texts like Gal. 3.1–3, 4.13–15. All is geared toward getting the Galatians to walk in the Pauline Gospel and reject the other Gospel.[61]

Quintilian also says that in the statement of facts it is appropriate to discuss external matters and "in deliberative speeches we may often begin with a reference either to ourselves or to our opponent" (*Inst. Or.* 3.8.8–10) which is precisely what we find for the most part in Gal. 1–2. Paul

---

59. Fairweather, "Galatians and Classical Rhetoric: Part 3," p. 225.

60. On 'comparison' as a rhetorical device in this section of Galatians see now B. Malina and J. Neyrey, *Portraits of Paul. An Archaeology of Ancient Personality* (Louisville: Westminster/John Knox, 1996), pp. 34–51.

61. Kennedy, *New Testament Interpretation*, p. 145 rightly points out that the narration in Gal. 1–2 does not function at all like a narration in a forensic piece of rhetoric – "the narrative of the first and second chapters of Galatians is not an account of facts at issue. It is supporting evidence for Paul's claim in 1.11 that the Gospel he preached was not from man, but from God, a topic which had been enunciated in the first verse of the salutation."

must establish his ethos here and at the same time remind his audience about the truth of the Gospel which will be what he offers as an alternative to circumcision and the keeping of the Mosaic Law. Notice how Gal. 1.10 bridges between the *exordium* and the *narratio*, by raising the matter of ethos and character. Paul is no people pleaser, nor is he seeking his audience's favor or approval, which is precisely what many rhetors and all sophists did in Paul's day. Paul is conveying a persona that is characterized by candor.[62] Most of all, in Gal. 1–2 Paul is presenting his own experience as an example to his converts both negatively (before conversion) and positively (after conversion).[63]

Fourthly, Paul is having this document delivered to the Galatian assemblies (ἐκκλησίαε – 1.2), and it is hard not to hear an allusion here to the traditional audience for a piece of deliberative rhetoric – namely the Greek assemblies. It was in these assemblies that policies and courses of action for the future were decided, and it is in the Christian assemblies that Paul seeks to perform similar acts of persuasion and dissuasion with his converts.[64] Though he is somewhat defensive about his past at the beginning of Galatians, this is because Paul must establish his *ethos* at the beginning of his address to the assemblies so that his audience will accept his authority and trust and take the advice he must give them in what follows. This document is not about defending Paul's apostleship, but about persuading the assemblies in Galatia to continue to follow the truth of the Gospel already received and reject the 'other Gospel'.

If Paul had believed that his authority really was in serious question in Galatia he would not be able to write the sort of things we find him writing in Galatians. He would indeed have had to offer not a largely paraenetic speech, but instead a judicial one attacking the opponents and defending himself. As Fairweather puts it, the debate that is meant to arise in the Galatian assemblies as a result of this document is not whether Paul was a true apostle or not, but rather 'The Galatians deliberate whether Gentile believers in Christ should be circumcised'.[65] The settling of this issue of course had implications for what

---

62. See Kennedy, p. 148.

63. Cf., e.g., Dunn, *Theology*, p. 5: "the autobiographical narrative in chapters 1 and 2 was intended to build up to and introduce the principal theological argument of the following chapters. The highly personal language of 2.14–21 and 6.11–17 is indication in itself of the degree to which Paul saw his own experience as an epitome of the Gospel." Or G. Lyons, *Pauline Autobiography*, p. 171: "Paul presents his 'autobiography' as a paradigm of the Gospel of Christian freedom".

64. Of deliberative rhetoric Quintilian says "The majority of Greek writers have held that this kind of oratory is entirely concerned with addressing public assemblies . . ." *Inst. Or.* (3.8.14).

65. Fairweather, "The Epistle to the Galatians and Classical Rhetoric: Parts 1 and 2," *TynBull* 45.1 (1994), pp. 1–38, here p. 5.

Paul's ongoing relationship would be with his converts, and it is notable that one of Paul's rhetorical moves in this letter is to begin the letter with the first person singular,[66] move to the second person plural and then conclude with the first person plural.[67] The goal of this rhetorical piece is to get the Galatians to reject the 'gospel' of circumcision and re-establish them in the Pauline Gospel for what counts is not circumcision but the new creation, as the climax of the speech says (6.15). If the goal is achieved, this in turn will effect reunion or harmony between Paul and his converts so he will not need to speak in terms of 'I' and 'you all', suggesting estrangment, but once again of 'we' who share the truths of the Pauline Gospel.

It will be worthwhile at this juncture to review a few other things Quintilian tells us about deliberative rhetoric because much of it is very apropos of what we find in Galatians. First of all, forensic rhetoric had no corner on the market of emotive and inflammatory verbage. All three major species of rhetoric resorted to emotional appeals, especially at the beginning and end of a speech, or in the sections of the speech where *ethos* and *pathos* come into play. In fact, Quintilian makes clear that it is not in forensic but rather in deliberative speeches where emotional language is most to be expected and is most effective, because the effectiveness of deliberative rhetoric depends on the audience accepting the speaker's authority[68] and "anger has frequently to be excited or assuaged and the minds of the audience have to be swayed to fear, ambition, hatred, reconciliation" (see *Inst. Or.* 3.8.12). In other words the author must both grab their attention and establish rapport with his audience at the beginning of the speech, and then at the end of the speech appeal to the deeper emotions such as pity or empathy. Polemics and strong emotional language do not in themselves indicate a forensic speech. One must ask what the intended effect of such language is, and in Galatians the emotional language is intended to make the Galatians rethink things and change their behavior if they are already Judaizing.[69]

Paul clearly follows the standard advice about arousing the audience's emotions so they will change their behavior by, on the one hand waking the Galatians up by calling them foolish and invoking various curses at the beginning of Galatians, and only then going on to show that he is a trust-

66. This statement must be somewhat modified since we do have the first person plural used before the end of the letter when Paul wishes to refer to 'we Jews' as opposed to the Galatian Gentiles. Kennedy, is however, correct that at the end 'we' is Paul and the audience reunited under one heading as fellow Christians.

67. See Kennedy, p. 150.

68. "But what really carries greatest weight in deliberative speeches is the authority of the speaker" (*Inst. Or.* 3.8.12).

69. After having written this I discovered that Hall "Rhetorical Outline," pp. 280ff. also sees the relevance of this material.

worthy guide for his audience as to what they must do because he himself has gone through the experiences or actions they have had (conversion to Christianity) or were contemplating undertaking (observing the Mosaic Law) and that he had always been true to the Gospel since his conversion.

Then at the end of his speech Paul quite clearly pulls on the heartstrings of his audience by referring to the marks on his body suffered in the service of Christ (6.17 cf. also 4.13–17). Both Cicero and Quintilian note that when one appeals to the deeper emotions such as pity in order to move and guide one's audience at the end of the speech, it was not uncommon for an orator to display wounds and scars of himself, or if speaking for another, of his client, to achieve the desired end (cf. Cicero *De Oratore* 2.28.124; Quintilian 6.1.21). It is interesting that Quintilian and Cicero suggest that such displaying of scars and use of emotion-charged language was an audacious ploy and not a tactic approved by Attic theorists, though it was not uncommon in Asiatic rhetoric (cf. Quintilian 6.1.7; Cicero *De Oratore* 2.28.124).

As Fairweather stresses, it is important to bear in mind when evaluating Paul's rhetoric that "Paul was no Athenian. In terms of the literary criticism of his day he would surely have been regarded as an *Asianus*, and not only for his disinclination to eliminate non-Attic elements from his diction."[70] Quintilian tells us that Asiatic rhetoric was viewed by Atticists as deficient in taste and restraint, "being naturally given to bombast and ostentation, . . . puffed up with a passion for a more vainglorious style of eloquence" (11.10.16–17). One suspects that Quintilian would have seen Paul's Galatians as clearly an example of Asiatic rhetoric, lacking somewhat in restraint and taste.

Quintilian might even be describing Paul in this letter when he speaks of "he whose eloquence is like to some great torrent that rolls down rocks and 'disdains a bridge' and carves out its own banks for itself, [and] will sweep the judge from his feet, struggle as he may, and force him to go wherever he bears him" (12.10.61). Paul of course is addressing those who would be most familiar with Asiatic rhetoric, and if we consider the Galatians' social level they were also probably a class of clientele that would be more apt to appreciate the more bombastic style of Asiatic rhetoric than the measured and restrained tones of the more scholarly and upper-class Attic rhetoric. Consider Quintilian's elitist complaint about declaimers who use the more florid style when giving a deliberative discourse: "they have always affected abrupt openings, an impetuous style, and a generous embellishment, as they call it, in their language . . . deliberative themes do not require an *exordium* . . . [so] I do not . . . understand why they should open in such a wild and exclamatory

---

70. Fairweather, "Galatians and Classical Rhetoric: Part 3," p. 229.

manner. When a man is asked to express his opinion on any subject, he does not, if he is sane, begin to shriek, but endeavors as far as possible to win the assent of the man who is considering the question by a courteous and natural opening" (3.8.58–59).

One can readily imagine how Quintilian would evaluate the abrupt *exordium* in Gal. 1.6ff. (which immediately follows the salutation without any intervening thanksgiving period): 'I am astonished that you are so quickly deserting the one who called you in the grace of Christ and are turning to a different Gospel – not that there is another Gospel ... If any proclaims a Gospel contrary to what you received, let that one be accursed!' or for that matter the equally abrupt and emotive beginning of the argument or *logos* section of the letter: 'You foolish Galatians! Who has bewitched you? It was before your eyes that Jesus Christ was publicly exhibited as crucified!' (3.1).

Quintilian makes clear that if one wants to cause someone to follow the proposed course of action suggested in a deliberative speech it is often necessary to point out "the appalling consequences that will follow the opposite policy" (*Inst. Or.* 3.8.39). "I am not sure that most people's minds are not more easily influenced by fear of evil than by hope of good, for they find it easier to understand what is evil than what is good" (3.8.40). Paul's deliberative rhetoric attests to this sort of strategy in Gal. 5.2–4 when Paul tells his audience that Christ himself will be of no value to them if they accept circumcision, indeed they will find themselves cut off from Christ. Notice also how Paul cites first the list of the vices of the flesh in 5.19–21 before he lists the fruit of the Spirit. It is important to bear in mind that there is no reason not to see the material in Gal. 5–6 as part of the arguments of proofs, rather than a separate section called an 'exhortation'. "Since the exhortations seek to persuade the Galatians to adopt the proposition of the letter, considered rhetorically they are part of the proof."[71] It is also important to point out that Gal. 5–6 involves more than exhortation, there are also arguments which are punctuated by exhortations, which is perfectly appropriate in deliberative rhetoric.

Much more could be said along these lines, but we must draw this portion of the introduction to a close and leave more detailed comments about the rhetoric of Galatians to the commentary itself. Suffice it to say that this entire Galatian discourse can be analyzed as an effective and powerful example of deliberative rhetoric, following Asiatic conventions and style which tended to be more abrupt, bombastic, and emotive. The following outline shows the basic structure of what we find in Galatians with indication of where there are major discussions on some of the key topics of the discourse:

71. Hall, "The Rhetorical Outline," p. 285.

EPISTOLARY PRESCRIPT: 1.1–5

EXORDIUM: 1.6–10 – TWO GOSPELS?

NARRATIO: THE ORIGIN AND CHARACTER OF THE GOSPEL OF GRACE – 1.11–2.14 (with 1.11–12 being transitional)
    I. The Gospel of Christ – 1.11–12
    II. A Narrative of Surprising Developments: Jerusalem, Antioch and Beyond – 1.13–2.14
    EXCURSUS: A CONVERSATION ON CONVERSION
    EXCURSUS: THE AGONY OF AN AGONISTIC CULTURE

PROPOSITIO: 2.15–21 – BY THE FAITHFULNESS OF CHRIST, NOT BY WORKS OF THE LAW

PROBATIO: 3.1–6.10
    ARGUMENT I: THE FAITH OF ABRAHAM AND THE FOOLISHNESS OF THE GALATIANS – 3.1–18
    DIVISION 1: The Appeal to Spiritual Experience – 3.1–5
    EXCURSUS: THE CONSTRUCTION OF A COMMUNITY
    DIVISION 2: The Appeal to Scripture – 3.6–14
    EXCURSUS: PAUL THE EXEGETE AND ALLEGORIZER
    EXCURSUS: DELIBERATING ABOUT RITUALS
    DIVISION 3: The Appeal to Legal Covenants – 3.15–18
    ARGUMENT II: THE GOAL OF THE GUARDIAN, THE FUNCTION OF THE FAITHFUL ONE – 3.19–4.7
    DIVISION 1: Why the Law was Added – 3.19–22
    DIVISION 2: The Guardian's Goal – 3.23–29
    EXCURSUS: THE LAW AS CHILDMINDER AND GUARDIAN
    EXCURSUS: DISSECTING A MILLENARIAN CONVERSIONIST SECT
    DIVISION 3: The Heirs Apparent – 4.1–7
    ARGUMENT III: SHARED EXPERIENCE – 4.8–20
    DIVISION 1: Déjà Vu – 4.8–11
    DIVISION 2: Paul's Labor Pains – 4.12–20
    ARGUMENT IV: THE ALLEGORY OF ANTIPATHY – 4.21–5.1[72]
    EXCURSUS: LAYING DOWN THE LAW
    ARGUMENT V: THE UNKINDEST CUT OF ALL – 5.2–15
    DIVISION 1: Testimony from the Top – 5.2–6
    DIVISION 2: What Cuts and What Counts – 5.7–12
    DIVISION 3: Freedom's Service, Love's Law – 5.13–15

---

72. It is perhaps possible to see this portion of the discourse as a *refutatio* if in fact it is the case that Paul is countering arguments of the agitators about Jerusalem and the Sinai covenant and Abraham at this point, but this is not certain.

ARGUMENT VI: ANTISOCIAL BEHAVIOR AND ESCHATOLOGICAL
    FRUIT – 5.16–26
    DIVISION 1: Foiling the Fulfillment of the Flesh – 5.16–21
EXCURSUS: THE VIRTUE OF VICE LISTS
    DIVISION 2: The Spirit's Fruit – 5.22–26
ARGUMENT VII: BEARABLE BURDENS AND THE YOKE OF CHRIST
    6.1–10
    DIVISION 1: The Law of Christ – 6.1–5
    DIVISION 2: Doing Good to Teachers and Others – 6.6–10

PAUL'S AUTOGRAPH: 6.11

PERORATIO: 6.12–17
    EXCURSUS: CIRCUMCISION AND DECISION

EPISTOLARY CLOSING: 6.18

It will be seen that the first part of this structural analysis is in agreement
with Betz about the extent of the *narratio* and the *propositio*, and the analysis
of the *exordium* is closely similar as well.[73] I am also in agreement about the
peroratio. This makes clear that one can agree with Betz on much of the
rhetorical structure of Galatians without being in agreement on the rhetorical
species of a discourse. There is a real sense in which there is only one theme in
Galatians, with a variety of permutations and facets. This letter is more of a
unity in its theme than many another of Paul's letters.[74] Yet it is right to point
out that Paul uses a variety of arguments to deal with what is essentially one
topic (should the Galatians continue along the path that Paul led them, or
should they be circumcised and commit themselves to observing the Mosaic
Law?). This variety of arguments is what the outline above is meant to
delineate.

Deliberative rhetoric was rhetoric often used to produce concord and
unity and to overcome discord and disunity.[75] It is clear enough that this is
a significant part of Paul's aim in penning Galatians. Discord has been
interjected into the situation in Galatia because of the agitators coming and
insisting on the observance of the Law. Paul finds himself in the awkward
position of having to argue with and in some cases even against some of his
own converts who may have begun 'Judaizing' and who appear to be
contemplating going all the way, accepting circumcision with its other
implications and obligations. The effects of this was to divide the Galatians

73. See Betz, *Galatians*, pp. 16–23.
74. See, e.g., C. K. Barrett, *Freedom and Obligation. A Study of the Epistle to the
Galatians* (Philadelphia: Westminster, 1985), pp. 32ff.
75. See M. Mitchell, *The Rhetoric of Reconciliation*, pp. 56ff.

over these matters and so Paul in the so-called ethical section of the discourse
must warn them against biting and devouring one another (Gal. 5.15) and
against the effects of enmity, strife, jealousy quarrels, dissensions, factions and
the like (5.20). As J. Barclay has noted "while some of these terms are paralleled
in other Pauline vice-lists, others are unique to this passage and their heavy
concentration suggests Paul has deliberately emphasized these features of
fleshly conduct. When this evidence is taken together with the direct warnings
against hostility and envy in 5.15 and 5.26 . . . , it can be seen that all the
relevant . . . criteria . . . point towards a situation of discord in the Galatian
churches."[76]

Paul also uses the illustration of what happened in Antioch in Gal. 2 to
show how the agitators' sort of proclamation produced discord and disunity
between Jewish and Gentile believers in Antioch, and was likely to do so again
in Galatia. In other words, Paul writes to the Galatians in an atmosphere of
discord, both in his own situation and in that of his converts. Concord between
the apostle and his converts will be re-established if he can persuade his
audience to ignore or renounce the advice of the agitators and resume
following the Gospel he had preached when first in Galatia.

Yet another piece of evidence that Paul is arguing for unity and concord
in this letter comes from a close examination of Gal. 3.15–18. Paul is arguing
about how his converts are already all *one* in Christ, and that they do not have
to add anything to what they received by grace through faith. In fact to do so is
to divide the already unified body of Christ. The seed is 'one', God is 'one' and
anything that in effect divides Gentiles from Jews and so tends to produce two
peoples of God is to be shunned or avoided.[77] One of the ultimate aims of
Paul's discourse in this document is to avoid the further fragmentation of the
body of Christ, and in fact restore harmony, concord and unity in the Galatian
assemblies disrupted by the agitators.

Galatians as a letter

It is clear enough, especially from the beginning and end of Galatians, that it is
not just a transcript of a speech but rhetorical arguments placed into an
epistolary framework because the rhetor is unable to be present to address his
audience. It must be stressed as Mitchell has shown that "deliberative rhetoric
was commonly employed within epistolary frameworks in antiquity (see, e.g.,

76. Barclay, *Obeying the Truth*, p. 153.
77. See the helpful exposition of N. T. Wright, in *The Climax of the Covenant*
(Edinburgh: T. & T. Clark, 1991), pp. 162ff.

especially Isocrates *Ep.* 1–3; Demosthenes *Ep. 1*; 1 Clement).[78] If we wish to become more specific about Galatians, it is possible to say that the sort of deliberative letter we find in this case is a rebuke–request letter not, as Betz argued, an apologetic letter.[79] This fact has been amply demonstrated by G. W. Hansen and it will be well to summarize some of his arguments against Betz's proposal and for the rebuke–request view.[80]

Before we turn to Hansen's arguments, however, something must be said about the importance of being able to distinguish between apologetics and polemics, the former has more to do with substance of a discourse, the latter with its tone. A discourse can of course be both polemical and apologetic, but it is also true that non-apologetic discourses can be polemical in tone.

Apologetics properly speaking involves the attempt to provide a reasoned defense of the faith, usually in a setting where it is under attack.[81] Apologetics may involve polemics but it can often also be irenic in tone. Polemics by contrast never involves an irenic tone. Polemics entails the use of strong, hyperbolic, and emotive language to aid in persuading or dissuading an audience in regard to a particular course of action. It is a tool that has more to do with pathos than logos or formal arguments (while apologetics most definitely has to do with arguments), and it is meant to create horror or revulsion in the audience about something or someone. We see this very sort of thing for example in Gal. 5.12 when Paul says he wishes the agitators would castrate themselves. Paul is not really arguing for them to undertake such a

78. M. Mitchell, pp. 21–22.

79. Betz, *Galatians*, pp. 14ff.

80. These arguments are found now in the published form of his doctoral dissertation entitled *Abraham in Galatians. Epistolary and Rhetorical Contexts* (Sheffield: Sheffield Academic Press, 1989). See also Longenecker, *Galatians*, pp. cv-cxix.

81. One must assess carefully whether one thinks the agitators in Galatia were actually deliberately attacking Paul or his Gospel, or simply arguing that it needed supplementing. It is doubtful they came to Galatia and questioned Paul's apostolic credentials, though they are likely to have disputed the notion that a Law-free Gospel was a fully adequate one. Nor is there any evidence that they were disputing fundamental issues like whether Jesus was the messiah, or whether his death on the cross affected human salvation. At issue was the question how Gentile Christians should live in order to be considered full converts to Christ by Jewish Christians, and in order to be full heirs of the promises made to Abraham. At issue more broadly was how all Christians were to relate to the Mosaic Law. It is not surprising that few people, prior to Paul, had worked out the full implications of the cross of Christ in so far as what it meant for the keeping of the Law. Paul of course does think a Law-free Gospel needs to be maintained and he is willing to argue to that end, but the aim of his arguments is so the Galatians will see the implications of their actual and potential Judaizing activities and refrain from such actions. He is not rehearsing his initial apologetics which he offered in Galatia for he assumes that his converts *still* believe in Christ and in the Gospel but have been led astray so that they do not see its implications for Christian living. In other words the social and deliberative aims of Paul's arguments throughout Galatians needs to be recognized.

drastic action; these words are addressed to Paul's converts not to the agitators, and they are meant to help the Galatians to decide to reject circumcision and reaffirm the Pauline Gospel previously accepted. These distinctions must be kept in mind when one is evaluating the emotive language in Galatians. The question of the character of the material in Gal. 1–2 is particularly at issue in this case.

After an extended discussion of the matter J. H. Schütz argues that what we find in Gal. 1–2 is not a defensive response to an attack on Paul's apostolic office but rather an aggressive and polemical explication of the fact that there is only one Gospel, the Gospel of grace and faith, which must not be compromised by attempting to tack on observance of the Mosaic Law to it.[82] The function of the autobiographical remarks in Gal. 1–2 is certainly not to defend Paul's pre-Christian past, nor for that matter to defend his Christian past. They rather show how God works (by grace through faith in calling and commissioning Paul), and they provide in the example of Paul a paradigm of appropriate conduct for other Christians to follow, and in the case of Peter or Barnabas, examples to shun.[83] The latter had not submitted themselves unswervingly to the truth of the Gospel, while Paul had, and he insisted his converts must follow his example, not theirs (for especially in Peter's case the actions were hypocritical) or that of the agitators. They must become as he is. In Paul's view Gospel truth leads to unity of Jews and Gentiles in Christ, but the Law leads to distinctions, separations, and discord.

In short, if the first two chapters reflect the themes with which deliberative rhetoric is concerned, no matter how polemical they are in tone, we should not see these chapters as an attempt to defend Paul's apostleship, but rather as part of the larger attempt to persuade and influence Galatian belief and conduct vis à vis the Gospel of grace.

What, however, of the view that Paul is defending his Gospel, rather than his apostolicity, in Gal. 1–2? The problem with this view is that Paul does not in fact defend his Gospel in Gal. 1–2, he simply asserts there is only one such Gospel which comes from God, and then in Galatians 3 he goes on to remind the Galatians how they came to be saved in the first place. No defense of grace, faith, or justification takes place in these chapters, in fact there are no formal arguments in Gal. 1–2 at all but rather we primarily find narrative with a paraenetic function in mind. The *propositio* is also not an apologetic argument but rather a careful statement by Paul of what he believes to be true. If Gal. 1–2 cannot be shown to be apologetics, it is even less likely that one can make the case for the rest of Galatians.

---

82. J. H. Schütz, *Paul and Apostolic Authority* (Cambridge: Cambridge University Press, 1975), pp. 128ff.

83. See Schütz, pp. 134ff.

Turning to the arguments of Hansen, as he points out there were always very serious problems with the suggestion that Galatians is an apologetic letter. Betz points to Plato's *Epistle* 7, Isocrates' *Antidosis*, Demosthenes' *De Corona*, Cicero's *Brutus*, and Libanius' *Oratio* as providing the evidence that this type of letter was an established literary type.[84] Unfortunately for this view Plato's *Epistle* 7 is not a real letter; it uses the letter format as a literary fiction so the author can set forth a kind of manifesto combined with a history. Furthermore, Isocrates' *Antidosis* is no letter at all, Demosthenes' *De Corona* is simply a transcript of a speech, Cicero's *Brutus* reviews Roman rhetorical practices, and finally Libanius' *Oratio* 1 is a direct imitation of the aforementioned work by Isocrates! In short, Betz has provided us with no evidence of an apologetic letter tradition that Paul might be following.[85]

By contrast, the evidence that there was such a thing as a rebuke–request letter is considerable. Hansen is able to provide numerous actual examples from the first to the fourth centuries A.D. of this type of letter from the papyri (cf. BGU 850.1–6 from A.D. 76; P. Baden 35.1–11 A.D. 87; P. Mich. 209.1–13; P. Merton 80.1–15 et al.).[86] These sort of letters follow the pattern of beginning with some form of the verb θαυμάζω followed by various rebuking remarks and then in the second half of the letter one or more requests are made as a result of or based on the rebuke or rebukes. This is what we find in Galatians. Notice not only do we find the astonishment and rebuke formulae in Gal. 1.6ff. but the rebuke continues through a series of questions in 3.1–5, statements about negligence that imply a rebuke (4.9) and only *after* all of this is there finally a request or demand made of the audience. The first imperative in Galatians does not come until 4.12 when Paul urges the Galatians to become as he is, but it is then followed by a string of other imperatives (4.27, 30; 5.1, 13, 14, 16; 6.1, 2, 5, 6, 7, 9, 10).[87] The question to be asked then is – in what condition is Paul that they should follow his example, and the answer is given clearly enough by the autobiographical remarks given both before and after this first imperative in 4.12 – namely he is one in whom Christ is formed, even to the point of bearing the marks of the Crucified one in his body (6.17), he is the one loyal to the truth of the Gospel (2.5, 14), the one dead to the law and alive in Christ (2.19; 3.25), the one living by faith and not annulling the grace of God (2.20–21).[88] The Galatians are meant to follow his present Christian example and shun his pre-Christian one. The letter has a paraenetic aim

---

84. Betz is largely followed in this line of argumentation by B. Brinsmead, *Galatians – Dialogical Response to Opponents* (Chico: Scholars Press, 1982), pp. 25ff.

85. See Hansen, pp. 25–27.

86. Various of these are cited in part or in whole by Hansen, pp. 34–43.

87. See Hansen, pp. 42ff. and p. 226 n. 81.

88. See Hansen, pp. 46–47.

throughout and ultimately even the Christological and soteriological remarks work toward that end.[89]

There are several other standard epistolary elements that we find in Galatians. There is of course, for example, the reference to the author adding a signature and a summary after having dictated the earlier part of the letter (6.11; cf. 1 Thess. 3.17; 1 Cor. 16.5). Also the opening salutation is followed by a doxology (1.5), and it may be that this is Paul's self-conscious way of drawing the epistolary section of the document to a close, especially since he does not plan to include the normal thanksgiving section. Though we do not really have a travelogue in this letter,[90] we do find a reference in Gal. 4 to Paul's previous travel in the Galatian province and the Galatians previous reception of him then, which serves much the same function as a travelogue, namely to encourage the Galatians to return to the sort of behavior they initially exhibited when Paul first visited. One can also point to certain stereotyped epistolary formulae such as 'I wish you to know' or 'you know that' (P. Giss. 11.4; cf. P. Mich. 28.16; cf. Gal. 1.11; 3.7; 4.13) or the request formula (BGU 846.10, P. Ent. 82.6; cf. Gal. 4.12), or the use of the vocative often to signal a transition in the letter (P. Mich. 206.4; cf. Gal. 4.19, 28, 31; 5.11, 13), or a closing benediction (Gal. 6.16). These sort of formulae tend to cluster at junctures where there is a transition from one part of the letter to the next, or from one argument to the next.

Whether we view this document as rhetoric or as letter it is a unity and involves a unified series of arguments that have been carefully structured. Hansen noticed the following parallels between the first and second halves of the document:

1.6 – rebuke	4.12 – request
1.13 – disclosure of autobiography	4.13 – disclosure of autobiography
3.7– appeal to Scripture	4.21 – appeal through Scripture
4.9 – rebuking question	5.1 – requested action
4.11 – expression of distress	5.10 – expression of confidence.[91]

The difficulty with this analysis is that it basically omits the last chapter and a half of the letter, and so is not really an analysis of the two halves of the letter. Nevertheless, it does show that there are certain repeated patterns to

---

89. Hansen's thesis will have to be modified somewhat when we discuss what we find in Gal. 5–6. See pp. 359ff. below.

90. Perhaps because Paul could not promise to be coming in the immediate future in view of the crisis in Antioch that was still unresolved, and would be until the crucial meeting in Jerusalem transpired.

91. Hansen, p. 50.

Paul's discourse and Hansen is right to stress about the material at the end of the letter that "the emphasis on freedom, the spelling out of a new relationship to the Law, and the contrast between the flesh and the Spirit are all themes which must be seen as intimately related to the larger context of the letter".[92] Paul in Galatians is not merely firing unrelated salvos at his audience, he has a plan and a direction he intends his series of arguments to tend towards. His words are carefully chosen and the arrangement of the material bears the mark not only of an orderly mind, but of one used to following certain rhetorical patterns of argumentation.

Galatians in its social setting

In comparison to epistles like 1 or 2 Corinthians, not a great deal has been done to analyze Galatians in terms of its social and cultural dimensions, using the tools of the social sciences and cultural anthropology to shed light on the text. This is in some respects surprising because this document, perhaps more than any other in the Pauline corpus, raises the questions about how one gets in, how one stays, and how one goes on in the Christian community (and also in the future kingdom of God; cf. Gal. 5) and what sorts of rites of passage are involved. It is also surprising in view of the evidence in the first two chapters of Galatians that honor challenges seem to have been undertaken by Paul and perhaps his opponents, and that Paul has chosen as one of his rhetorical strategies in this document the bold approach of shaming his converts into rejecting the proposals of the agitators in Galatia. Then too, this document has something to say about social networks between Jerusalem and Antioch, power structures in the early church, and what 'the right hand of *koinonia*' and also what expulsion might amount to in the early church as forms of social interchange. What does Paul mean when he insists he is Christ's agent to the Gentiles? What sort of authority and power does Paul envision himself having, especially when in an unguarded moment he expresses the fear that he might have been running in vain if the Jerusalem pillars had not recognized the legitimacy of what he was doing? One must also ask how Paul's advice in Galatians would have been heard in the social setting of the Galatian churches, especially in view of the fact that 1 Cor. 16.1 and the very preservation of this letter suggests that Paul was heard and heeded by the Galatians.

By way of background for the discussion of these sorts of issues in the commentary let us consider several factors that may illuminate the social setting of the Galatian churches and of Paul's own immediate social

92. Hansen, p. 51.

matrix.[93] If in fact this letter was written in about A.D. 49 it is in order to point out that it was written at a time when the eastern half of the Empire was feeling the effects of a significant food crisis, caused in part by a famine which resulted in a shortage of grain production in Egypt in the mid and late 40s.[94] Famines were not uncommon, but food crises were even more common and in fact can be said to have been of a chronic nature in the mid-first century A.D. and regularly affected various parts of the Mediterranean world.[95] This helps to explain the request in Gal. 2.10 and Paul's eagerness to respond to the request. By means of collecting for famine relief and giving it to the poor in the Judean church, Paul and his co-workers would set up a reciprocity situation and a social network that would implicitly suggest the acceptance of the Pauline largely Gentile churches by the mother church. This larger aim is something Paul clearly desired (cf. 1 Cor. 16.1–3; 2 Cor. 8–9). In this way, not only Paul would have a social network and *koinonia* with the Jerusalem Church but so also would his congregations.

It is interesting, however, that at least this plan of connecting the Galatian churches to Jerusalem may have failed because in his later discussions of the matter in Rom. 15.25–28 he does not mention that the Galatian churches have been pleased to share with the poor among the saints in Jerusalem. Perhaps the Galatians had taken a little too seriously the rhetoric in Gal. 4 where Paul suggests that it is not the earthly Jerusalem but the Jerusalem which is above that really matters. Perhaps they had been cautious knowing that they too could suffer the serious and debilitating effects of a famine.

Consider the Latin inscription set up by Domitian's legate in Galatia from the slightly later period of A.D. 91–93 found at the site of Pisidian Antioch which reads in part:

93. It is my view that Paul, as Gal. 2.11–14 suggests, was some sort of authority figure in the Antioch church probably both before and after his second journey up to Jerusalem. This helps to explain why he may have thought he had the authority to rebuke even Peter and also Barnabas. The *narratio* breaks off with events in Antioch and it is therefore plausible to assume that this is the locale of Paul when he wrote this document. Notice that though they are anonymous, Paul sends greetings to the Galatians from all the 'brothers' who are with Paul (1.2). In other words Paul does not write this document while alone or on the road but out of the setting of an established Christian community that is not in Galatia.

94. See B. W. Winter, "Secular and Christian Responses to Corinthian Famines," *TynBull* 40 (1989), pp. 86–106.

95. See P. Garnsey, *Famine and Food in the Graeco-Roman World. Response to Risk and Crisis* (Cambridge: Cambridge University Press, 1988). One must be able to distinguish between genuine famine which always produced a food crisis, and food crises which could be caused by a host of factors including the hoarding of grain by the well-to-do. Famines were less frequent than food crises. See Garnsey, pp. 3–40.

Since the duoviri and decurions of the most splendid colony of Antioch have written to me that because of the harsh winter the market price of grain has shot up, and since they have requested that the people have the means of buying it, with Good Luck on our side, all those who are either citizens of the colony of Antioch or are inhabitants of it shall openly before the duoviri of the colony of Antioch within thirty days of the time when this edict of mine has been posted, [state] how much each person has and in what place, and how much for seed or for annual allowance of his family he deducts, and the rest of the grain, the whole supply, he shall make available to buyers of the colony of Antioch . . . since it is most unjust for the source of anyone's profit to be the hunger of his citizens, exceeding one denarius for one modus as the price of grain (is a practice) I forbid. [Lucius Antistius Rusticus, legate of Imperator Caesar]

A second social issue that may inform our reading of Galatians is the state and status of Jews in Roman colonies in Asia Minor, especially in light of the expulsion of Jews and apparently Jewish Christians from Rome in A.D. 49 (cf. Acts 18). Were the Jews in Asia Minor in A.D. 49 feeling marginalized enough that any attempts at proselytism pointed in their direction or the very existence of a local Christian congregation which had led people out of the synagogue was likely to be met with a hostile response by at least some? This question must be raised in view of Paul's passing remarks to the effect that the Galatians themselves were being persecuted by 'the child who was born according to the flesh' (i.e., Jews) whether he is referring to the Judaizers or non-Christian Jews in Galatia. It may also be raised in view of the various expulsions and restrictions of Jews during the reigns of Caligula and then of Claudius leading up to this point in time.[96] Notice in Gal. 6.12 the reference to the agitators *themselves* being persecuted for the cross of Christ, and that this is why they are insisting on the Galatians being circumcised. These references certainly comport with the picture painted in Acts 13–14 in which Paul and his co-workers are attacked by some Jews from the synagogue, particularly in Pisidian Antioch and in Iconium. Galatians suggests this was an ongoing problem and that apparently the agitators were seeking to solve it by appeasement, by making the Christian community follow Jewish practices to stop the persecution.

Another social factor that may have come into play is the increasing pressure brought to bear throughout the Empire by the cult of the Emperor. We know for a fact from inscriptional evidence that the 'god' Augustus and the goddess 'Roma' were worshipped in the Roman province of Galatia already as early as during the reign of Tiberius.[97] This cult was becoming increasingly popular and prominent throughout the first century and nowhere outside of

96. See my *The Acts of the Apostles*, pp. 506ff.
97. See the translation of the inscription in R. K. Sherk, *The Roman Empire: Augustus to Hadrian* (Cambridge: Cambridge University Press, 1988), pp. 73-74.

Italy was there more devotion to it than in Asia Minor. Partly the popularity of the Imperial cult, as the inscription OGIS 533 suggests, was due to the public banquets, lavish spectacles, and gymnastic competitions sponsored, but also partly due to the distribution of important commodities, such as oil, in a variety of places.

The Romans were wise enough to make the Galatians themselves the high priests of this cult to ensure local interest and devotion to the cult.[98] The reason this matter could have affected fledgling Christians in Galatia is that if it could be shown that they were *not* Jews, they would not be exempt from offering or at least participating in the sacrifices and celebrations of the Imperial Cult, especially in the Roman colony cities such as Pisidian Antioch and Iconium. The most dominant building in Pisidian Antioch when Paul will have visited it would have been the Temple of divine Augustus in the center of the city.[99] One possible solution to this problem would be to claim that the church was the true Israel of God (see Gal. 6.16) a claim that non-Christian Jews might have been prepared to resist even with violence, or alternatively Christians could 'Judaize', practicing circumcision and the like so that it would appear clear that Christians were Jews, and thus there would be no social pressure or persecution if they did not participate in the Imperial Cult. Either of these scenarios might be behind the elliptical remarks about agitators urging Gentile Christians in Galatia to practice Judaism, but then why does Paul refer only to the persecution of the agitators themselves?

In any case, one must not under-estimate the importance of the Emperor cult as a social factor in everyday Galatian life. As S. Mitchell says "one cannot avoid the impression that the obstacle which stood in the way of the progress of Christianity, and the force which would have drawn new adherents back to conformity with the prevailing paganism, was the public worship of the emperor. The packed calendar of the ruler cult dragooned the citizens of Antioch into observing days, months, seasons, and years which it laid down for special recognition and celebration."[100] It is believable that the Judaizers were offering the Galatians a way out of observing the Imperial cult's calendar, by substituting the Jewish calendrical celebrations, which would be seen as a legitimate substitute and would not cause Gentile Galatian Christians to lose all their status and standing in Galatian society, as would participating in a novel unsanctioned *superstitio* like 'Gentile Pauline Christianity'. Nevertheless, we will see reasons in the commentary to

---

98. Sherk, p. 38 n. 3 points out that the names of most of the listed high priests in this inscription are Celtic names.

99. See G. W. Hansen, "Galatia", *AIIFCS Vol. 2*, p. 394.

100. S. Mitchell, *Anatolia: Land, Men and Gods in Asia Minor. Vol. 2: The Rise of the Church* (Oxford: Clarendon Press, 1993), p. 10.

doubt that the Imperial Cult is the ultimate reason for the agitators' pressure on the Galatians.[101]

It is appropriate to ask what we know about Judaism in the Galatian province apart from what can be discerned from the book of Acts. It must be admitted that the evidence is not plentiful,[102] but Josephus tells us that during the reign of the Seleucid ruler Antiochus III Jews were removed from Mesopotamia and Babylon to Phrygia and Lydia in order to help pacify the area and help insure a stable, normal hard-working populus in the region (*Ant.* 12.3). There is also inscriptional evidence from northern Galatia of houses of prayer and worship of the one Almighty God and of the same in Pisidia but the evidence is not plentiful.[103] There is, however, no good reason to doubt that there were Jews and Jewish assemblies in the cities Paul visited in south Galatia, not least because Josephus informs us that Jews had been coming to the region since at least the time of the Seleucids, and Acts may provide independent evidence to this fact. There is in addition inscriptional evidence for God-worshippers or God-fearers elsewhere in Asia Minor where there was a Jewish presence and there is no reason why Galatia should be any different on this score.[104] It is, however, possibly significant that the inscriptional evidence for women playing important roles in Judaism in Galatia is non-existent, unlike the case with other parts of Asia Minor. Acts 13.50 is possibly, but probably not, evidence to the contrary.[105]

The issue of leadership structures is an important one and there are important clues in Galatians that help us get an inside glimpse of some of the things going on in early Christianity. We notice the stress at the outset on Paul's apostolic status. Clearly enough Paul's authority rested on his claim that God had singled him out for a particular mission, and the evidence that his preaching was blessed by God as evidenced by conversions, miracles, the presence of spiritual gifts. His authority did not arise from his connection with Jesus' family or with the Twelve. This was not problematic when Paul was venturing into new mission territory or relating to his own converts, but it apparently was problematic when Paul tried to relate to other leaders in early Christianity, and particularly those who had ties with Jesus' family or were

---

101. See pp. 205ff. below.

102. As W. M. Ramsay, *A Historical Commentary on St. Paul's Epistle to the Galatians* (New York: Putnam's, 1900), pp. 192–93.

103. See the discussion by P. Trebilco, *Jewish Communities in Asia Minor* (Cambridge: Cambridge University Press, 1991), pp. 136–37, and the further evidence of Jews in northern Galatia on p. 243 n. 49.

104. See Trebilco, *Jewish Communities*, pp. 152–65.

105. On women assuming important roles in Diaspora synagogues, including in other parts of Asia Minor see B. Brooten, *Women Leaders in the Ancient Synagogue* (Atlanta: Scholars Press, 1982), p. 23 and notes.

members of the Twelve or of the Jerusalem church. Paul was never a regular participant in the Jerusalem church, and though he was known to its leaders and perhaps in some of the house churches in Jerusalem itself that he had persecuted years before, we must take very seriously the fact that Paul says his face was not familiar in the Judean churches (1.22).[106] It is difficult to have 'face' in such congregations when one's face is unknown, or possibly feared even several years after one's conversion.

Though Paul's rhetoric in Gal. 1–2 suggests that the pillars added nothing to Paul's *auctoritas*, it is fair to say that they were in a position to take something away, if his work was not recognized by the leaders of Christianity's mother church. It was critical to develop certain social networks between the Jerusalem church and Paul's churches if Paul's converts were to be in partnership with the mother church in various ventures. In fact, we will see that Paul acts like many other ancient Mediterranean persons in that he needs corporate affirmation of his work and sense of identity.[107]

It is difficult to know how much to make of the fact that James is mentioned first by Paul in Gal. 2.9, but the reference to persons who came from James in 2.12 suggests a bit more strongly that the titular head of the Jerusalem church was James, an impression Acts, especially in Acts 15, gives as well, though the reference to Peter, James and John as pillars suggests there was an inner circle of three top leaders. It appears, however, that Peter also was extremely important, for Paul goes to see him in particular (Gal. 1.18), and he in particular is said to be entrusted with the missionary work to Jews (Gal. 2.7). It may be that James was the ongoing leader in Jerusalem in a sense by default, for Peter was away much of the time (cf. Gal. 2.11–14).

What all of this suggests is a somewhat fluid situation, and nothing whatsoever is said about laying on of hands of anyone at this point. Paul is looking for endorsement for and co-operation with his already inherently valid ministry, not 'ordination', to speak anachronistically. Christianity at this point is more of a sect than an institutional church, even though it is willing to speak of pillars (of the Christian temple?) already standing in the persons of Peter, James, and John.

Much more reflection is needed on the social networks exhibited in Galatians including the relationship between Paul and his converts, the relationship between the Galatians and the converts elsewhere including in Antioch, the relationship between Paul, Barnabas and Titus, the relationship between Paul and Peter, the relationship between Paul and James, the relationship between James' emissaries and the leadership of the Antioch

---

106. About these matters cf. Dunn, *Jesus, Paul, and the Law. Studies in Mark and Galatians* (Louisville: Westminster/John Knox, 1990), pp. 108–28.

107. See pp. 107ff. below.

church, the relationship between Paul and James' emissaries, and of course the relationship between Paul and the agitators in Galatia. For example, the passing reference to Paul's going up to Jerusalem with Barnabas and Titus in Gal. 2 suggests Paul is part of a delegation to Jerusalem, not making a private trip. We will attempt to discuss some of these webs of power in the commentary.

Two scholars have argued at some length that we need to reflect on the development in early Christianity from reform movement within Judaism to independent sect. P. Esler has applied sect typology primarily to Luke-Acts, while F. Watson applied it to Paul's letters.[108] We will have more to say about sect analysis in the commentary itself, but here it is worthwhile to state a major thesis of this particular commentary. A major reason for the tensions between Paul and the Jerusalem church, especially its more conservative Jewish members, was that when he wrote Galatians Paul was already thinking in terms of Christianity being a sect, while the agitators and perhaps James and others of the Jerusalem church invisioned the church as an extension of or a reform movement within Judaism.[109] For Paul, the church was Jew and Gentile united in Christ and this *was* the Israel of God, something separate from non-Christian Jews, while others such as the Judaizers thought more in terms of a reform movement, and still others such as Peter were in principle in agreement with Paul, but were subject to pressure and retrenchments on pragmatic grounds, perhaps to keep peace in the church.

There are a variety of honor and shame issues raised by Galatians involving the relationship between Paul and the pillars in Jerusalem. We intend to address these issues at various points. These will include why it is that Paul chooses to shame the Galatians during his rhetorical discourse, why it is that Paul also chooses to use polemics when speaking of the agitators and the 'spies' but is more restrained when speaking of others such as Peter or James. We must also discuss P. Esler's theory that Paul had offered an honor challenge to the Judaizers in Jerusalem and had won, and thus they sought revenge against him both in Antioch and elsewhere.[110] The vice and fruit lists must also be examined closely in the light of ancient concepts of honor and shame. It will also be necessary to discuss the egalitarian rhetoric found in Gal. 3.28 and ask what its actually practical and social implications seem to have been in Paul's

---

108. P. Esler, *Community and Gospel in Luke-Acts. The Social and Political Motivation of Lucan Theology* (Cambridge: Cambridge University Press, 1987), and F. Watson, *Paul, Judaism and Gentiles: A Sociological Approach* (Cambridge: Cambridge University Press, 1986). Both are drawing on the important work of B. R. Wilson cf. his *Religion in Sociological Perspective* (Oxford: Oxford University Press, 1982).

109. I do not subscribe to Watson's theory that Paul was first a failed missionary to Jews, before he and Barnabas tried evangelizing Gentiles.

110. See P. Esler, "Making and Breaking an Agreement Mediterranean Style: A New Reading of Galatians 2.1–14," *Biblical Interpretation* 3 (1995), pp. 285–314.

mind. The language of zeal is important in Paul's discussion of his past and we must discuss what sort of behavior Paul had actually seen as honorable – had he been a Zealot before his conversion? Finally, it will be important to discuss the in-group and out-group language found throughout Galatians, and the accompanying discussion of rites of inclusion and exclusion, and of course the related matter of conversion. How was Paul able to convince Gentiles that conversion to a particular Jewish sect focusing on a crucified messiah was a good, noble, honorable, right, and beneficial thing to do? These are just some of the issues Galatians raises for us. After a bibliography we will turn to the commentary itself.

Bibliography

This bibliography is not intended to be exhaustive by any means and in fact should be seen as a complement to the one found in my *Conflict and Community in Corinth: a Socio-Rhetorical Commentary on 1 and 2 Corinthians* (Grand Rapids: Eerdmans; Carlisle: Paternoster 1995). I am indebted to my research assistants Don Ebert, John Wadhams and Jared Treadway for their help in preparation of this work. The abbreviations for journals and series are the standard JBL abbreviations and I have omitted reference to the standard dictionaries, lexicons and grammars. There are a few items in this bibliography which have unfortunately appeared too recently for me to assess.

Commentaries

Becker, J. *Die Briefe an die Galater* (Göttingen: Vandenhoeck & Ruprecht, 1981).

Betz, Hans D. *Galatians: A Commentary on Paul's Letter to the Churches in Galatia* (Philadelphia: Fortress, 1979).

Bligh, J. *Galatians* (London: St Paul, 1969).

Borse, Udo. *Der Brief an die Galater* (Regensburg: Pustet, 1984).

Bruce, F. F. *The Epistle of Paul to the Galatians* (Grand Rapids: Eerdmans, 1982).

Burton, E. De Witt. *A Critical and Exegetical Commentary on the Epistle to the Galatians* (Edinburgh: T. & T. Clark, 1921).

Calvin, J. *The Epistles of Paul the Apostle to the Galatians, Ephesians, Philippians and Colossians*, trans. T. H. L. Parker (Grand Rapids: Eerdmans, 1965).

Cousar, Charles B. *Galatians: Interpretation Commentary* (Atlanta: John Knox, 1982).

Dunn, J. D. G. *The Epistle to the Galatians* (Peabody: Hendrickson, 1993).

Fung, Ronald Y. K. *The Epistle to the Galatians*, NICNT (Grand Rapids: Eerdmans, 1988).

Lagrange, M. J. *Saint Paul Epître aux Galates* (Paris: Gabalda, 2nd ed., 1925).

Lietzmann, H. *An die Galater* (Tübingen: Mohr, 1910).

Lightfoot, J. B. *Saint Paul's Epistle to the Galatians* (London: Macmillan, 1896).

Longenecker, Richard N. *Galatians* (Dallas: Word, 1990).

Luhrmann, D. *Galatians*, Continental Commentaries (Minneapolis: Fortress, 1992).

McKnight, S. *Galatians. The NIV Application Bible Commentary* (Grand Rapids: Zondervan, 1995).

Matera, Frank J. *Galatians*, Sacra Pagina 9 (Collegeville, Minnesota: Liturgical Press, 1992).

Mussner, F. *Der Galaterbrief* (Freiburg: Herder, 3rd ed., 1977).

Osiek, Carolyn. *Galatians* (Wilmington: Glazier, 1980).

Ramsay, William M. *A Historical Commentary on St. Paul's Epistle to the Galatians* (Grand Rapids: Baker, reprint 1979).

Ridderbos, H. N. *The Epistle of Paul to the Churches of Galatia* (Grand Rapids: Eerdmans, reprint 1981).

Schlier, H. *Der Brief an die Galater* (Göttingen: Vandenhoeck & Ruprecht, 1965).

Witherington, B. III. *Conflict and Community in Corinth. A Socio-Rhetorical Commentary* (Grand Rapids: Eerdmans, 1995).

Witherington, B. III. *Friendship and Finances in Philippi* (Valley Forge: Trinity Press International, 1994).

Witherington, B. III. *The Acts of the Apostles. A Socio-Rhetorical Commentary* (Grand Rapids: Eerdmans, 1997).

Zahn, T. *Der Brief des Paulus an die Galater* (Leipzig: Deichert, 1922).

Ziesler, J. *The Epistle to the Galatians* (London: Epworth, 1992).

Monographs, Dissertations, Articles and Lectures

Abegg, M. "Paul, 'Works of the Law', and MMT," *BAR* 20.6 (1994) 52–55.

Arnold, James P. "Jewish Christianity in Galatians: A Study of the Teachers and Their Gospel," PhD diss., Rice, 1991.

Atkins, R. *Egalitarian Community. Ethnography and Exegesis* (Tuscaloosa: University of Alabama Press, 1991).

Baarda, T. "*Ti eti diokomai* in Gal. 5:11: Apodosis or Parenthesis?" *NovT* 34 (1992) 250–56.

Baasland, Ernst. "Persecution, A Neglected Feature in the Letter to the Galatians," *ST* 38 (Oslo 1984) 135–50.

Bachmann, Michael. *Sunder oder Ubertreter: Studien zur Argumentation in Gal. 2:15ff.*, WUNT 59 (Tübingen: Mohr, 1992).

Bahr, G. J. "The Subscriptions in the Pauline Letters," *JBL* 87 (1968), 27–41.

Balsdon, J. P. V. D. *Romans and Aliens* (London: Duckworth, 1979).

Balthasar, Hans Urs von. "Der sich für mich dahingegeben hat" (Gal. 2:20): *Geist und Leben* 53 (1980) 416–19.

Bammel, E. "Galater 1, 23," *ZNW* 59 (1968) 108–12.

Bammel, E. "Gottes ΔΙΑΘΗΚΗ (Gal. 3.15–17) und das jüdische Rechtsdenken," *NTS* 6 (1960) 313–19.

Bandstra, A. J. *The Law and the Elements of World: an Exegetical Study in Aspects of Paul's Teaching* (Kampen: Kok, 1964).

Barclay, J. M. G. "Mirror-reading a Polemical Letter: Galatians as a Test Case," *JSNT* 31 (1987) 73–93.

Barclay, J. M. G. *Obeying the Truth* (Edinburgh: T. & T. Clark, 1988).

Barker, P. G. "Allegory and Typology in Galatians 4:21–31," *StVladTheoQuart* 38 (2, 1994) 193–209.

Barrett, C. K. "The Allegory of Sarah and Hagar," in *Essays on Paul* (Philadelphia: Westminster, 1982), 154–70.

Barrett, C. K. *Freedom and Obligation* (London: SPCK, 1985).

Barrett C. K. "Paul and the Pillar Apostles," in *Studia Paulina*, J. De Zwann Festschrift, ed. J. N. Sevenster (Haarlem: Bohn, 1953), 15–19.

Barrett, C. K. *The Signs of an Apostle* (London: Epworth, 1970).

Bauckham, R. J. "Barnabas in Galatians," *JSNT* 2 (1979) 61–71.

Bauckham, R. J. "James and the Gentiles," in *History, Literature, and Society in the Book of Acts*, ed. B. Witherington (Cambridge: Cambridge University Press, 1996), 154–84.

Bauckham, R. J. *Jude and the Relatives of Jesus in the Early Church* (Edinburgh: T. & T. Clark, 1990).

Beker, J. C. *Paul the Apostle: The Triumph of God in Life and Thought* (Philadelphia: Fortress, 1980).

Belleville, Linda L. "'Under Law': Structural Analysis and the Pauline Concept of Law in Galatians 3.21–4.11," *JSNT* 26 (1986) 53–78.

Berchman, R. M. "Galatians (1.1–5): Paul and Greco-Roman Rhetoric," in *New Perspectives on Ancient Judaism. Volume Three: Judaic and Christian Interpretation of Texts: Contents and Contexts*, eds. J. Neusner and E. S. Frerichs (Lanham: University Press of America, 1987), 1–15.

Berenyi, Gabriella. "Gal. 2:20: A Pre-Pauline or a Pauline Text?" *Biblica* 65 (1984) 490–537.

Betz, H. D. "In Defense of the Spirit: Paul's Letter to the Galatians as a Document of Early Christian Apologetics," in *Aspects of Religious Propaganda in Judaism and Early Christianity,* ed. E. Schüssler Fiorenza (Notre Dame: University of Notre Dame Press, 1976), 99–114.

Betz, H. D. "Galatians, Epistle to the," *ABD* II, 872–75.

Betz, H. D. "The Literary Composition and Function of Paul's Letter to the Galatians," *NTS* 21 (1975) 353–79.

Black, David A. "Weakness Language in Galatians," *GraceTJ* 4 (1983) 15–36.

Blessing, K. "Yet without Sin: the Meaning of the Barren Woman at Galatians 4.27," 1996 SBL lecture.

Bligh, J. *Galatians in Greek* (Detroit: University of Detroit Press, 1966).

Boers, Hendrikus. "We who are by inheritance Jews, not from Gentiles, sinners," *JBL* 111 (1992) 273–281.

Borchert, G. L. "A Key to Pauline Thinking – Galatians 3:23–29: Faith and the New Humanity," *RevExp* 91 (2, 1994) 145–51.

Boring, M. E. et al. eds. *Hellenistic Commentary to the New Testament* (Nashville: Abingdon, 1995).

Botha, P. J. J. "Letter Writing and Oral Communication in Antiquity: Suggested Implications for the Interpretation of Paul's Letter to the Galatians," *Scriptura* 42 (1992) 17–34.

Bowersock, G. W. *Roman Arabia,* Cambridge: Harvard University Press, 1983.

Boyarin, D. "Was Paul an 'Anti-Semite'? A Reading of Galatians 3–4," *UnSemQuartRev* 47 (1–2, 1993) 47–80.

Brinsmead, B. H. "Galatians as Dialogical Response to Opponents," PhD diss., Andrews, 1979.

Brinsmead, B. H. *Galatians – Dialogical Response to Opponents* (Chico: Scholars Press, 1982).

Brooten, B. *Women Leaders in the Ancient Synagogue* (Atlanta: Scholars Press, 1982).

Buckel, John. "'The curse of the law': An Exegetical Investigation of Galatians 3:10–14," PhD diss., Leuven, 1988.

Byrne, B. *'Sons of God' – 'Seed of Abraham': a Study of the Idea of Sonship of God of all Christians in Paul against the Jewish Background* (Rome: Biblical Institute Press, 1979).

Callan, Terrence. "Pauline Midrash: The Exegetical Background of Gal. 3:19b," *JBL* 99 (1980) 549–67.

Campbell, T. H. "Paul's 'Missionary Journeys' as Reflected in his Letters," *JBL* 74 (1955) 80–87.

Clemens, J. S. "St. Paul's Handwriting," *ET* 24 (1912–13) 380.

Cohn-Sherbok, D. "Paul and Rabbinic Exegesis," *SJT* 35 (1982), 130–37.

Cole-Turner, Ronald S. *Anti-heretical Issues in the Debate Over Galatians 2:11–14 in the Letters of St. Augustine to Jerome*, Augustinian Studies 11 (Villanova, 1980), 155–66.

Collins, J. J. "A Symbol of Otherness: Circumcision and Salvation in the First Century," in *To See Ourselves as Others See Us: Christians, Jews, "Others" in Late Antiquity*, ed. J. Neusner and E. S. Frerichs (Chico: Scholars Press, 1985), 163–86.

Cook, David. "The Prescript as Programme in Galatians," *JTS* 43 (1992) 511–19.

Corley, B. "Reasoning 'By Faith': Whys and Wherefores of the Law in Galatians," *SWJournTheol* 37 (1, 1994) 17–22.

Cosgrove, C. H. "Arguing Like a Mere Human Being: Galatians 3:15–18 in Rhetorical Perspective," *NTS* 34 (1988) 536–49.

Cosgrove, C. H. *The Cross and the Spirit: A Study in the Argument and Theology of Galatians* (Macon: Mercer, 1988).

Cosgrove, C. H. "The Law has Given Sarah no Children (Gal. 4.21–30)," *NovT* 19 (1987) 219–35.

Cosgrove, C. H. "The Law and the Spirit: An Investigation into the Theology of Galatians," PhD diss., Princeton Theological Seminary, 1984.

Cosgrove, C. H. "The Mosaic Covenant Teaches Faith: A Study in Galatians 3," *WestTJ* 41 (1978) 146–64.

Cranford, L. L. "A Rhetorical Reading of Galatians," *SWJournTheol* 37 (1, 1994) 4–10.

Cranford, M. "The Possibility of Perfect Obedience: Paul and an Implied Promise in Galatians 3:10 and 5:3," *NovT* 36 (3, 1994) 242–58.

Cronje, J. "The Strategem of the Rhetorical Question in Galatians 4:9–10 as a means toward persuasion," *Neotestamentica* 26 (1992) 417–24.

Dahl, N. A. "Der Name Israel: Zur Auslegung von Gal. 6.16," *Judaica* 6 (1950) 161–70.

Daube, D. "Rabbinic Methods of Interpretation and Hellenistic Rhetoric," *HUCA* 22 (1949) 239–62.

Dautzenberg, Gerhard. "'Da ist nicht mannlich und weiblich': zur Interpretation von Gal. 3:28," *Kairos* 24 (1982) 181–206.

Davies, W. D. *Jewish and Pauline Studies* (London: SPCK, 1974).

Davies, W. D. *Paul and Rabbinic Judaism. Some Rabbinic Elements in Pauline Theology*, 4th ed. (Philadelphia: Fortress, 1980).

De Vries, C. E. "Paul's 'Cutting Remarks' about a Race: Galatians 5.1–12," in *Current Issues in Biblical and Patristic Interpretation* ed. G. F. Hawthorne (Grand Rapids: Eerdmans, 1975), 115–20.

Denton, Peter T. "'No longer a slave but a son': A Model for Pauline Ethics," PhD diss., Durham: Duke, 1991.

Derrett, J. Duncan M. "'Running' in Paul: The Midrashic Potential of Hab. 2:2," *Biblica* 66 (1985) 560–67.

Dodd, C. H. "Ἔννομος Χριστοῦ," in *More New Testament Studies* (Manchester: Manchester University Press, 1968), 134–48.

Dodd, C. H. *The Mind of Paul: Change and Development* (Manchester: John Rylands Library, 1934).

Dolamo, R. T. H. "Rhetorical Speech in Galatians," *Tviat 17* (Sovenga: SAf 1989), 30–37.

Donaldson, T. L. "The 'Curse of the Law' and the Inclusion of the Gentiles: Galatians 3:13–14," *NTS* 32 (1986) 94–112.

Donaldson, T. L. "Zealot and Convert: The Origin of Paul's Christ-Torah Antithesis," *CBQ* 51 (1989) 655–82.

Du Toit, A. B. "Alienation and Re-Identification as Pragmatic Strategies in Galatians," *Neotestamentica* 26 (2, 1992) 279–95.

Du Toit, A. B. "Galatians 6:13: A Possible Solution to an Old Exegetical Problem," *Neotestamentica* 28 (1, 1994) 157–61.

Dunn, J. D. G. *Christology in the Making* (Philadelphia: Westminster, 1980).

Dunn, J. D. G. "Echoes of an Inter-Jewish Polemic in Paul's Letter to the Galatians," *JBL* 112 (3, 1993) 459–77.

Dunn, J. D. G. "4QMMT and Galatians," *NTS* 43 (1997) 147–53.

Dunn, J. D. G. "The Incident at Antioch," *JSNT* 18 (1983) 3–57.

Dunn, J. D. G. *Jesus, Paul, and the Law. Studies in Mark and Galatians* (Louisville: Westminster/John Knox, 1990).

Dunn, J. D. G. ed., *Paul and the Mosaic Law* (Tübingen: Mohr, 1996).

Dunn, J. D. G. "The Relationship Between Paul and Jerusalem According to Galatians 1 and 2," *NTS* 28 (1982) 461–78.

Dunn, J. D. G. "The Theology of Galatians." SBL Seminar Papers 1988, 1–16, and also "The Theology of Galatians," in *Pauline Theology Vol. I,* ed. J. M. Bassler (Minneapolis: Fortress, 1991), 125–46.

Dunn, J. D. G. *The Theology of Paul's Letter to the Galatians* (Cambridge: Cambridge University Press, 1993).

Dunn, J. D. G. "Works of the Law and the Curse of the Law (Galatians 3:10–14)," *NTS* 31 (1985) 523–42.

Dupont, J. "Pierre et Paul à Antioche et à Jerusalem," *Recherches de Science et Religieuse* 45 (1957) 42–60, 225–39.

Duvall, J. S. "'Identity-Performance Result': Tracing Paul's Argument in Galatians 5 and 6," *SWJournTheol* 37 (1, 1994) 30–38.

Duvall, J. S. "Pauline Lexical Choice Revisited: A Paradigmatic Analysis of Selected Terms of Exhortation in Galatians 5 and 6." *FilolNT* 7 (13, 1994) 17–31.

Easton, B. S. "New Testament Ethical Lists," *JBL* 51 (1932), pp. 1–12.

Ebeling, Gerhard. *Die Wahrheit des Evangeliums: eine Lesehilfe zum Galaterbrief* (Tübingen: Mohr, 1981).

Elliott, J. K. "Paul, Galatians, and the Evil Eye," *CurrTheoMiss.* 17 (1990) 262–73.

Elliott, J. K. "The Use of ἕτερος in the New Testament," *ZNW* 60 (1969) 140–41.

Ellis, E. E. *Paul's Use of the OT* (Edinburgh: Oliver & Boyd, 1957).

Ellis, E. E. *Prophecy and Hermeneutic in Early Christianity: New Testament Essays* (Tübingen: Mohr, 1978).

Eshbaugh, H. "Textual Variants and Theology: a Study of the Galatians Text of Papyrus 46," *JSNT* 3 (1979) 60–72.

Esler, P. F. *Community and Gospel in Luke-Acts. The Social and Political Motivation of Lucan Theology* (Cambridge: Cambridge University Press, 1987).

Esler, P. F. "Family Imagery and Christian Identity in Gal. 5.13–6.10," *Constructing Early Christian Families: Family as Social Reality and Metaphor*, ed. H. Moxnes (London and New York: Routledge, 1997), 121–49.

Esler, P. F. *The First Christians in their Social Worlds* (London: Routledge, 1994).

Esler, P. F. "Group Boundaries and Intergroup Conflict in Galatians: A New Reading of Galatians 5.13–6.10," 1994 SBL lecture.

Esler, P. F. "Making and Breaking an Agreement Mediterranean Style: A New Reading of Galatians 2.1–14," *Biblical Interpretation* 3.3 (1995) 285–314.

Fairweather, J. "The Epistle to the Galatians and Classical Rhetoric: Parts 1 and 2," *TynBull* 45.1 (1994) 1–38.

Fairweather, J. "The Epistle to the Galatians and Classical Rhetoric: Part 3," *TynBull* 45.2 (1994) 213–43.

Farmer, William R. "Galatians and the Second-century development of the Regula Fidei," *SecC* 4 (1984) 143–70.

Fee, G. D. "Freedom and the Life of Obedience (Galatians 5:1–6:18)," *RevExp* 91 (2, 1994) 201–17.

Fee, G. D. *God's Empowering Presence. The Holy Spirit in the Letters of Paul* (Peabody: Hendrickson, 1994).

Ferguson, E. *Backgrounds of Early Christianity* (Grand Rapids: Eerdmans, 2nd ed. 1993).

Fitzgerald, J. T. *Cracks in an Earthen Vessel* (Atlanta: Scholars Press, 1988).

Fitzmyer, J. A. "Some Notes on Aramaic Epistolography," *JBL* 93 (1974) 201–25.

Fitzmyer, J. A. "The Use of Explicit Old Testament Quotations in Qumran Literature and in the New Testament," *NTS* 7 (1961) 297–333.

Fletcher, Douglas K. "The Singular Argument of Paul's Letter to the Galatians," PhD diss., Princeton 1982.

Forbes, C. "Comparison, Self-Praise and Irony," *NTS* 32 (1986) 1–30.

Fowl, S. "Who Can Read Abraham's Story? Allegory and Interpretive Power in Galatians," *JSNT* 55 (1994) 77–95.

Fraser, J. "Inheritance by Adoption and Marriage in Phrygia," *Studies in the History and Art of the Eastern Provinces of the Roman Empire*, ed. W. M. Ramsay (Aberdeen: Aberdeen University Press, 1906) 140–50.

Fredricksen, P. "Judaism and Circumcision of Gentiles, and the Apocalyptic Hope: Another Look at Galatians 1 and 2," *JTS* 42 (1991) 532–64.

Fung, Ronald Y. K. "A Note on Galatians 3:19–4:7," *JETS* 25 (1982) 53–62.

Furnish, V. P. *The Love Commandment in the New Testament* (Nashville: Abingdon, 1972).

Furnish, V. P. *Theology and Ethics in Paul* (Nashville: Abingdon, 1968).

Gardiner, E. N. *Greek Athletic Sports and Festivals* (Oxford: Clarendon Press, 1955).

Garnsey, P. *Famine and Food in the Graeco-Roman World. Response to Risk and Crisis* (Cambridge: Cambridge University Press, 1988).

Gaston, L. "Angels and Gentiles in Early Judaism and in Paul," *SR* 11 (1982) 65–75.

Gaston, L. *Paul and the Torah* (Vancouver: University of British Columbia Press, 1987).

Gaventa, B. R. *From Darkness to Light: Aspects of Conversion in the New Testament* (Philadelphia: Fortress, 1986).

Gaventa, B. R. "Galatians 1 and 2: Autobiography as Paradigm," *NovT* 28 (1986) 309–26.

Gaventa, B. R. "The Maternity of Paul: an Exegetical Study of Galatians 4.19," in *The Conversation Continues: Studies in Paul and John* (Grand Rapids: Eerdmans, 1990), 189–201.

Gaventa, B. R. "The Singularity of the Gospel: A Reading of Galatians," SBL Seminar Papers 1988, 17–26.

Goddard, A. J. and S. A. Cummins. "Ill or Ill-Treated? Conflict and Persecution as the Context of Paul's Original Ministry in Galatia (Galatians 4:12–20)," *JSNT* (1993) 93–126.

Gordon, T. D. "A Note on ΠΑΙΔΑΓΩΓΟΣ in Galatians 3.24–25," *NTS* 35 (1989) 150–54.

Gordon, T. D. "The Problem at Galatia," *Int* 41 (1987) 32–43.

Grabe, P. J. "Paul's Assertion of Obedience as a Function of Persuasion," *Neotestamentica* 26 (2, 1992) 351–58.

Grant, R. M. "Neither Male Nor Female," *BibRes* 37 (1992) 5–14.

Gregersen, V. "Pagan and Jew. Literary-critical Investigation of the Letter to the Galatians," *DanskTeolTids* 56 (1, 1993) 1–18. [Danish]

Griffin, B. W. "The Paleographical Dating of p46," Nov. 1996 SBL lecture.

Gromacki, Robert G. *Stand Fast in Liberty: An Exposition of Galatians* (Grand Rapids: Baker, 1979).

Hall, J. "Paul, the Lawyer, and the Law," *JLawRel* 3 (St. Paul, 1985) 331–79.

Hall, R. G. "Arguing like an Apocalypse: Galatians and an Ancient Topos outside the Greco-Roman Rhetorical Tradition," *NTS* 42 (1996) 434–53.

Hall, R. G. "Circumcision," *ABD* I, pp. 1025–34.

Hall, R. G. "Epispasm and the Dating of Ancient Jewish Writings," *Journal for the Study of Pseudepigrapha* 2 (1988) 71–86.

Hall, R. G. "Historical Inference and Rhetorical Effect," in *Persuasive Artistry. Studies in New Testament Rhetoric in Honor of George A. Kennedy,* ed. D. F. Watson (Sheffield: JSOT Press, 1991), 308–20.

Hall, R. G. "The Rhetorical Outline for Galatians: A Reconsideration." *JBL* 106 (1987) 277–87.

Hansen, G. W. *Abraham in Galatians. Epistolary and Rhetorical Contexts* (Sheffield: Sheffield Academic Press, 1989).

Hansen, G. W. "Galatia", in *The Book of Acts in its First Century Settings Vol. 2,* ed. D. Gill and C. Gempf (Grand Rapids: Eerdmans, 1994), 377–95.

Hansen, G. W. "Paul's Three-Dimensional Application of Genesis 15:6 in Galatians," *Trinity Theological Journal* 1 (Singapore 1989), 59–77.

Hanson, A. T. "The Origin of Paul's Use of *paidagogos* for the Law," *JSNT* 34 (1988) 71–76.

Harrisville, R. A. "Πιστίς Χριστοῦ: Witness of the Fathers," *NovT* 36 (1994) 233–41.

Hays, R. B. "Christology and Ethics in Galatians: The Law of Christ," *CBQ* 49 (1987) 268–90.

Hays, R. B. *Echoes of Scripture in the Letters of Paul* (New Haven: Yale University Press, 1989).

Hays, R. B. *The Faith of Jesus Christ: An Investigation of the Narrative Structure of Galatians 3.1–4.11* (Atlanta: Scholars Press, 1983).

Hays, R. B. *The Faith of Jesus Christ: An Investigation of the Narrative Substructure of Paul's Theology in Galatians 3:1–4:11*, PhD diss., Emory, 1981.

Hays, R. B. *The Moral Vision of the New Testament* (San Franscisco: Harper, 1996).

Hays, R. B. "Recent Books on Galatians," *QRMin* 5, 3 (Nov. 1985) 95–102.

Helminiak, Daniel A. "Human Solidarity and Collective Union in Christ, " *AnglTR* 70 (1988) 34–59.

Hemer, C. *The Book of Acts in the Setting of Hellenistic History* (Winona Lake: Eisebrauns, 1990).

Hengel, M. *Judaism and Hellenism*, 2 vols. trans. J. Bowden (Philadelphia: Fortress, 1974).

Hengel, M. *The Pre-Christian Paul* (Philadelphia: Trinity Press International, 1991).

Hengel, M. and A. M. Schwemer. *Paul Between Damascus and Antioch: The Unknown Years* (Louisville: Westminster/John Knox, 1997).

Hester, J. D. "Placing the Blame: The Presence of Epideictic in Galatians 1 and 2," in *Persuasive Artistry*, ed. D. F. Watson (Sheffield: JSOT Press, 1991), 184–208.

Hester, J. D. "The Rhetorical Structure of Galatians 1:11–2:14," *JBL* 103 (1984) 223–33.

Hester, J. D. "The Use and Influence of Rhetoric in Galatians 2:1–14," *TZBas* 42 (1986) 386–408.

Hill, C. *Hebrews and Hellenists* (Minnesota: Fortress, 1992).

Hirsch, Richard A. "Paul's Use of Scripture in Galatians 4 and Romans 9, and Related Rabbinic Materials," in Brauber, Ronald A., *Judaism and Christianity: Jewish Civilization 3* (Philadelphia: Reconstructionist Jewish College, 1985), 113–33.

Hodgson, R. "Paul the Apostle and First Century Tribulation Lists," *ZNW* 74 (1983) 59–80.

Hofius, O. "Gal. 1:18: ἱστορῆσαι Κηφᾶν," *ZNW* 75 (1984) 73–85.

Holmberg, B. *Paul and Power. The Structure of Authority in the Primitive Church as Reflected in the Pauline Epistles* (Lund: C. W. K. Gleerup, 1978).

Holtz, Traugott. "Der antiochenische Zwischenfall (Galater 2:11–14)," *NTS* 32 (1986) 344–61.

Hong, I.-G. "Does Paul Misrepresent the Jewish Law? Law and Covenant in Gal. 3:1–14," *NovT* 36 (2, 1994) 164–82.

Hong, I.-G. "The Law and Christian Ethics in Galatians 5–6," *Neotestamentica* 26 (1992) 113–30.

Hong, I.-G. *The Law in Galatians* (Sheffield: JSOT Press, 1993).

Hong, I.-G. "The Perspective of Paul in Galatians," *Scriptura* 36 (Stellenbosch, 1991), 1–16.

Hooker, M. D. "ΠΙΣΤΙΣ ΧΡΙΣΤΟΥ" *NTS* 35 (1989) 321–41.

Howard, George. *Paul: Crisis in Galatia; A Study in Early Christian Theology*, SNTS Monograph Series, No. 35 (Cambridge: Cambridge University Press, 1979).

Howard, J. K. "The New Eve: Paul and the Role of Women," *Journal of the Christian Brethren Research Fellowship* (Wellington, NZ, 1990), 19–26.

Hübner, H. "Der Galaterbrief und das Verhältnis von antiker Rhetorik und Epistolographie," *TRE* 12 (1983) 5–14.

Hübner, H. *Das Gesetz bei Paulus: Ein Betrag zum Werden der paulinischen Theologie* (Göttingen: Vandenhoeck & Ruprecht, 1978), in English as *Law in Paul's Thought* (Edinburgh: T. & T. Clark, 1984).

Hughes, F. W. "The Gospel and its Rhetoric in Galatians," in *Gospel in Paul: Studies on Corinthians, Galatians and Romans for Richard N. Longenecker*, ed. L. A. Jervis and P. Richardson (Sheffield: Sheffield Academic Press, 1994), 210–21.

Hultgren, A. J. "Paul's Pre-Christian Persecutions of the Church: Their Purpose, Locale and Nature," *JBL* 95 (1976) 97–111.

Hultgren, A. J. "The *Pistis Christou* Formulation in Paul," *NovT* 22 (1980) 248–63.

Hurtado, L. W. "The Jerusalem Collection and the Book of Galatians," *JSNT* 5 (1979) 46–62.

Irwin, K. M. "The Use of Astronomical Imagery by Roman Religions of late Antiquity," 1996 SBL lecture.

Jaquette, J. L. "Paul, Epictetus, and Others on Indifference to Status," *CBQ* 56 (1, 1994) 68–80.

Jegher-Bucher, Verena. "Der Galaterbrief auf dem Hintergrund antiker Epistolographie und Rhetorik," PhD diss., Basel, 1988.

Jewett, R. "The Agitators and the Galatian Congregation," *NTS* 17 (1970–71) 198–212.

Jobes, K. H. "Jerusalem, Our Mother: Metalepsis and Intertextuality in Galatians 4:21–31," *WestTJ* 55 (2, 1993) 299–320.

Johnson, H. Wayne. "The Paradigm of Abraham in Galatians 3:6–9." *TrinJ* 8 (1987) 179–99.

Johnson, J. F. "Paul's Argument from Experience: A Closer Look at Galatians 3:1–5," *ConcJourn* 19 (3, 1993) 234–37.

Jones, D. L. "The Imperial Cult in Roman Pergamum," Nov. 1996 SBL lecture.

Judge, E. A. "Paul's Boasting in Relation to Contemporary Professional Practice," *Australian Biblical Review* 16 (1968) 37–48.

Judge, E. A. "The Social Identity of the First Christians," *Journal of Religious History* 11 (1980) 201–17.

Kanter, R. *Commitment and Community* (Cambridge, Mass: Harvard University Press, 1972).

Kennedy, G. A. *New Testament Interpretation through Rhetorical Criticism* (Chapel Hill: University of North Carolina Press, 1984).

Kern, P. H. "Rhetoric, Scholarship and Galatians: Assessing an Approach to Paul's Epistle," PhD diss., University of Sheffield, 1994.

Kertelge, K. "The Assertion of Revealed Truth as Compelling Argument in Galatians 1:10–2:21," *Neotestamentica* 26 (2, 1992) 339–50.

Kertelge, K. "Gesetz und Freiheit im Galaterbrief," *NTS* 30 (1984) 382–94.

Kieffer, Rene. *Foi et Justification a Antioch: Interpretation d'un Conflit* (Paris: Cerf, 1982).

Kilpatrick, G. D. "Peter, Jerusalem and Galatians 1:13–2:14," *NT* 25 (1983) 318–26.

Kim, S. "The Mystery of Rom. 11.25–26," SNTS lecture, August 1996.

Kim, S. *The Origin of Paul's Gospel* (Grand Rapids: Eerdmans, 1981).

Kim, Y. K. "Paleographical Dating of p46 to the Late First Century," *Biblica* 69 (1988) 248–57.

King, Daniel H. "Paul and the Tannaim, A Study in Galatians," *WestTJ* 45 (1983) 340–70.

Kline, M. *By Oath Consigned* (Grand Rapids: Eerdmans, 1968).

Klumbies, P.-G. "Zwischen Pneuma und Nomos: Neuorientierung in den galatischen Gemeindem," *Wdienst* 19 (1987) 109–35.

Knobloch, F. W. "Adoption," *ABD* I, 76–79.

Koptak, P. E. "Rhetorical Identification in Paul's Autobiographical Narrative: Galatians 1.13–2.14," *JSNT* 40 (1990) 97–113.

Kraftchick, Steven J. "Ethos and Pathos Appeals in Galatians Five and Six: A Rhetorical Analysis," PhD diss., Atlanta: Emory, 1985.

Kraftchick, Steven J. "Why Do the Rhetoricians Rage?" in *Text and Logos: The Humanistic Interpretation of the New Testament*, Theodore Jennings, ed., Homage Series (Atlanta: Scholars Press, 1990), 55–79.

Kramer, W. *Christ, Lord, Son of God* (London: SCM Press, 1966).

Kruger, M. A. "Law and Promise in Galatians," *Neotestamentica* 26 (2, 1992) 311–27.

Kuck, D. W. "'Each Will Bear His Own Burden,' Paul's Creative Use of an Apocalyptic Motif," *NTS* 40 (2, 1994) 289–97.

Lambrecht, J. "The Line of Thought in Gal. 2.14b-21," *NTS* 24 (1978) 484–95.

Lambrecht, J. "Transgressor by Nullifying God's grace: A Study of Gal 2:18–21," *Biblica* 72 (1991) 217–36.

Lategan, B. C. "The Argumentative Situation of Galatians," *Neotestamentica* 26 (2, 1992) 257–77.

Lategan, B. "Is Paul Defending his Apostleship in Galatians? The Function of Galatians 1:11–12 and 2:19–20 in the Development of Paul's Argument," *NTS* 34 (1988) 411–30.

Lea, T. D. "Unscrambling the Judaizers: Who Were Paul's Opponents?" *SWJournTheol* 37 (1, 1994) 23–29.

Legrand, L. "'Il ny a ni esclave ni homme libre, ni homme ni femme': St. Paul et l'emancipation sociale," *Spiritus* 22 (1982) 395–415.

Lemmer, H. R. "Mnemonic Reference to the Spirit as a Persuasive Tool (Gal. 3:1–6 within the argument 3:1–4:11)," *Neotestamentica* 26 (1992) 359–88.

Levick, B. M. "The Augustan Restoration" in *The Cambridge Ancient History Vol. X* (Cambridge: Cambridge University Press, 2nd ed. 1996), 650–51.

Levick, B. M. *Roman Colonies in Southern Asia Minor* (Oxford: Oxford University Press, 1967).

Levinskaya I. *The Book of Acts in its First Century Settings: Volume V Diaspora Setting* (Grand Rapids: Eerdmans, 1996).

Levinsohn, S. H. "Phrase Order and the Article in Galatians: A Functional Sentence Perspective Approach," *OPTAT* 3, 2 (Dallas 1989) 44–64.

Lincoln, A. T. *Paradise Now and Not Yet. Studies in the Role of the Heavenly Dimension in Paul's Thought with Special Reference to his Eschatology* (Cambridge: Cambridge University Press, 1981).

Litfin, D. A. *St. Paul's Theology of Proclamation. 1 Corinthians 1–4 and Greco-Roman Rhetoric* (Cambridge: Cambridge University Press, 1994).

Loewe, R. *The Position of Women in Judaism* (London: SPCK, 1966).

Longenecker, R. N. "Ancient Amanuenses and the Pauline Epistles," in *New Dimensions in New Testament Study*, ed. Longenecker and M. C. Tenney (Grand Rapids: Zondervan, 1974), 281–97.

Longenecker, R. N. "Graphic Illustrations of a Believer's New Life in Christ: Galatians 4:21–31," *RevExp* 91 (2, 1994) 183–99.

Loubser, J. A. "The Contrast Slavery/Freedom as Persuasive Device in Galatians," *Neotestamentica* 28 (1, 1994) 163–76.

Luedemann, G. *Paul, Apostle to the Gentiles. Studies in Chronology* (Philadelphia: Fortress, 1984).

Lührmann, Dieter. "Gal. 2:9 und die katholischen Briefe: Bemerkungen zum Kanon und zur regula fidei," *ZNW* 72 (1981) 65–87.

Lull, David J. "'The Law was our Pedagogue': A Study in Galatians 3.19–25," *SBL* 105 (1986) 481–98.

Lull, David J. *The Spirit in Galatia: Paul's Interpretation of Pneuma as Divine Power*, SBL Dissertation Series, No. 45 (Chico: Scholars Press, 1980).

Lutjens, R. "You do not do what you want: What does Galatians 5.17 really mean?" *Presbyterion* 16.2 (1990) 103–17.

Lux, W. *Zur Freiheit begreit: zur Wirkungsgeschichte des Galaterbriefs*, Studienhefte Religion 3 (Stuttgart: Calwer, 1982).

Luz, U. *Das Geschichteverständnis des Paulus* (Munich: Kaiser, 1968).

Lyons, G. "The Function of Autobiographical Remarks in the Letters of Paul: Galatians and 1 Thessalonians As Test Cases," PhD diss., Emory, 1982.

Lyons, G. *Pauline Autobiography: Toward a New Understanding* (Atlanta: Scholars Press, 1985).

MacDonald, Dennis R. *There is no male and female: The Fate of a Dominical Saying in Paul and Gnosticism*, Harvard Dissertations in Religion (Philadelphia: Fortress, 1986).

McKnight, S. *A Light among the Gentiles* (Minnesota: Fortress, 1991).

McLean, B. H. "Galatians 2.7–9 and the Recognition of Paul's Apostolic Status at the Jerusalem Conference: a Critique of G. Luedemann's Solution," *NTS* 37 (1991) 67–76.

Magie, D. *Roman Rule in Asia Minor to the End of the Third Century. Vol. I: Text* (Princeton: Princeton University Press, 1950).

Malan, F. S. "The Strategy of Two Opposing Covenants, Gal. 4:21–5:1, *Neotestamentica* 26 (1992) 425–40.

Malina, B. *The New Testament World: Insights from Cultural Anthropology* (Atlanta: John Knox, 1981).

Malina, B. and J. Neyrey, *Portraits of Paul. An Archaeology of Ancient Personality* (Louisville: Westminster/John Knox, 1996).

Marshall, P. *Enmity in Corinth: Social Conventions in Paul's Relations with the Corinthians* (Tübingen: Mohr, 1987).

Martin, D. B. *Slavery as Salvation. The Metaphor of Slavery in Pauline Christianity* (New Haven: Yale University Press, 1990).

Martyn, J. L. "Apocalyptic Antinomies in Paul's Letter to the Galatians," *NTS* 31 (1985) 410–24.

Martyn, J. L. "Christ, the Elements of the Cosmos, and the Law in Galatians,' in *The Social World of the First Christians*, ed. M. White and L. Yarbrough (Minnesota: Fortress, 1995), 16–39.

Martyn, J. L. "The Covenant of Hagar and Sarah," in *Faith and History: Essays in Honor of Paul W. Meyer* (Atlanta: Scholars Press, 1990), 160–92.

Martyn, J. L. "Events in Galatia" in *Pauline Theology Vol. I*, ed. J. M. Bassler (Minnesota: Fortress, 1991), 160–79.

Martyn, J. L. "A Law-observant mission to Gentiles: The Background of Galatians," *MichQR* 22 (1983) 221–36.

Matera, F. J. "The Culmination of Paul's Argument to the Galatians: Gal. v.1–vi.17," *JSNT* 32 (1988) 79–91.

Matera, F. J. "The Death of Christ and the Cross in Paul's Letter to the Galatians," *LouvStud* 18 (4, 1993) 283–96.

Mavrofidis, Sotirios. "Gal 2:10: Various Aspects of Scholarship Between 1893–1979," *DeltioVM* 15, 1 (1986) 20–34.

Mayer, Friedrich. *Die Gerechtigkeit aus dem Glauben: der rechtschaffene Gaube: Betrachtungen über den Galaterbrief und den Jakobusbrief* (Metzingen: Franz, 1986).

Meagher, Patrick. "Faith active through *agape* (Gal 5:6): A Study of the Formation of a Christian Community of agape according to the Letter to the Galatians," PhD diss., Pontifical Institute, Rome, 1984.

Meeks, W. A. "Breaking Away: Three New Testament Pictures of Christianity's Separation from Jewish Communities," in *To See Ourselves as Others See Us: Christians, Jews, "Others" in Late Antiquity*, ed. J. Neusner and E. S. Frerichs (Chico: Scholars Press, 1985), 93–155

Meeks, W. A. "The Image of the Androgyne: Some Uses of a Symbol in Earliest Christianity," *History of Religions* 13 (1974) 165–208.

Meeks, W. A. "The Social Context of Pauline Theology," *Int* 36 (1982) 266–77.

Meeks, W. A. "Toward a Social Description of Pauline Christianity," in *Approaches to Ancient Judaism II*, ed. W. S. Green (Missoula: Scholars Press, 1980), 27–42.

Mitchell, M. *Paul and the Rhetoric of Reconciliation* (Tübingen: Mohr, 1991).

Mitchell, S. *Anatolia: Land, Men and Gods in Asia Minor. Vol. 2: The Rise of the Church* (Oxford: Clarendon Press, 1993).

Mitchell, S. "Galatia," *ABD* II, 870–72.

Mitchell, S. "Population and the Land in Roman Galatia," *ANRW* 2/7/2 (1980) 1053–81.

Moo, D. J. "Law, 'Works of the Law', and Legalism in Paul," *WestTJ* 45 (1983) 73–100.

Moore-Crispin, D. R. "Galatians 4.1–9: The Use and Abuse of Parallels," *EQ* 60 (1989) 203–23.

Moule, C. F. D. "Fulfilment Words in the New Testament: Use and Abuse," *NTS* 14 (1967–68) 293–320.

Moule, C. F. D. "Fulness and Fill in the New Testament," *SJT* 4 (1951) 79–86.

Moule, C. F. D. *The Origin of Christology* (Cambridge: Cambridge University Press, 1977).

Moulton, J. H. and G. Milligan, *The Vocabulary of the Greek Testament* (Grand Rapids: Eerdmans, 1930).

Moxnes, H. "Honor, Shame, and the Outside World in Paul's Letter to the Romans," in *The Social World of Formative Christianity and Judaism*, ed. J. Neusner et al. (Philadelphia: Fortress, 1988), 207–18.

Munck, J. *Paul and the Salvation of Mankind* (Richmond: John Knox, 1959).

Murphy-O'Connor, J. *Paul: A Critical Life* (Oxford: Clarendon Press, 1996).

Murphy-O'Connor, J. "Paul in Arabia," *CBQ* 55 (4, 1993) 732–37.

Neitsel, Heinz. "Zur Interpretation von Galater 2:11–21," *TuTQ* 163 (1983) 13–39.

Neufeld, Edmund K. "Christ and the Spirit in Galatians and 2 Corinthians 1–5: An Eschatological Comparison," PhD diss, Milwaukee: Marquette, 1987.

Neyrey, J. "Bewitched in Galatia: Paul and Cultural Anthropology," *CBQ* 50 (1988) 73–100.

Neyrey, J. *Paul in other Words* (Louisville: Westminster/John Knox, 1990).

Nock, A. D. *Conversion* (Oxford: Oxford University Press, 1933).

Nock, A. D. *St. Paul* (London: Butterworth, 1938).

O'Neill, J. C. *The Recovery of Paul's Letter to the Galatians* (London: SPCK, 1972).

Pelser, G. M. M. "The Opposition Faith and Works as a Persuasive Device in Galatians (3:6–14)," *Neotestamentica* 26 (1992) 389–405.

Perriman, A. C. "The Rhetorical Strategy of Galatians 4:21–5:1," *EQ* 65 (1, 1993) 27–42.

Pfitzner, V. C. *Paul and the Agon Motif: Traditional Athletic Imagery in the Pauline Literature* (Leiden: Brill, 1967).

Pretorius, E. A. C. "The Opposition *pneuma* and *sarx* as Persuasive Summons," *Neotestamentica* 26 (1992) 441–60.

Räisänen, H. "Galatians 2:16 and Paul's Break with Judaism," *NTS* 31 (1985) 543--53.

Räisänen, H. *Paul and the Law* (Philadelphia: Fortress, 1983).

Ray, C. A. "The Identity of the 'Israel of God,'" *TheolEduc* 50 (1994) 105–14.

Reugg, U. "Paul et la rhetorique ancienne," *BCentProt* 35, 7s (1983) 5–35.

Roberts, J. H. "Paul's Expression of Perplexity in Galatians 1:6: The Force of Emotive Argumentation," *Neotestamentica* 26 (2, 1992) 329–38.

Rollins W. G. "Greco-Roman Slave Terminology and Pauline Metaphors for Salvation," *SBL 1987 Seminar Papers*, ed. K. H. Richards (Atlanta: Scholars Press, 1987), 100–10.

Rusam, D. "Neue Belege zu den στοιχεῖα τοῦ κόσμου (Gal. 4:3, 9; Kol. 2:8, 20)," *ZNW* 83 (1–2, 1992) 119–25.

Russell, W. B. "Does the Christian Have 'Flesh' in Gal. 5:13–26?" *JETS* 36 (2, 1993) 179–87.

Russell, W. B. "Paul's Use of Sarx and Pneuma in Galatians 5–6 in Light of the Argument of Galatians" (Philadelphia: Westminster Theological Seminary, 1991).

Russell, W. B. "Rhetorical Analysis of the Book of Galatians, Part 1," *BiblSac* 150 (599, 1993) 341–58.

Russell, W. B. "Rhetorical Analysis of the Book of Galatians, Part 2," *BiblSac* 150 (600, 1993) 416–39.

Russell, W. B. "Who Were Paul's Opponents in Galatia?" *BS* 147 (1990) 329–50.

Ryan, E. E. "Aristotle's *Rhetoric* and *Ethics* and the Ethos of Society," *Greek, Roman, and Byzantine Studies* 13 (1972) 296–302.

Sampley, J. P. "Before God I do not Lie' (Gal. 1.20): Paul's Self Defense in the Light of Roman Legal Praxis," *NTS* 23 (1977) 477–82.

Sampley, J. P. *Pauline Partnership in Christ* (Philadelphia: Fortress, 1980).

Sanders, B. "Imitating Paul: 1 Cor. 4.16," *HTR* 74 (1981) 353–63.

Sanders, E. P. "Jewish Association with Gentiles and Galatians 2.11–14," in *The Conversation Continues. Studies in Paul and John*, eds. R. T. Fortna and B. R. Gaventa (Nashville: Abingdon, 1990), 170–88.

Sanders, E. P. *Paul, the Law, and the Jewish People* (Minnesota: Fortress, 1983).

Sanders, E. P. *Paul and Palestinian Judaism* (London: SCM Press, 1977).

Sanger, D. "'Verflucht ist jeder, der am Holze hängt' (Gal 3:13b). Zur Rezeption einer frühen antichristlichen Polemik," *ZNW* 85 (3–4, 1994) 279–85.

Sasson, J. M. "Circumcision in the Ancient Near East," *JBL* 85 (1966) 473–76.

Schmithals, Walter. "Judaisten in Galatien?" *ZNW* 74 (1983) 27–58.

Schafer, P. "Die Torah der Messianic Zeit," *ZNW* 65 (1974) 27–41.

Schütz, J. H. *Paul and Apostolic Authority* (Cambridge: Cambridge University Press, 1975).

Schwartz, Daniel R. "Two Pauline Allusions to the Redemptive Mechanism of the Crucifixion," *JBL* 102 (1983) 259–68.

Schweizer, E. "Slaves of the Elements and Worshippers of Angels: Gal. 4:3, 9 and Col 2:8, 18, 20," *JBL* 107 (1988) 455–68.

Scott, J. M. *Paul and the Nations* (Tübingen: Mohr, 1995).

Segal, A. F. "The Cost of Proselytism and Conversion," *SBL 1988 Seminar Papers* (Atlanta: Scholars Press, 1988), 336–69.

Segal, A. F. *Paul the Convert* (New Haven: Yale University Press, 1990).

Seifrid, M. A. "A Select Bibliography of Commentaries on Galatians," *RevExp* 91 (2, 1994) 219–24.

Sherk, R. K. *The Legates of Galatia from Augustus to Diocletian* (Baltimore: Johns Hopkins Press, 1951).

Sherk, R. K. *The Roman Empire: Augustus to Hadrian* (Cambridge: Cambridge University Press, 1988).

Sherk, R. K. "Roman Galatia: The Governors from 25 B.C. to A.D. 114," *ANRW* 2/7/2 1980, 954–1052.

Silva, Moises. "Text and Language in the Pauline Corpus: With Special Reference to the Use of Conjunctions in Galatians," *Neotestamentica* 29 (1990) 273–78.

Smiga, George M. "Language, Experience and Theology: The Argumentation of Galatians 3:6–4:7 in Light of the Literary Form of the Letter," PhD diss., Pontifical University Gregoriana, 1985.

Smit, J. "The Letter of Paul to the Galatians: A Deliberative Speech," *NTS* 35 (1989) 1–26.

Snyman, A. H. "Modes of Persuasion in Galatians 6:7–10," *Neotestamentica* 26 (1992) 475–84.

Standaert, B. "La rhetorique antique et l'epître aux Galates," *FoiVie* 84/5 (1985) 33–40.

Stanley, C. "'Under a Curse': A Fresh Reading of Galatians 3.10–14," *NTS* 36 (1990) 481–511.

Stanton, G. N. "The Law of Moses and the Law of Christ. Galatians 3.1–6.2," in *Paul and the Mosaic Law*, ed. J. D. G. Dunn (Tübingen: Mohr, 1996), 99–116.

Steindl, Helmut. "Gott, Mensch und Gesetz: zur Unerfüllbarkeit des Gesetzes nach Luthers Grosser Galaterbriefvorlesung," *FreibZ* 30 (1983) 2385–401.

Stendahl, K. *Paul among Jews and Gentiles* (Philadelphia: Fortress, 1976).

Strelan, J. G. "Burden-Bearing and the Law of Christ: a Re-Examination of Galatians 6.2," *JBL* 94 (1975) 266–76.

Strobel, Karl. "Die Galater im hellenistischen Kleinasien: historische Aspeckts einer hellenistischen Staatenbildung," In *Hellenistische Studien: Gedenkschrift Hermann Bengston*, ed. Jacob Seibert (München: Maris, 1991).

Styler, G. M. "The Basis of Obligation in Paul's Christology and Ethics," in *Christ and the Spirit in the New Testament. Studies in Honour of C. F. D. Moule*, ed. B. Lindars and S. S. Smalley (Cambridge: Cambridge University Press, 1973), 175–87.

Suggs, M. J. "The Christian Two Ways Tradition: Its Antiquity, Form and Function," in *Studies in the New Testament and Early Christian Literature*, ed. D. E. Aune (Leiden: Brill, 1972), 60–74.

Sumney, J . L. *Identifying Paul's Opponents: The Question of Method in 2 Corinthians* (Sheffield: JSOT Press, 1990).

Taylor, G. M. "The Function of PISTIS CHRISTOU in Galatians," *JBL* 85 (1966) 58–76.

Taylor, N. H. "Paul's Apostolic Legitimacy. Autobiographical Reconstruction in Gal. 1:11–2:14," *JournTheolSAfric* 83 (1993) 65–77.

Taylor, N. H. *Paul, Antioch, and Jerusalem. A Study in Relationships and Authority in Earliest Christianity* (Sheffield: JSOT Press, 1992).

Thielmann, F. "From Plight to Solution: A Jewish Framework for Understanding Paul's View of the Law in Galatians and Romans," *VT* Supp. 61 (1989).

Thielmann, F. *Paul and the Law* (Downers Grove: InterVarsity Press, 1994).

Tolmie, D. F. "*ho nomos paidagogos* . . . The Persuasive Force of a Pauline Metaphor (Gal. 3:23–26)," *Neotestamentica* 26 (1992) 407–16.

Treblico, P. *Jewish Communities in Asia Minor* (Cambridge: Cambridge University Press, 1991).

Treblico, P. "Women as Co-workers and Leaders in Paul's Letters," *Journal of the Christian Brethren Research Fellowship* (Wellington, NZ, 1990), 27–36.

Turner, N. *Grammatical Insights into the New Testament* (Edinburgh: T. & T. Clark, 1965).

Verseput, D. J. "Paul's Gentile Mission and the Jewish Christian Community: A Study of the Narrative in Galatians 1 and 2," *NTS* 39 (1, 1993) 36–58.

Vögtle, A. *Die Tugend und Lasterkataloge im Neuen Testament* (Munster: Aschendorff, 1936).

Vorster, J. N. "Dissociation in the Letter to the Galatians," *Neotestamentica* 26 (2, 1992) 297–310.

Vos, J. S. "Die hermeneutische Antinomie bei Paulus (Galater 3:11–12; Römer 10:5–10)," *NTS* 38 (1992) 254–70.

Vos, J. S. "Paul's Argumentation in Galatians 1–2," *HTR* 87 (1, 1994) 1–16.

Vouga, F. "La construction de l'histoire en Galates 3–4," *ZNW* 75 (1984) 259–69.

Vouga, F. "Zur rhetorischen Gattung des Galatersbriefes," *ZNW* 79 (1988) 291–92.

Walker, William O. "Why Paul Went to Jerusalem: The Interpretation of Galatians 2:1–5," *CBQ* 54 (1992) 503–10.

Wallace, D. B. "Galatians 3.19–20: *A Crux Interpretum* for Paul's View of the Law," *WestTJ* 52 (1990) 225–45.

Watson, F. *Paul, Judaism, and the Gentiles* (Cambridge: Cambridge University Press, 1986).

Webster, J. B. "Christology, Imitability and Ethics," *SJT* 39 (1986) 309–26.

Weima, J. A. D. "Gal. 6:11–18: A Hermeneutical Key to the Galatian Letter," *CalvTheoJourn* 28 (1, 1993) 90–107.

Wessels, G. F. "The Call to Responsible Freedom in Paul's Persuasive Strategy, Galatians 5:13–6:10," *Neotestamentica* 26 (1992) 461–74.

Westerholm, S. "On Fulfilling the Whole Law," *SvEx* 51s (1986) 229–37.

Westerholm, S. *Israel's Law and the Church's Faith. Paul and his Recent Interpreters* (Grand Rapids: Eerdmans, 1988).

Wibbing, S. *Die Tugend- und Lasterkataloge im Neuen Testament und ihre Traditionsgeschichte unter besonderer Berücksichtigung der Qumran Texte* (Berlin: Topelmann, 1959).

Wilckens, U. "Die Bekehrung des Paulus als religionsgeschichtliches Problem," in *Rechtifertigung als Freiheit: Paulusstudien* (Neukirchen-Vluyn: Neukirchen Verlag, 1974), 11–32.

Wilcox, M. "The Promise of the Seed in the NT and the Targumim," *JSNT* 5 (1979) 2–20.

Williams, S. K. "Again *Pistis Christou*," *CBQ* 49 (1987) 431–47.

Williams, S. K. "The Hearing of Faith: ΑΚΟΗ ΠΙΣΤΕΩΣ in Galatians 3," *NTS* 35 (1989) 82–93.

Williams, S. K. "Justification and the Spirit in Galatians," *JSNT* 29 (1987) 91–100.

Williams, S. K. "Promise in Galatians: A Reading of Paul's Reading of Scripture," *JBL* 107 (1988) 709–20.

Wilson, B. R. *Religion in Sociological Perspective* (Oxford: Oxford University Press, 1982).

Winger, M. "Unreal Conditions in the Letters of Paul," *JBL* 105 (1986) 110–12.

Winger, M. "Tradition, Revelation, and Gospel: A Study in Galatians," *JSNT* 53 (1994) 65–86.

Winter, B. W. *Are Paul and Philo among the Sophists?* (Cambridge: Cambridge University Press, 1997).

Winter, B. W. "Secular and Christian Responses to Corinthian Famines," *TynBull* 40 (1989) 86–106.

Winter, B. W. *Seek the Welfare of the City* (Grand Rapids: Eerdmans, 1994).

Wischenmeyer, O. "Das Gebet der Nächstenliebe bei Paulus," *BZ* 30 (1986) 161–87.

Witherington, B. III. "Editing the Good News," in *History, Literature, and Society in the Book of Acts*, ed. B. Witherington (Cambridge: Cambridge University Press, 1996), 324–47.

Witherington, B. III. "The Influence of Galatians on Hebrews," *NTS* 37 (1991) 146–52.

Witherington, B. III. *Jesus, Paul, and the End of the World* (Downers Grove; InterVarsity Press, 1992).

Witherington, B. III. "Not so idle thoughts about *eidolothuton*," *TynBull* 44.2 (1993) 237–54.

Witherington, B. III. *Paul's Narrative Thought World. The Tapestry of Tragedy and Triumph* (Louisville: Westminster/John Knox, 1994).

Witherington, B. III. 'Rite and Rights for Women – Galatians 3:28," *NTS* 27.5 (1980) 593–604.

Witherington, B. III. *Women in the Earliest Churches* (Cambridge: Cambridge University Press, 1988).

Witherington, B. III. *Women in the Ministry of Jesus* (Cambridge: Cambridge University Press, 1984).

Wright, A. G. "The Literary Genre Midrash," *CBQ* 28 (1966) 113–20.

Wright, N. T. *The Climax of the Covenant* (Edinburgh: T. & T. Clark, 1991).

Wright, N. T. "Paul, Arabia, and Elijah," *JBL* 115 (1996) 683–92.

Yaron, R. *Gifts in Contemplation of Death in Jewish and Roman Law* (Oxford: Clarendon Press, 1960).

Yates, R. 'Saint Paul and the Law in Galatians," *IrTQ* 51 (1985) 105–24.

Young, Norman H. "Paidagogos: The Social Setting of a Pauline Metaphor," *NovT* 29 (1987) 150–76.

Ziesler, J. A. *The Meaning of Righteousness in Paul: A Linguistic and Theological Inquiry* (Cambridge: Cambridge University Press, 1972).

Epistolary Prescript: 1.1–5

Paul, apostle, not from human beings, nor through a human being but through Jesus Christ and God the Father who raised him from the dead, and those with me, all the brothers, to the assemblies of Galatia. Grace to you and peace from God our Father and the Lord Jesus Christ who gave himself for our sins, so that he might deliver us out of the present evil age according to the will of our God and Father, to whom be glory unto the ages of ages, Amen.

In some respects this is one of the more unusual beginnings to a Pauline letter. Paul starts with two negations about his apostolic status and he concludes this section not by moving on into a thanksgiving prayer but with a doxology followed by Amen. This demonstrates, if we needed any such demonstration, that Paul felt free to modify the epistolary conventions of his day, and it is also the case that there is a certain flexibility in the way he handles the rhetorical conventions of his day.[1] Yet these are variations on a theme, because equally clearly Paul does work within the general framework of the epistolary and rhetorical guidelines of his day.

The letter begins in vs. 1 with the mention of the name of the addressor – Παῦλος. This is not a Jewish name but rather a Greek one, meaning 'little', and if it is true that Paul was a Roman citizen this would have surely been his

---

1. On Paul's flexible use of epistolary and rhetorical conventions see R. M. Berchman, "Galatians (1.1–5): Paul and Greco-Roman Rhetoric," in *New Perspectives on Ancient Judaism Volume Three: Judaic and Christian Interpretation of Texts: Contents and Contexts*, eds. J. Neusner and E. S. Frerichs (Lanham: University Press of America, 1987), pp. 1–15. I must say, however, that this study is far too atomistic, finding different rhetorical genres within one verse, and is probably wrong in seeking to find such extensive use of rhetorical conventions in the epistolary introduction to the discourse.

cognomen, not his family or clan name (the *nomen*), or the personal *praenomen*. Neither of Paul's other two Roman names is ever mentioned in the NT. What is mentioned in Acts is that Paul as a Jew was named after the first king of Israel – Saul (cf., e.g., Acts 9.1), a notion which certainly comports with what Paul tells us in Phil. 3.5, namely that he is from the tribe of Benjamin.

Paul immediately introduces the issue of the social status and authority which he has in the Christian communities that are addressed in this letter. The term he uses to describe this status and role is ἀπόστολος. There has been considerable discussion by scholars as to the meaning or import of this term. The term as it was used in classical Greek was not a technical term for some sort of official, in fact it was used largely in an impersonal way.[2] The term is found only once or twice in Josephus (*Ant.* 17.300, possibly in *Ant.* 1.146), and it carries a verbal sense of 'to send out' in accord with its etymological sense. It is because the NT usage of this term cannot be very readily paralleled in the Greek and Hellenistic Jewish writings of the day, and indeed few parallels can be found in all of Greek literature from the second century B.C. and through the second century A.D. that might suggest that the term means something like delegate, envoy, or messenger that it has been often suggested that a Hebrew or Aramaic term and concept may lie behind the use of ἀπόστολος in the NT, and especially in Paul's letters.

The term which most often surfaces is the term *shaliach*. Normally cited in this discussion is the Mishnaic material, especially 'a man's agent is as the man himself' (M. Ber. 5.5). The agent in question was a person to whom authority had been delegated to transact some sort of agreement for the one who had sent him, whether it be a property transaction, the concluding of a marriage agreement, or the performing of some ceremonial ritual. There is some Biblical precedent for this suggestion for *shaliach* is translated as ἀπόστολος in 3 Kgdms. 14.6 (LXXa).

This concept of agency could possibly lie behind Paul's reference to agents of churches (2 Cor. 8.23), for in that instance, like the Hebrew concept, we are probably talking about agents whose commission is of a specific nature and of a limited duration. This might also explain the use of ἀπόστολος in Acts 14.4, 14 where interestingly enough we have the only example in Acts where Paul is called an apostle. In this text Paul and Barnabas are commissioned and sent out by the church in Antioch. It needs to be said, however, that the term *shaliach* is never used of missionaries and in general was not usually used in a religious context.[3] In short, the usage of ἀπόστολος in the

---

2. See the discussion in Longenecker, *Galatians*, p. 2.
3. See C. K. Barrett, *The Signs of an Apostle* (London: Epworth, 1970).

NT of those who had some sort of permanent commission or authorization to perform certain religious tasks seems to be without clear precedent.[4]

A conjecture at this point is in order. If I am right that Galatians is written by Paul from Antioch shortly after his first missionary journey, and indeed may be his very first letter written to any of his converts, then this prescript may be intended to establish that Paul is *not* a mere 'apostle' of churches, an agent sent out by a church such as the Antioch church on a mission of a specific nature and limited duration and with humanly derived authority, but rather an apostle of Christ with an enduring commission and authority. In other words, the use of the term apostle, without such qualifications as we find here, would not have conveyed to the Galatians the status and authority Paul wanted to make clear to them he had. Perhaps they had been told that Paul and Barnabas had been sent out by the Antioch church. If this conjecture has merit, then it is unnecessary to conclude that Paul is defending his apostleship against the aspersions of his opponents. It is the ambiguity or lack of clarity in the meaning of the term itself, not the assertions of opponents that called forth the two negations which follow the term 'apostle'.

It needs also to be said at this point that if Paul were intending to defend his apostleship in this letter, it is passing strange that after the initial part of this letter the term ἀπόστολος does not arise again. The term ἀπόστολος and its derivatives occur only four times in the entire letter, the last being at 2.8, while εὐαγγέλιον and its derivatives occur some fourteen times spread throughout the first four chapters of this document. Both in the *exordium*, *narratio*, and the *propositio* the main topic turns out to be the Gospel, not Paul's apostleship.[5] There is not a shred of evidence that the Galatians had ceased to recognize Paul's apostolic authority, or even necessarily that the 'agitators' had questioned that authority.[6] As R. G. Hall has pointed out, and as

---

4. See my discussion in *The Acts of the Apostles* (Grand Rapids: Eerdmans, 1997), pp. 413ff.

5. See rightly, B. Lategan, "Is Paul Defending his Apostleship in Galatians?" *NTS* 34 (1988), pp. 411–30, here p. 417.

6. Cf. J. Schütz, *Paul and Apostolic Authority* (Cambridge: Cambridge University Press, 1975), p. 127: "The opponents do not accuse Paul of dependence on Jerusalem, but blame him for not demanding the custom of circumcision and adherence to the law in his gospel." It is one of the non sequiturs of those who engage in excessive mirror-reading of this prescript and other parts of Galatians, that they suggest that the agitators were arguing that Paul was dependent on Jerusalem and no true apostle. This is hardly credible, for dependence on Jerusalem is precisely what Judaizing opponents, especially if they were from the Jerusalem church, would *not* have objected to if it were true of Paul's ministry. Dunn, *Galatians*, p. 26 who wishes to argue that it is the questioning of Paul's apostolic status which has led him to assert it strongly at the beginning of this letter, does so in part on the basis of the fact that he assumes that 1 and 2 Thessalonians are letters written earlier and Paul does not introduce himself in this fashion there at the beginning of those

we shall see in the discussion of the *narratio* and the arguments, Paul in fact implies his need for the recognition of his ministry by the Jerusalem authorities by mentioning that he went up to lay before them his Gospel lest he be running in vain, and if "Paul needed to show his independence from the Jerusalem apostles, one would expect an argument for his independence in the proof (3.1–6.10), but none appears. Instead in the proof Paul argues that God's recent act in Christ places Jews and Gentiles in a new sphere of God's activity; they should stand fast in the new sphere and not return to the old."[7] It is, in any case, a mistake to evaluate Paul and his actions as if he were a modern Western person, with Western values about maintaining his individuality and independence.[8]

The assumption of Paul lying behind the writing of this letter is that the Galatians do still respect his authority and advice and Paul is hoping to correct their errors by writing to them. The issue or *stasis* in this letter is what Paul takes to be the apostolic message or Gospel, as opposed to the message of the agitators which Paul says is not a version but rather a perversion of the true Gospel.[9] A telltale sign that the major issue is the message Paul preaches is that of the nineteen occurrences of the verb εὐαγγελίζομαι in the undisputed Paulines, seven occur in Galatians, and six in this very first chapter.

---

letters. This involves at least three questionable assumptions: (1) that Paul only became sensitive about his apostolic status when it was attacked. But to judge from 1 Cor. 15, since Paul saw himself as the last to become an apostle of Christ and was seen as one 'untimely born' he was likely to be sensitive about this matter from the outset; (2) that 1 and 2 Thessalonians were written before Galatians. But if Galatians comes before 1 and 2 Thessalonians then the progression from less defensive to more defensive falls by the wayside; (3) that Paul is not concerned to assert his apostolic authority in the Thessalonian correspondence. But Paul most certainly does assert his status as apostle of Christ in 1 Thessalonians (see 1 Thess. 2.7). If one wants to see Paul in a defensive mode about his apostolic status one should turn to 2 Cor. 10–13, not Galatians. Lastly, Paul sometimes refers to his apostolic status in the prescript and sometimes does not (cf. Phil. 1.1; Philem. vs. 1). There is no definite pattern. I doubt we can tell anything about how defensive Paul was feeling about his apostolic status by whether or not he mentions it in the prescript.

7. R. G. Hall, "Historical Inference and Rhetorical Effect," in *Persuasive Artistry. Studies in New Testament Rhetoric in Honor of George A. Kennedy*, ed. D. F. Watson (Sheffield: JSOT Press, 1991), pp. 308–20, here p. 317.

8. See now Malina and Neyrey, *Portraits of Paul*, pp. 34ff.

9. Rhetorical issue and rhetorical aim are related but are not one and the same. The issue is the main bone of contention, and here the *stasis* has to do with definition – what is the content of the true Gospel (see the *propositio* in 2.15–21) and as a result of that, how does one define the true people of God. The rhetorical aim of this discourse is to persuade the Galatians to continue to follow Paul's Gospel and understanding of God's people and to reject the message of the agitators who urge circumcision and submission to the Mosaic Law.

The first negation Paul makes is that his apostolic status is not from human beings. In other words, it is divine in origin, not human. He is not merely an agent of another human being or group of human beings. The second negation indicates that he did not receive his apostolic commission through human beings, which may be to counter an assumption made by the Galatians that since Paul had been sent out by the Antioch church, he had indeed received his apostolic commission from them. A second possibility would be that Paul is here distinguishing himself from the 'men who came from James' especially if they were identical with the agitators in Galatia. The men who came from James were clearly commissioned through a human being and sent on a specific task. They were the ones who could be called 'apostles' with a small 'a'.[10]

There may in fact be in these negations an echo of OT remarks about prophetic calls, as seems to be the case later in this chapter. For example, one may point to Amos 7.14–15, 'I am no prophet, nor am I a prophet's son, for I am a herdsman . . . but the Lord took me . . .' One may also wish to compare what is placed on Moses' lips by Philo: 'I did not of my own free will choose to superintend and preside over public affairs, nor did I receive the office through appointment by some other of humankind, but when God by clear oracles . . . made evident his will to me . . ." (*Virt.* 63). In neither case is the negation a response to the attacks of opponents. F. Matera puts the matter thus: "the emphasis upon Paul's apostleship has the rhetorical function of grounding the Torah-free Gospel in God and Jesus rather than of defending Paul from the attacks of opponents."[11]

What follows the negations is the indication that Paul was an apostle through Jesus Christ and God the Father. The ἀλλά is strongly adversative here and indicates that in contrast to human commission, Paul's was divine in origin and character. The order of mention of Christ and then the Father is somewhat odd (cf. the usual order in Rom. 1.7; 1 Cor. 1.3; 2 Cor. 1.2; Phil. 1.2), but is perhaps to be explained by the fact that Paul is already thinking of the fact that he received both his call and conversion through a Christophany (see below). Lest there be any doubt of which God called Father, Paul has in mind there is a further clause declaring that this God is the one who raised Jesus from out of the realm of the dead. The fatherhood of God plays an important role in Galatians (cf. 1.3, 4; 4.2, 6), and as Betz says this is in part because Paul wants to speak about adoption (3.7, 26; 4.4–7, 22–31).[12] In fact he wishes to

10. Betz, *Galatians*, p. 39 is right to caution against any and all attempts to judge what the opponents were 'charging' Paul with on the basis of this prescript. Rather, what we have here is an assertion, not a rebuttal – a "carefully composed definiton of the concept of apostle" (p. 38).

11. Matera, *Galatians*, p. 41.

12. Betz, *Galatians*, p. 39 n. 27.

assert the paternity of God in regard both to Jews and to Gentiles through the agency of Jesus Christ. As we will see this is in contrast to the notion of paternity in relationship to only one particular ethnic group – Jews. In Paul's view, one does not have to become a Jew to be a son or daughter of God, indeed a son or daughter of Abraham. All that is required is having the same faith and faithfulness as Abraham. The reference to resurrection is important for it signals that what really matters in the discussion that follows is the eschatological state of affairs. If resurrection has already happened then the new creation has begun (cf. Gal. 6.15), and one cannot assume that what has applied in the past to God's people still applies. This impression is reinforced in vs. 4 as we shall see.

Verse 2 indicates that Paul is not alone when he writes this letter. He refers to those with him, and uses the phrase 'all the brothers'.[13] Probably the intended rhetorical effect of this last phrase is that it is meant to indicate that there are various other Christians at Paul's location who are in agreement with what he is about to tell the Galatians. He is not promulgating *his* Gospel, but *the* Gospel, and he has plenty of other Christians who agree with his views. What is not mentioned here is who these 'brothers' are. The phraseology of the first part of this verse is very close to what we find in Phil. 4.21, and there it is not secretaries but other Christians, perhaps even Paul's ministerial co-workers, who seem to be meant. It may, however, be significant that Paul does not mention any of his co-workers by name in this prescript.

I incline to the suggestion of R. Bauckham who argues that the lack of reference to Barnabas in this prescript is telling.[14] Surely if Paul could have cited in this prescript the other major missionary who first visited the Galatians as one supporting Paul's views he would have done so. The prescript here bespeaks a situation where Paul's social and support networks are weak or under-developed. There had been a falling out between Paul and Barnabas as a result of the incident at Antioch and now, while Paul was not alone, he was not able to cite other apostles or prominent co-workers who agreed with him and would co-write this letter with him. This is perhaps all the more telling when we look at the other early letters of Paul, 1 and 2 Thessalonians and 1 and 2 Corinthians, where Paul is very careful to mention by name other well-known Christians and Pauline co-workers who are with him and may be assisting or contributing in the production of the letter (in Thessalonians, Paul and Silas and Timothy; in 1 Corinthians, Paul and Sosthenes; in 2 Corinthans, Paul and Timothy).

John Chrysostom was right in his Commentary on Galatians to stress the sparseness of the way the addressees are referred to in vs. 2. Paul "does not say

13. This may in fact of course mean both male and female believers but it is difficult to tell.

14. R. Bauckham, "Barnabas in Galatians," *JSNT* 2 (1979), pp. 61–72.

'to the beloved' or 'to the sanctified' and this omission of all names of affection or respect, and speaking of them merely as a society without the addition 'of God', for it is simply 'assemblies of Galatia' is strongly expressive of deep concern and sorrow".[15] Paul has nothing to praise about the Galatian assemblies, hence the sparseness of the address and the lack of a thanksgiving section.

It is also important to note that Paul refers to assemblies *plural*. This letter is intended as a circular letter, and this also means that Paul assumes that the agitators' message has infected and affected not just one congregation but several. The situation is all the more grave in Paul's view because of the scope of the problem. Lastly, it may be of some significance that Paul has chosen to use the term ἐκκλησία here, the term used for Greek assemblies where matters of policy would be debated and decided. It was the place where deliberative rhetoric was *the* form of persuasion to be used. As we shall see, this is the form of rhetoric used throughout this particular letter as Paul seeks to persuade the Galatians not to have themselves circumcised and place themselves under the requirements of the Mosaic Law, and instead to continue to follow the dictates of the Gospel he proclaimed to them when he first visited Galatia.

There is no reason why Paul could not have referred to the residents of Derbe, Lystra, Iconium, and Pisidian Antioch as Galatians, as Paul does use Roman provincial designations elsewhere in his letters.[16] It is also possible to suggest that the fact that the plural is used here of ἐκκλησία slightly favors the suggestion he is writing to the churches founded on his first missionary journey, for we have no evidence that he founded multiple churches in Galatia in subsequent visits to the region, or in other parts of the province. Furthermore, Paul speaks of them quickly departing from the Pauline Gospel (cf. below).

In vs. **3** Paul offers his characteristic greeting of 'grace' and 'peace' (cf. Rom. 1.7; 1 Cor. 1.3; 2 Cor. 1.2 etc.). 'Grace' is probably an adaptation of the traditional Greek greeting which involves χαίρειν (cf. 1 Macc. 12.6; Acts 23.26), while peace would be the equivalent in Greek to the Hebrew greeting *shalom* (cf. 1 Sam. 25.5–6; Dan. 4.1). But Paul is not simply offering perfunctory greetings for he makes clear that the source of what he is conveying here is God the Father and the Lord Jesus Christ. In other words, Paul is talking about some of the benefits the Galatians have and can continue

---

15. My translation differs slightly from that of G. Alexander found in *The Nicene and Post-Nicene Fathers of the Christian Church Vol. XIII*, ed. P. Schaff (Grand Rapids: Eerdmans, 1976 rpr.), p. 4. Here and in what follows I will from time to time be citing Chrysostom, and if there is a quotation one may assume it comes from Chrysostom's teaching on that particular verse unless otherwise indicated. The reader is encouraged to consult the Alexander translation if the Greek text is not available to him or her.

16. See the Introduction, pp. 5ff. above.

to receive from God if they continue to 'walk according to the Spirit'. The greeting is especially pointed here as it is precisely the matters of grace and peace that are at issue in the Galatian assemblies. They have not understood the implications of the Gospel of grace and instead of peace there is strife, and quarrels and divisions exist in these assemblies. Under such conditions, Paul must take it upon himself to use 'political' rhetoric, deliberative rhetoric which tries to produce concord and harmony and unity in a factious and fracturing situation.[17] He must argue against divisive actions and beliefs, in this case submitting to circumcision and the Mosaic Law which will divide those Christians who submit to such requirements from those who do not.[18] He can show the divisive character of submitting to Judaizing suggestions by appealing to the example of the incident in Antioch which divided that congregation and, as Acts 15.1 says, caused no small dissension and debate.

Galatians says very little about the resurrection of Jesus, but it is clear that what Jesus accomplished on the cross is very important to Paul's overall argument in this document and so it is not surprising that already in vs. 4 we hear that 'he gave himself for our sins in order to deliver us out of this present evil age according to the will of God the Father'. This is a very important phrase on several grounds. It seems likely that Paul is quoting here a fragment of an early Christian confession for Paul uses very similar terms elsewhere and says that he had received the Christian message in the form that Christ died for our sins (1 Cor. 15.3). Verse 4 indicates that Christ voluntarily submitted to death on the cross (cf. Phil. 2.8). Furthermore, it indicates that Christ's death is some sort of necessary sacrifice for human sins. The use of ὑπὲρ here probably has the same significance as we find in 3 Kgdms 16.18f. (LXX) where it must be translated 'because of'. Since we do not have ἀντί we do not have the notion of a vicarious act (in our stead) being clearly stressed here,[19] though that idea is probably implied (cf. Gal. 3.13). What is clearer is that God required such an atoning act for human sins in order that fallen humanity could be saved. Both the death and the rescue were 'according to the will of God' which tells us something profound about Paul's view of God. In Paul's view, suffering and even death is by no means outside the will of God for a person, indeed in the Son's case this was at the very heart of what God sent the Son to do on earth. Then too, redemption is the larger aim of God for humankind.

The verb ἐξέληται is found here for the only time in the Pauline corpus, but its use in Acts 7.10, 34; 12.11; 23.27; 26.17 makes it clear enough that the sense of the verb is 'rescue'. The notion here is of rescue from the evil of the age (on which cf. 4 Ezr. 6.9; 7.12–13; 2 Bar. 14.13; 15.8; CD 6.10, 14), not removal

---

17. See M. Mitchell, *Paul and the Rhetoric of Reconciliation* (Tübingen: Mohr, 1991), pp. 60–64.

18. For example, this will divide Paul from his own converts in Galatia.

19. See the discussion in Lightfoot, *Galatians*, p. 73.

from the age itself. Christians are to live in but not of the world. Betz says that "Paul speaks of the liberation out of the evil aeon and not the change of the aeons themselves".[20] But clearly enough Paul believes that while this present fallen age continues, yet the new creation has already broken into its midst, such that Paul can speak of the eschatological Kingdom of God being both an already and a not yet proposition in this world (cf. Rom. 14.17 and Gal. 5.21).[21] I quite agree with J. L. Martyn and B. R. Gaventa that the antinomies or antitheses that we are going to see in abundance in Galatians are a reflection of Paul's belief about things apocalyptic, in particular his conviction that "the Christ event constitutes an invasion of the world. The revelation (apocalypse) of Christ is not simply one more act in a string of revelations. It is rather a new creation and there is no 'through-train' connecting the old creation with the new."[22] In such circumstances it would be better to speak of the beginning of the eschatological age caused by the death and resurrection of Jesus and seen in the lives of the converted in the midst of the present evil age.[23] That rescue is required makes quite clear that salvation is not seen by Paul as a human self-help program. Salvation is of God and through the action of Christ.

Verse 5 provides us with a doxology to God the Father. Praise and glory should go to God forever and ever for what God accomplished in Christ. Possibly Paul has quoted part of a confession that ended with this doxology.[24] In short there should be eternal praises for the eternal life wrought by God in Christ.[25] It is quite possible that Paul places a doxology here to mark off clearly the epistolary section of this document from the rhetoric which follows.

---

20. Betz, *Galatians*, p. 42.

21. See my *Jesus, Paul, and the End of the World* (Downers Grove: InterVarsity Press, 1992), pp. 52ff.

22. The quotation is from Gaventa's "The Maternity of Paul: an Exegetical Study of Galatians 4.19," in *The Conversation Continues: Studies in Paul and John* (Grand Rapids: Eerdmans, 1990), pp.189–201, here p. 198. She is following and drawing on the metaphor of J. L. Martyn, "Paul and his Jewish Christian Interpreters," *USQR* 42 (1988), p. 6.

23. Paul, however, does not think that the eschatological event of the death and resurrection of Jesus simply affects the lives of believers, for he is also prepared to speak of the 'schema' of this world already passing away (1 Cor. 7.31).

24. So Longenecker, *Galatians*, p. 9.

25. Glory here could refer to an essential attribute of God but it is far more likely that the term has here the sense of honor or praise which humans should give to God, but cf. Lightfoot, *Galatians*, p. 75.

Exordium: 1.6–10   Two Gospels?

I am amazed that so quickly you have been changed over from the one calling you in grace[1] unto a different Gospel, not that there is another one, but some are disturbing you and wishing to distort the Gospel of Christ. But even if it were possible that we or an angel from heaven should proclaim [something] to you contrary to what we proclaimed to you, let that one be anathema. As we said before and say again to you: if anyone proclaims [something] to you contrary to what you received, let that one be anathema. For now do I persuade human beings or God? Or seek to please human beings? If I still was pleasing human beings, I would not be Christ's slave.

W. Hansen has documented the epistolary conventions of a rebuke–request letter at some length, and Galatians seems to comport with these conventions to some extent.[2] It is clear enough, however, that the paragraph above also suits the requirements for an *exordium* in a deliberative piece of rhetoric. The main function of an *exordium* was to introduce the major topic or topics that are going to be discussed in what follows. A further function was to get the attention of the listeners so they will be disposed to hear what follows. Lastly, there was always a concern in the *exordium* to establish the speaker's ethos or authority so that what follows will be received as words from an important

---

1. It is not clear whether Χριστοῦ is original or is a later addition after 'in grace', especially since it is omitted in p46, the earliest papyri containing Galatians. Cf. B. M. Metzger, *A Textual Commentary on the Greek New Testament* (London and New York: United Bible Societies, 1971), p. 589. The way Paul speaks of the 'change over' here suggests that while the Galatians are in large measure responsible for their own behavior, nevertheless he believes they have been duped or bewitched. See p. 197 below on Gal. 3.1.

2. See the discussion in the Introduction pp. 36ff. above and see also Longenecker, *Galatians*, pp. cv-cix.

and reliable source. More often than not in an *exordium* the establishment of contact and rapport with the audience was made by way of praise or flattery or thanksgiving, but if the case was serious or dangerous enough the *exordium* could also begin with blame or rebuke, in short the splash of cold water in the face of the audience to get their attention and wake them up to what their situation really was and to the fact that they needed to take action to correct the situation. Paul chooses to follow the latter approach here. He has already in part established his ethos in the prescript but he adds to it here by proceeding in a manner that indicates he is an authority figure: (1) he is one who can define what is and is not the true Gospel; and (2) he is a figure of power, one who can pronounce an anathema.

Quintilian reminds us that in deliberative oratory the people would frequently demand a certain impetuosity of eloquence (*Inst. Or.* 8.3.14), and Paul meets this expectation with vigor in this exordium.[3] As Quintilian says "appeals to the emotions . . . are especially necessary in deliberative oratory. Anger has frequently to be excited or assuaged and the minds of the audience have to be swayed to fear, ambition, hatred, reconciliation" (*Inst. Or.* 3.8.12). By stating things the way he does, Paul is preparing the audience to make a decision about their future. They must either choose the Gospel which Paul had already proclaimed to them or the message which the agitators had offered them. They could not have it both ways.

Persuasion and/or dissuasion must be accomplished in a rhetorical piece and it is important to note that deliberative rhetoric serves the purpose of addressing questions where some doubt exists in the mind of the audience as to what the proper course is to take (*Inst. Or.* 3.8.25). The Galatians are at a crossroads and Paul speaks passionately to try to show them how to go forward in their Christian lives. This rhetorical piece is *not* about 'getting in' or even about 'staying in' but about how Christians should 'go on', and especially how they should not 'go off' the right track and so commit what Paul views as apostasy. There is doubt about the proper course they should take and Paul must offer arguments to convince them of the right road. These arguments will be of a variety of sorts, theological, ethical, social, personal, even political. It is true enough that Paul will remind his audience about how they got in, and how they received the Spirit and on what basis miracles happened in their midst, but the function of this reminder is that the Galatians will properly know how to go on with their Christian lives.

Far from the main issue of this document being 'how may one be saved' (by grace rather than by works) Paul is concerned with telling those already saved how they can avoid becoming lost or even apostate. Getting out, not

---

3. A deliberative speech did not always require an *exordium* (cf. Quintilian *Inst. Or.* 3.8.6), but it was certainly allowed and frequently used.

getting in is the concern, hence all the language about curses, casting out intruders, being bewitched and the like. The Galatians are indeed testing the boundaries, but from the inside out, not the outside in. Nevertheless, confusion about boundaries in general and rites of passage in particular requires of Paul that he explain: (1) how entrance was achieved to the community; (2) what the rite of passage was (cf. Gal. 3.28); (3) what the implications are of the means of entrance and maintenance; (4) why other boundary and mainten- ance rituals are not required; (5) what these other rites signify and commit the initiate to. It must be stressed, however, that Paul does not have a 'magical' view of these rituals. As he says, neither circumcision nor uncircumcision amounts to anything. What counts is the new creation. However, Paul is gravely concerned with the theological, ethical and social commitments associated with these rituals, and this is the main reason why his arguments take the form they do.

Quintilian says that an *exordium* in a deliberative speech should be but a brief prelude that prepares for what follows (*Inst. Or.* 3.8.10), and Gal. 1.6–10 nicely meets these requirements. The listener hearing this *exordium* would conclude that there is basically only one topic to be discussed in what follows – What is the true Gospel and what does it entail and require of its receivers? This impression left by the *exordium* is the correct one, for the rest of Galatians is not a polyglot of discussions on disparate topics but rather a series of arguments and variations on one theme. Even the narration of events which follows this *exordium* is not intended to be a personal defense of Paul's apostleship. Rather as Kennedy says it "is supporting evidence for Paul's claim in 1.11 that the Gospel he preached was not from man, but from God, a topic which had been enunciated in the first verse of the salutation."[4] All of Galatians is one unified rhetorical piece meant to head off the Galatians' march towards having themselves circumcised and submitting to the Mosaic Law and covenant, and by contrast to aid them to continue to walk in the Spirit and according to grace, according to the Gospel Paul first preached in Galatia.

Though Paul is following a convention in vs. **6** when he expresses amazement or surprise, the tone of what follows makes clear that Paul is not merely mouthing clichés. He is genuinely amazed and upset and believes his audience needs to be rebuked. Cicero says that in a rhetorical speech an expression of amazement or perplexity is in order as a means of regaining favor with one's audience if one finds they have been won over by the opposition (*De Invent.* 1.17.25). This is basically the situation we find in Galatians.

The words οὕτως ταχέως are important for they make clear that one of the causes of the apostle's surprise is that so short a time has elapsed between

4. Kennedy, *New Testament Interpretation*, p. 145.

when the Galatians were converted and when they are contemplating a change in direction. It is not completely clear whether we should translate this phrase 'so soon' (indicating the shortness of time between two events) or 'so quickly' indicating the speed with which they capitulated to another view.[5] Even if it is the latter, the briefness of the amount of time is implied and this must not be dismissed or overlooked. It is very possible, as F. Mussner suggests, that the language here echoes several OT passages which speak of God's people, in fact some of the first Israelites, quickly abandoning the covenant or committing apostasy (cf. Ex. 32.8; Deut. 9.16).[6] It is very likely then, and certainly is the most natural reading of these words, that in Paul's mind there has been only a short period of time between when he first preached to the Galatians and when he is now writing to them.

It is important to note the present tense of the verb μετατίθεσθε. The Galatians have not yet completely defected from the true Gospel, but they are in the process of doing so when Paul writes.[7] This verb has the sense of transferring from one state to another or changing over from one condition to another. It is not found elsewhere in Paul's letters but the overtones of desertion, changing one's mind, or even committing apostasy are clear enough from usage elsewhere in Greek literature (cf. Polybius 24.9.6 where the term has a political sense;[8] Sir. 6.9; 2 Macc. 7.24; Josephus Ant. 20.38). It is interesting that the substantive form of this word ὁ μεταθέμενος is used to refer to a person who leaves one philosophical school of thought for another (Diogenes Laertius 7.1.37; 4.166).

Notice, however, that Paul speaks here of leaving someone behind (the one who called you) in exchange for something (a different Gospel). The agitators were not offering a different God or Christ or Spirit (contrast what Paul says in 2 Cor. 11.4), but they were offering a different message. Probably Paul has in mind God here as ultimately the one who called them in grace, though Paul was the agent of God in this. Paul does not distinguish 'call' from conversion, rather he identifies the two both in the case of his converts and of himself (cf. below on 1.15).

Verse 6 and vs. 7 refer to 'a different' Gospel and Paul uses two different terms to refer to it – ἕτερον and ἄλλο. The older commentators tried to make certain distinctions of meaning between the two terms here, based on classical usage. On this showing the former term would refer to a difference in kind,

5. See Dunn, *Galatians*, p. 40.
6. F. Mussner, *Der Galaterbrief* (Freiburg: Herder, third ed. 1977), p. 53.
7. See Burton, *Galatians*, pp. 18–19.
8. It is worth pointing out that there are a variety of basically political terms that Paul uses in Galatians, or better said terms usually used in political discussions. Among other clues, this supports the case that we are dealing with a piece of deliberative not forensic rhetoric here.

while the latter would mean another alongside of the first.[9] But elsewhere in Paul's letters the apostle seems to use the terms interchangably (cf. 2 Cor. 11.4; 1 Cor. 12.9–10), and generally speaking in Koine Greek they are interchangeable.[10] The point in any case is that in Paul's view there is only one true Gospel, the Gospel of grace, from which the Galatians are defecting. There are, however, some (τινές) who are disturbing the Galatians and are misrepresenting or perverting[11] (notice again the present tenses here – εἰσιν, θέλοντες) the Gospel of Christ. It is probable that this last phrase means the Gospel about Christ (cf. Gal. 1.12, 16), for it is God who does the revealing.

Verse 8 refers to a future more probable condition ('even if', with ἐάν), which suggests a possibility, while vs. 9 begins with a simple condition which assumes a reality. Paul says that even if an angel from heaven should proclaim a Gospel to the Galatians contrary to what 'we' (presumably Paul and Barnabas is meant) proclaimed, that one should be cursed or banned. There may be a point to the reference to a messenger from heaven. Later in this document Paul is going to refer to the fact that it was believed that the Law was delivered to Moses by angels (3.19). Paul will also refer to the fact in 4.14 that he was received as an angel of God when he first came to Galatia. The former of these two references may be germane here. The Gospel of Moses, even though mediated through angels should not be received. In Paul's view it is no Gospel at all. This verse is also crucial because it makes clear that Paul thinks it is the message not the messenger which matters and is the issue in this crisis.

The term ἀνάθεμα used twice in the space of two verses (vss. 8–9). This is the Koine variant of the classical term ἀνάθημα. It is important to understand that this term is the regular translation of the Hebrew term *harem*, which means ban (cf. Lev. 27.28–29; Deut. 7.26; 13.17 Josh. 6.17–18). The idea here is of something which is set aside for destruction, and in this case destruction by God. Paul is not himself banning or cursing the agitators but asking God ('let him be . . .') to act against them. Less probable, though not impossible, is the suggestion that Paul has in mind the Galatians banning or

9. See Lighfoot, *Galatians*, p. 76.

10. See J. K. Elliott, "The Use of ἕτερος in the New Testament," *ZNW* 60 (1969), pp. 140–41.

11. Another verb which begins with μετά (μεταστρέψαι) indicating a change from one thing or state or condition or person to another. All the language here points to the Galatians being on the fence or about to cross the boundary. As Betz *Galatians*, p. 50 points out this verb is also most often used in political contexts and refers to turning of things upside down. It suggests revolutionary activity. It is the sort of rhetoric we would expect Paul to use in an unstable social situation which he is trying to stabilize using deliberative rhetoric.

expelling the agitators from their assemblies, a suggestion which comports with the probable implication of Gal. 4.30.[12] Verse **9** suggests that Paul had previously told his Galatian converts about rejecting other so-called Gospels and invoking a curse on their proclaimers. It is more likely that this refers to something Paul said to his converts when he first visited them rather than that vs. 9 is simply alluding back to vs. 8. The point of the repetition and the strongly polemical language is to reinforce to the Galatians the seriousness of this situation and try to jolt them into rejecting the message of the agitators. We have already seen the remark of Quintilian that strong and emotive language was characteristic of deliberative rhetoric and Paul wishes to make very sure his converts understand that by using these curses he is not simply following rhetorical convention or striving to make a mere rhetorical impression, rather he is in deadly earnest.

He accomplishes this aim in vs. **10** by offering two rhetorical questions focusing on the tasks of a rhetor – to persuade or to please. The debate about rhetoric was how much it was in fact the art of persuasion and how much it might degenerate into a mere attempt to please the audience.[13] The answer to the question 'Am I still trying to please human beings?' is an emphatic no, though Paul admits that in the past (presumably before his conversion, note the ἔτι) he had acted in this fashion. Rather, his task is to persuade human beings, not merely tickle their ears. The verb πείθω has as its normal meaning, especially in a rhetorical piece such as this, to persuade. The issue here is persuasion not seeking approval, as should be clear from a comparison with 2 Cor. 5.11 where we find the only other example of the transitive form of the verb in Paul's writings.[14] There Paul plainly admits 'we persuade human beings'.

If the expected answer to the first rhetorical question is also no, then Paul could be saying he is not merely using the art of persuasion on humans or God here, this is no mere exercise in rhetoric, even though Paul will follow the rhetorical conventions. The reference to God perhaps arises because of the curse in the previous verses. A curse is an attempt to persuade God to do something against someone else. Note that the particle γὰρ connects this verse to the immediately preceding one about cursing.

---

12. See Ziesler, *The Epistle to the Galatians*, p. 5.

13. See the discussion in Litfin, *St. Paul's Theology of Proclamation*, pp. 37ff. about the difference between sophists and serious and responsible rhetors. The crucial point is to stress that there were two different approaches to the rhetorical task, one that would use any rhetorical tack to win over or please the audience, the end justifying almost any means including falsification of facts and arguments, and the other which felt that one must persuade the audience using appropriate ethical means, not hesitating to speak about things the audience needed to hear, but might not be pleased to hear.

14. See Bruce, *Galatians*, p. 84.

Alternatively, and more probably, one could take the answer to the first rhetorical question to be yes. Paul is trying to persuade both the Galatians and God to act.[15] But his is a serious minded rhetoric. The second question makes clear that his form of rhetoric should not be read as a mere attempt at pleasing the audience.[16] It is not impossible that already here we have the subtle suggestion that people-pleasing is what the agitators have been doing (cf. Gal. 4.17; 6.12–13), but we cannot be sure about this. Thus Paul, both here and elsewhere, stresses that he does not speak to his audience as a people-pleaser or flatterer (cf. 1 Thess. 2.4–5; 1 Cor. 10.33; Col. 3.22). This is not his intent or style when he uses rhetoric.

The last clause of vs. 10 contrasts being a people-pleaser and being a servant of God. Clearly enough, in terms of rhetorical strategy Paul could not resort to a form of rhetoric, sophistic rhetoric, that would be 'full of sound and fury' but 'signifying nothing'. That sort of rhetorical approach was ruled out by the seriousness of the content of Paul's message. Thus what Paul is attempting to accomplish in vs. 10 is to make clear that while he is trying to persuade, he will not stoop to mere people-pleasing. He is a slave of Christ, seeking to please him, and so is not a slave of his audience, seeking to please them.[17] Thus what he says to the Galatians, he means. The exordium closes with the proper rhetorical signals about what sort of rhetoric the audience should expect in what follows.[18]

15. A third possibility is raised by Matera, *Galatians*, p. 47 namely that ἤ in vs. 10a is disjunctive rather than copulative, in which case Paul could be contrasting his behavior towards God and towards human beings. Lyons, *Pauline Autobiography*, pp. 136–46 opts for the disjunctive interpretation, but also for the translation 'curry favor with'. Paul is trying to curry favor with God, but not with human beings. The problem with this interpretation is that the letter itself bears witness that Paul is trying to appeal to and win back the Galatians, whether we call it currying favor or something else. He does indeed care how his converts react to him, not least because he sees them as his spiritual children (cf. Gal. 4.19).

16. Cf. the polemical definition of rhetoric in Plato, as part of the debate between philosophers and rhetoricians. Rhetoric says Plato is "something to gratify people" (*Gorg.* 462D).

17. As D. B. Martin, *Slavery as Salvation* (New Haven: Yale University Press, 1990), pp. 51ff. rightly points out, being the slave of an important figure, especially a slave who was the dignitary's agent, conferred a certain status on a person. In a surprising way then, we could have here a claim to a leadership role, under Christ's direction of course.

18. It should be noted at this point that there was a mixed opinion among those who were experts in rhetoric as to where to place the *propositio*. Aristotle (*Rhet.* 3.13) speaks of the proposition following the *exordium* rather than following the *narratio*. Quintilian by contrast suggests that the normal practice was for the *propositio* to follow the *narratio* (*Inst. Or.* 3.9.2). Paul is flexible and uses both patterns. For example, in 1 Corinthians we find what Aristotle spoke of, whereas here in Galatians the *propositio* does not appear until after the *narratio*.

Bridging the Horizons

Several major issues of modern import are raised for the church today by the material just discussed. The first of these is whether the church has, and believes it has, a definite Gospel message to which believers should adhere at all costs. It is clear enough that Paul believed there was such a message, and as we shall see when we examine the major 'proposition' of this rhetorical piece it has to do with believing certain things about Jesus Christ and the saving effects of his death (see 2.15–21). Our own pluralistic Western culture has a difficult time with the notion of Truth with a capital T. This is because of a commitment to the notion of relativism, the concept that we all only have partial glimpses at the truth, sometimes also entailing the belief that there is no such thing as or at least we cannot know absolute truth. Paul by contrast believes in a God who is capable of revealing himself adequately and accurately to human beings by a variety of means – through personal encounter, through words, through deeds. For Paul, the Gospel is not the sum of human reflections about God, trying to reach out and grasp the meaning of the divine, rather it is a gift from God. Paul is then not suggesting that his own opinions should be seen as the Truth, but rather that God's views and Word, coming as they do from an all-knowing Being not subject to the relativisms and partial knowledge humans must live with, are Truth. This Truth is seen as transcending and transforming all partial human knowledge and calling for an absolute commitment. Paul is not like the arrogant intellectual zealot who thinks that he or she personally has a corner on the market of Truth. Rather Paul believes God is the all-knowing one, and that since God is also all powerful, God is able to reveal the divine nature, plan and will both accurately and adequately. The Church then must decide today whether it still believes in the concept of revelation from God or not. If it does, then Paul's rhetoric here about no other Gospel must be taken to heart, and not dismissed as the ravings of a religious fanatic. What would it mean for the church once again to take seriously its commitment to a definite Gospel message centered on the definitive saving work of Christ?

In order to bridge the horizons from the first-century text to today, it will also be necessary to take into account the very different values many of us have in regard to what amounts to acceptable forms of dialogue and discourse compared to what was acceptable in antiquity. S. McKnight puts the matter well:

> The ancient world simply loved inflammatory language for expressing its differ-
> ences. I can document a great deal of such language in their literature, but I have not
> been able to document any who thought such language was personally biased or out
> of line. The ancients delighted in overstatement, and overstatements were effectively
> countered with similar overstatements. Today, however, we have become, if

anything, over-sensitized to offending special interest groups. So today we have editors who, admirably, reread our texts to see if they will offend racial, religious and gender-sensitive groups. Ours is not the ancient world.[19]

The modern reader then must be sensitized to how very different our own culture views proper modes of discourse and discussion as opposed to how the ancients viewed such matters. One must not be put off by the volume or the tone of Paul's rhetoric.

A third issue raised by this material concerns the notions of call and conversion, and behind that the notion of salvation, or being rescued out of the darkness of our world. Sometimes in the modern church the concept of conversion has been looked at askance, and the concept of call has been trivialized into taking a personal inventory of what one is able and feels inclined to do as one's life work. We must ask ourselves hard questions such as – Do we really believe in the fallenness of human culture, and thus the need for redemption and rescue? Do we really believe that God singles out individuals for specific tasks, or in fact that God calls all human beings both to conversion and to follow a divinely directed vocation? In a world full of crime, drugs, wasting of resources, greed, racial prejudice, deadly viruses and the like it is hard not to believe our world is a fallen place. The question then becomes where to look for help.

Whatever else one may say about Paul, he is surely a clear example that even in the case of adults the old adage 'you can't teach old dogs new tricks' is far from an absolute truth. Change, even radical change for the better, is possible in a human life, and Paul is telling us that in his case it came through an encounter with Jesus Christ on the road to Damascus. We must of course be careful to remember that neither Paul nor Acts suggests that all Christians have the exact same sort of conversion experience as Paul did. For some the change is far less dramatic and far from instantaneous. Furthermore, Paul warns in this very letter that a change for the worse is also possible – not all change is good change. Nevertheless, Paul holds to the dictum that all persons may be changed by God, all persons need to be changed by God, and that when such change happens what comes with it is a new sense of vocation – a call to serve God and others in some form. In this respect, Paul's words to us today have an especial appropriateness in a Western world that is becoming increasingly more secular and self-centered.

The urgency for transformation has never been greater in this century. One final example will have to do. There has been much effort made in recent years to warn our children about harmful drugs of various sorts. In America

---

19. S. McKnight, *Galatians. The NIV Application Commentary* (Grand Rapids: Zondervan, 1995), p. 60.

this has taken the form of a campaign with the slogan 'Just say no'. The theory is that if children are well enough educated and warned about the dangers of heroin or alcohol or cocaine or nicotine that they will make the right choices. In other words it is assumed that ignorance is the basic problem and more information is the answer to the drug problem. I would like to suggest that this assumption is at best a half truth. Information without personal transformation is insufficient. The real root of the problem lies in the hearts and minds of those who desire to try various things, even though they often are very well aware of the potential dangers. As Shakespeare has one character in *Macbeth* say, 'Who can minister to a mind diseased?' Who can root out fallen desires in the human heart? Paul's answer is that Jesus Christ can do this, and Paul spoke from personal experience as one who formerly had violently persecuted Christians but who now loved them. Are we compelled to reject his testimony about the validity and value of conversion to and through Christ? I think not.

Narratio: 1.11–2.14   The Origin and Character of the Gospel of Grace

I: 1.11–12

THE GOSPEL OF CHRIST

For I make known to you brothers, the Gospel, the one proclaimed by me that it is not according to human beings, for neither did I receive it from human beings nor was I taught it but [I got it] through a revelation of Jesus Christ.

Verses **11–12** are clearly transitional and show that despite the passion behind Paul's arguments here, Paul is attending to what will make for a rhetorically effective communication. The *narratio* proper does not begin until vs. 13.[1] It was the mark of a good orator that his transitions from one part of a speech to another were smooth and natural ones. Paul here links together a theme already briefly touched on in the prescript in 1.1, which he plans to elaborate on in detail in the *narratio* which follows in 1.13–2.14. Paul will present his life and actions as a paradigm of his Gospel of grace. This is not because his Christian life and experiences or his apostleship were being questioned but because his Gospel was being challenged or at least supplemented by the agitators. Lyons sums up matters well:

> That Paul offers his autobiographical narrative in 1.13–2.21 as substantiation of his claim in 1.11–12 concerning the nature and origin of his Gospel suggests he considers himself in some sense a representative or even an embodiment of that gospel. As in the ancient philosophical lives, the consistency between his . . .

1. See B. Lategan, "Is Paul Defending his Apostleship in Galatians?" *NTS* 34 (1988), pp. 411–30, here pp. 419–20.

'conduct', and ... 'deeds', and his ... words demonstrates the truth of his philosophy, the Gospel of Jesus Christ. He is a paradigm of the Gospel he preaches to the Gentiles. The formulation of Paul's autobiographical remarks in terms of 'formerly-now' and '[hu]man-God' serves the paradigmatic function of contrasting Paul's conversion from Judaism to Christianity with the Galatians inverted conversion, which is really nothing other than a desertion of 'the one who called [them] in the grace of Christ (1.6) and a surrender of Christian freedom for the slavery of the law (see 2.4; 3.28; 4.1–9, 22–31; 5.1,13).[2]

There is some debate as to whether the connecting particle γάρ or δὲ is the original reading in vs. 11. P46, א, A and others read the latter, while B, D, G and others read the former. Clearly enough the connective preferred in both the preceding and the following clauses is γάρ, which might favor the suggestion that scribes were more likely to change a δὲ here to a γάρ.[3] Also tipping the scales in favor of δὲ here are the parallels we find in 1 Cor 15.1, 2 and 2 Cor. 8.1 where there is the same combination of δὲ and the verb γνωρίζω.[4] The significance of accepting the reading δὲ is that it is a mildly disjunctive connecting word, suggesting a new beginning or section at 1.11.

Paul uses the verb γνωρίζω to introduce a solemn statement about some truth that he feels is crucial to bear in mind (cf. 1 Cor. 15.1, 2; 2 Cor. 8.1). This statement affirms the proposition of the divine origin and character of Paul's Gospel, a thesis Paul intends to illustrate in the *narratio*. This is *not* the main thesis of this work, but rather the one which undergirds the main thesis. The essential proposition to be promulgated in this work is not announced until after the *narratio* at 2.15–21, where we hear the first full expression of the *content* of this Gospel. The Gospel of grace proclaims the acceptance and acceptability of both Gentiles and Jews on the basis of trust in the faithful work of Jesus Christ which justifies (or sets right) sinners, and not on the basis of works of the Mosaic Law. Therefore works of the Mosaic Law are not merely unnecessary or redundant. If they are pursued by those who are Christians as the proper manner of Christian living, as if Christians were obliged to obey the Mosaic covenant's requirements, they amount to a fall from grace, a devaluation of what Christ accomplished on the cross. The origin, character and content of the Gospel determines the origin, character and behavior of the people of God, who are Jew and Gentile united in Christ and his finished work on the cross.

It can be shown that the thesis stated in vss. 11–12 is the main one underlying the *narratio,* as Matera does with the following outline: (1) 1.11–12 the theme announced – the Gospel is not of human origin; (2) 1.13–17 –

---

2. Lyons, *Pauline Autobiography,* p. 171. See also B. R. Gaventa, "Galatians 1 and 2: Autobiography as Paradigm," *NovT* 4 (1986), pp. 309–26.

3. See Lighfoot, *Galatians,* pp. 79–80.

4. See Longenecker, *Galatians,* p. 22.

first proof that Paul received the Gospel through a revelation of Christ; (3) 1.18–20 – second proof – that the Jerusalem church didn't commission Paul; (4) 1.21–24 – third proof – that those in Judea glorified God because of Paul; (5) 2.1–10 – fourth proof – Paul defended his Gospel at Jerusalem; (6) 2.11–14 – Paul defended his Gospel at Antioch.[5] All this is meant to show Paul's consistency and the divine character and origin of his message. His life has been a public demonstration of the Gospel of grace.

It is doubtful that Paul means in vs. 11 that the Galatians have heard nothing about what he is about to narrate. Indeed 1.13 will inform us that the Galatians had already heard about the before and after of Paul's conversion experience, and so presumably also about how his views on the Gospel changed. He is, however, using a disclosure formula here to make known to them the divine origin of the message, even though they already knew its content. The disclosure formula is appropriate and will be reinforced by the apocalyptic language we find at the end of vs. 12.

Two things need to be noticed at this juncture. Firstly, it is at this point (vs. 11) that Paul goes into the first person singular, which makes clear to us that while Paul and his Gospel appear to have supporters where he is (Antioch?) as the prescript suggests, in essence this is a personal letter from Paul alone, not a joint communication. Secondly, Paul still calls his audience brothers and treats them as such. The family language which he uses here is not just conciliatory but it makes clear a fundamental conviction of Paul's. That conviction is this – that the family of God is composed on the basis of faith, not heredity or other factors. Those whom Paul considers brothers and sisters in Christ are those who share the same faith in Christ and what he accomplished through his death and resurrection (cf. the prescript above). While it is certainly true that Jews spoke of those of their ethnic group as brothers (Lev. 19.17; Deut. 1.16; 2 Macc. 1.1 cf. Acts 7.2; Rom. 9.3), it is likely that this is not the origin of the Pauline usage. More probable is the suggestion that it ultimately goes back to Jesus' own remarks about the basis and character of God's family – namely that it is constituted by faith (Mk. 3.31–35 and par.; Mt. 23.8), though Paul himself probably first picked it up from the early Christians with whom he himself first came into contact after his conversion.[6] It is also crucial to bear in mind the social function of this language. It is boundary-defining language, suggesting who is and is not family, and furthermore it suggests that Paul sees some relationship between the norms and values of the family and the family of faith.[7] The second clause of vs. 11 provides us with the disclosure itself. The Gospel that Paul

5. Matera, *Galatians*, p. 55.
6. See Longenecker, *Galatians*, p. 22.
7. See now P. Esler, "Family Imagery and Christian Identity in Gal. 5.13–6.10."

gospeled (noting the deliberate redundancy here in the Greek) was not κατὰ ἄνθρωπον. The basic meaning of κατὰ is 'according to' and the point being made is that Paul's Gospel does not stem from a human source or mere human ideas or customs. This will be made more clear in vs. 12.

Verse 12 entails two specific denials. Paul neither received his Gospel from human beings, nor was he taught it. Rather it came through an apocalypse or revelation of Jesus Christ. The question is what is Paul denying here? How should we read the final clause? Is it an example of the use of an objective genitive or a subjective genitive? Is Christ seen as the mediator of this revelation or the content of it? The first denial involves the semi-technical term 'received' often used for the transmission of sacred tradition in early Jewish and Jewish Christian circles (cf. 1 Cor. 15. 3). What follows this verse in Gal. 1–2, make quite clear that Paul is not denying that he had received some informaton about Jesus from other human beings. Things could perhaps be clarified somewhat if we could decide whether the final clause involves an objective or subjective genitive. On the one hand, Gal. 1.1 might be thought to favor the suggestion that the phrase refers to a revelation that came from or through Christ, but there the issue is Paul's apostleship, not his Gospel. On the other hand, 1.16 speaks of a revelation of which Christ is the content. On the whole it seems likely that Paul in vs. 12 is referring to a revelation about Christ.[8] If this is correct then Paul must have something specific in mind about Christ or his ministry, an insight or idea he had not received from other Christians. In view of the subject matter of what precedes and follows 1.12, the most reasonable suggestion is that Paul is referring to his Law-free Gospel for the Gentiles which focuses on and is based on faith in the finished work of Christ on the cross which provides one with right standing before God. This distinctive Gospel message about Christ Paul admits is not the sort of thing human beings could come up with on their own. It had to be revealed by God for it to be known at all.

The term ἀποκάλυψις is primarily found in the Pauline epistles in the NT (thirteen out of eighteen times it occurs in the NT), and must be seen for what it is. It refers to a revelation of a hidden and heavenly secret about God's plan for the redemption of human beings. It can refer to the eschatological things God has already accomplished in Christ, or it can refer to future eschatological actions involving Christ (Rom. 2.5; 8.19; 1 Cor. 1.7; 2 Thess. 1.7). In Paul's view this revelation or apocalypse provides a key to understanding the relationship between God and humankind now that Christ has come and salvation has been made available to all.[9] "Paul has

8. Further support for this conclusion comes from noticing that it is God, according to 1.16, who does the revealing, not Christ. See the still helpful discussion of Burton, *Galatians*, pp. 41–43; see Matera, *Galatians*, p. 56.

9. See Dunn, *Galatians*, p. 53.

taken as his leading subject not the Law but rather the Gospel of Christ and the history that this Gospel has created and continues to create . . . the Teachers' [i.e., Agitators'] fundamental issue is covenantal nomism, if you like; Paul's is evangelical, cosmic, history-creating christology."[10]

This message is definitely not one that is 'according to human beings' or 'human tradition'. Paul will present in what follows vss. 11–12 "two case studies to illustrate the claim that the Gospel is not κατὰ ἄνθρωπον".[11] Paul's theology is not merely some theory, but rather implies a definite way of living for Christians. The imperative grows out of the indicative in Paul's thought world. And Paul's thought world is a narrative thought world full of stories about major figures, and these figures provide examples, either negative or positive, of how Christians should not or should behave (e.g., Paul, Peter, Barnabas, the agitators, Abraham, Jesus).[12] Paul assumes that his audience is and will be caught up in the stories of Abraham and Christ and Paul and find them recapitulated in their own past and present experience. Even the narrative and theological sections of this letter have social and paraenetic aims, as we shall see.

There is general agreement among Greek and Roman rhetoricians that examples or παραδείγματα are most appropriate in and most often found in deliberative rhetoric (cf. Aristotle *Rhet.* 1.9.40; *Rhet. ad Her.* 3.5.9; Cicero *De Or.* 2.335; Quintilian *Inst. Or.* 3.8.36, 66).[13] As the last reference to Quintilian makes clear, the sort of examples the rhetoricians primarily have in mind are actual historical examples, and all other things being equal the more current ones the better. One particular form that the appeal to example takes is the appeal to imitation, in particular the imitation of the speaker. Again, the form of rhetoric that the appeal to imitation is most common in is deliberative oratory (cf., e.g., Isocrates *Or.* 8.36–37; Dio Chrysostom *Or.* 41.9–10). Paul's rhetorical strategy in the *narratio* is to present himself as a positive example for the Galatians to follow, and others as negative examples. Having done this, he is then later in the midst of the argument section of his discussion able to appeal directly for the imitation of himself when he returns to a narrative mode of discourse (Gal. 4.12).[14]

---

10. J. L. Martyn, "Events in Galatia" in *Pauline Theology Vol. 1*, pp. 160–79, here pp. 164–65.
11. Lategan, "Is Paul Defending?" pp. 424–25.
12. See Lategan, pp. 425ff.
13. See the discussion in Mitchell, *Rhetoric of Reconciliation*, pp. 39–46.
14. The otherwise interesting rhetorical analysis of this material by J. D. Hester is marred by failure to recognize the deliberative species of this material and so the function of these narrative episodes as providing examples. But see his "The Rhetorical Structure of Galatians 1.11–2.14," *JBL* 103 (1984), pp. 223–43.

This last appeal is one more sign that we must be dealing with a deliberative form of argument in this document, because not surprisingly the appeal to imitate oneself is not really appropriate in the rhetoric of defense, when one's character is thought by the audience to be in doubt. To put it the other way around, Paul's appeal in Gal. 4.12 suggests strongly that Paul assumes that the Galatians do basically trust and admire Paul, and would be willing to follow his example. This must be borne in mind as we consider 1.13–2.14.

II: 1.13–2.14

A NARRATIVE OF SURPRISING DEVELOPMENTS: JERUSALEM, ANTIOCH AND BEYOND

For you heard about my former manner of life, how that I in Judaism persecuted exceedingly the church of God and was laying it waste, and I was progressing further in Judaism than many of my contemporaries among my race, being even more zealous [than them] about the traditions of my fathers. But when he was pleased, the one who set me apart from my mother's womb and called [me] through his grace, to reveal his Son in me, in order that I might proclaim him among the [Gentile] nations, immediately I did not consult with flesh and blood, nor did I go up unto Jerusalem to those who were apostles before me, but I went into Arabia and again went back unto Damascus.

Then after three years I went up unto Jerusalem to make the acquaintance of Cephas and stayed with him fifteen days, but other apostles I did not see except James the brother of the Lord. Now what I write to you, surely before God [I swear] that I do not lie. Then I went unto the district of Syria and of Cilicia. And I was unknown by sight to the assemblies of Judea, those in Christ. But they kept hearing that 'The one formerly persecuting us now is proclaiming the faith who formerly laid [us] waste', and they were glorifying God because of me.

Then after fourteen years again I went up unto Jerusalem with Barnabas also taking along with me Titus. Now I went up according to a revelation and I laid before them the Gospel which I proclaim among the [Gentile] nations, but separately to those well thought of, lest I might be running or have run for nothing. And not even Titus who was with me, being Greek, was compelled to be circumcised. But because of false brothers brought in surreptitiously, who intruded to spy out the freedom which we have in Christ Jesus in order that we would be enslaved, to them not for a moment did we yield in submission, in order that the truth of the

Gospel would continue unchanged for you, but from those considered to be something, whatever they were it does not matter to me, God does not accept the 'face' of a human being, for to me those considered to be something added nothing, but on the contrary seeing that I was entrusted with the Gospel for the uncircumcised just as Peter for the circumcised, for the One who worked in Peter for apostleship of the circumcised also worked in me for the [Gentile] nations, and having recognized the grace given to me, James and Cephas and John, those who are considered to be pillars, gave to me and Barnabas the right hand of common participation in order that we [might go] unto the [Gentile] nations, but they unto the circumcision, only that we might continue to bear in mind the poor, which same thing I also was [already] eager to do.

But when Cephas came unto Antioch I opposed him face to face because he stood condemned. For before certain ones from James [came], he was eating with the Gentiles. But when they came he made a move to draw back and was separating himself being afraid of those from the circumcision, and the rest of the Jews also joined him in a pretense, so that even Barnabas was actually carried away in their play-acting. But when I saw that they were not on the right road toward the truth of the Gospel, I said to Cephas in front of all 'If you being a Jew, living Gentile like and not Jew like, how can you compel the Gentiles to Judaize'?

Strictly speaking, a *narratio* was not absolutely necessary in a deliberative speech, but it would often be included if it could serve to set the stage for the essential proposition and the advice the rhetor wished to give his audience, or if the marshalling of facts could serve to correct mistaken impressions about the speaker and so improve his *ethos*, making the audience more receptive to the advice he would give following the *narratio* (cf. Dio Chrysostom *Or.* 40.8–19; 41.1–6).[15] Quintilian says that statements about external matters that are nonetheless directly relevant to the discussion at hand could be introduced in a *narratio* in a deliberative speech (*Inst. Or.* 3.8.10–11). A close scrutiny will show that all three of these statements very adequately describe some of the major functions of the narrative in 1.13–2.14. For example, it is clear enough that the material, especially in 2.11–14 prepares for the material in 2.15–21, so much so that some have even thought that the latter is a continuation of the former despite some signals in the narrative that we should separate the two paragraphs (cf. below). It is better to say that the narrative leads one up to the essential summary of the argument or proposition found beginning in 2.15. Betz puts the matter succinctly: "It cannot be accidental that at the end of the *narratio* in Gal. 2.14, when Paul formulates the dilemma which Cephas is in, this dilemma is identical with the issue the Galatians have to decide 'why do you compel the Gentiles to judaize?'"[16]

15. See Mitchell, *The Rhetoric of Reconciliation*, pp. 200–1.
16. Betz, *Galatians*, p. 62.

Secondly, notice that while Paul says that his audience knows about his former life as a Pharisee and persecutor, it is clear enough that they do not know enough about his life during the years immediately after his conversion and call. This is why the former period of his life can be summed up in two verses but the post-conversion period must be given much fuller treatment, with the correction of possible misperceptions along the way as to where Paul got his Gospel and how much contact he may have had with the Jerusalem authorities. This approach conforms to what the rhetoricians say such a *narratio* was meant to accomplish in a piece of deliberative rhetoric. A *narratio* is only supposed to include the facts that are germane to the presentation the speaker wants to make to his audience, "not saying more than the case demands" (*Inst. Or.* 4.2.43). This is in part why we find Paul's remarks maddeningly brief at certain points. But Paul is not writing an autobiography here; he is arguing a particular case and trying to persuade his audience to adhere to the one true Gospel of grace, adhering to his own personal example. He is, in short, adhering to the rhetorical requirements for clarity, brevity, and plausibility in a *narratio*, leaving out all material that is not directly relevant to the case.[17]

One important feature of a *narratio* is that of characterization of the major players. The use of pejorative language was in order to dispose the audience in a particular direction toward one's own viewpoint and against that of others. Hence we hear about 'false brothers' 'secretly brought in' who 'spy things out', or about 'those *reputed* to be pillars', or about Peter's and Barnabas' 'hypocrisy'. This use of pejorative and emotional language is not accidental. It is meant to raise animus against the opposing viewpoint, and sympathy for the speaker's case.[18]

It should also be noted that the events Paul recounts in the *narratio* do not transpire in Galatia but rather in Jerusalem, Arabia, Antioch, and elsewhere. These are clearly external matters to the immediate situation in Galatia, but Paul sees them as providing necessary parallels and clues to help the Galatians understand the argument that he is about to present, and so follow the right sort of examples in regard to the Gospel of grace. Quintilian tells us that the proper way to signal the beginning of a *narratio* when the audience knows something of the facts is with some such phrase as 'I know that you are aware that . . .' or 'you remember' or 'you are not ignorant of the fact . . .' (*Inst. Or.* 4.2.21-22). It will be seen that we have 'you have heard' at the beginning of vs. 13, and we may also note the disclosure formula in vs. 11, 'I make known to you'. The audience would have picked up the rhetorical

---

17. On this whole matter see R. G. Hall, "Historical Inference and Rhetorical Effect: Another Look at Galatians 1 and 2," in *Persuasive Artistry*, pp. 308-20.

18. See rightly Betz, *Galatians*, p. 61.

signal in vs. 11 of the transition to a new section, and would have been prepared for the reminder of facts already known in vss. 13–14. If we ask why familiar facts would be repeated, Quintilian properly answers that the function of the *narratio* is not just to inform or remind, but to persuade by placing the facts in a certain context and presenting them in a certain light. Finally, it was the proper and normal rhetorical convention in a *narratio* to list events in chronological order, though on rare occasions a logical order might be used that did not follow the actual sequence of events.[19] If the latter was going to be the case, however, it was expected that one would announce or signal this fact in some manner. In fact Quintilian says that if one presented events out of order that he would be expected to state to the audience or judge at some point what the proper order of events was (*Inst. Or.* 4.2.83–85). Paul's use of temporal designations of sequence (cf. below) strongly suggests he is following the normal rhetorical practice at this point. Certainly, his audience listening to 1.13–2.14, would assume that the incident at Antioch followed the second meeting in Jerusalem, in the absence of hints or statements to the contrary.[20]

The first major subsection of the *narratio* is found in vss. **13–17**. As Lyons says, the stress in this section is to contrast what was formerly the case with Paul and what now is the case. "The formulation of Paul's auto-biographical remarks in terms of 'formerly-now' and '[hu]man-God' . . . serves a paradigmatic function, to contrast Paul's conversion from Judaism to Christianity with the Galatians inverted conversion . . . Even the verb μετατίθημι which describes their desertion of Paul and his Gospel in 1.6 has the connotation of a reverse conversion, apostasy, treachery, desertion."[21] Paul's trajectory is to be the paradigm, other models are to be abandoned or ignored.[22]

19. Clearly Quintilian states that one ought to "follow the order of events as a general rule" (*Inst. Or.* 4.2.87). In fact *Inst. Or.* 4.2.83 suggests that Quintilian knows he is swimming up stream against the prevailing tide of opinion when he allows occasionally for a non-chronological arrangement of the facts. The majority opinion was clearly against him as is shown by examining Cicero *De Invent.* 1.20.29; *Rhetor. ad Alex.* 31.1438b.19–23; *Rhet. ad Her.* 1.9.15. The Latin tradition differed in some small ways from the Greek tradition, and Paul clearly follows the Greek rhetorical tradition.

20. See Betz, *Galatians*, p. 61. Once one accepts that Paul is following rhetorical conventions in this narrative, then the case for rearranging the Jerusalem visit and the Antioch incident becomes very weak indeed, but see J. Dupont, "Pierre et Paul à Antioche et à Jerusalem," *Recherches de Science et Religieuse* 45 (1957), pp. 42–60, 225–39.

21. Lyons, *Pauline Autobiography*, p. 150.

22. On this entire section one should see B. R. Gaventa, *From Darkness to Light: Aspects of Conversion in the New Testament* (Philadelphia: Fortress, 1986), pp. 22–28.

Perhaps the first point of note to make about vs. **13** is the contrast between 'Judaism' and the assembly of God.[23] Paul was previously involved in the former entity and now in the latter. The term Ἰουδαϊσμός is rare in the NT, in fact it only appears in this verse and the next one. It is used in Jewish literature of this general period (cf. 2 Macc. 2.21; 8.1; 14.38; 4 Macc. 4.26) to describe a Torah-true Jewish lifestyle and belief system as contrasted to Seleucid Hellenism.[24] M. Hengel has aptly defined the term: "The word means both political and genetic association with the Jewish nation and exclusive belief in the one God of Israel, together with observance of the Torah given by him."[25]

Here Judaism is contrasted with living a life in accord with the Gospel and within the assembly of God. To be sure, Paul continues to regard himself as ethnically a Jew, so that he can speak of his kinsmen and kinswomen according to the flesh, or of 'my people' (cf. 1.14; 2.15), but his point is that he is no longer a part of the social and religious and political system known as Judaism. The issue then and now is of course how one defines what a true Jew is (cf. Rom. 9). In Paul's view, birth or ethnic identity is not sufficient, indeed it is not necessary, to make one a true member of the people of God. That comes through faith. More to the point in this document, Paul believes that observance of the Torah is neither necessary nor sufficient to make or keep one a member of the people of God. The people of God are no longer under the Mosaic covenant in Paul's view, rather they are under the new covenant which is grounded in the earlier Abrahamic one.

Paul's approach is a sectarian one, and in this he differs from various Christians in Jerusalem. At the ecclesiological level he does not see continuity between those who are currently under the Mosaic covenant and outside of Christ, and those who are within the Christian assembly. In Paul's view Jew and Gentile united in Christ *are* the assembly of God, not merely in continuity

---

23. The term Judaism is an appropriate translation of the Greek but it sometimes conveys the notion that we are speaking of later rabbinic Judaism, which is not the case. This is why some scholars have suggested the translation Judeanism. Much depends on the origins of this term. If it is the case that it is a term that non-Jews chose to use of the Jewish religion, then it is in order to point out that "non-Israelites as a rule, believed all Israelites came from Judea, [and] hence called them Judeans and their customs 'Judaism'" (Malina and Neyrey, *Portraits of Paul*, p. 38). However, the use of the term 'Judaism' in the Maccabean literature as a form of self-description by Jews indicating they were Torah true, suggests that the geographical component is not to the fore here when used by someone like Paul, but rather the religious and social component.

24. See the discussion of Y. Amir, "The Term *Ioudaismos*: A Study in Jewish-Hellenistic Self-Identification," *Immanuel* 14 (1982), pp. 35–36, 39–40.

25. M. Hengel, *Judaism and Hellenism*, 2 vols. trans. J. Bowden (Philadelphia: Fortress, 1974), Vol. I, pp. 1–2.

with the assembly of God.[26] This entity must be distinguished from 'Judaism'. The heritage of Israel is seen by Paul as being claimed by and fulfilled in the Christian assembly and not elsewhere.[27] This is not the view of some in the Jerusalem church. As we shall see, Paul will argue that it is in the Christian assembly that the promises of God to Abraham are being fulfilled. In fact, Paul will go so far as to say in a later letter (in Rom. 9–11) that non-Christian Jews have been at least temporarily broken off from the people of God, with the hope that they might be grafted back in on the same basis as Gentiles, namely through faith in Christ. While this sort of approach should not be called anti-Semitism, as Paul certainly is not manifesting prejudice against Jews as a race of people, it is not inappropriate to call it a radical critique of Judaism. Paul's days of being bound to observe Torah as someone under the Mosaic covenant were over. It was what he 'formerly' (πότε) did.[28]

Notice that Paul chooses the term ἀναστροφήν to describe his former life. The term refers more to orthopraxy and social existence than to orthodoxy and belief systems and is properly translated 'manner (or way) of living'. It is a truism to say that Judaism was more concerned with matters of orthopraxy than orthodoxy, but clearly enough certain particular beliefs undergirded the praxis. Paul will go on to speak of the proper manner for Christian living as 'walking according to the Spirit', which is an adaptation and alteration of what we find in the OT where we hear 'walk in all my commandments' (1 Kngs. 6.12; cf. Test. Ash. 6.3 which refers to taking the Law as one's way of life). The reason this matter comes up at this juncture is that Paul's entire argument in Galatians is about how the Galatian Christians should or should not live now and in the future. It is not about getting in, or staying in, but about the right and wrong ways of going on, one leading towards unity, community harmony, and progress in the Christian life, the other leading to disunity, discord, and

26. Here and elsewhere Dunn, *Galatians*, p. 57 misses the point. The sectarian mindset sees its group as the legitimate heirs to the religious legacy of the group they have come out of, and other Jews as illegitimate, at least at present. This is the reason for all the antitheses and antinomies in Galatians, as Martyn has rightly stressed. True enough, Paul sees the church as continuous with the Biblical heritage, especially as manifested in Abraham. He does not see the church, however, as continuous with the synagogue, or with contemporary Judaism. In this he differs with various of his fellow Christians in the Jerusalem church.

27. There is of course a certain parallel with the Qumran sectarians at this point who anathematized the Jerusalem hierarchy and temple apparatus and saw true Israel as being or to be manifested in their community and midst. Paul's views are, however, even more radical because the Qumran community believed that it was incumbent on them still to observe the Law, indeed observe it more scrupulously than other Jews. Paul believed that the Mosaic covenant was now obsolete, since Christ came.

28. Gaventa, *From Darkness*, pp. 25ff. misses the signals in the sectarian use of common language, and so is also inclined to deny that Paul really underwent a conversion.

even apostasy. One's way of life involves beliefs, behavior, and social interaction. It involves certain rites of passage and not others, certain beliefs about salvation and not others, certain forms of behavior and not others among Christians.

Paul gives further description to his former way of life in vs. 13b by saying that on the one hand he persecuted exceedingly the assembly of God, no doubt because he believed it to be beyond the pale, an apostate community and not a Torah-true Jewish one, not the assembly of God at all, and on the other hand he himself was heading in the opposite direction from the assembly of God, advancing and progressing in Judaism beyond most of his Jewish contemporaries. The key to both the negative and positive behavior of Paul was what he describes in vs. 14 as his exceedingly great zeal for the traditions of his ancestors.

The verbs ἐδίωκον and ἐπόρθουν[29] are both in the imperfect and refer to past repeated actions, not one time aberrations from a person's normal conduct. The two verbs must be interpreted together with the latter making more explicit what is implicit in the former. These are political terms, with the latter regularly used to refer to the sacking or destroying or devastating of a city, and the former in this sort of context referring to persecution, not mere pursuit (cf. Josephus *War* 4.534 and 1 Macc. 2.47; 3.5 where in a close parallel it refers to the pursuit and persecution of apostate Jews). This action on Paul's part was something he was clearly ashamed of (cf. 1 Cor. 15.9; Gal. 1.13, 23; Phil. 3.6), but only after his conversion. There is no hint in the NT that Saul had an uneasy conscience about such actions before his encounter on Damascus Road. The adverbial phrase καθ' ὑπερβολὴν indicates the level which this persecution reached. Paul went to extremes, the persecutions being not merely extensive (in and beyond Jerusalem) but also intensive. As Hengel says, when one takes these two verbs together one must conclude that Paul used violence or brute force against some Christians.[30] The adverbial phrase may even suggest the use of excessive force leading to the death of some Christians through the zealous taking of the law into his own hands (cf., e.g., Acts 6–7).[31] Paul is speaking of more than just vigorous dialogue and debate here, and it is important to take this seriously in attempting to evaluate what Paul will say elsewhere about Jewish persecution of Christians (cf. Gal. 6.12).

29. That this verb only occurs here in Galatians 1 and in Acts 9.21 and only to refer to Paul's persecuting activities, is a rather strong hint that the author of Acts knew either Paul or at least the Pauline tradition about his pre-Christian life. See my discussion in *The Acts of the Apostles*, pp. 306ff.

30. Against Gaventa, pp. 24ff.

31. M. Hengel, *The Pre-Christian Paul* (Philadelphia: Trinity Press International, 1991), pp. 71–72.

There is no reason to doubt that such actions did from time to time take place against Christians, even though there is no evidence of an organized Empire-wide attempt to eliminate Christians either by Jews or Romans in the middle of the first century. Paul will accuse the agitators of insisting on circumcision due to fear of Jewish persecution. We must take this evaluation seriously, especially in view of texts like 2 Cor. 11.24 which refers to multiple disciplinary whippings Paul received at the hands of Jews. In short, the social context out of which Christianity arose, especially during the period when there was close association or at least regular contact with the synagogue was a volatile one, which may explain a good deal about the behavior and suggestions of the Jerusalem church to other churches.

Verse **14** informs us about Paul's progress in Judaism. As in Josephus *Life* 8, the term προκοπή refers to either moral and spiritual development and/or progress in education, more likely the latter than the former, as is clearly the case in the Josephus text. If Paul is speaking about moral development he is clearly being ironic here, since he is writing this as a Christian who regrets having persecuted Christians. Perhaps the parallel use of the term in Lk. 2.52 in what is clearly a pedagogical situation favors the suggestion that advancement in education is meant here, as does the reference to the traditions of the ancestors. It is in order to point out, then, that among the advanced subjects which students of Jewish teachers studied in Jerusalem during this period was rhetoric, the art of persuasion.[32] Paul says of himself that he was far more zealous for the traditions of his fathers than various of his Jewish contemporaries, by which he probably means his fellow Jewish students of the Law who studied in Jerusalem, who also were making progress in Judaism, since vs. 14 must be taken together as one continuous thought.

The question then becomes as to whether Paul's use of the term ζηλωτής here warrants the conclusion of Lightfoot and others that Paul, far from being like Hillel or Paul's mentor Gamaliel (at least as portrayed in Acts 5.33–42 cf. Acts 22.3),[33] was in fact part of the extreme faction of Pharisees.[34] This thesis has recently been given new life by N. T. Wright who argues that Paul before his conversion was a Shammaite Pharisee who saw himself as being in the tradition or line of other 'men of zeal' such as Phineas, or Elijah, and the Maccabees and was prepared to take violent action even and perhaps especially against fellow Jews that he saw as destroying or apostasizing from the true

---

32. See D. Daube, "Rabbinic Methods of Interpretation and Hellenistic Rhetoric," *HUCA* 22 (1949), pp. 239–62. Note that Paul's instructor Hillel, in turn had instructors from Alexandria where rhetoric was a staple of all education.

33. See my discussion of this material in *The Acts of the Apostles*, pp. 641ff.

34. See Lightfoot, *Galatians*, pp. 81–82.

Jewish manner of life.[35] He goes on to hypothesize, that seeing himself in this mold, when he was converted, he went off to Mount Sinai in Arabia, as Elijah had done to see what a zealot ought to do next, in view of the change in his life. This thesis has some very attractive features, and would explain not only why Paul acted as he did, but why the church in Judea was so fearful of Paul even after his conversion (cf. Gal. 1.21; Acts 9.26). The thesis has some weaknesses, however. When Paul goes on to characterize how God had set him apart from birth and called him, he speaks of his call and commission not in Elijah- or Phineas-like terms but in terms reminiscent of what was said about Jeremiah and the Servant of God in Isaiah, as we shall see.

Secondly, in view of 2 Cor. 11.32–33 it is far more likely that when we are told Paul went off to Arabia what is meant is that he went to certain populated parts of the Nabatean kingdom and tried out his Gospel for the Gentiles. This is why Aretas sent his official after Paul while he was in Damascus (which at the time was part of the Nabatean kingdom). Whatever we conclude about Wright's thesis, it is important to recognize that Saul was not just zealous for the Law in principle, he was prepared to take violent political action against those whom he saw as Lawbreakers and apostates. Both before and, as manifested clearly in Galatians, after his conversion, Paul was strongly concerned in preserving the boundaries of the community of God, because the boundaries help make clear the core identity of the group. Defining boundaries is part of the act of self-definition. Before his conversion Paul was zealously maintaining the boundaries of Judaism, now he is zealous to maintain the boundaries of the assembly of God in Galatia, hence all the discussion about boundary issues and rituals, even though he is addressing those who are already Christians. The Galatians are, however, confused Christians, who do not understand the implications of what happened when they received the Spirit and what they committed themselves to then, and what sort of persons of faith they became when they became Christians. Nor do they grasp the implications of how taking on the duties of the Mosaic Law will violate that past.

As we conclude our discussion about Paul as a zealot, it is important to bear in mind how much of a clue 'zeal' is to the mind of Paul both before and after his conversion.[36] The fundamental study of T. L. Donaldson has shown

---

35. In a series of lectures on Paul's career as going from Zeal to Zeal, given in the spring of 1996 at Asbury Seminary. The first of these, 'The Agendas of Saul of Tarsus' is where one will find these ideas most readily. This lecture is now published as "Paul, Arabia, and Elijah," *JBL* 115 (1996), pp. 683–92.

36. Notice how an epideictic approach to this material overlooks the way this material actually functions rhetorically. It is not about praise and blame, but about advice and consent, but cf. Hester, "Placing the Blame: The Presence of Epideictic in Galatians 1 and 2," in *Persuasive Artistry*, pp. 281–307.

that any study of Paul's view of the Law that does not take into account the 'zeal' factor will not do justice to the issue. Donaldson's basic thesis is that both before and after his conversion Paul saw a fundamental antithesis between the Law and Christ as the basic means of defining the boundaries of the community of God. "The incompatibility of Christ and Torah was the constant element in the syllogism that on the one side of the conversion experience led to persecution of the church, and on the other resulted in fierce resistance to the Judaizers. In this approach, then it is assumed that a tight convictional or cognitive connection can be found to link together Paul's persecution of the church, his conversion, and his later pattern of thought."[37] Donaldson shows the basic flaws in various views that do not recognize this close connection.[38] The following factors need to be taken into account: (1) the evidence that we have suggests strongly that Paul persecuted Christians precisely because he saw their convictions and way of life as a threat to the understood boundaries and social cohesion of the Jewish community and a violation of Torah piety; (2) it is not adequate to argue that Paul's zeal was directed only against some Jewish Christians who took too liberal approach to Torah observance. Besides the fact that Paul does not say this, were this the case we would have no explanation for why *after* his conversion Paul didn't simply become like those mentioned in Acts 21.20 who were followers of Christ *and* zealots for the Law; (3) Paul's argument in Galatians would have been in serious jeopardy had it been true that after his conversion he had initially preached circumcision and a Gospel to the Jews, and only after that failed, a Gospel to the Gentiles. This ignores the strong case presented by U. Wilckens that in Gal. 1 and in Phil. 3 Paul presents his conversion as involving a break with Torah piety, and presents his call like that of Jeremiah and the Servant, which involved being a light to the nations;[39] (4) The view of H. Räisänen that Paul after his conversion gradually came to a view that the Law was an *adiaphoron* fails precisely because it fails to take into account Paul's zeal for the Law before his conversion. "The idea that someone with zealous commitment to the Torah would after his conversion casually abandon it as an *adiaphoron* without having come to a conviction that this was a necessary corollary of his new faith in Christ, is

---

37. T. L. Donaldson, "Zealot and Convert: The Origin of Paul's Christ-Torah Antithesis," *CBQ* 51 (1989), pp. 655–82, here p. 656.

38. Donaldson's critique dismantles the suggestion of A. J. Hultgren, "Paul's Pre-Christian Persecutions of the Church: Their Purpose, Locale and Nature," *JBL* 95 (1976), pp. 97–111, that Paul's persecution was directed at only some more Hellenized Jewish Christians.

39. U. Wilckens, "Die Bekehrung des Paulus als religionsgeschichtliches Problem," in *Rechtfertigung als Freiheit: Paulusstudien* (Neukirchen-Vluyn: Neukirchen Verlag, 1974), pp. 11–32.

unthinkable."[40] The above should be sufficient to make clear how impcrtant the zeal factor is in understanding Paul's view of the Law.[41] It must never be forgotten that unlike other Jewish Christians, Paul came to faith in Christ in the midst of a career as a persecutor, as one who saw a fundamental distinction between being a Torah-true Jew and being a Jewish follower of Jesus Christ. "Before he came to the conviction, then, that salvation is through Christ, he had already become convinced that Christ and Torah represented mutually exclusive ways of describing the community and sphere of salvation."[42] Galatians then articulates what amounts to a long-held conviction of Paul's about Law and Christ.

The phrase 'the traditions of the fathers' has been taken by Dunn and others to refer to the oral *halakah* which was an extrapolation beyond the Mosaic Law though based on it, not a reference to the Mosaic Law itself.[43] It would then be similar to the phrase found in Mk. 7.5 'the tradition of the elders'. It must, however, be remembered that Paul is writing in this letter primarily if not almost exclusively to Gentiles. The phrase 'ancestral traditions' to them would have surely connoted the Mosaic Law, and perhaps also any oral extrapolations, but in any case would not have excluded the Law itself. Here a close comparison with Acts 22.3 is very relevant. There Paul claims to his fellow Jews that he has been 'instructed in accord with strictness of our ancestral *law* (νόμου), being a zealot for God'. One may also wish to compare 1 Macc. 2.27 where Mattathias is seen as the model of zeal and he is said to be 'zealous for the Law' and also the covenant. There as here, Paul's zeal does not have to do just with oral Torah, but also and perhaps primarily with the written Mosaic Law passed down by God's people.[44] Betz is right to paraphrase here that Paul is saying he was an ardent observer of the Torah.[45] Paul's pre-Christian zeal was 'not according to knowledge' not just because he followed and pressed the observance of oral *halakah*, but because he felt the Mosaic covenant and the keeping of its requirements was the proper means of defining who God's people were.

Perhaps a significant part of why Paul puts things the way he does is to punctuate the fact that his conversion was miraculous. "As a Jew he had no reason to leave Judaism."[46] Indeed, as Betz says he was heading in the opposite

40. Donaldson, p. 662. He is critiquing Räisänen's *Paul and the Law* (Tübingen: Mohr, 1983).

41. See pp. 341ff. below.

42. Donaldson, p. 668.

43. See Dunn, *Galatians*, p. 60; Longenecker, *Galatians*, p. 30.

44. See Matera, *Galatians*, p. 59.

45. Betz, *Galatians*, p. 68. He points to the useful parallel in Acts 21.20. There it is Jewish Christians zealous for and strict observers of the Mosaic Law. This was precisely the problem in the Christian community because it required Gentiles to follow suit if they wanted to have fellowship with such Christians.

46. Betz, *Galatians*, p. 68.

direction from Christianity. He was a person of integrity and he believed that one should pursue one's faith wholeheartedly, and be intentional about keeping the entire Law in detail. Paul is making clear that he had no second thoughts about his manner of life before he converted. Indeed he was excited about it and angry with those whom he perceived as betrayers of the true faith. Thankfully, the days of psychologizing this narrative seem to have largely passed, for we seldom hear remarks like those of C. H. Dodd any more, who suggested that Paul, in order to eliminate the doubts in his own heart and repress inclinations toward more humane tendencies, took up persecuting to vindicate the claims of 'legal absolutism'.[47]

Nothing in Gal. 1, or in Acts for that matter, suggests that Paul was struggling with doubts about Judaism or the Law prior to his conversion. As K. Stendahl has said, this sort of analysis of Paul is a result of the 'introspective consciousness of the West' and not a product of uncovering actual hints in this direction in the text. No one, looking back on his life as Pharisee and saying his behavior in regard to righteousness under the Law was *blameless* (Phil. 3.6), was likely to have been struggling with guilt or self-doubt about his abilities to keep God's commandments when he was a Pharisee, or for that matter worrying about excessive zeal against infidels (cf. Phil. 3.6b).[48]

Verse **15** refers to the action of God, though it is probable that the words ὁ θεὸς were not an original part of this text.[49] God set Paul apart from the time of birth (literally here, 'from my mother's womb'). This may be an attempt to make clear that Paul was a 'separated one' before he ever became a 'Pharisee'(which means those set apart).[50] More certainly we should probably hear an echo of Jerm. 1.5: 'Before I formed you in the womb I knew you, and before you were born I consecrated you; I appointed you a prophet to the nations' and perhaps parts of Is. 49.1–6. Paul then refers to his call by grace, which is also a reference to his conversion (cf. below). The point of this remark is that God had his hand on Paul from the time of his birth, and had in mind

---

47. C. H. Dodd, *The Mind of Paul: Change and Development* (Manchester: John Rylands Library, 1934), p. 36.

48. See K. Stendahl, *Paul among Jews and Gentiles* (Philadelphia: Fortress, 1976), pp. 78–96.

49. It is omitted by the earliest papyri p46, and also by B, F, G and other manuscripts, but it is included by ℵ, A, D and various other manuscripts. See Metzger, *TC*, p. 590. There is no good reason why these words should have been omitted if they were original.

50. See Bruce, *Galatians*, p. 92; Dunn, *Galatians*, p. 63 puts it differently: "The point would be that his attempt at separatism within Judaism had been superseded by God's separating him for the Gospel (Rom. 1.1) – and from before his birth so that his time as a Pharisee (1.13–14) had been merely an interlude between the major phases of God's purpose." Dunn also suggests Paul is countering here the notion that he was merely commissioned at and by the Antioch church.

for him to be God's mouthpiece to the nations. Paul's current occupation was not a result of his own choice or careful career planning. Indeed it was in spite of his previous life, it was a result of grace and God's own plan and will and good pleasure. The sequence here, however, is God's plan, the setting apart, then the calling by grace. It will be seen from this way of putting things that the focus is not on the personal benefits of God's action (Paul was converted or saved), but on the basis of Paul's ministry and message. This is a task-centered description of what happened to Paul.

In an insightful study, Malina and Neyrey point out not merely the numerous parallels between the way Paul speaks of his call and the versions of similar prophetic calls in the OT (cf. Jerm. 1.5–6; Is. 49.1, 6; Is. 6; Ezek. 1) but stress that Paul is claiming a special role and status among God's people that is given by God directly. Furthermore, "his present role was not so much a change as simply a return to where he originally should have been. Because his former 'manner of life' set him against God's revealed purposes, it was incumbent upon him finally to take up what God wanted for him. Thus he was not an opportunist, a fickle person, or a flatterer! By invoking God as the agent of change, Paul claims that his new manner of life was ordained by God and thus should be regarded as highly honorable . . ."[51] In other words, Paul has framed his discussion of these life changing events in a rhetorically effective way so as to fend on the criticisms that often were leveled in the Greco-Roman world against chameleon-like behavior.

Lest we think that Paul is only describing a call of God to be some sort of prophetic witness, Paul hastily adds vs. 16 which speaks of God's revelation of the Son to and perhaps in him. Grammatically it is possible to translate the preposition ἐν either 'to' or 'in', but probably the latter is the correct interpretation here, especially in the light of Gal. 2.20 where Paul speaks of Christ living in him, and of 4.6 where it is said the Spirit of the Son resides in our hearts. Paul does speak of Christ as Son of God or the Son some fifteen times in the undisputed Paulines (Rom. 1.3–4, 9; 5.10; 8.3, 29, 32; 1 Cor. 1.9, 15.28; 2 Cor. 1.19; Gal. 1.16; 2.20; 4.4, 6; 1 Thess. 1.10). Interestingly there are no examples in either the Captivity Epistles or the Pastorals. If we compare the usage of this term or title to titles such as Lord or Christ it is immediately apparent that these last titles are far more prevalent, with more than a hundred examples of each usage.[52] There is some evidence that Son of God was a title used of messiah in early Judaism (4QFlor. on 2 Sam. 7.14; 4 Ezr. 7.28–29; 13.32; 14.9), and so Paul may have derived it either from his Jewish past or his Christian present. I would stress that this title is a relational term. It is God's Son that has been revealed in Paul, which suggests Christ's special relationship

51. *Portraits of Paul*, p. 40.
52. See W. Kramer, *Christ, Lord, Son of God* (London: SCM Press, 1966), p. 183.

to God the Father, and also the means through which Paul came to have a somewhat analagous relationship with the Father, such that he could address God as Abba just as Jesus did (Gal. 4.6).

The verb ἀποκαλύψαι 'to reveal' coupled with the 'in me' phrase suggests that Paul is referring to his having received an apocalyptic vision of Christ. The terminology is different from what we find in 1 Cor 9.1 where we hear of 'seeing' Christ (cf. also 15.8). Paul in all likelihood would not agree with modern distinctions between objective and subjective revelations. If such terms had to be used he probably would have insisted that his encounter on Damascus Road was both objective and subjective.[53] It was objective in that it came from God and from outside Paul's psyche. It was not an example of wish projection or fantasizing or dreaming, or even a mystical experience where the mystic achieves a certain kind of spiritual state of mind or being and then reaches out for something beyond himself or herself and sees something. On the other hand, it was also subjective because it was deeply personal. The revelation took place in Paul, in the very depths of his being, and not in others who may have been with him at the time. The language of vision (from heaven, and so something which has to be unveiled or otherwise it would not be seen or known) comports with the accounts in Acts which suggest that Paul saw Christ *after* he ascended to heaven, and so *from* heaven (cf. the later debate about this vision in Pseud. Clement. *Hom.* 17.13–19).[54]

The purpose of this revelation in Paul is said to be so that Paul might preach Christ among the nations. Notice that the verb 'preach' is in the present tense, whereas 'set apart' and 'called' are aorists. Paul is of course referring to his ongoing task that was given him from the time of his call and conversion. Here it will be in order to enter in some detail into the debate about whether the Damascus Road experience was a call or a conversion or both, and in the process we must consider the nature of and conceptions about conversion in antiquity.

Excursus: A Conversation on Conversion ─────────────────

I have undertaken elsewhere to discuss the matter of ancient views about salvation and health,[55] here I am focusing more narrowly on views of how one converts from

---

53. See Betz, *Galatians*, p. 71.

54. Here is not the place for a detailed analysis of the threefold accounts in Acts of Paul's Christophany, or for a comparison of them with Galatians. See my *The Acts of the Apostles*, pp. 302ff. and on the form critical and editorial issues see my "Editing the Good News," in *History, Literature, and Society in the Book of Acts*, ed. B. Witherington (Cambridge: Cambridge University Press, 1996), pp. 324–47.

55. See my *The Acts of the Apostles*, Appendix One.

one religion or philosophy of life to another. What was the process involved? How did Jews view the relationship of initiation and conversion? How does Paul view the matter? What does this sort of data tell us about Paul's experience and how he evaluates it? Are there insights from sociological studies that help us to understand and define what conversion is?

Since at least the time of A. D. Nock's classic study of conversion,[56] it has been widely recognized that conversion is not a word that applies simply to early Christianity and early Judaism. With hindsight, what one can say, however, is that most of the conversionist sects and groups in the first century A.D. were developments of one or another form of an eastern religion, not the traditional Greco-Roman religions, whether one is talking about conversion to Judaism, Christianity, the cult of Isis, or another of the eastern religions which, like the cult of Isis, had adopted and adapted the Greek practice of initiation in a 'mystery'.[57] This is important to bear in mind when we discuss Paul's conversion. The ideological distance that Paul traveled was from one party or movement in early Judaism to an offshoot of early Judaism. It was not as if he had converted from the worship of Yahweh to the worship of Astarte or Jupiter Optimus Maximus. Yet nonetheless it involved a dramatic religious change.

The difficulty with Nock's study can be said to be at least twofold. Firstly, he was thinking of conversion too much in the light of the nineteenth-century seminal work of W. James about the varieties of religious experience, especially about radical or profound emotional experiences. The psychological side of the matter was to the fore, and perhaps in some cases too much to the fore. The relationship of conversion and initiation needed to be further explored, as also did the social and communal component. Secondly and as a consequence of the first difficulty, Nock's understanding of conversion to Christianity, in the light of his own study of Acts, but especially in the light of his interest in Paul's conversion, focused too much on the experiential side of conversion (visions, encounters, the reception of the Spirit) and perhaps not enough on the ideational and practical side of the matter.[58] Nock, however, rightly saw that conversion could happen not just from one religion to another, but also from one philosophy to another. It is a mistake to confine the notion too narrowly to 'religious' conversion. A Copernican revolution in one's thinking, feeling and lifestyle, in other words one's basic mental and social existence, can be called a conversion whether it involves a recognized religion or not. Nevertheless, in Paul's case we are speaking of a religious transformation.

It is important to keep steadily in view that by and large Greco-Roman culture "valued stability and constancy of character. Hence, 'change' of character was neither expected nor praiseworthy. Normally adult persons were portrayed as living out the manner of life that had always characterized them."[59] In some cases, for instance in the historical works of Tacitus, we see a variant on this theme. Tacitus stresses when

---

56. A. D. Nock, *Conversion* (Oxford: Oxford University Press, 1933).

57. See the helpful discussion in E. Ferguson, *Backgrounds of Early Christianity* (Grand Rapids: Eerdmans, 1993 2nd. ed.), pp. 235ff.

58. See the helpful critique of A. Segal, "The Cost of Proselytism and Conversion," *SBL 1988 Seminar Papers* (Atlanta: Scholars Press, 1988), pp. 336–69, here pp. 336–37.

59. Malina and Neyrey, *Portraits of Paul*, p. 39.

talking about persons, particularly Emperors, that eventually their true personality will come out, even if it has been disguised along the way in order to succeed and gain power. The idea is that they had always had this personality but had successfully disguised the facts.[60] Even more pointed was the Stoic view of things. Cicero says "The [Stoic] philosopher surmises nothing, repents of nothing, is never wrong, and never changes his opinion" (*Pro Murena* 61). In this environment it is not surprising that many people looked askance at conversions or claims of conversion. Some thought such drastic changes didn't really happen, others thought that if they did, it was unlikely to be a good thing. The suspicions of the Judean church about Paul's conversion are in fact typical of more widely held attitudes about conversion.

One way of approaching the issue of the change in Paul's life is to consider what amounted to conversion *to* Judaism from paganism in the first century. As Segal says, conversion to early Judaism almost always was a gradual process.[61] We can see this fact in the distinction between God-fearers who are not seen as full converts nor as pure pagans, and proselytes.[62] Futhermore, its completion was necessarily signalled by the willingness to submit to circumcision and the requirements of the Law. This process is not identical to what we find in the description by Josephus of his own life where he speaks of trying out and becoming an adherent or disciple of one or another of the Jewish parties (*Life* 7–12). Josephus goes through various initiations and commitments but it is doubtful one can call this conversion, not least because he is simply moving from one recognizable form of early Judaism to another, all of which shared a belief in the obligation to keep the Mosaic Law in one fashion or another. If a current analogy is not inappropriate, what Josephus was doing is not unlike a Christian changing denominations within the Christian church, with perhaps the closest analogy being between going from a paedo-baptistic group to a group that practices adult immersion, and so a new initiation ritual is usually required (cf. Josephus' adaptation of water ablutions of a specific kind while following Banus). This is a matter of adherence not conversion. Full conversion to Judaism involved initiation in the form of a circumcision ritual. This was what chiefly distinguished a proselyte turned Jew from a mere God-fearer.

It is of course true that Paul was not the only person ever to seek the conversion of Gentiles to a religion that at least had roots in Judaism. There is some evidence that there were Jews, perhaps especially in Diaspora, who were interested not just in receiving converts, but in making converts. Valerius Maximus tells us already in 139 B.C. that Jews were being expelled from Rome because they were attempting to transmit the Jewish holy rites to Romans. It is likely this was why Jews were expelled

---

60. A good example of this phenomenon can be seen in the case of P. Cornelius Sulla.

61. Segal, "Proselytism and Conversion," p. 341: "one general rule which differs significantly from the Christian stereotype can be promulgated at the beginning; gradual conversion was the typical and expected pattern for virtually every sectarian group in Judaism, though sudden and emotional conversion may have occurred occasionally."

62. See my discussion of the viability of the category of God-fearers in *The Acts of the Apostles*, pp. 330ff.

under Tiberius.[63] "Jewish proselytism was therefore both real and controversial. Jews gained proselytes but did not overwhelm the pagan world because its message was for a sophisticated minority. Becoming a Jew was never merely a decision to join another religious club. Judaism was exclusive . . . [it] was primarily a decision to join another *ethnos*, which was not self-evidently possible to everyone . . . and often viewed with some suspicion".[64] It is wrong simply to dismiss texts like Mt. 23.15 or the story of the conversion of the royal house of Adiabene (Josephus, *Ant.* 20.2.3–4), or the Qumran evidence about converts as providing us with clues as to the attempts of Jews, and in particular Pharisees, to convert both non-Jews and in some cases Jews, who were deemed beyond the pale, to Judaism. Though such efforts were likely only undertaken by a minority of first-century Jews, the point is they were undertaken, and Saul of Tarsus would have understood what such actions entailed and meant, and on the other hand what crossing the boundaries of Judaism heading in the other direction (apostasy) also involved. Conversion was not an alien concept to him. Indeed as a Jew if he was one who drew the boundaries of Judaism quite clearly and narrowly, conversion or apostasy would have been seen as alternately a possibility or a threat for a large group of people. The smaller number of true Jews in Paul's mind, the greater the need to prevent apostasy and perhaps even to encourage conversion. Paul lived in a social world where conversion was deemed possible and apostasy also possible and in fact a real danger in a Hellenized Judea with a foreign power ruling the land.

In one of the more important sociological studies of conversion, R. Kanter made the distinction between affective commitment, instrumental commitment, and moral commitment. The first category has to do with one's attachment to the members of a particular group, the second to the organization and rules of the group, and the third the commitment to the ideas of the group to which one is converting.[65] She stresses that generally speaking, whether one's conversion is sudden or gradual,[66] one is converted into a community, and so commitment must be discussed in social and not just in individual terms. However intensely personal Saul's experience on Damascus Road, sooner or later he saw that experience as leading to his adherence to the group he calls 'the assembly of God', using the language of the OT but also of the Greco-Roman world to describe the group he joined. He saw it as a distinct and distinguishable entity. I would submit that analysis of Paul's conversion in terms of all three forms of commitment mentioned above makes clear that we must speak of what happened to Paul as a conversion. Paul's primary commitment is to his brothers and sisters in Christ, he recognizes that the group he is a part of has specific rules which he needs to follow (e.g., church discipline [cf. 1 Cor. 5], or when he sought the endorsement of his Gospel and the right hand of fellowship from the Jerusalem church, and of course 'the Law of Christ'), and thirdly he is committed at an

---

63. See my discussion of these matters in the context of the expulsion under the reign of Claudius about A.D. 49 in my *The Acts of the Apostles*, pp. 507ff.

64. Segal, p. 346.

65. R. Kanter, *Commitment and Community* (Cambridge: Harvard University Press, 1972), pp. 61–74.

66. Sociologists have generally distinguished between these two forms of socialization, one which occurs more suddenly, the other more slowly.

ideological level to a redefining of terms – the Israel of God is Jew and Gentile united in Christ, the Shema can be redefined as incorporating both one God, the Father and one Lord, Christ (1 Cor. 8.6), salvation is to be found in Christ and not elsewhere.

In sociological terms, one would have to say that Paul underwent a thorough re-socialization. His symbolic universe was not merely altered, in some respects it was turned upside down, for example in regard to his view of the Mosaic Law before and after conversion. What is also interesting about Paul is that there is precious little evidence in the Pauline letters about his ever being integrated into a Christian community of faith, and equally little or nothing about his going through a rite of passage when he became a Christian, though Acts provides us with a little information on both scores. That Paul does not talk about a faith community of which he was a part, but only about communities which he helped found, and likewise he does not speak of spiritual mentors or his instructors in the faith (unless Peter counts, cf. below), but only about those he has mentored and the co-workers he has chosen or with whom he has done missionary work is striking. One gets the strong sense of Paul not being socialized or at least not well socialized into existing Christian communities at the point of his conversion. To the contrary Paul says he immediately went to the mission field in Arabia. From Gal. 2, one does get the sense that later Paul was a part of the Christian community in Antioch, something Acts confirms, but even here Paul says very little about the community or his life in that community. He largely leaves the impression of being an isolated holy man. Sociologists would want to ask how much of Paul's independent spirit seems to have derived from a lack of thorough integration into a faith community after his conversion. How much of this isolation also contributed to his being seen as a maverick by various other Christians, perhaps especially by members of the Jerusalem church? These are questions worth pondering, and certainly one must say that Paul's independence of a 'home' community suggests he could not be seen as a typical example of dyadic personality if by that term one means someone whose identity is almost completely defined for him or her by the community of which he or she is a part.[67]

Yet another way to approach the conundrum of Paul's thoroughgoing resocialization is to ask the question – Who is a true Jew from Paul the Christian's viewpoint? On this score one must be able to make a distinction between: (1) being ethnically a Jew (these Paul calls his brothers and sisters according to the flesh); (2) being an adherent of one or another form of early Judaism which involved an *obligation* not merely an *option* to be Torah-true (Paul's view of the agitators in Galatia); (3) being part of a breakaway sect that drew on the sacred texts and language of early Judaism (though often using them in very different ways than other Jews), but was busily defining itself and distinguishing itself from early Judaism in regard to the matter of the necessary observance of the Mosaic covenant and Law. I submit that the latter is what we see Paul advocating and working for in Galatians and the way in which he would define who a true Jew is.

If Law observance could be seen as a matter of adiaphora ('neither circumcision nor uncircumcision matters . . .'), the terms of the discussion have changed radically. To be sure Paul was happy to allow some degree or forms of Law observance so long

67. See N. Taylor, *Paul, Antioch, Jerusalem* (Sheffield: JSOT Press, 1992), pp. 62ff.

as it did not entail the division of Jewish and Gentile Christians, and the preventing of them from having fellowship including table fellowship, which is to say so long as it did not involve requiring observance of the Mosaic Law. The unity of all in Christ took precedence over the optional observance of the Law by some Christians. For Paul a true Jew was a messianic one who followed the example of the faith of Abraham, but also followed Christ, and this necessarily led to a different view of the role of the Law in the life of the true Jew.

The Law was precisely the rub between Paul's vision of the Christian community and that of many other Jewish Christians. The agitators in Galatia, the false brothers, and perhaps a large number of members of the Jerusalem church were not prepared to see observance of the Mosaic Law as *optional* or adiaphora for followers of Christ. They were not comfortable with the idea of merely being a Jew to the Jew but also being able to be a Gentile to the Gentile. That for them was going beyond the pale, was violating the Law. The basic assumption of such Christians was that followers of Christ must continue to observe Torah and be under the Mosaic covenant. These Christians saw themselves as part of a renewal or reform movement within Judaism. They saw themselves as Torah-observant messianic Jews. This is not how Paul saw himself or his Gentile converts, and this in large measure must go back to the profundity of his conversion.

It tells us something fundamental about Paul's new view of the people of God that he sees the Jewish rite of passage as something that is not of fundamental importance in signaling who is in the 'assembly of God'. Joining that assembly was not a matter of joining Judaism. What sets Christians apart is a new act of creation, or if we must speak of matters of initiation what sets them apart is the inclusive ritual, both for females and for males, of baptism, not circumcision. Part of the non-Jewishness of Paul's approach is that he does not identify the rite of circumcision as the completion and sign of conversion. While he seems to have seen conversion as leading to initiation, a conversion was 'to Christ' not to Judaism and initiation involved baptism. Initiation and conversion were distinguished by Paul with conversion and faith being more critical. Paul is perfectly prepared to devalue baptism if one invests too much significance in it (cf. 1 Cor. 1). Paul was not an advocate of sacramental salvation. The upshot of all this is that Paul does not hold the view that a willingness to submit to circumcision is the evidence or even the means of defining and determining who is and is not among the people of God.

It has become common since the work of K. Stendahl and others to refer to what happened to Paul on Damascus Road as simply a call experience, not a conversion from Judaism to some other form of religion.[68] Stendahl is right in what he affirms; certainly what happened to Paul was a call experience. However, he is wrong in what he denies. Even with all the diversity that was tolerated in early Judaism and even with all the movements and parties, no truly Jewish group, whether we think of the Pharisees, or Sadducees, or Qumranites, or even the Samaritans, was prepared to say in the first century that observance of the Mosaic Law was no longer obligatory for God's people. None was prepared to call the Mosaic covenant glorious,

---

68. See, e.g., Stendahl, *Paul among Jews and Gentiles*, pp. 7–23.

but nonetheless a glorious anachronism as Paul does (2 Cor. 3). Nor were any prepared to say that converts to their form of Judaism would not have to observe the Mosaic Law, though of course there were disagreements in regard to details and extent. Segal is quite right that if one assesses the full measure of the change in the life of Saul of Tarsus, from a Jewish point of view it would surely have appeared to have been an apostasy, a going *beyond the pale*, beyond the social boundaries that defined early Judaism.[69] In other words in more positive language it was a conversion, as well as a call. Not incidentally 'apostate' appears to be precisely how Saul during his time as a Pharisee had viewed those in the church of God. This in turn led to his zealous actions against such Jews. It is impossible to believe that Paul the zealot for the Law and persecutor of the church could ever have taken the attitude that 'neither circumcision nor uncircumcision matters' without as radical a change in his life as conversion connotes. C. K. Barrett is right when he says "If the transformation of a persecutor into a preacher of the faith he formerly persecuted is not a conversion, a radical turning round so as to adopt a course opposite to that previously followed, I do not know where one is to be found. What must be added is that every true conversion carries with it a call."[70]

The change in Paul's life involved a fundamental paradigm shift in the life and in the semantic universe of Paul whereby Law is replaced by Christ as the determinative prism through which all must be viewed. "Christ, rather than Torah, is understood as the divinely given means of determining membership in the community destined for salvation."[71] It "cannot be denied that Paul's experience resulted in decisive shifts of values, orientation, and commitment of a kind more appropriately associated with a 'conversion' than a 'call'. No Isaiah was ever called to a change of direction as dramatic as that of the persecutor turned apostle (Gal. 1.13–16). No Jeremiah ever transvalued his past the way Paul does in Phil. 3.4–8."[72]

As Segal rightly says "apparently other Jews advocated that the Gentiles need only live moral lives. The problem that Paul stimulated among Jews and Jewish Christians was not one of universalism so much as the recommendation that the distinctions between Jews and Gentiles be removed entirely. This first of all shocked Paul's fellow Christians."[73] "Paul should be seen as an example of the phenomenon of conversion in first century Jewish sectarian life. What is particularly interesting about Paul's terminology is that he evinces the high commitment state of the radical conversion sectarian communities, but he also recommends that no Gentile needs a conversion in the technical Jewish sense of the word, in terms of the Law . . . Paul changes the definition of what a conversion is. He does not see ritual status as important for this process . . . This is understandable given his personal journey from Pharisaism to Gentile Christianity."[74]

---

69. See A. F. Segal, *Paul the Convert* (New Haven: Yale University Press, 1990).
70. C. K. Barrett, *Freedom and Obligation*, p. 110, n. 7.
71. Donaldson, "Zealot and Convert," p. 682.
72. Donaldson, "Zealot and Convert," p. 681.
73. Segal, "Proselytism and Conversion," p. 359.
74. Segal, "Proselytism and Conversion," pp. 361–62.

The upshot of this discussion is that we must see the change in Paul's life as both call and conversion. Stendahl overlooked the rhetorical purpose and function of the material in Gal. 1–2. The function of this material was not to offer auto-biographical reflections on Paul's status as a Christian but to explain the origin and divine character of his call and Gospel. Paul only tells us enough to let us know what he felt called and committed to do as a result of the conversion. The rhetorical function of this material is quite different from the three accounts of Paul's conversion found in Acts. Paul says nothing about being saved, or forgiven not because he does not believe he has had such an experience, just like his Gentile converts, but because his remarks are intended to have another function – supporting his deliberative argument about the Gospel they must follow and the examples they must look to in doing so. In particular Paul is presenting himself as the paradigm of one called in grace, for the task of proclaiming grace to the Gentiles, and called to live a life on the basis of grace.

One final question needs to be addressed before we close this discussion. The question has been raised as to how much of the distinctive aspects of Paul's Gospel can be traced back to his Damascus Road experience, and how much is theology forged in the furnace of controversy during his ministry to the Gentiles. Several factors in Galatians help point us in the right direction. Firstly, as we have already said, Donaldson was right to point out if it were not the case that Paul's Gospel in its essentials was there from the beginning, then the entire argument of Galatians would be in serious jeopardy not only because Paul would have falsely claimed that he got his Gospel from God when God revealed his Son in him *before* he ever met with any Jerusalem officials, but also because if he had preached 'the other Gospel' for the first decade or so of his ministry the agitators could easily have refuted the document we are now examining, and accused Paul of the same inconsistency of which he accuses Peter and others.[75]

Secondly, Galatians as a document stands or falls on the truth of Paul's claim that when he preached to the Galatians, what he preached to them was the Gospel of grace, the Law-free Gospel, and that it was through the reception of this Gospel that they received the Spirit and other benefits of salvation. If Paul in fact had preached some other message when he was there, if for example he had allowed for circumcision in Galatia and not objected to the observance of certain Jewish feast days and the like, his argument in this letter has no real force. This letter can serve as an act of persuasion precisely because Paul has not changed his tune. He is just reinforcing the message the Galatians have already heard.

Thirdly, Paul is presenting himself as a faithful paradigm of the Gospel – he received this Gospel at his conversion and call and he has been faithful to proclaim and live by it ever since that time. This is his essential argument.[76] This means it is exceedingly unlikely that Paul himself had not worked out in his own mind the

75. See Donaldson, p. 664.
76. Cf. Dunn, *Galatians*, p. 72: "Paul's understanding of the revelation 'to preach him among the Gentiles' was already firmly established before he ever went near Jerusalem . . . his gospel to them is the gospel he received on the Damascus Road, established by divine revelation well before he made direct contact with Jerusalem."

implications of the relationship of faith in Christ to Torah observance not only before he wrote to the Galatians but also before he visited them. To be sure some of Paul's arguments in this letter are quite likely generated in response to the crisis in Galatia. This is not, however, the issue. One must be able to distinguish between one's basic views and position and the arguments one uses to defend such a view. It is some of the latter that are ad hoc, not Paul's basic world view.

Fourthly, I think Donaldson is right that it appears likely that the antithesis in Paul's mind between faith in Christ and obedience to the Law goes back to *before* his conversion, and continued after it. This explains his zeal about these things on both sides of the Damascus Road experience better than any other explanation.

The upshot of this is that I find myself in fundamental agreement with S. Kim and the case he has repeatedly made and recently strengthened about the origin of Paul's Gospel going back in essence to his own conversion experience and the revelation from God he believed that he received then.[77] As I have said elsewhere, it is essentially incorrect to suggest or assume that Paul's thought arises out of or primarily in response to particular situations in his congregations. "The situations Paul addresses cause him to articulate his thoughts in one way or another, but those thoughts have *arisen* as a result of his deep and ongoing reflection on the narrative that molds all of his thoughts. One must always bear in mind that we have in all of Paul's letters the words of a mature Christian person who, even in the case of the earliest letter we have, has had at least ten [or more likely fifteen] years to reflect on the Christian faith. Whatever development Paul's thought has undergone seems to have taken place almost entirely before any of these letters were written. Even in regard to the crucial subject of Christology, there is precious little evidence of new developments in Paul's later letters. The contingent situations affect how Paul articulates his thoughts, but those thoughts are basically not ad hoc in character."[78] In other words, contingency has to do with when and how Paul articulates his beliefs and contingent situations cause him to draw out the implications of his thought in various ways he has not done before. It even causes him to generate new and ad hoc arguments for his basic position. Again however arguments for and articulation of one's symbolic universe differs from the generation of that thought world. Paul's Gospel of grace is bound up with Paul's experience of grace and is grounded in the content of God's revelation of his Son in Paul, which Paul then worked out the implications of for his beliefs about God, messiah, Law, salvation, who God's people are and a host of other subjects.

Bearing in mind that the function of this material is to make evident where Paul's Gospel came from, and where it did not come from, vs. **16b** is easily

77. S. Kim, *The Origin of Paul's Gospel* (Grand Rapids: Eerdmans, 1981), and more recently his SNTS lecture in Strasbourg in August 1996 "The Mystery of Rom. 11.25–26". One must be able to distinguish Paul's Gospel, and factors which contributed to the way he articulated it. Paul's Gospel did not come to him before he was converted, but his pre-conversion disposition to believe in an antithesis between the Law and following Christ contributed to the way he understood their relationship after Damascus Road.

78. Witherington, *Paul's Narrative Thought World*, pp. 3–4.

understandable. The point is that the distinctive aspects of Paul's Gospel were not received in consultation with any human beings ('flesh and blood' is deliberately used to make clear that no human being was involved, only God in the giving of this Gospel). The verb προσανατίθεσθαι is rare, and complicating matters is that the term appears to have a different sense in Gal. 2.6. Here it seems to mean something like confer or consult with.[79] Dunn suggests, on the basis of texts like Diodorus Siculus 17.116.4 where the verb refers to consulting a seer, that the verb means consult in order to gain an authoritative interpretation.[80] This may be correct, but there is reason for doubt. The examples Dunn cites do not prove his case, because it is the context of them, not the technical nature of the verb that conveys such an idea.[81] Commentators differ as to what the word 'immediately' modifies here. Does it go with what precedes, only with the reference to consultation, or with the whole phrase up to the word Arabia? The word would seem to have an emphatic position and go with what follows it. Paul is denying any immediate consulting with humans including any immediate going up to Jerusalem, and by contrast an immediate departure to Arabia.[82]

In vs. 17 Paul admits that there were those in Jerusalem who had become apostles before him (on the phrase cf. Rom. 16.7). He does not call them so-called or pseudo-apostles (contrast 2 Cor. 11.13), there is no pejorative tone to this mention of these persons. In view of 1 Cor. 15.5–7 it is probable that in Paul's view the apostles is a wider circle of persons than the Twelve, but it is not impossible that it would include them. It is very likely that this reference includes James, the brother of Jesus. In any case this is a tacit admission of the legitimacy of these persons, and that they had a certain pre-eminence over Paul as authorities having been commissioned before Paul. The point is, however, that Paul didn't get his distinctive Gospel from them, it had a divine source and character.

Recently a strong case has been made by Malina and Neyrey that we must read Paul's whole presentation of his conversion and subsequent behavior in the light of what we know about how first-century personality normally worked. For example, Paul's concern that he should not be running in vain, is typical of those who seek and need validation from the larger group of which they are a part.

79. See Betz, *Galatians*, p. 72.

80. Dunn, *Jesus, Paul and the Law* (Louisville: Westminster/John Knox, 1990), pp. 109–16.

81. See the helpful discussion and critique of Dunn's view by M. Silva, *Explorations in Exegetical Method. Galatians as a Test Case* (Grand Rapids: Baker, 1996), pp. 58–62 and also Malina and Neyrey, *Portraits of Paul*, p. 42.

82. See Dunn, *Jesus, Paul, and the Law*, pp. 110–11.

Paul presented himself as the quintessential group-oriented person, controlled by forces greater than he: a) God ascribes roles, status, and honor at birth; b) Paul presents himself in terms of group affiliation, a Pharisee, a member of a specific group; c) he claims to have learned nothing on his own but to have been taught by another, a truly noble teacher, namely God; d) he demonstrated the group virtues of loyalty, faithfulness, and obedience; he sought only the honoring of his patron, not his individual benefit; and e) most important, he is ever sensitive to the opinion others have of him: either his detractors, his Galatian audience, or the Jerusalem 'pillars'. Acknowledgment by the Jerusalem church becomes a matter of the highest importance to this group-oriented person.[83]

Paul tells us nothing whatsoever here about what he did in Arabia, and of course it is debated what locale Paul means by Arabia. Strabo, who certainly should have had his facts straight as he was in a position to know, says that in his day the Nabateans, like the Syrians, were subject to the Romans (16.4.21), which means this territory was part of a Roman province. This refers to the state of affairs at about the turn of the era, and we know that between about 8 B.C. and somewhere around or shortly before A.D. 37–38 Aretas IV ruled the kingdom of the Nabateans. This territory sometime in the late 30s would seem to have included Damascus, in view of 2 Cor. 11.32–33. Did the territory return to more direct Roman control after A.D. 40?[84] It would appear not, as Aretas had a successor, Malichus II, and we have his coins into the A.D. 60s. The clear establishment of the Roman province Arabia post-dates the time of Paul. This means that Paul is not using a provincial designation here. J. Murphy-O'Connor has shown that to Jews Nabatea was considered part of Arabia. In fact the term also referred to the territory east of the Jordan and as far south as the Sinai penisula.[85] J. Murphy-O'Connor rightly points to Josephus who makes clear enough that Nabatea was included in Arabia, as is shown by the fact that Petra was called Arabia Petrea (cf. *War* 5.4.3; *Ant.* 18.5.1). The Nabateans had very stormy relationships with Jews.

It is very plausible that the reference in 2 Cor. 11 to Paul's being tracked down by the ethnarch of Aretas in Damascus gives us the necessary clue to explain Paul's reference to Arabia here. The Nabateans would not have been seen by Paul as Jews or even Semitic cousins of the Jews (unlike the Idumeans). Paul had to have done something to raise the ire of Aretas and the best

83. Malina and Neyrey, *Portraits of Paul*, p. 51.
84. See the discussion in G. W. Bowersock, *Roman Arabia* (Harvard: Harvard University Press, 1983), pp. 66–71.
85. J. Murphy-O'Connor, "Paul in Arabia," *CBQ* 55 (1993), pp. 732–37. Interestingly, Justin Martyr in his *Dialogue with Trypho* refers to Damascus as belonging to Arabia in the time before the second century A.D. Cf. Lightfoot, *Galatians*, p. 88.

explanation for the reference in 2 Cor. 11 is that Paul had immediately gone to begin his evangelistic career among the Nabateans. He had gone from Damascus to Nabatea, had probably stayed only for a short time due to a hostile response, had returned to Damascus, and at some point was tracked down by Aretas' ethnarch, perhaps at a point in time when Damascus was under Aretas' control.[86] Paul's reference to 'again returning' to Damascus provides us with the only Pauline clue that his conversion took place in or near that city. The overall impression left by vss. 16–17 is that Paul was nowhere near Jerusalem when he received his Gospel nor for about three years thereafter. Indeed, he was nowhere near any Jewish Christians either once he left Damascus, and surely nowhere near any apostles or any of the Twelve. His call, his message, his initial mission was not born out of Jerusalem or the Jerusalem church.

Verse **18** begins with the word ἔπειτα which must surely be seen to indicate temporal sequence. It is also found in vs. 21 and again at 2.1, and what it means in one of these instances is surely what it means in all of them. It will be noted that the first and third of these uses of the term is followed by a rather specific indication of a span time (cf. the use of the term in 1 Cor. 15.23 as a part of an attempt to make clear a chronological sequence of events). It is natural in the wake of these three uses of ἔπειτα, which should be translated 'then', that we take the ὅτε δὲ ('but when') in 2.12 to indicate further developments (cf. the identical phrase at 1.15) that took place after the sequence of three events, unless there are strong reasons in the context to think otherwise, and there are not. The efforts of Luedemann and others to argue to the contrary and place the Antioch incident before the meeting described in 2.1–10 must be deemed special pleading.[87]

The phrase μετὰ τρία ἔτη should be compared to the similar phrase in Mk. 8.31, 10.34. In each case the phrase in all likelihood must be seen as an example of the ancient practice of inclusive reckoning – i.e. 'in the third year', not 'after three full years'. If the period began at the end of the first calendar year and ended early in the beginning of the third calendar year, the amount of time could even be less than two full years. The question really is what is the point of reference from which Paul is reckoning this passing of time. From his conversion? From the time of his return to Damascus? In all likelihood it is the

---

86. On the chronological issues see my *The Acts of the Apostles*, pp. 69ff. One must date the incident in Damascus before A.D. 40 but after the likely date of Paul's conversion, perhaps about A.D. 34 or 35. Thus this incident must have happened about 37 when Aretas controlled the city, once Caligula became Emperor. Paul then presumably will have made his first visit to Jerusalem as a Christian no sooner than A.D. 37 or 38.

87. Luedemann, *Paul, Apostle to the Gentiles*, pp. 56ff.

former, and so we cannot tell precisely how long Paul spent either in Arabia or in Damascus.[88]

Paul says he 'went up' to Jerusalem, which presumably reflects the fact that the city is in the Judean hills. The purpose of going has to do with 'Cephas'. This Aramaic word is the way Paul normally refers to Peter (cf. Gal. 2.9, 11, 14; 1 Cor. 1.12; 15.5). Only in Gal. 2.7–8 does Paul call him Peter.[89] The key verb here is ἱστορέω. Probably the earliest commentator on this document, Chrysostom, translates this verb 'to visit' (PG 61.651), but in commenting on this verse he says that Paul "does not say to 'see' . . . but to visit and survey (ἱστορῆσαι), a word which those, who seek to become acquainted with great and splendid cities, apply to themselves".[90] He goes on to add that it does not mean to get information or knowledge from Peter. This may not be right, however. Polybius 3.48.12 uses the verb to refer to inquiring and learning about something, and Plutarch uses it to refer to one engaged in the study of Socrates and his philosophy (*Moralia* 516C; cf. Epictetus 3.7.1). The problem with these examples is that they basically do not involve the use of this verb with a personal object as in Gal. 1.18. In passages where such a combination occurs (Herodotus 2.19; 3.77) it can mean 'to ask' someone, but a closer parallel to our text is found in Josephus *War* 6.81 where it refers to making someone's acquaintance (cf. also Plutarch *Theseus* 30, *Pompey* 40; Epictetus *Diss.* 2.14.28; 3.7.1). As Dunn rightly concludes it is not really possible to exclude the notion of inquiry or gaining of information here, even if we translate the verb 'to make the acquaintance' as above.[91]

---

88. Cf. Longenecker, *Galatians*, p. 37; Lightfoot, *Galatians*, p. 84 says the 'immediately' in vs. 16 leads to the conclusion that Paul is figuring this period from the time of his conversion. Matera, *Galatians*, p. 66 argues that this conclusion is likely and may suggest that Paul spent a considerable time in Arabia. 2 Cor. 11 would suggest he was there at least long enough to get himself into hot water with Aretas.

89. The term Κηφᾶς is found outside of the Pauline corpus only at Jn. 1.42, but of course the term presumably lies behind Mt. 16.18 even though no transliterated Aramaic is present there. Some Western and Syrian manuscripts followed by the Textus Receptus change Cephas to Peter at Gal. 1.18 (D, F, G, K, L, P, S2). The reading Cephas however has good support here in p46 and 51, א, A, B and others. Cf. Metzger, *TC*, p. 591.

90. It is possible that Ambrosiaster actually preceded Chrysostom in commenting on Galatians if one can date Ambrosiaster's work on Galatians to somewhere between A.D. 380–90.

91. Dunn, *Jesus, Paul, and the Law*, pp. 112–13. It was apparently C. H. Dodd who first remarked that we may be sure that Paul did not spend fifteen days talking to Peter about the weather. O. Hofius, "Gal. 1:18: ἱστορῆσαι Κηφᾶν," *ZNW* 75 (1984), pp. 73–85, followed by R. Y. K. Fung, *The Epistle to the Galatians* (Grand Rapids: Eerdmans, 1988), p. 74 argues that the verb simply means 'to get to know' (personally) when in the sort of grammatical construction we find here. I agree this is how the verb is to be translated, but this personal information without question must have involved learning something about Peter's relationship with Jesus, about Jesus' message and the like.

This conclusion, that Paul sought information, even if only from and in part about Peter himself, runs counter to the notion that Paul was trying to defend himself here against the charge that he was dependent in any way on such Jerusalem church luminaries. The aim in Galatians is not to defend Paul's apostolic office nor attack anyone else's apostolicity. Chrysostom is right that verses such as 1.17–18 show that Paul has no intent to speak disparagingly of the apostles nor is he reluctant to acknowledge any debt he may have to them. His only overarching concern is the integrity of his Gospel which the Galatians received.

The question about vs. **19** is whether Paul is including James among the apostles or not. Lightfoot is surely right that we must link the word ἕτερον ('other') with εἰ μὴ and that means it is also linked with 'apostles'. I would suggest that here as in Gal. 1.6 ἕτερον is enumerative and not comparative or differentiative.[92] Paul then is suggesting James was indeed one of the apostles, which would not necessarily make him one of the Twelve, since Paul does not equate the two groups (cf. 1 Cor 15.7). In view of the way Paul refers to him, this James is surely not James son of Zebedee or James son of Alphaeus, but rather the one known as James the Just who was killed in A.D. 62 through the instigation of Annas the High Priest during the period between the rule of two Roman governors (Josephus *Ant.* 20.200). Josephus makes clear he had a reputation for ascetical piety and devotion to the Jewish faith. This is surely the James mentioned first among Jesus' siblings in Mk. 6.3 (cf. Mt. 13.55), but to judge from texts like Mk. 3.21, 31–35 and Jn. 7.3–5 he was not a disciple of Jesus during his earthly ministry. Yet he is mentioned at the beginning of Acts (1.14) as being part of the inner circle in the upper room, and most would rightly attribute this to his having seen the risen Jesus (1 Cor. 15), though the Gospels do not mention this fact. His prominence in the Jerusalem church is evident not only in Gal. 1–2 but also in Acts 12.17, 15.13, and 21.18–19.[93]

Perhaps it is possible to read between the lines of our text here and the one in Acts 12. If Paul went up to make the acquaintance of Peter but only saw James in addition, this may be because at this period, Peter was seen as the titular head of the Jerusalem church, with James also considered one of the pillars. Sometime after this Peter left Jerusalem to do missionary work, a fact probably recorded in Acts 12 but also suggested by Peter's presence in Antioch (Gal. 2; cf. also 1 Cor. 1.12; 3.22), after which James was in charge, which is apparently the situation when Paul wrote Galatians, and even before that when 'men from James' came to Antioch. On the other hand, Paul may have wished to see Peter not because he was the main pillar, but because of his long

92. See Longenecker, *Galatians*, p. 38; Lightfoot, *Galatians*, pp. 84–85.
93. On Jesus' relatives see R. Bauckham, *Jude and the Relatives of Jesus in the Early Church* (Edinburgh: T. & T. Clark, 1990).

association with Jesus' ministry. In other words, this verse may tell us nothing specific about the pecking order of power in the Jerusalem church.

A brief discussion of the question of James' relationship to Jesus is perhaps in order. There is certainly nothing in any of the references to James in the NT which would suggest that he was other than a full brother of Jesus. Tertullian (A.D. 160–220) is the earliest post-canonical writer to commentate on the situation to any degree and he speaks of James and the other brothers as other children of Joseph and Mary (*Adv. Marc.* 4.19; *De Car.* 7), a view later supported by Helvidius of Rome somewhere around A.D. 380. It is my view that it was probably the growing Christian ascetical movement which fostered a conviction about Mary's perpetual virginity and this in turn led to the sort of thing that we hear in documents like the Protoevangelium of James where these 'brothers' are sons of Joseph by a previous marriage (9.2), a view later supported by Epiphanius (A.D. 315–403). A third view of the matter arose with Jerome (A.D. 347–420) who argued that these brothers were simply first cousins of Jesus, being the children of Alphaeus and Mary of Clopas. Though the views of Epiphanius and Jerome cannot be absolutely ruled out, nothing in the NT text really suggests such a view any more than the NT suggests the perpetual virginity of Mary. Indeed, to judge from Lk. 2.22 not only was the birth of Jesus perfectly normal, but his parents assumed that the Jewish post-partum purification ritual was in order, something that would seem unlikely if they had believed that Mary continued to be holy (e.g., ritually clean) and a *virgo intacta* even after the birth of Jesus. It is also probable that Mt. 1.25 suggests that Mary and Joseph had sexual relations after the birth of Jesus and that Lk. 2.7 probably suggests she had more children as well.[94] Thus, Dunn's comment may be on target when he reminds us that in the Middle East, the line of inheritance passes horizontally from one brother to another, and so it is quite understandable how after the death of Jesus, the Jerusalem church might look to James for leadership.[95]

When one contrasts the main verb in vs. **19** with that in vs. 18, we must conclude that whatever Paul did with Peter, he only saw James, he did not consult with him. Thus, the emphasis may lie on the fact that Paul owes nothing of his Gospel to James. Paul would say the same about Peter, whatever details he may have learned from him about the life and ministry of

94. See the discussion in Lightfoot, *Galatians*, pp. 252–91 and my *Women in the Ministry of Jesus* (Cambridge: Cambridge University Press, 1984), pp. 94–95 and notes, and also the more extended discussion in my 1981 Durham dissertation *Women in the Gospels and Acts*.

95. Dunn, *Galatians*, p. 76. It is even possible and may indeed be probable to conclude from Acts that James was one of the three main leaders from the first, perhaps the primary one, and this status was only enhanced when Peter left town. See my *The Acts of the Apostles*, pp. 422ff.

Jesus.[96] Paul's Gospel is basically *not* about the day to day events of the earthly ministry of Jesus, but rather about the soteriological effects and benefits of his life, death, resurrection, and appearances. Paul's focus and distinctive message has to do with Christ crucified and risen, and mainly focuses on the now exalted Lord.

There is, however, no disrespect reflected toward James in this verse, for Paul calls James the *Lord's* brother, a very interesting phrase, and a highly honorific one at that. The one who had become Paul's Lord and James' Lord through a resurrection appearance was also, in terms of the flesh, James' brother, but now had become James' spiritual kin as well. The humanness and yet more than humanness of Jesus is expressed in this phrase 'the Lord's brother'. What is also expressed here is the high privilege and status of James, which Paul does not dispute. If Paul had really believed that deliberate attacks were coming against his Gospel from James himself, it is very doubtful that he could have spoken in this way about James, whom he clearly distinguishes from the false brothers, who receive a pejorative label unlike the label 'the Lord's brother'.

Verse **20** presents us with an oath, and of course the question arises as to what prompts this oath. Was there someone disseminating a story that Paul owed his Gospel to James or Peter or even his apostleship? Was dis-information being spread by the agitators in Galatia about Paul? We cannot know why exactly Paul chooses this point to offer an oath, but perhaps an analogy is in order. As J. Paul Sampley has pointed out,[97] it was the custom in the Greco-Roman world not only to offer oaths within a courtroom situation, but in a manner similar to the modern practice of a sworn deposition one could also swear an oath outside the courtroom to warn the other party that one was prepared to stand trial on the veracity of one's claims. I suspect this is the case here. Paul does not know exactly what the agitators are arguing in Galatia, though he may suspect they were questioning his character and ethos.[98] In order to forestall having to go into a defensive mode in relating to his converts, he swears an oath now in advance of such a forensic situation that he is prepared to attest to the truthfulness of his *narratio*.[99] He is not here offering

96. See Longenecker, *Galatians*, p. 38.

97. See J. Paul Sampley, "'Before God I do not Lie' (Gal. 1.20): Paul's Self Defense in the Light of Roman Legal Praxis," *NTS* 23 (1977), pp. 477–82.

98. Probably the situation is that Paul is trying to forestall any such possible later attacks rather than respond to existing ones.

99. Quintilian *Inst. Or.* 5.6.2 says that in order to win one's case one may offer to take an oath as a culminating proof of a clear conscience. Clearly the rhetorical function here is to improve Paul's ethos and establish his character with his audience as a truth teller in advance of presenting his formal arguments to them. The logic is, if he is credible about his own story, then presumably his persuasion could be trusted about other matters about to be discussed.

such a defense, he is simply recounting the facts as an attempt to persuade his audience to act in a certain way. Nonetheless, he serves notice that he is prepared to defend himself if necessary.

The concern about Paul's ethos surfaces again and again in Gal. 1–2, and some have even seen Paul as presenting an encomium here in praise of himself.[100] The function, however, of this material is not to praise or lay blame, it is to make clear Paul has always had a good ethos, and so can be relied upon to tell his converts the truth when he begins his arguments in earnest. Paul portrays himself as a virtuous, God-loving and God-directed person who has his audience's best interests at heart (cf. Menander Rhetor 1.361.17–25). In these regards he presents himself as an exemplar for his audience. He also portrays himself as one having high status (as an apostle and prophet of God), a status given by God and recognized by the Jerusalem church, and demonstrated by his having a commission on a par with no less than Peter himself. The missionary world in a sense was divided between the two of them.[101]

It is in order to compare other places where Paul uses the affirmation that before God he does not lie. The first of these is in a very similar place in the *narratio* in 1 Thess. 2.5 where also Paul is reminding his converts what he did and did not do and say while among them. If it is not necessary to assume that Paul is combating already extant charges and criticisms in Thessalonica, especially since 1 Thessalonians is another example of deliberative rhetoric, it is not necessary to conclude that here either. The other two examples (2 Cor. 1.23 and 2 Cor. 11.31) do, however, come in pieces of forensic rhetoric. The point I am making is that the oath in itself could occur in either deliberative or forensic rhetoric and it does not in itself signal that Paul is necessarily rebutting known charges here.[102] Paul must assure his audience in his *narratio* of his truthfulness. This is a major part of the function of a *narratio*, as it builds confidence in the character of the speaker before he makes his arguments. Since the truth of the Gospel and how one should follow it is in Paul's mind at issue, it is not surprising that Paul insists he is telling the truth about it and other matters. He cannot present himself as a paradigm to his audience for imitation otherwise.

Verse **21** provides us with the second ἔπειτα and here Paul does not tell us how long a period of time was involved. As Chrysostom says in commenting on this verse it is quite possible to conclude that Paul passes over a

---

100. See now Malina and Neyrey, *Portraits of Paul*, pp. 34–51.
101. See the entire discussion in Malina and Neyrey, pp. 34–51.
102. On the function of oaths in rhetoric see ps.-Aristotle *Rhet. ad Alex.* 17, p. 1432a33.

considerable expanse of time in just a few words here.[103] Paul's point is to
make clear that he was not in Jerusalem during this time. The term κλίματα
may be used here in a general and non-political sense of districts or territories
(notice the repetition of the article τῆς cf. Rom. 15.23; 2 Cor. 11.10), though
it has been argued by Ramsay that it is a technical term referring to the
adminstrative subdivisions of a Roman province.[104] What is clear enough is
that both Syria and Cilicia were included within one Roman province at this
time, indeed had been for over half a century, and so we may see here Paul's
shorthand way of referring to the fact that he went to various regions within
this Roman province. As Longenecker points out, it is clear from the remarks
that follow about Judea that Paul does not include Judea as part of Syria, and if
as is usually the case Paul is using the provincial designation 'Judea' it is in
order to point out that this would include Galilee, Samaria, as well as Judea
proper.[105] Antioch was the capital of the Roman province of Syria-Cilicia at
this time and the next most prominent city therein was Tarsus, and so we
should probably compare this text to what is said in Acts 9.30, 11.25–26.[106]

Verse 22 refers to Paul being unknown by 'face' to the Christian
assemblies in Judea. This has sometimes been seen to contradict the account
in Acts 8.3. It must be seen, however, that the difficulty is not just with what
Acts says, but with what Paul himself claims in Gal. 1.13. How can he have
both persecuted the church of God and not be known to them? Several
points are germane. Firstly, Acts 8.3 does not suggest that Paul ever persecuted
any house group of Christians outside of Jerusalem itself, nor does Gal. 1.13.
Paul's persecution transpired during the earliest days of the existence of the
church when it was just forming in Jerusalem. Secondly, one must reckon on
some church expansion between that time of persecution and the time when
Paul went off to the regions of Syria and Cilicia. At least three or four years had
gone by from the time of Paul's conversion. During that time the early church
may have established various new house churches in outlying areas in Judea.
Notice that whereas Paul speaks of 'church' (singular) in 1.13 he speaks of
congregations (plural) in 2.22. Thirdly, note Paul speaks of 'remaining
unknown by face'. This means that in these churches he was previously
unknown as well. Fourthly, note that the following verse seems to provide us
with a report of the Jerusalem church about Paul's conversion to these other

---

103. There is nothing here to suggest a ministry far afield from Syria and Cilicia in
either Macedonia or Greece during this period. On the other hand we must put the
ministry in Galatia at some point and it would seem to belong either to this period before
the second visit up to Jerusalem or not long after returning from there, probably the latter.
See my discussion of chronological matters in *The Acts of the Apostles*, pp. 413ff.

104. Ramsay, *Galatians*, pp. 278–80.

105. Longenecker, *Galatians*, p. 40.

106. See my discussion in *The Acts of the Apostles*, pp. 431ff.

churches. They had learned of this only second hand. I thus conclude it is not necessary to see a contradiction here between what is said in 1.13 and what is said in 1.22, or with Acts either.[107]

Paul was known by some members of the Jerusalem church both before and after his conversion. It was the household congregations in Jerusalem that he had ravaged when he was a persecutor. His was an urban strategy of persecution – first Jerusalem, then Damascus, just like his later urban strategy of evangelism. Paul had not dealt with the outlying congregations and of course he had not persecuted those who were only converted in Judea after Paul's own conversion. Paul's point in saying what he does is in part to make clear that he owed nothing of his Gospel or ministry to these other churches in Judea either.[108] Finally, notice that Paul speaks here of these assemblies being 'in Christ', which seems to have a locative sense here.[109] Just as Paul had previously been 'in Judaism' so now he and Christian congregations were 'in Christ' as a distinct and distinguishable bounded social entity.[110]

Verse **23** is important because it appears to include an early report of the Jerusalem church to its satellites in Judea about Paul.[111] The verbal form of 'hearing' is imperfect periphrastic suggesting hearing over a considerable period of time.[112] The phrase 'proclaiming the faith' is important on several scores. Firstly it shows that Paul is perfectly capable of using πίστις in the sense of the content of the Gospel that is believed ('the faith' cf. 1 Cor 16.13), rather than just of the act of believing or trusting. This choice of words here is to be explained by the fact that Paul thinks the content of his proclamation is being challenged in Galatia. This document is intended to argue for that content and against the alternative offered by the agitators. As Dunn notes the

107. Acts 9.26–30 does speak of Paul trying to join the disciples when he comes to Jerusalem from Damascus, but we are told they were afraid of Paul and in essence did not accept him even in Jerusalem until Barnabas paved the way. Nothing is said here about Paul visiting Judean churches outside of Jerusalem, and the way the report reads in Gal. 1.23 these outlying churches only heard the report from the Jerusalem church about Paul's conversion. They still had not met him face to face. Hengel, *Paul between Damascus and Antioch*, pp. 36ff. suggests Paul uses "Judea" in Gal. 1.22 in the provincial sense, which would even include Galilee and Samaria.

108. See Dunn, *Galatians*, p. 80.

109. See C. F. D. Moule, *The Origin of Christology* (Cambridge: Cambridge University Press, 1977), p. 56.

110. See Dunn, *Galatians*, p. 82; Burton, *Galatians*, p. 63.

111. Not as Betz, *Galatians*, p. 81 suggests the report of these Judean churches themselves. We must take seriously that the text says they were only *hearing* this report about Paul. The persons speaking are other than the persons hearing the report. Then too the phrase 'The One persecuting *us*' most naturally refers to members of the Jerusalem church proper. On this being an early report of this church see E. Bammel, "Galater 1, 23," *ZNW* 59 (1968), pp. 108–12.

112. Cf. BDF no. 353; rightly Dunn, *Galatians*, p. 83.

word 'faith' occurs some twenty-two times in Galatians, which means that proportionately he uses the term more in this letter than in any other Pauline letter (out of 243 total uses in the NT, 142 are in Paul's letters).[113] Here is another clue that this document is about the content of the Gospel, rather than being a defense of Paul's apostleship. The reference to Paul's persecuting of 'the faith' is likewise important. As we have already noted above, Paul saw some sort of fundamental antithesis between faith in Christ and his teachings and being a Torah-true Jew. This verse provides a bit of further confirmation that Paul's persecuting was not just socially but rather also ideologically motivated.[114]

It is these Judean churches, perhaps also with those who told them the story in the Jerusalem church, that are said in vs. 24 to have glorified God 'in me' "He says not, they admired me, they applauded me or were astonished at me, but [he] ascribes all to divine grace by the words 'they glorified God in me'" (Chrysostom on 1.24). 'In me' here would presumably mean 'on acccount of' 'because of' or 'for' me.[115] Lightfoot suggest an echo here of Is. 49.3: "You are my servant, Israel, in whom I will be glorified".[116] Bearing in mind the echo of Isaiah noted above when Paul speaks of his call and conversion, this text may lie in the background here.

The third major section of the *narratio* runs from 2.1–10 and recounts the second trip of Paul up to Jerusalem. This section is difficult to interpret not least because of the grammar. There appears to be a significant anacoluthon at the beginning of vs. 4, and in any case vss. 3–5 appear to be parenthetical, with the main subject being raised in vss. 1–2, and then being resumed in vss. 6–10. In addition vss. 6–10 are apparently one long convoluted sentence in the Greek.[117]

Here again ἔπειτα is used as a temporal marker indicating this event happened after the time Paul spent in Syria and Cilicia. The reference to 'fourteen years' prefaced with διά and followed by the word πάλιν has led to various conclusions about the time period Paul meant. It is not clear what event begins this fourteen-year period. Is this a reference back to Paul's conversion experience or is it a reference to his last visit to Jerusalem, or even to his time spent in Syria and Cilicia? The word 'again' would seem to support the view that the fourteen years is since Paul's last visit to Jerusalem, a view which would also seem to be supported by the fact that the main issue in both the preceding and present paragraph is the duration and nature of Paul's visits to Jerusalem. Dunn points out that the διά here also probably favors the

113. Dunn, *Galatians*, p. 84.
114. See Matera, *Galatians*, p. 70.
115. See Burton, *Galatians*, p. 65.
116. Lightfoot, *Galatians*, p. 86.
117. See Longenecker, *Galatians*, p. 44.

view that the starting point was Paul's last visit to Jerusalem. Paul would be saying that throughout or during the fourteen years following his first visit to Jerusalem he was absent from there.[118] Having drawn this conclusion, however, we must still deal with the problem of inclusive reckoning with the 'fourteen years' just as we did with the 'three' years. Fourteen years could mean as little as twelve years and a few months (twelve full years plus parts of two others), and when added to the previous number mentioned, we could in fact arrive at a total of fourteen years for the entire period since Paul's conversion (one and a half years plus twelve and a half years). On the other hand, it could be as much as seventeen years. I suspect it is closer to the former than to the latter.[119]

One of the keys to understanding this section is to recognize that Paul is using the terminology of political or deliberative rhetoric here to characterize in pejorative terms an adversarial situation in the church.[120] He is seeking to influence a similar situation and the decision making procedure among his Galatians on the basis of this precedent. He will discuss a meeting of the ἐκκλησία in Jerusalem to settle future matters of policy in regard to the mission to the Gentiles. In this meeting there are in fact not two parties involved as Paul presents the matter but three: (1) Paul, Barnabas, and Timothy representing the Gentile mission and presumably also the Antioch church;[121] (2) the pillars of the Jerusalem church; (3) the 'spies' or intruders.[122] The adversarial relationship exists with, and the polemics seem to be directly primarily if not exclusively against, the third group.

The political rhetoric is largely used to characterize this third group in good propaganda fashion. They are 'spies', they seek to 'enslave' others, they have been 'secretly smuggled in', or 'infiltrated' a private meeting, they are 'false brothers'. Paul, however, and his group refused to act like a conquered people. They refused to 'yield in submission' to these false ones. Rather they have come for a different political action – 'to submit for consideration' their message and mission to the pillars, and perhaps the Jerusalem church as a whole as well. The picture here is of an embassy from one group to another, seeking to reach some sort of agreement or concordat. It is then not surprising

118. Dunn, *Galatians*, p. 87.

119. This conclusion is based on my more detailed work on Pauline chronology in connection with Acts chronology. See my *The Acts of the Apostles*, pp. 69ff.

120. It is a surprise that while Betz, *Galatians*, pp. 83ff. quite properly recognizes that Paul is drawing on political terminology in this section he does not draw the appropriate conclusion from this clue about the rhetorical species of this document. On political terms in 1 Corinthians as a proper clue to the sort of rhetoric involved in that letter cf. Mitchell, *Rhetoric of Reconciliation*, pp. 68ff.

121. See the discussion in N. Taylor, *Paul, Antioch, and Jerusalem. A Study in Relationships and Authority in Earliest Christianity* (Sheffield: JSOT Press, 1992), pp. 88ff.

122. It is in fact possible there were two meetings on this occasion – a small private and a larger public one.

that the outcome of this meeting is also described in social and political terms. The result of the meeting is some sort of agreement made binding by the giving and receiving of the right hand of κοινωνία.

Paul says in **2.1** that he went up to Jerusalem 'with Barnabas taking along also Titus'. That Paul does not put matters the other way around (that Barnabas went with Paul) may well suggest that at this point in time Barnabas is still seen as the senior partner in this relationship. Notice that the order of names here is the same as in Acts 11.30 and 12.25. Titus is most likely seen here as a Pauline co-worker whom Paul decided to take along to Jerusalem. The question is why he would intentionally take Titus along, especially in view of the fact that Paul is going to make clear that he is an uncircumcised Greek.

I would suggest that Paul's plan was to press the issue of the status of Gentiles in the church and raise the issue of what was necessary for them to have full participation with Jews in the body of Christ. He would be presenting Titus as a test case to the leaders of the Jerusalem church. As things turned out, however, Paul had not reckoned on the presence of 'false brothers' at the meeting and *they* took the presence of Titus as a provocation, an honor challenge, to which they must respond in kind or give up their own views. The 'pillars' basic ruling was in Paul's favor, which meant in an agonistic culture that the 'false brothers' had been shamed and would have to respond to save face. Paul for his part thinks that the whole matter of face and honor challenges is not merely counterproductive to the aims of the ἐκκλησία but against the essence of the Gospel which is grace. He indicates this is his view in three ways in this section: (1) by distancing himself from the honor ratings that some were bestowing on the pillars; (2) by stressing that God does not accept face, that is, he does not judge matters on the basis of human reciprocity and honor conventions, and pays no heed to human credentials; (3) he stresses that the pillars added nothing to Paul's personal honor rating or status;[123] rather they recognized the unmerited favor given Paul by God. God shows no partiality, and the Gospel of God likewise does not – it is a matter of pure grace. Hence, the ἐκκλησία and its mission should not be 'showing face' either in its mission to Jews and Gentiles, or in its own community life to those who had close connections of one sort or another with Jesus before his death. This explains Paul's dismissive remark about the pillars – 'what they *were* (i.e., before Easter and seeing the risen Lord) matters nothing to me'. Neither blood ties nor social relationships matter in the Kingdom, but rather grace.[124] A few words are in order at this point about agonistic cultures.

---

123. Notice that Paul says they added nothing 'to me', he is not referring primarily to them adding some stipulations to his Gospel or mission.

124. See for a slightly different reading, but one which raises some of the right issues. P. Esler, "Making and Breaking an Agreement Mediterranean Style: A New Reading of Galatians 2.1–14," *Biblical Intepretation* 3.3 (1995), pp. 286–314.

Excursus: The Agony of an Agonistic Culture ─────────────

Understanding agonistic cultures should in some regards not be difficult for those moderns who have grown up in western societies where competition plays such a large role in business, sport, and indeed everyday life. But competition in antiquity was not chiefly for money or fame as we know it, but rather for 'honor', and by the same token one was prepared to go great lengths to avoid shame. P. Esler puts matters succinctly: "Honor means both someone's claim to worth and the public acknowledgement of the merit of that claim by a relevant social group. Its opposite is shame. Honor may be either ascribed, that is, obtained without any personal effort (for example by being born into a noble family) or acquired, that is gained actively, through various forms of social interaction. In Mediterranean culture relationships among people who are not kin are governed not merely by self-interest but by the object of obtaining honor from vanquishing or even deceiving non-kin . . . In this context all social interactions, including gift-giving, sporting contests, dinner invitations, commercial transactions, discussions in taverns, and around wells, arranging marriages and *settling agreements*, offer those involved an opportunity, eagerly seized upon, to enhance their honor at someone else's expense."[125] In short, competition was the essence of such a culture, not least because it was believed that honor was a limited good, that is in short supply, such that for one person to have it, another would have to be deprived of it.

It is interesting that in matters not touching the heart of the Gospel Paul was perfectly willing to talk about honor and shame and even competition. He will use in this very text the language of athletics to speak about 'running in vain', an agonistic motif.[126] The Christian life is seen as a struggle which requires one to be a moral athlete, and Christian missionary work is seen in the same light. Paul uses the language of 'running in vain' to speak about a social consequence that could have arisen if the Jerusalem church leaders had not agreed with him about the legitimacy of the Gentile mission. While Paul did not see their endorsement as an authorization of his Gospel or mission or apostleship, he did fear that if they rejected or censured him and his mission it would adversely affect not only his missionary work but the prospects of their being a unified people of God, Jew and Gentile united in Christ. In Paul's view, the issue is not authorization, but recognition of one already authorized, and co-operation in the future.

In the Greco-Roman world honor was closely bound up with authority and power. If Paul was shamed by the Jerusalem church he would lose clout with his converts, and the agitators would gain the upper hand in Galatia. It was important for Paul to establish better social networks with the Jerusalem church not least because his honor rating was and would continue to go down with his converts if he could not show he had at least the moral support of the Jerusalem leaders. It needs also to be borne clearly in mind that it was difficult to shame someone of higher social status or

125. Esler, p. 290, emphasis mine. He is of course following B. Malina, *The New Testament World: Insights from Cultural Anthropology* (Atlanta: John Knox, 1981), pp. 32ff.
    126. See V. C. Pfitzner, *Paul and the Agon Motif: Traditional Athletic Imagery in the Pauline Literature* (Leiden: Brill, 1967), pp. 82ff.

considerable authority and power. Paul has no qualms about attempting to shame the false brothers, or 'the men from James' or the agitators in Galatia, or even his own converts (cf. Gal. 3.1–5)[127] but he is on the whole more circumspect in the way he speaks of the pillars, while still distancing himself from them in some ways. He *does* attempt to shame Peter directly by confronting him in Antioch, and we must judge that in view of his attempt to be more circumspect in this letter, that he saw the provocation of Peter's hypocrisy as so great that he had to go against decorum and speak out in Antioch. In other words, the incident at Antioch was certainly not over some minor matter such as whether or not Gentiles should wash their hands before dinner. This incident may well also suggest that Paul sees himself, at least in regard to his work as an apostle, as Peter's equal, for it was rare for a subordinant ever to try and shame a superior, and certainly never in public so that they lost face with their clientele.

The rhetorical culture of which Paul was a part fostered the comparison of speakers and philosophers, and normally this included debates and competitions. It is clear enough that Paul sees himself as in competition with the agitators over the hearts and minds of the Galatian converts. At stake was their future and of course also Paul's reputation. It would appear likely that the Galatians were being urged to make a 'comparison' συγχρίσις between Paul's message and that of the agitators. Paul must respond with both polemics and also clear teaching as to what the Galatians should believe and do in the future.

In the agonistic struggle, the agitators had the upper hand at the time Paul wrote for two reasons: (1) they had been in Galatia more recently, and may well have still been there when Galatians was written, and at the same time Paul was not present to represent his Gospel; (2) religion in the ancient world had at its very heart ritual. It was a matter of rites and sacrifices and meals and observances and processions and festivals. This was as true of Greco-Roman religion as it was of Jewish religion. The problem for Paul was that in his advice to the Galatians as to how to go on with their Christian life, he had not provided them with honorable and repeatable rites and duties (or at least not provided sufficient on-going ones) that they could easily follow and so have a concrete means of responding to what they believed God had done in their lives. In short, in the agonistic competition for the souls of the Galatians, the agitators had offered them a way of living that made perfectly good religious and social sense given their background. The proper way to honor and respond to God and God's blessing was through observance of months, days, seasons, and through rituals like circumcision.

Paul's social strategy in Galatia, as would also be the case in Corinth and elsewhere, was to redraw the lines of honor and shame. He is not in the business of simply baptizing the larger values of Greco-Roman society. In fact he undermines many of those fundamental values by touting a crucified messiah as the model of honorable conduct. Being in Christ was in Paul's view what brought real status – the status of being sons and daughters of God on a permanent basis. In Paul's view only

127. One way he will attempt to shame his converts into coming around to his view again is by suggesting that they were shaming him (cf. 4.11).

God really bestows permanent honor or lasting shame, and so there is a sense in which he is attempting to set up a counterculture which uses many of the terms of the dominant culture, but in different ways.[128] This is typical of someone who is fostering a breakaway sect, but what is interesting is that not only does Paul take over the terminology of early Judaism and alter its meaning, he does this with the terminology of the dominant Greco-Roman culture as well, redefining honor and shame, good and evil and the like. Paul is especially concerned with the issue of how Christians live, not only in Galatians but also in his other letters, and so H. Moxnes is right to conclude that "apparently it is within the area of 'lifestyle' that Paul wants to establish the distinctive characteristics of a specific Christian identity".[129] We see this especially in Paul's detailed advice about how to walk in the Spirit and about following the 'Law of Christ'. Paul is not simply working with a modified version of the Mosaic Law, but attempting to set up something different that comports with the new creation that exists in Christ while drawing on some terms and ideas from both the world of Judaism and the Greco-Roman world. We will have occasion to say much more on this front as the commentary progresses.

Paul tells us at **2.2** that he went up to Jerusalem on the basis of an ἀποκάλυψις. It is most unlikely this is a reference to the revelation Paul received at his conversion, for if that were the case we would have expected a grammatical signal that what was meant was the one mentioned in 1.12, namely we would have expected a definite article before 'revelation' here.[130] When Paul speaks of revelation he sometimes is referring to something received by means of a vision (cf. 1.12; 2 Cor. 12.1ff.), but he also believed revelation came through prophecy (cf. 1 Cor. 14.6, 26, 30), and there is no reason why this could not be the case in this instance. If this is so, then Paul would probably be referring to a prophecy directed to him and perhaps also to Barnabas and Titus (and perhaps others) that they needed to go up to Jerusalem for some reason.[131] This conclusion comports with the thesis that Paul is alluding to the episode recorded in Acts 11.27–30 in which Agabus a prophet from Jerusalem came to Antioch and revealed there would be a severe famine, which prompted the disciples to send relief funds to the Christians in Judea by means of Barnabas and Saul. It also comports with what Paul says in Gal. 2.10, namely that he was asked by the Jerusalem leaders to continue to remember the poor, something he was already eager to do. In other words, this last verse implies that part of the purpose of the trip referred to in 2.1–10 was

128. See my *Conflict and Community in Corinth*, pp. 154–55.

129. H. Moxnes, "Honor, Shame, and the Outside World in Paul's Letter to the Romans," in *The Social World of Formative Christianity and Judaism*, ed. J. Neusner et al. (Philadelphia: Fortress, 1988), pp. 207–18, here p. 213.

130. See rightly Dunn, *Galatians*, p. 91.

131. Notice Paul does not say that he as a prophet personally received this revelation, but rather that he went in accord with a revelation. We would have expected some such phrase as 'a revelation given to me' if that was what he meant here.

to aid the poor, and Paul promised to continue this charitable work (cf. below on this verse). No doubt too, Paul wants his own Galatian audience to know that he did not go up to Jerusalem because he was summoned by the leaders there, but rather because of a prompting from God. But beyond that why more precisely did Paul feel a need to go?

One clue comes from those with whom he goes. Barnabas, a Jewish Christian who, according to Acts, had both close ties with the church in Jerusalem and in Antioch and could bear witness to Paul's work and message and the fruit of these up to this point in time, and in fact had introduced Paul to the Jerusalem church in the first place, and for that matter to the church in Antioch as well (cf. Acts 4.32–37; 9.26–29; 11.22–29).[132] Titus could hardly have been more different from Paul or Barnabas; he was a 'Greek', uncircumcised, and presumably had not ever even been a God-fearer. In other words, it would appear he was a convert from paganism. Paul must have known that bringing such a person to Jerusalem, not least if he was to stay and eat with members of the Jerusalem church, would bring matters to a boil on the issue of the social relationships between Jewish and Gentile Christians in the church. He must have been brought as exhibit A, or as a test case, for the point Paul would want to make about his Gospel for the Gentiles, while his presence will without doubt have been taken as a provocation by the more hard line of the Judaizing Christians in Jerusalem. Barrett sums things up rather aptly:

> It would make no sense that after so long he [i.e. Paul] should develop cold feet and wonder if what he was preaching, the message that had converted men and women, changed their lives, and gathered them into churches, was perhaps a mistake. He does not say he was seeking either correction or validation. It is nearer the truth to say he could see that trouble was blowing up (the next few verses will show how near it was) and went to lay his cards on the table recognizing that though Jerusalem authorities could not prove him wrong or right they could ruin his life's work (2.2). Perhaps what he wanted was a show-down and he took Titus with him as a deliberate provocation. Jerusalem was evidently a divided church, for we leave the authorities and come first to the false brothers (2.4) . . .[133]

Verse **2b** is complex. Does it refer to two meetings, one more public, one more private, or only one? On the one hand the αὐτοῖς has been taken by some commentators to refer to a larger group than those mentioned as the δοκοῦσιν later in the verse and thus to allude to two meetings. I would suggest that this is unlikely. Paul did not go up to Jerusalem to present his Gospel to two different groups but rather to one. As his previous trip to Jerusalem

---

132. Cf. below for a fuller discussion of Barnabas and his importance to Paul, and see my *The Acts of the Apostles*, pp. 378ff.

133. Barrett, *Freedom and Obligation*, pp. 10–11.

suggests, he dealt only with the leaders of the Jerusalem church when he made such visits, and that was all the more likely to be the case on this visit when he was to present the Gospel he preached to the Gentiles. The only ones who could truly be said to make his efforts fruitless if they did not accept his message and ministry would be the leaders of the Jerusalem church. I thus must conclude that the 'them' is not different from the δοκοῦσιν mentioned later in the verse. This means there was only one meeting on this occasion, intended to be a private one, not least because of the volatility of the subject matter of the meeting.[134]

Notice that Paul speaks of the 'Gospel I preach' (present tense) not 'the Gospel I preached'. He is making a claim that he has not changed his mission or message along the way, a point highly relevant for his Galatian audience who needed to be able to trust that Paul's message had not changed through the years, and that what they had heard and believed was not different from what other converts to Christianity had heard and believed.

The verb ἀνεθέμην is in the middle voice and has the sense of 'present' or 'lay out for consideration' or even 'communicate with a view to consultation'.[135] It suggests a significant and perhaps even formal meeting that was to produce definite ratifiable results (cf. Acts 25.14; 2 Macc. 3.9; Mic. 7.5 LXX). Betz says of this verb the "use of official political language shows the event had an official and legally binding character. The task of the delegation was to 'submit for consideration' . . ."[136]

Especially in view of the following comment about fearing that he might be running in vain, it becomes clear that we are dealing with an asymmetrical social relationship here, even though Paul asserts the independence of origin of his Gospel and apostleship. The Jerusalem leaders did not come to Paul, he went to them, and it is doubtful they would have feared their ministry was in vain if Paul had not approved of its character or direction. In other words, *de facto* Paul finds himself in a role socially inferior to the Jerusalem leaders in the social network of the church. This position he finds awkward at least because he feels he was commissioned and given a message by Christ, and so is not beholden to the Jerusalem church for his authority or ministry or message. Practically, however, he knows that if the church is to be Jew and Gentile united in Christ, as he will say in Gal. 3.28, this requires that he must make some effort to contribute to the social unity of the larger body of believers. It is not

134. And this, I would suggest, is why Luke does not mention this meeting in his account in Acts 11–12. It was a private meeting which resulted in a private agreement, or at least it would have been private had there not been those who slipped into the meeting, and apparently made matters both uncomfortable and then later public when they did not get their way.

135. See Longenecker, *Galatians*, p. 47.

136. Betz, *Galatians*, p. 86.

satisfactory to have a Gentile church divided from a Jerusalem based Jewish church.

In this asymmetrical relationship Paul can impose or require nothing of the Jerusalem leaders and there are some requirements or tasks he will not accept from the pillars. There are others tasks, however, to judge from 2.10, he is happy to accept as it will contribute to the 'sharing in common' which is essential between Christians if they are to be a united body of believers. One gathers that Paul draws the line at those things that he sees would compromise the truth of the Gospel.

The word δοκοῦσιν is a significant term in a culture where ascribed honor is one of the paramount cultural values (cf. the excursus above). The term comes from political rhetoric and refers to 'those reputed to be important' (cf. Xenophon *Cyr.* 7.1.41; Demosthenes *Or.* 21.213). The term can be used positively (cf. Josephus *War* 3.453; 4.141, 159), but it can also be used negatively, especially in an ironic sense (cf., e.g., Plato *Apology* 21b – 'those reputed [τῶν δοκοῦντων] to be wise'). The question here is reputed by whom? In view of what Paul will go on to say, it is surely not Paul who is giving the Jerusalem leaders this honor rating, as he will go on to say that 'whatever they were' matters nothing to him.[137] One suspects that Paul alludes to either the 'false brothers' or more likely 'the men who came from James' or most likely the agitators in Galatia as bestowing reputation on the Jerusalem leaders, because we must bear steadily in mind that these autobiographical remarks are given because of their bearing on the Galatian situation. Paul is not reminiscing to no purpose here.

Verse 2c expresses poignantly Paul's apprehensiveness going into this meeting – 'lest somehow I should or had run in vain'. Paul is concerned not just with the verdict on his past work, but what a negative response would do to his present and future ministry. The expression εἰς κενὸν is always an adverbial one indicating result in Paul's letters (cf. 2 Cor. 6.1; Phil. 2.16; 1 Thess. 3.5). Paul is worried about 'running' uselessly or without effect, or as we would say 'for nothing'.

The grammar and syntax begins to break down in vss. 3–4, perhaps because of Paul's agitation when he remembers some of the things that happened in Jerusalem on this occasion. First he blurts out a fact which no doubt he was greatly relieved to be able to report to the Galatians – 'not even Titus was compelled to be circumcised, though he was a Greek'. This is the first mention of the major issue on which Paul will be attempting to address

---

137. Notice that we are talking about ascribed rather than achieved honor here. Here Bruce, *Galatians*, p. 109 is not convincing when he suggests there is no ironic tone here, but rather only a positive one. Paul clearly puts no stock in human credit ratings, because he believes God doesn't do so either.

the Galatians and exercise persuasion about in the remainder of this document. Titus is not just exhibit A for the Jerusalem church, Paul is using him as a paradigm for the Galatians as well, as if the Jerusalem church leaders would say the same things about and to the Galatians that they had said about and to Titus on this occasion.[138] The question is – Who could have compelled Titus to be circumcised? The answer must surely be the Jerusalem church leaders. If one reads between the lines it is possible to conclude that they might have preferred for him to be circumcised, but they would not go so far as to compel the act. We may suspect that some at the meeting may have argued vigorously for compulsory circumcision. This may have distinguished the position of the 'false brothers who would enslave' and also the agitators in Galatia who indeed were trying to require that the Galatians be circumcised from that of the Jerusalem leaders. What one should *not* conclude from this verse is that Titus was circumcised voluntarily, not under compulsion.[139] That would make a nonsense of what Paul will say afterwards in vss. 5–7 (e.g., that he did not submit, that nothing was added, that his gospel for the uncircumcised was recognized, cf. below).

Verses **4–5** are difficult because of the fact that vs. 4 is a sentence fragment. Longenecker suggests that we must insert at the beginning of the verse 'Now this happened' followed by the text as we have it.[140] Bruce on the other hand suggests adding after the first clause of vs. 4 'that this question later arose'.[141] A. D. Nock once suggested that vs. 4 should begin 'but the pressure for this arose . . .'[142] This matter is in part affected by when and where one thinks these 'false brothers' slipped in. Was it in Jerusalem? Was it in Antioch? In this matter close attention needs to be paid to the connection between the reference to the fact that the meeting Paul went to was private (vs. 2 – κατ᾽ ἰδίαν) and the phrases 'secretly brought in' and 'slipped in to spy out'. These latter phrases are only really apt if those being discussed are intruders or interlopers who appear somewhere where they had not been invited. Now this is an unlikely description of an official delegation sent by James to Antioch. One could not

138. There is a textual problem in vs. 3 In D* and other Western manuscripts, in the Latin version of Irenaeus, and in a number of the works of several Latin church Fathers (e.g., Tertullian) the words οἷς οὐδὲ are omitted, but the generally received reading is well supported.

139. However, even this has been suggested, see A. D. Nock, *St. Paul* (London: Butterworth, 1938), p. 109; D. W. B. Robinson, "The Circumcision of Titus, and Paul's Liberty," *Aus BibR* 12 (1964), pp. 24–42. Robinson does, however, make the valid point that for Paul liberty or freedom does not merely mean freedom from the Law, but freedom to act in whatever way is most conducive to leading people to Christ, provided of course one was acting in accord with Christ-like conduct.

140. Longenecker, *Galatians*, p. 50.

141. Bruce, *Galatians*, p. 106.

142. Nock, *St. Paul*, p.106.

say of them that they were 'secretly brought in' to Antioch. There was nothing illegitimate about James sending representatives to meet with the Antioch church any more than Paul and Barnabas as representatives of the Antioch church were interlopers at the Jerusalem meeting. I must thus conclude that Paul is referring to something that happened at that private Jerusalem meeting that should *not* have happened. In other words, Longenecker's insertion is nearer the mark than Bruce's.

The issue of compelling Titus to be circumcised apparently arose because of certain false brothers who were 'secretly smuggled in'. This is military language later used in political rhetoric as here. In Polybius 1.18.3 and 2.7.8 (cf. Diodorus Siculus 12.41.4; Plutarch *Mor.* 261B) the term παρεισάγω describes a conspiracy. One may wish to ask who smuggled them into this private meeting in Jerusalem. Apparently they had a sympathizer among those of repute, who was perhaps worried about how this meeting might go. Was it Peter, or James, or John? We cannot know, and it may have even been someone else if those of repute included the pillars but was not limited to them. Paul is clear enough by using this emotive language what he thinks about their actions – they were illegitimate and underhanded. In fact, he is prepared to call them false brothers, though obviously they would not have seen themselves that way, and one must assume that whoever smuggled them in also did not feel that way.

Paul also describes them as those who infiltrated (cf. Polybius 1.7.3; 2.55.3) to spy out[143] 'our freedom'. Paul sees them as like undercover agents and conspirators whose plan is to expose what happened in this private meeting and cause mayhem. More than that, Paul sees as their goal 'to enslave us' by which he means not just himself and Barnabas and Titus, but also Paul's converts. The language of slavery, like the earlier reference to circumcision is telling, as it is meant to prepare for the arguments that follow addressing the situation in Galatia. Paul obviously sees a clear connection between the two situations, a fact which becomes even more abundantly clear at the end of vs. 5 when Paul refers directly to the audience ('for you').[144] It raises the question of whether the 'false brothers' and the agitators in Galatia are one and the same. Even if they are not, Paul sees the *modus operandi* and the goals of the two groups as the same – they will attempt to impose the Mosaic Law upon his Gentile converts or else say that Gentiles cannot have fellowship (in particular table fellowship) with Jewish Christians. In short they

143. The verb, κατασκοπῆσαι, like the verb 'smuggled in' is a hapax legomenon in the NT, and shows that Paul has especially chosen these military/political terms because of the sort of rhetoric he wants to offer here.

144. Cf. the helpful discussion by P. Esler, *The First Christians in their Social Worlds* (London: Routledge, 1994), pp. 60ff.

want a church that is either united in the strict observance of the Mosaic Law, and so a church that is seen as part of Judaism, or else two churches. To neither of these options will Paul accede.

It is probable that in vs. **4b** we get a glimpse of the heart of the message Paul laid before the Jerusalem authorities – the freedom which we have in Jesus Christ. This phrase in some ways could be said to be the theme of this entire act of persuasion. The noun ἐλευθερία appears five times in the letter (here, 5.1; 5.13 twice), the adjectival form some six more times (3.28; 4.22, 23, 26, 30, 31) and the verb once (5.1), to which one may add the related concept 'redeem' found at 3.13 and 4.5.[145] This is social and political language once again and as Dunn says for a Gentile readership "this was an emotive chord to strike, since the distinction between slave and free was fundamental in Greek thought and the idealization of freedom was axiomatic in Hellenistic self-perception".[146] Paul must surely mean that he presented to the Jerusalem authorities the fact that he had been preaching the positive benefits one has in Christ, including being set free from various things that can enslave human beings, including the Mosaic Law. The key here must surely be what Paul says in vs. 2 – he laid before them what he preached to the Gentiles. Had Paul gone to Jerusalem and said that neither Jews nor Gentiles should keep the Mosaic Law, there can be little doubt that those of repute would have rejected this message. The issue at the conference was what Gentiles must or must not do to be considered full-fledged Christians by everyone.[147]

Verse **5** brings us to a further problem, this time a textual one. Some manuscripts and early Christian writers omit οἷς οὐδὲ at the beginning of this verse (the Western text, Tertullian, Irenaeus).[148] This results in Paul saying just the opposite of what we might expect – 'we gave in for a moment'. However, all Greek uncial manuscripts except D* include these words, as does our earliest papyrus p46, as do all but it(d, e) among the versions and all the Greek Fathers except Irenaeus in translation. In sum, the longer reading must be preferred.[149] Paul says he did not yield in submission to these false brothers even for an hour, or as we would say even for a moment.[150]

145. See Longenecker, *Galatians*, p. 51.

146. Dunn, *Galatians*, p. 100.

147. Yet Matera, *Galatians*, p. 82 may be right in stressing that Paul says 'our freedom' also implying his own. In other words, Paul already lived like a Gentile and would see a return to works of the Law as being enslaved as well, and would perforce separate him from his converts unless they did what the agitators were urging them to do.

148. Others simply omit οἷς (Marcion).

149. See Metzger, *TC*, pp. 591–92.

150. Dunn, *Galatians*, p. 86 n. 2 plausibly insists on the translation hour, not just because it is literally correct here (the hour being the smallest real unit of time in this era), but also because it rightly suggests that Paul was under more than just a moment's sustained pressure.

Verse **5** concludes with a ἵνα clause that is important for understanding why Paul is telling his Galatian converts about all of these far-flung happenings. It will be remembered that a *narratio* is not required in a deliberative speech but it could be included if it presented facts relevant to the case at hand or as Quintilian puts it 'external matters which are relevant to the discussion' (*Inst. Or.* 3.8.10; cf. 4.2.11). Had Galatians been a piece of forensic oratory we would have expected a narration of Paul's activities in *Galatia*, not a travelogue of his adventures in Arabia, Syria and Cilicia, Jerusalem, and Antioch.[151] Paul says in this purpose clause that the reason he did not yield to pressure on the circumcision question is in order that 'the truth of the Gospel might remain for *you*'. The verb indicates that at the time Paul is writing, the Galatians had already responded favorably to Paul's Gospel of freedom, therefore it was a matter of remaining in this truth, staying the course, going on on the same track, which is the essential positive advice Paul is giving in this deliberative speech.[152] Now Paul is probably not suggesting that he already had converts in Galatia at the time of the second visit to Jerusalem, although that is not entirely impossible. He is most likely saying that he stood on principle about a Law-free Gospel so that his Gentile converts wherever they were or would be could be benefited. Paul sees as at the core of the truth of the Gospel a fundamental commitment to the freedom we have in Christ. That this subject is a major theme in Galatians explains why some have called Galatians the Magna Carta of Christian freedom.

Verse **6** returns to the matter of what transpired between Paul and those of repute at the Jerusalem meeting, and so to the main line of discussion begun in vss. 1–2. Here Paul calls them 'those who *are* reputed to be something'. Lightfoot is right that the present tense of οἱ δοκοῦντες is important here. Paul is not just concerned with what these persons *were* reputed or esteemed to be at the time of the Jerusalem meeting. He is concerned with what they are now, at the time of writing, reputed to be.[153] So again we must ask – Reputed by whom? And one must assume it is by those agitators in Galatia who are troubling Paul's converts. It is interesting then to note the contrast between the present tense of 'being reputed' with what Paul says next – 'whatever they *were* doesn't matter to me'. The best explanation of this juxtaposition is that the honor rating which the Jerusalem leaders were currently receiving was based on their past, presumably their past associations with the historical Jesus.

The enclitic ποτε here coupled with the imperfect verb 'were' refers to a particular point in the past (cf. 1.13, 23). Now it is quite unlikely that Paul

---

151. See rightly, Esler, *The First Christians*, p. 60.
152. See Longenecker, *Galatians*, p. 52.
153. See Lightfoot, *Galatians*, p. 107.

means by 'were' what they were at the time of the meeting mentioned in 2.1–10. Had this been his meaning we would most certainly have expected τότε ('then') not ποτε here. Paul would have said 'whatever they were then, now matters not to me'.[154] That we do not find τότε here means that those who wish to posit a major rift or break down in relationship between Paul and the pillars, *after* this Jerusalem meeting, perhaps caused by the Antioch incident are probably wrong.[155] Nor do we have any evidence that Paul also during his earlier Christian life once put stock in such honor ratings of the pillars but when he wrote he does so no longer. So far as we can tell, he has always respected them, but placed no stock in merely human evaluations of them.

The basic problem Paul has when he writes this letter is with the agitators in Galatia, not with the pillars in Jerusalem. Even the Antioch incident is viewed by Paul not as a reneging by Jerusalem on the deal struck and its basic principles, but as an example of hypocrisy on the part of Peter and others due to social pressure from very conservative Jewish Christians (cf. below). An important part of the problem when Paul is writing has to do with the way the agitators are touting the Jerusalem leaders, giving them high honor ratings. Paul does not wish to discredit these Jerusalem leaders, indeed he has admitted he sought and desired their approval and co-operation with his missionary work, but he does wish to discredit those who are touting them, and he wishes to make clear that the normal sort of criteria used to determine human honor ratings do not and should not apply in the church.

This is why Paul walks a tightrope in this passage in the language he uses about the pillar apostles. His pejorative language he reserves for the false brothers and those like them. He uses ironic language of the pillars because he believes them to be touted using merely human criteria. He wishes to discredit the touters and the touting, not the ones being touted. Had he done the latter, he would have undermined a goodly part of the argument in the *narratio* which speaks of him consulting and gaining support from these Jerusalem authorities. Betz puts it this way: "This expression [i.e., those reputed to be something] . . . allows Paul both to acknowledge the fact that these men possess authority and power and to remain at a distance with regard to his subservience to such authority."[156]

Paul enunciates a basic principle that affects how he views the whole matter of human honor rating systems at vs. 6b – literally 'God does not accept the face of human beings'. This is clearly enough a Hebrew expression that comes out of a culture where giving and accepting of face is an important

---

154. See Longenecker, *Galatians*, p. 53.
155. Dunn, *Galatians*, pp. 102–03.
156. Betz, *Galatians*, p. 92.

value. It was also a culture where God's people were reminded God has no regard for the status, ascribed or achieved, of human beings (cf. the LXX passages where 'face' is discussed – Lev. 19.15; Deut. 1.17; 16.19; 2 Chron. 19.7; Job 13.10; Ps. 81.2; Prov. 18.5; Mal. 2.9). The meaning of this key phrase is not so much that God *shows* no partiality as a judge although that is a Biblical notion as well, but that he does not evaluate human beings on the basis of their 'face', their honor rating or credentials. It is interesting that in the NT 'accepting face' is seen as a bad thing. As Lightfoot says it signifies giving regard to the external features of a person's life – wealth, status, rank, power, authority, gender, race and the like.[157] The opposite of this is considering a person's real intrinsic character, or from a Christian point of view considering what they are by and through the grace of God. By placing the word Θεὸς in an emphatic position Paul is contrasting human ways of evaluating people with God's way. He is suggesting that he is following God's lead in this matter, unlike the agitators in Galatia and perhaps various others.

At the end of vs. 6 Paul says that those being reputed highly in Jerusalem 'added nothing to me'. Commentators have often disputed whether this meant they added no additional requirements to his Gospel, or no additional restrictions on his mission field or the like, but this is missing the point of the mention of 'face' in the previous verse. Paul is saying that the Jerusalem authorities added nothing to (and subtracted nothing from) his own status or honor rating. This came to him from God by grace.[158] He was not beholden to them for the fact that he was a Christian and a Christian apostle. They added nothing to what God had already done in his life. It would have been untrue to say they had added no tasks, and made no distinctions about fields of service, as vss. 7–10 makes clear.

Verse 7 begins with the contrasting connective ἀλλὰ. Paul is indicating that not only did the Jerusalem authorities add nothing to him, they in fact 'saw' (ἰδόντες) that God had already done the adding, having entrusted to Paul the Gospel for the 'uncircumcision', just as Peter had been entrusted with the Gospel for the 'circumcision'. The verb 'entrusted' is in the perfect tense indicating a commission given prior to this Jerusalem meeting and of ongoing, indeed permanent duration (contrast the usage in Rom. 3.2). Furthermore, Paul is not talking here about two sorts of Gospels (a Gospel of circumcision versus a Gospel of uncircumcision), not least because he does not admit there is more than one true Gospel (cf. 1.6–7) but rather two audiences or spheres that are to be addressed by the one Gospel. This is made clear in vs. 9 when Paul says that the concordat reached involved him and the Pauline co-workers

---

157. Lightfoot, *Galatians*, p. 108.
158. Notice the ἐμοὶ in the emphatic position.

going to the 'Gentiles', while the pillars (presumably chiefly in the person of Peter) were going to 'the circumcised'. That the terms for circumcised and uncircumcised keep coming up in the discussion shows that this boundary marking rite was a major issue at this meeting.[159]

The question still remains whether we should see this primary division of labor as chiefly racial, or chiefly geographical or some of both. The terminology Paul uses in these verses ('the uncircumcised', the 'Gentiles' as opposed to the 'circumcised') refers, primarily to people not places.[160] One must bear in mind, however, that there were Jewish colonies all over the Roman Empire including in both Antioch and Galatia, and this meant that Peter's missionary work would necessarily overlap with Paul's in the Diaspora, with both of them going to some of the same cities such as Antioch or Corinth or Rome (cf. Gal. 2.11–14; 1 Cor. 1.12; 3.22; Rom. 15.14–29). One must also recognize that since Paul says not only that he became the Jew to the Jew in order to win some Jews (1 Cor. 9.20) but also that he suffered punishment from synagogues (2 Cor. 11.24), he probably had preached in synagogues both to Jews and to Gentiles. There was probably considerably more overlap in these Petrine and Pauline spheres of ministry than one might suspect on a superficial inspection of the matter.[161] In other words, Paul did not take this agreement to mean that he would never preach to Jews, or that Peter would never address Gentiles. We are speaking of the major focus and purpose of their respective ministries. Paul tried on the whole to stay out of territories already evangelized by others (for example the province of Judea), though he was prepared to write to and visit the Roman Christians,[162] but even in this latter case his aim was so that they could send him out farther west where the Gospel had not yet been preached (Rom. 15.23–24). Surely, one of the main reasons Paul was irritated with the agitators in Galatia is because they were Jewish Christians seeking primarily to influence Gentile Christians to become like them, which Paul saw as a violation of the Jerusalem agreement. Gentiles were Paul's and his co-workers' target audience. The agitators were intruding on Paul's turf.

Verse **8** confirms what we have already noted on the basis of the use of the passive of 'entrusted' in vs. 7. Paul believes that it is God, not the Jerusalem church that selects apostles and calls them to specific fields of ministry. It is God who was effectively at work when Peter exercised his 'apostleship', just as it was God who was effectively at work ('energizing') in Paul when he

159. See Dunn, *Galatians*, p. 107.
160. See rightly, Longenecker, *Galatians*, p. 59.
161. It is probably true, however, that even in the synagogues, Paul saw it as his main task to address the Gentiles that were there.
162. And probably also the Colossian Christians, though in this case they were probably converted by a Pauline co-worker.

evangelized Gentiles.[163] In both these cases we are talking about missionary work already undertaken before this Jerusalem meeting, and about the Jerusalem leaders simply seeing and recognizing what God was already doing through these men. In other words, we are not talking about a planned missionary strategy set in motion by the leaders or the Jerusalem leaders, but an *ex post facto* recognition of what was already happening. Paul's perspective on these matters is essentially the same as that of the author of Acts, who sees the Spirit as prompting, guiding, empowering the missionary work of the church.

The term ἀποστολή is rare in the NT (cf. Acts 1.25; Rom. 1.5; 1 Cor. 9.2), and nothing should be made of the fact that the term 'apostleship' is not predicated in this particular phrase of Paul. As Matera says we have a balance in the use of ellipsis in these two verses "Paul entrusted with the Gospel to the uncircumcised, Peter to the circumcised; Peter entrusted with apostleship to to the circumcised, Paul to the uncircumcised".[164] Paul is indicating equality between himself and Peter by this way of putting things, not inequality.[165] Furthermore, Dunn is right that while Paul is probably alluding to the final agreement struck between the Jerusalem leaders and himself and Barnabas, it is unlikely he is quoting the agreement here, for it is not plausible that the agreement drawn up by the Jerusalem church would have used 'Peter', the Grecized form of his name, rather than Cephas.[166] Furthermore, it is likely that this was an oral contract sealed with a handshake, not a written one.

Verse 9 continues along the same lines of what has already been said. Those reputed to be pillars, here identified as James and Cephas and John, knew the grace given to Paul. This must surely mean that they recognized not only his mission, but the work of grace done in Paul's life and so also his apostolic status (cf. 1 Cor. 3.10 and Rom. 15.15–16 where this phrase is used to refer to his apostleship).[167] Again notice that this reputation is not something the

---

163. On the issue here of Paul and power (and authority), it is clear enough that Paul is and sees himself primarily as an example of a charismatic leader, not one raised up by some institution or body of believers. It is interesting that he speaks of Peter in the same sort of terms. On this issue in general see B. Holmberg, *Paul and Power. The Structure of Authority in the Primitive Church as Reflected in the Pauline Epistles* (Lund: C. W. K. Gleerup, 1978), pp. 114ff.

164. Matera, *Galatians*, p. 77.

165. See now Malina and Neyrey, *Portraits of Paul*, pp. 47–48.

166. Dunn, *Galatians*, p. 105; cf. Betz, *Galatians*, pp. 96–98.

167. See B. H. McLean, "Galatians 2.7–9 and the Recognition of Paul's Apostolic Status at the Jerusalem Conference: a Critique of G. Luedemann's Solution," *NTS* 37 (1991), pp. 67–76, here p. 75. McLean shows that Luedemann's theories about the non-recognition of Paul's apostleship at Jerusalem will not do (cf. Luedemann, *Paul, Apostle to the Gentiles*, pp. 64–80).

pillars were necessarily claiming for themselves. It was an attributed honor rating, one given by others (with Paul certainly not being the source of such an attribution).

The term στῦλοι is interesting and would seem to suggest that this Jerusalem triumvirate were seen as the main supporting columns in the eschatological and 'spiritual' Temple of God currently under construction by God through the Gospel about Christ. As Barrett rightly points out, the word 'pillars' frequently appears in the LXX in reference to the supports of the tabernacle and later the columns of the Temple. Note especially the language about the Solomonic temple in 1 Kngs. 7.15–22; 2 Chron. 3.15–17 (cf. 2 Kngs. 23.3; 2 Chron. 34.31 on the names of the columns – Jachin and Boaz). This conclusion is supported by what we find in Rev. 3.12 (cf. 1 Clement 5.2).[168] It must be remembered that there was considerable speculation about the destruction and reconstitution of the Temple in the eschatological age (Ezek. 40–48; Jub. 1.17–28; 1 En. 90.28–29; 11QTemple; Test. Ben. 9.2), and Jesus himself seems to have had something to say on this very matter (Mk. 14.58; Jn. 2.19; Acts 6.14), as did Paul who saw the body of Christ as also the Temple of God (1 Cor. 3.16–17; 2 Cor. 6.16 cf. Heb. 3.6; 10.21; 1 Pet. 2.5).[169] In other words, calling these three men the pillars was no small honor rating. It meant they were holding up and holding together the people of God being now renewed and restored in Christ. It invested in these men an enormous importance and implied they had tremendous power and authority.

Notice that our earliest and best manuscripts have James mentioned first among the pillars, and then Peter, while several mainly Western manuscripts (D, G, it (a, b), Marcion, Jerome) have Peter first (presumably because of his later significance for the Western church).[170] It may also be that this arrangement of names was caused by scribes who remembered the order 'Peter, James, and John' in the Synoptics (Mk. 5.37; 9.2), failing to recognize that James here is not James son of Zebedee.[171]

The gesture referred to in vs. **9b** is of great significance for several reasons. First, notice that it is the Jerusalem authorities who 'gave the right hand' which may indicate their superior position in the existing social structure of the church. While the Hebrew phrase 'to give the hand' is common (cf. 2 Kngs. 10.15; Ezr. 10.19; Ezek. 17.16; 1 Chron. 29.24; 2 Chron. 30.8; Lam. 5.6). it is not at all clear that this material is directly relevant here, for the last three of these references implies the submission of the ones

---

168. On all this see the discussion by Barrett, "Paul and the Pillar Apostles," in *Studia Paulina*. J. De Zwann Festschrift, ed. J. N. Sevenster (Haarlem: Bohn, 1953), pp. 15–19.

169. Here I am following Dunn, *Galatians*, p. 109.

170. Metzger, *TC*, p. 592.

171. See Dunn, *Galatians*, p. 86 n. 3.

giving the hand,[172] which is certainly not the case here with the pillars extending the handshake to Paul and Barnabas. Furthermore, it is the 'right hand of κοινωνία' that is being extended here, and one might judge from Phil. 1.5 that Paul sees this more of a symbol of partnership, something closer to equality in the sharing of the Gospel. The evidence about the phrase 'to give the right hand' suggests it refers to a gesture implying friendship and acknowledging an agreement that is something offered by a superior to an inferior (cf., e.g., Josephus *Ant.* 18.328–29 – a king offers it toward some Jews), but also sometimes between equals (cf. Xenophon, *Anab.* 1.6.6; 2.5.3). Could Paul have interpreted it the latter way, and others interpreted it the former way? The gesture is known among Jews even though it seems to have arisen first in a Persian context (cf. 1 Macc. 6.58; 11.50, 62, 66).

The term κοινωνία is important here and probably has its active sense as elsewhere in Paul,[173] referring to a sharing of something in common or a participating with others in something. In this case the proclamation of the Gospel must be what Paul says they agreed to share or participate in together. The term κοινωνία in fact can even refer to a formal treaty,[174] and in any case the gesture suggests a formalizing of an agreement. J. Paul Sampley may be right that Paul is using the language of *societas* here, indicating a binding agreement or partnership between friends, or at least that this is how Paul viewed the agreement.[175] The agreement would include one stipulation that Paul was happy to accept, as vs. 10 shows.[176]

Careful attention must be paid to vs. **10**. This verse brings to a conclusion the sentence which began in vs. 6. The first word of the verse μόνον indicates the *only* further requirement laid upon Paul and his mission on this occasion, namely that the poor be remembered. In view of the similarities between this verse and Rom. 15.27 it seems quite clear that Paul does not mean the poor in general, and surely not the spiritually poor (for how would taking up a collection improve that condition?), but rather the poverty-stricken among the saints in the Jerusalem church. Their condition seems to have been caused perhaps in part by the combination of famine, food shortage, and sabbatical

172. See Burton, *Galatians*, p. 95.

173. See my discussion in *Conflict and Community*, pp. 224–25.

174. See Betz, *Galatians*, p. 100 n. 411.

175. J. Paul Sampley, *Pauline Partnership in Christ* (Philadelphia: Fortress, 1980), pp. 29–30. This text has more promise of reflecting such an agreement between 'equals' than that which Sampley points to in Philippians. See my critique in *Friendship and Finances in Philippi* (Valley Forge: Trinity Press International, 1994), pp. 123–24.

176. P. Esler has suggested to me that κοινωνία here refers to table fellowship. The question is, why is Titus not also mentioned at this point if this is the case? Is Paul implying that the Jerusalem church was not yet prepared to have table fellowship with an uncircumcised Titus? Esler has also pressed the issue from the standpoint of where Titus might have been eating and drinking while in Jerusalem if not with his fellow Christians. I

year that affected the area in the late 40s A.D., 46–48 in particular.[177] The food shortage had apparently overtaxed the system of food distribution in the Jerusalem church (cf. Acts 4.32–37; Acts 6.1–7) that may have still been in place at this time.[178] In view of Acts 4.35–36 one would assume that Barnabas would be very ready to agree to this sort of request, as was Paul.[179] One wonders if there is a closer connection between vss. 9–10 than is usually thought. It will be remembered that Acts 2.44–45 and 4.32–34 speaks of the Jerusalem church as sharing all things in common, such that there were no needy ones among them. Could it be that the right hand of κοινωνία refers to an agreement to participate in the economic sharing in common that already existed in Jerusalem?

Certainly vs. 10 suggests that the agreement included an economic component, regardless of whatever else it may have included.[180] Some have also suggested that James and the pillars have proposed here that Paul and Barnabas undertake the Mosaic requirement in regard to almsgiving to the poor (Deut. 24.10–22; Ps. 10.2, 9; Is. 3.14–15; Amos 8.4–6). Such an obligation was seen as central to covenant righteousness in early Judaism (cf. Dan. 4.27; Sir. 3.30; 29.12; Tob. 4.10). In other words, it would make Paul and Barnabas appear to remain in compliance with the Mosaic Law. If this is how the pillars saw the matter, it would not appear that Paul agrees as he says nothing to this effect here. When he does speak about the matter in Rom. 15.25–29 what he seems to suggest is that instead it is part of the eschatological action of God where Gentiles will go up to Zion and contribute to what is going on there with Jews, having shared in the spiritual blessings offered to them.[181]

---

would suggest it is perfectly possible that Titus ate with Paul and Barnabas, perhaps at the house of Paul's sister (see Acts 23.6), but *not* with members of the Jerusalem church during this visit. In other words, I am not convinced that this agreement also included the issue of table fellowship, though it may well be that the deal to recognize the legitimacy of Paul's Gentile mission was sealed by Paul and Barnabas dining with the pillars. One must be careful not to read too much between the lines here.

177. See my discussion in *The Acts of the Apostles*, pp. 506ff., and cf. Dunn, *Galatians*, p. 112.

178. Or perhaps not, if the one reads the summaries in Acts as retrospectives that refer to practices that did not continue into Luke's day. Cf. *The Acts of the Apostles*, pp. 149ff.

179. Notice the '*we* continue to remember' which could in fact allude back, at least in part to Barnabas' previous generosity.

180. What it most likely did not mean is an agreement to share in table fellowship in or with the Jerusalem church (cf. below on 2.11–14).

181. Dunn *Galatians*, p. 114 tries to argue that Paul soldiered on with the agreement, making the collection, even after there had been a significant rift between himself and the pillars, because of a desire to maintain continuity with Judaism. If this were so we would expect some hint of anger or sorrow in Rom. 15 when the matter of the

Μνημονεύωμεν is an auxiliary verb in this sentence and is in the present subjunctive, as part of ἵνα clause. The present tense indicates an ongoing action and is best translated 'so that we might continue to remember . . .' This must be compared to the main verb ἐσπούδασα which is in the aorist and has a pronominal suffix. Here Paul is focusing on his own reaction to this requirement or request, and so the suffix should not be taken to indicate anything about the time of the action spoken of in the verb, whether past, present, or future.[182] Possibly we should take the καὶ which precedes the verb to mean 'also'. For the time of the action one must focus on the tense of the verb, and the tense is aorist indicating a punctiliar event, a completed action, in the past. In other words, Paul refers to an attitude about this matter which he already had in the past and we may translate 'which very thing I also was (already) eager to do'.[183] In other words, Paul makes clear that this was a priority not only for 'us' (Barnabas and Paul), but also for Paul in particular. He wishes his converts to know he personally was eager to support the Jerusalem church in such a matter.

Here it is in order to sum up what we may learn about this meeting from this passage: (1) this was a private meeting between the luminaries of the Jerusalem church and Barnabas, Paul and Titus, into which some 'false brothers' intruded.[184] This third group was not invited but rather was smuggled in. (2) the main subject of the discussion was Paul's Gospel for the Gentiles, which also involved a discussion of circumcision, fields of service, and the

---

collection comes up, but we find there nothing of the kind. Further, Paul is not interested in continuity of covenant and salvation history with Israel here. The issue is unity within the body of Christ the new humanity of Jew and Gentile united in Christ (cf. 2 Cor. 8.19ff.). Neither in Galatians nor in Corinthians nor in Romans does he ever suggest that there is a fundamental, ongoing and irreparable rift between himself and the pillar apostles. This is making far too much of the incident at Antioch, and is based on the assumption that that incident occurred after the Acts 15 council.

182. See rightly, Longenecker, *Galatians*, p. 60 against Burton, *Galatians*, pp. 99–100 and others who have followed him.

183. In view of the fact that the time frame for the auxiliary verb is the point at which the agreement was struck, it is surely likely that the same is true for the main verb. In other words, when Paul says 'I was eager' he does not mean 'was' from the point of view of the time at which he wrote the letter, but rather from the time of the agreement itself, hence the insertion of 'already' after 'was' is warranted here to indicate this. Paul is sharing what his feelings were about the matter at that time.

184. I would suggest that the private nature of the meeting is partly why Luke really doesn't refer to it directly in Acts 11, but perhaps also because the matter of circumcision was not officially laid to rest at this meeting. That only transpired after the Antioch incident which is referred to as the immediate precursor to the Acts 15 council in Acts 15.1–3. In my view Galatians was written not long after the Antioch incident while Paul was still smarting from that encounter, and just before he and others went up to Jerusalem for the the apostolic council.

problem of the poor in the Jerusalem church. Nothing seems to suggest that table fellowship or meals or Gentile eating habits (or for that matter Jews' eating habits) was a major subject of discussion at this meeting or had anything to do with the agreement struck at this meeting. This conclusion favors the view that we are not talking about the same meeting as described in Acts 15, which is basically a public meeting and matters are resolved with a Decree about Gentile habits in regard to food, among other things.[185] The latter was a meeting more likely to have transpired after the incident over table fellowship in Antioch. Both the reference to remembering the poor, and the reference to going up by a revelation better suits the account found in Acts 11.27–30, than that in Acts 15 which says nothing about action in response to a revelation and nothing about remembering the Jerusalem poor;[186] (3) Paul distances himself from the human credentialing that was going on in relationship to the pillars, but he does not polemicize against the pillars themselves not least because he wants their continued co-operation. Note the contrast between the 'ironic' language used of the pillars and Paul's pejorative language used against the false brothers.[187] (4) Paul sees himself as having independent authorization, he simply seeks co-operation lest his work prove fruitless. (5) Titus is presented as a test case. If he was not compelled to be circumcised, then the Galatians didn't need to be either; (6) the upshot of (5), is that the false brothers were the big losers in the debate and in the honor struggle over circumcision that went on at this meeting. It is unlikely that they were going to let the matter rest, especially since there had not been a public discussion and resolution of the matter taking all parties into the debate; (7) the toing and froing between I and 'we' in this passage is partly due to what Paul wants to stress to the Galatians about his own attitudes and actions in this matter, presenting himself as a paradigm of how to resist the pressure to give in to the appeal for circumcision, but it may also reflect the current estrangement between himself and Barnabas. Paul writes Galatians in the aftermath of the Antioch incident as a rather isolated figure, and one who fears he and his work is in danger of being marginalized on several fronts; (8) the outcome of this meeting, if Paul reports it at all accurately, must mean that the pillars, though certainly not as

185. This is of course why some have argued that the Decree comes from another and yet later occasion (cf. Acts 21.25). The problem with this argument.is that nothing in Paul's letters suggests that the Decree came later, and Acts 15 says it did not. In fact, I have argued that 1 Cor. 8–10 very clearly reflects a knowledge of the decree already. See my *Conflict and Community in Corinth*, pp. 221–29.

186. See further my discussion of this matter in *The Acts of the Apostles*, pp. 429ff.

187. See Matera, *Galatians*, p. 77 who points out that Paul does not speak of the pillars in a sarcastic tone, not least because their recognition of his work is important to the case he is making to the Galatians.

radical as Paul, must be seen as moderates in the debate compared to the false brothers and the agitators in Galatia. In other words, the Jerusalem church was divided over these issues, and the pillars did not simply side with the hardline conservative Jewish Christians who insisted on circumcision for Gentile converts.[188]

The concluding segment of the *narratio*, 2.11–14, is in some ways the most interesting, but also the most elliptical and frustrating. It is frustrating not least because no one knows for sure either how Paul's confrontation with Peter turned out (did Paul lose this honor challenge or did Peter and the others stop and rethink things?), or what the sequel was to this event. Obviously, it makes a great deal of difference whether this event followed or preceded the meeting spoken of in Acts 15, not least because it too had something to do with issues of food and fellowship. It also makes a great deal of difference whether 'the certain ones who came from James' represented or misrepresented James' views, and whether or not what they were suggesting amounted to a reneging on the agreement mentioned in Gal. 2.1–10, or if they were dealing with another matter. Further, are these ones from James the same persons Paul has earlier called the false brothers and/or the same persons who were causing trouble in Galatia? The text does not give clear answers to these questions, and much hinges on the answers.

Various scholars, going back at least to F. C. Baur have seen the Antioch incident as more than an incident, indeed as the great watershed event that separated Jewish from Gentile Christianity, or at least precipitated that rift. I am quite unconvinced on this latter score, precisely because of what we hear in Paul's later letters, namely that Paul and his converts are still in contact with the Jerusalem church, the Collection is still being made and will be delivered by Paul and some of his converts, and Paul will continue to see Peter, Barnabas and others as legitimate fellow apostles and missionaries (cf. 1 Cor. 1–3, 9.5–6; 2 Cor. 8–9; Rom. 15.22–29; Col. 4.10).

Thus, while one may wish to say that this is a crucial episode in the history of early Christianity, it is well not to give way to highly rhetorical and grandiose claims such as that this incident was the turning point which led to the rift between Jewish and Gentile Christianity.[189] I would suggest that other historical forces, including the Jewish war leading to the destruction of Jerusalem in A.D. 70 and the rapid increase of Gentiles into the church between the 40s and the end of the century did far more to change the relationship between Jews and Gentiles in Christ than the incident at Antioch.

Paul, after all is said and done, writes this letter and restrains his criticism of the pillars compared to his polemics against the false brothers. He also still

---

188. So Matera, *Galatians*, p. 81.
189. See, e.g., Taylor, *Paul, Antioch, and Jerusalem*, p. 139; Dunn, *Galatians*, pp. 130–31.

has colleagues who support and presumably agree with him on these matters (1.2), and he has not raced off immediately to Galatia to fix the damage done. Indeed, I would suggest he is still in Antioch when this letter is written, preparing to go off to yet another meeting in Jerusalem over the latest crisis and he will go with Barnabas (and perhaps even with Peter), if Acts 15 is to be believed. In other words, Paul sees this incident as a crisis that must be dealt with, but he writes before the matter has been resolved. I would also suggest that if even half of what Paul says about walking in the Spirit and the fruit of the Spirit and being Christ-like was true in his own life, that it is not stretching things to suggest that there was a mending of fences between Paul and the other apostles after this blow up and its resolution. The above conclusions have arisen only after I have dealt for a long time with the details of the text, but I state them in advance because often readers get distracted looking for what someone will say about these historical questions in a commentary and do not give the proper attention to the details which we must do at this juncture.

Verse **11** begins with an indeterminate temporal particle ('when'), exactly the same as we found at 1.15. It is not clear when Peter came to Antioch, but since the previous paragraph had him in Jerusalem we may suppose he came from Jerusalem, unless of course these events are recorded out of sequence. J. Dupont has made a telling critique of the suggestion that 2.1–10 happened after 2.11–14, and one must say that with the text as it is, unless they had additional information from another source, the Galatians would never have guessed these events are recorded out of order, especially in view of 1.15 where Paul uses this same temporal marker to indicate an event that *followed* his days of persecuting the church.[190] Indeed, in view of the rhetorical conventions in regard to the statement of facts, they would expect them to be recorded in order unless there were signals in the text and strong reasons behind them for not doing so (cf. above).

Thus, it is reasonable to conclude that Peter came to Antioch from Jerusalem. From what follows in the text we must assume that he spent more than just a brief period of time there. He must have been there long enough for: (1) him to have established a pattern of 'living like a Gentile' including eating with Gentiles in Antioch; (2) the church in Jerusalem to have heard about this and sent some representatives to speak with Peter directly about the matter; (3) that encounter to have led to a gradual (cf. below) pulling back by Peter, and then others, from table fellowship with Gentiles in Antioch; and (4) for Paul to have confronted Peter in a public assembly about the matter.

---

190. See J. Dupont, "Pierre et Paul à Antioche et à Jerusalem," *Recherches de Science et Religieuse* 45 (1957), pp. 42–60, 225–39.

It may be that once the concordat was struck in Jerusalem, Peter and Paul almost immediately began to take up their respective tasks of mission outside of Jerusalem. These tasks took Peter to Antioch and its surrounding environs,[191] a very logical place for him to begin his missionary work outside Judea, for it was an area where the largest group of Jews in the eastern end of the Empire outside of Palestine could be found.[192] I suspect that Paul was not in Antioch when either Peter came to town or when the certain ones from James showed up,[193] for had he been he would surely have confronted and opposed not just Peter, but the certain ones who came from James. The alternative is to suppose that Paul bided his time until the representatives from James left, and until Peter and then others withdrew from eating with Gentiles, and *then* he pounced on Peter. This second alternative seems much less likely, especially in view of how strongly Paul obviously felt about the matter. If he could have stopped the withdrawal while it was in progress, or even better yet once it was suggested by the ones from James but before it started, surely he would have done so. For him, a matter of principle regarding the character of the Gospel and of God's people was at stake. It was not merely a social or pragmatic issue. I suggest then that Paul was out of town away on missionary work at the time. Since one cannot imagine the process described in four steps above happening overnight, one suspects Paul was gone for a considerable period of time, and came back to find that Peter had withdrawn, under pressure from table fellowship with Gentiles. It was perhaps while Paul was away evangelizing Galatia that this encounter between Peter and the persons from James transpired.[194]

191. Perhaps in part because of the episode recorded in Acts 12, he was in a sense driven to move on.

192. See the discussion by Longenecker, *Galatians*, pp. 65–78 on the large Jewish colony in Antioch, and my discussion in *The Acts of the Apostles*, pp. 360ff.

193. It is interesting that p46 has 'before a certain *one* came from James'. This may be caused by another variant in this verse which has the verb 'came' in the third person singular.

194. If Acts 13–14 provides us with essentially accurate information at this point in regard to Paul and Barnabas, then we must also suppose that Barnabas, who is mentioned last among the withdrawers, did so after he and Paul returned to Antioch, and Barnabas had had time to assess what Peter and other Jewish Christians had done. To be fair to Barnabas, one must bear in mind that he had close ties with and had been a part of the Jerusalem church well before he became part of the Antioch community. Indeed Acts 11.22 says he was specifically sent to Antioch by the Jerusalem church, presumably to watch over the progress of church growth and make sure things happened in a way that would be consistent with the Jerusalem Christian community. We have no good historical reason to doubt the account in Acts 11.22 or in Acts 4.35–37 both of which tell us of Barnabas' subservience to the apostles in Jerusalem (in the former text it is in regard to an important matter of material support). Furthermore, Acts 4 also informs us Barnabas was a *Levite*, which is to say one who could probably be appealed to effectively about the importance of Jewish Christians following Jewish food laws and customs.

In any case, Paul was not going to stand for this sort of behavior on the part of Peter, because it set a very bad example in Antioch where there was clearly a significant number of Gentile converts, indeed so many that Acts tells us this is the first place where the followers of Jesus were called Χριστιανοί (Acts 11.26), presumably by outsiders who could tell a difference between this religious group and those who met in the synagogue. Furthermore, Paul in recording this example in this letter wants to urge his Galatians *not* to give way to Judaizing pressure, not to follow the lead of Peter or Barnabas or the agitators in Galatia, but to follow his lead and resist such Judaizing pressure.

Paul first announces his action in vs. 11, and then explains what led to it in vss. 12–14. To oppose someone of the importance of Peter to his face and in a public meeting of believers (cf. below on vs. 14a) tells us that Paul probably saw himself as Peter's equal and so felt it would not be wrong to confront him, especially in view of the damage his example had done among the other Jewish Christians in Antioch. This was a bold attempt to shame Peter into rethinking his actions. This sort of action would cause one or another of these two to 'lose face'. If Peter did not respond to the challenge he would lose face, *unless* it was the view of the Antioch church that Paul was Peter's inferior, in which case Peter could probably ignore the challenge as not touching his *dignitas*, and so shame Paul in the process. If Peter responded negatively, and his fellow Jewish Christians approved, Paul would also lose face in Antioch. This action on Paul's part was a gamble in any case.

The verb ἀντέστην was originally a military and political term, but came to be used more broadly of any deliberative situation where opposition to actions or beliefs were involved. Elsewhere in the NT it is used to refer to action against heretics or charlatans. (cf., e.g., Acts 13.8; 2 Tim. 3.8).[195] The previous paragraphs have already made clear the importance of the language about face in this passage when one takes into account the honor and shame culture and how it provides the context for understanding such honor challenge situations. The phrase κατὰ πρόσωπον means literally 'according to face' or just 'to (the) face', but in fact if one compares 2 Cor. 10.1 and Acts 25.16 it becomes clear that it has the idiomatic sense of 'face to face'. In other words we are talking about a 'face off' in which someone will lose and someone will gain face. The reason for this confrontation is said to be because he was condemned. The verb once again comes from political life, more particularly this one comes from the law court (cf. Josephus *War* 2.135 cf. Plutarch *Alcib.* 202E). Peter's actions are on trial before the assembly of the faithful and in the presence of God, and Paul is saying he is already condemned before the divine tribunal. The translation 'is blameworthy' is not adequate here to convey the seriousness of the tone of this scene, nor will 'is self-condemned' be

195. See Betz, *Galatians*, p. 106 and n. 443.

adequate.[196] The verb is a divine passive here. The Ebionites who later attacked Paul and his action against Peter understood very well the tenor of this sentence (cf. Pseud. Clem. *Hom.* 17.19). Notice that the verb is in the perfect, indicating an already existing state which Peter was in before Paul ever confronted him. In short, Paul's action is taken because he believes that God condemns what Peter has done. What precipitated this awkward and sad state of affairs?

Verse **12** is a complex sentence, where careful attention must be paid to details, including verb tenses and prepositional phrases. We are made to understand in no uncertain terms that in Paul's view things were fine 'before certain ones from James came'. They are seen as the catalysts precipitating a bad situation in Antioch. Paul does not name these persons, which may be a shaming device, as he does not regularly mention his antagonists by name. It is hard to doubt that he had found out rather specifically who these persons were, when he returned to Antioch and was informed about what happened. They were not likely to have been mere couriers or anonymous messengers. In such an important matter James was not likely to send someone who was not known and respected by Peter so that the instructions would be taken with the utmost seriousness. It is interesting, however, and perhaps important that Paul does not call these persons 'false brothers who came from James'. He treats them with more respect perhaps, than the false brothers.

Before these representatives of James came Peter was eating with the Gentiles. The verb συνήσθιεν is in the imperfect and suggests that Peter was regularly eating with the Gentiles before the 'James gang' came to town. In view of the usage in vs. 14b 'Gentiles' here surely means Gentile believers. The question is whether we are talking about ordinary meals,[197] meals that were part of Christian meetings and/or eucharistic meals. Paul says nothing about Peter withdrawing from house church meetings, which presumably would regularly have included both Jews and Gentiles, as probably vs. 14 and Acts 11 certainly suggests. Nothing whatsoever is said here about circumcision or other issues. *The* issue is eating with Gentile believers, something which according to Acts 10.24–11.18 Peter had done before, and had been criticized for in the past.

One can understand why Torah-observant Jewish Christians would be especially critical of Peter for this sort of behavior. The Jerusalem church had recognized that God had set him apart for missionary work among Jews, and here he was fraternizing with Gentiles over meals which would cause many of those in his target audience to raise questions about his Jewishness. From the point of view of these members of the Jerusalem church, Peter was being a bad witness, and acting in conflict with the character of his calling.

---

196. See rightly, Longenecker, *Galatians*, p. 72 and cf. Josephus *War* 1.635; 7.154; 7.327.

197. So, e.g., Burton, *Galatians*, p. 73.

It will be noticed that Paul says nothing whatsoever about Peter violating the agreement mentioned in Gal. 2.1–10. Nor does he say anything about Barnabas violating the agreement. Schütz's question is apt: "Why would Barnabas, the most visible member of the Antioch missionary movement, succumb so quickly to Jerusalem's position if Jerusalem . . . reneged on an earlier agreement? Barnabas' action makes it almost impossible to construe the Antioch affair as a simple act of bad faith on Jerusalem's part."[198] So far as we can tell, that agreement didn't say anything about whether Jewish Christians should eat with Gentiles or not. That agreement had three parts: (1) circumcision was not compelled even in the case of one like Titus; (2) two spheres of ministry were approved, involving missionary work with both Jews and Gentiles; (3) Paul's Gentile mission was to remember the poor in Jerusalem. To say that the agreement involved more than this is simply an argument from silence.

What Paul accuses Peter of is violating his own previously chosen manner of living, and probably by implication Paul is accusing him of violating the implications of a Law-free Gospel to the Gentiles (cf. below).[199] In other words the crisis in Antioch was not simply the crisis in Jerusalem part two, nor was it

198. Schütz, *Paul and Apostolic Authority*, p. 151.

199. There are at least two problems with Dunn's suggestion that Peter's 'living like a Gentile' only meant he was being less strictly observant as a Jew, which is usually coupled with the suggestion that Antioch Gentiles and Jewish Christians were following some requirements of the Kosher food laws, but just not strictly enough to satisfy Jerusalem. Firstly, it does not make sense of the language about Peter and Barnabas 'withdrawing' or play-acting. There was something about this action that Paul saw as *inconsistent* with their former behavior, something that could constitute living like a Gentile. If the problem had merely been an insufficient attention to food law details, the solution would surely have been not 'withdrawal' from table fellowship with Gentiles but more restrictions on or more rigor in the already accepted practice of basically following Jewish dietary laws. Withdrawal is what the men from James precipitated on charges of living like a Gentile. This charge surely meant being non-observant of Kosher requirements, for they are not charged with merely living like a God-fearer or proselyte. (Cf. Sanders' critique of Dunn in "Jewish Association with Gentiles," pp. 170ff.)

Secondly, Dunn's view totally ignores the Cornelius episode in Peter's life. Unless one is prepared to argue there was no such episode prior to Paul's writing of Galatians, or that if there was, it had nothing to do with Peter's receiving a vision declaring all foods (and persons) clean, or at least no foods and persons ritually unclean, this tradition must be accounted for. I suspect that Paul is able publicly to accuse Peter of being inconsistent primarily because he knew Peter himself had for some time already been prepared to have table fellowship with Gentiles, in Gentile homes on their own terms. He knew Peter's own convictions on these matters because he knew about Peter's own experiences with Cornelius. It wasn't just that Peter had given notional assent to Paul's Gospel of grace in Jerusalem; it was that Peter had already begun to live out such a Gospel himself, as had Barnabas and Paul, when they had fellowship with Gentiles. This is what I would suggest lies behind Paul's explosion at Antioch and his charges of inconsistency.

a matter of reneging on the bargain made in Jerusalem. The issues were different though not unrelated, and those on whom stipulations were being placed were different. It is telling that vs. 13 says that the rest of the 'Jews', by which is meant Jewish Christians in Antioch, withdrew as a result of Peter's actions. The aim of the ones who came from James must have been to get Jewish Christians in Antioch to be more Law-observant in regard to their eating habits, in particular in regard to eating with Gentiles and their visit had its intended effect.

Vs. 12b gives more specific information about what happened. When the ones came from James, Peter 'began to draw back and separate from' the Gentiles. The two verbs here give a clearer picture of what happened. They suggest a gradual, perhaps even a reluctant or uneasy withdrawal on the part of Peter. The verb ὑποστέλλω is once again a military or political term describing a retreat or a retrenchment to an inconspicuous sheltered position (cf. Polybius 1.16.10; 6.40.14; 7.17.1; cf. Plutarch *Demetrius* 47, 912E). As Betz suggests, this may mean that Paul views Peter's action as pragmatic, or a tactical manoeuver, not one based on convictions.[200] The second verb ἀφορίζειν may be a Jewish technical term coming from the discussion about ritual purity and referring to separating from unclean persons or things. "The separation of the mission to the Jews from that of the Gentiles would imply that Peter would retain his Jewish way of life, and this included first of all the dietary and purity laws."[201]

What are we to make of the phrase 'fearing those ἐκ περιτομῆς'? Obviously this refers to some group of Jews, but are we to think of Jewish Christians or non-Christian Jews? On the one hand the structure of the sentence might be taken to suggest it could refer to 'those who came from James' and the group they represented. After all the sentence is about what Peter did when these people came to town, namely withdraw from eating with Gentiles, and without additional information one would naturally assume that Peter's 'fear' had to do with them. Perhaps he was fearful of displeasing them, or disappointing them, or being shamed by them as a less than observant Jew. The rest of Galatians will be dealing with Christians who are insisting on other Christians being circumcised. It is plausible Paul would call such people those of the circumcision party. If Acts 15.1 is about this same episode we can see even further why Paul would call them 'those of the circumcision'. By this he would mean more than that they were Jews, he would mean that they were of the circumcision party who wanted Jews to be Law-observant and wanted Gentiles to be circumcised and also be Law-observant.

---

200. See Betz, *Galatians*, p. 108 n. 460 for many more references.
201. Betz, p. 108.

The focus in the discussion in Gal. 2.11–14 is on the effect of this party on Peter and Jewish Christians, not on Gentiles, though the implications for Gentiles are seen clearly by Paul (cf. vs. 14b). It is unlikely that Paul means that those who came from James were Jewish Christians of a non-partisan sort, for then their encounter with Peter and his response becomes rather inexplicable. Thus, we must choose between the phrase 'those from the circumcision' referring to partisan Law-observant Jewish Christians or referring to non-Christian Jews of whom Peter was afraid for some reason. In favor of the latter conclusion would be the fact that ἡ περιτομή certainly refers to non-Christian Jews in Gal. 2.7–9, and this is usually the meaning of the term περιτομή in Paul's letters (cf. Rom. 3.30; 4.9, 12; 15.8; Col. 3.11; 4.11).

Scholars have also often pointed to Gal. 6.12 where we hear of the agitators in Galatia trying to compel the Galatians to be circumcised so they, the agitators, will not be persecuted for being followers of the crucified Christ. A rather elaborate argument has been put forward by various scholars, including R. Jewett, to the effect that pressure and persecution from Jews was causing Jewish Christians to try and force Gentile Christians to Judaize. "Jewish Christians in Judea were stimulated by Zealotic pressure into a nomistic campaign among their fellow Christians in the late 40s and early 50s. Their goal was to avert the suspicion that they were in communion with lawless Gentiles. It appears that the Judean Christians convinced themselves that circumcision of Gentile Christians would thwart Zealot reprisals."[202] But all Jewish persecution of Jewish Christians was not motivated by 'Zealotic' pressure, to judge from Acts, especially not in the Diaspora where the political situation was surely not as volatile for Jews or Jewish Christians as in Jerusalem. Nevertheless, Jewett's explanation has some plausibility because it is certain that the men who came from James were closely connected to the situation in Jerusalem in the late 40s, and it would appear the agitators may have been as well, even if they were not the same group. Notice that in Gal. 6.12 the issue is so 'they (i.e., the agitators) may not be persecuted', not the Galatians themselves. If the agitators were closely connected with Jerusalem and concerned about their own fate and that of Judaism and Jewish Christianity, then Jewett's thesis may well apply in the case of the agitators as well as the men who came from James, even if the pressure or persecution the agitators feared was from Jews in Galatia.

Two added factors may support Jewett's suggestion. Josephus tells us that in A.D. 49 thousands of Jews were killed in Jerusalem during the feast of the Passover, that is in the spring of A.D. 49 (War 2.224–27; Ant. 20.112). Josephus says the disturbance which led to this massacre was instigated by

202. R. Jewett, "The Agitators and the Galatian Congregation," NTS 17 (1970–71), pp. 198–212, here p. 205.

Zealots.[203] Writing not long after A.D. 49, Paul says in 1 Thess. 2.14–16 that judgment had fallen on some Jews for the persecution of Christians in Judea. These accounts show the volatility of the situation in Judea (and elsewhere in the Empire),[204] and provide a reasonable explanation for a certain amount of xenophobia among Jews in Judea, and more to the point a rationale for a nomistic campaign by Jews against Jewish Christians, which in turn led to pressure by Law-observant Jewish Christians on Gentile Christians to Judaize.

I thus conclude that we cannot know for sure whether Peter's fear was of zealotic Jews or zealotic Jewish Christians, or zealotic Jewish Christians who had raised the spectre of angry Jews causing major trouble for the assembly of Christians in Jerusalem.[205] I suspect that the first of these is what Paul means in vs. 12b by 'those from the circumcision', as this is probably how the Galatians would have understood it in the light of the immediately preceding usage in 2.7–9. I think, however, that it was indeed Torah-true Jewish Christians who raised the spectre of persecuting Jews, namely the ones who came from James. Paul characterizes Peter's actions, as we shall see, as out of character and done out of fear, and so as inconsistent with Peter's own beliefs and chosen life-style. In other words, he characterizes them as not done on the basis of principle or logic, but rather yielding to pressure and emotional arguments. If this assessment by Paul is correct, then it means that Peter (or for that matter Barnabas) probably did not share the views of those who came from James if they were Judaizers, they only shared a love for the mother church and did not want to see it dismembered.

Verse **13** informs us that the rest of the Jewish Christians joined with Peter, which included even Barnabas. Paul characterizes this action as τῇ ὑποκρίσει, play-acting or a charade or a pretense, whereby one appears and outwardly acts one way, but in fact believes another. He says that Barnabas was 'led away' in this charade. The noun ὑποκριτής means simply an actor, and the compound verb συνυποκρίνομαι is found only here in the NT. It is probably another example of Paul's predilection for adding συν to words to indicate a joint effort. The idea behind both the noun and the verb is that someone is acting in a way that belies their true nature. They are concealing their true feelings or thoughts under a guise. The compound verb came to have the secondary sense of join someone in playing the hypocrite (cf. Polybius 3.52.6; 3.92.5; Plutarch. *Marius* 14.8; Josephus *War* 1.569; 5.321). This sort of behavior was all too typical in a culture saturated with a love for entertainment

203. A.D. 49 appears also to have been the year that Jews were expelled by Claudius from Rome. Cf. my *The Acts of the Apostles*, pp. 507ff.

204. One could also cite the terrible pogrom against Jews in Antioch in A.D. 40 in the third year of Caligula's brutal and anti-Semitic reign. Cf. Longenecker, *Galatians*, p. 69.

205. See Longenecker, *Galatians*, p. 75.

including entertaining rhetoric, for people admired those who in chameleon-like fashion could act a part that was not theirs, who could adapt to the circumstances and say and do what was required of them. Exhibit A of such behavior was an actor or a rhetor, both of whom performed for money. This problem of course also plagued the realm of politics as well. Consider what Polybius says "for all persons are given to adapt themselves and assume a character suited to the times, so that from their words and actions it is difficult to judge of the principles of each, and in many cases the truth is quite hidden from view" (3.31.7). Even more telling is the reference Betz points to from Epictetus commenting on a Gentile influenced by Judaism "whenever we see someone wavering between two faiths we say 'He is not a Jew, he is play-acting'" (ὑποϰρίνεται – *Diss.* 2.9.20).[206]

Paul is more charitable in his interpretation of Barnabas. He was *led* astray into *their* charade, and would appear to have been the last to capitulate after all the other Jews followed Peter's example. The ὥστε is followed here by an indicative verb in a consecutive clause, something which happens only one other time in the NT (Jn. 3.16). The force of this construction is that it makes the statement emphatic.[207] The clause should read 'so that even Barnabas was carried away in their charade!' Paul could hardly believe it. Apparently Barnabas could not bring himself to act against the instructions of the church which sent him to Antioch. Paul is suggesting that he too, like Peter was acting irrationally and against his better judgment, carried away by an emotional appeal. In short he was a victim of effective rhetoric and polemics.[208]

Verse **14** indicates that Paul did not act until he saw clearly where all this was leading. The verse begins with the strong adversative ἀλλα which sets it in contrast to what has come before it. Where it was leading was in the opposite direction from where they should have been heading in Paul's view. The verb ὀρθοποδέω is interesting.[209] Its fundamental meaning is walking in a straight or upright manner (as opposed to limping), or more metaphorically proceeding down the right road, going straight toward the proper goal. This is precisely what Paul wants his converts to do, and characterizes such action later in the letter as walking in the Spirit (5.16). Unfortunately, all of these Jewish Christians in Antioch were doing just the opposite and are presented

---

206. It is interesting that Chrysostom thought (see his comment on Gal. 2.12 in his commentary) that Peter and Paul were together play-acting in a common scheme or plan (οἰϰονομίας), so that Paul could have an opportunity to proclaim the true Gospel in Antioch. This was also the view of Jerome. Paul's tone in Galatians makes this suggestion, however interesting, truly unbelievable.

207. See Robertson, p. 1000.

208. See Betz, *Galatians*, p. 110.

209. It is the basis of the English word 'orthopedics'.

here as negative paradigms for Paul's converts in Galatia. Peter and those who followed his example are not walking in a straight manner toward the truth of the Gospel.[210]

It would appear that Paul waited to confront Peter until the time of an assembly of all Christians. Betz suggests we should see this as a parallel occasion to the Jerusalem meeting, but in fact this was a public meeting before everyone. No one was smuggled into this meeting. Paul then quotes what he said to Peter on that occasion: "If you being a Jew, are yet not living like a Jew but like a Gentile, how can you compel the Gentiles to 'judaize'?"[211] It is a very good question. Betz rephrases the matter thus – "by attempting to preserve the integrity of the Jewish Christians as Jews, Cephas destroyed the integrity of Gentile Christians as believers in Christ".[212]

What Paul is trying to do is bring out the implications of Peter's actions for the Gentile Christians whose table fellowship he has now forsaken. If all the Jewish Christians withdraw from having table fellowship with Gentile Christians then, in Paul's view, the unity of the body of Christ could not be preserved. 'Separate but equal' really meant inherently unequal and certainly not united. By withdrawing from Gentile fellowship, Peter was forcing the Gentiles to Judaize if they wanted to continue to have table fellowship with him or other Jewish Christians in Antioch. If one asks why Paul would directly attack Peter but not James, C. Hill has provided a plausible answer. The "issue in Antioch was *Jewish* and not Gentile obedience. On this matter Peter had reversed himself, but on the issue of Gentile obedience James had not."[213] Whatever else one may say, it is very unlikely, in view of Gal. 2.1–10, that James is behind what was happening in Galatia.

In Paul's view one would have to choose between Jewish purity or body unity. The church could not have both, because it had already been agreed by Peter and the pillars that circumcision was not required of someone like Titus, which to Paul meant observance of the Law was not required of Gentile converts. Body unity could only happen one of two ways – the Gentiles could be required to Judaize, or the Jews could be asked to recognize that observance of the Law was only optional, not required even of Jewish Christians. Even if a Jewish Christian chose to be Law-observant he or she

---

210. This phrase may intimate that Paul was prepared for a gradual progressive move in the direction of the 'truth of the Gospel' by his fellow Jewish Christians, but he could not abide a move in the opposite direction.

211. Longenecker, *Galatians*, p. 78 is right that the present tenses of the verbs in the protasis strongly imply that Paul believed that Peter had not abandoned his non-legal lifestyle on a permanent basis, but only as a matter of expediency.

212. Betz, *Galatians*, p. 112.

213. C. Hill, *Hebrews and Hellenists* (Minnesota: Fortress, 1992), p. 134 n. 128.

should not withdraw from fellowship with Gentiles.[214] The truth of the Gospel involved Jew and Gentile united in Christ. In other words, Paul is arguing that the 'truth of the Gospel' is the only real basis for true unity in the Christian church.

The word Ἰουδαΐζειν is a significant term which occurs nowhere else in the NT, meaning to adopt Jewish customs and practices, which would include sabbath observance, observing food laws, and even being circumcised. In other words the term focuses on the orthopraxy of early Judaism. This is clear enough from the use of the term in Josephus *War* 2.454 and by Ignatius (*Magn.* 10.3) where he says "it is monstrous to talk of Jesus Christ and to 'Judaize'" (i.e., *practice* Judaism).[215] Paul's view, however, is that the Law is a package deal, as Gal. 5.3 makes abundantly clear.

The verb ἀναγκάζεις is the same verb we have already seen in 2.3, and this is surely no accident. Paul is pointing to the implicit inconsistency between what happened in Jerusalem, and what Peter's actions suggested in Antioch. It is doubtful that Peter was in fact 'compelling' Gentiles to Judaize, this is just Paul's polemical way of indicating that Peter left the Gentiles no choice if they wanted to have fellowship with him and other Jewish Christians than to act like Jews if they wanted to be fully accepted as Christians. Paul's objection to this is fundamental because he does not see Christianity as simply a subset of early Judaism. He sees it as involving the creation of a new eschatological community.[216]

What happened after this confrontation? Paul does not tell us. Does silence mean that Peter consented or does silence mean that Paul lost this battle? I am among those who are inclined to conclude that Paul lost this battle or at least the matter was not yet resolved to his satisfaction when he wrote this letter.[217] If Paul could have claimed that even one of these Jewish Christians, whether Peter or Barnabas or any of the rest of the Jewish Christians in Antioch had been swayed to return to their former practice by Paul's logic surely he would have done so since it would have considerably strengthened his argument to his wavering converts in Galatia. That he cannot do so suggests that Paul is now basically alone among the apostles in his position on these matters. Yet there is a rhetorical fitness to ending the *narratio*

214. Presumably this might mean that a Jewish Christian would wish to go through ritual purification after such occasions with Gentiles, especially if non-Kosher food was involved. Paul, however, would argue the more radical case that the Law was obsolescent, and that there was no more ritually unclean food or persons, only morally unclean persons – sinners, both Jew and Gentile.

215. See Plutarch *Cicero* 7.5; Esther 8.17 LXX.

216. One might say that his sectarian views amounted to admitting that Christianity came out from Judaism, but was not of it, because it was not under the Mosaic covenant.

217. See Nock, *St. Paul*, p. 110: "Had Peter conceded the justice of Paul's position, Paul must have said so; it would be a trump card in his hand."

at this point. Paul's interlocutors have no answer to the truth of the Gospel, the argument in Paul's question is presented as irrefutable, for Peter is rendered silent.[218]

We must sum up at this juncture. It is a mistake to read the Antioch incident as simply part two of the Jerusalem meeting, or as its reversal. The issue of Gentile circumcision is raised at the first meeting, the issue of Jewish Christians in Antioch being Law-observant is raised at Antioch. These of course are not separate matters if there is going to be a united body of Christ, both have implications for each other. What both meetings have in common is that the ultimate issue is whether Gentiles have to become Jews to be considered full-fledged Christians.[219] The result of the first meeting would seem to have been no, but the implications of Peter's actions would have suggested the contrary. Paul implies that Peter and Barnabas both agreed in principle with him that there was no problem in having table fellowship with one's fellow Gentile Christians, but irrationally withdrew due to pressure brought to bear by those who came from James.

It is believable that James, himself a devout Law-observant Jewish Christian, especially if there was threat of the dissolution of the church in Jerusalem due to persecution, might request his fellow Jewish Christians to be Law-observant.[220] It is possible, however, that all he was really requesting was *Peter* be Law-observant since his mission was to Jews.[221]

---

218. See rightly Matera, *Galatians*, p. 90.

219. See rightly Ziesler, *Galatians*, p. 19.

220. See Barrett, *Freedom*, p. 13 who argues that James had agreed that there should be a Gentile mission and that Gentiles didn't need to be circumcised to be saved but had "probably not contemplated the existence of mixed churches . . . and reacted with horror to the notion that Jews should so far relax their legal observance as to eat with Gentiles". That James had not reckoned with the possibility of mixed churches seems hard to believe, especially in view of the number of Gentiles already in synagogues in the Diaspora. The question would be on what terms would they eat together. If they ate in a Jewish home with Jewish food this might not be a problem. I am unpersuaded by Esler's argument that there was an absolute prohibition of Jews eating with Gentiles in early Judaism. But see his *The First Christians*, pp. 62ff. As E. P. Sanders, "Jewish Association with Gentiles and Gal. 2.14," in *The Conversation Continues*, pp. 170–88 shows, the Letter to Aristeas 181–294 is clear evidence that such sharing of meals took place. One must not mistake the issue of food with the issue of people. As Sanders says "There was no barrier to social intercourse with Gentiles as long as one did not eat their meat and drink their wine" (p. 178). To be sure there were hard-liners such as those who wrote Jubilees or Joseph and Aseneth who wanted a more absolute ban of such fraternizing between Jews and Gentiles, but there was no Jewish ban of the practice.

221. See Sanders "Jewish Association," p. 186: "It was . . . probably not [the case] that James sent a message to the Jewish members of the church there, prescribing their behavior in general. He apparently sent a message to Peter – *You* should not eat with Gentiles – and the other Jewish members followed him. This particular message is best

It is also possible that the men from James went beyond their writ in this matter and insisted that it would be proper and good for other Jewish Christians to follow Peter's lead as well. It is, if Acts 15.1 is any clue, also possible that they did indeed wish to undo or at least sabotage the agreement made in Jerusalem about circumcision, by also arguing for Gentiles Judaizing, perhaps not arguing directly but indirectly because they knew that Judaizing would be required if Gentiles were to stay in fellowship with Law-observant Jewish Christians. It is also possible that the men who came from James were indeed the false brothers, only James had not viewed them in the same way Paul (later) did. If this latter possibility was the case then there may be merit to the suggestion that now these men were returning the favor of the honor challenge that Paul offered when he brought Titus to Jerusalem, by offering one of their own, shaming Peter into a retrograde action.[222] I doubt that James himself had such an intent, especially in view of Acts 15.24 and Acts 21.20–26 where James seems caught in the middle and tries to act as a mediating figure, keeping the church together.[223] Perhaps James' word even to Peter alone was offered on pragmatic grounds because of 'nomistic pressure' in Jerusalem, not because he objected to 'the truth of the Gospel'.

The *narratio* has neatly accomplished its rhetorical functions. So far as Paul's ethos is concerned, it has established him as one who does not involve himself in charades or play-acting, rather he is one who is faithful to live out the 'truth of the Gospel'. He is not a mere politician or a pragmatist or a chameleon-like rhetor. Furthermore, he is one who was acknowledged by the pillar apostles both in terms of the grace working in his life and his missionary tasks. Even the Judean churches praised God for what had happened to him. In a series of episodes his converts have seen how in both Jerusalem and Antioch he has been true to the divine revelation he received, and has resisted false brothers and wavering fellow apostles when the implications of the truth of the Gospel were about to be or were being compromised. Paul wishes for his converts to follow his example and resist the blandishments of the agitators in Galatia. It is not clear whether Paul sees the false brothers, the men from James and the agitators in Galatia as the same persons or not, but rhetorically speaking it does not matter, all he wishes to do is make clear the parallels in their actions and critique each in turn. They, along with the withdrawing Peter,

---

explained by a theory of general concern on the part of James. He feared that it might be said of Peter that he fraternized too much, and thus was generally suspect, not that he had violated some individual rule".

222. See Esler, "Making and Breaking," pp. 306ff.

223. It needs to be seen that Paul too was capable of being pragmatic, as long as he did not perceive some basic principle of the Gospel being at stake. He was prepared to be the Jew to the Jew. He was not prepared to require Jewish Christians to be Law-observant, much less Gentile ones.

Barnabas, and Jewish Christians provide the negative paradigms in this *narratio* while Paul provides the positive one, as one divinely called and divine graced to bring the truth of the Gospel to Gentiles like the Galatians.[224] Paul is *not* exercised to defend his apostleship in this *narratio*, but what he does want to make clear is that his Gospel is from God, not of human origin. In Paul's view, the ethos of the true Gospel as well as his own personal ethos is at stake in this discussion. He makes clear the divine source of his Gospel not only by recording how he received it, through a visionary experience, but also by making clear how and where he did not receive it (in Jerusalem and from the pillars). His conversion is presented as a call precisely because the issue is where Paul got this Gospel he claims he was called to preach. Paul's autobiographical remarks are intended to prepare for the deliberative argument which follows, urging the Galatians to be like Paul – true to the Gospel they first received and resisting the urgings of the non-Gospel of circumcision and works of the Law. They are not intended to *defend* Paul's past actions or his apostleship. One must look to texts like 2 Cor. 10–13 to see how Paul would go about such a defense, a text which reads very differently from this one, though they both involve polemics and emotive rhetoric to achieve their aims.

This *narratio* then is an attempt to clarify Paul's ethos. Paul's character and the character of the Gospel he preaches and embodies come from the same source – God through Christ. Therefore, the Galatians should listen closely to the acts of persuasion that are about to follow before they walk down the wrong path rather than walking in and by the Spirit.

It will become clearer in the arguments that follow that Paul is not simply arguing for a less strict combination of Gospel plus covenantal nomism than his interlocutors. Dunn's theory that Paul will argue for faith in Christ plus observance of major tenants of the Law relieved of its restrictive and ritualistic aspects,[225] fails to come to grips with the radical character of Paul's Gospel of grace.[226] As J. L. Martyn has aptly put it, Paul's "main concern is the singularity of the Gospel, as he focuses his attention specifically on what the Gospel of Christ has done and is doing to the world. The Teacher's [i.e., agitators'] fundamental issue is covenantal nomism, if you like; Paul's is evangelical, cosmic, history-creating Christology."[227] These two messages are basically not on a continuum but rather on a collision course. One represents reform within Judaism, the other is a sectarian message that creates a new community of Jew and Gentile united in Christ, and not united under Torah. If it is true that the

---

224. See Gaventa, "Galatians 1 and 2: Autobiography as Paradigm," pp. 309ff.

225. See, e.g., Dunn's "The Theology of Galatians," in *Pauline Theology Vol. I*, pp. 125–46.

226. Indeed it ends up making Paul sound more like his opponents than like himself.

227. Martyn, "Events in Galatia," in *Pauline Theology Vol. I*, pp. 160–79, here p. 165.

Jerusalem pillars recognized and endorsed Paul's Gospel of grace when he visited Jerusalem, it is also true that they did not clearly understand its implications, as the Antioch incident makes quite apparent. Peter and other Jewish Christians in Antioch had made a start in the direction of Christian unity that the Pauline Gospel of grace suggested, only to pull back under pressure and for pragmatic or even emotional reasons. They were not, or not yet, prepared as Paul was so to identify with Gentiles and so to live by grace which all shared, that they became part of a sectarian offshoot of Judaism rather than a development within it.

Finally, it is worth reflecting for a moment as to what this episode tells us about the social structure of the early church. It suggests, as Holmberg noted, that it was possible for the Jerusalem church to exert influence over those in churches outside Judea, although it may be that there was only an attempt to exert direct influence on Peter, and others simply followed his example.[228] Notice also that the Antioch Jewish Christians, and perhaps the church as a whole did not seem to see this as interference in their autonomous existence. On the other hand, the fact that Jerusalem felt it had to send a delegation urging a change of course suggests that it had not been keeping a close watch on the situation in Antioch previously. It is hard to know whether Peter's power and authority, or simply the effect of his example is exhibited in this episode, probably the latter. As for Barnabas, it would appear that his longer association with the Jerusalem church matters counted more than his recent association with Paul and the Gentile mission.[229] What is also shown by this episode is that Paul was willing to stand alone among the Jewish Christians, and confront Peter, suggesting he saw himself as Peter's equal. This also suggests that Paul more closely identified with the Gentile Christians in these matters, and is certainly not willing to be subservient to the Jerusalem church, even to James, if he believes the truth of the Gospel is at stake. He is a charismatic leader, not an institutional functionary. Yet it would appear that he does not think that James ultimately intended to invalidate his Gospel, for he surely would not have cited James and the pillars as endorsing that Gospel in this letter, if he believed or knew that James tried to undermine it later. Furthermore, he accuses Peter and Barnabas not of sabotage but of charades, of not living according to what they knew to be right. Paul apparently does not wish to believe that there is an unbridgable rift on principle between himself and other apostles. How could there be if they had agreed earlier to preach the one true Gospel, only to different audiences?

228. Holmberg, *Paul and Power*, p. 33.
229. Even ignoring Acts we should assume such an involvement on the part of Barnabas on the basis of Gal. 2.1–10, and on the basis of Paul's shock at what Barnabas did at Antioch.

The early church had plenty of growing pains and crises. Its social structure seems to have developed over time, with its webs of power and influence only slowly becoming clear, being revealed by crises like those described in the *narratio* in Galatians. It must always be kept steadily in view that Galatians is but part of a conversation and a situation that was ongoing. It is not the last shot fired by Paul, nor does it represent the end of his relationship with Peter or Barnabas or the Jerusalem church. These events, however, may have propelled Paul thereafter into spending more of his time heading west and breaking new ground, rather than continuing to butt heads with those in already existing churches in Antioch and Jerusalem. Much depends on assumed and conjectural answers to questions about the date when Galatians was written and what followed the writing of this document. More certain is the character of Paul's Gospel and the arguments he uses to re-present it to his converts. To these we must turn after a discussion of the contemporary relevance of this section of the letter.

Bridging the Horizons

It has been said that a society that loses its sense of shame also loses its sense of honor. These two primal values do not exist in modern western society in the same way as they did in the Ancient Near East and in the ancient Mediterranean world, and yet we can still see what such societies are like by reflecting a moment on colleges or universities who still have an actively enforced honor code, or on the honor codes that exist in the military (cf., e.g., *A Few Good Men*), or on the honor codes involved in the martial arts and in general on the growing influence of oriental culture on Western society. Honor in the society of which Paul was a part had to do with having and giving face, and there is a very real sense in which this concept can be understood in our own culture. Those who have 'face' in our own society tend to be sport and movie stars or occasionally a charismatic leader, or on the local level those who are notably successful in what they do, whether doctors, lawyers, teachers, ministers, or business men and women. Paul says in our passage that God judges by a very different standard, he does not regard human means of measuring worth or status.

One of the things that is most instructive about this passage for us today is the way Paul reacts to the honor and shame conventions and the way he believes God is deconstructing human efforts at gaining face. For Paul God's point of view should be that of the believer and this means not being beguiled by a person's 'accomplishments' or wealth or reputation. All humans are equal in the eyes of God – equal in the disgrace of sin, and also equal in their need for grace. This means that human pecking orders often need to be deconstructed or relativized in the light of the Gospel.

For Paul, grace is what breaks the cycle of endless honor challenges or cycles of competition to gain more face than one's neighbor, or to protect one's own and one's family's honor. Grace is the great equalizer which relativizes the importance of all natural bases for establishing human hierarchies, whether they are based on race, gender, social status, wealth or other factors. In Paul's view the basic issue is what a person is in Christ and on the basis of grace – namely sons and daughters of God and brothers and sisters of each other. In the Christian community, or as we would say, in the church, Paul carefully tries to tear down and do away with societal values that he sees are at odds with the Gospel.

In Paul's view, Christ on the cross and the Spirit in the church are the basis of human freedom, and nothing not even God's former revelation in the form of the Law of Moses, should be allowed to curtail that freedom or re-establish barriers between one group of persons and another. In Paul's world view, honor and shame have to do with behavior (see Gal. 5–6) not heredity, or gender, or social status, but even more than this, honor has to do with what God has done for and in the believer. Grace and grateful responses to it are meant to take the agony out of an agonistic cultural situation and place all Christians on the same level playing field with the same freedoms and obligations.

It has been said that a foolish consistency is a hobgoblin of small minds, and yet as Paul makes clear in this text, it is far preferable to its opposite, namely inconsistency or even worse, hypocrisy. Of course, Paul is particularly concerned here with a specific kind of consistency, namely living out what one professes to believe, or in Peter's case the reverse, professing what one is in fact already living. Paul believes that Peter's life reflects his real creed, and so his withdrawal from fellowship with Gentiles is not merely an act of inconsistency but of hypocrisy – it is play acting of the worst sort. This text raises for us the question of what sort of charades we play in our lives. Do we, like Peter, give in to pressure, in our case perhaps peer pressure, or pressure from an employer, and do things that we later despise ourselves for? Do we play games in order to please those whose approval we seek? Do we even play these charades with our families? Paul's sense of moral outrage here is in part due to the fact that Peter had already been treating Gentiles as family, and now he was reneging on that commitment. One often finds out where one's ultimate loyalties lie when pressure is brought to bear in our lives.

There is indeed a freedom in living in accord with what one believes. It frees one from having to hide or dissemble or even lie about one's behavior or words or choices. The hardest part about lying or living a lie is that one thereafter must be extremely careful to say and do things that are consistent with that lie, and so life becomes an endless game of calculation. In short, it becomes slavery rather than freedom. Sometimes a person even begins to believe the lie, or at least engages in creative rationalization. Human beings, it has been said, have an infinite capacity for self-justification, but when one has been justified by Christ, one has been and can be set free from all such charades, lies, rationalizations, self-protective and at the same time self-destructive behavior.

Whatever else one learns from the incident at Antioch, it should be clear that the early church was just as complex as the church is today, and social struggles and church conflicts were just as messy then as they are now. These early Christians had as much trouble with consistently living out the implications of the Gospel as we do today, and so often we must learn to 'go and do otherwise' when we look at them as exemplars, not simply go and do likewise. NT texts must be handled carefully when we go looking for models for Christian behavior. Not all examples are positive examples, and even when we are dealing with basically positive characters in the Biblical narratives, they are often shown to have feet of clay, as in the portrayal of Peter in Gal. 2.

Paul has sometimes been faulted for confronting Peter publicly in this matter, but sometimes hypocrisy must be exposed in public if it is to be finally done away with. Even some modern tele-evangelists whose public confessions of wrongdoing have sickened many, nevertheless understood the truth behind the warning 'be sure your sins will find you out'. There are some principles so important to the Christian faith that one cannot compromise them even for the sake of friendship or peace in the 'family'. Paul understood this, and he was prepared to pay the price of ostracism and isolation for telling the truth, which in fact he appears to have been suffering when he wrote this letter. His witness raises the question of whether we are likewise prepared to pay such a price for Christian principles we consider non-negotiable. John Wesley once said that one of the chiefest of Christian virtues was the ability to avoid turning small things into great ones, and also the converse. In Paul's view the freedom that we have in Christ and by the power of the Spirit was no small thing, and he was willing to pay no small price to uphold it. Yet it bears mentioning that Paul also highly prized co-operation with other Christians, otherwise he would never have gone to Jerusalem to lay before the pillars his Gospel.

To a real extent we become what we admire, and in this narrative section of Galatians Paul parades before our eyes positive and negative examples of Christian actions. He also presents us with a remarkably self-effacing portrait of himself as both zealous opponent of and now proponent of the Gospel. His story raises once again the old question about the power of personal testimonies about human transformation. Our own culture still has a place for such testimonials, even if it can take them only in small doses or limits them to places like Alcoholics Anonymous meetings or divorce support group meetings. Paul is saying to his own converts that he had been down the Mosaic road before and that his converts should really benefit from his own experience and take another route in the Christian life.

Recently, I had occasion to go out to dinner with a close friend of mine. He recounted his own personal testimony to my children. He had been a musician in a major rock band in the 1970s and had indulged in the usual excesses in the areas of drugs and alcohol that were all too common then, as now. One evening he was seized with massive chest pains, and when rushed to the hospital the X-rays and further tests revealed a malignant tumor near his heart. The doctors informed him he had probably six months to live if the cancer was already spreading. They urged surgery. This young man was shattered by this news, and he went to visit his devout grandparents who had been praying for his conversion, and now also for his healing. His time with them was eventful in that he gave his life to Christ, and felt prepared to go and face whatever the surgery would bring. When he arrived at Duke medical center in Durham N.C. for the surgery, one final X-ray was taken to guide the doctors. When my friend met with the doctors just prior to the scheduled surgery, he was told the shocking news that the tumor had simply disappeared and they had no explanation. He had, however, his own explanation – the miraculous grace of God had transformed his life both spiritually and physically. He is now one of the leading Methodist pastors in my own conference, pastoring the fastest growing church in that conference. He has remained true to the revelation of the Son that happened in his own life. There are still testimonies that have power and persuade, and they bear listening to, especially in this jaundiced world which thinks there is never anything new under the sun.

Propositio: 2.15–21   By the Faithfulness of Christ, not by Works of the Law

We by nature are Jews and not sinners from the [Gentile] nations, and seeing that a human being is not acquitted from works of the Law but through the faithfulness of Jesus Christ even we began to believe in Jesus Christ, in order that we might be justified by the faithfulness of Christ and not by works of the Law, because 'by works of the Law will no flesh be justified'. But if seeking to be acquitted by Christ we ourselves were found to be at the same time sinners, then is Christ a servant of sin? Absolutely not! For if I build up again what was destroyed, I show myself to be a transgressor. For I through the Law died to the Law in order that I might live to God. I have been crucified with Christ. I no longer live, but Christ lives in me. But now living in the flesh, I am living in the faith – that of the Son of God who loved me and gave himself for me. I do not render invalid the grace of God, for if through the Law [there is] justification, then Christ died for nothing.

It was proper rhetorical procedure for the statement of facts to lead smoothly into the issue to be determined or the statement of the question at issue (the *propositio* – cf. Quintilian, *Inst. Or.* 4.2.132) and this is what we find here. At the end of the *narratio* we were left with the poignant question – how can you compel the Gentiles to Judaize? We were left with a picture of Peter and Barnabas impersonating their former selves, by returning to a more Law-observant lifestyle.[1] The question is, should they be doing it, and even more to

---

1. On impersonation and deliberative rhetoric cf. Quintilian *Inst. Or.* 3.8.49–52. Impersonation involves the assumption of a role or the playing of a part that is not really one's own. This is what Paul is accusing Peter and Barnabas of. They are not acting out of conviction but rather play-acting for prudential or emotional reasons. Paul feels this way because he believes they had previously accepted the 'truth of the Gospel' and had begun to live by it.

the point in this letter should the Galatians be following their example, Judaizing so that they can be considered full-fledged Christians and have fellowship with Jewish Christians? As Quintilian says "deliberation is always concerned with questions where some doubt exists" (*Inst. Or.* 3.8.25), and it is clear from this letter that Paul is trying to persuade his converts not to Judaize, not to follow bad examples and the urgings of the agitators, but rather good examples like his own. This means there was some doubt in Galatia as to what the proper course to take was. The question is not just what arguments Paul will use to convince his audience not to submit to circumcision and the Law, these we will begin to find at Gal. 3.1, the question is – What underlying principle or truth or issue is at stake in the decision? Paul will try to clarify in short form the fundamental issue in 2.15–21.

In order to make a smooth transition, it was proper to make the *propositio* both backward and forward looking in character. "The function of the *propositio* is twofold: it sums up the . . . content of the *narratio* by this outline of the case and provides an easy transition to the *probatio*."[2] The *Rhetorica ad Herrennium* stresses that two kinds of remarks are appropriate in a *propositio*: "we ought to make clear what we and our opponents agree upon, if there is agreement on points useful to us, and what remains contested" (1.10.17). These two sorts of remarks we find enumerated in vss. 15–16 and in vss. 17–18 respectively. Then in very succinct fashion, using brief theological formulae, Paul in vss. 19–21 sums up in advance the terms and ideas to be elaborated upon in the arguments that are to follow, in part giving a personal testimony in these climactic verses. Paul follows the advice that the *propositio* should be brief, concise and relatively complete, providing a preview of what is to come (cf. Cicero *De Invent.* 1.22.32; Quintilian, *Inst. Or.* 4.5.26–28).[3] The terms and ideas must be unpacked in what follows, they are not explicated at this point, but a clue to how they should be explained is given here.

The insight that an understanding of the rhetorical function of this section brings to the discussion of 2.15–21 is severalfold. In the first place, it

---

2. Betz, *Galatians*, p. 114.

3. At this point, but not on most others, I must disagree with Kennedy, *New Testament*, p. 148 that what we have here is an epicheireme rather than a *propositio*. It is not so much argumentative, as it provides a preview of the arguments which are to come, which is appropriate in a *propositio*. J. Smit, "The Letter of Paul to the Galatians: a Deliberative Speech," *NTS* 35 (1989), pp. 1–26, here p. 3, seems to assume that a proposition must give a point by point outline in advance of the arguments to come. However, if there is only really one major issue under debate, it was perfectly appropriate to present the basic issue and some of the key terms of the coming arguments rather than summarizing all the arguments to come. The latter is Paul's rhetorical strategy here.

makes clear why there has been debate as to whether this subsection goes with what precedes or with what follows. It is transitional, but it is not simply a continuation of Paul's address to Peter. This *propositio* is addressed to the Galatians, even though it may sum up some of the things Paul said or, with hindsight, would like to have said to Peter when he confronted him. Notice that while this section begins with 'we' as if Paul were still addressing Peter, by vs. 18 we have a series of 'I' statements. Secondly, it makes clear that Paul is assuming he is on common ground in vss. 15–16 when it is stated that 'we know a person is not justified by works of the Law but rather by the faithfulness of Christ'. As Betz says what Paul states here "is thoroughly Pauline, but Paul's claim that he shares this doctrine with Jewish Christianity should be taken seriously."[4] This is the common ground he believes he stands on with Peter and Barnabas, and also with his Galatian converts. This is surely some of the essence of what Paul means by the truth of the Gospel, a truth which was recognized in the Jerusalem meeting. Paul is assuming his converts will not dispute this proposition.

It is what follows the remarks in vss. 15–16 that is under debate. What are the implications of this belief in being set right with God through Christ's death? If this is true, why then the Law? Does the Law still have a function in the new economy of God? Should one add obedience to the Law to faith in Christ as the agitators were urging in Galatia? Should the Galatians submit to circumcision, and if they do what are the implications of doing so? Are they nullifying the grace of God expressed and given through and because of the death of Christ by submitting to the Law? The *propositio* simply tries to set these kind of questions going in the mind of the Galatians before Paul actually gets to his proper arguments. Notice how some of the key terms and ideas that will be used in the rest of Galatians are introduced here in the *propositio*.

Δικαιοσύνη – 2.21; 3.6, 21; 5.5.

Δικαιόω – 2.16 (thrice), 17; 3.8, 11, 24; 5.4.

Νόμος – 2.16 (thrice), 19 (twice), 21; 3.2, 5, 10 (twice), 11, 12, 13, 17, 18, 19, 21 (thrice), 23, 24; 4.4, 5, 21 (twice); 5.3, 4, 14, 18, 23; 6.2, 13.

Ἔργον – 2.16 (thrice); 3.2, 5, 10; 5.19; 6.4.

Πίστις – 2.16 (twice), 19 (twice), 21; 3.2, 5, 10 (twice), 11, 12, 13, 17, 18, 19, 21(thrice), 23, 24; 4.4, 5, 21(twice); 5.3, 4, 14, 18, 23; 6.2, 13.

Ζάω – 2.14, 19, 20 (twice); 3.11, 12; 5.25.[5]

---

4. Betz, *Galatians*, p. 114.

5. I owe this chart to Matera, *Galatians*, p. 98. Ramsay, *Paul's Epistle to the Galatians*, pp. 305–6 rightly notes "But the address is practically an epitome of the theme which is set forth in the following chapters . . . in 2.14ff. [one] finds . . . the whole truth in embryo." He does not, however, recognize the rhetorical reasons why this is so and how it functions here.

The issue as raised in the *propositio* is – What should the role of the Mosaic Law be in the life of a Christian believer, whether Gentile or Jew, and as a subset of that question, should the Galatians submit to circumcision and the various other boundary-marking rituals of Judaism? Lying beneath all of this is the question – Who are the people of God, and what constitutes them as such?

It cannot be stressed enough that throughout all of Paul's acts of persuasion that follow, Paul is arguing with *Christians* about the proper and improper ways of getting on with their Christian lives. In other words, even though Paul will at points give his converts a reminder about how they got into the ἐκκλησία of God, this argument is not basically about getting in, nor even about how one stays in, but rather about how one goes on in Christ and with the aid of the Holy Spirit. In fact Paul is concerned about the Galatians crossing the community boundary in the other direction – getting out, or committing apostasy.[6] The argument is theological, ethical, and social throughout, and at stake is the unity and equality of Jew and Gentile in the church of God, in the new creation that exists in the midst of this present evil age.

The argument is misperceived if it is seen as some sort of general polemic in favor of faith and against 'works righteousness' or a works mentality or a works religion, or the human attempt to feel after God and find God. Paul is not even arguing against the general concept of 'legalism'. He has something much more specific in mind when he speaks of works, namely 'works of *the Law*', obedience to the Mosaic Law and seeking to be part of the community that relates to God on the basis of the Mosaic covenant. As we shall see Paul is not anti-works, not anti-obedience to God, not even anti-Law, indeed he will argue for the 'Law of Christ' as the guiding principle for Christians. His complaint has to do specifically with the Mosaic Law and the covenant of which it is a part. The Mosaic Law and obedience to it is not, in Paul's view, how one got into Christ, how one stays in Christ, or how one goes on in Christ.[7] It is no longer what defines and delimits who the people of God are and how they ought to live and behave.

Verse **15** begins as if Paul were still addressing Peter, or more generally Jewish Christians. He speaks of those who are 'by nature' Jews. The sentence begins with an emphatic 'we', so here Paul is distinguishing himself and other Jews from the majority of his audience.[8] The term φύσει is found elsewhere in the Pauline corpus and is used similarly at Rom. 11.21–24 (cf. Gal. 4.8) to refer

---

6. This is why one must read cautiously the boundary language in Galatians and not assume too quickly the issue is how one 'gets in'.

7. The latter being particularly at issue in this letter.

8. See Bruce, *Galatians*, p. 137.

to what a person is by physical nature (cf. the more extended sense in Rom. 2.27). As Burton says, this opening clause is concessive 'though we are Jews by nature . . . yet even we . . .'[9] This natural condition of Jews is contrasted with what they are not – 'sinners from the Gentiles' (or nations). Is Paul talking about the 'natural' moral condition of Gentiles, or their ritual status of being 'unclean' from a Jewish point of view, or both? Probably he has in mind something similar to what we find in Ephes. 2.12. The idea is that Gentiles by nature are outside the circle of the old covenant, do not have the Law (cf. Rom. 2.14; Ps. 9.17; Tobit 13.6; Jub. 23.23–24; Mt. 5.47), and therefore are by definition (but also by nature and choice), beyond the pale – sinners.[10] Here it is instructive to compare a text like 2 Macc. 6.12–17, that distinguishes the sinfulness of Jews as opposed to the sinfulness of Gentiles, the latter leads to destruction, the former to discipline. Paul, however, though addressing his fellow Jewish Christians in language they would be used to, in fact believes that God takes Jewish sinfulness as seriously as Gentile sinfulness. In either case it can lead to destruction (cf. Gal. 5.17–21; 1 Thess. 2.14–16).

Verse **16** continues this sentence with another subordinate clause about what Paul would take as common knowledge between himself as his fellow Jewish Christians. 'We know' that human beings are not δικαιοῦται from 'works of the Law'. Notice that Paul here broadens the discussion to refer to what is true of human beings in general. It must be considered unlikely that Paul considers it a common opinion among Jews in general that human beings are not δικαιοῦται by works of the Law, but rather he assumes it is the proper and normal view of Jewish Christians, in light of what they know and believe about the work of Christ.

The term δικαιοῦται brings us to the point of discussing one of the more crucial word groups and concepts which Paul will use in this letter.[11] The verbal form of this word occurs some eight times in Galatians (2.16 three times, 2.17; 3.8, 11, 24; 5.4),[12] and in addition we also have the noun form δικαιοσύνη at the end of the *propositio* in vs. 21. This language is clearly Pauline, as 27 of the 35 occurrences of the verb in the NT occur in

---

9. Burton, *Galatians*, p. 119.

10. That it is not just a matter of being ritually beyond the pale is clear enough from the way Paul contrasts Gentile life and behavior before conversion (cf. 1 Cor. 6.9–11; 1 Thess. 1.9–10) to what it is like now.

11. See my longer discussion of this matter in *Paul's Narrative Thought World*, pp. 255–62.

12. It appears some fifteen times in Romans, and only twice in 1 Corinthians, and twice more in the Pastorals. In other words, it is a major theme in two of Paul's letters, but not in all of Paul's letters. However, the importance of an idea to Paul cannot be determined simply on the basis of a word count.

Paul's letters. Especially because this word group occurs repeatedly in the *propositio*, the thesis statement of the document, it deserves our close attention, not least because it has been the subject of repeated controversy since at least the Reformation. This word group comes from the Law court,[13] and if we are looking for OT background we should consider texts which speak of a judge acquitting or vindicating the innocent or righteous (cf. Ex. 23.7; Deut. 25.1, 2; 2 Sam. 15.4; Mic. 6.11). To be acquitted by God in these sorts of texts has to do with being found faithful to the covenant and the demands of its Law. If this, however, is the basic sense in the OT and other early Jewish literature, one must say that the nuances have changed by the time we get to Pauline literature. Here it is the unrighteous and the sinners who are acquitted, because in fact in Paul's view 'all have sinned and fallen short of God's glory' (Rom. 3.23; cf. 3.9–26), and both Jew and Gentile outside of Christ will be judged for their sin (Rom. 2.12–13). Instead of the translation 'vindicated' we often find 'reckoned as righteous' or 'acquitted' in the Pauline corpus, because the legal judgment stands in variance with the actual fact that all are by nature and choice sinners. 'Vindicated' suggests that one is innocent or righteous and so deserves to be acquitted. It is not, however, the righteous that are being acquitted in Paul's view, for 'none are righteous, no not one'.

Thus the verb δικαιόω is used forensically and relationally by Paul to indicate the status or standing in relation to God of a person who is in Christ. For such a person there is now no condemnation (Rom. 8.1). Paul, however, does not just use the δικαιόω language and related terms to refer to someone at the point of entry into the body of Christ. He will also talk about final justification before the divine tribunal as well (cf. Gal. 5.5 'we . . . await the righteousness [δικαιοσύνης] for which we hope' cf. Rom. 6.16), and it is clear enough that this involves an assessment of the Christian's behavior and works (cf. 1 Cor. 3.12–15; 2 Cor. 5.10; Phil. 3.8–14). He even discusses 'righteousness' or 'right standing' as an ongoing status or relationship (Rom. 5.21). As it turns out, Paul can use the noun δικαιοσύνη and the adjective δίκαιος with behavioral nuances. Paul then "joins forensic and ethical categories in his understanding of righteousness, with the one always involving the other . . . For while the aorist ἐπιστεύσαμεν ('we have believed') of vs. 16 refers to a once-for-all response that results in a transfer of status (cf. ἵνα δικαιωθῶμεν) the four uses of the verb in vv. 16–17 and the noun in vs. 21 cannot be treated as simply 'transfer terms' when the

---

13. This should not be taken to mean that Paul is signaling here that a piece of forensic rhetoric will follow, any more than the prevalence of this term in Romans signals such a thing. Paul is giving advice to his converts about whether or not to follow the Mosaic *Law*, and this requires the use of some juridical language. It does not mean he is offering a defense here.

issue at both Antioch and Galatia had to do with the lifestyle of those who were already believers in Jesus."[14]

I must reiterate here what I have said before. Paul's primary concern in this letter is with how the Galatians will go on in Christ, and indeed he even discusses the possibility of their going out of Christ, committing apostasy. The language about how they entered the Christian community is used in the service of this larger discussion, reminding them how they got in, but also discussing how they should now walk in Christ. Justification is not the main subject of this letter, it is brought into the discussion about how the Galatians should behave as Christians and whether they should 'add' obedience to the Mosaic Law, to their faith in Christ. Paul's response is that precisely because they did not come to be in Christ by obeying the Law (initial salvation and justification was by grace through faith), they should *not* now add obedience to the Mosaic Law to their faith in Christ. Rather they should continue as they started in Christ, walking in the Spirit and according to the Law or Norm or Example of Christ.

To a real extent the question Paul is addressing is a matter of honor. Paul is saying that all Christians have already ascribed honor through justification by faith and therefore they do not need the acquired honor thought to be the result of doing works of the Law. Paul reacts in this letter as one who has been shamed in Antioch, and must re-establish his ethos, especially in the eyes of his converts. He does this not by trying to acquire honor but by stating that he has from God all the honor and status he could possibly need, as do the Galatians themselves.[15]

This leads us to discuss another crucial phrase which appears for the first time in Galatians at vs. 16, namely 'works of the Law'.[16] There is little dispute among scholars that when Paul speaks of 'the Law' here he means the Mosaic Law. The debate primarily centers on what sort of 'works' he has in mind. Does Paul mean any and all sorts of 'works of the Law' by this phrase, or some particular subset, say for instance those works which served as boundary markers, those which set Jews apart from others – circumcision, sabbath observance, food laws? Or is in fact Paul focusing in this phrase on some

14. Longenecker, *Galatians*, p. 85. The definitive study which establishes that while the relational sense and idea is probably primary, there are also behavioral nuances as well, in particular when the noun and adjective are used is J. A. Ziesler, *The Meaning of Righteousness in Paul: A Linguistic and Theological Inquiry* (Cambridge: Cambridge University Press, 1972).

15. See the discussion by W. B. Russell, "Paul's Use of Σάρξ and Πνεῦμα in Galatians 5–6 in Light of the Argument of Galatians" (Westminster Theological Seminary, Philadelphia, 1991), pp. 113–18.

16. We will reserve our larger discussion of Paul's view of the Law for later in the commentary, when Paul discusses at length the question 'Why then the Law?'

particular attitude toward the Law (e.g., legalism)? It would seem clear from the fact that Paul uses the phrase 'works of the Law' interchangeably with just the word 'works' to speak about the same subject (cf., e.g., Rom. 4.2 to Rom. 3.20; or Rom. 4.6 to Rom. 3.28 where 'works' plus the same preposition occurs in both cases), and from the fact that ἔργον is regularly used of actions rather than attitudes,[17] that it is unlikely that Paul is focusing on the problem of legalism when he uses the phrase '*works* of the Law', however much he may have disapproved of legalism.[18]

Of specific relevance is the use of the phrase 'works of the Law' or closely similar phrases in early Jewish literature. It is interesting on this score that the specific phrase 'works of the Law' is not found in the OT, not even in the Greek translation (the LXX), and for that matter it is not used by any NT author except Paul. There is one clear parallel from the Qumran material in 4QFlor. 1.7, but one must also take into account other closely parallel phrases such as 'his works in the Law' (1QS 5.21; 6.18), or more distantly 'works of righteousness' (1QH 1.26; 4.31) and from 2 Bar. 57.2 'works of the commandments'. It is also of relevance that in the Mishnah and Talmuds the word 'works' most often refers to works of the Mosaic Law.[19]

Dunn has tried to argue on the basis of some of the Qumran evidence that a particularly sectarian approach to the Law is implied in the use of phrases like 'works of the Law', and that it particularly refers to the sect's distinctive understanding and practice of the Law. By implication Dunn wishes to argue that the same is true of Paul's use of the phrase (e.g., that it refers to, or at least focuses on, the distinctive boundary-marker practices which are at issue in Galatia).[20] He points especially to 4QMMT and to the fact that it includes a series of distinctive Qumran rulings on the Law's disputed points, under the heading 'Some of the Deeds of the Law'. Now the problem with this argument is that the title is '*some* of the deeds of the Law'. That the Qumranites took a sectarian approach to the Law is not in dispute, but that they used the phrase 'deeds or works of the Law' to refer particularly to their sectarian views or rulings or attitude about the Law is very doubtful. The phrase 'deeds of the Law' is not a technical phrase in any of these Qumran texts. Certainly, the phrase would *include* their distinctive practices and ways of doing the Law, but the point is that the phrase was not limited to such distinctive practices, nor is there any evidence that the phrase 'works/deeds of the Law' usually or mainly

---

17. See U. Luz, *Das Geschichteverständnis des Paulus* (Munich: Kaiser, 1968), p. 147 and n. 3.

18. See the important discussion by D. J. Moo, "Law, 'Works of the Law', and Legalism in Paul," *WestTJ* 45 (1983), pp. 73–100. See especially the chart on p. 93.

19. See Moo, p. 91.

20. See, e.g., most recently, Dunn, *Galatians*, pp. 136–37; and his *The Theology of Paul's Letter to the Galatians* (Cambridge: Cambridge University Press, 1993), pp. 88ff.

referred to those practices *in particular*. I thus conclude that the Qumran evidence does not provide adequate support, indeed it may not provide support at all, for the conclusion that "'works of the law' . . . was probably used initially in a polemical context . . . to denote particularly those *obligations* of the law which were reckoned especially crucial in the maintenance of covenant righteousness . . ."[21]

Dunn also makes the further claim that at issue is a particular sectarian interpretation of these 'boundary marker' obligations. But there was nothing sectarian about what the agitators were asking the Gentiles to do in Galatia so far as we can tell. Urging them to be circumcised and keep the Law was what God-fearers and proselytes were *normally* urged to do if they wanted full participation in Israel. Nothing is said in Galatians about any peculiar or specifically sectarian practices of some Jews.

There is another line of approach to this question which must be briefly mentioned at this juncture, and dealt with more fully later. It has often and rightly been noted that Paul deals with the Law: (1) as a corporate entity and (2) as connected to a specific covenant which must be evaluated in light of recent salvation historical developments. That Paul deals with the Mosaic Law as a whole when he speaks of it is shown not only by the fact that he never once speaks of 'Laws' (plural) but only of 'the Law' (119 times), but also from such statements as 'the whole Law is fulfilled in one word . . .' (Gal. 5.14), or more crucially 'all persons being circumcised are under obligation to do the whole Law' (5.3). In other words Paul connects the ritual Law, including the distinctive boundary rituals to the rest of the Law and says that one entails the other. As regards (2) above, it is enough to say at this point that Paul distinguishes being under the Law and being in Christ as having to do with two separate eras of salvation history. This is especially clear in texts like 'When the fullness of time came God sent his Son . . . in order that he might redeem those under the Law' (Gal. 4.4, 5), or 'the Law *was* our guardian *until* Christ came . . . but now . . . we are no longer under a guardian' (Gal. 3.24–25). We must thus conclude that by 'works of the Law' Paul means actions performed in obedience to the Mosaic Law, or more specifically acts performed in response to any and all commandments of the Law.[22] He is not simply concerned with specific laws, nor with the social function and effect of the Law of separating Jews from Gentiles.[23]

---

21. Dunn, *Galatians*, p. 136. To overcome the obvious criticism of this view Dunn adds that while the whole Law was meant in principle by this phrase, that in practice it referred to the test cases or specific laws that set a Jew apart from a Gentile.

22. Cf. the conclusions of Moo, p. 92.

23. Contra Dunn, *Jesus, Paul and the Law*, p. 213 n. 11: "The laws which Paul specifically excludes are precisely those which separated Jews from Gentiles in the Greco-Roman world, which uniquely characterized the Mosaic covenant and the Jews." Now

One final caveat. There is in Paul's mind a difference between some essential principle in, or underlying, the Law (and mentioned in the Mosaic Law) on the one hand being fulfilled by a Christian through following the 'Law of Christ', and on the other hand obeying or being under the Mosaic Law. Fulfillment has to do with a salvation historical argument about the consummation of God's purposes in and for human beings, obedience has to do with being in and under obligation to a particular covenant and its strictures. Paul affirms the former and rejects the latter.

Paul says in vs. **16b** that Jewish Christians know that they are not acquitted or given right standing with God by means of doing works of the Mosaic Law. Rather, there is an alternate means. Here again we run into a controversial phrase – ἐὰν μὴ διὰ πίστεως Ἰησοῦ Χριστοῦ. In dealing with this phrase one must bear in mind that Paul is talking about the proper means by which justification or acquittal comes to anyone male or female, Jew or Gentile (ἄνθρωπος), since it does not come by means of works of the Law. The first critical problem one must deal with is whether ἐὰν μὴ (literally 'if not') should be taken as exceptive in force, as in Gal. 1.19, or as adversative. The former would lead to the translation 'except' or 'but only' the latter to the translation 'but'. It must be said, however, that even in an adversative sense, ἐὰν μὴ surely must be taken to mean 'but only'[24] and so in effect the exceptive sense is the same as the adversative sense. Taking it in an exceptive sense the question becomes whether the exception is to all of what precedes or to some particular part of what comes before.[25]

The real question is how the phrase 'works of the Law' functions here in regard to the exception. Dunn wishes to argue that the sentence could mean 'a person is not justified by works of the Law except through faith in Christ'. In other words, a person *can* be justified by works of the Law if this covenantal nomism is supplemented with or accompanied by faith in Christ. Dunn admits, however, that Paul goes on in the latter half of this verse to set up a clear antithesis,[26] and so this sense is unlikely. In part, Dunn's argument

---

even under this formulation Dunn's view will not work, because surely part of what most distinguished Jews from Gentiles was not just their distinctive ritual practices, but their strict monotheism and equally strict sexual codes. In other words, it is not just the social, but also the theological dimension that distinguished them. Cf. the more balanced conclusion of Ziesler, *Galatians*, pp. 25–26: "We may therefore agree that two of the identity markers are what spark off the debate behind this letter, but need not go on to accept that the focus is on them throughout the argument. They are the specific cases which lead to the general question and *it is the general question which finally dominates Galatians*"(emphasis mine).

24. See rightly Dunn, *Jesus, Paul, and the Law*, p. 212 n. 9.
25. See Burton, *Galatians*, p. 121.
26. See Dunn, *Jesus, Paul*, pp. 188ff.

hinges on his view that Paul is here formulating in vs. 16a a statement geared to gain Peter's assent.[27] However, whatever the pre-history of this material in Gal. 2.15–21, and it is not at all clear it was ever addressed to Peter (cf. above), its function in this letter is to address the Gentile Galatians, to set forth the essential theological proposition about which he wants them to be persuaded. It is hardly believable that Paul would have said to the Galatians that 'works of the Law' plus faith in Christ could justify. Indeed, it is precisely this sort of combination that he is arguing against in the remainder of this letter! In short, Paul is saying here no justification by works of the Law, only through 'the faith of Christ'. This leads us into the next hornet's nest of scholarly contention.

Should the phrase, which if translated literally reads 'faith of Jesus Christ', be taken as an objective genitive or a subjective genitive? This has been a matter of no little scholarly debate in the last fifteen years, and to judge from the recent articles and commentaries on Galatians the debate is not abating. It is fair to say at this point that scholars, at least in North America, are fairly evenly divided on the objective versus subjective genitive issue, whereas it is a minority view elsewhere that we should take the phrase as involving a subjective genitive. Briefly summarized, the objective genitive view involves taking the phrase to mean the faith of which Christ is the object, and so faith in Christ, while the subjective genitive view refers to Christ's own faith or faithfulness. A good deal hangs in the balance of what one decides about this matter.[28] On the one hand, the traditional view that Paul is referring to faith in Christ has a long pedigree (cf., e.g., Chrysostom's comment on this verse in his Galatians commentary). There is also no doubt that Paul not only affirms faith *in* Christ, but sees it as an important matter (cf. Rom. 10.14; Phil. 1.29),[29] as this very paragraph of Galatians shows.

The complaints against the subjective genitive view have been recently ably summarized by Dunn: (1) to take Paul to mean 'the faithfulness of Christ' by this phrase requires a great deal of further explanation that Paul never gives; (2) one would expect the verbal form of πίστις (i.e. πιστεύω) to function in equivalent fashion to the noun, but what we find, for example, here in 2.16ff. and in 3.5–9, 22 is Paul speaking about believing *in* Christ, not Christ's own faith or faithfulness. In fact we never read about Christ himself believing (verbal form) in the Pauline corpus; (3) the issue here and in other texts where this 'faith of Christ' phrase arises is about how a person is justified or acquitted, and the key background text for this discussion is clearly Gen. 15.6 (Gal. 3.6;

---

27. See Dunn, *Galatians*, p. 138.

28. See my discussion of this matter in *Paul's Narrative Thought World*, pp. 268–71.

29. Despite the exegetical gymnastics of S. K. Williams, "Again *Pistis Christou*," *CBQ* 49 (1987), pp. 431–47, Christ is seen as an object of faith by Paul.

Rom. 4.3) which refers to Abraham being justified by his own faith in God; (4) finally, as an antithesis to works of the Law one would naturally expect Paul to pose an alternative human response to God's gracious initiative.[30]

Let us consider each of these objections by Dunn in turn. The first objection in fact fails almost immediately because Paul does indeed unpack what he means by this phrase, not only in this very context but in other texts where the phrase arises. He refers to the crucifixion of Christ not only in Gal. 2.19, but also again in 2.21. Compare also for example Phil. 2.5–11 where we hear of the faithful obedience of Christ even unto death, after which Paul uses the phrase in question in Phil. 3.9 to refer to this very event. Furthermore, just as no one would dispute that Paul uses the OT in an allusive or echo fashion, one also should not dispute that Paul could use the story of Christ in a similarly allusive fashion, and allude to that familiar story of the death and resurrection with a catch phrase like 'the faithfulness of Christ', especially when there are hints in the context that this is what he is alluding to by using this phrase.

The second objection seems at first more substantive, that is until we realize that it often happens that a noun and a verb get used in somewhat different ways in the very same sentence. Suppose a fifth-century Greek-speaking Christian had wanted to say 'I trust that you will be faithful to affirm the faith when we next recite the Symbol (Apostles' Creed) in church, saying 'I believe in . . .' What words would he have used? Certainly he would have used πιστεύω/πίστις and done so drawing on the full semantic field of these words so he could speak of trusting (an act of faith in someone or something), 'believing', 'the faith' (something believed), and finally being trustworthy or faithful. The verbs would refer to actions and the nouns would refer to things or concepts which are the subject or object of actions. In other words, the verbs and nouns would often carry different though related nuances. Paul is certainly not compelled to use the noun and the verbal form of this key word 'faith' in the same fashion even in the same text. Indeed what we know of Paul suggests that he was quite capable of using the same root word in a variety of ways. His Greek was not merely of the rudimentary sort with limited vocabulary. The question is whether Paul was simply being redundant in some of these key texts and speaking in two different ways about faith in Christ, or whether the difference between the noun phrase and the use of verbs signals a difference in ideas. I suggest the latter is more plausible.

Another objection along this sort of semantic and grammatical line has also been raised in regard to the use or rather absence of the definite article before the noun πίστις in our key phrase (cf. Gal. 2.16; 3.22; Rom. 3.22, 26; Ephes. 3.12; Phil. 2.9). Before considering this argument it must be kept

30. Dunn, *Galatians*, p. 139.

steadily in view that elsewhere we do find in Paul a phrase like τὴν πίστιν τοῦ Θεοῦ (Rom. 3.3), which surely must be seen as a subjective genitive and translated 'the faithfulness of God'. Paul can certainly use πίστις to mean faithfulness in such a phrase with a subjective genitive.

A. J. Hultgren has argued that it is notable that in contrast to the phrase just quoted from Rom. 3.3 and elsewhere where there is a subjective genitive following the word πίστις and Paul speaks of Christ, he never uses the definite article to begin the phrase, he never says ἡ πίστις τοῦ Χριστοῦ.[31] As Williams has shown, however, in the NT while a noun with a following genitive pronoun is normally articular, the rule is generally observed that when governed nouns are articular so are the governing ones, and when the governed nouns are not articular neither is the governing noun.[32] Thus, since 'Christ' has no article before it in our key phrase, we would not expect one before 'faith' either.

In fact, we find anarthrous and articular nouns used interchangeably to refer to the same thing. For example, in Rom. 3.3–7 the phrases 'the faithfulness of God' and 'the truth of God' are the functional equivalent of θεοῦ δικαιοσύνη in 3.5. Furthermore, we also find δικαιοσύνη θεοῦ at 3.21 and Rom. 1.17, but in Rom. 10.3 we find the very same phrase with the definite article – 'the righteousness of God', *without a difference in meaning*. If one examines other similar phrases in Paul's letters where both nouns lack the article but which require a translation with a definite sense, we will see that it is perfectly feasible for Paul to mean 'the faith(fulness) of Christ' by πίστις Χριστοῦ. For example, consider the phrases 'the power of God', 'the righteousness of God' and 'the wrath of God' in Rom. 1.16–18, or more importantly 'the grace of Christ' in Gal. 1.6 (χάριτι Χριστοῦ),[33] or 'children of the slave woman' at Gal. 4.31. All of this leads to the conclusion that if Paul wanted to speak of 'the faithfulness of Christ' he certainly could have done so using either πίστις Χριστοῦ or ἡ πίστις τοῦ Χριστοῦ.[34]

In response to Dunn's third objection, what he states here is true. Paul is concerned with how one is justified or acquitted. Unfortunately Dunn does not mention that there is both a subjective and an objective component to how this happens. It happens through faith on the subjective side, but on the objective side it happens through or because of the death of Christ. The Abrahamic text of course speaks to only one side of this faith

31. A. J. Hultgren, "The *Pistis Christou* Formulation in Paul," *NovT* 22 (1980), pp. 248–63.

32. There are a few exceptions to this rule: cf. Gal. 3.29.

33. Cf. this phrase to that at the end of Gal. 1.7 – the Gospel of Christ, where the governed noun is articular so the governing one is as well.

34. See the helpful discussion by Williams, pp. 431–33.

equation.[35] The question is which side of the discussion is being focused on by 'the faith of Christ'.

Finally, Dunn argues that the natural antithesis to works of the Law is faith in Christ. This, however, is debatable. If Paul were only interested in the subjective side of this issue, then yes faith in Christ is a natural antithesis to works of the Law. But this overlooks that the larger antithesis which stands behind works versus faith, is Law versus Christ. Paul's emphasis when he discusses justification, as vs. 21 makes clear, is on what Christ accomplishes on the cross, namely what the Law could not accomplish. The Law could not give life, it could not make a person good, it could not sanctify or empower the believer to do God's will. It could only inform a person of God's will. Paul's basic concern, as is shown by the climactic sentence in the *propositio* is to make clear that if justification could have come through the Law, Christ died for nothing. Thus for Paul, the objective means of justification is Christ's death on the cross, not the Law, and the subjective means of appropriating justification or right standing with God is faith in the faithfulness of Christ, not works of the Law. I conclude, not least because of where the emphasis lies in Paul's thought when he discusses justification (namely on the Godward side of things, not on the side of the human response), that the phrase 'faith of Christ' is a shorthand allusion to the story of the faithful one who was obedient even unto death on the cross, and so wrought human salvation.[36]

Paul, still speaking as and for a Jewish Christian perspective, says in vs. **16b** that 'even we have believed in Christ Jesus in order that our acquittal might come from the faithfulness of Jesus Christ and not from works of the Law.' The καὶ ἡμεῖς needs to be properly translated. Here we have the explicative use of καὶ which makes ἡμεῖς emphatic.[37] Paul, going back to his opening clause in this complex sentence, is saying that *even we* Jews have obtained right standing with God through the finished work of Christ

---

35. One might want to argue that Paul actually means at Rom. 4.12 'the faithfulness of our father Abraham', in which case he might be thinking of the Akedah. He would see Abraham, presumably in his offering of his son Isaac, as the prototype of Christ, of one being faithful and obedient even unto death. I think, however, in light of Rom. 4.3 this is probably not a correct translation here.

36. Further support along these lines can be found in R. B. Hays, *The Faith of Jesus Christ: An Investigation of the Narrative Structure of Galatians 3.1–4.11* (Atlanta: Scholars Press, 1983); and more recently his *The Moral Vision of the New Testament* (San Franscisco: Harper, 1996), pp. 27ff.; M. D. Hooker, "ΠΙΣΤΙΣ ΧΡΙΣΤΟΥ" *NTS* 35 (1989), pp. 321–41; Longenecker, *Galatians*, pp. 87–89; Witherington, *Paul's Narrative Thought World*, pp. 268–71. For the evidence from the Greek church fathers, who were rather unanimous in interpreting the phrase to mean faith in Christ, see now R. A. Harrisville, "Πιστίς Χριστοῦ: Witness of the Fathers," *NovT* 36 (1994), pp. 233–41.

37. Cf. Longenecker, *Galatians*, p. 88.

on the cross. The premise behind this of course is that Jews needed to be put in right standing with God just as Gentiles did. The verb 'believed' is in the aorist and refers to the initial response of a person to the Gospel message.

In the final clause of vs. 16, Paul provides a warrant for the proposition he has just put forth, by quoting Ps. 143.2 (142.2 LXX), though clearly Paul has modified it for his own purposes.[38] This obviously is an important text for Paul as he cites it again in Rom. 3.20 in a similar context. It is in order to remind ourselves that in a rhetorical piece such as Galatians is, it was important to cite external authoritative sources.[39] This was not just any sort of text, but a text recognized by both Paul and his audience as a sacred text, one which had inherent authority. If Paul is still having his imaginary conversation with Peter here, the citation would presumably have even more clout.[40] The source Paul is drawing on reads 'because every living being shall not be acquitted/justified before you'. Paul has modified his source in three ways: (1) Paul substitutes 'all flesh' for 'every living being'; (2) he omits the phrase 'before you'; (3) he adds a clause about means – 'from works of the Law'. The emphasis on 'flesh' is probably intentional. Paul is suggesting that humans by their nature (perhaps Paul means by their fallen nature) cannot justify or acquit themselves before God. Obviously the most important change here is the addition of the phrase 'from works of the Law'. This addition shows the importance of the phrase for Paul (on its meaning cf. above). Works of the Law are works done by humans who are 'flesh', and precisely because of this they do not produce justification. Paul's form of argument suggests that this would be a new insight for Jews. Non-Christian Jews, and presumably the agitators as well, would not have read Ps. 143.2 in the way Paul does, as making a comment on lack of efficacy of works of the Law. In Rom. 3.20 and elsewhere in Romans Paul will attempt to explain more fully why no one is justified by works of the Law.

It must always be kept steadily in view that Paul is concerned not only with initial justification (as seems to be the *main* emphasis here), but also with the final verdict of God on human life and human works at the return of Christ. I would suggest that since the verb 'justified' in the quotation is in the future, that Paul has at least in part this final justification in view here.[41] This is

38. Ὅτι here could be *recitativum*, functioning as a veritable quotation mark, but probably we should see it as in the main causal 'because . . .'.

39. On the use of documentary evidence in or as support for proofs cf. Quintilian, *Inst. Or.* 5.7.1ff.

40. See rightly, Lightfoot, *Galatians*, p. 115: "This sentence indeed would be an unmeaning repetition of what had gone before, unless the Apostle were enforcing his own statements by some authoritative declaration."

41. Notice that final justification or acquittal is not surprisingly the subject of such discussions in early Jewish literature since non-Christian Jews by and large did not agree with Paul that the eschatological age had already dawned. There was rather widespread

important because it gets at the heart of the problem in Galatia. Paul is addressing those who are already Christians and have already passed across the boundary into the Christian community. Initial justification has to do with that crossing. The problem for them was how they should go on in their Christian life, whether or not they should add works of the Law to faith in Christ in order to gain the final approbation or acquittal of God in the future.[42] Paul is concerned both with the social effects on the community of following the agitators' (or Peter's) approach, and with the theological underpinning that supports such an approach. He is assuming that if carefully explained with proper acts of persuasion, fellow Christians would agree with Paul's understanding of justification.[43]

In his helpful study of Paul's autobiographical remarks, G. Lyons argues that what we are dealing with in 2.15–21 is a continuation of Paul's attempts to present both negative and positive paradigms to his audience. He does this by way of a comparison (σύγκρισις) of Paul's and Peter's behavior in 2.11–14, and more generally by speaking about Paul and Jewish Christians in 2.15–21.[44] Furthermore, the function of this material is not to defend Paul against charges, but to make clear how he has experienced and embodied the Gospel of divine grace which he preaches and therefore is worthy of imitation by the Galatians. It is interesting that if one reads 2.19–21 in conjunction with 1.13–16a that we see some rather striking similarities to the pattern of autobiogaphical remarks in Phil. 3.4–22. There too, Paul begins with his Jewish past and ends with his renunciation of all privileges for the sake of Christ.[45] This reminds us that we must take the 'I' (vs. 18ff.) seriously here, even if Paul is speaking on behalf of Christians or Jewish Christians generally, and we must also take very seriously the 'formerly'/'now' language by which Paul emphasizes the notable changes in his life caused by his conversion. It will be noted that

---

agreement that no one could claim to be sinless and so worthy of final acquittal by God; cf. Job 9.2; Ps. 14.1–3; Is. 59.2ff.; 1 En. 81.5; 1QH 9.14–15. Cf. Betz, *Galatians*, p. 119 on the future reference in vs. 16.

42. I take seriously the suggestion by Ziesler, *Galatians*, p. 27 that the agitators and indeed even Peter and other Jewish Christians in Antioch may well have not understood the implications of their behavior in terms not only of its social effect on the Christian community (creating division) but also in terms of its theological implications (namely that Christ's death was at best insufficient in itself for justification, and at worst was for nothing). In other words, they may have been more guilty of a sort of unreflective partisanship for a Jewish way of viewing things, than of malice aforethought.

43. See Betz, *Galatians*, p. 115 who rightly stresses that justification by grace through faith was not only a Pauline idea in early Jewish Christianty. Cf. Jam. 2.14–26; Justin *Dial.* 46.1; 47.1; 116; Mt. 12.37; Lk. 15.11–32; Acts 13.39 Pseud. Clem. 8.5–7.

44. Lyons, *Pauline Autobiography*, p. 135.

45. See Lyons, p. 147, who is following N. Dahl at this point.

these changes have to do chiefly, though not solely, with Paul's relationship to the Law, which he 'died' to, through his encounter with Christ.

As Betz, suggests, we should probably see vs. **17** as the beginning of a brief section where Paul discusses matters about which various others, in particular other Jewish Christians, would not agree with Paul.[46] There are in essence three propositions here, one to do with seeking to be justified in Christ, one about being found sinners, and one about Christ as a servant or minister of sin. The first two are part of the protasis of this conditional sentence. By type we are dealing with a first class condition with εἰ, which normally means we are meant to assume that *both* of these two propositions are true.[47] Paul's point seems to be this – if one grants that we Christians are seeking to be justified in Christ (locative sense)[48] and not elsewhere, and in the process even we Jewish Christians are found to be operating and acting outside of the sphere of the Law, living and acting beyond the pale and so subject to the complaint that we are like Gentile sinners (cf. 2.14), then the question becomes, is Christ a minister of sin?

Close attention needs to be paid here to the καὶ αὐτοὶ, '*even* ourselves' which strongly suggests Paul is still speaking as and for Jewish Christians like himself and Peter. In view of this, it is likely that we should take the word 'sinners' in the same sense as at vs. 15, which is to say that it is a comment more on a person's position (outside the Law, and so lawless), than on a person's condition (immoral), though the latter is certainly not excluded.[49] The terminology here is important because Paul is going to go on to use a very different term in vs. 18. Paul will go on to say that if one re-establishes the Law as the basis of Christian community then he himself and many others will be found to be not merely beyond the pale, but actually lawbreakers, 'transgressors'. In a tour de force argument, he will contend that those who try to rebuild or re-establish the Law as that which defines and confines the Christian community are in fact the ones who are committing sin. They are sinning against the finished work of Christ on the cross, by suggesting it was insufficient to justify and define a people.

Verse **17b** gives us the apodosis of this conditional sentence, and there is a question as to whether or not we should take the ἆρα as having a circumflex

46. Betz, *Galatians*, p. 119.

47. See Longenecker, *Galatians*, p. 89.

48. It is true that Paul could be using ἐν to mean 'by' here, but the ἐν Χριστῷ formula normally carries a locative sense, and Paul is here contrasting life within two spheres – the sphere of the Law and the sphere of Christ.

49. The logic here is similar to what one finds in places like Rom. 3.9–26 and Rom. 11.32, where Paul is arguing that all have been placed into the category of sinner, all have been imprisoned in disobedience, all have sinned and fallen short so that God may have mercy on all through Christ. The righteousness of God has now been manifested *apart from the Law*, and in Christ.

making this an interrogative particle here. Against the notion is the fact that nowhere else in Paul do we find the interrogative particle, whereas ἄρα as an inferential particle ('then') is quite common in Paul's letters including in Galatians (cf. Gal. 2.21; 3.7, 29; 5.11; 6.10). Thus the inferential particle is more likely, but it is still probable that we have a question here rather than a statement as follows – 'Is Christ, then (in that case), a minister/servant of sin?'[50] The vast majority of translations and commentators assume that the sentence is in fact a question for the very good reason that it is followed by μὴ γένοιτο. These words regularly follow a rhetorical question (cf. Gal. 3.21; Rom. 3.4, 6, 31; 6.2, 15; 7.7, 13; 9.14; 11.1, 11; 1 Cor. 6.15, though see Gal. 6.14 where nonetheless it still sets up a sharp contrast), and 2.17b should surely not be seen as an exception to this rule.

Rhetorical questions are, according to Quintilian, the most common of rhetorical 'figures' and are used not to seek information but rather are intended as devices to enhance the cogency of one's argument (*Inst. Or.* 9.2.6ff.). In this case Paul is throwing odium on his opponents' point of view or shaming them, by showing the absurd conclusions that their sort of approach leads to (cf. *Inst. Or.* 9.2.9).[51] The phrase 'Christ, a minister of sin'[52] should be compared to the objection raised elsewhere that Paul, by his Gospel of grace, is promoting sin (cf. Gal. 5.13; Rom. 3.7–8 and 6.15).

Paul emphatically denies such a suggestion by means of μὴ γένοιτο. This phrase is interesting and also difficult to translate. It is a very strong exclamation, not dissimilar to the modern slang 'No way!', or to use more proper English 'Absolutely not!' It is interesting that the positive γένοιτο is found in the LXX to render the Hebrew 'Amen' (cf. Ps. 72.19; 71.19 in the LXX), and thus the negation of 'Amen' would mean something like 'I strongly disagree' or even 'may it certainly not be so'. As Bruce says, Paul seems particularly prone to say μὴ γένοιτο when it is suggested that freedom from the Law will encourage people to sin (cf. Rom. 6.1ff.; 6.15).[53] This suggests two things: (1) Paul was certainly one who thought that Christ had set his people free from observance of the Mosaic Law; and (2) he was rather regularly having to fend off suggestions that this made his Gospel anti-nomian, or that his message fostered immorality.

---

50. See the helpful discussion by J. Lambrecht, "The Line of Thought in Gal. 2.14b-21," *NTS* 24 (1978), pp. 484–95, here pp. 489ff.; cf. also Bruce, *Galatians*, p. 141. Matera, *Galatians*, p. 95 seems to assume that for there to be a question here, the interrogative particle is required, but that is not so.

51. Quintilian also speaks of rhetorical questions functioning as a way of making an assumption of that which in a dialogue would take the form of a question (*Inst. Or.* 5.11.5).

52. Dunn, *Galatians*, p. 141 may be right that διάκονος here carries the overtones of one who waits at table, in light of the previous discussion in 2.11–14.

53. Bruce, *Galatians*, p. 141.

In vs. **18** Paul turns, not for the first or last time, to a metaphor about constructing and demolishing buildings (cf., e.g., 1 Cor. 3.10–15; 2 Cor. 10.4). The metaphor is important in deliberative rhetoric where the ultimate issue is what makes for the building up of community and what makes for its destruction. What produces concord or unity, and what does not?[54] Here Paul is using the metaphor negatively to speak of the reconstruction of a Torah-observant lifestyle and community, after that sort of approach was dismantled by the death of Christ, or more to the point (since Paul will speak in the first person here), dismantled by his encounter with the crucified and risen Christ on Damascus Road. Scholars have puzzled over why we have here not a contrary to fact condition, but rather a first class condition which would suggest that this is actually being done by the speaker. Is Paul thinking here of what Peter and other Jewish Christians were doing in Antioch, building up again a Law-observant Christian community?[55] If Paul is speaking here for his fellow Jewish Christians in Antioch as a group and as a member of that group, then we must bear in mind that apparently all of them except Paul had in fact capitulated to the pressure or request that came from the 'men from James'. Paul then would be the lone exception, but otherwise, for members of this group, this statement would be true. Paul wishes them to see the consequences of such actions for *him*. 'If I rebuild what I once destroyed then I demonstrate or reveal myself to be a 'transgressor' or 'Law-breaker'.

The word παραβάτην does not just refer to a sinner, but to a transgressor, one who stands within a community bound by a particular form of Law, and violates that Law.[56] It is in fact a legal term, as is true of many terms in this subsection (e.g., 'annul', 'acquit').[57] Paul in Rom. 2.25 closely connects circumcision with being bound to obey the Law (writ large), and says that if you are circumcised, this is of value if you obey the Law, but if not you are a Law-breaker. Notice also Rom. 4.15 where the statement is made that where there is no Law there is no transgression (cf. below on Gal. 3.19). Paul is not speaking of being lawless here but of violating the Mosaic Law, which assumes it is in force on the Christian. The word order in the apodosis is intentionally dramatic – 'a transgressor myself I demonstrate'.

Notice that the verb 'destroy' is in the aorist, referring to an event which was done or happened in the past. Probably Paul is alluding to the point of conversion when the Law was set aside as either a means of justification or a *modus vivendi*, though it is just possible this is an allusion to the point in time when it was decided to have table fellowship with Gentiles and to allow them

54. See the discussion by Mitchell, *Rhetoric of Reconciliation*, pp. 99ff.
55. Cf. Lambrecht, "The Line," p. 493; Longenecker, *Galatians*, p. 90.
56. Lightfoot, *Galatians*, p. 117.
57. Betz, *Galatians*, p. 121.

to participate fully with Jews in the community of Christ without requiring them to be Law-observant. In any case, as Lambrecht says the "transgression consists precisely in the act of building up again; the restoration of the Law is the negation of God's initiative in Christ (cf. vs. 21a)."[58]

Verse 18 should be seen as transitional to the final section of the *propositio*. It was in the first person, but it was Paul speaking as a member of a group. Beginning in vs. **19**, however, things appear to become more personal, with Paul giving something of a testimony about his own experience. This is signalled by the emphatic ἐγώ which begins the verse.[59] What follows is about 'I myself'. The rhetorical function of this material is not defense, but rather to provide Paul's converts with an example of how they too should interpret their conversion experiences. Paul knows of course that the unique and peculiar experiences Paul has recounted in Gal. 1.1–2.11 cannot be reduplicated in the lives of his converts, but what he says in 2.19–21 is of another and more universalisable character. Gaventa puts the matter aptly:

> What the Galatians can imitate is Paul's single-minded response to the gospel that was revealed to him. When he 'immediately' returned to Damascus (1.17) he also discarded his Zeal for maintaining the Law and the tradition. He died not only to the Law but also to the traditions and customs he had previously served. It is the reversal of those prior commitments that the Galatians are to imitate, although their commitments may be of a quite different sort (cf. 4.1–11). To become as Paul means to allow Christ to live in oneself (cf. 2.20) to the exclusion of the Law or of any other tradition or category (cf. 3.27–28).[60]

On any showing, vs. 19a is difficult – 'for I myself through the Law died to the Law, in order that I might live to God. I have been crucified with Christ'. It is perhaps helpful if we consider for a moment Paul's discussion in Rom. 7.1–4 about dying to the Law. There Paul reminds his audience that the Law is binding on a person so long as they live. Verse 4 is crucial where Paul says that his audience has died to the Law (cf. vs. 6 discharged from the Law) through the body of Christ, so that they might belong to another (i.e., to Christ) in order that they might bear fruit.

---

58. Lambrecht, *Galatians*, p. 494.

59. It is in my judgment in the main a mistake to read this section of Galatians in the light of Rom. 7, or vice versa. In the latter text Paul has not just offered an autobiographical *narratio* as is clearly the case in Gal. 1–2. One can say this about both texts, however: in each case, Paul writes as a Christian describing a pre-Christian state of affairs that led to conversion. Rom. 7 is in all likelihood not a description of the Christian life, especially in view of what Paul goes on to say in Rom. 8.1ff.

60. Gaventa, "Galatians 1 and 2," p. 322. As we shall see, Gal. 3.27–28 stands at the very heart of Paul's deliberative case for concord and unity in Christ, as he argues against the fragmentation of the Galatian community which will happen if they take up the yoke of the Law.

Some commentators have suggested that Paul's argument here in Gal. 2.19a is rather strictly personal. Paul was a persecutor of the church because of his zeal for the Law, and it was precisely that zeal which led him down Damascus Road to his head-on collision with Christ. This is what 'through (my zeal for) the Law, I came to die to the Law' is sometimes thought to mean.[61] I would suggest that we must take seriously the parallel in Rom. 7.4, and the fact that Paul is speaking here as a paradigm.[62] Even more importantly the statement 'I have been crucified *with* Christ' is probably part of vs. 19, and provides a clue to Paul's meaning.[63] The place where the Law was abolished or set aside was on the cross of Christ. It was Christ himself, taking on the curse of the Law who died to the Law for all, through the execution of the Law's curse on him. Inasmuch as Paul or any Christian was crucified 'with' Christ on that occasion (Christ being both representative and corporate head of his group of followers), he or any Christian also as a result died to the Law. This meant they were no longer under the Law's jurisdiction, no longer obligated to keep the Law, no longer under the Law's power, free from the Law's curse and its demands. It also meant that the "distinction between sinner and righteous is no longer determined by Torah".[64] They now lived in a new sphere of influence, namely Christ, or to put it another way they were now part of the eschatological new creation. They were now under a new mandate, namely the Law of Christ, which meant first and foremost following the example of Christ, of his self-sacrificial community-creating obedience and faithfulness expressed pre-eminently on the cross.

Verse **19b** suggests that one must die to the Law, in order to live to God. This no doubt would be seen as a paradoxical statement by the agitators in Galatia or the false brothers in Jerusalem, or the men who came from James. After all, there are statements in early Judaism such as we find at 4 Macc. 7.19 and 16.25 where 'living to God' refers to life beyond death, namely life beyond the grave. Yet Paul is speaking about having this life while still in the flesh, and having it quite apart from the Law.[65] For the normal Jew, life comes through or

---

61. See, e.g., Dunn, *Galatians*, p. 143.

62. The reference to the body of Christ in Rom. 7.4 may indeed be a reference to Christ's crucifixion.

63. See rightly, Matera, *Galatians*, p. 103: "But since the Law is binding only during a person's lifetime (Rom. 7.1), Paul concludes that Christ and those *in* Him are free from the Law because of Christ's death . . . Paul has died to the Law *through* the Law by his co-crucifixion with Christ. He is dead to the Law because he is alive to a new eschatological reality."

64. Ziesler, *Galatians*, p. 27.

65. See Ziesler, *Galatians*, p. 29: "What is remarkable here is that instead of seeing the Law as representing the regime or power of God Paul sees it as an alternative . . .".

at least consists of obeying Torah (cf. Gal. 3.12), but Paul now believed that the Law could not give life or make one alive (Gal. 3.21). Only God in Christ could do that. In short, the death and resurrection of Christ has put to death all old means of trying to live or obtain life, here or hereafter, and has offered a new means of life and living.

It is important to note the tense of the verb 'crucified with' at the end of vs. 19. It is in the perfect, suggesting an action which began in the past and has continuing and ongoing effects in the present.[66] Paul is not merely talking about imitating Christ here, though that is a part of the matter, nor even just that Paul suffered in Christ, when Christ died on the cross. Had the latter been the sole focus here we might have expected an aorist verb here. Paul is suggesting that he is now being conformed to the sufferings of Christ in his own person when he is persecuted for Christ's sake (cf. Gal. 6.17) and so depicts the suffering Christ in his own life and person. Furthermore, he can even speaking in Phil. 3.10–11 of sharing in common Christ's suffering and becoming like him in his *death*. As was the case with the Master, so will be the case with his servants.

Furthermore, it is not just that outwardly in the events and pattern of his life that Paul is being conformed to the image of Christ. Verse **20** says that Paul can no longer speak about himself living (it is not 'I' who live), rather it is Christ who lives in Paul. In short there is also inward conformity to the life and nature of Christ as well. As Hansen says, this does not amount to a loss of human personality but rather a Christological renewal of true personality.[67] Paul usually speaks of being in Christ, rather than the reverse (Christ being in him), but the latter idea is found from time to time in his letters (cf. Rom. 8.10; 2 Cor. 13.5; Col. 1.27; Ephes. 3.17). A good deal more frequent is the notion that the Spirit indwells the believer (Rom. 5.5; 8.9, 11, 15, 16, 23, 26).[68]

Lest all this 'in Christ' and 'Christ in me' mysticism sound totally otherworldly, Paul quickly adds that all this is true while he is still living in the flesh. The νῦν here speaks of what is true of the believer after conversion and before physical death. The believer still lives in the body though he or she may be full of Christ and the Spirit (cf. 2 Cor. 4–5). Not only is the world in a dialectical tension between already and not yet, but so is the believer by the very fact that the believer is still in the unredeemed and unrenewed human

66. As Dunn, *Galatians*, p. 144 says, it is hardly likely this is a reference to baptism. Paul means he was nailed to the cross with Christ and he is still hanging there, not that he is still immersed. This is what comes of reading Gal. 2 in light of the later material in Rom. 6, as H. Schlier, *Der Brief an die Galater* (Göttingen: Vandenhoeck & Ruprecht, 1965), pp. 99–101 does.

67. Hansen, *Galatians*, p. 76.

68. See rightly, Dunn, *Galatians*, p. 145.

body he or she always had.[69] This verse also means, as Longenecker points out that Paul is referring to what is true after he has died to the Law and while Christ lives in him.[70]

In vs. **20b** we have another phrase where we must decide whether we are dealing with an objective or subjective genitive. Hays suggests we translate here 'I live by the faith of the Son of God who loved . . .'[71] On the other hand, even Longenecker who elsewhere is an advocate of the subjective genitive approach to 'the faith of Christ' thinks that here we have an objective genitive.[72] The following factors must be taken into consideration. Here πίστις is preceded by the preposition ἐν. Secondly, while the reading 'Son of God' here is likely to be preferred, there are various good witnesses that support the variant reading 'God and Christ' (p46, B, D*, G and others), and certainly this is the more difficult reading, for it is not found elsewhere in Paul.[73] Whatever the origin of this variant, it appears clear that these scribes did not understand the subject here to be 'the faithfulness' of God or Christ, but rather faith in them. A sort of combination view is suggested by Williams who

---

69. Dunn, *Galatians*, p. 146 wishes to read the term 'flesh' here as a reference to Paul's ethnic origin, his Jewishness (citing Rom. 1.3; 4.1; 9.3, 5, 8; 11.14). This is because Dunn wishes to stress that Paul does not renounce his continued Jewishness in order to live as a Christian. I doubt that Paul's Jewishness is at all alluded to here, especially since he is presenting himself as an example of and paradigm for all Christians, including his Gentile converts in Galatia. As for Paul not renouncing his continued Jewishness, while he certainly does not deny his Jewish origins, he says very clearly in Phil. 3.7–10 that he counts his Jewish credentials in the loss (and gone) column, and indeed he even says that he regards them as σκύβαλα, 'crap'. Cf. Hays, *Moral Vision*, p. 30.

The question that must be raised is – What does Jewishness mean for Paul the follower of Christ if he is prepared to say that circumcision counts for nothing, and he himself is prepared to live without regard to things like the food and sabbath laws? Can he really be said to be in continuity with early Judaism under these circumstances, or is he a sectarian person, who has taken on a new identity which leaves behind various things the vast majority of early Jews would see as essential to one's Jewish identity? I would suggest that the latter is a fairer assessment of where Paul is when he writes Galatians; cf. H. Räisänen "Gal. 2.16 and Paul's break with Judaism," *NTS* 31 (1985), pp. 543–53, here p. 53: "Paul's attack on covenantal nomism – largely implicit but nonetheless real – signals such a discontinuity or such a change of values that it is hardly too much to speak of a break." (Cf. E. P. Sanders, *Paul and Palestinian Judaism*, London: SCM Press 1977), p. 551). Dunn's assessment sounds more like a description of the agitators, or the men from James, or perhaps even of James himself at this juncture, though I would suggest that if James had accepted 'the truth of the Gospel', namely that all were given right standing with God through faith in the faithful work of Christ, he too might have been considered beyond the pale by many if not most early Jews.

70. Longenecker, *Galatians*, p. 93.

71. Hays, *Moral Vision*, p. 32.

72. Longenecker, *Galatians*, pp. 93–94.

73. See Metzger, *TC*, p. 593.

translates here 'I live in faith – that of the Son of God who loved me . . .'[74] If ἐν is taken as instrumental here ('by') then one could translate 'I live by the faithfulness – that of the Son of God'. Perhaps a slight preference should be given to this last reading in view the presence of τῇ after 'I live' and the presence of the following qualifying clauses which follow it, where it is clear that the action of Christ is in view.[75]

Verse **20c** affirms that the Son of God 'loved' me and 'gave himself' for me. These participles are in the aorist suggesting a particular event in the past, namely the death of Christ. This is where Christ's faithfulness (obedience) and faith and love were fully and climactically shown. Dunn may well be right that the main inspiration for these phrases comes from the Jesus tradition (cf. Mk. 10.42–45; Jn. 10.11; 15.13). In any case, it is right to emphasize that Paul has personalized things in a radical way here – Christ gave himself over to death for me, hence the intimacy of the connection between Christ's death, the believer's life, and also the cruciform shape of the believer's life.[76] There is, as Lategan says, a clear echo of Gal. 1.4 in Gal. 2.20. Furthermore, it is this echo and vss. 19–20 which more than any other part of this *propositio* prepare the way for what is to follow in Gal. 3–4.[77]

In vs. **21** Paul makes a simple assertion. He is not going to say or do anything to 'nullify' the grace of God. The language here is legal (cf. 1 Macc. 11.36; 2 Macc. 13.25; Gal. 3.15; 1 Cor. 1.19; 1 Tim. 5.12), coming from the realm of wills, testaments, and covenants. Paul's view is that a new covenantal situation has been set up by the death of Christ (cf. 2 Cor. 3), and this covenant is based on God's gracious work in Christ. Anything which compromises or constricts the efficacy or character of that work is seen by Paul as an attempt to invalidate or annul this new gracious covenant. Paul's implication is that there are those who are annulling the grace of God, by insisting on Christians, in particular Gentiles in this case, keeping the Mosaic Law. This is why the *propositio* ends with a bang in the form of a conditional statement. Here again we have a first class condition – 'for if righteousness/justification [comes] through the Law, then Christ died for nothing!' It is, however, in view of vs. 16, surely not a real condition.[78] It must be said on this score that by Paul's day,

---

74. Williams, p. 445.

75. The issue must remain uncertain, not least because of the placement of ζῶ between 'in faith' and what follows. But, on the other hand, the τῇ after ζῶ seems resumptive (i.e., 'By faith I live, that faith of the Son of God . . .').

76. Dunn, *Galatians*, p. 147. While the Gospel cannot be reduced to Paul's own experience, and it can be said that Paul reads his biography in light of the Gospel, there is some sort of symbiotic relationship between Paul's reading of his own experience and Paul's understanding of the Gospel.

77. Lategan, "Is Paul Defending," p. 428.

78. See Betz, *Galatians*, p. 126.

contrary to fact conditions in the indicative with εἰ did not require an ἄν in the apodosis to signal this fact. We see examples of this sort of phenomenon for example in Gal. 4.15 and also in Jn. 15.24, and I would suggest that Gal. 5.11 is simply another example of the unreal or contrary to fact condition with εἰ and without ἄν.[79] The grammarians agree that though it is rare, there are occasions where the indicative can be used in a protasis without ἄν in the apodosis to refer to an unreal condition.[80] It is clear from vs. 16 that Paul does not think Christ died for nothing and consequently he does not think righteousness or justification comes through the Law. Christ's action (not our faith) is here set over against the Law as that which puts the believer in right relationship with God, and in fact one has this ongoing relationship with God because of what Christ did.[81]

The word δωρεά has as its basic meaning gift. One may wish to compare Rom. 3.24 and 2 Cor. 11.7. The accusative form here is used as an adverb meaning 'in vain' or 'for nothing'[82] or 'to no purpose' or 'without a cause' (cf. Job 1.9; Ps. 34.19, i.e., 35.19 in the LXX; and on the last meaning Jn. 15.25). In Paul's view, any idea or any practice which takes away from or seeks to eclipse or to invalidate or to suggest the insufficiency of what Christ did on the cross, must be countered and rejected. If grace and the cross and being in Christ are the basis and guiding principles of the new covenant, then Mosaic requirements are not, not least because in Christ there is meant to be a unity of Jew and Gentile, slave and free, male and female. "The unity and equality of all believers in Christ is the foundational principle and overarching aim of Paul's entire argument."[83]

That is to say, Galatians is one large deliberative act of persuasion for the unity of the body of Christ in Galatia, with the theology of freedom from the Law and freedom in Christ found here and in Gal. 3–4 preparing for and providing a basis for the exhortations and ethical advice that follows in Gal. 5–6 about factionalism and divisive behavior and practices (such as, for instance, circumcision), and about walking in the Spirit as opposed to doing works of the flesh, or attempting works of the Law.

Paul has established his ethos and identity in Gal. 1–2 as a trustworthy paradigm for his converts to imitate, in contrast to Peter, Barnabas, the

79. On this latter text see pp. 372ff. below.

80. See BDF no. 360.

81. In other words δικαιοσύνη is not just about how the relationship began, but about its continuance as well. This is why Ziesler (*Galatians*, p. 30) plausibly suggests the translation righteousness here, meaning living as God's people ought to live. Cf. above pp. 173ff.

82. I.e., Gratis, as J. Calvin, *The Epistles of Paul the Apostle to the Galatians, Ephesians, Philippians and Colossians*, trans. T. H. L. Parker (Grand Rapids: Eerdmans, 1965), p. 44. Chrysostom suggests translating it something like 'superfluous'.

83. Hansen, *Galatians*, p. 73.

agitators, and others. His story since conversion shows, as he is conformed to the image of the crucified Christ, that he embodies the truth of the Gospel, that he models non-factious self-sacrificial behavior. Paul must go on to unpack the *propositio*, providing arguments to support the assertions he makes here. Most of all he must not only emphasize the great freeing and equalizing capacity of grace and how it creates community in the midst of diversity, but he must explain why the Law existed before Christ came. We must begin to examine his λόγοι or arguments at this juncture.

Bridging the Horizons

For some today the entire discussion in Gal. 2.15–21 will seem a bit esoteric or far too legal to be interesting to anyone but lawyers. For others, it will appear from this passage that God is not the loving God we otherwise have been led to assume exists. What kind of God requires his only son to die a hideous death on a cross? I have even heard of one case of a seminary professor arguing that the cross is evidence that God practiced child abuse! All of these attitudes grow out of fundamental misunderstandings about the human condition and also about the nature of God.

It was Paul's belief that all human beings had sinned and fallen short of God's will for human life and behavior. More than this, he believed that without divine help, human beings could not be extricated out of the quicksand of their fallen condition. This was one side of the divine–human equation. The other side is that Paul believed that God was both righteous and merciful, both just and loving, both holy and prepared to forgive. We often have trouble with holding these concepts together, but hold them in tension we must if we are to begin to understand how Paul could have thought that it was God's plan that his Son should die for the sins of the world.

In Paul's understanding, God could not simply forgive sin, both the reality and the effects of sin had to be countered if there was to be reconciliation between God and human beings. The big question was how God could both be just, not renouncing the divine character, and still be the justifier of sinful human beings. Paul's answer was that God must provide an atonement for sin in the person of his Son who was born as a human being for this very purpose. He was, as Dorothy Sayers used to say, the man born to die. Once sin was dealt with effectively and definitively on the cross, then the door was open to the possibility of normalizing relationships between God and humankind.

The story is told of William Herschel. As a young boy he loved military music, and growing up in Hanover in Germany he joined a military band. When his nation went to war, he was one of those leading the military band. As a young man he was totally unprepared for the horrors of war, and the result was that before long he deserted his military unit and fled the battle scene during an intense period of fighting.

He fled to England, and began to pursue further training in both music and science. Thinking he was in the clear, he grew and prospered in his new country. In fact he made various scientific discoveries that made him famous, and he gained great renown for his musical abilities. However, after Herschel came to the British Isles, another Hanoverian also came to live there – George who in fact became the King of England. King George knew of Herschel's past desertion of the army and summoned the great musician and scientist to appear before the royal court. Herschel went with fear and trembling, and when he arrived in the palace he was told to wait a considerable time in an ante-chamber to the throne room. Then finally, one of the King's servants came to Herschel and handed him a document and told him to read it. He opened it with fear, only to discover that it read 'I George pardon you for your past offenses against our native land'. George had pronounced the verdict of no condemnation on William Herschel, and in fact the document went on to say that for his outstanding service to humankind as a musician and a scientist, he was now to become Sir William Herschel: he was to be knighted! He had gone from criminal to honored dignitary in an instance, quite apart from what he might have deserved according to German law (the penalty for desertion was death). Paul is saying that this is what God's pronouncement of pardon does for all of us who accept it. It not only removes the source of alienation; it places us in a favored relationship with God.

This story perfectly illustrates Paul's concept of justification – it is a matter of God pronouncing a verdict of no condemnation on the sinner, or, put positively, it is a matter of declaring that the person in question was justified, in right relationship to the Law and the Law giver, even though he was in fact far from perfect. With the legal judgment of no condemnation (cf. Rom. 8.1ff.) comes the implication that sins have been forgiven, and so one need no longer be estranged from God. Yet estrangement is not overcome merely by a pronouncement from above. One must respond in faith to such a pronouncement. One must accept forgiveness. Forgiveness offered is not the same as forgiveness received.

Of course there are many people today who think we live in a no fault world, a world where no one is to be blamed for anything, no one need take responsibility for anything they have done wrong. From this point of view, there is no sin to atone for, only guilt feelings that need to be assuaged. The human problem is not that we are sinful, we just struggle with feelings of low self esteem! But it is worth asking why we have guilt feelings at all if there is no such thing as sin, or absolutes in matters of right and wrong. Why has God created human beings with the capacity of having a conscience unlike all other creatures? Perhaps then there is such a thing as accountability for human actions. Perhaps we really do live in a moral universe where it is true ultimately that what a person sows, that also shall they reap (Gal. 6). Perhaps there really was a need for God to provide a means of salvation and forgiveness; perhaps Christ's death really was both the necessary and sufficient means to atone for and deal with the sin problem and human estrangement from God.

If this is so, then it is understandable why Paul felt that nothing should be allowed to compromise the importance of or annul the effects of the death of Christ. Not even things that were good in their time, namely the Mosaic Law, should be allowed to obscure the sufficiency and importance of Christ's death for humankind. Paul believed that he had expressed the heart of the Gospel in 2.15–21 and nothing should be allowed to compromise it, not even well meaning attempts to help Gentile Christians be more moral persons. This explains both Paul's earnestness and his sense of urgency as he sums up in advance the heart of his Gospel. The question is whether we also are prepared to hear and receive this message as the Galatians originally did, hear and receive it as Good News.

Probatio: 3.1–6.10

Argument I: 3.1–18

THE FAITH OF ABRAHAM AND THE FOOLISHNESS
OF THE GALATIANS

*O foolish Galatians! Has someone cast the evil eye on you, before whose
eyes Jesus Christ was publicly exhibited as having been crucified? This
only I wish to ascertain from you: was it from works of the Law or from
hearing (that is, faith) that you received the Spirit? Thus you are
foolish, you began with the Spirit, now will you be completed in the flesh?
Have you experienced so much for nothing, if indeed it was even for
nothing? So then the One bountifully supplying you the Spirit and doing
mighty works among you, [was it] from works of the Law or from hearing
(i.e., faith)?*

*Just as 'Abraham believed God and it was reckoned to him for
righteousness'. For you know that those [living] from faith, these are
children of Abraham. But [because] the Scripture foresaw that by faith
God would justify the [Gentile] nations, it gave the good news before hand
to Abraham that 'all the nations will be blessed in you' so that those from
faith are blessed with the faithful Abraham.*

*For those who are [living] from works of the Law, are under a
curse. For it is written that 'Accursed are all who do not persevere in
all the things written in the Book of the Law, those putting it into
practice'. Because from works of the Law no one shall be justified before
God, it is clear that 'the righteous one from faith will live'. But the Law is
not from faith, but 'those doing it will live in them'. Christ ransomed us
from the curse of the Law being for us a curse, because it is written 'Cursed
be all those hanging upon a cross', in order that the blessing of Abraham
could be extended to the Gentile nations in Christ Jesus, in order that we
might receive the promised Spirit through faith.*

197

Brothers, I speak from a merely human point of view, in the same way a person's legally confirmed will can neither be annulled nor have a codicil added to it. But to Abraham were made the promises and to his seed. It does not say 'and to his seeds', as to many but as to one, 'and to your seed' who is Christ. But this I say, the Law which came into being 430 years later did not nullify the covenant that had been ratified before by God so as to render ineffective the promise. For if [it was] from the Law or by legal inheritance, it was no longer from the promise. But to Abraham through the promise God for all time granted a favor.

At Gal. 3.1 Paul begins the section of the letter where he will present his formal arguments to his converts so that they will not pursue a Judaizing course, and will instead continue to walk in the Spirit. Paul's arguments have an urgency to them not least because he knows that if even some of the Galatians do listen to the agitators it will mean the division of the churches in Galatia – disunity and discord are bound to result. Thus, throughout what follows in the remainder of Galatians Paul will be arguing against beliefs and behavior that lead to discord and disunity and for beliefs that lead to unity and harmony in the Galatian churches. In other words his arguments are of a deliberative, not a forensic nature.

In a deliberative piece of rhetoric the 'proofs' or arguments seek not to prove something true or false, but to provide reasons for the audience to take up a certain course of behavior. Deliberative rhetoric points out examples, such as that of Abraham or Paul himself (cf. Gal. 3.1 to 4.12), and asks the audience to emulate their behavior. What the rhetor must do is to show his audience that the course of conduct or action he is proposing is or will be beneficial, useful, honorable, and, by contrast, to pursue an alternate course of action or behavior will bring strife, will be useless, will be foolish (3.1) and the like.

If one is looking for signals in Paul's arguments for the rhetorical character of this material one must look out for terms such as 'benefit' or 'use' such as we find in Gal. 5.2, or for the language of building up and tearing down of community (cf. Gal. 2.18), or for warnings against behavior that produces discord or disunity (5.15, 20–21), but in fact one needs look no further than the very first remark of the very first argument in 3.1 to find a succinct clue as to where these arguments are leading. The Galatians are acting foolishly, having been 'bewitched' and 'bewildered' by some agitators, and so Paul must offer a mid-course correction and provide a rationale for continuing along the path they had begun when he was with them. The theological rationale, so to speak, is provided largely in Gal. 3–4, while the concrete advice about how to go forward is provided mainly in Gal. 5–6, though one must see 4.30 as transitional, for already there Paul begins to tell them what they must do to correct matters – cast the agitators out of the Galatian churches!

An interesting clue to the rhetorical aim of this document is found in paying close attention to the personal pronouns and how they are used as Paul's rhetoric progresses. As Kennedy points out, Paul "moves from the first person singular in earlier parts of the letter [I – cf. 2.18–21] to the second person plural [you all – cf. 3.1ff.] to a first person plural identification of himself and the Galatians" [we – cf. 5.25–26; 6.9–10].[1] This remark must be modified somewhat by saying that when 'we' occurs in the earlier part of the letter it consistently refers to 'we' Jews or more often 'we' Jewish Christians rather than uniting Paul and the audience. The goal of reunion between Paul and the audience is only achieved literarily near the end of the discourse. It must be stressed that the goal of the letter is reunion not just among the Galatians, but between the Galatians and the apostle, who is at present somewhat estranged from them and fearful about their future (cf. 4.19–20). The Galatians must return to that course of conduct which produces unity, bearing one another's burdens (6.2), working for the good of all, especially those of the household of faith (6.10). This is the sort of conduct for which Paul's arguments beginning in 3.1 will provide undergirding.

Paul's deliberative arguments in this letter are of both the inartificial and artificial sort. The former are usually the stronger sort of arguments and include "decisions of previous courts, rumors, evidence extracted by torture, documents, oaths and witnesses" (*Inst. Or.* 5.1.2). In Gal. 3 alone we will find an appeal to the Galatians' own experiences (they themselves are witnesses to what Paul is claiming) and to documents (Scripture and human wills, though the latter may be seen as an analogy with standing legal precedent or customs). Artificial arguments were generally thought to be less persuasive but often they would reflect the creativity of the rhetor. An excellent example of the latter is the innovative allegorical interpretation of the Sarah and Hagar story in Gal. 4. Undergirding all of his arguments is Paul's appeal to the supernatural work of God already done among and within the Galatians. This sort of argument was considered extremely strong by the ancients, it provided "evidence of the highest order" (cf. *Inst. Or.* 5.7.35).[2] It will be seen that Paul plays this trump card from the very first (3.1–5) so that he immediately has the Galatians on the spot. Unless they are prepared to renounce their own experiences of God, they must listen to Paul's arguments about what conclusions they should draw on the basis of those experiences.

Paul is not above appealing to the emotions in the λόγοι section of this document. We see this clearly in Gal. 4.13–20, where the appeal to pathos is clear (cf. also the final tug on the heart strings in Gal. 6.17b). In general such emotional appeals are more dependent on vivid imagery and emotive language than on logic. At the very outset of his arguments Paul is going to remind his

1. Kennedy, *New Testament Criticism*, p. 150.
2. Betz, *Galatians*, p. 130.

audience of his own 'pathos'-filled presentation of Christ crucified when he was first with the Galatians (3.1b).

Finally, in terms of rhetorical strategy, Paul shrewdly begins by using the inductive method, no doubt because he is dealing with a controversial subject (whether keeping the Law will benefit the Galatian Christians or not). As Cicero says "induction is a form of [indirect] argument which leads the person with whom one is arguing to give assent to certain undisputed facts; through this assent it wins his approval of a proposition about which there is doubt, because this resembles the facts to which he has assented" (*De Invent.* 1.31.51).[3] There are formally speaking three divisions to Paul's first argument (3.1–5, 3.6–14 and 3.15–18) or one could say that we have three arguments here, but the καθώς closely links 3.6 with 3.5, and so the faith of Abraham is closely linked to that of the Galatians.[4]

Argument I, Division 1: 3.1–5

THE APPEAL TO SPIRITUAL EXPERIENCE

Gal. 3.1 begins with a bang in the form of an exclamation followed by a series of questions (first apparently a real one and then a series of rhetorical

3. As one works through Betz's commentary on Galatians, it is notable how his argument for the forensic character of this document becomes less and less convincing once Gal. 1–2 is left behind, indeed it becomes nearly impossible by the time one reaches Gal. 5–6 and Betz has to admit that 'exhortations' were not the stock and trade of forensic rhetoric, but rather deliberative rhetoric. Betz admits the difficulty in analyzing the logic of the rhetoric of Gal. 3–4, but resorts to the rather weak argument that Paul's logic of defense and attack is not plain because he diversifies his argument with various interruptions using 'figures' or tropes of various sorts (dialogue, proverbs, examples, quotations); cf. Betz, *Galatians*, p. 128.

But all of these figures are quite natural in a deliberative piece of rhetoric where one is trying to persuade someone by various means to pursue a certain course of action in the future. One doesn't normally or naturally adorn a forensic speech by dialoguing with the judge or telling 'allegories'; rather one defends one's past actions and attacks one's opponents. It will be noted that the 'agitators' are decidedly in the background in Gal. 3–6, unless one engages in rather massive amounts of mirror-reading. What is in the foreground is the Galatians and their present and future beliefs and behavior. Paul's *modus operandi* in Gal. 3–6 is very appropriate if he is trying to persuade an assembly (ἐκκλησία) about what they must think and do through dialogue and discourse, through 'figures' and facts.

4. Chrysostom in commenting on Gal. 3.2 says that Paul uses concise arguments and a summary method of proof here.

ones).[5] The exclamation is 'O you foolish Galatians!' ᾿Ω with the vocative, as here, is very emphatic. The word for foolish here, ἀνόητοι, is found elsewhere in Paul at Rom. 1.14 where it is contrasted with being wise. The word should not be translated 'ignorant' for Paul is not castigating his converts for something they do not know. It is not lack of knowledge, or lack of intelligence but lack of moral or spiritual judgment (wisdom) that is at issue. But there may be more involved as well. In his helpful study of first-century cultural anthropology, B. Malina stresses that the 'fool' in first-century Mediterranean culture was not only the moral failure, but also one who lacks respect for or understanding of social boundaries, and so is capable of being guilty of crossing these boundaries from time to time and so bringing shame upon himself.[6] It is clear enough that Paul sees his converts as being about to or in danger of crossing such a social boundary by accepting circumcision and he sees it as his duty to persuade them and if need be shame them so they will not commit this social error. The issue here in part is violation of community boundaries, and in Paul's view to enter the community bounded by the Mosaic Law is to exit the community bounded by allegiance to Christ. In short, Paul sees apostasy looming on the horizon and he will marshal all his arsenal of arguments to prevent it. Underlying his arguments is a clearly sectarian view of the Christian community, which he does not see as simply a reform movement within early Judaism.

The first of Paul's questions is 'who has bewitched you?' Or perhaps more likely one should translate it 'who has cast the evil eye on you?' It is unlikely that Paul is suggesting that the Galatians have been beset by magicians or sorcerers,[7] but it may well be that Paul is referring to the ancient concept of the evil eye. The verb βασκαίνω is found only here in the NT and it is clear enough that originally it was used to refer to the casting of the evil eye on someone (cf. Plutarch, *Quaest. Conviv.* 680C-683B). Furthermore, Chrysostom,[8] commenting on this verse says that Paul means 'who has cast an envious eye on you?' and says the question implies "that their previous conduct had excited jealousy and that the present occurrence arose from the malignity of a demon, whose breath had blasted their prosperous

---

5. Though it is not uncommon for Paul to cloak his opponents in the garb of anonymity, in this case I would suggest that there are enough signals in the letter to suggest that Paul is not certain who precisely is bothering the Galatians. He apparently has some hearsay evidence that they are either from Jerusalem or they make much of Jerusalem, Jewish tradition, and in particular circumcision and Abraham. Cf. pp. 21ff. above.

6. B. Malina, *The New Testament World* (Louisville: Westminster/John Knox, 1993), p. 60.

7. But cf. Schlier, *Galaterbrief*, p. 119, who appears to think the Galatians have actually fallen under a spell.

8. The first major Christian commentator on Galatians who still lived in a culture much like that of Paul's day and understood the nuances of Paul's Greek.

estate".[9] Paul, he says, is referring to those who had looked enviously on the Galatians with evil intent and out of moral depravity.[10]

The idea of the evil eye is known in earlier Jewish literature (cf. Deut. 28.54; Sir. 14.6, 8; Wis. 4.12) and it is common in the papyri (cf., e.g., P. Oxy. II. 292[12] from about A.D. 25 cf. P. Oxy. 6.930[23]).[11] Basically the concept is that certain persons (or even certain animals or demons or gods) have the power of casting an evil spell on someone or causing something bad to happen to them by gazing at them. The eye was seen as the window of and to the heart, the channel through which one's innermost thoughts, desires, intentions could be conveyed.[12] This concept was closely connected with notions about envy, jealousy, greed, stinginess, as Plutarch makes clear (*Quaest. Conviv.* 680C-683B). In first-century society there was great fear of the evil eye, and there were various practices, such as curses, the use of amulets, spitting, that were thought to ward off or neutralize the effects of the evil eye. Especially children or the unwary were thought to be vulnerable to the malign influence of the evil eye. For example Virgil bemoans what has happened to some children saying "I do not know what eye is bewitching my tender lambs" (*Ecol.* 3.103). Broadly speaking the casting of the evil eye fell under the category of sorcery, and there was of course a widespread belief in these sorts of black arts in the Greco-Roman world.

Luther, in his exegesis of this text states clearly that Paul is speaking about the evil eye here (*LW* 27.244) and in fact says "Paul does not deny that witchcraft exists and is possible; for later on in the fifth chapter (vs. 20) he also lists sorcery, which is the same as witchcraft, among the works of the flesh. Thereby he proves that witchcraft and sorcery exist and are possible" (*LW* 26.190).[13] Several scholars have picked up on this idea and discussed at some length the characteristics of a 'witchcraft' society or sect and how this concept might apply to the Galatian situation.[14]

There are a variety of good insights that come from this sort of line of thinking, but at the end of the day one must ask whether Paul is literally suggesting that someone had cast a spell on the Galatians, or if Paul is using

9. One can point to the even earlier evidence in Ignatius *Rom.* 3.

10. This comment is made toward the end of his discussion of Gal. 3.1a.

11. See the discussion in Moulton and Milligan, *Vocabulary of the Greek Testament*, p. 106.

12. See J. K. Elliott, "Paul, Galatians, and the Evil Eye," *CurrTheoMiss* 17 (1990), pp. 262–73.

13. Lightfoot, *Galatians*, p. 133, is one of the more recent commentators who recognizes the cultural concepts Paul is dealing with here, and prefers the translation 'who has fascinated you' with the technical sense of fascinate, from Latin 'being in mind' (i.e., one who could cast the evil eye was called in the Middle Ages a 'fascinator').

14. J. Neyrey, *Paul in Other Words* (Louisville: Westminster/John Knox, 1990), pp. 181ff.; cf. J. H. Elliott, "Paul, Galatians, and the Evil Eye," pp. 262–73.

this well-known concept, but speaking metaphorically here. I would suggest the latter is the case. As a good rhetor Paul would know that there was real fear of the evil eye among his Galatian converts from paganism, and one of the best ways he could demonize the agitators would be to suggest that they cast the evil eye on his converts. The question is, would this implied accusation be deemed plausible by the Galatians?

Firstly, as Elliott points out, Gal. 4.15 in speaking of how the Galatians received Paul says, if we translate it literally, 'though my physical condition was a trial to you did not scorn me or spit'.[15] What Paul is talking about is that it was widely believed that sick persons or deformed persons were that way because of the evil eye having been cast upon them, and it was thought that even a victim of the evil eye might be a carrier of the bad influence. What this passage shows is that Paul and his audience were well familiar with this idea, and the implication is that if they did not see Paul in this negative light then, they certainly had no reason to see him that way now, unless they had become the victims of *someone else's* evil eye. Again this is an effective way to demonize one's opponent by implication. Is there other evidence in Galatians which might suggest Paul is drawing on the constellation of ideas surrounding the concept of the evil eye?

Let us consider what Paul suggests about the agitators' motives and conduct. It does not appear the agitators were envious of the Galatians' freedom, indeed they thought it shameful and immoral and wished to remedy the problem so that they could thereafter boast in 'the flesh' (and the circumcision) of the Galatians (Gal. 6.12–13). Paul also has earlier said that the agitators make much of the Galatians but to no good end and try to 'exclude' them (Gal. 4.17). What these passages suggest is that they were envious or jealous of Paul's success with the Galatians, and were trying by flattery and persuasion, which is to say by various forms of rhetoric (cf. Gal. 5.8) to win them over so they could boast about the Galatians and deprive Paul of his boast, and so shame Paul. They were greedy, wanting all the plaudits in Jerusalem for themselves (contrast Gal. 1.24; 2.9). Possibly the agitators were even some of the false brothers from Jerusalem and having failed to get their way in the Jerusalem meeting, having lost the honor challenge there, they plotted revenge, wanting to demonize Paul (cf. Gal. 4.16 'have I become your enemy?').

Paul plants the seed in the minds of his audience that they might be susceptible to the influence of the evil eye from these people when he speaks of his converts as little children who need protection (Gal. 4.19–20). The invoking of the curse on those preaching another Gospel in 1.8–9 also fits in with the typical sort of response to the influence of the evil eye. Notice too the repeated emphasis on eyes, first in 3.1 when Paul will talk about the

15. Elliott, p. 269.

Galatians having seen with their own eyes Christ portrayed, then again in 4.15 where Paul says they would have plucked out their eyes and given them to Paul.[16] All of this is effective rhetorical technique to cause suspicion about the agitators. It seems clear enough from texts like Gal. 5.8 that Paul believes he is dealing with people who are wielding an opposing persuasive campaign among his converts, not those who were actually practising sorcery. Paul never actually accuses his opponents of witchcraft, precisely because he does not believe he is dealing with magic, but rather with Judaizing, and so the discussion of witchcraft societies while interesting is not directly germane here, because Paul is using the evil eye language polemically and metaphorically.

That we are on the right track here is perhaps also shown by paying attention to the textual variant at 3.1 which provides a clue as to how some of the very earliest readers of this text understood it. C, D, K, L, P and a host of other manuscripts and versions and the Textus Receptus add τῇ ἀληθείᾳ μὴ πείθεσθαι which should probably be translated 'not to be persuaded of the truth'.[17] This variant understands that Paul is using 'bewitched' in a metaphorical sense here not to speak of an actual act of sorcery or even to conjure up the idea of the evil eye, but to castigate or demonize one's rhetorical opponents. Betz is probably right to say that the term 'bewitch' is used "to characterize opponents and their sophistic strategies" (cf. Demosthenes *De Corona* and 8.19; 16.19).[18] The point then is that the Galatians have been sucked in by the 'sophistical' rhetoric of the agitators and so have been led astray.[19] Paul must offer a different sort of rhetoric grounded in the facts of the Galatians' experience to get them back on course. Notice that even here Paul gives a charitable interpretation to the actions of the Galatians like he does with Barnabas, they had been *led* astray by others.

16. See Elliott, pp. 266ff.

17. It could be translated 'not to obey the truth', but this translation ignores the rhetorical context here. Cf. Longenecker, *Galatians*, p. 99.

18. It is interesting that Chrysostom knows this is a possible interpretation even though he mentions it only to reject the translation 'Who has been sophistical with you?'

19. On sophistic rhetoric, cf. my *Conflict and Community in Corinth*, pp. 46ff., and B. W. Winter, *Are Paul and Philo among the Sophists?* (Cambridge: Cambridge University Press, 1997). Sophistic rhetoric was far more ornamental in character than ordinary deliberative rhetoric and more interested in pleasing the audience and catering to their fears and predelictions. It is possible that the agitators had come to Galatia and had preyed on the Galatians' fears that they were not doing enough to be real Christians. For Greco-Roman persons ritual, ceremonies, festivals, sacrifices were of the essence of true religion and were seen as the proper manner to express one's piety. The agitators may have come to Galatia and discovered their audience was primed for the very sort of arguments they wanted to present.

In vs. **1b** Paul will remind his converts of how things were when he first presented the Gospel to them. Before their very eyes Jesus Christ was publicly portrayed or displayed as crucified. The verb προεγράφη means literally written beforehand, but unless Paul means he displayed drawings of the crucifixion of Christ,[20] this verb too is probably meant to be seen as metaphorical in character. The "crucified Christ was so vividly represented to the Galatians that they could see him on the cross with their own eyes".[21] In other words, Paul acted as an ancient orator when he came to Galatia and delivered his speech with such vivid language that the audience imagined that 'we were there when they crucified the Lord'.[22] It is quite possible that we should conclude that Paul used the technique of impersonation.[23] He portrayed Christ to them.[24] Paul may give us a clue to what he means at the very end of Galatians (6.17). There he speaks of bearing the marks of Christ on his own body. The following scenario is plausible: Paul, when he presented Christ in Galatia, was one who already had been persecuted and in his presentation in fact displayed some of his wounds he suffered for the cause of Christ, wounds he referred to as suffering with Christ or filling up the suffering of Christ or part of his being crucified with Christ, to appeal to the emotions of his audience.[25] It is clear enough from passages like Gal. 4.13–20 that Paul was not reticent to use rhetorical techniques that could stir the deeper emotions. One final remark about this verse is in order. Once again as at 2.19 the verb 'crucified' is in the perfect, indicating a past fact that has enduring influence and effects. It is perhaps appropriate, before our discussion goes any further to ask what sort of image of the Galatian community is conveyed by Paul's remarks here and elsewhere in this letter.

Excursus: The Construction of a Community ——————————

As I have already had occasion to say, the signals we get from Galatians suggest that Paul is addressing a group of neophytes, those who are rather recent converts to the Christian faith and are not yet fully socialized or clear on the nature and limits of

---

20. See Quintilian *Inst. Or.* 6.1.32, though he thinks bringing such gruesome pictures into the courtroom is going too far.

21. Dunn, *Galatians*, p. 152 and cf. Betz, *Galatians*, p. 131.

22. See Betz, *Galatians*, p. 131.

23. On which cf. pp. 25ff. above.

24. Calvin in commenting on 3.1 not surprisingly thinks that Paul is simply referring to his teaching (i.e., his words) which conveyed the living image of Christ.

25. If this letter is addressed to the congregations formed on the first missionary journey through south Galatia, then it may be germane to consider what is said at Acts 13.50; 14.5, 19. Could Paul be referring to his near death experience when he was stoned in Lystra, but was seen alive again by the Lystrans thereafter (14.21)?

their new identity. This impression of newness comes not merely because Paul speaks of the Galatians in 1.6 as so quickly after their conversions contemplating a change in direction, but because there is almost no evidence whatsoever of any sort of social network or leadership structure or web of power set up in these Galatian churches to which Paul could appeal. Gal. 6.6 is perhaps the sole hint that there may have been some established teachers in Galatia, but on the whole, Paul has neither local leaders nor co-workers to appeal to, to help him deal with the problems arising because of the agitators.[26] Rather he must appeal directly to the Galatian converts to act, even in so difficult a matter as how to handle the agitators (4.30).

Furthermore, the repeated references to the Spirit and the guidance of the Spirit coupled with the warning against various sorts of behavior thought to be typical of pagans suggest we have a community that is pneumatic in character and has not yet developed anything remotely like offices or institutions or set practices. Being Gentiles, this lack of structure and clearly defined roles and tasks (or 'grid' see below) made them vulnerable to the appeal of the agitators because the latter could give the Galatians a much clearer sense of identity and social boundaries by the suggestion that they should now follow the Mosaic law. Greco-Roman persons in general saw ritual and regularized symbolic actions as the heart of religion, and so they were probably doubly vulnerable at this stage in their development.

The notion of conversion if separated in time or distinguished from some kind of ritual initiation might well be confusing for them, and it seems clear enough from Gal. 3 that Paul is arguing that conversion, not some kind of ritual initiation is what made them Christians and set them apart for God. Gal. 3.27 is the sole reference to a ritual that Paul performed on behalf of the Galatians, and of course this ritual was not a repeatable one, but rather symbolized getting into Christ, something that had already been actualized when they received the Spirit through the hearing of faith. It is quite surprising that we hear little or nothing in this letter about what might be going on in Galatian worship (contrast 1 Cor. 11–14). One gets the impression that Paul had not offered the Galatians sufficient ongoing liturgical duties that they could regularly perform, and the agitators had taken advantage of this situation.

Paul views the state of his converts as one of spiritual immaturity. They are rather easily led astray, need to be reminded about some of the basics of the truth of the Gospel, and have admitted into their community those who are introducing pollutants or poisons into the body there (cf. Gal. 5.9; 6.7–8). If this poison and its source is not expelled from the community they will have been running in vain. Worse still, Paul sees them potentially going in a negative direction towards apostasy, by which he means denying the efficacy of Christ's death through the assumption of the Mosaic requirements substituting slavery and stratification and social status for freedom and equality in grace.

Neyrey points out that if one simply examines the language Paul uses, Galatians bristles with the discussion of rivalry, competition, hypocrisy, jealousy, boasting,

---

26. See rightly Neyrey, *Paul in Other Words*, p. 199: "In the churches in Galatia there appears to be a vaccuum of leadership . . . there is apparently no mechanism in Galatia to sort out the competing claims of Paul or his opponents."

society. Rather there was an attempt to fit into it, at least into larger Jewish society. (2) Routinized symbolic action which constantly reaffirmed the identity of the group was the order of the day. Some of the Galatians may have already accepted or were inclined to accept this part of the agitators' agenda to reconstruct the communities in Galatia in a Jewish mold. This is what Paul is complaining about in Gal. 4.10 – you are observing special days, months, seasons, and years. (3) There were group oriented goals of action, but they were centered not just on the local group, but on the larger group or the mother community in Jerusalem led by the pillars, and the even larger community of the 'children of Abraham' in general. They saw themselves as always and already part of the Israel of God, a larger entity and probably they believed this included non-Christian Jews. It was their agenda to make sure that all Christian Gentiles also became full proselytes into this larger society or community. (4) Unlike the case of the Galatians themselves, the agitators had a very elaborated symbolic universe and symbol system which they were rapidly teaching to the Galatians. It was closely tied to the routinized symbolic actions. In short, they were trying to construct a Quadrant C group or type of community in Galatia.

Again Atkins is helpful in summing things up.

> The social environment of Quadrant C is dominated by the large group [in this case not just the Jerusalem Church, but perhaps also Jerusalem centered Judaism writ large]. The group justifies both its own existence and the strong classifications of individuals in roles in the group . . . Individuals understand their place and purpose in society in terms of the greater good of society [e.g., The Galatians should conform so the Jerusalem Jewish Christians, or the agitators or both, won't be persecuted] . . . Specific tasks are reserved for special classes of participants. These are not achieved roles, but are ascribed to categories of status [e.g., the pillars, those of repute]. The stability for the individual is the security of knowing his or her place within the social system and of having a purpose in the cosmos."[28]

It is also crucial to note that a Quadrant-C group uses nature to justify actions. One does not go against 'nature'. Such a group, with a male-only initiation rite, was almost inevitably going to be a male dominated group, which did not handle pneumatism and other pressures toward a more egalitarian model of society well. There were more asymmetric than symmetric relationships in such a group and they could be based on ethnic, social, or gender factors or all three. A group with high grid is a group which has more degrees of social control through classification by sex, race, etc. and so more degree of role specification.

What is described above is two dueling models of community, that have more to disagee about than to agree about at the level of social existence. One is attempting to be a sect, the other a movement or party within a larger society. In such a situation a clash was inevitable.

---

28. Atkins, p. 71.

GROUP-GRID COMMUNITY MODEL

QUADRANT A	QUADRANT B
Society and nature separate, which is negatively evaluated	Society part of nature, which is positively evaluated
Routinized symbolic action	Routinized symbolic action
Ego-oriented goals of action	Group-oriented goals of action
Unelaborated symbolic system	Elaborated symbolic system

QUADRANT C	QUADRANT D
Society and nature separate, which is positively evaluated.	Society part of nature, which is negatively evaluated.
Personalized symbolic action	Personalized symbolic action
Ego-oriented goals of action	Group-oriented goals of action
Elaborated symbolic system	Unelaborated symbolic system

The vertical line in the above model represents the 'grid' with increasing stratification and individuation the higher up the line one goes. The horizontal line represents the 'group' with the progression from weak to strong group moving from left to right. Both Paul and the agitators were working toward a strong group concept, though with significant differences.[29]

While 3.1 may be a rhetorical question, though I doubt it, the questions we find in **3.2** through to 3.5 are certainly rhetorical. Notice that Paul's approach in 3.2 is indirect. He does not make an observation or a charge, he asks a rhetorical question. Paul, of course, knows the answer to the question but he wishes to lead his converts through a process of thinking that leads them to certain definite conclusions about what they are contemplating doing. That Paul does not say 'I wish to learn from *some* of you' suggests that he considers the problem rather widespread.

The first question reads literally 'From works of the Law did you receive the Spirit or from hearing of faith?' Notice the emphasis put on 'works of the Law' by placing it first in the sentence.[30] This is the bone of contention and the cause for writing this letter.

The verb 'received' is in the aorist indicating a definite event in the past. Paul is referring to what happened to the Galatians at the point of their conversions. As Dunn points out, the phrase about receiving the Spirit is something close to a technical phrase for early Christians when they wanted to talk about conversion (cf. Rom. 8.15; 1 Cor. 2.12; 2 Cor. 11.4; Gal. 3.14; Jn.

---

29. See the discussion in Atkins, *Egalitarian Community*, pp. 70ff.
30. On the meaning of this phrase cf. pp. 175ff. above.

7.39; Acts 2.38; 10.47; 19.2). "It focuses the fact that for Paul and the first Christians this was the decisive and determinative element in the event or process of conversion and initiation; hence the nearest thing to a definition of 'Christian' in the NT, in Rom. 8.9 makes possession of the Spirit the *sine qua non*. Moreover it cannot really be understood in other than experiential terms (as though 'receiving the Spirit' was a matter of purely rational conviction, or simply a deduction to be drawn from the fact of their having been baptized). The appeal is clearly to an event which Paul could expect them vividly to remember . . ."[31] G. D. Fee emphasizes that Paul is referring to what he deems to be unimpeachable evidence, which suggest he is surely referring to some dynamic experiences of the Spirit in Galatia that could have been neither forgotten nor denied.[32] The point of this appeal is of course that Paul takes the reception of the Spirit as irrefutable evidence that God had accepted these Gentiles, and had accepted them without their having to submit to the Law of Moses and do 'works of the Law'.

It is hard to overestimate the importance of the appeal to the 'Spirit' for Paul in this letter. As D. J. Lull has noted we find this appeal in interrogatives (3.1–5), in arguments from Scripture and tradition (3.6–14; 4.1–7, 21–31), and in paraenesis (5.1–6.10), which is to say that Paul uses it in each of the rhetorical forms of material he draws upon in Gal. 3.1–6.10.[33] Notice that Paul does not mention the Spirit before he begins the argument or proof section of the letter, and thereafter it becomes a crucial part of the discussion until the rhetorical portion of this document is complete and Paul returns to epistolary conventions (cf. 6.11, 18). In other words, Paul's discourse on the Spirit is not just a matter of Paul using traditional language or formulae. The Spirit is at the heart of matter and so plays a vital role in his acts of persuasion. A measure of the importance the appeal to the Spirit has for Paul is shown by what Paul sets the Spirit over against: (1) 'works of the Law' as here in 3.2; or (2) just 'the Law' as in 4.5–6 and 5.18; or (3) 'desires of the flesh' as in 5.16–17, 24–25 or (4) 'works of the flesh' as in 5.19–23 or finally (5) just 'flesh' (cf. 3.3 and 6.8).[34] What (1) and (4) have in common is that they are dealing with merely human actions rather than divine ones. As Ziesler puts it: "For Paul, the indisputable fact that they have the Spirit is proof that they are God's people [cf. Ezek. 36.22–27], and his argument is that the Law had nothing to do with it. It therefore cannot be a necessary condition for being the people of God."[35]

31. Dunn, *Galatians*, pp. 152–53.
32. See G. D. Fee, *God's Empowering Presence. The Holy Spirit in the Letters of Paul* (Peabody: Hendrickson, 1994), pp. 384ff.
33. D. J. Lull, *The Spirit in Galatia* (Chico: Scholars Press, 1980), p. 25.
34. Lull, p. 27.
35. Ziesler, *Galatians*, p. 32.

Lull has helpfully summed up matters as follows:

> The letter to the Galatians itself gives evidence that Paul's use of the term πνεῦμα
> was historically conditioned by the fact that the Spirit was a primary datum of
> experience for the Galatians, and not simply by the polemic against Jewish-Christian
> nomists: Paul mentions the problem with Jewish-Christian nomists in Jerusalem
> (2.1–10) and Antioch (2.11–14) without ever mentioning the Spirit . . . Paul's
> statements about the Spirit serve to remind the Galatians that they were 'eye-
> witnesses' that salvation and freedom came from the crucified Christ and his
> Spirit; for they had received the Spirit, the 'highest evidence', from Paul's gospel.
> The Spirit, therefore, proves Paul's gospel and Galatian Christianity had no need of
> the law of Moses, since they had received the Spirit from Paul's message about the
> crucified Christ before they had opportunity to perform any of the rites of the law of
> Moses.[36]

The question remains about the proper translation of the final phrase in 3.2 – ἐξ ἀκοῆς πίστεως. It could be rendered in one of four or five ways: (1) from hearing with faith; (2) from hearing, that is from faith; (3) from hearing the faith; (4) from the message that results in believing; (5) from the message about the faith.[37] If one is looking for other Pauline phrases that appear at least on the surface to say the same thing as this phrase Rom. 10.17 immediately comes to mind where Paul speaks of ἡ πίστις ἐξ ἀκοῆς. There the context (cf. 10.17b) favors the translation 'faith comes by or from hearing', as Paul is speaking about a chain of events – preaching the word about Christ is followed by hearing and proper hearing leads to believing what has been heard. That this conclusion is correct is reinforced by what follows in 10.18 where Paul quotes Is. 29.10 – 'Have they not heard?' and also 10.14 where it is asked 'How are they to hear without someone to proclaim?' In other words, while the translation of ἀκοῆς here as 'what is heard' (i.e., 'faith comes from what is heard' [the message]) is possible, the context suggests it is less likely than the translation we have suggested. The question is, however, does the slightly different phrase in Gal. 3.2 (ἀκοῆς πίστεως) have the same nuances as the phrase in Rom. 10.17?

In Gal. 3.2 though the contrast here is between faith and Law and not between hearing and doing, it should be noted that the contrast of importance here is between observing the Law that is doing works of the Law[38] and something, and that something is most naturally seen not as 'what is heard' but another human activity of the Galatians, namely 'hearing'.[39] Secondly, as Fung points out, usually in Paul's letter the preposition ἐκ is used to denote a

---

36. Lull, pp. 39–41.
37. See the discussion in R. B. Hays, *The Faith of Jesus Christ* (Chico: Scholars Press, 1983), pp. 143ff.
38. On the meaning of this cf. pp. 175ff.
39. See rightly Lightfoot, *Galatians*, p. 135.

direct not a remote causal relationship.[40] The Gospel message is not the *direct* cause of the Galatians receiving the Spirit, rather hearing and believing the Gospel is. Thirdly, the active sense 'hearing' is supported by the larger context for as the καθώς suggests at the beginning of 3.6, Paul intends to draw a comparison between what was true of Abraham and what is true of the Galatians. Abraham is said to be justified not by a message about faith or even a message which produces faith, but rather by faith. Verse 14 must be compared to vs. 5 as part of an ongoing single argument.[41] S. K. Williams' critique of R. B. Hays' view on this phrase is telling.[42] Ἀκοή as a noun never seems to lose its primary passive sense and focuses on the receiving or appropriating action rather than on the origin of something (i.e., what has been heard). It is no argument to say that we must translate this word 'message' because it is ridiculous to think that Paul believes that God supplies the Spirit or works miracles on the basis of some human action such as hearing. This overlooks that even if one translates the word message, preaching the Gospel is no less a human action than hearing it. In short God does depend in either case on a human activity for miracles to happen or the Spirit to be received.[43]

In conclusion, Williams may also be right that we should see a sort of epexegetical sense to this phrase ('hearing' that is 'faith'), for faith is a kind of hearing and receiving of what God is giving.[44] If this is correct, then there is a very close parallel to what follows in 3.6ff. Just as Abraham was justified by responding in faith, so the Galatians received the Spirit the same way – by faithful hearing or the 'hearing' that is more than listening but in fact believing and heeding (cf. Rom. 1.5) the word spoken (cf. 1 Kngs. 22.19–23; Is. 6; Jerm. 1.11–16; Ezek. 1; Amos 7.1–9; 8.1–3; 9.1–4). Jesus himself appears to have emphasized this sort of believing hearing – 'let the one who has ears, hear' (Mk. 4.9 and passim).[45] A second alternative would be simply to translate the phrase as is often done 'hearing with faith'.

Verse **3** begins with οὕτως which points to what follows, a series of rhetorical questions. Notice the use of invective again, or παρρησία (free speech), with Paul calling his converts fools once more.[46] That Paul feels free

---

40. Fung, *Galatians*, p. 132.

41. Not *pace* Betz, *Galatians*, pp. 137ff. Two separate arguments.

42. Cf. Hays, *The Faith*, pp. 143–50 to S. K. Williams, "The Hearing of Faith: ΑΚΟΗ ΠΙΣΤΕΩΣ in Galatians 3," *NTS* 35 (1989), pp. 82–93.

43. See Williams, pp. 86ff. rebutting Hays, pp. 147ff.

44. Williams, p. 90.

45. On hearing meaning obeying cf. Ex. 6.12, 15.26; Deut. 4.30; 27.10; Josh. 1.18; Is. 1.19.

46. The Cynics were especially known for their 'free speech', but this was also characteristic of a certain kind of blunt and direct rhetoric as well. Cf. Betz, *Galatians*, p. 133.

to address the Galatians this way may suggest the strength of their relationship, as Paul does not seem to assume that this sort of address will alienate his converts, but rather give them a wake-up call. Paul wants to know if they are going to be so spiritually undiscerning that having begun[47] with the Spirit, they now are going to bring their Christian life to completion with the flesh. These two verbs occur together elsewhere in Paul (2 Cor. 8.6; Phil. 1.6), and in each case, the reference is to the beginning and end or completion of a process. For this reason, it is probably a mistake to bring into the discussion extraneous notions about 'being made perfect'. This brings up a crucial point. Paul's subject in this letter is not how one gets into the Christian fold, nor how one stays in the Christian fold, but how one goes on with one's Christian life until either the Lord returns or the person dies. The Galatians are thinking of adding obedience to the Law to faith in Christ. In Paul's view this is changing horses in the middle of the stream. Paul uses the word 'flesh' here no doubt because he is thinking of the entrance ritual for the Mosaic covenant, circumcision.[48] Circumcision was sometimes called 'the covenant in the flesh' (Gen. 17.13; Sir. 44.20). Both 'flesh' and 'Spirit' seem to be used here in the instrumental sense.

The idea being critiqued here could be rather easily defended by Jewish Christians, even using the example of Abraham as is shown by Jam. 2.22 which speaks of Abraham's faith being made perfect by works, and the author would presumably include circumcision among those works since Genesis does go on to refer to Abraham's submission to circumcision.[49] But Paul will having nothing to do with the notion that Christians ought to add obedience to the Mosaic Law to faith in Christ. "Christian life is one that starts, is maintained, and comes to culmination only through dependence on the activity of God's Spirit",[50] not by relying on 'works of the Law' to complete one's Christian life. Notice that ἐπιτελεῖσθε is in the present continual tense. This is the issue Paul must primarily discourse on in what follows, how they will go on in the present and into the future as Christians, not how they began.

Verse 4 brings us to yet another controversy – how to translate ἐπάθετε. Does it mean 'suffered' or does it have a more general sense 'experienced'? On the one hand it might seem obvious that the verb ought to be translated 'suffered' here. After all, always in the LXX and also always elsewhere in the NT

---

47. The aorist inceptive is used here referring again to conversion, the beginning of the Galatians' Christian lives.

48. It is also possible that Paul means to introduce a pejorative note into the discussion as well.

49. See J. Bligh, *Galatians in Greek* (Detroit: University of Detroit Press, 1966), p. 127. I also think that Bligh is probably right that we hear an echo of the controversy being debated in Galatians at Heb. 7.19 – 'for the Law made nothing perfect'.

50. Longenecker, *Galatians*, p. 104.

some forty-one times, this verb is always used in an unfavorable sense, meaning 'suffered' (cf., e.g., Lk. 22.15; 24.46; Acts 1.3; 3.18; 17.3; 1 Cor 12.26; Heb. 2.18; 1 Pet. 2.20). Yet this is not the only thing this verb can mean, it can indeed be used in a positive sense (cf. Josephus *Ant.* 3.15). Furthermore, as Betz points out, the verbal pair μαθεῖν/παθεῖν has a long history in Greek thought, and we do find the former verb in 3.2 meaning to learn and in such a tandem the latter verb normally means 'to experience'.[51] However, in the one text in the NT where we find this tandem more closely joined, Heb. 5.8, πάσχω surely means suffered. Thus it is not certain how we should translate the verb here, but the context certainly favors the translation 'experienced' with reference to the spiritual experiences of the Galatians.[52] Nowhere else in Galatians do we hear about these converts suffering (6.12 refers to the 'agitators' being persecuted, not the Galatians). The second half of this verse suggests that Paul strongly hopes they have not experienced so much for nothing. As Lightfoot says "the Apostle hopes better things of his converts. Εἴ γε leaves a loophole for doubt, and καὶ widens this implying an unwillingness to believe on the part of the speaker."[53]

The first division of this argument is brought to a closure in vs. 5, as the οὖν, which is resumptive, suggests. Verse 5 is a restatement of the one question that Paul initially asked in vs. 2. The restatement, however, places stronger emphasis on the source of the Spirit – it came to the Galatians from the One who so bountifully supplies all good things. The verb here probably does not mean merely 'gives' but rather 'bountifully supplies'.[54] One may wish to compare Phil. 1.19, but as Lightfoot says the compound form of this verb which we find here especially conveys the notion of liberality (cf. 2 Pet. 1.5). This indicates that the Galatians had, in Paul's view, some remarkable spiritual experiences when they were converted, and presumably vs. 4 suggests that such experiences continued beyond conversion. These experiences would presumably include the manifestation of various spiritual gifts (ecstatic prayer? – cf. Gal. 4.6), and perhaps visions as well. Also mentioned are miracles ('works of powers' – the plural indicating miracles),[55] and these presumably continued well beyond the time of the Galatians' conversions,[56] as the present tense of the participles 'supplies' and 'works'

---

51. Betz, *Galatians*, p. 134.
52. See rightly Fee, *God's Empowering Presence*, p. 387 n. 69.
53. Lightfoot, *Galatians*, p. 135.
54. See Lightfoot, *Galatians*, p. 136.
55. See Dunn, *Galatians*, p. 158.
56. Bligh, *Galatians*, p. 129 wishes to insist that since vs. 5 is resumptive of vs. 2 that Paul must be referring only to what happened at conversion. But it will be seen that vs. 5 resumes, and goes beyond what vs. 2 says, and in any case 'supplying' is not in the aorist here but rather in the present.

suggests. Paul does not mention miracles very often in his letters, but there are sufficient references to let us know that the work of the Spirit from time to time took this form in Paul's churches (cf. Rom. 15.19; 2 Cor. 12.12). There is no indication that these miracles were all performed by Paul and/or his co-workers when he was present with the Galatians. Paul concludes this first division of his first argument by reminding his converts of the obvious – these things did not occur through works of the Law but rather from hearing and believing the Gospel message.

Argument I, Division 2: 3.6–14

THE APPEAL TO SCRIPTURE

Quintilian, in his discussion of the use of παραδείγματα or examples in the proof section of a rhetorical speech, reminds us that this is an inductive method of persuasion (*Inst. Or.* 5.11.2–3). He associates it with "that which takes the form of a question in dialogue", that is, he associates it with the so-called diatribe style, which some have seen as in evidence in 3.1–5. This style of argument involves dialogue with an interlocutor not immediately present. Often it proceeds to a conclusion on the basis of a series of questions (frequently rhetorical ones), usually moving from one which involves a thought the audience will readily assent to, to questions that involve ideas the audience will agree to only when they have seen that the logic of assenting to the former questions leads to assent on the latter ones as well.

The most important sort of proof from analogy is said to be the proof from example, especially historical example (*Inst. Or.* 5.11.6–8), and this is the way our inductive argument proceeds in 3.6ff., appealing to the example of the greatest of all the patriarchs and 'father' of Israel – Abraham. As Mitchell reminds us, the appeal to examples is especially appropriate in deliberative rhetoric, though it is not unknown in forensic rhetoric.[57] Aristotle puts it this way "examples are most suitable for deliberative speakers, for it is by examination of the past that we divine and judge the future" (*Rhet.* 1.9.40). It was the way of deliberative rhetors to put forward a person whom the audience respects or admires as the example, on the assumption that one seeks to become like what one admires (cf. Aristotle *Rhet.* 1.6.29 – "all things that those whom they admire [they] deliberately choose to do").

57. Mitchell, *Rhetoric of Reconciliation*, p. 42.

Deliberative examples are used to show that some course of action will be advantageous and beneficial if pursued bringing concord and peace and unity, or if the audience is considering doing something the speaker wishes to warn them against, that the track they are pursuing is disadvantageous, ruinous, or unprofitable. Paul uses Abraham to make the positive point that the Galatians already have and will continue to receive the divine benefits they need on the basis of faith, just as Abraham did. Pursuing the Law at this point would be not only unnecessary but positively foolish and disadvantageous. Thus while Abraham is used largely to make the positive point, Paul is also cognizant that he must make the negative point about pursuing the Law along the way as well. In Paul's view faith in Christ unites all sorts of people of various races, a variety of social statuses and both genders (Gal. 3.28), and by contrast pursuing the Law is a divisive approach to Christian living, as the example of the incident at Antioch showed, causing factions and turmoil especially among Gentile converts.

It is quite clear that Paul is using Abraham here in the prescribed manner to make the sort of points deliberative rhetoric wishes to make. Paul is not defending his or the Galatians' past, but rather drawing on their own experience and that of Abraham to guide his converts about how they should live now and in the future. As such, what we find in Gal. 3–4 prepares us quite nicely for the material in Gal. 4–6 where Paul will argue more directly about the sort of conduct the Galatians should be pursuing, but even the arguments in Gal. 3–4 have a paraenetic aim.

Paul has not changed his mode of argument here (i.e., it is still inductive), and in fact he sees 3.6ff. as a continuation of the argument begun in 3.1–5. This is shown by the fact that 3.6 begins with the word καθώς, which should be translated 'just as'. Despite the argument of Betz,[58] this is not an introductory formula such as 'as it is written'.[59] In the first place, Paul nowhere uses just the word καθώς to express such an idea, and in the second one must ask the question of whether vss. 6–7 are two parts of one sentence or two separate sentences. Against the notion that 3.6 is the protasis and 3.7 the apodosis of one sentence is the fact that elsewhere in Galatians where ἄρα introduces the apodosis of a sentence, the protasis is an 'if' clause, unlike here (cf. Gal. 2.21; 3.29; 5.11). This means that we should probably treat 3.6 and 3.7 as two separate sentences, which in turn means that the καθώς does not refer forward, but rather backward being conceptually dependent on

58. Betz, *Galatians*, p. 140 n. 13.

59. Several scribes also made this mistake, adding γέγραπται to καθώς here (cf. G and Ambrosiaster), but this is clearly not the original reading here. It is interesting to note that at Qumran we never find the sort of abbreviated citation formula Betz assumes we have here. Cf. J. Fitzmyer, "The Use of Explicit Old Testament Quotations in Qumran Literature and in the New Testament," *NTS* 7 (1961), pp. 297–333.

vs. 5.[60] In short, Paul will compare the faith of the Galatians and what they received when they believed, to the faith of Abraham and what he received when he believed.[61]

Perhaps no greater paradigm could have been appealed to because not only was Abraham seen as the font of the people of God, but he was also widely regarded as the greatest example of faith in the OT. If the Galatians' experience of grace and faith could be said to be analogous to that of Abraham, the question would then become – What more does one need to be part of the people of God? In fact, Paul will not merely compare these two acts of faith, he will closely link them using some interesting exegesis of Genesis and some equally remarkable hermeneutical moves thereafter, both of which have led to no end of controversy among scholars on the legitimacy of the way Paul handles the OT.[62]

T. L. Donaldson has complained that Gal. 3.6–14 is "a maze of laboured exegesis, puzzling illustration, and cryptic theological shorthand"[63] while C. K. Barrett has urged that the only way to make sense of why Paul chooses and uses the texts that he does here is because the agitators were already using at least some of them to bolster their case and so Paul must take up these texts and give them a different interpretation.[64] I am not at all sure that either of these two scholars is entirely right. The former comment comes out of the frustration of trying to evaluate Paul's handling of Scripture upon the basis of modern canons of historical critical exegesis. But surely Paul must be interpreted on the basis of the methods and approaches available in his own day, and when one does this his argument makes a great deal more sense. For example, Abraham is not a puzzling example at all when one considers both how examples function in deliberative rhetoric, and how Abraham was repeatedly used as an example in earlier Jewish literature, for example in Sir. 44.19–21 (cf. 1 Macc. 2.52). Furthermore, it is not at all clear to me that Paul knew the precise arguments of the agitators in Galatia. Since they were arguing for circumcision one would expect that they would have argued on the basis

60. See rightly, S. K. Williams, "Justification and the Spirit in Galatians," *JSNT* 29 (1987), pp. 91–100, here p. 93.

61. Cf. Lightfoot, *Galatians*, p. 136: "The answer to the question asked in the former verse is assumed, 'Surely of faith: and so it was with Abraham.'" Notice that various versions have recognized that Paul is citing a example here using καθὼς – cf. JB, NEB, NIV, NRSV.

62. It is interesting that Marcion, no doubt because of his allergic reaction to the OT, in his recension of this Pauline letter leaves out vss. 6–9, finding it unseemly to rely on OT examples to make one's point. See Tertullian *Adv. Marc.* 5.3.

63. T. L. Donaldson, "The 'Curse of the Law' and the Inclusion of the Gentiles: Galatians 3.13–14," *NTS* 32 (1986), pp. 94–112, here p. 94.

64. Barrett, "The Allegory of Sarah and Hagar," in *Essays on Paul* (Philadelphia: Westminster, 1982), pp. 154–70.

of texts like Gen. 17.9–14 or Lev. 12.3 but Paul is completely silent on texts like these that mention circumcision. It is far more likely that Paul has chosen texts to suit his own arguments about faith and blessing and righteousness on the one hand and Law and curse on the other. Perhaps he had a general knowledge that the agitators were making much of Abraham and Mount Sinai and Jerusalem. Since it is true to say that apart from Gal. 4.21–30 no other portion of Galatians is so Scripture laden as Gal. 3.6–14 is,[65] something needs to be said at this point in more detail about Paul's handling of Scripture.

Excursus: Paul the Exegete and Allegorizer

It is quite impossible in a brief excursus to discuss even the major lines along which Paul uses the Hebrew Scriptures. We must settle for the more modest goal of explaining some of the ways he uses it here in Galatians while referring to the larger context for discussing these matters. Bound up in this question is of course Paul's view of the Law which we will reserve for a later discussion in this study.[66]

The question of Paul's view of the Scripture becomes especially urgent when one discovers that Paul can simply omit any dealing with texts from the Abraham narratives which would seem to call his conclusions about the Law into question. For example, entirely missing is any discussion of Gen. 17.9–14 where membership in the family of Abraham is connected to circumcision, nor does Paul deal with direct commands like Lev. 12.3 where circumcision is required of God's people. This is all the more surprising since if the agitators were arguing for the circumcision of the Galatians and their submission to the Mosaic Law, it seems likely they would have appealed to such texts. To this E. P. Sanders adds the complaint that Paul "can also find two different righteousnesses in Scripture and say that one of them (by implication, not the other) saves (Rom. 10.4–10). He also manages to have the Law condemn those who are under it (Gal. 3.10, quoting Deut. 27.26),"[67] a surprising move since the Deuteronomy text in question would seem to be arguing for a curse on those who *don't* observe the Law. In short, it is not difficult to see why some modern scholars have thrown up their hands and concluded that Paul's handling of Scripture is arbitrary, and his views on the Law confused, inconsistent, and involving contradictions.[68] Further complicating the matter is the fact that Paul can use the term νόμος to mean simply Scripture (cf. Rom. 3.19; 7.1; 1 Cor. 14.21), making a rather neat division

---

65. In vs. 6 Paul quotes Gen. 15.6; in vs. 8 he quotes Gen. 12.3; in vs. 10 we hear from Deut. 27.26; in vs. 11 from Hab. 2.4, in vs. 12 we have Lev. 18.5, in vs. 13 we find Deut. 21.23. There are other partial citations or merged quotations as well, not to mention allusions. Cf. Matera, *Galatians*, p. 121.

66. See pp. 341ff. below.

67. E. P. Sanders, *Paul, the Law, and the Jewish People* (Minnesota: Fortress, 1983), pp. 160–61.

68. See, e.g., H. Räisänen, *Paul and the Law* (Tübingen: Mohr, 1983).

between Paul's positive evaluation of Scripture apart from the Mosaic Law and his negative evaluation of the Law more than a little difficult.[69] How can Paul cite the Law within the Scriptures as an authority to strengthen his argument and make his case, when he will also say that the Law has had its day, and that day is done?

Our particular concern here is to discuss how Paul uses Scripture, including the Law, but it is only possible to focus on this if one first says something about how Paul *views* Scripture, namely he views *all* of it as God's Word. He is even happy to cite a portion of the so-called ritual or ceremonial Law to make a point that he thinks God wants to make to Paul's converts (cf. 1 Cor. 9.8–9). Paul cites this particular law as of divine authority, though he uses this citation to make a point about human beings rather than oxen, presumably because he assumes that the principle underlying this law applies equally to humans. There is no evidence that he makes some sort of hermeneutical distinction between the ritual Law and the moral Law in Scripture, when he wishes to use the Hebrew Scriptures to reinforce an argument or persuade his Christian converts.

Saying that Paul sees all the Hebrew Scriptures as God's divine Word, however, fails to explain much of why he uses the Scriptures the *way* he does. It is more helpful to recognize that Paul reads the Scriptures in the light of certain central convictions: (1) "he and his readers are those upon whom the ends of the ages have come. They are God's eschatological people who, in receiving the grace of God through Jesus Christ, become a living sign, a privileged clue to the meaning of God's word in Scripture";[70] (2) because of this realized eschatology, Paul believes it is crucial to read the OT in the light of where God's people *now* are in the progression of salvation history, namely they are beyond the era when God's people were under the Law, and are now to be living in Christ. (3) If the eschatological age has come, it follows that now one can and should go back and look for pre-figurements and types and prophecies and promises of what was to come in the Scriptural record of all previous ages of the history of Israel. This also implies that all of that which has come before is preliminary, not final. Even the revelation which came before was partial not final and pointed beyond itself; (4) the Law, and indeed all of the Hebrew Scriptures are to be read not just ecclesiologically but also and perhaps primarily Christologically. Though previously Paul had read all of life through the lens of the Law, now he reads it all from the viewpoint of his faith in the eschatological Christ.[71] If one does not subscribe to these central convictions, it is only to be expected that one will not find Paul's Christological or ecclesiological or typological or allegorical handlings of Scripture very convincing.

69. Enhancing this problem is the fact that Paul is quite happy to say that the Mosaic Law itself is by no means sin or evil (Rom. 7.7), but rather is holy, just and good (7.12).

70. R. B. Hays, *Echoes of Scripture in the Letters of Paul* (New Haven: Yale University Press, 1989), p. 121.

71. See rightly, Sanders, *Paul, the Law*, p. 162 who rightly points to the fact that behind Paul's reading of Scripture lies certain great convictions which determined his career: "God has appointed Christ for the salvation of the world, for the salvation of all without distinction. God always intended this – he proclaimed it in advance to Abraham – and his will is uniform and stated in Holy Writ. That salvation is being accomplished now, in the last days, with himself, Paul, unworthy though he is, as the apostle whose task is to bring in the Gentiles."

Bearing these things in mind we can say more about Paul's exegetical and hermeneutical techniques.

It is a commonplace of scholarly treatments of Paul's handling of Scripture to say that Paul "employed standard techniques of Scriptural exegesis, occasionally even using some of the rules of 'rabbinic' hermeneutics".[72] This statement of course involves a certain amount of anachronism, for it assumes that Paul's efforts can and should be compared to the mostly later material found in the Talmuds and Mishnah. I would suggest it would be more helpful to compare Paul's techniques to those found for instance in the Qumran material, the Maccabean corpus (the parts which pre-date Paul), the late Wisdom literature (e.g., Sirach, Wisdom of Solomon), and perhaps also to Philo's use of Scripture, for unlike the rabbinic material Paul does not cite catenas of the views of other Jewish Scripture scholars on one or another text.

An example of the attempt to read Paul's handling of Scripture in the light of Jewish techniques, including later rabbinic techniques, can be seen in the discussion of Gal. 3 where we are told that Paul is doing a midrash on Abrahamic history.[73] But what does this mean? The term midrash has been so over-used and misused that it is often unclear what is meant in any specific instance. A. G. Wright laments: "The word midrash at present is an equivocal term and is being used to describe a mass of disparate material. Indeed, if some of the definitions are correct, large amounts, if not the whole of the Bible, would have to be called midrash. Hence, the word as used currently in biblical studies is approaching the point where it is no longer meaningful."[74] The word 'midrash' is of course a transliteration from the Hebrew word meaning 'interpretation', and so the word by itself does not signify a particular kind of exegetical or hermeneutical technique. As G. F. Moore says, midrash starts with the text of Scripture and will interpret words, phrases, clauses, and sentences independently of their literary and historical context, often in combination with words, phrases and the like from other texts.[75]

Let us consider what can and cannot be said about Paul's exegetical and hermeneutical technique on the basis of a close scrutiny of Gal. 3–4. On the one hand, Paul does use introductory formulae with some quotations as we also find in rabbinic literature (cf. Gal. 3.10, 13), and like that same rabbinic corpus Paul does sometimes personify Scripture (cf. Gal. 3.8). This, however, has nothing to do with midrashic *interpretation*. Citation formulae are not interpretations. Furthermore, it is doubtful, as we have already noted that we have a citation formula in 3.6 at all (cf. above).[76]

---

72. D. Cohn-Sherbok, "Paul and Rabbinic Exegesis," *SJT* 35 (1982), p. 132; cf. E. E. Ellis, *Paul's Use of the OT* (Edinburgh: Oliver & Boyd, 1957), p. 38; W. D. Davies, *Jewish and Pauline Studies* (London: SPCK, 1974), pp. 176–77.

73. So Ellis, *Paul's Use*, p. 119; cf. J. C. Beker, *Paul the Apostle: The Triumph of God in Life and Thought* (Philadelphia: Fortress, 1980), p. 47.

74. See his "The Literary Genre Midrash," *CBQ* 28 (1966), pp. 113–20, here p. 108.

75. G. F. Moore, *Judaism Vol. I* (New York: Schocken, 1971), p. 248.

76. Notice that the citation in 3.6 does not begin until after the word Abraham, which is not in the original text of Gen. 15.6.

On the negative side, unlike what we find in rabbinic midrash we do not find Paul citing other interpreters or offering catenas of their interpretations here in Gal. 3–4 or elsewhere in the Pauline corpus, nor is Gal. 3 a collection of independent units of interpretation, nor does Paul have more than one interpretative comment per Scriptural citation. I agree with Hansen that when one places Gal. 3 side by side with midrashim they appear to reflect different interpretative strategies.[77] In my judgment perhaps the one salient way in which Paul's handling of Scripture in Galatians resembles later midrashic technique is in his atomistic exegesis of the term 'seed' in Gal. 3.16. In most regards, however, Paul's eschatological orientation places him much closer to the Qumran pesher sort of exegesis, as he not merely wishes to show the text's contemporary relevance to the group he sees as the people of God, but he believes this hermeneutical task is both necessary and relevant because of the eschatological situation.

Having said this, I do not wish to suggest that Paul's handling of Scripture does not bear some resemblance to Jewish techniques that are found not only at Qumran, but also elsewhere in early Jewish literature. Paul certainly uses a chain of quotations in 3.6–16 (seven texts quoted) as we find in rabbinic literature, and this chain seems to be mainly welded together by certain key terms such as faith, blessing, Law and the like. In other words, the quotations are chosen because they contain the key terms in them. Furthermore, Paul accepts the fundamental Jewish principle that Scripture should be used to interpret Scripture (cf. how in Gal. 3.8 Paul uses Gen. 12.3 and 18.18 to interpret his use of Gen. 15.6 in Gal. 3.6).[78] Paul also uses merged quotations such as in Gal. 3.8, which seems to be more characteristic of Qumran literature than it is of rabbinic literature, but it is a widely used technique.[79]

Not everything Paul does, however, necessarily reflects an indebtedness to Jewish techniques. It is my own judgment that Paul's use of a 'from the lesser to the greater' kind of argument or vice versa is probably not a reflection of specific indebtedness to Jewish exegetical techniques, since this was also a common technique used in Greco-Roman rhetoric and also in philosophical discussions.[80] The same can be said about his appeal to examples. If Paul was an effective communicator with his largely Gentile audience we would expect some effort on his part to use some more universal forms of argument.

Something should be said here about the question of typology and allegory. Scholars are divided as to whether Gal. 4.21–31 is in fact an allegory or an example of typology,[81] or perhaps some of both. It needs to be borne in mind, however, that ἀλληγορεῖν can mean either to speak or to interpret allegorically, and there is a difference between allegory and the allegorical interpretation of a text which is not

77. See Hansen, *Abraham in Galatia*, p. 202.

78. Here I am following Hansen, p. 205.

79. See Ellis, *Prophecy and Hermeneutic in Early Christianity: New Testament Essays* (Tübingen: Mohr, 1978), pp. 177–81.

80. On the indebtedness of Jewish teachers, including teachers in Jerusalem in the first century to Hellenistic rhetoric and its techniques cf. D. Daube, "Rabbinic Methods of Interpretation and Hellenistic Rhetoric," *HUCA* 22 (1949), pp. 239–64.

81. See the discussion on this text pp. 321ff. below.

originally an allegory. I would suggest that in the main the latter is what Paul is doing with this text, though he does it within a salvation historical framework, which makes it similar to the way typology works.[82] The allegorizing interpretation allows Paul to apply the story directly to the situation in the church in his own day, for he is making correspondences that are not finally grounded in the historical story itself but in the situation in the Galatian church as he is writing. Typology is more firmly grounded in the actual characteristics of the type and the antitype displayed in the narratives and it is normally persons not places that are set up as type and antitype (cf., e.g., Melchizedek and Christ in Hebrews). In allegory, however, persons, places, and things can all take on symbolic or secondary connotations. I suspect if asked, Paul would be most willing to allow that Hagar was not really a 'type' of either Mount Sinai or the present Jerusalem. Only the concept of bondage or slavery binds them together, and it is this linkage that allegorizing the text brings to light. Here, Paul is not so much doing exegesis as we know it, but rather presupposing a basic understanding or knowledge of the content of these texts and then using them for pastoral hermeneutics and applications. I would call this a homiletical use of the Scripture, and as such it should not be evaluated as failed or bizarre attempts at contextual exegesis. Paul's allegorizing of the historical narrative is perhaps closest to what we find at Qumran. Consider for example the allegorization of Num. 21.18 found in the Damascus Document, an allegorization which is guided by eschatological assumptions about living in 'the end of days':

> The Well is the Law, and those who dug it were the converts of Israel who went out of the land of Judah to sojourn in the land of Damascus . . . The Stave is the Interpreter of the Law of whom Isaiah said, He makes a tool of his work (Is. 54.16); and the nobles of the people are those who come to dig the Well with the staves with which the Stave ordained that they should walk in the age of wickedness – and without them they shall find nothing – until he comes who shall teach righteousness at the end of days (CD 6.3–11).[83]

Here as in Gal. 4.21–31 it is contemporary events or ideas outside the story that dictate how the story is used and applied, and this approach is at the heart of allegorizing.

The story in Gal. 4.21–31 calls forth a few final comments on Scripture and Paul's narrative framework of thought. If we were to take into account not only the quotations of Scripture by Paul in Galatians, but also the echoes of Scripture, we would discover what a very large role Scripture actually plays, often beneath the surface, in all of Paul's arguments. It is not just that Paul speaks a Scriptural language and clothes his own thoughts in Biblical phraseology. Rather, much of the basic matter that goes into forming Paul's symbolic universe comes from Scripture. This is of course not the whole 'story' for in important ways Paul's mental furniture indeed his whole

---

82. The standard way typology works is with a type and an antitype, but this hardly seems to adequately describe the relationship between Hagar and Mount Sinai, which then is also said to relate to the present Jerusalem (Gal. 4.25).

83. Cf. The discussion by Hansen, *Abraham*, pp. 211ff.; and Longenecker, *Galatians*, p. 206.

framework was rearranged when Paul accepted the story of the crucified and risen
One into his way of thinking about various Scriptural matters. The important thing to
bear in mind is that when Paul uses terms like Law or faith he is thinking of entire
Scriptural stories about Moses or Abraham.[84] Paul is not just cutting out Scriptural
terms or ideas from the OT and pasting them into the Gospel story, or gathering up all
the pertinent references in the OT to a particular word like 'faith' or 'righteousness'
and pasting them together in a collage. This means that his approach to Scripture is
fundamentally *not* a midrashic approach, if one accepts Moore's definition of what
midrashic interpretation entails.[85] It is far more complex than that. It is one part
Jewish, one part Greco-Roman, and in all of this he is working toward a distinctively
Christian and Christocentric mode of interpreting the Word.

The story that matters more to Paul than any other and most effects his handling
of Scripture is the story of Christ, a story that is taken more from Christian tradition
than from Holy Writ. It is not only the story which guides his interpretation of what
has gone before and the record of it in the Hebrew Scriptures, but also what has come
since in the lives of Jesus' followers, including his own life. The faithfulness of Jesus
Christ is not only the key to Scriptural interpretation but the paradigm for Christian
life. It is *the* story that is used as both a lens to read the text and also a litmus test for
the Christian life. This should not surprise us in light of Gal. 3.1–5 and 3.6ff. where we
see first the appeal to Christian experience and then the appeal to Holy Writ as two
parts of one argument, joined together by καθώς and meant to be compared to each
other. The middle term linking the two together which allows and indeed first
suggested this comparison was Christ, whom Paul will go on to call the seed of
Abraham, and the one in whom even Gentiles become the heirs of Abraham and
through whom they have received the Spirit. No account of Paul's use of Scripture
will be adequate if it does not take into account this Christ script.

Paul's citation of Gen. 15.6 in vs. 6 agrees almost entirely with the LXX version
of the text, except Paul introduces the quotation with a mention of Abraham
by name. It is crucial to keep in mind as we examine all that follows in this
chapter that Paul, like many of his contemporaries operates on the assumption
that the more ancient a notion is, the greater the authority and significance it
is likely to have. It is clearly important to Paul to be able to use a text which
shows that Abraham's faith, his being reckoned as righteous, *and* the promise
of blessing (cf. already Gen. 12.2) all came before there is any mention whatsoever of circumcision as a covenant sign (Gen. 17) or of Abraham's faithful
and obedient deed in regard to the offering of Isaac in sacrifice (Gen. 22), and
most importantly it came centuries before the giving of the Mosaic Law and
covenant. From this it follows in Paul's mind that right-standing with God
and the promise of God cannot be said to be dependent on keeping the Mosaic
Law, but rather on faith. Paul will make much of the principle of historical

84. See my discussion of these matters in *Paul's Narrative Thought World*, passim.
85. Cf. For instance the careful unfolding of Paul's use of the promise to Abraham
theme in Hays, *Echoes*, pp. 105ff.

precedent in direct contrast to the way the Abraham tradition was used elsewhere in early Judaism where Abraham is specifically said to be reckoned as righteous because he was found faithful (in offering Isaac; cf. 1 Macc. 2.52), or it is said that the promise to multiply his descendants and be a blessing to the nations was given because Abraham "kept the commandment of the most High and entered into covenant with Him; in his flesh He engraved him an ordinance, and in trial he was found faithful" (Sir. 44.19–21 cf. Jub. 23.10), or it is said 'he was accounted a friend of God because he kept the commandments of God' (CD 3.2). In short, two "emphases with regard to Abraham are constantly made in the literature of Judaism: (1) that Abraham was counted righteous because of his faithfulness under testing; and (2) that Abraham's faith spoken of in Gen. 15.6 must be coupled with his acceptance of circumcision as referred to in the covenant of Gen. 17.4–14 . . . Furthermore, Abraham's faithfulness under testing is always presented as being meritorious both for Abraham himself and for his posterity."[86] In short, there is no evidence that Paul got his particular interpretation of the Abraham material from this Jewish heritage, even if he shows some indebtedness at the level of the general way he approaches Scripture. If anything, Paul's approach seems more faithful to the progression of the narrative than the anachronistic approaches found in Sirach and other early Jewish sources. Gen. 12 and 15 do both suggest that Abraham believed and trusted God and received promises and right-standing before and apart from any act of circumcision or offering of Isaac in sacrifice. For Paul, Abraham is an example of trust or faith in God and God's Word and its consequences, while in the other Jewish literature he is an example of faithfulness, even meritorious faithfulness to God (cf. even Philo *Abr.* 262–74 and *Praem.* 27).

There is, however, one particular line of Jewish reasoning about Abraham to which Paul does seem indebted. I am referring to the view that Abraham should be seen as the prototype of the first proselyte and first convert to Jewish monotheism who abandoned idols at the call of God. This theme is in evidence in a variety of early Jewish sources (cf. Jub. 12; Apoc. Ab. 1–8; Philo *Abr.* 60–88; Josephus *Ant.* 1.155). Paul's rhetorical move here will be not to follow the Jewish approach of interpreting Abraham's faith in light of his later faithfulness in regard to Isaac and submission to circumcision, but rather to focus on what was true about Abraham at and from the beginning of his walk with God, which is to say what was true about his life that Paul could readily parallel in the lives of the Galatians.

Notice that the text quoted does not say 'Abraham believed *in* God' but rather 'he believed God'. Faith in Abraham's case means something like trusting

---

86. See the excursus in Longenecker, *Galatians*, pp. 110–11 and also in Hansen, *Abraham in Galatia*, pp. 200–5.

or taking God at his Word. The verb ἐλογίσθη comes from the realm of calculations involved in transactions (such as wages credited to a worker) and refers to something being credited or reckoned (cf. Ps. 105[106].31 and 1 Macc. 2.52).[87] The larger question is what Paul means here by δικαιωσύνην. Does Paul take the text of Gen. 15.6 to refer to righteousness, or is the term used forensically to refer to right-standing? If we consider for a moment the parallel text in Ps. 105.30–31 there we hear about Phineas who stood up and interceded with God for God's people whom God was judging by means of a plague and 'that has been reckoned to him as righteousness from generation to generation forever.' Reckoned by whom? In this case it would seem to be subsequent generations of Jews. Here as in the case with Abraham one thing is credited or reckoned to a person for another. The use of the verb ἐλογίσθη followed by the preposition εἰς probably leads to the translation 'reckoned for' rather than 'reckoned as' and in both cases the word δικαιοσύνη *means* righteousness, not right-standing, but if this state is only 'reckoned', then a statement is not being made about the rectitude of one's character. Faith is counted as righteousness in the case of Abraham, or if one wishes to stretch the statement a bit because of his faith, Abraham was reckoned as if he were righteous.[88] The term here would seem to have a positive connotation, and not simply mean acquittal or not deserving of condemnation.[89] God will count Abraham's faith for righteousness.

Verse 7 begins with the verb γινώσκω which could be translated either as an indicative ('you know') or as an imperative ('consider' or 'recognize'). Is Paul teaching the Galatians something they do not know here, or is he reminding them? Since γινώσκετε ἄρα ὅτι is a common disclosure formula in Hellenistic letters,[90] and ἄρα means 'then' here, the translation 'you know' is to be preferred with 'then' being a reference back to vs. 6. This means vs. 7 is seen as the logical consequence of vs. 6. What they are said to know is that 'those living from faith, *these* persons are the sons of Abraham'. The phrase οἱ ἐκ πίστεως is elliptical (literally 'those from faith'). We should probably contrast this phrase with the fuller one found in vs. 10 which reads literally 'Whoever is from works of the Law'. Paul in each case is talking about one's basic life orientation, the basic or guiding principle by which one lives, and so it is probably appropriate to translate our phrase in vs. 7 'those who live from or out of or on the basis of faith'.

---

87. It translates the Hebrew equivalent which can mean 'think' but it can also mean 'account' or 'credit'.

88. See my discussion in *Paul's Narrative Thought World*, pp. 254–62.

89. See Matera, *Galatians*, p. 114: "The noun expresses more than acquittal; it is the gift of God's justice."

90. See Longenecker, *Galatians*, p. 114.

The novelty of Paul's argument here has rightly been noted by Longenecker. "Paul's habit in addressing Gentiles was not to commend Christ to them on OT grounds or to explain how they were related to Abraham and the Jewish nation (cf. esp. 1 and 2 Corinthians, Philippians, Colossians, 1 and 2 Thessalonians)."[91] This suggests that the situation Paul is addressing in Galatia has generated this form of argument. This may in part be because the agitators were speaking to the Galatians about how they might become true children of Abraham by means of circumcision, but in any case Paul's form of argument presumes a lot of his audience. It suggests that he assumes they already know about Abraham and his progeny, and at least the general contours of this kind of Jewish discussion. This in turn may well suggest that the majority of Paul's converts in Galatia, even though they were Gentiles, had come out of the synagogue or had some previous association with Jews and the synagogue, a suggestion which could be supported from texts like Acts 13.43, 48 and 14.1. Gentile persons of faith relate to God as did Abraham, and in part because of this they may be counted as Abraham's sons or heirs. This, however, is not the whole story, for Paul will go on to say that Christians are heirs of Abraham through Christ, not just because like Abraham they have faith in God. The assertion in vs. 7 is meant to remind the Galatians of the common ground they already share with Abraham, quite apart from circumcision and the Mosaic Law.

Verse **8** presents us with the personification of Scripture. It is said that Scripture foresaw what was going to happen in regard to Gentiles being included in God's people in the NT era, and that therefore it pre-preached[92] the Good News to Abraham about this matter. Paul sees the Scriptures as alive, active, speaking, even locking people up under sin (Gal. 3.22).[93] Paul is able to say this because he identifies what Scripture says with what God says. Verse 8 could as easily be read 'God, foreseeing what was going to happen to the Gentiles . . . spoke to Abraham in advance'. Scripture is seen as a written transcript of the living divine Word that comes directly from the mind and mouth of God,[94] and so can be personified as it is here. Verse 8 then says that it was always in the mind of God to justify the Gentile nations 'out of faith' (ἐκ πίστεως), that is by means of faith. Scripture is said to foresee this outcome and as a result to tell Abraham in advance that 'all the nations will be blessed in you'. This form of the promise differs a little from any of the forms found in

91. Ibid.
92. Προευηγγελίσατο is a hapax legomenon, found only here in the NT. The translation 'pre-preached the gospel' is suggested by Hays, *Echoes*, p. 105.
93. See Hays, p. 106.
94. Whether by Paul or a Paulinist, 1 Tim. 3.16 very accurately sums up Paul's view of the matter – The Hebrew Scriptures are God-breathed, which is to say they express exactly what God wants to and does say.

the OT (cf. Gen. 12.3; 18.18; 22.18; 26.4; 28.14; Ps. 71.17 LXX; Sir. 44.21 LXX; Acts 3.25). It appears to be largely indebted to the first two of these texts. Paul's concern here is not just to establish that a universal and all-inclusive Gospel requires justification by grace through faith,[95] but that there is an inherent link, indeed a double one, between Abraham and Gentile believers. It is not just that Gentiles receive a blessing through faith just as Abraham did, but that in fact they are the objects of blessing referred to in the original promise to Abraham. They are Abraham's heirs through faith. The implicit negative point is that Gentiles need not become Law-observant to get in on the promises or blessings. They already have these things by faith.

Paul knows that the text of Genesis says not only 'in you all the tribes of the earth will be blessed', but also in Gen. 22.18 'in your seed all the nations [i.e., Gentiles] of the earth will be blessed'. The logic underlying what follows Gal. 3.9ff. seems to be this: The Gentiles are blessed in Abraham, but the means of this happening is that they are blessed in the seed of Abraham, which Paul will argue is Christ. The connection between Gentiles and Abraham then is not simply that they both have faith. The Gentiles are connected to Abraham through faith in Christ the 'seed' of Abraham and the benefits they receive from Him. Hays is right that Paul is stressing that the promise given to Abraham was inclusive in scope, already including Gentiles simply on the basis of faith.[96] Williams has argued convincingly that to say that the nations are blessed in Abraham is to say that they are blessed as he was, namely to be reckoned righteous, and thereby not required to render themselves righteous by observing the Law.

In other words, the reception of the Spirit through faith and the reception of being reckoned as righteous by faith are seen as distinguishable yet parallel phenomena, this is why Paul is able to draw an analogy between the Galatians' experience and that of Abraham. The "experience of the Spirit and the status of justification are, for the apostle, inconceivable apart from each other. Each implies the other. Those persons upon whom God bestows the Spirit are justified; the persons who God reckons righteous have the Spirit poured out upon them."[97] Notice that Paul does not ask the Galatians whether they were justified on the basis of faith or on the basis of works. Rather, he declares that this is the way things work as is demonstrated by Scripture when it speaks of the case of Abraham. Rhetorically this is a much more powerful move than if he had asked the Galatians what they thought on the matter.[98]

The important theological point implied by the comparison of the initial experience of Abraham and that of the Galatians deserves to be reiterated.

---

95. See Ziesler, *Galatians*, p. 39.
96. Hays, *Echoes*, p. 106.
97. Williams, "Justification of the Spirit in Galatians," p. 97.
98. Ibid.

"For Paul, a new status before God implies a life transformed by the working of God's Spirit and vice versa. It would not occur to him that a Christian would claim the status if the signs of the Spirit were lacking. Justification and the Spirit: in Paul's mind one necessarily implies the other, and to claim the one without evidencing the other would be to misapprehend the nature of the Christian life."[99] The Spirit is not a blessing received as a result of justification, rather it is the subjective side of the one blessing in which God at one time both reckons a person righteous through faith and bestows on them the Spirit that transforms their lives. The analogy with Abraham is only fully apt if this is the logic which underlies the comparison.

Verse **9** provides a conclusion on the basis of what Paul has argued in vss. 6–8. Those who live from faith are blessed with faithful Abraham. There is a sense in which Paul believes that Abraham was the first one to hear the Gospel of justification by grace through faith and accept it, and thus a sense in which he is seen as a prototype of the Christian, even more daringly a prototype or antitype of the Galatian Gentile Christians. In other words, if this Gospel was good enough for Abraham providing him with the full blessing it should be good enough for the Galatians as well. Those who live from faith "are blessed with Abraham because they *are* Abraham's promised descendants"[100] but this is not just any sort of faith we are talking about, it is faith in Christ, the seed of Abraham (cf. below).

Excursus: Deliberating about Rituals ───────────────────

As the arguments or proofs of Paul proceed in Gal. 3–6 it becomes clearer and clearer that their rhetorical function is not to discuss theology or ethics in the abstract but to provide undergirding and rationale for the exhortation that the Galatians should not submit to circumcision and the Mosaic Law. In other words what is at issue here is what was often at issue in deliberative rhetoric – a debate about changing or maintaining religious rituals or practices. In the *Rhetoric to Alexander* 1423a religious ritual is the very first topic mentioned as the proper subject for a deliberative speech in the ἐκκλησία.

It is of importance to realize that Paul's arguments in Gal. 3–4 basically fall into the category of dissuasion, trying to head off a proposed course of action that the Galatians are contemplating or are about to undertake. We must assume that the acts of persuasion performed by the agitators in Galatia were having some effect, and it appears likely that they argued in the classical manner on the basis of what would be advantageous or expedient for the Galatians. Consider for a moment what is said in *Rhetoric to Alexander* 1423b on this very matter: "Arguing from expediency, we shall

---

99. Williams, p. 98.
100. Matera, *Galatians*, p. 123, emphasis mine.

say that the performing of the sacrifices [or other religious rituals] in the ancestral manner will be advantageous either for individual citizens or for the community on the ground of economy, and that it will profit the citizens . . . [and] on the ground of practicability if there has been neither deficiency nor extravagance in the celebrations. These are the lines we must pursue when we *are advocating the established order . . .*"

It must be borne in mind that the agitators had established Jewish practice on their side. They could appeal to the antiquity of the rituals and Law they were urging on the Galatians and how beneficial the practice of such things had been in previous generations. They could easily argue that observing the Mosaic Law was a matter of continuation of an already existing practice among Christians in the mother church in Judea, and that the Galatians' Christian life would not really be complete without the taking on of the yoke of the Law and its covenant sign circumcision.

Paul's acts of dissuasion required him to argue for a *change* of practice in these matters. In other words, he is definitely swimming upstream throughout the argument section of Galatians. The *Rhetoric to Alexander* 1423b is again helpful when it discusses those who will argue for an *alteration* of established religious practice. We "shall find plausible arguments for changing the ancestral institutions in saying . . . *that even our forefathers used not to conduct the sacrifices always on the same lines . . .*" Paul in Galatians 3 is indeed going to argue that if one goes back *ad fontes*, to Abraham himself, that the basis of establishing and maintaining a relationship with God involved faith. Since ritual was at the heart of almost all ancient religion in the Greco-Roman world his case was a difficult one because on the one hand he was going to argue that the ritual was not at the heart of the matter, faith was, and on the other hand, while he will mention in passing an alternative ritual, baptism (Gal. 3.26ff.), he clearly does not wish to put the emphasis on that ritual, but rather on faith.

What Paul must do is show what benefits accrue if the Galatians continue along the track that they had begun on when Paul was with them, and on the other hand he must show them that following the exhortations of the agitators will not only not be beneficial or advantageous but in fact will be detrimental to their Christian lives. "One dissuading must apply hinderance by the opposite means: he must show that the action proposed is not just, not lawful, not expedient, not honorable, not pleasant, and not practicable; or failing this, that it is laborious and not necessary . . ." (1421b). It will be seen that Paul uses several of these approaches in Gal. 3–6. He will argue that the practice is not necessary – the Galatians already have the benefits they need through the Spirit, and cannot gain them through the observance of the Law. He will argue that in fact the Law is not finally practicable, because one must observe all the Law. He will imply that submitting to circumcision commits one to a laborious process of observing many more Laws. He will even suggest that if they submit to the Law that what they have gained thus far will be in vain, profiting nothing.

It is said of arguments from expediency that what "is expedient is the preservation of existing good things, or the acquisition of goods that we do not possess, or the rejection of existing evils, or the prevention of harmful things expected to occur. Things expedient you will classify under body, mind, and external possessions" (1422a). The author goes on to state that for a group or state what is expedient is what brings concord rather than disunity, discord, and factionalism. It is reasonably clear that Paul is urging the expedient course on his converts to preserve the exciting good things they already have through faith, and on the other hand to avoid the potential curse that will fall on those who fail to observe all the Law. In other words he will use several forms of the argument from expediency to achieve his aims here.

In giving primacy to arguments from expediency Paul is following the direct advice of Aristotle who stresses that 'expediency' is the primary basis for appeals in deliberative rhetoric. "The [deliberative] orator aims at establishing the expediency or harmfulness of a proposed course of action: if he urges its acceptance he does so on the ground that it will do good; if he urges its rejection [as in Galatians] he does so on the ground that it will do harm; and all other points, such as whether the proposal is just or unjust, honorable or dishonorable, he brings in as subsidiary and relative to the main consideration" (*Rhetoric* 1.3.21–25).

It is important to note that Gal. 5 is not a departure from what has been argued in Gal. 3–4 but rather a continuation of the same exhortation, only here Paul will argue deliberatively more for behavior that produces unity and concord in the group than he has heretofore. It must be stressed that Paul's arguments are directed to and at his converts, he is not holding a debate with the agitators.[101] He has already pronounced a curse on the latter group in Gal. 1, and he is not trying to persuade or dissuade them of anything. In the main, throughout Galatians Paul seems to focus on arguments about necessity, expediency, and practicability when he is arguing against submission to the Law, and all of this falls well into the described parameters of how deliberative rhetoric is supposed to proceed.[102]

Verses **10–14** provide a second portion of the second division of Paul's argument, an argument that as a whole ranges from 3.1 to 3.18. It is in some ways the most debated and complex portion of the argument, dealing as it does with the issue of the Law's curse. Having established the positive example of Abraham's faith, he now must deal with the issue of why it will be

101. Cf., e.g., L. Gaston, *Paul and the Torah* (Vancouver: University of British Columbia Press, 1987), p. 209 n. 8 "Paul does not argue with his opponents, even at second hand, but only calls them names (Gal. 5.10–12; 1.6–9) and urges them to be cast out (1.6–9; 4.30). All of Paul's arguments in Galatians must be understood as directed to the Galatian Judaizers and not to those who 'court zealously' (4.17) or 'trouble' (1.7; 5.10, 12) or 'compel' (6.12–13) them." Excessive mirror-reading has led many down dead-end paths in the interpretation of the argument section of Galatians.

102. See the conclusion of C. Stanley, "'Under a Curse': A Fresh Reading of Galatians 3.10–14," *NTS* 36 (1990), pp. 481–511, here p. 491: "Thus Paul's letter to the Galatians represents a clear example of 'deliberative' rhetoric, a piece of argumentation designed to persuade his hearers to take (or not to take) a particular course of action in the immediate future. In actual practice, of course, Paul's argumentation most often reveals a strategy of *dis*suasion, as he seeks to counter the 'persuasion' (5.8) that the Galatians have already received from the mouths of the 'Judaizers'. Generally speaking, he sets forth no new positions, nor does he commend any truly new actions to his hearers. Instead, he repeatedly calls the Galatians back to 'the Gospel of Jesus Christ . . . which we proclaimed to you' (1.7–8)."

inexpedient and impracticable to submit to the Law. Paul states that those who are (living) on the basis of works of the Law are under a curse. In order to support this conclusion he quotes a text that on the surface might seem not to be entirely helpful in establishing or supporting such an argument. The text is Deut. 27.26 and Paul quotes it as follows: 'Cursed are all who do not remain in all that is written in the book of the Law, doing it.' It will be seen that this is a widening of the field of focus for the LXX simply has 'cursed are all persons who do not remain in all the words *of this Law.*' It is possible that Paul has assimilated his quotation to the form customary in legal documents of the day, a form with which his converts might be familiar,[103] but it seems more likely to me that Paul is deliberately trying to speak in more general terms about the Law, not just about particular Laws. Paul does not wish to focus just on a curse appended to a particular set of Mosaic Laws, but one which pertains in general to those 'under the Law'.

This modification of the OT quotation must count against any suggestion that the primary bone of contention is simply boundary marker Laws or practices which would socially separate Jews from others.[104] Paul's argument is salvation historical, he believes that people 'under the Law' need to be redeemed from under the Law and its curse (cf. Gal. 4.5) by Christ, and this means Jews, and presumably also Gentiles who happen to be Torah-observant. It has been suggested by D. R. Schwartz that the redemptive mechanism Paul has in mind is that of the scapegoat. The curse that once was upon the Law breaker has been laid upon Christ the scapegoat, and so the Jews have been redeemed from the curse.[105]

It is not just the non-observance of particular laws that Paul is inveighing against in Galatians. Nor is his argument against 'works' or 'doing' in general. As J. Barclay makes abundantly clear, in Gal. 5–6 Paul is very happy to insist on the importance of various sorts of works and deeds, indeed on obedience to 'the Law of Christ'.[106] Paul's argument is against observance of a specific kind of works – works of the Mosaic Law in general.

103. See Bligh, *Galatians in Greek*, p. 134.

104. Also against such a suggestion is the fact that Paul nowhere mentions any debate about food laws in Galatia or for that matter sabbath observance, unless Gal. 4.10 is a reference to such a practice there, but this is unlikely (cf. below pp. 299ff. and note the reference to 'days' not the sabbath day and contrast Col. 2.20–22). See Stanley, "Under a Curse," p. 490 n. 34, against Dunn, *Jesus, Paul and the Law*, pp. 215ff. Deut. 27.26 in its original context is of course the last of twelve curses which were part of a covenanting ceremony which Israel was to perform once in the Holy Land. "Paul however, takes the text of Deut. 27.26 in a broader sense by applying it to the prescriptions of the entire Mosaic Law." (Matera, *Galatians*, p. 123.)

105. See D. R. Schwartz, "Two Pauline Allusions to the Redemptive Mechanism of the Crucifixion," *JBL* 102 (1983), pp. 259–68, here pp. 261–63.

106. See Barclay, *Obeying the Truth*, pp. 94ff.

The quotation of Deuteronomy makes clear enough that the curse falls on *all* those who are under the Law and do not remain in *all* of it so as to do all of it. This curse has nothing to do with general human fallenness but more specifically with being a Mosaic Law breaker, and thus it applies only to those who are 'under the Law'. If the Galatians submit to the Mosaic Law they will also indeed be subject to such a curse, if, that is, they fail to keep all the Law.

Probably C. Stanley is right that Paul's basic argument here is this: "Anyone who chooses to abide by the Jewish Torah in order to secure participation in Abraham's 'blessing' is placed in a situation where he or she is threatened instead with a 'curse' since the Law itself pronounces a curse on anyone who fails to live up to every single one of its requirements."[107] In other words, we must see the argument in vs. 10 as falling into the category of a rhetorical threat "intended to induce the Galatians to reconsider their contemplated course of action by pointing out possible negative consequences and so inducing a sense of fear regarding its outcome."[108] Aristotle reminds us that when attempting a deliberative argument that it is important not just to appeal to positive motives for the course of action proposed, but also to appeal to the more primitive emotions such as fear and anger in order to get the audience not just mentally but also emotionally on the right track as well (*Rhetoric* 2.5.1ff.).[109] The argument here is about a possibility for the audience addressed, not an already existing reality, unless the Galatians submit to and do not 'remain in' the Law.[110]

Paul has prepared for this argument well in Gal. 1 – the agitators who preach another Gospel have already been cursed, and by implication Paul's audience stands in danger of falling into the same state if they submit to the Law and do not keep it all.[111] Furthermore, he will go on to say that Christ already has endured a curse for them, so they would *not* have to submit to the Law and end up being cursed.

---

107. Stanley, "Under a Curse", p. 500. In other words the curse is provisional or only potential, and is incurred only upon non-compliance with the demands of the Law.

108. Stanley, p. 501.

109. "[A]ll things must be fearful that appear to have great power of destroying or inflicting injuries that tend to produce great pain" (2.5.2). "And those who have commited some wrong, when they have power, . . . are afraid of retaliation, which was assumed to be feared" (2.5.9). In our case, the Galatians had not merely a human reprisal to fear, but rather the curse of God, which would be the most fearsome of prospects. This sort of argument of course depends for its efficacy on a climate where not only God is believed in, but divine judgment is believed to be a regular occurrence, which is certainly the case with the social environment and context to which this argument is addressed.

110. On the deliberative argument about future possibilities see Aristotle, *Rhetoric* 2.19.1ff.

111. Notice how Paul will state quite plainly in Gal. 6.13 that even the agitators don't keep all the Law.

Verse 11 makes another fundamental or principial assertion – 'But precisely because no one is justified before God by the Law, it is clear that the righteous one will live from faith'. The δέ which begins this verse is surely adversative, not merely a connective, and the discussion here is still surely about the Mosaic Law, not about law in the abstract or universal sense.[112] Justification clearly enough, in view of vs. 10, has to do with the verdict of the Mosaic Law and so also the verdict of God who gave the Law on human beings as to whether they are in compliance with the divine requirements for relationship with God, which of course entails a judgment on human conduct. The point to which this argument is leading, however, is that in light of the Christ event, the judgment of God about those in Christ is different than the judgment of the Law about sinners.[113]

In vs. 11b Paul quotes Hab. 2.4 in some form. There is certainly no hint that Paul is referring to Christ here. The discussion is about what is or should be the case with the Galatians. This text was obviously important to Paul, as he cites it again in Rom. 1.17 in his 'thesis' statement addressed to the Roman Christians. The Hebrew of Hab. 2.4 reads 'the righteous shall live by his faith/faithfulness'. The question is who is referred to by 'his'? LXXa understands the Hebrew to mean 'My righteous one shall live on the basis of faith/faithfulness', while LXXb understands it to mean 'the righteous shall live on the basis of "my" (i.e., God's) faithfulness'. It is interesting that in some later Jewish sources Hab. 2.4 is sometimes seen as the summation of the whole Mosaic Law in one principal statement taken to mean that faithfulness is rewarded as meritorious with faith (cf. Mid. Ps. 17A.25; BT Mak. 24a). Even more intriguing is what 1QpHab 7.14–8.3 says about Hab. 2.4: "This concerns all those who observe the law in the house of Judah, whom God will deliver from the House of Judgment because of their suffering and *because of their faith in the Teacher of Righteousness*."[114] I agree with Longenecker that in view of the fact that Paul does not include or discuss at all the pronominal suffix found in the Hebrew text, that the issue must be that righteousness in the life of the believer is associated with faith alone not with the Law. God's righteousness or Christ's faithfulness is not under debate, but rather the status of those who have faith like Abraham's. 'Righteousness' or right relationship

112. Contra Mussner, *Galaterbrief*, p. 228.
113. Cf. Burton, *Galatians*, p. 165.
114. It will be seen that even this Qumran text provides no encouragement for the suggestion that the faithfulness of Christ is referred to by this quotation. The Qumran text is about faith *in* the Teacher, not about his faithfulness. In the first place, had that been Paul's meaning he would surely have made it more clear. Christ is nowhere mentioned in vss. 6–12. In the second place, this entire argument is about how the Galatians shall live in the future, and we must take the future tense of ζήσεται seriously here. This is not about how God's Righteous Son did or does live, but about how the Galatians should and will live.

with God is something that is reckoned by God because of faith, not because of attempts to keep the Law. Indeed curse rather than blessing accrues to those who try and fail to keep the Law.[115]

Verse 12 begins as did vs. 11 with an adversative δὲ. But the Mosaic Law is not 'from faith'. We should probably see vs. 10 and vs. 12 lining up on one side of the argument here, with vs. 11 on the other side.[116] Law and curse stand on one side of the argument, the negative side. Righteousness and faith stand on the other side. The issue is how God's people shall live, how they shall go on in their Christian life.

Paul chooses to quote Lev. 18.5 about the Law – 'the one doing it shall live in them'. The larger context of this quotation in the LXX is most likely in Paul's mind: 'and you shall observe all my commandments and all my decrees and do them; the man who does them shall live by them'. Paul seems to be saying that the Law is not based on faith, but has as its basic *modus operandi* living by carefully observing the commandments or instructions. Perhaps here we can understand Paul's logic by anticipating what he will go on to say later in Gal. 3 and in Gal. 4. Under-age children require rules and regulations to keep them in bounds as they do not understand the basic rationale which underlies certain kinds of human conduct and they are not old enough to exercise critical moral judgment. When a person matures, however, they may be trusted to act in the proper way without laying down the Law, they may be trusted to act on the basis of good judgment and in good faith.

The Law was not given to govern those who were already mature in the faith, much less those who already had the Spirit to guide and empower proper Christian living. The Law was given to those whose life needed to be structured by following certain clear precepts. One needed to live by careful observance of the commandments, not by making faith judgments on one situation or another. In other words, Paul is commenting on the basic purpose of the Law here, and its divinely intended social function. He will go on to explain further that function when he uses the analogy with the παιδαγωγὸς and speaks about 'we' Jewish Christians who were under the 'elementary principles of the world' when we were heirs but nonetheless minors (cf. 3.23–25; 4.1–7). The Law's function, according to Paul, was to keep God's people in line and in bounds, it could not, however, empower them to observe it. They were to live by the Law, but they could not be enlivened or empowered by it.

At vs. 13 and not before, Paul finally introduces Christ into his first major argument. Here Paul speaks of Christ redeeming 'us' from the curse of the Law, becoming for us a 'curse' and then he quotes Deut. 27.26. Paul is driving

---

115. See Longenecker, *Galatians*, p. 119.
116. Against Betz, *Galatians*, p. 147.

toward the conclusion of this division of his argument in vs. 14, and it will only become clear there, when one compares vs. 5 and vs. 14 that this is all part of one large argument. The major question which needs to be answered about this verse is who the 'we' are who have been redeemed from the curse of the Law, which in turn requires us to ask who is under the Law with its potential curse. Is Paul referring to we Jews; is he referring to we Jewish Christians; is he referring to Gentile Christians; is he referring to everyone? This issue must be addressed at this juncture because it will continue to plague us throughout the rest of Gal. 3–4.

If we look elsewhere at how the phrase 'under the Law' is used, clearly in 1 Cor. 9.20 the term is restricted to Jews. In Rom. 6.14–15 Gentiles may be included, however, only after the sort of qualifiers we find in 2.12–14. In other words, no clear answer can be derived from these parallels. Some have pointed to Gal. 4.1–11 in order to insist that Paul does have in mind that everyone, Jew and Gentile, is under the Law and its potential curse. This conclusion is based on the assumption that 'the elementary principles of the universe' is simply synonymous with the Law. As we shall see when we discuss στοιχεῖα,[117] this conclusion is more than a little doubtful. It is far more likely that Paul sees the Law as a particular expression of the larger category of the 'elementary principles of the universe'.

If we look carefully at the text at hand, however, there are good reasons for concluding that as in Gal. 2.14–21, 'we' means 'we' Jews or more particularly 'we' Jewish Christians.[118] Firstly, consider the narrative flow of the argument on the basis of the following chart:

(1) The Group and its Plight
 – 'we' were under the Law's curse (3.10,13)
 – 'we' were confined under the Law, our guardian (3.23–24)
 – 'we' were under Law, slaves of the elementary principles (4.3, 5)

(2) Identification of Christ with the Plight
 – he became 'a curse for us' (3.13)
 – the Faith/ Christ 'came' (3.23–35)
 – he was 'born under the Law (4.4)

(3) Redemption of the Group
 – Christ 'redeemed us' (3.13)

117. See pp. 284ff. below.
118. Here I will be following to a considerable extent the case laid out in full by T. L. Donaldson, "'The Curse of the Law' and the Inclusion of the Gentiles: Galatians 3.13–14," *NTS* 32 (1986), pp. 94–112.

– 'now that the Faith has come, we are no longer under a guardian'
(3.25)
– 'to redeem those under the Law' (4.5)

(4)   Blessings Accruing to All Believers – cf. 3.14; 3.26–29; 4.5b-7.[119]

Secondly, we note the emphatic placement of ἡμᾶς at the first of vs. 13 and of τὰ ἔθνη in vs. 14 suggests a possible intended contrast between the two groups. Note also that those subject to the curse from which Christ is the redeemer would seem to be the same group as those living from the law mentioned in vs. 10. Paul is arguing against the notion that Torah observance is required to participate in the blessing of Abraham. The "status of uncircumcised and unbelieving Gentiles is not under dispute here; they do not enter the picture at all".[120] Of course it is true that Paul is warning some uncircumcised believing Gentiles against placing themselves into the category of those under the Law. As we have said, in the light of the thesis statement in 2.15–21, we should certainly expect that in the arguments 'we' might continue to mean 'we' Jewish Christians. Paul would seem to be arguing that Christ redeemed at least a remnant of Israel, and he did so in part so that promises to Abraham might come true and that the Gentiles might then and thereby be blessed.

Paul's argument, as we have already had occasion to say, is apocalyptic or eschatological or even to some degree salvation historical in character. As Donaldson reminds us,[121] we should therefore consider carefully how early Jews argued about the eschatological salvation of Gentiles. The argument, based in part on texts like Is. 2.2–4 or Is. 45.20–23, can be seen played out in a variety of places. For instance, Tobit 14.4–7 speaks of what will transpire after the exile including the rebuilding of the Temple, and "then all the Gentiles will turn to fear the Lord God in truth and will bury their idols". The point to be emphasized here is the sequence of events. First God's people will return from exile and the Temple will be restored, *then* Gentiles will turn to the Lord.

Far more important, however, for our purposes is the argument found in Acts 15.14–19 where we find the text of Amos 9.11–12 on the lips of James.[122] As R. Bauckham says "the Jewish Christian exegete who created the text in Acts 15.16–18 understood the eschatological Temple, not as a literal building, but as the eschatological people of God composed of both Jews and Gentiles."[123]

---

119. An adaptation with some slight modifications of Donaldson, p. 95.
120. Donaldson, p. 97.
121. Donaldson, pp. 98–99.
122. On the likelihood of the substance of this speech actually going back to James, cf. my *The Acts of the Apostles*, pp. 423ff. and also R. Bauckham, "James and the Gentiles," in *History, Literature and Society in the Book of Acts*, pp. 154–84.
123. Bauckham, p. 164.

Now to judge from the context of the discussion in Acts 15, James is also being portrayed as one who subscribed to the idea that first there would be a restoration of the tent of David and then, as the experience of Peter and others showed, Gentiles would be joined to this restored tent. I would furthermore suggest that there is an allusion to this whole way of thinking in Gal. 2.9 where Paul alludes to those deemed to be 'pillars', namely Peter, James, and John. As we said when we discussed this text, the question is deemed by whom, and the answer must be other Jewish Christians in Jerusalem, and presumably this would also include the agitators if they are from Jerusalem as well. The logic then is that the mother church, the Jerusalem community of Jewish Christians is the restored tent or temple of Israel with Peter, James and John as its pillars. Gentiles must be integrated into this community. Paul agrees that there cannot be two peoples of God, and he also agrees that Christ came to redeem those under the Law first.

The question then becomes – on what basis are Gentiles integrated into and live as part of God's people? Paul argues, and he claims that James and Peter and John agreed, that the Gentiles would be accepted on the basis of faith, and circumcision would not be required. What is not in dispute in Paul's mind, however, is that the Gospel is to the Jew *first* and also to the Gentile (cf. Rom. 1.16 cf. Rom. 9–11). In other words, the logic that we have suggested above where 'we' means we Jewish Christians, makes perfectly good sense on Paul's lips, and especially so in a context where he is arguing about how one becomes part of and lives as the people of God. What is of importance is stressed by N. T. Wright. Paul is suggesting here, not that particular individuals might not keep the Law even in detail (cf. Phil. 3.6), but that the Jewish people as a people had not kept all the Law, indeed had repeatedly failed to do so, and so were under the curse of the Law. Accordingly, the Jewish people as a people were in need of redemption from the curse of the Law.[124] We can now attend to some of the details in vss. 13–14.

The verb ἐξηγόρασεν is found here and comes up again at 4.5. The aorist tense here points to the event of Christ's death. The term 'redemption' or 'redeem' comes into religious discussion from the realm of commerce, in particular from the discussion of the emancipation of slaves. Paul is in fact going to use a great deal of this sort of commercial language in what follows, including his use of the term slaves, his use of the phrase 'for freedom' (Gal. 5.1), and his speaking of the yoke of slavery.[125]

---

124. See N. T. Wright, *Climax of the Covenant*, pp. 145ff. Paul's sense of the people of God as a collective will reappear again when he uses the concept of being 'in Christ', but even more clearly when Paul uses the concept of 'seed' both to describe Christ and those who are in Christ (cf. Gal. 3.16, 19 to 3.29).

125. See below and cf. *Hellenistic Commentary to the New Testament*, ed. M. E. Boring et al. (Nashville: Abingdon, 1995), pp. 463ff.

The second half of vs. 13 speaks of Christ becoming a curse. We might have expected, in view of the quotation of Deut. 21.22–23, that Paul might say that Christ became cursed or endured a curse for us. The logic of this portion of vs. 13 is not perfectly clear, but perhaps we should not press the first phrase too literally and be content to think that Paul's meaning is more clearly expressed in the quotation. Mussner compares Jerm. 24.9; 42.18 and Zech. 8.13 and suggests that 'become a curse' is just a more vivid way of saying 'become accursed'.[126] Christ on the cross endured the curse of the Law, indeed the curse of God that falls on Lawbreakers, his execution being the carrying out of the curse. There is no need to talk about the exchange of one curse for another, rather we must talk about the exchange of one object of the curse for another.[127] Christ was born under the Law, and endured the curse that fell on Lawbreakers, not because Paul thinks he was such, but on behalf of those who were. The evidence or proof Paul gives that Christ endured such a curse is seen in the fact that he was crucified on a cross or tree. Paul no doubt knows the original context of Deut. 21.22–23, and that in its original setting the saying was about the hanging of a corpse on a tree after execution, as a shaming device. However, Paul may also have known about the use of the text in early Judaism, for example in 11QTemple 64.6–13 where the language of this text is used to speak of execution on a tree, that is of crucifixion (so also 4Q169 psNah 1.17–18). This is certainly how he uses the text here. In any case, the implications of this verse have been aptly summed up by Donaldson: "the redemptive road passes through the territory of the Law (and its people): 'Christ redeemed us from the curse of the Law'. It was not possible to make an end run around the Law and those in its domain. Rather, the way forward for both Jew and Gentile required the redemption of Israel from its plight ὑπὸ νόμον."[128]

Verse **14** presents us with two ἵνα clauses. The question is whether they are to be seen as co-ordinate or whether the latter clause is dependent on the former. The most fundamental point to be made is that Paul here returns to the theme enunciated in vs. 5, which makes clear that all of Gal. 3.1–14 is part of one argument. It would appear that we have here two purpose clauses, which means they must be connected to what has gone before in vs. 13. Paul then would be arguing that Christ had to endure the curse of the Law to redeem those under the Law, so that it would then be possible for the blessing of Abraham to be realized among the nations. In short, part of the purpose of redeeming Israel was so that Gentiles also might join the people of God by means of faith in the crucified Christ.

126. Mussner, *Galaterbrief*, p. 233.
127. See Matera, *Galatians*, p. 124: "The Christ in whom we believe . . . freed us from the Law's curse by assuming the curse of the Law for us."
128. Donaldson, p. 102.

Notice how Paul puts the matter – the blessing of Abraham comes to the Gentile nations, but only in Christ. He will amplify on the meaning of 'in Christ' in what follows. He also says that Christ's death was so that the promise of the Spirit might be received through faith. Is Paul in these two ἵνα clauses simply saying the same thing in two different ways, namely that the blessing of Abraham is the same as the promise of the Spirit? Clearly enough the first clause refers to what the Gentiles get. It is quite possible that the second clause refers to what the Jews get since Paul says 'in order that *we* might receive the promise of the Spirit'. It is true to say that the blessing of Abraham, namely inclusion of the nations in the people of God by faith, comes to the Gentiles through or with the reception of the promised Spirit. Here faith and the reception of the Spirit are closely linked in the believer's life, just as we saw a parallel between these two things mentioned in reverse order in 3.5 and 3.9. Nevertheless, if Paul is being consistent in his use of 'we' in this passage, Paul will be seeking to emphasize that Christ's death not only opened the door for the Gentiles to receive the blessing but for Jews to receive the Spirit, just as he had already said the Galatian converts did at 3.5 (cf. Acts 2.32).[129] This concludes Paul's complex argument from Scripture, but it is not by any means the end of this first main argument, only the end of its second main division.

Argument I, Division 3: 3.15–18

THE APPEAL TO LEGAL COVENANTS

Quintilian reminds us that it was the normal practice to begin with one's strongest arguments or proofs and finish with the weakest ones (*Inst. Or.* 5.12.14). Paul is following this procedure carefully as he brings his first major argument to a close. What we find in 3.15–18 is an analogy between human and divine covenants and more technically what we have here is a *similitudo* or simile. A simile is a bit different from an example (*exemplum*), though it has a force or rhetorical effect very similar to an example (*Inst. Or.* 5.11.22). Basically the force of the argument is strengthened to the degree that the things being compared are equal or nearly so. This form of proof is less powerful than for example the appeal to the Galatians' experience, not least because it involves an artificial, or humanly devised proof.[130] Paul himself alerts his audience at the outset of vs. 15 that the argument which will follow will be

---

129. See Matera, *Galatians*, p. 120.
130. See Betz, *Galatians*, p. 154, though Betz seems to confuse examples and similes.

κατὰ ἄνθρωπον. Burton has suggested this means 'from common human practice'[131] and Betz that we should translate it 'from common human life',[132] but both of these translations ignore the rhetorical function of the phrase. Paul is about to offer a humanly devised or artificial proof. What will follow will be speaking 'according to human beings' and so humanly generated as opposed to that which comes from God.[133] Paul has presented his two divine proofs, one from supernatural experience and one from the sacred Scriptures, and now he will turn to more mundane, merely human arguments, or as Chrysostom put it, Paul now uses human examples.[134] Martin Luther understood quite well what was going on here: "Paul adds another [argument], one that is based on the analogy of a man's will; this seems to be a rhetorical argument."[135] Almost completely missing the point of the phrase is Dunn who comments that Paul's use of the phrase κατὰ ἄνθρωπον indicates that Paul understood that his analogy here was a weak one.[136] Paul is not signalling the weakness of the analogy, only the humanness of the argument.[137] It would have been rhetorically inept to suggest an argument was lame, and then offer it![138]

131. Burton, *Galatians*, pp. 177–78.
132. Betz, *Galatians*, p. 154.
133. T. Zahn, *Der Brief des Paulus an die Galater* (Leipzig: Deichert, 1922), p. 161 was right that in Paul this phrase normally contrasts something human with that which comes from God or revelation. This is precisely how the phrase is used here as well. Cf. Rom. 3.5; 1 Cor. 9.8. See also Paul's use of the similar phrase κατὰ σάρκα for example in 2 Cor. 5.16 where it means 'from a human point of view'. Missing the point is C. H. Cosgrove, "Arguing like a Mere Human Being: Gal. 3.15–18 in Rhetorical Perspective," *NTS* 34 (1988), pp. 536–49 who assumes we have an *argumentum a persona* (*Inst. Or.* 5.10.23–31) and that Paul is adopting the argument or premises of his opponent here and turning them against them. He is, however, quite right (p. 538) that the phrase κατὰ ἄνθρωπον is not equivalent to the much later Latin phrase *argumentum ad hominem* (which is not attested during the Empire).
134. This comment is found at the beginning of Chrysostom's comment on Gal. 3.15. Longenecker, *Galatians*, p. 125 suggests this is an *ad hominem* argument, which is partly on the right track, though he also misses the rhetorical signal the phrase sends.
135. This is found in his 1535 commentary on this verse.
136. Dunn, *Galatians*, p. 181.
137. See C. H. Cosgrove, "Arguing like a Mere Human Being: Galatians 3.15–18 in Rhetorical Perspective," *NTS* 34 (1988), pp. 536–49, who is right on this point, but I would disagree that Paul is citing here the view of the agitators.
138. Note Chrysostom's interesting remark at this point: "he proceeds to common usages; and this he does invariably in order to sweeten his discourse, and render it more acceptable and intelligible to the duller sort." This segment of Paul's argument makes especially clear the difficulties of mirror-reading. For example, Mussner, *Galaterbrief*, p. 241 suggests that the opponents made the Sinai covenant a mere addendum to the Abrahamic one, or even wanted to nullify the Abrahamic covenant. As Betz, *Galatians*, p. 159 n. 56 says this is a difficult, indeed I would say highly improbable, thesis. We have no evidence that Paul even knew the details of the agitators' arguments.

It is to be noted that Paul begins this particular argument by calling his audience ἀδελφοί, a clear signal that he sees his audience as still Christian, albeit they are confused Christians. As Matera says, the rhetorical force of this term of endearment is to remind the audience of the close relationship it has with Paul. Notice that Paul uses the term increasingly, the further the argument progresses (cf. 4.12, 28, 31; 5.11, 13; 6.1, 18). This is part of his overall rhetorical strategy to move from alienation to reunion, so that by the end of the letter Paul can speak of 'we' and refer to himself and his audience.[139]

The word ὅμως an adverb which then is followed by the generic form of the noun 'human being' in the genitive, probably signals that Paul is arguing from the lesser to the greater, from what is true with a human 'covenant' to what is true with a divine one.[140] The word διαθήκη is an important term, and Paul will play on the various meanings of the term which range from 'testament', in the case of a human being, to 'covenant' in the case of God. In both cases the translation 'contract' or even 'agreement' would not really be adequate for we are not talking about a concordat between equals, nor a negotiated settlement, but a unilateral arrangement set up by one individual which affects others. More particularly Paul wants in each case to talk about an arrangement that once set up was unalterable.

The word διαθήκη appears first here, although Paul has been in fact talking about this matter since vs. 6. The basic meaning of the term in Greek literature is 'testament' or 'will', and it is intriguing that Josephus always uses this Greek word to mean this, and never uses it to mean covenant.[141] The LXX, however, does regularly use διαθήκη to translate the Hebrew word *berith* (270 out of 286 occurrences) which we regularly render covenant. When speaking of what God sets up, it seems clear that Paul follows the LXX. In any case a covenant is a declaration of an individual, not an agreement between two parties.[142]

Enormous debate has been undertaken about what known human practice, Roman, Greek, or Jewish, Paul could be referring to. On the one hand Betz was wrong that there was no such things as an irrevocable agreement in the first century about which the Galatians might have known,[143] for certainly there were irrevocable dispositions of property known both in Jewish circles and Greco-Roman ones.[144] The problem, however, is that these sorts of

---

139. Matera, *Galatians*, p. 126.

140. See Longenecker, *Galatians*, p. 126.

141. See, e.g., *War* 1.451, 573, 588, 600; *Ant.* 13.349, 17.53, 78, 146.

142. See Matera, *Galatians*, p. 126.

143. Betz, *Galatians*, p. 155.

144. Cf. BGU 993 and the discussion by R. Yaron, *Gifts in Contemplation of Death in Jewish and Roman Law* (Oxford: Clarendon Press, 1960), pp. 46ff. See also E. Bammel, "Gottes ΔΙΑΘΗΚΗ (Gal. 3.14–17) und das jüdische Rechtsdenken," *NTS* 6 (1960), pp. 313–19.

agreements are not identified by the term διαθήκη. Furthermore, the argument of G. Taylor that Paul is drawing on the Roman procedure known as *fidei commisum* must face the weakness that the term πίστις is not found in this argument nor other technical terms that might signal this is what Paul has in mind.[145] In the human realm, the latter seem always to have been alterable. Longenecker has made the suggestion that perhaps Paul is saying that whether we are talking about covenants or last wills and testaments, they were not alterable by an outside or third party.[146] Only the testator could later alter his will. Of course in Paul's view, God was not capricious and so God would not alter a covenant that was divine in origin. This may be what Paul has in mind, but there are two other possibilities.

Paul could be arguing in a truly 'artificial' manner, namely he could be speaking purely hypothetically at the human level – 'imagine a human will or testament that was irrevocable, like a covenant set up by God'. Secondly, it seems to have been overlooked that Paul's argument is surely grounded in his covenant theology. In Paul's view the Abrahamic covenant is a *separate* covenant from the Mosaic covenant, and thus one could not say that the stipulations of the Mosaic Law could simply be added to the Abrahamic covenant (see 4.24). These were different arrangements. This is in fact the basic assumption underlying vss. 17–18, and the reason why Paul can distinguish between a covenant previously ratified (the Abrahamic one) and the Law which came 430 years later, and also distinguish between the inheritance that comes from the 'promise' covenant as opposed to what comes from the Law covenant. In short, if one allows Paul's assumptions about the distinguishability of the Abrahamic and Mosaic covenants, his argument makes good sense and is stronger than is sometimes realized. We must now consider some of the details of the argument in vss. 15–18, bearing in mind the legal language Paul is using throughout (e.g., will/covenant; ratify; annul; inheritance).

Verse **15** uses the word ὅμως to introduce the argument itself, and in view of 1 Cor. 14.7 where we find the only other use of the term, it is probably the case that this term is used to set up or signal the comparison. We would expect it, in that case, to precede the latter member of the comparison but in fact Paul does not place it there in 1 Cor. 14.7 where a comparison is clearly going on. We should thus translate 'As with a human testament . . . so it is in the case . . .'[147] Paul is saying that no one annuls or adds to a ratified human testament. The tense of the participle κεκυρωμένην is perfect indicating that

145. Cf. G. M. Taylor, "The Function of ΠΙΣΤΙΣ ΧΡΙΣΤΟΥ in Galatians," *JBL* 85 (1966), pp. 58–76 and the critique by Cosgrove, "Gal. 3.14–18," pp. 538–39 n. 2.

146. Longenecker, *Galatians*, p. 130.

147. See rightly, Longenecker, *Galatians*, p. 127. In fact it is not impossible that ὅμως is mis-accented in our modern Greek testaments and could reflect the older ὁμῶς which meant equally, likewise.

the agreement is irrevocable, and the passive mood of the verb indicates it was a unilateral arrangement. This prepares us for what Paul wants to say about how God established a relationship with Abraham.

Verse **16** states plainly that 'the promises' were spoken to Abraham and to his 'seed'. The word 'promise' does not occur in Genesis, but the concept is surely implied in the Abraham story.[148] The notion was first mentioned in our text at 3.14 and it becomes a significant theme in the discussion from 3.16 through to the end of Gal. 4 (cf. 3.16, 21 for the plural; 3.14, 17, 18, 22, 29; 4.23, 28 for the singular). It has been suggested that the use of the plural (promises) has in mind Gen. 17.1–9 where God promises land, descendants, and to be Abraham's God.[149] This may be correct. The more important issue is the content of the promise. In a convincing argument, Williams has suggested that promise "on the one hand . . . refers to the divine pledge to Abraham that he would have innumerable descendants. But since God keeps his word, fulfills his pledge, through the operation of his Spirit, the promise of many descendants is, at the same time, the promise of the Spirit – that is, the promise of the *means* by which sons of Abraham would be created out of people who have been enslaved."[150]

The second half of vs. 16 involves an exegetical argument which hangs on the fact that σπέρμα is in the singular not in the plural. Paul has often been pilloried for exegetical legerdermain here, but in fact as Dunn says, this is not only anachronistic,[151] but it fails to note that the promise as given to Abraham referred intially to a particular individual, Isaac, and then also to Abraham's more remote descendants "so a rhetorical play on the ambiguity is invited".[152] Furthermore, Paul will use the term 'seed' to refer not only to Christ, but to believers at 3.29, indicating he is well aware that it was a collective noun which was also in the first instance used of an individual. There is also perhaps some evidence (cf. Jub. 16.17f.) that some Jewish interpreters had already referred 'seed' in the promise to Abraham to a particular person.[153] Finally, it must be borne in mind that Paul really does believe that the exalted Christ is an inclusive personality. He really believes that Christians are 'in Christ', and that in some sense and to some degree what has been given to Him has also been

---

148. See rightly, Dunn, *Galatians*, p. 183 who says the word promise summarizes the various passages where God says 'I will give' (cf. Gen. 15.2–3; 17.16).

149. See Schlier, *Galaterbrief*, p.143.

150. Williams, "Promise in Galatians: A Reading of Paul's Reading of Scripture," *JBL* 107 (1988), pp. 709–20, here p. 716.

151. See the discussion in the Excursus above pp. 219ff. about Paul's handling of Scripture.

152. Dunn, *Galatians*, p. 184.

153. Cf. M. Wilcox, "The Promise of the Seed in the NT and the Targumim," *JSNT* 5 (1979), pp. 2–20; Bruce, *Galatians*, pp. 172–73.

given to them. Thus Paul clearly identifies the 'seed' in the primary sense as not Isaac, but Christ. The "intention is not to deny that Abraham's seed is multitudinous in number, but to affirm that Christ's pre-eminence as that 'seed' carries with it the implication that all 'in Christ' are equally Abraham's seed (3.26–29)."[154]

In vs. **17** Paul speaks not on the authority or basis of the Galatians' experience, or on the basis of Scripture, or on the basis of the analogy, but on his own authority. Here his basic salvation historical argument comes to light. The covenant previously ratified by God by no means is annulled by the Law which was given 430 years later. This calculation is surely based on Ex. 12.40 LXX which says that the Israelites dwelled in Egypt for this length of time. What Paul is especially concerned with is that this Law did not annul or nullify the promise previously given to Abraham.[155] He is also suggesting the Law came on the scene a very long time after the promise was given.[156]

Verse **18** provides the conclusion that Paul wishes to draw on the basis of his historical observation and analysis.[157] The γὰρ indicates we are meant to connect the previous sentence to this one. Here again, though Paul uses εἰ plus an implied indicative verb, he is clearly dealing with what he considers to be an unreal condition: 'If the inheritance [comes] from the Law, then it does not come from the promise. But God graciously gave it to Abraham through (or by) the promise.' Here promise and Law are set over against each other as the essence or heart of two separate covenants. As Lightfoot says 'Law' and 'Promise' "are used without the article, as describing two opposing principles".[158]

Paul at this juncture introduces into the discussion for the first time, the concept of inheritance, which he will build upon later when he speaks of heirs and inheriting (3.29; 4.1, 7; 4.30; 5.21). The literal meaning of κληρονομία is legal portion or inheritance. Also important is the verb χαρίζομαι which is properly translated 'to give graciously or freely', and its perfect tense here signals that the effect of the giving is still ongoing.[159] This verb "lays stress on the character of the inheritance given – that is, it was an expression of God's

---

154. Dunn, *Galatians*, p. 185.

155. It is interesting that the Textus Receptus and various later uncials (D, G, I, K) and most minuscules add εἰς Χριστόν after 'by God' suggesting that the Abrahamic covenant was ultimately one that was made between God and the seed of Abraham, Christ. See Metzger, *TC*, p. 594.

156. Ziesler, *Galatians*, p. 44.

157. Here Cosgrove, pp. 548–49 is quite right. The issue here is not about getting in, but about how the heirs get their inheritance, and it is through Christ the seed of Abraham.

158. Lightfoot, *Galatians*, p. 144.

159. Mussner, *Galaterbrief*, pp. 242ff. may be right that this verb should be seen as another example of Paul's use of legal language.

grace and not a commercial transaction."[160] It is intriguing that Philo when he is discussing Gen. 17.2 says: "Now covenants (διαθῆκαι) are drawn up for the benefit of those who are worthy of the gift, so that a covenant is a token of the grace which God has set between Himself who proffers it and human beings who receive." Herein we see the difference between Philo and Paul. Paul would not affirm that the recipients were worthy of God's gracious gift.[161]

Paul's first major argument or proof has now come full circle. Paul began by discussing the gracious gift of God to the Galatians in the form of the Spirit in 3.1–5 and he concludes this first main argument by speaking of the initial gracious gift of a status and a promise to Abraham which was to be the source of that later 'Spiritual' blessing to the Gentiles. Paul has given here a strong rationale for rejecting the appeals of the agitators for the Galatians to submit to the Law, for he has appealed to the Galatians' experience, to Scripture, and to human reason and reflection using an analogy between human and divine covenants. Paul has contended that the Galatians already have (through Abraham), promise, Christ, the Spirit – in short the status and the spiritual benefits they need. Submitting to the Law would be neither necessary nor beneficial in such a situation. Paul then must answer the question which would surely follow from his first argument – Why then was the Law given at all if this is the case? To this task Paul turns in his second argument or proof, beginning at 3.19 and continuing on until 4.7. As we shall see, these arguments are meant to be cumulative in effect and they depend upon one another to accomplish Paul's rhetorical aims.[162]

Bridging the Horizons

For the modern reader, Paul's first argument will be seen as both straight forward and also confusing. His appeal to religious experience strikes a familiar note, but the way he handles Scripture does not, nor is his analogy with human covenants self-evident in our contemporary setting. Paul is one who was seeking to persuade a particular audience at a particular time about a particular matter, using the rhetorical techniques which were found persuasive in that day. Doubtless he would tell us to do the same if we are to be effective communicators of God's Word today. While I doubt we can or should simply

160. Longenecker, *Galatians*, p. 134.

161. Betz, *Galatians*, p. 156 shows that several of the major terms in the discussion in Gal. 3 are found in Gen. 17.1–11 LXX including διαθήκη and σπέρμα.

162. For example, the reason Paul must go on to say what he does about ethics and obedience in Gal. 4–6 is precisely because his second major proof would raise the question of how one should live, if one ought not to submit to the Law.

repeat Paul's hermeneutical techniques in handling the OT, we can never-theless, as Paul does, have a high view of Scripture and look for ways to draw analogies between the stories of the OT and our own stories today. My own suggestion is that when one is using ancient texts addressing situations rather different from those we find today, it is nonetheless possible to ask several probing questions of a text such as Gen. 15 or Gen. 17.

For example we may ask what the text tells us about God, what it tells us about human beings, and what it tells us about the way God seeks to relate to human beings. On this score the trust that Abraham had in God and in God's promise, still provides us with an excellent example of how a person of faith can and should live today, and the story of Abraham also reminds us that there are enormous benefits to living a life of trust, not the least of which is that by doing so we are accepted by the Almighty.

Paul's appeal to the dynamic work of the Holy Spirit in the lives of the Galatians, including the working of miracles will strike a chord, especially among those who gravitate towards more charismatic circles in the church. Yet we should not miss the fact that Paul is saying that the experience of the Spirit as saving presence in our lives is that which constitutes anyone a Christian. Paul is not talking about spiritual experiences for the few, while other Christians are viewed as 'pneumatically challenged', he is speaking about the dramatic transforming work that changes any convert from a non-Christian to a Christian. Christian belief and behavior are only possible if God has done a work in the individual in question. It is also noteworthy that Paul gives no encouragement to those who want to parse Christian experience into neat stages (stage one – trust in God, stage two – receive the Holy Spirit). In his view justification and reception of the Spirit are things that transpire at the same time at the beginning of one's Christian life. In Paul's thought there is no such person as a Christian without the Spirit of God in their life transforming it.

As this commentary develops it should become clearer all the time that Paul does indeed operate with a two- or perhaps even three-covenant theology (depending on whether one sees the new covenant as the fulfillment of the Abrahamic one and therefore part of it, or as its fulfillment without being a part of it). Paul believes that God is capable of starting afresh with the people of God, and that he did so in sending Jesus Christ. This is not because Paul thinks the Mosaic Law is a bad thing, but because he believes that Law has had its day and has ceased to be the standard that Christians must live by. If this is a correct reading of Paul's thought, it follows that the Christian cannot unreflectingly apply this or that verse of the Mosaic covenant to the lives of Christians without asking if this or that imperative or principle has in fact been reaffirmed in the new covenant.

In other words, when the question arises about obligation and obedience to God's Word, it is appropriate to ask which covenant Christians are under, and what obedience looks like under that particular covenant. We will have more to say on this subject when we discuss the Law of Christ. Here it is enough to remark that Paul encourages us all to read the OT both christologically and eschatologically, that is, in terms of promise and fulfillment, in terms of the new creation that has broken into the present evil age, in terms of God's Son who was born under the Law but came to redeem those under the Law from its power. The Gospel was certainly the sequel to the Law, but it certainly was not simply the Law Part Two, or just a renewal of the Law covenant. This is in part why Judaism and Christianity to this day appear to most to be rather different religions, and why some Jewish scholars, such as Jacob Neusner, have even suggested that Jesus intended to set up a new religion.

I do not think this last conclusion is right. There is no evidence that either Jesus or Paul or other early Christians thought in terms of their being two different peoples of God. Nevertheless, Jesus did set things in motion and Paul furthered his initial thrust suggesting a very different interpretation of what it meant to be a true heir of Abraham. We are still wrestling with these redefinitions even today, and we must wrestle with them carefully and prayerfully in a century which has seen not only the extermination of millions of Jews due to violent anti-Semitism but also increasing hostility toward Christianity as the west becomes increasingly neo-pagan and more secular.

Argument II: 3.19–4.7

The Goal of the Guardian, The Function of the Faithful One

Why then the Law? It was added because of transgressions (until the time when the seed came to whom promise was given), ordained through angels by the hands of a mediator. But the mediator is not [a mediator] of one, but God is one. Is then the Law against the promises of God? Absolutely not! For if a Law had been given which was able to make alive, then righteousness would actually be from the Law. But the Scripture confined all under sin, in order that the promise due to the faithfulness of Jesus Christ might be given to those who believe.

Before the Faith came, we were confined under the Law being guarded until the destined Faith was to be revealed, so that the Law was our guardian unto Christ, in order that we might be righteous from faith. But when the Faith came we were no longer under the guardian. For you are all sons of God through faith in Christ Jesus. For whoever was baptized into Christ clothed himself in Christ. Not any Jew or Gentile, not any slave or free, not any male and female, for all are one in Christ Jesus. But if you are of Christ, then you are seed of Abraham, and inheritors according to the promise.

But I say as long as the legal heir is a minor, he differs not at all from a slave of the master, but he is under the guardian and household steward until the date set by the father. So also we, when we were minors being under the elementary principles of the world, were enslaved. But when the fullness of time came, God sent out his Son, born from woman, born under the Law, in order that he might ransom those under the Law, so that we might receive adoption as sons. But because you are sons God sent out the Spirit of his Son into our hearts crying 'Abba, Father', so that you are no longer a slave but a son. But if a son then also a legal heir through God.

It was the task of any good rhetor to anticipate any questions or objections to one's arguments that might be raised by one's audience, and to forestall them by answering them in advance. Paul does this here, once again drawing on the diatribe style involving a question to an imaginary interlocutor followed by the speaker's answer.[1] Quintilian reminds his hearers that it is a mistake to trivialize or ignore the possible objections that may be raised to one's arguments (*Inst. Or.* 5.13.36). He also warns declaimers that "they should not put forward objections that can easily be met or assume that their opponent is

---

1. On which see pp. 25ff. above.

a fool" (5.13.42). Paul could not be accused of either fault in what follows in his second argument. He takes seriously the question he raises in 3.19 and takes care to explain the purpose of the Law, in view of what he has maintained in the first major argument of the *probatio*.[2]

As Betz says, the discussion of the Law and of its nature and purpose was indeed a standing topic for philosophers, theologians, but also for orators as well. Quintilian says that both lawyers and also those who study in the rhetorical schools "raise the question of the letter and the intention of the law, in fact a large proportion of legal disputes turn on these points" (7.6.1). It is intriguing that under the heading of how to speak properly about the intention of the law, Quintilian says "in cases concerned with wills (or testaments) it sometimes happens that the intention of the testator is clear, though it has not been expressed in writing . . . A second heir had been appointed in the event of a posthumous son dying while a minor. No posthumous son was born. The next of kin claimed the property. Who could doubt that the intention of the testator was that the same man should inherit in the event of the son not being born who would have inherited in the event of his death? But he had not written this in his will" (7.6.9–10). Besides the fact that Paul draws on the language of this sort of discussion beginning in Gal. 3 and continuing into Gal. 4, as well as on the standing topic 'what is the intent of the law?', it should be also noted that there is a further intriguing parallel between the case Quintilian mentions and the one with which Paul is dealing. Paul knows full well that the Mosaic covenant does not place itself under a time limit, nor does it suggest that the Gentiles might inherit Abrahamic blessings through faith alone. Accordingly, Paul must argue that the intent of the testator (i.e., God) in giving the Mosaic covenant and Law, while not revealed in that document itself, is revealed by a study of the larger history of God's people, both during the Abrahamic period before Moses, and now in the era since Christ has come. In particular, the intent of the testator in giving the Law and the fact that the Law had a limited purpose and function become clear in and through the Christ event and so outside the Mosaic Law itself. Also, who the proper heirs are, and on what basis they may inherit is not given final definition in the Mosaic covenant itself, but in Paul's view is revealed in part in the earlier Abrahamic covenant, and more clearly in the Gospel. Paul then must

---

2. Kennedy, *New Testament Interpretation*, p. 149 remarks: "His anticipation of objections involves difficult philosophical or theological concepts which are very succinctly stated, and though they may have been clear to him, their rhetorical function in the letter is perhaps more to seem to recognize the possibility of objections and to be prepared to answer them confidently than to provide a developed response." This underestimates the force and logic of Paul's salvation historical schema in which he can give the Law an important role in the history of God's people, without admitting that it would always be applicable to them.

appeal to the true intent of the testator as revealed in the story of Abraham and of Christ.

As he has done with his first argument, Paul will press his case until he can reach a proper conclusion about who the heirs are and how they inherit (cf. 3.18 to 4.7). Also as with his previous argument he will lead up to a positive statement of 'Good News' speaking of promise and inheritance, or in the case of the second argument, possession of the Spirit and being an heir (4.6–7). Notice too that Paul's second major argument has three subdivisions as did his first argument (3.19–22; 3.23–29; 4.1–7), and further more in both cases: (1) the first division of the argument is carried forward by rhetorical questions; (2) the second division of the argument relies on a discussion of the progression of salvation history and draws on traditional material (the Scriptures in the former case; Christian tradition in the latter); (3) the third division of the argument has to do with inheritance or being heirs and that one does not receive the inheritance through or while under the Law. The following chart sums up the parallels.

ARGUMENT I	ARGUMENT II
DIVISION 1 – 3.1–5	DIVISION 1 – 3.19–22
RHETORICAL QUESTIONS	RHETORICAL QUESTIONS

LEADING TO CONCLUSION THAT WHAT
WAS PROMISED IS RECEIVED THROUGH FAITH (cf. 3.5, 22)

DIVISION 2 – 3.6–14	DIVISION 2 – 3.23–29
USE OF SACRED TRADITIONS	USE OF SACRED TRADITIONS
(OT)	(CHRISTIAN)

LEADING TO CONCLUSION THAT GENTILES RECEIVE
BLESSING OF ABRAHAM AND ARE HIS OFFSPRING THROUGH
FAITH IN AND BELONGING TO CHRIST (cf. 3.14, 29)

DIVISION 3 – 3.15–18	DIVISION 3 – 4.1–7
ANALOGY WITH ORDINARY	ANALOGY WITH ORDINARY
HUMAN AFFAIRS	HUMAN AFFAIRS

LEADING TO CONCLUSION
THAT ONE IS AN HEIR AND HAS INHERITANCE BECAUSE OF
GOD'S PROMISE TO ABRAHAM[3]

---

3. Notice the same sort of pattern of argumentation in 1 Cor. 11.2ff. where Paul first appeals to sacred arguments from Scripture and then from nature, and finally from human custom.

In short Paul's arguments have been carefully crafted to lead to a positive conclusion; they are not haphazardly thrown together. They also deal along the way with objections raised about or on the basis of the Law. It becomes clear that, as with the example cited above from Quintilian, Paul is arguing about covenants or testaments and the dispensing of inheritance to those who may have seemed not to be directly in line to inherit according to the Mosaic Law. Paul's view is that the Galatians have already received both the status of heir and at least in part the promised inheritance. They have no need to come under the Mosaic covenant, and it is in any case no longer incumbent upon God's people, for the Law has had its day and has become, since Christ has come, a glorious anachronism, but an anachronism nonetheless. In any case it did not provide either the basis for or the inheritance itself.

It will be seen from what has just been said that it is a significant mistake to relegate 3.19ff. to the role of a digression (*digressio*) as Betz does, for discussing the purpose of the Law is critical to Paul's overall argument.[4] The question raised in 3.19 is not just an aside, or about a minor issue. The second argument is intended in part to prevent the hearers from wrongly concluding that the Law had no purpose or function in God's divine economy since it did not provide the basis of right relationship with God or provide the Spirit and life. This second argument explains for the first time the positive though limited (in time and scope) role the Law was intended by God to play in the life of God's people and it does so by comparing and contrasting that role with the role Christ plays in the life of the believer.

Argument II, Division 1: 3.19–22

WHY THE LAW WAS ADDED

It is is scarcely an exaggeration to say that how one views Gal. 3.19–20 will go a long way to determining how one understands Paul's view of the Mosaic Law. This can be seen, for example, in the treatments of this passage by H. Hübner, H. Räisänen, and E. P. Sanders, to name but three. Hübner's hypothesis is that Paul's view of the Law developed and changed significantly between the time of writing Galatians and the time Romans was written. Briefly Hübner suggests that as opposed to what we find in Romans, Paul argues in Galatians that the Law is not divine in origin, in fact it comes from evil angels or

---

4. Betz, *Galatians*, p. 163.

demons.[5] H. Räisänen does not agree with Hübner's assessment but he too concludes that in regard to the issue of the origin and purpose of the Law Galatians 3.19ff. is at odds with other Pauline passages.[6] It is characteristic of Räisänen's argument that he finds internal contradictions in Paul's arguments both here in Galatians and in Romans. By contrast with both of these views, E. P. Sanders while agreeing that Gal. 3.19–20 is a *crux interpretum,* argues that Paul's views are internally coherent but not systematic. His view is that Paul's argument can be made sense of when one realizes that Paul is arguing from 'solution to plight' viewing the Law through the lens of Christ, who is seen as the solution to the human dilemma.[7] In short, these two verses require close scrutiny.

The first issue to be raised is whether we should translate τί οὖν as 'Why then' or as 'What then'. Scholarly opinion is divided on this matter, but the following clues suggest an answer to the question. The οὖν is retrospective, which tells us that the question being raised is raised because of what has been said in the first argument. It is fair to say that the first argument did not raise questions so much about the nature or essence of the Law, but rather what *purpose* it could possibly have if one gets promise, Spirit, inheritance through faith in Christ and not by works of the Law. The question left hanging after the first argument was – Is the Law superfluous since it does not provide the sort of soteriological benefits the Galatians already enjoy quite apart from any observance of Torah? Secondly, it should not be objected that τί can't be taken adverbially, for clearly enough it can and is used this way in the Pauline corpus when τί is not accompanied by a preposition (cf. Rom. 3.7; 14.10; 1 Cor. 4.7; 10.30; Gal. 5.11; Col. 2.20). There are in fact no real stylistic or grammatical reasons why we cannot translate this phrase 'Why then . . .'.[8] We must then discern from what follows whether Paul thinks the Law has or ever had any real *raison d'être,* and if so if its purpose is merely negative in character, or also positive.

In the second half of vs. **19** Paul states succinctly the purpose or at least a purpose of the Mosaic Law – 'it was added because of transgressions until the Seed came . . .' Whatever Paul means by this elliptical remark, he places the statement of purpose under a time constraint. The word ἄχρις indicates that 'it was added . . . *until* . . .' This is a remarkable statement by a first-century Jew,

---

5. See H. Hübner, *Das Gesetz bei Paulus: Ein Betrag zum Werden der paulinischen Theologie* (Göttingen: Vandenhoeck & Ruprecht, 1978), now available in English as *Law in Paul's Thought* (Edinburgh: T. & T. Clark, 1984).

6. H. Räisänen, *Paul and the Law* (Tübingen: Mohr, 1986).

7. See Sanders, *Paul, the Law, and the Jewish People,* his main treatment of Gal. 3.19–20 can be found on pp. 65–70.

8. See rightly, D. B. Wallace, "Galatians 3.19–20: A *Crux Interpretum* for Paul's View of the Law," *WestTJ* 52 (1990), pp. 225–45, here pp. 231–32.

for we can provide plenty of evidence that early Jews believed that the Law had a permanent, indeed an eternal purpose and significance for the life of God's people (cf. 2 Bar. 4.1; 1 En. 99.2; Wis. 18.4; Jub. 1.27; 3.31; Josephus *Ap.* 2.277). Furthermore, there is nothing in the way Paul puts this matter that suggests that he talking about the cessation of only *some* of the purposes of the Law. Paul's argument has to do with eras of salvation history, and in his view the coming of the Seed changed the eschatological state of affairs and brought to a close the age when the Law had a necessary and indeed crucial function in the life of God's people. As I.-G. Hong has argued, the Law is seen by Paul as an important parenthesis between the Abrahamic covenant and the fulfillment of the promises to Abraham in Christ, but a parenthesis none-theless, a temporary means of God's dealing with the chosen people.[9] L. Belleville is right to stress that the series of analogies Paul uses to describe the role of the Law suggest a temporary, not a permanent role. Paul does not picture "a no-exit situation. Otherwise the analogies of a παιδαγωγός, ἐπίτροπος, and οἰκονόμος, as well as the parallel with τὰ στοιχεῖα τοῦ κόσμου, become meaningless."[10]

We must now deal with the word παραβάσεων which appears at the very beginning of the answer about the Law's purpose. Clearly enough the word means transgression, but the question is whether it is seen as simply a synonym with ἁμαρτία (sin) or even with παράπτωμα (trespass) or has some distinct meaning. This matter can be debated precisely because on the one hand Paul says explicitly in Rom. 4.15 that where there is no Law there is no transgression (παράβασις). This text has suggested to most that by 'transgression' Paul must mean a violation of an existing and known law. However, D. J. Lull has pointed to Rom. 5.14 where Paul speaks of Adam's sin as a 'transgression' (παράβασις).[11] This citation, however, does not necessarily mean that Paul is not consistent in his usage of the term. Paul is well aware that the Genesis story says that God had given an explicit commandment to Adam and Eve (cf. Rom. 7.7–12).[12] Paul nowhere says that the Mosaic Law is the only law God ever gave to any human being. Thus, we may conclude that παράβασις in Gal. 3.19 surely does mean a violation of an existing law, just as the statement in Rom. 4.15 sugggests, and it is the context which in this case lets us know that Paul has in mind a rather specific law, the Mosaic one.

---

9. I.-G. Hong, *The Law in Galatians* (Sheffield: JSOT Press, 1993), pp. 149–56.

10. L. Belleville, "'Under Law': Structural Analysis and the Pauline Concept of Law in Galatians 3.21–4.11," *JSNT* 26 (1986), pp. 53–78, here p. 71. On these analogies see the discussion that follows.

11. D. J. Lull, "'The Law was our Pedagogue': A Study in Galatians 3.19–25," *SBL* 105 (1986), pp. 481–98, here p. 484.

12. On this text being a dramatic presentation of the Genesis story see my *Paul's Narrative Thought World*, pp. 14ff.

The verb προσετέθη is an aorist passive verb with a suffix, and the appropriate question to be asked is: 'added' by whom? The context does not say specifically, but it is surely most natural to take this as another example of the divine passive, especially when in the very next clause we find ἐπήγγελται, a passive which clearly implies God is the agent. Paul *had* previously said that God gave the promises. Hübner has tried to argue that Paul is saying that the (evil) angels were ultimately responsible for the Law, but this suggestion not only makes less sense in view of ἐπήγγελται, but also surely Paul would have mentioned the angels not in the subordinate construction near the end of the verse but with the main verb.[13] There is no reason to doubt that when in Rom. 7.12 Paul says the Law is holy, just and good, and when in Rom. 8.7 he speaks of *God's* Law, he had always believed this was the case. This is not a new view that only surfaces after he wrote Galatians; it was a view Paul had strongly held both before and after his conversion.

As a final comment on the verb 'added' I see no reason to suggest that this implies inferiority. What it *does* imply is subsequence to the promises, which is the point already made in vss. 15–18. What it surely does *not* imply is that "the role of the Law . . . is integrated into that of the promise".[14] This is precisely what Paul argues *against* in Gal. 3.15 when he says no one adds a codicil to or annuls an already existing testament (or covenant)! As Gal. 4.24 makes abundantly clear, Paul sees the Abrahamic covenant and the Mosaic covenant as two separate covenants, not two parts of one covenant. One is added to Israel's story after the other, and Paul is trying to maintain their separation, while the agitators presumably were seeing them as blended together.[15] Furthermore, it is added *until* Christ came: "The temporality of the Law includes an *end* as well as a beginning in history, a point made five times in 3.19–25 (vv. 19c, 23a and c, 24a, 25)."[16]

Comment must also be made on the word χάριν, a following preposition. The question is whether we should take this word and its appended phrase in a causal sense 'to cause or increase transgressions' or in a cognitive sense 'to bring about a knowledge of or point out transgressions'. Was the purpose of the Law to make sin known or to increase or multiply sin? Here several comments are in order. Firstly, in view of Paul's consistent use of the term 'transgressions' the meaning here is unlikely to be 'because of already existing transgressions', or 'to multiply transgressions' because no transgressions against the Mosaic Law existed before it was 'added'. It is well to ask, as Longenecker does, why God would wish to increase the number of

13. See rightly Wallace, "Galatians 3.19–20," p. 235.
14. Contra Dunn, *Galatians*, p. 192.
15. See pp. 21ff. above.
16. Lull, "The Law was our Pedagogue," p. 483.

transgressions leading up to the time of Christ.[17] Furthermore, our interpretation of the purpose and role of the Law here must comport with the
role predicated of the Law in the 'guardian' analogy (cf. below), and it is
unlikely that that analogy is meant to portray an entirely negative view of the
Law.

I would suggest that what Paul means is that the Law turns sin, which
certainly already existed before and apart from the Law, into transgression.[18]
That is, the Law makes quite clear that every sin is a sin against God. Lull is on
the right track when he says "the Law identifies sin for what it is, imputes
sinful deeds to those who do them, and in that sense increases the tresspass".[19]
This is an increase not in number, but in responsibility, because sin has been
identified for what it is and shown plainly and in writing to be against God's
will (cf., e.g., the NEB 'to make wrong-doing a legal offence'). It should also be
added that this is not a *negative* function of the Law, for from God's point of
view it is a positive thing for humans to be made aware that they have sinned
and fallen short of God's glory.

It is worth adding at this point that there is a difference between the
purpose of the Law and its effect on fallen human beings. In Romans Paul
will talk in some detail about what the effects of the Law are, not the least of
which is that with a fallen person a perfectly good law can be a stimulus to sin,
an impetus to try a new form of rebellion. Here Paul will talk about the
Law's intended purpose which was to keep God's people under custody,
confined, giving them the status of a minor until Christ came. It was to be
their παιδαγωγός. In other words, it was to guard them, when necessary
discipline them, and to inform them about the rudimentary rules and ways of
God. The social consequence and one might even say the social intent of this
Law was to separate God's people from the nations. One can see this social
consequence played out in the Antioch episode (Gal. 2.11–14), and Paul
believes strongly that the Law will continue to divide Jew from Gentile, even
when they are Christians, if the Law is insisted on as the necessary *modus
vivendi* within the Body of Christ. This Paul cannot abide, and he offers his
alternative theologically in the two major arguments in Gal. 3–4, and socially
in Gal. 3.26–28.

In some ways, the final two clauses of vs. 19 are the most puzzling, and
what follows in vs. 20, which seems to amplify on the matter, is only a partial
help. The clauses probably are to be translated 'ordained through angels by the
hand of a mediator'. Ever since Jerome, there have always been those who have
argued that the mediator that is being referred to is Christ, rather than Moses,

17. Longenecker, *Galatians*, p. 138.
18. See the helpful discussion of N. T. Wright, *The Climax of the Covenant*, pp.
160ff.
19. Lull, p. 484.

which is the usual view.[20] This view, however, finds little support in the context. Christ here is called the Seed, not the mediator, and though Paul is not averse to occasionally mixing metaphors it is doubtful this is an example of such a practice.[21]

A further point is that Paul, when he wishes to speak of evil supernatural beings, calls them demons, not angels (cf. 1 Cor. 10.20–21). There is absolutely nothing in this context to suggest Paul is viewing these angels in a negative light. We must also consider the use of διά here. Though occasionally this preposition can have the force of ὑπό, this is quite rare. If Paul had wanted to make the angels ultimately responsible as the source of the Law, ὑπό is surely the more natural choice. Διά normally expresses intermediate agency, and this is likely to be the case here. The Law was ordained by God, but came to Moses through angels. This latter interpretation finds ample support in other texts which speak of the angels having a positive role in the giving of the Law (cf. Deut. 33.2 LXX; Ps. 67.18 LXX; Jub. 1.27–29; Acts 7.38, 53; Heb. 2.2).

The phrase ἐν χειρὶ (literally, in the hand) is a Hebraism meaning by means of (cf. Lev. 26.46; Acts 11.30). There is plenty of evidence that Moses was seen as and called a mediator in early Judaism (cf., e.g., Philo *Vit. Mos.* 2.166; *Assump. Mos.* 1.14; Heb. 8.5–6). We must conclude then that Paul is referring here to the giving of the Law, which was ordained by God, and given to God's people through the agency of both supernatural and natural beings. There is nothing here that necessarily implies a criticism of the Law. But this material must be seen in tandem with vs. 20 to which we now turn. Paul's point is not to deny that the Law is God's word, but to deny that it is his last and definitive word. It was a word in due season and *pro tempore*.

Verse 20 is clearly elliptical. Literally the text says 'But a mediator is not "of one", but God is One'. It is possible to fill in the blank as follows 'But a mediator is not [a mediator] of one, but God is one'. The NEB may be on the right track in translating 'an intermediary is not needed for one party acting alone, and God is one.' Wright is correct that it is important to see this entire discussion in the light of the stress on unity throughout this context. Paul has just argued that there is one Seed, and that the promises have been given to this one seed. He is going to go on to argue in the second division of this second argument that in Christ all Christians are one person (3.28), or as we might say one family. Here in the verse at hand Paul stresses the oneness of God, alluding no doubt to the Shema in Deut. 6.4, something he does elsewhere as well (cf. 1 Cor. 8.6; Rom. 3.29–31).

20. See Wright, p. 160 n. 17 for a list.
21. The later material found in 1 Tim. 2.5 is surely not germane here. Paul's audience couldn't be expected to think along these lines unless there was some clue in Galatians to suggest such a view, and there is not. One must also ask why ἑνὸς is in the genitive here ('of one'). See Wright, p. 160.

The reason for the stress on unity is precisely because the introduction of the Law and its observance into the discussion in Galatia has created division there, and threatens to sever the body of Christ into two parts, as it seems to have done in Antioch (cf. Gal. 2.11–14). In other words, Paul is concerned with the social effect or consequences of requiring Torah observance in Galatia, and he uses theological arguments to deal with this problem.[22] He is also, however, concerned with right thinking about the Law and the faith, and right living as well and so it is not just the social issues which exercise him.

With the translation 'but a mediator is not a mediator of one, but God is one' in the phrase 'of one', the question becomes – 'one' what? Often Paul's argument has been assumed to be that while on the one hand God dealt with Abraham directly, face to face so to speak, on the other hand the Mosaic covenant came to God's people through a mediator and through angelic helpers as well. On this reading the issue is one of immediacy and intimacy. Longenecker puts this view of the Law as follows: "Its point has to do with the inferiority of the Law because of its indirect introduction into the people's existence."[23] It seems clear enough that the concept of a mediator implies a duality or plurality of parties or groups between whom the mediator must mediate, and so Paul may indeed be saying that a mediated revelation is inferior to an immediate one. This would comport with his emphasis that the Law came later than the promise and was for a specific duration, unlike the promise. "The Law is therefore to be understood not as a restriction of the Abrahamic promises to one race – that is the mistake Paul's opponents are making – but as a temporary measure introduced for certain specific purposes which, in the long run, would not prevent but rather facilitate the creation of the single family spoken of in the promise."[24]

Wright suggests that we must read Gal. 3.20 in a similar fashion to what we find in Rom. 3.29–31. God is one, which is also to say that God is the one God both of Jews and of Gentiles and God desires to create one family out of humankind involving both Jews and Gentiles, not two families. Moses is not the mediator 'of the one *family*' precisely because the Law he mediated created and was intended to create a separate people, the Jews, setting them apart from the rest of humanity. This sort of argument makes good sense of what Paul is saying here, but would the Galatians have understood the elliptical 'of one' to refer to 'of one *family*' or would they have understood it to be a basic statement about a mediator standing between two groups? I incline to the latter view.[25] In any case, that the Law was given through a mediator certainly

---

22. Here Watson, *Paul, Judaism, and the Gentiles*, pp. 70ff. is on the right track.
23. Longenecker, *Galatians*, p. 142.
24. Wright, *Climax*, p. 167.
25. See Dunn, *Galatians*, p. 191 and n. 1.

suggests a certain separation or distance between the Holy God and the people God has chosen.[26] Intimacy such as Abraham experienced comes only through faith and by grace.[27]

The Law's function was to confine and guard God's people until 'the Faith' could come (cf. below), making them aware that sin was transgression against God and that God required holiness of heart and life. It shut up all Jews under sin and under a curse, not because the Law was wicked in intent but because God's people, as a collective entity, were not faithful or careful to keep the Law. This condition lasted until Christ the faithful one came and exhausted the curse on God's people by dying on the cross.

In view of vs. **21**, it appears Paul feels that something he had just said could be interpreted to mean that the Law opposed or compromised or altered the promises. Paul strongly wishes to deny such an implication and does so using the familiar exclamation μὴ γένοιτο – absolutely not![28] The point is that the Law wasn't meant to give what the promises promised, it wasn't meant to 'make alive' or give a person a right relationship with God. Here Paul is offering a contrary to fact condition. This is signaled by εἰ with a past tense verb in the protasis followed by ἄν with a past tense verb in the apodosis (cf. Gal. 1.10b; 1 Cor. 2.8; 1 Jn. 2.19). The verb ἐδόθη ('had been given'), suggests again that the Law he has in mind originates with God. But even so, this Law was not able to make a fallen sinful person alive (ζῳοποιῆσαι), which was what was needed, only the Spirit could do that (cf. 2 Cor. 3.6). This was not the purpose of the Law, and indeed the effect of the Law on fallen persons was quite the opposite of making live.[29]

26. Wright, *Climax*, pp. 169–72.

27. It perhaps does not need to be said that Paul did not see Christ as a mere mediator of a covenant, or at least not as a mediator of the same order and ilk as Moses. Christ is seen as the one who actually performs the divine saving tasks, not merely delivers the Word.

28. See pp. 186–87 above on this phrase.

29. While Paul does not want to say that the Law is against the promises, nonetheless the Mosaic Law and the promises are two separate things, given at different times to God's people, being part of different covenants and serving different purposes, or as Hong, *Law in Galatians*, p. 150 says when the promise was given there was no Mosaic Law, but when the promise was fulfilled in Christ, it presupposed a people under the Law, under its curse, needing redemption. He adds "the Law came to help the promise to find fulfillment through Christ by producing transgressions, not by preventing them." I would prefer to say it turned sins into transgressions (cf. Barrett, *Freedom*, p. 34: "Its effect was . . . To make sin everywhere observable in the form of transgression"). In Paul's view the Law and the promises should not be blended or integrated together. Dunn is right to speak of "the limited power of the Law . . . it was not so ultimate and important a factor in the divine purpose as grace and Spirit, as promise and inheritance received through faith; nor so ultimate and powerful as sin . . ." (p. 195).

Paul says in vs. 22 that 'The Scripture locked up all things' under the power of sin so that what was promised might be given to those who believe in Christ and rely on the faithfulness of Jesus Christ.[30] The verb συγκλείω when used figuratively means to confine, hem in, imprison, or lock up. Possibly Paul personifies the Scripture here as a guardian or even a jailor. The question is whether by 'the Scripture' he is referring to a particular text here, such as Deut. 27.26 (the definite article before Scripture perhaps pointing us to some particular unnamed passage),[31] or whether by Scripture here he simply means God's Word in general,[32] or whether he is speaking about the Law in general.

Wright, for example, assumes Paul means the Law and argues "the fact that the Law has the effect of shutting up [people] under sin (cf. Rom. 11.32) does not mean it is not a good Law, but simply that all human beings are sinful and therefore can find membership in the people of God only through faith in Jesus Christ."[33] There may, however, be a problem with drawing an analogy with Rom. 11.32, for there quite clearly it is God who is doing the imprisoning. The parallel is close enough to raise the subject again of whom Paul sees as confined here in Galatians. In Rom. 11 Paul is clearly talking about all human beings, both Jews and Gentiles being confined to disobedience. Here, however, τὰ πάντα means literally 'all things' and while the focus may be particularly on humans the parallel usage in Col. 1.20 and Ephes. 1.10 suggests a broader nuance including 'things in heaven' as well as 'things on earth'. Barrett notes that the neuter of 'all' here rather than the masculine form of the word expresses comprehensiveness and universality.[34]

It is possible then to take this statement apocalyptically. Paul would mean that all of the created order including humans was under the power of sin and feeling the effects of the fall. This comports with the reference to the present evil age in Gal. 1.4. If this is the meaning, then Paul may simply be alluding to the story in Genesis 3 about the fall and its effects not only on humans but on

30. On the translation of the key phrase here as 'the faith/faithfulness of Christ' see pp. 179ff. above. This phrase in fact prepares us for what follows in vs. 23 where we hear about the revelation of 'the coming Faith'.

31. Ἡ γραφὴ does normally mean some particular Scripture elsewhere in Paul (cf. Gal. 3.8; 4.30; Rom. 4.3; 9.17; 10.11; 11.2), but it is not impossible that this text is an exception.

32. See Matera, Galatians, p. 135 who points to Gal. 3.8 and says Scripture here is not a synonym for Law, but for God's will. Betz, Galatians, p. 175 clearly distinguishes between the Scripture and the Law, with only the former seen as an agent of salvation, though he also says Torah or Law does have a positive part to play in the process, not in conveying life or salvation, but in confining God's people so that the promises might go to those who believe when Christ appeared.

33. Wright, p. 172.

34. Barrett, Freedom, p. 34. He adds "It may in theory offer a way of life; in practice it signifies a sentence of death. There is no way to the presence of God by works of the Law, obedience and virtue; that way is bolted, barred, and barricaded."

the earth and other things as well. In this case Paul may mean the action and sentence of God taken against humankind in general. The reference to the Law doing this in Gal. 3.23, where the Law is seen as the jailor, is not necessarily against this conclusion, for Paul can sometimes use the term Law to refer to material in parts of the Pentateuch not directly associated with Moses or the Mosaic Law.

It is also possible to conclude that 'under sin' is a broader category than being 'under the curse', for it would include everyone, but those under the curse are those under the Law, namely Jews and those Gentiles who have submitted to the Law. The human dilemma for all is sin, the human dilemma for those under the Law is also transgression and the curse of the Law. Paul subscribes to the theory that to whom more is given more is required, and perhaps also that judgment falls firstly upon the house of God, and so likewise redemption comes to that house first as well.[35] To sum up, all persons, whether under the Law or not have been imprisoned or confined in sin, and the only way out for either Jew or Gentile was faith in the faithful one Jesus Christ. This is the means by which the promises and the benefits they offered could be partaken of. Once again Paul has drawn a division of his argument to a climax by making clear that it was through faith and promise, not through Law and works that the blessings were inherited.[36]

Argument II, Division 2: 3.23–29

THE GUARDIAN'S GOAL

If it was not clear up to this point, it should be clear from this portion of Paul's argument that Paul's view of the Law is conditioned by his view of salvation history, and the place he believes he and his audience are in the eschatological timetable. In fact temporal terms abound throughout the second argument,

35. Precisely at this point, Sanders' argument (*Paul and the Law*, p. 68) does not hold up when he suggests that Paul simply puts everyone, whether Jew or Gentile, in the same position having the same status, enduring the same sinful condition. It is true that Paul argues that all alike need salvation from sin, but his description of 'those under the Law' is not identical to those without the Law. Only those under the Law are under the curse and must deal with transgressions of the Mosaic Law. Cf. below pp. 262ff.

36. It is even possible to conclude that Paul means that the Law confined God's people under the curse and under sin *in order that* they could only plug into the promises by means of God's grace and mercy and through faith.

which as we have seen begins at 3.19 with the rhetorical question 'Why then the Law?' Consider the following list: (1) ἄχρις – 3.19; (2) πρὸ – 3.23; (3) εἰς τὴν μέλλουσαν πίστιν – 3.23; (4) εἰς Χριστόν – 3.24; (5) ἐλθούσης δὲ τῆς πίστεως – 3.25; (6) οὐκέτι – 3.25; (7) ἐφ' ὅσον χρόνον – 4.1; (8) ἄχρι – 4.2; (9) ὅτε – 4.4; (10) οὐκέτι – 4.7.[37] Paul is trying to make clear in as many ways as is possible that the Law is *pro tempore* and in none of this temporally pregnant discussion does Paul suggest that only a portion or one aspect of the Law falls under this time constraint.

Something must be said about Paul's use in this second argument of the rhetorical figure called προσωποποιία. This particular rhetorical device often involves impersonation of an important person, but personification also fell into this category of rhetorical device as well. Quintilian says "we often personify the abstract as Virgil does with Fame, or as Xenophon records that Prodicus did with Virtue and Pleasure, or as Ennius does when in one of his satires, he represents Life and Death contending with one another" (*Inst. Or.* 9.2.36). The rhetorical function of such a device was to lend both variety and animation to one's discourse, but as Quintilian stresses, it was also to get to the heart of the matter or reveal the inner substance of something or someone by "lending a voice to things to which nature has denied it" (9.2.30–32). In our case Paul in a short span of verses in this second argument personifies Sin, Scripture, and the Law, and most revealing of all is his personification of the Law as a παιδαγωγός. In this manner, Paul presents in a vivid fashion the essence of his argument about the limited purposes or functions of the Law and the limited time duration of the Law.

Excursus: The Law as Childminder and Guardian

There is a great wealth of data in the classical sources and in the inscriptions about 'guardians', and on occasion we even find them portrayed in ancient art, for example on vases. It is important to bear in mind that this data is not all of one sort, and it is even more important to bear in mind that the portrait we get of 'pedagogues' from this data contains both positive and negative aspects. It is a mistake to draw conclusions about Paul's use of this social metaphor largely if not solely on the basis of the caricatures of pedagogues that we sometimes find for instance in plays,

---

37. I owe this list to N. H. Young, "*PAIDAGOGOS*: The Social Setting of a Pauline Metaphor," *NovT* 29.2 (1987), pp. 150–76, here p. 174. It will be noted that the one section of this material without temporal references is Gal. 3.26–28, widely regarded as a pre-set piece which Paul uses here. The absence of such temporal references which reflect the hand of Paul and his unique view of the Law provides one more argument for the conclusion that a source is involved in 3.26–28.

particularly in the New Comedy from the age of the Empire. For example, Betz's assessment that "pedagogues had the bad image of being rude, rough, and good for no other business . . .Understandably, the public did not have much respect for this pedagogue . . ."[38] is much too one-sided. There were both bad and good pedagogues and the latter were not rare exceptions to a rule. One must consider the source of the evaluation before believing the upper class rhetoric of those who were cultured despisers of slaves and foreigners in general, and all the more so when they had become necessities of life in upper class homes throughout the Empire.[39]

It has been suggested by Ramsay that the way Paul speaks of the guardian here tells us something about his audience. In particular, he argues that Paul's description better fits the older Greek model of the pedagogue than the later Roman one, which was more subject to caricature as the Romans were not as careful in choosing their child minders. Ramsay suggests that Paul's use here supports the south Galatia hypothesis for only in south Galatia would we find the harvest of Hellenism, including such institutions as the Greek-styled pedagogue. There may be something to this suggestion, but on the other hand, two of the cities Paul visited in south Galatia were Roman colonies, where the Roman institution may have been more to the fore.[40]

The word παιδαγωγὸς means literally a boy or child leader[41] and it refers to a member of the household entrusted with the care and guardianship of a minor. The practice of using 'pedagogues' dates to at least the fifth century B.C. (originating in Greece in Attica) and lasted until late Imperial times. This person was almost always a slave,[42] and very often in the first century A.D. was a foreigner.[43] Generally speaking these persons were taken captive during a war, sold at a slave auction, and were bought by well-to-do heads of households looking for slaves who had some knowledge of

---

38. Betz, *Galatians*, p. 177.

39. On this entire matter one should consult Young, "The Social Setting," pp. 150ff.; D. J. Lull, "The Law was our Pedagogue: A Study in Galatians 3.19–25," *JBL* 105 (1986), pp. 481–98, here pp. 486–98, and Longenecker, *Galatians*, pp. 146–49; T. D. Gordon, "A Note on ΠΑΙΔΑΓΩΓΟΣ in Galatians 3.24–25," *NTS* 35 (1989), pp. 150–54; L. L. Belleville, "'Under Law': Structural Analysis and the Pauline Concept of Law in Galatians 3.21–4.1," *JSNT* 26 (1986), pp. 53–78; H. I. Marrou, *A History of Education in Antiquity* (New York: Sheed & Ward, 1956), pp. 142–44; 221ff.

40. But see Ramsay, *Historical Commentary on Galatians*, pp. 382–85.

41. It must be kept steadily in mind that normally it was only boys in the Greco-Roman world who got any form of outside the home education, and accordingly they were the prime candidates to have a 'boy-leader' who would escort them through the streets to and from school.

42. As Young "Social Setting," p. 167 notes, references to 'pedagogues' who were freedmen are rare, and normally they refer to someone who has been freed in gratitude for his previous service as a slave who had the role of a 'pedagogue'. Cf. CIL 6.8967, 8970, 8988; Dio Cassius 48.33.1; Aristides *Or.* 12.83.

43. It is surely not an accident that there are far more references to pedagogues in Latin inscriptions than in Greek ones. It was for the most part the rulers of the Empire who were taking the captives and selling and buying the slaves in the first century, and it was the upper class among those Romans who sought to procure the services of slaves who could be pedagogues, or chose to turn over such functions to their older slaves.

Greek, and perhaps some smattering of philosophy so they could aid in the moral upbringing of the 'master's' children, in particular his male heirs. They were not by and large teachers, despite what the word 'pedagogue' has come to mean in English. As Longenecker puts it "in antiquity a *paidagogos* was distinguished from a *didaskalos* (teacher) and had custodial and disciplinary functions rather than educative or instructional ones."[44]

In view of the widespread practice of pederasty, a father was usually careful to choose an older man as his son's 'guardian', indeed not infrequently an old man who had outlived his usefulness in performing some of the more strenuous physical activities required in the managing of an estate or household. This is no doubt why the pedagogue is so often depicted as aged in vase paintings and terra cotta figures.[45] Stobaeus in fact complained that fathers too often gave what was most valuable by nature (he is referring to the training of sons) to the least valuable (monetarily speaking) household members – old or injured slaves (*Ecl.* 121).

Generally speaking a child came under the supervision of a guardian at about age six or seven and continued under that supervision until he (or occasionally she) was in his late teens. Plautus suggests that from the seventh until the twentieth year of a minor's life were the years a pedagogue supervised (*Bacc.* 422–39). This in effect meant he was in control of and largely responsible for the safety and day to day care of the child for some eleven or twelve years of his life. It is not surprising under these circumstances that many children often bonded more with their pedagogues than with their parents, if the pedagogue was at all congenial and affectionate. Cicero says quite plainly that a man's nurse and pedagogue are often the first persons a young man truly loves (*De Amicitia* 20.74). No less a person than Alexander the Great is said by Plutarch to have risked his life to stay with and care for his worn out pedagogue Lysimachus (*Alex.* 24.6).

If we examine more closely the functions of the 'pedagogue' we may list the following tasks: (1) as Plato says, he was to be the shepherd of the flock (*Laws* 808D), or at least of one sheep, though often a pedagogue would oversee several sons in one family; (2) he was to walk the child back and forth to school and in fact anytime he went out in public the pedagogue was expected to come along to protect the child from harm along the way, which included, when the child reached puberty, fending off both male and female suitors (see Lucian *Vit. Auct.* 15);[46] Libanius puts the matter succinctly: "For pedagogues are guards of the blossoming youth, they are keepers, they are a fortified wall, they drive out the undesirable lovers . . . they beat off the lovers' assaults, becoming like barking dogs to wolves" (*Or.* 58.7). (3) Because in the Greco-Roman world children were normally viewed as those who were driven by passions rather than reason or conscience, one of the chief functions the pedagogue was to serve was a moral guide or compass for the child. Plato draws an analogy between the way a pedagogue functions and the function of a horse's bridle (*Laws*

---

44. Longenecker, *Galatians*, p. 146.
45. See Young, pp. 152–53.
46. Interestingly, Aeschines, *Tim.* 9–10 suggests that the law required a pedagogue to stay at school with his charge, because of the possibility that a teacher's morals might prove suspect.

808E). The pedagogue then was to guide the child as he or she morally matured in the path of virtue, and usually these virtues were the well-known ones – self-control, honor, respect, discipline, putting one's best foot forward in public and the like.[47] It was not unusual for the pedagogue to chide or even beat a child on occasion to achieve the desired form of behavior; (4) The pedagogue did have a limited educational role, he might help a child with his homework, rehearsing the things that were to be memorized on the given day, or correct a child's grammar or speech, and it was also his task to carry the tools of education for the child to school (e.g., the box of writing tablets and styli; books or scrolls; perhaps a lyre if music was part of the education – see Pseudo-Lucian *Amor.* 44). (5) Since the attending to 'junior' was a full time affair this often involved menial tasks like drawing his bath, seeing that he was properly dressed and combed before going out, seeing that he ate and slept properly, attending to his health needs (see, e.g., Epictetus *Diss.* 3.19.5). As Libanius says, while the teacher's job terminates at midday, the pedagogue is on the job from early rising until bedtime (*Or.* 58.8–9). Though the pedagogue had an almost all-encompassing role in the child's life for eleven or twelve years, nevertheless, when the child came of age, the pedagogue no longer had any official control over the child.[48] He might occasionally advise, but he could not control once the child became a man. Notice how Xenophon puts the matter: "When a boy ceases to be a child, and begins to be a lad, others *release* him from his 'pedagogue' and from his teacher; he is then *no longer under them*, but is allowed to go his own way" (*Laced.* 3.1).

What then should we conclude from this data about Paul's use of this interesting social metaphor? Firstly, it is a mistake to assume that Paul was thinking of all the functions of the pedagogue when he chose this metaphor to illustrate his point about the Law. In any metaphor there are points of similarity and difference between the two objects compared, and this example is no different. One must look for clues in the text for the aspects of being a pedagogue that Paul is focusing on. Clearly enough, from all the temporal language in this entire section, one of Paul's points of emphasis is that the pedagogue has a role to play, but it is of limited duration. There comes a time when the pedagogue can no longer command and serves no longer as a guardian of a boy because he has become a man.

Secondly, it is to be noted that Paul is completely silent about any educational roles the pedagogue might play. He is not depicted here as a tutor, much less a teacher. Also nothing is said about the pedagogue leading a person to a teacher, and so it is in all likelihood unwarranted to speak of the Law leading a person to Christ. As T. D. Gordon says "if the role of this particular discipline is to 'drive us to Christ',

---

47. Cf., e.g., Aristides' catalog of typical nagging comments: 'It is not proper to stuff yourself full'; 'Walk on the street in a seemly way'; 'Rise for your elders'; 'Love your parents'; 'Do not be noisy'; 'Do not play dice'; 'Cross your legs' (*Or.* 2.380).

48. That control and not just guidance is the proper word is shown by examples like the famous dialogue between Socrates and a youth quoted by Plato in *Lysis* 208C: "'But someone controls you?' 'Yes' he said 'my παιδαγωγός here.' 'Is he a slave?' 'Why certainly; he belongs to us' he said. 'What a strange thing, I exclaimed; a free man controlled by a slave! But how does this παιδαγωγός exert his control over you?' 'By taking me to the teacher', he replied."

how is it that in Galatia Paul perceives it to be driving people *away* from Christ . . . ?"[49]
Εἰς in Gal. 3.24 is used in the same fashion as it is in vs. 23 to mean 'until', not 'to'. In fact, Paul believes that the keeping of or doing of works of the Law could never lead to Christ. Christ had to intervene in the history of Israel and redeem God's people. Paul's view of 'salvation history' is not developmental or evolutionary but apocalyptic or interventionist.[50]

Thirdly, careful attention must be paid to the actual verbs which are used to describe the role of the pedagogue. Verse 23 speaks of being guarded and confined and it is said at 4.2 that the condition of the person under a guardian is no different from that of a slave as long as he is a minor. As Young says, "Paul's emphasis in vv. 23–24 falls on the confining and restrictive rather than either the corrective or protective functions of a pedagogue"[51] although 'guarded' may also suggest the protective function.[52] If we ask why God's people were locked up under the Law the simplest answer is because all things, even God's people, were under the reign of sin already and the Law made clear to them that they were sinning against God. The Law turned sins into transgressions during the period from the time of Moses until the time of Christ. Lull sums up "the Law was intended to serve as a 'pedagogue' during the period when everything was in bondage to sin, a period which the Law did not create and which Jesus Christ 'the offspring' of Abraham, brought to an end."[53]

Paul says nothing in Gal. 3–4 about any ongoing functions of the Law past the time when Christ arrived on the scene. In fact Paul implies that the pedagogue is replaced in the life of the Christian by other things, namely: (1) the example of Christ; (2) the 'Law' or principle of Christ; and (3) the Holy Spirit. The former two inform the Christian's life, the latter transforms it into a Christ-like image and gives 'life' and the power to follow Christ and his example. Notice that it is the Holy Spirit, instead of the pedagogue which forms the virtues in the life of the Christian (Gal. 5) and Paul is pointed in stressing that this is a matter of the one guide or guard being replaced by the other. This is precisely what Gal. 5.18 is about 'If you are led by the Spirit, you are not under the Law'. It is no accident that the verb 'led' (ἄγεσθε) here is the verbal form of ἀγωγός, part of the word pedagogue.[54]

We will have occasion to say more about this when we discuss Galatians 5–6, but for now it is enough to say that the social metaphor of the pedagogue does not

49. T. D. Gordon, "A Note on ΠΑΙΔΑΓΩΓΟΣ in Galatians 3.24–25," *NTS* 35 (1989), pp. 150–54 here p. 153.

50. Young rightly stresses that Paul is talking about a group of people, the Jews, and not about the process in an individual's life which leads to conversion, as if the Law led or drove an individual to Christ. He says: "It would be entirely erroneous to see in Paul's usage a reference to the so-called second use of the Law whereby the individual is so oppressed by the Law that he flees to Christ for release. Paul is addressing a change in the historical process of the Jewish nation, not the conversion of an individual whose conscience has been smitten by the discipline or threats of the Law" (p. 171). It is a mistake to equate the discussion here with what we find in Rom. 7.

51. Young, p. 171.

52. Cf., e.g., Phil. 4.7 and 1 Pet. 1.5 where φρουρέω seems to refer to protection.

53. Lull, p. 488.

54. See Lull, p. 495.

encourage us to think that Paul after all of his arguments presented to the Galatians against submitting to the Law and performing its works and against the agitators' insistence that they do so, decided after all to allow a role for the Mosaic Law in the life of the Christian. On the contrary, Paul's metaphor here suggests that the pedagogue was for *Jews* before the time of Christ, and now that Christ has come no one *needs* or is *required* to submit to it for getting in, staying in, or going on in the Christian life. Neither circumcision nor uncircumcision counts in the new era, what counts is the new creation.[55] In Paul's mind there is a difference between submitting to the Mosaic Law and its requirements, and so becoming a Jew, and learning from Scripture what God's Word or will is for humankind. Paul believes that God's plan or will is indeed partly revealed in the Hebrew Scriptures, but it is more fully and finally made clear in Christ, who proves to be the hermeneutical key for properly understanding both the Scriptures and the role of the Law recorded in the Scriptures. It is no longer the Law, but Christ (and being in Christ) that defines who God's people are.

Careful attention must be paid to the use of pronouns throughout Paul's arguments in Gal. 3–4, and this subdivision of Paul's second argument is no different. In vss. 23–25 we have the first person plural 'we' which is distinguished from 'you all' in vss. 26–29. Once again, in 4.3–5 Paul goes back to the first person plural, but returns again to the second person plural in 4.6–10. In the 'we' passages Paul is describing the situation of those under the Law, namely Jews, which of course included Paul before his conversion to Christ. In the 'you' passages Paul is directly addressing the Galatians, who were apparently overwhelmingly Gentile in terms of ethnic extraction. Paul is indeed arguing that salvation brought by Christ came to the Jews first, but also that it came to them so that they might fulfill their proper role of being a light to the Gentiles. As Matera puts it, because "of the Messiah's work of redeeming his own people from the Law, the Galatians have received sonship and the gift of the Spirit",[56] and this has been made possible because of Jewish Christian evangelists like Paul and Barnabas.

Verse **23** begins a new subdivision of the argument which will provide us with another argument based on a temporal or eschatological point of view. Paul says that before 'the faith' came 'we' were confined under the Law. This is an odd way to speak if Paul means that before Jewish people began to believe in Christ, they were confined under the Law. The definite article before πίστις is especially peculiar if this is Paul's meaning. If one translates the definite article 'this', which is certainly not required, one then supposes that the term is retrospective and may be seen as defined in the previous verse. Even so, there is still debate as to whether the reference is to 'those who believe'

55. Which is to say, neither Jewishness nor Gentileness has soteriological or social significance in Christ; cf. below on Gal. 3.26–28.

56. Matera, *Galatians*, p. 143, see also p. 144.

or to 'the faith of Jesus Christ' in vs. 22. On the whole it seems more logical to see the subordinate clause in vs. 23 as more clearly defining what is meant in the main clause in that verse, since they are two parts of the same sentence. This being the case, the phrase 'the coming faith to be revealed' is a further explication of 'the faith'.

Furthermore, as Longenecker says, due attention must be paid to the temporal dimension of this sentence 'before the coming' and 'about to be' which indicates Paul is referring to something that began or was revealed at a specific point in time after the Law had been given. "Paul could not have spoken of faith in qualitative terms as only recently come about in the course of salvation history, since as he has argued from 3.6 on, faith is at least as old as Abraham, the man who epitomized faith qualitatively."[57] It is thus likely that 'the faith' refers to something which did not exist on earth before or during the time of the Law. We have already seen in Gal. 3 the personification of the Law, and here we see the reverse rhetorical process, here a person is described as the very definition of an abstract concept faith or faithfulness, and that person is Christ. In short, 'the Faith' here refers to Christ.[58] In fact, we have already clearly seen a similar rhetorical move applied to Christ in Gal. 3.16 where Christ is called 'the Seed'. This is in fact a very clever rhetorical way of contrasting Law and Christ. The Law is personified, but Christ is epitomized as Seed or Faith.

Attention must be paid to the verb tenses in vs. 23. We have the imperfect passive of the main verb 'confined' and the present passive participle 'being guarded'. Paul is talking about a condition that originated in the past, beginning before 'the Faith' (i.e., Christ) came. Verse 24 continues this sentence providing us with a clause introduced with ὥστε, which signals a result clause, or simply a consequence of what has just been said, probably the latter. Literally then the clause reads 'therefore the Law has been our 'guardian'.[59] We have stressed in the Excursus above that Paul is focusing on the confining and restrictive function of the Law, in his use of this social metaphor.

To this we may add that in the light of 3.19 (cf. above) Paul also sees the Law as that which makes clear the existence of sin, and in particular makes clear it is against God, by turning sin into a willful violation of an already existing Law, namely a transgression. This comports very well with the function of a pedagogue whose essential job was not teaching but making one's charge aware of the moral consequences of their actions. Of course the social effect of moral chiding could be the opposite of the intended effect. It

---

57. Longenecker, *Galatians*, pp. 145–46.

58. This makes very good sense in light of the verb 'revealed', a verb Paul has already used in 1.16 to describe what God did with his Son.

59. Notice that in p46 and B we have ἐγένετο ('it was'), and this is probably the sense here, with the perfect being used like a historical aorist.

could goad a rebellious teenager into doing the very thing he was warned against. Paul, however, does not say this here, but in his later discussion of the Law in Romans we do find remarks of this sort and about the Law's condemning or chiding function (cf. Rom. 4.15; 5.20; 7.7–8). But the Law as the pedagogue of God's people lasted only until Christ came. Here εἰς Χριστόν is surely to be taken in a temporal not a telic sense, especially in view of vs. 25. Paul says that God's purpose (ἵνα) in doing things this way is 'in order that we might be justified by faith'. Paul here is stressing that Jews in fact are justified in the very same manner as Gentiles are (cf. 2.16).

Verse **25** could just as easily have read 'But with the coming of the Christ we are no longer under the Law', but Paul is continuing in the metaphorical mode and so instead he speaks in terms of 'the Faith' and 'the Guardian'. It is hard to overstress the radical character of this remark. Paul is saying that not merely Gentiles, but in fact 'we' Jews are no longer under the Law. It was one thing for Paul to argue that the Gentiles did not have to submit to the Mosaic law to be Christians, much less full-fledged Christians. It is another thing entirely to say that 'we Jews' (which probably here means 'we Jewish Christians') are no longer under the Law.

In this opinion Paul would probably have found himself in disagreement not just with the agitators and false brothers, but also with the men who came from James, and probably even at this point with James himself.[60] 'We *are* no longer under the Law' means that Paul indeed is arguing for a truly sectarian and restrictive view of the Law. What he proposes as an alternative way of defining and delimiting the people of God becomes evident in 3.26–28. Speaking of Christ the seed, T. D. Gordon puts matters this way: "The identifying symbol is no longer that which separated Jew from Gentile but the one in whom the two are united. Christ must have pre-eminence. He identifies God's people, not in an age of preparation, but in an age of fulfillment, 'when the time had fully come' (4.4)."[61]

Up to this point in his argument Paul has been alternating between discussing what is true of everyone ('all'), what is true of Jewish Christians ('we'), and what is true of Paul's largely Gentile audience ('you' plural). All persons, Jew or Gentile, and indeed all things were imprisoned under sin by the Scriptures (vs. 22), 'we' were confined under the Law (vss. 23–25), and now once again Paul turns to discussing what is true of all his audience ('you all'), but of course in this case he would say the same about 'we all' as well.

Verse **26** speaks of all the audience being sons of God through faith in Christ. Paul's choice of terminology here is not accidental. The designation 'sons of God' was seen in Jewish circles as something that should be predicated

---

60. See pp. 111ff. above on the views of James and Paul on these matters.
61. T. D. Gordon, "The Problem at Galatia," p. 39.

exclusively of Israel. Israel was, and the nations were not, God's 'sons'. This terminology designated what God's people believed they were because of God's electing and calling them.[62] Though the terminology is not frequent in the OT (cf. Ex. 4.22–23; Deut. 14.1–2; Hos. 11.1), it is telling that in early Judaism the phrase 'sons of God' occurs frequently and in a wide variety of sources (cf. Sir. 36.17; 3 Macc. 6.28; 4 Ezr. 6.55–59; Ps. Sol. 17.26–27; Jub. 1.22–25). Note that the phrase is found especially in eschatological contexts, and so Byrne is probably right in concluding "it was an epithet felt to be particularly applicable to the ideal Israel of the end-time, the holy and purified people of God, the citizens of [God's] eternal kingdom."[63] The point then Paul is making is that the Gentiles now enjoy a title that formerly had belonged exclusively to Jews.[64] Here Paul says this status is obtained through faith; in Gal. 4.6–7 (cf. Rom. 8.14) Paul associates it with having the Spirit of God.

Verses **27–28** have been widely regarded as part of a pre-Pauline baptismal formula. There are close parallels in form and in thought in Col. 3.10–11 and 1 Cor. 12.13, and in Galatians itself we see this sort of contrasting of opposites in 5.6 and 6.15. What all these texts have in common is that they all refer to rites of passage. What Gal. 3.28, Col. 3.10–11 and 1 Cor. 12.13 all share is: (1) the language of baptism presented in one form or another; (2) contrasting pairs; (3) unity in Christ, whether that is expressed as being part of one body, one person, or all being filled with one Christ.[65] It is not only possible that we have a baptismal formula here, but it may well have been one meant to distinguish the followers of Christ from other religious groups, in particular from Judaism, but also from Gentile religious and social notions. In other words, the formula may well have a sectarian thrust. I say this in the light of a variety of traditions with which our verses may be formulated to stand in contrast. For example, Diogenes Laertius attributes the following expression of gratitude to Thales and Socrates: "that I was born a human being and not a beast, next a man and not a woman, thirdly, a Greek and not a barbarian" (*Vit. Phil.* 1.33).[66] This saying, which surely pre-dates our text, speaks about what a person is by birth, but ours is about what a person is on the basis of 'rebirth' and resocialization. The Jewish sayings all come from a later era, but at least

62. See on this whole matter B. Byrne, *'Sons of God'- 'Seed of Abraham': a Study of the Idea of Sonship of God of all Christians in Paul against the Jewish Background* (Rome: Biblical Institute Press, 1979), pp. 62ff.

63. Byrne, pp. 62–63.

64. See rightly, Matera, *Galatians*, p. 141.

65. See my detailed study on these verses "Rite and Rights for Women – Galatians 3.28," *NTS* 27 (1980–81), pp. 593–604.

66. Interestingly, this same saying is attributed to Plato in Plutarch's *Marius* 46.1 and also by Lactantius *Div. Inst.* 3.19.17.

one of them is likely to date ultimately to the first century – the three blessings that occur at the beginning of Jewish morning prayers: 'Blessed be He that He did not make me a Gentile; blessed be He that He did not make me a slave (or ignorant peasant); blessed be He that He did not make me a woman' (cf. JT *Ber.* 13b attributing the saying to R. Meir; BT *Ber.* 7.18 to R. Judah b. Elai). Though it is likely to be of later provenance than our text Seder Eliahu Rabba 7 is also worth quoting: 'I call heaven and earth to witness that whether Gentile or Israelite, man or woman, slave or handmaid reads this verse . . . the Holy One, blessed be He, remembering the binding of Isaac . . .' In both of these Jewish sayings the subject is, as in the Greek saying quoted above, about what one is by birth, except possibly in the case of the slave/free person pair, though even in this case it was of course possible to be born a child of slaves and so a slave.

What we are dealing with in all these sayings are the basic social divisions in society as seen from a Greek or Jewish point of view. What is assumed is that birth to a large extent determines one's destiny or roles and status in society. The Jewish sayings assume this is also true within the people of God, and so one can praise God that God did not make a person, a Gentile, a slave, or a woman. Our saying assumes that these distinctions are *not determinative* of whether one can be in the people of God and what one's status will be once in the body of Christ. What ultimately matters in Paul's view is not creation but the new creation.

It is my view that Paul is using this traditional material in Gal. 3.27–28 to aid in constructing a conversionist sect, one with its own rites, rules, and definition of who is and is not the people of God and on what terms they are a part of the group. The important thing to bear in mind is that he is defining the group largely over against ethnic Israel (hence the emphasis on not under the Law) but also to a lesser extent he is playing off against some Greco-Roman notions as well. As Dunn says the "language implies a radically reshaped social world as viewed from a Christian perspective".[67] What Paul is *not* doing is offering up the idea of an androgynous Christ, or body of Christ, or androgynous individuals within that body as ought to be especially clear from the fact that Paul says there is no male *and* female combination in Christ for all are one person (indeed εἷς is in the masculine here) in Christ (cf. Ephes. 2.15; Justin *Dial.* 116).[68] At this point we need to speak in more detail about conversionist sects.

---

67. Dunn, *Galatians*, p. 207.
68. However, see D. R. MacDonald, *There is no Male and Female. The Fate of a Dominical Saying in Paul and Gnosticism* (Philadelphia: Fortress, 1987), pp. 113–26; Betz, *Galatians*, pp. 197–200. Nor do I think Paul was working with an assumption that Adam was androgynous either, but cf. W. A. Meeks, "The Image of the Androgyne: Some Uses of a Symbol in Earliest Christianity," *History of Religions* 13 (1974), pp. 165–208.

Excursus: Dissecting a Millenarian Conversionist Sect ————————

Sociologists have struggled with the definition of a sect. Partly, the problem has arisen because most of the earliest sociological studies on this subject focused on groups that split off from some larger church body, especially Protestant ones, and not enough attention has been paid to the differences between these groups and sects from much earlier periods of history. There was always the danger of anachronism when a model based on sectarian developments in the last 150 years was then applied to ancient phenomena. There was furthermore the difficulty that the term 'sect' has often carried a pejorative connotation (i.e., of a heretical group).[69]

I would suggest that it will be useful to distinguish between a party within a religious group, a reform movement within a religious group, and finally a sect that splits off from a religious group, whether due to expulsion or secession. Once a sect splits off from the larger religious body, thereafter "joint membership of both will no longer be possible. If such a split takes place in a religious context it is appropriate to call the group which has departed a 'sect'."[70] I agree with P. Esler that as long as a movement remains within the larger group it is best described as a reform movement. As I have already suggested, at the social level, one of the main reasons for Paul's conflict with the agitators, the false brothers, and perhaps even the men who came from James is that all these three groups (if they are in fact separate groups and not one and the same) were striving to preserve the Christian movement as a movement within early Judaism, whereas Paul was not.[71] His view was that a new entity had been brought into existence, indeed, as Paul puts it there is a new creation because of the eschatological and apocalyptic action of God in Christ. Already in Galatians, perhaps the earliest letter we have from Paul, we find the Apostle attempting to construct a symbolic universe that will give meaning and stability to the new group he is nurturing in Galatia.

Bryan Wilson in his analysis of sects mentions the following traits: (1) they tend to be exclusivistic "in the sense that they do not admit of dual allegiances: a sectarian is committed to only one body of religious teaching, and has only one membership"; (2) sects tend to claim they have a monopoly on the religous truth; (3) sects tend to be anti-sacerdotal and lay-oriented, believing all persons have equal possibility of access to the truth; (4) sects are noted for their voluntarism. "An individual chooses to be a sectarian." (5) sects generally exercise sanctions against the

---

69. See, e.g., B. Wilson, *Religion in Sociological Perspective* (Oxford: Oxford University Press, 1982), pp. 89ff.

70. P. Esler, *The First Christians in their Social Worlds* (London: Routledge, 1994), p. 13.

71. See Esler, p. 62. He is probably also right that different parts of the Christian group developed in different ways and at different rates in their relationship with wider Judaism. It would not be surprising if the closer a Christian group was in locale to Jerusalem the less quickly it would develop sectarian views, while the further one was from Jerusalem and the more one's group was populated by Gentiles rather than Jews the more quickly a sectarian approach materialized. I am suggesting that there are probably two factors at work here, geographical location and social make-up of the particular group.

wayward or against intruders who seek to change the sect and this can often involve expulsion.[72]

If we compare these traits to the rhetoric of Paul in Galatians we discover the following: (1) throughout this letter Paul is trying to urge the Galatians not to submit to circumcision and the Mosaic Law because that would be tantamount to forsaking Christ and joining a different religious entity (cf. Gal. 5.2–3); (2) Paul claims that there is only one true Gospel, the one he preaches (Gal. 1.6–8); (3) there is hardly a hint in this letter of a concern about sacraments in Galatia unless Gal. 3.27 is such evidence, and likewise there is precious little evidence of a leadership structure in place in the Galatian churches, though Gal. 6.6 may be an exception;[73] (4) this letter is full of the language of voluntarism about receiving the Spirit by means of believing what is heard (3.5) about being free in Christ to choose a godly course of life (5.1, 13), about running purposefully in a chosen direction (5.7), about obeying commandments (5.14), about walking in the Spirit (5.16) and the like; (5) we see the urging of expulsion of the agitators in Gal. 4.30, which should be compared to what we find in 1 Cor. 5.1–5. In short, all the major features of a sect we find Paul inculcating in this document.

How then does one mold a group of new converts into a sectarian group, especially if, as is likely, some of them, perhaps some Jews and more probably various Gentiles, have come over into the Christian group from Diaspora synagogues? How does Paul create what can be called social cohesion among his converts? Firstly, he must inculcate a set of strongly held beliefs about what is real and what is valuable, "different in some salient aspects from beliefs commonly held in the general society". Secondly he must create or draw on "emotionally effective symbols for those beliefs".[74] Thirdly, he must use symbols and terms that are familiar to at least a goodly number of his converts, though, as is characteristic of sects, he will use them in new ways or give them new referents.[75] In particular, he will take over symbols, terms and concepts from Judaism and apply them to the new group. Fourthly, what often most typifies a new sect is intensity of commitment,[76] so the founder of the group must insist on this high level of commitment by urging avoiding or eliminating other potential rival commitments and demanding exclusive alliance to the new group in no uncertain terms.

We see Paul throughout this letter inculcating certain fundamental and non-negotiable ideas or behaviors such as justification by grace through faith, or walking

72. Wilson, pp. 91–92.

73. However, see pp. 430ff. below on this text.

74. I am quoting W. A. Meeks, "The Social Context of Pauline Theology," *Int* 36 (1982), pp. 266–77, here p. 271.

75. See rightly, Barclay, *Obeying the Truth*, p. 98: "Any sect in the process of breaking away from the parent religion will endeavor to justify its existence as the sole legitimate heir of the religious tradition while also introducing a host of reinterpretations which define its difference from the rest of the religious community. In this respect, as has often been pointed out, Paul's methods of Scriptural exegesis are closely analogous to those employed at Qumran, since both groups were sectarian movements with roots in Jewish traditions."

76. See Wilson, p. 94.

by the Spirit and not submitting to circumcision and the Mosaic Law. In order to set up clear boundaries for the new group it was necessarily to be quite clear on what the central beliefs and values of the group were. It was important to Paul that his theology and ethics support the fundamental notion that salvation is available to all on the same terms, and that Christian behavior depends on resources available to all believers everywhere regardless of their gender, ethnic extraction or social status, namely on the resources of the Word and the Spirit. Theology and ethics both had to be grounded in the central object of belief, Christ and the Christ event (e.g., his death and resurrection), so that a clear belief and behavior structure could be constructed. It was also critical if this was to be a sect that potentially could have universal appeal that it used symbols that were inclusive of all, not just some, members of the group – such symbols as baptism, which was not gender or ethnic or status specific, and the family meal, the Lord's Supper which was for all, and to be shared by all at the same time (cf. 2.11–14 to 1 Cor. 11.17–34).[77] As for the taking over and transformation of familiar religious concepts and terms consider the following: (1) the 'assembly of God' applied to the church and distinguished from Judaism (1.13); (2) the identification of Abraham's seed as Christ (3.16); (3) the identification of Paul's largely Gentile audience as the 'sons of God' (3.26); (4) the use of the phrase 'Law of Christ' to refer to something other than the Mosaic Law (6.2); (5) the identification of Mount Sinai with Hagar and slavery (4.25); (6) possibly the 'Israel of God' refers to the church or at least its Jewish Christian members. As for the inculcation of exclusive alliance we need look no further than Gal. 5.6 and 6.15 where Paul says emphatically that in Christ neither circumcision nor non-circumcision matters at all, and then he reinforces this exclusivity by insisting that those who submit to circumcision will discover that Christ is no longer of benefit to them (5.2). In short, Paul makes his audience make a sectarian kind of either/or decision between the cross of Christ and its benefits and circumcision and the Mosaic Law. Measuring by the usual traits or elements that typify sects (exclusivity, total commitment voluntarism, insistence on transformation of its adherents life style as well as beliefs),[78] it seems clear enough that Paul is trying to build a sectarian consciousness among his converts.

It will not be surprising to learn that sects are the religious groups who tend to insist most strongly on conversion, rather than just adherence or partial allegiance. Paul's churches do not seem to have formalized anything similar to the God-fearer status we find in early Jewish synagogues. "Conversion is a process of resocialization to distinctive ideas and values. The convert learns a language and a life-style which becomes a part of himself as he takes on a new definition of his own individuality and personality and of the social collectivities in which he participates".[79] But not all sects share the same sort of views as to how salvation is to be obtained or maintained. For example there are reciprocity concepts of salvation and also gift concepts of salvation. Salvation in the former case is seen as something that can be attained or obtained by certain actions, ritualistic or ethical and exchange for which God will bless them. This

---

77. See my discussion of this material in *Conflict and Community in Corinth*, pp. 241ff.

78. See Wilson, p. 94.

79. Wilson, p. 119.

approach has often been called the salvation by works approach as opposed to the salvation by grace approach. In the Greco-Roman world with its reciprocity conventions it was far more likely that the former concept of salvation would be understandable and the latter less popular and less well understood. It is not an accident that Paul sets up an antithesis between works of the Mosaic Law and faith in Christ. He wishes to suggest that the Galatians already have the salvific benefits by faith that they are contemplating obtaining or retaining through circumcision and works of the Law.

Surely part of the reason Paul must use and explain ideas like grace and faith over and over again is precisely because he is swimming against the social tide in the views of salvation he is promulgating. The essence of almost all forms of ancient religion was rituals, festivals, sacrifices, augury, astrology and the like. That Paul spent little time dealing with these sorts of practices and more time dealing with theological and ethical concepts likely made his converts susceptible to the appeals of people like the agitators who offered them opportunities to concretize their Christian faith through ritual actions including both rites of passage, and periodic observances (4.10). This would have seemed much more straightforward and religious to Gentiles than apparently abstract advice like 'walk in the Spirit'.

Finally, something should be said about the 'millenarian' aspect and atmosphere of Pauline Christianity. This aspect is not as overtly in evidence in Galatians as in 1 Thessalonians, but it certainly is not absent here. The sectarian view of the world tends to be that the world is an evil and dark place which one gains shelter from in the supportive community of light and love where true life-affirming values are evident. One even needs shelter from other forms of religion, which tend to be anathematized. Often the sect will believe that only direct divine intervention can finally change the world, an intervention that signals the end of the world in the sense of the end of the present social order. A moment's reflection on phrases like 'set free from this present evil age' (Gal. 1.4) or 'the new creation is everything' (Gal. 6.15) or the language about the revelation of the Son (1.16; 3.23), or the discussion about the Jerusalem which is above (4.26), or the affirmations about the coming of the Christ and the reception of the Spirit or the periodization of history, show that Paul is expressing his message in eschatological and apocalyptic terms. He believes, and wishes his audience to be aware what time it is. It is past time to put the Law to rest, for the fullness of time has arrived, the Messiah has come, the Spirit has been bestowed, those under the Law have been redeemed from under its rule, those suffering under the στοιχεῖα other than the Law have also been liberated in Christ, and so it is high time to get on with life in the new eschatological community of God made up of a kaleidoscope of opposites all of whom relate to God on the basis of faith.

Paul's basic sectarian message is as follows: (1) the boundaries of the community have already been crossed (by initiation and conversion) and no other boundaries need to be crossed – the Galatians are already 'in'; (2) the benefits of salvation have already been obtained through faith by the Galatians including the inheritance or blessing promised to Abraham; (3) the time for submission to the Law is past, but the time for walking in the Spirit or following the example of Christ is now; (4) those who trouble or cast the evil eye on the community should be expelled; (5) the relationship with the founding apostle should be strengthened or renewed and other competing voices should be ignored or silenced; (6) the Galatians should follow good examples (e.g., Abraham, Christ, Paul); (7) the body of Christ is an egalitarian body with universal scope where social, sexual, ethnic differences do not determine entrance or status and are not the basis for unity and cohesion of the group. In this last point, the Pauline community would not have been totally unique in Asia Minor, as we find statements about universal access to a god in an inscription of the second or first century B.C. from Philadelphia where we hear "Dionysius . . . grants free access to his house for men and women, free and slaves . . ."[80] And one can also point to what Philostratus says at the end of the first century A.D. about the Temple of Artemis in Ephesus: "Your temple is thrown open to all who would sacrifice, or offer prayers, or sing hymns to suppliants, to Hellenes, barbarians, free persons, to slaves" (*Vita Apoll.* Letter 67).

It is not entirely clear whether the source Paul is using includes both vss. 27–28 or is simply limited to vs. 28. The latter verse certainly can stand on its own, and at least as we have it, vs. 27 is connected to vs. 26 by γὰρ, which appears here to be more than an incidental connective. The logic of vss. 26–27 seems to run 'All are sons of God through faith in Jesus Christ *for* as many as have been baptized into Christ have put on Christ.' Here we would seem to have an example of the use of γὰρ in which one clause confirms another (cf. Rom. 6.14; 8.2–3).[81] The real question to be raised about vs. 27, however, is whether Paul is actually talking about what happens through or in the rite of baptism or whether Paul is using baptismal language to refer to what happens in conversion, a spiritual event of which baptism is only the appropriate symbol. Dunn rightly asks if this verse involves "a metaphor drawn from the ritual act, but not identical with it"?[82]

The question is appropriately asked especially in view of the close parallel in 1 Cor. 12.13 and one must also compare Rom. 6.3.[83] In the text in 1 Cor. 12.13 Paul seems clearly to be referring to what the Spirit accomplishes in the believer. It is the Spirit, not water baptism that joins a person to the body of Christ. That this is in fact Paul's view is especially clear from 1 Cor. 1.14 where Paul can actually say he thanks God he didn't baptize more than a few of the Corinthians. Now Paul certainly could not have said 'I thank God I did not convert more of you . . .'[84] This should give us pause before too quickly assuming that in Gal. 3.27 Paul is describing what happens during initiation.

---

80. This is most coveniently found in *Hellenistic Commentary to the New Testament*, ed. M. E. Boring, K. Berger, C. Colpe (Nashville: Abingdon, 1995), pp. 468–69.

81. See Longenecker, *Galatians*, p. 154.

82. Dunn, *Galatians*, p. 203.

83. These two close parallels may suggest that Paul is the originator of Gal. 3.27, and that only 3.28 is drawn from a source.

84. See my discussion in *Conflict and Community in Corinth*, p. 258.

Conversion and initiation are not identical in Paul's view, the former is something that happens to a person by grace and through faith, the latter depicts and provides a means of formally recognizing the transformation before the congregation. In other words the former spiritually integrates a person into the body of Christ, the latter socially does so, reinforcing the convert's experience of conversion.[85] Finally, conclusions about Paul's view of baptism must be compared to what we know about Paul's view of salvation about which there is a great deal more evidence. There is little or nothing in the Pauline corpus, unless we read it into a text like Gal. 3.27 or Rom. 6.3, to suggest Paul saw baptism as a magical sacramental act which converts persons, but there is much evidence that Paul believed that salvation came from hearing with faith the Gospel message (cf. Gal. 3.2; 1 Cor. 1.17; Rom. 10.14–15).[86] Burton rightly says: "if, in denying all spiritual value to such a physical rite as circumcision, he ascribed effective force to baptism, his arguments should have turned, as they nowhere do, on the superiority of baptism to circumcision."[87] Accordingly, it is more likely that Paul is talking about a spiritual transformation in vs. 27 and its social consequences in vs. 28.

Verse **27** stresses that those who have been truly converted, who have been spiritually joined to Christ and his body, have also at the same point in time been 'clothed' with Christ. It has often been conjectured that this is an allusion to the baptismal practice of unrobing and rerobing, perhaps with a new robe after the baptismal event, but it is not clear that this was the practice during NT times.[88] Ἐνδύω here is in the aorist indicative referring to a particular event in the past, and is probably a middle, leading to the translation 'you all clothed yourselves with Christ'. The metaphor is in fact a common one in the LXX (cf., e.g., Job 29.14 'clothed with righteousness', or other similar abstract qualities such as strength, glory, salvation; cf. 2 Chron. 6.41; Ps. 131.9; Prov. 31.25; Is. 51.9; 52.1; Zech. 3.3–5). Paul himself uses the metaphor to refer to clothing one's self with certain virtues or spiritual attributes (cf. 1 Thess. 5.8; Col. 3.12; putting on spiritual armor, Rom. 13.12; Ephes. 6.11–17) or even to be clothed with immortality when Christ returns (1 Cor. 15.53–54). In none of these instances do we have a mention of 'putting on' a person as we find here and it is appropriate then to ask what this metaphor signifies.

---

85. It may not be accidental that this process of conversion and then initiation is how Paul's own conversion is depicted in Acts 9. See my discussion in *The Acts of the Apostles*, pp. 295ff.

86. See the discussion of W. G. Rollins "Greco-Roman Slave Terminology and Pauline Metaphors for Salvation," *SBL 1987 Seminar Papers*, ed. K. H. Richards (Atlanta: Scholars Press, 1987), pp. 100–10.

87. Burton, *Galatians*, p. 205.

88. See Lightfoot, *Galatians*, pp. 149–50; Dunn, *Galatians*, p. 204.

As Dunn rightly points out, texts like Rom. 13.14, Col. 3.10–12, Ephes. 4.24 all speak of 'putting on Christ' as the epitome of Christian ethical practice.[89] It is not accidental that the verb here is indicative and probably middle ('you clothed yourselves with'). In Romans the reference is not to the past and is in the imperative, being contrasted with the deeds of the flesh. Both the Colossian and Ephesian texts suggest that when a person converted and was baptized there was instruction about living a new life, bearing the likeness of God and not of the old self. I would suggest that what Paul is referring to here is the basic instructions the Galatians received when they were converted. They had just been joined to Christ, and this in turn made incumbent upon them the task of donning the mantle of Christ, acting as Christ acted, following the pattern of his life as presented by Paul.[90] To live in Him meant to live like Him. Chrysostom in his comment on vss. 27–28 puts it this way: "you who have the Son within you, and are fashioned after His pattern, have been brought into one kindred and nature with him . . . 'You are all One in Christ Jesus', that is you have all one form and one mould, even Christ's." This pattern, and not the Mosaic Law, is what Paul means when he speaks later of the 'Law of Christ' which is fulfilled when one acts in Christ-like fashion, bearing one another's burdens (Gal. 6.2).[91]

Set in this context vs. 28, whatever its orginal intent in its pre-Pauline settings, spells out the social consequences of being joined to Christ and his body. It is critical that we recognize that Paul is not simply suggesting that this is God's view of matters, namely that all ethnic, social, and sexual divisions do not matter because all Christians are one person in Christ. This is of course true, but not the whole point. Most pressingly, Paul is trying to hammer home to his own converts that they do not have to become Jews, submitting to circumcision and the Mosaic Law, to be fully-fledged Christians, or Christians in good standing with the mother church in Jerusalem. It is in some ways the ultimate sectarian statement to say that 'there is not any Jew or Gentile' among the true people of God, for being a Jew was seen as the very definition of what it meant to be a part of God's people not only in early Judaism, but surely also by the agitators, the false brothers, and perhaps also the men who came from James. Paul's deliberative argument for concord in the body of Christ is based on a belief that there is a unity in Christ that transcends (in terms of who may be saved and what there standing is with God and among God's people) and also transforms these ethnic, social and sexual categories. What is really of

89. Dunn, *Galatians*, p. 205.
90. Paul has in mind in fact a two-way process: Christ is being formed spiritually in the converts (Gal. 4.19), transforming their mind, attitudes, will, emotions, and they in turn are attempting to live out of this transformation by imitating Christ in their behavior and practices.
91. On which cf. pp. 423ff. below.

enduring significance is the new creation. We see Paul attempting to implement this social transformation in various places and ways, whether we reflect on Philemon where he argues that a slave is actually a brother or sister in Christ, should be treated as such, and even requests Philemon to set him free, or on 1 Cor. 7 where Paul argues for equality in the marriage relationship, or on this passage in Galatians where he strives to make clear to his Gentile converts that they already have in and through Christ all the benefits Jews or Jewish Christians were offering them through observance of the Mosaic Law. In "conscious contrast to such Jewish and Greek chauvinistic statements [cf. above], early Christians saw it as particularly appropriate to give praise . . . that through Christ the old racial schisms and cultural divisions had been healed."[92]

It has often been debated why Paul breaks the pattern parallelism in Gal. 3.28c and instead of saying 'not any male or female' he chooses to say 'not any male and female'. This question needs to be raised not least because elsewhere when Paul speaks in these sort of terms, for instance in 1 Cor. 12.13 or Col. 3.10–11, he does not mention the male–female tandem at all. This may suggest, though we cannot be sure, that Paul has added it to the existing formula he took over. But in any case we must ask why it is here, for even if Paul did not add it to a pre-set piece, he cites it here because he feels it is apt as a part of his present discourse. It is normally pointed out that the *and* is probably the residual effect of the fact that Paul is consciously drawing on Gen. 1.27 LXX here, but elsewhere Paul is not loth to tailor a citation to suit his own purposes, and so again we must assume Paul cites it approvingly and to some purpose. We must bear in mind that ἄρσεν and θῆλυ are not the Greek words for man and woman, but specifically focus on the gender distinctiveness of the sexes.

I would suggest that we consider the possibility that Paul cites this clause because of the social implications of the Galatians adopting a nomistic lifestyle. It would mean a fostering of inequality of men and women in Christ, for women could not and would not be expected to respond to the exhortation to be circumcised, and in fact they would not be expected to fulfill various parts of the Law incumbent on men because they were periodically unclean due to menstruation. In other words, for the Galatians to take up the Law would, in Paul's eyes, make Christian women second-class citizens. I have tentatively suggested elsewhere that it is even possible that agitators were suggesting, in order to alleviate this problem of status inconsistency created when a nomistic lifestyle would be assumed, that women needed to be married to Christian men who were adopting such a lifestyle.[93] In this way they would be in full compliance with the Scriptural mandates which include the command that

92. Longenecker, *Galatians*, p. 157.
93. See "Rite and Rights," pp. 599ff.

humankind should be fruitful and multiply which immediately follows the statement that God made human beings male and female (Gen. 1.27–28). The agitators were insisting on obedience to the Mosaic Law and fulfilling the creation mandate. Paul replies that in Christ the coupling of male and female is not mandatory.

This view garners support from what Paul says elsewhere, for example in 1 Cor. 7 where he states quite plainly that neither women nor men needed to marry; it was acceptable, indeed in some ways even preferable to remain single in Christ if one had the 'charisma' to do so.[94] Perhaps one of the reasons Paul was adamant about his converts not submitting to the Mosaic Law was because he knew the social consequences for Gentiles in doing so (it would suggest that being Gentile is not good enough in God's eyes), for women in doing so, and one may also conjecture that he knew the social consequences for slaves in doing so, for the Mosaic Law does not abolish slavery.[95]

The final clause in vs. 28 is connected with the first part of the verse with a γὰρ which may suggest that we should read the verse as follows. 'There is not any Jew or Gentile, slave or free, no male and female *for* you are all one person in Christ Jesus.' Paul certainly could have chosen to use the neuter form of 'one' here but instead he gives us εἷς because he wishes to speak about union, not merely in some entity, but a personal union where people are united in the body of Christ. In other words, since it is Christ with whom they are clothed and into whom they have been baptized, the one person referred to is Christ himself. Christ is seen here as an incorporative personality into which various people can be joined. Indeed, Christ is seen as the basis of the unity of humanity, the One in whom there is a new creation, the race starting over in and with the last Adam (cf. 1 Cor. 15; Rom. 5.12–21). R. Loewe understood well the social vision of human unity Paul is articulating here: "The sociological basis on which Christianity rests is not ties of kinship, as in the case of Judaism, but that of fellowship – fellowship in Christ . . . Such fellowship may acknowledge kinship as a potential ally; it may regard it indifferently, as consisting of an equivocal force; or it may repudiate it, as being a distracting encumbrance. Whichever the position it adopts, the ties of kinship are, for Christianity, in the last resort expendable."[96]

Gal. 3.28 has sometimes been called the Magna Carta of Humanity and there is a sense in which that label is apt, but it is also well to be aware that Paul is not suggesting here the obliteration of the distinctions he mentions in this verse, but rather their redemption and transformation in Christ. The new creation is the old one transformed and transfigured. These ethnic, social, and

94. See my *Conflict and Community*, pp. 170ff.
95. See Ziesler, *Galatians*, p. 51.
96. R. Loewe, *The Position of Women in Judaism* (London: SPCK, 1966), pp. 52–53.

sexual distinctions continue to exist but in Christ they are not to determine one's soteriological or spiritual or social standing in the body of Christ. It is also fair to say that being in Christ and being led by the Spirit also affects what roles one may play in the Christian community, just as it affects one's roles and standing in Christian family life as well.[97] Thus, here at the very heart of this letter and in the middle of all his arguments, Paul articulates a vision of humankind and human unity that still challenges us today. It explains a good deal about why Paul is so vociferous in rejecting the appeal that his converts should take up the yoke of the Mosaic Law.

Verse **29** should not be seen as an afterthought, but rather as a conclusion to this subdivision of the second major argument. Paul returns to the theme that they have in Christ the heritage of Abraham, indeed they *are* in Christ the 'seed' of Abraham. Christ had previously been called the seed of Abraham (3.16) but since Paul views Christ as an incorporative personality, and since they are in Christ, they are also that seed promised to Abraham, having become in Christ the legal heirs of Abraham and the promises given to him. This verse reminds us, especially when coupled with vs. 26, that Paul is once more transferring the language applied formerly only to Jews to Gentiles, and claiming they already have the benefits that accrue from being brought into the family of Abraham.

Notice that while we have a conditional statement (if . . . then) here, it is a first-class or real condition, which assumes the truth of what it states. "Thus the 'mechanism' is explained whereby the eschatological blessing promised also to the Gentiles was realized, in accordance with the character of its first giving and receiving ('from faith'). And those believers in Galatia who had been told that they could not share in the blessing of Abraham without sharing in Abraham's seed by means of circumcision could be reassured that their share in that inheritance was already secure."[98]

Argument II, Division 3: 4.1–7

THE HEIRS APPARENT

In the final section of this particular argument Paul once again turns to familiar human customs, as he did in the third division of the first argument (cf. 3.15–18), to round off this part of his discourse. There has been

97. See the Pauline portion of my *Women in the Earliest Churches*.
98. Dunn, *Galatians*, p. 208.

considerable debate as to what sort of social conventions Paul is thinking of in
the analogy he presents in vss. 1–2. Is he referring to Jewish, Roman, or Greek
customs, and what does this tell us, if anything, about the social and
geographical location of his audience?

Most scholars have recognized that the least likely view here is that
Paul is appealing to Jewish customs. Neither legal guardianship nor adoption
were normal social practices of early Jews, nor is provision really made
for them in Mosaic Law.[99] Perhaps the majority view has been that Paul is
alluding to practices referred to in Roman law. This is certainly possible,
whether one thinks Paul is addressing a north or south Galatian audience,
perhaps more so in the latter case since two of the cities where Acts says Paul
set up congregations were Roman colonies (Pisidian Antioch and Iconium).
Nevertheless, it is also true that in the eastern provinces the Romans on the
whole left local law, including inheritance law alone, and furthermore, if this
letter is written to south Galatia, Paul is not just addressing converts in Roman
colony cities. What is of importance for our purposes is that the investigation
of inscriptional and legal evidence shows that no "trace of any non-Hellenic
system of inheritance for sons is known in the whole range of Phrygian
epigraphy".[100] Thus one must consider both Roman and Hellenistic Law as
viable options to explain the origin of this analogy.

Several clues in the text suggest that Paul has Hellenistic law in mind. For
one thing Paul seems to envision God as the adopter who provides the
purchase price. But in Roman law someone other than the adopter provided
the purchase price.[101] For another thing, Paul seems to have guardians (plural)
and trustees (plural) in view, and the normal Roman practice was to have one
of each, and furthermore Paul envisions being free of both these sorts of
supervisors at the same time, while the Roman practice was that a fatherless
boy was under the *tutor* until fourteen but he remained under a *curator* much
longer, usually until twenty-five.[102] Notice the evidence in P. Oxy 491 where
the testator nominates guardians (plural) for a son if the father dies before the
son comes of age. Then too, Paul does not envision an adoptive father making
a fictive purchase from the natural father, which was the Roman practice. The
Roman practice involved the peculiar procedure whereby a child was sold into
bondage three times and freed three times after which the child could be

---

99. See D. R. Moore-Crispin, "Galatians 4.1–9: The Use and Abuse of Parallels,"
EQ 60 (1989), pp. 203–23. On adoption and its absence from Mosaic Law see F. W.
Knobloch, "Adoption," *ABD* I, pp. 76–79.

100. J. Fraser, "Inheritance by Adoption and Marriage in Phrygia," *Studies in the
History and Art of the Eastern Provinces of the Roman Empire*, ed. W. M. Ramsay (Aberdeen:
Aberdeen University Press, 1906), p. 149.

101. See Moore-Crispin, p. 215.

102. See Moore-Crispin, pp. 206–7, Matera, *Galatians*, p. 148.

adopted, the *patria potestas* finally having no more legal force. Paul here seems to envision the death of the father and the appointment in a will of guardians and trustees, a normal Greek procedure. On the whole then, it would appear that Paul is alluding to practices in a cultural setting where Hellenistic law still determined such matters as adoption and inheritance.[103] This analogy then was more likely to suit the background and clientele Paul would have found in south Galatia where the Greek influence was considerable than in north Galatia.

One other legal point is of importance. Paul distinguishes between a minor child (νήπιος) and an adopted son, and he uses the term υἱοθεσία, the normal technical Greek term for adoption. As Moore-Crispin says, in ordinary human affairs certainly "the νήπιος of Gal. 4.1 could not be said to 'receive adoption' at a time set by his father", and there is no good reason why υἱοθεσία, which has a regular and clearly defined sense in Greek, should be translated 'receive the full rights of sons', as if Paul were speaking about the enhancement of those who were already God's 'sons'.[104] The conclusion one must draw is that Paul views the status both of Jews under the Law and of Gentiles outside of the Law as the same in regard to the matter of redemption, namely that they both needed redemption and adoption as sons, neither had this as a birthright. In Paul's view it is Christ who is the 'natural' son and heir, the true seed of Abraham and true son of God, and others can be included in his inheritance only by adoption, whether they are Jews or Gentiles. Nevertheless, Paul distinguishes somewhat between the natural child in vss. 1–2 and the slave in vs. 7 in regard to the kind of 'slavery' they endured, and perhaps in regard to what they might expect to happen once they were set free from their bondage (see below).

It is important also to bear in mind that in various regards an adopted child had an equal or in some ways better condition and status than that of a natural child under Hellenistic law as is shown by both P. Oxy. 1206 and P. Lips. 28. For one thing the adopted child became 'just as one from blood' with no legal difference. For another the adopter could not repudiate his adopted son or reduce the child to slavery. Furthermore, adoption established the right of the adopted child to inherit.[105]

It is clear enough from the way that **4.1** begins ('but I say') that we are dealing with a new division in Paul's argument, distinguished from what has come before by δέ. He is saying that as long as the 'legal heir' is a child he is not superior to a slave, although in prospect he is lord of all. This statement

---

103. See Ramsay, *Historical Commentary*, pp. 391ff. Ramsay notes that it is clearly a Greek touch to use the terms 'son' and heir almost interchangably here, a practice one finds readily in the inscriptions in Asia Minor.

104. See Moore-Crispin, p. 214.

105. Moore-Crispin, p. 216.

must be read as another metaphorical way, parallel to what has already been said about the 'pedagogue', of referring to the condition of those under the Mosaic Law, which is to say the condition of Jews, or in this case Jewish Christians.

The word προθέσμια in vs. 2 is the normal legal term for an appointed day or time when the stipulations of a contract or covenant have been fulfilled after which certain things cease to be true or begin to be true (cf. P. Oxy. 728.18; IG 6.1208.29; OGI 509.21). Paul has in mind an eschatological time set by God and also referred to in vs. 4 (cf. below). It is the father who sets this time in his will, leaving his child in the hands of guardians and trustees until he comes of age should the father die. The term ἐπίτροπος is a virtual synonym in some contexts with 'pedagogue', but here it has a more specific meaning of a guardian of an *orphaned* child. The word οἰκονόμος on the other hand refers to an estate manager, normally a trusted slave in the master's household (cf. Lk. 12.42). This person was different in social status from a guardian, the latter usually being someone of considerable social status who was a friend of the family. The steward had no choice but to do his job; the guardian did his voluntarily. Perhaps Paul means us to think of the former overseeing the person and education of the minor, the latter the minor's property.

The beginning of vs. 3 makes clear Paul is drawing an analogy – 'so also we', he says. Paul says that when 'we' Jews were children we were under the στοιχεῖα τοῦ κόσμου. The meaning of this last phrase is certainly one of the most debated issues in all of Pauline studies. Part of the problem is that outside the Pauline corpus, we do not find this precise phrase, and it is not clear that the term στοιχεῖα *simpliciter* has the same sense as this whole phrase. The context in which we find this phrase here suggests that it has some relationship to other recently used phrases which begin with ὑπό such as 'under the Law' (3.23), 'under a pedagogue' (3.24–25), and 'under guardians and stewards' (4.1–2). The original sense of the term στοιχεῖον was something which was part of a series or larger entity. Thus for instance it could refer to a letter in the alphabet, or a part of a word, such as a syllable, or degrees on a sundial. In all cases it had the sense of something rudimentary and simple, something basic or elementary.

The basic options for the meaning of the phrase in Gal. 4.3 can be narrowed to four: (1) the basic elements of the universe (e.g., earth, air, fire and water); (2) the fundamental or elementary principles or teachings of the world; (3) the heavenly bodies composed of the basic elements of the universe; (4) the elementary spirits of the universe (e.g., demons, gods, spirits, angels). One of the major drawbacks in arguing for either option (3) or (4) is that there is absolutely no lexical evidence that στοιχεῖα has such a meaning before or during NT times. The earliest attestation of meaning

(3) is from the middle of the second century, and we have no clear evidence for meaning (4) before the third or fourth century A.D.[106] This contrasts with the meaning 'elements of the universe' for which there is plentiful evidence before and during NT times (cf., e.g., Wis. 7.17; 19.18; 2 Pet. 3.10, 12; 4 Macc. 12.13).[107] In other words, the burden of proof must be on those who wish to argue for meanings (3) or (4) since there is no contemporary evidence to support such a translation. It is also the case, however, that to argue for meaning (1) requires that we ignore the apparent connection with phrases like under the Law, under a pedagogue and the like. Dunn, for instance, has pointed out the close parallels between 3.23–29 and 4.1–7 in which 4.3 is to be compared to 3.23 which refers to the Law as the Jewish person's custodian or pedagogue.[108] The context here requires that we come up with a meaning that has something to do with the status or condition of a minor as opposed to a mature adult, and the larger context suggests that it has something to do with submitting to or being under some kind of teaching or rules. One also must bear in mind Paul is talking about spiritual status as much as, or more than, legal status.

Meaning (2) in fact has a long pedigree; for example, Aristotle uses στοιχεῖον to refer to an elementary principle (*Pol.* 1309b16), Plato to refer to a fundamental assumption (*Laws* 7.790C), Xenophon speaks of instructions about what to eat as part of the elementary principles that one should educate a youth about (*Mem.* 2.1.1), and finally Philo uses τὰ στοιχεῖα to refer to the letters in grammar, which is seen as part of elementary education (*Op. Mundi* 126).[109] Then too, we have Heb. 5.12 where the meaning clearly is 'elementary teaching'. This last example may in fact reflect the earliest non-Pauline interpretation of Paul's use of this phrase, as there is considerable evidence that Hebrews reflects a knowledge of and is indebted to Galatians in various ways.[110] It is also helpful to compare the use of the verbal form of this word (στοιχέω), for instance in Acts 21.24 where it refers to living a regulated lifestyle according to a specific set of rules, and similarly in Gal. 6.16 where it refers to keeping to the rule of life or ordering life in accordance with the dictates of the Spirit (5.25).[111] The pedagogical and discipleship context of all this material is to the fore.

---

106. See rightly, Longenecker, *Galatians*, p. 165.

107. See E. Schweizer, "Slaves of the Elements and Worshippers of Angels: Gal. 4.3, 9 and Col. 2.8, 18, 20," *JBL* 107 (1988), pp. 455–68.

108. Dunn, *Galatians*, p. 210.

109. See the discussion in L. Belleville, "Under Law: Structural Analysis and the Pauline Concept of Law in Galatians 3.21–4.11," *JSNT* 26 (1986), pp. 53–78, here pp. 67–68.

110. See my discussion in "The Influence of Galatians on Hebrews," *NTS* 37 (1991), pp. 146–52.

111. See Belleville, p. 68.

It has often been the case that scholars have read 4.3 in the light of 4.9, and this is what has led to a preference for either option (3) or (4), especially when coupled with a certain kind of reading of Col. 2.8 and 20. Methodologically, however, the later uses of the phrase (e.g., in Colossians) should be interpreted in the light of the earlier ones, and the first occurrence of the phrase in 4.3 is important because it is fuller and less enigmatic than what we find in 4.9. If Col. 2.8, 20 helps us at all, it suggests pedagogical overtones should be heard in this phrase, for 2.8 says quite clearly that στοιχεῖα has something to do with philosophy and human traditions and 2.21 makes quite clear the author has in mind basic rules and regulations, or as vs. 22 puts it human commands and teachings. I thus must conclude that meaning (2) is lexically very possible and contextually the most likely in Gal. 4.3.[112]

It would appear that Paul's view is as follows. There are elementary teachings that are found throughout the world, and one form of these elementary teachings is the Mosaic Law.[113] Jews were under one form of these elementary teachings while Gentiles were under another, but both shared a common condition of being enslaved and under subjection because of these teachings.[114] For a Gentile Christian to submit to the Mosaic Law would be *like* going back under the elementary pagan teachings of the world, which they left behind when they became Christians.[115] God has even liberated Jewish Christians from under the Law, these basic teachings which were appropriate

112. See the conclusion of Belleville, p. 68: "This use of τὰ στοιχεῖα to mean basic or elementary rules that closely regulate one's life fits well the context of Gal. 4.1–11. A period of spiritual minority in vv. 1–2 suggests the notion of necessary regulation."

113. See the similar conclusion of Lightfoot, *Galatians*, p. 167, who follows Jerome in translating the key term 'elementary teaching'.

114. There is something to be said for the view of J. L. Martyn, "Christ, the Elements of the Cosmos, and the Law in Galatians," in *The Social World of the First Christians*, ed. M. White and L. Yarbrough (Minnesota: Fortress, 1995), pp. 16–39 that Paul has in mind liberation from the elemental pairs of opposites Jew and Gentile, Law and non-Law. Paul's emphasis here however is on the means which creates these distinctions, namely the Law, and other such elementary teachings which are deconstructed in Christ. The στοιχεῖα are not these pairs of opposites, but they are the teaching which create such opposites. See now the discussion by G. N. Stanton, "The Law of Moses and the Law of Christ. Galatians 3.1–6.2," in *Paul and the Mosaic Law*, ed. J. D. G. Dunn (Tübingen: Mohr, 1996), pp. 99–116, here p. 114.

115. See rightly, Matera, *Galatians*, pp.155–56: "In referring to the *stoicheia tou kosmou*, Paul is undoubtedly adopting a concept familiar to the Galatians and applying it to the situation of his Jewish co-religionists. In effect, he says to the Galatians." Even we Jews were under the powers which you call the *stoicheia tou kosmou*. But whereas you experiences the *stoicheia* by worshipping false gods (4.8), we experienced them by living under the Law; . . . Consequently, being under the Law does not result in the completion and perfection of faith (3.2) but in a state of servitude and minority."

for God's people during the period of spiritual minority but not after the eschatological condition of new creation came to pass, not after Christ came.[116] Therefore, Gentiles should not consent to submit to teachings which even Jewish Christians were no longer required to observe.[117]

Paul then in vs. **3b** describes life under the elementary teachings of the Mosaic Law as a form of being enslaved. The verb tenses are imperfect and refer to what was previously the case when those who were Jews were under the Law. Paul's concern, however, is with what is the case with his Gentile converts and what they are doing or will do, as we will see when Paul brings his argument to a close in vss. 6–7.

As J. B. Lightfoot long ago noted, vss. **4–5** are a chiasm[118] as follows:

> A. God sent his Son
> > B. Born under the Law
> > B.' To redeem those under the Law
> A.' That we might receive adoption as sons.

It has often been suggested that Paul is drawing here on a pre-Pauline formula or confession, and in particular one reflecting indebtedness to Jewish ideas about the pre-existence and sending of Wisdom (cf. Wis. 9.10 to Gal. 4.4 and Wis. 9.17 to Gal. 4.7).[119] Dunn has countered these arguments by suggesting that here we find Adam Christology with no implication of pre-existence. Instead he sees indebtedness to the idea of prophetic sending by God, and perhaps in particular indebtedness to the parable in Mk. 12.1–12.[120] Several things must be said against Dunn's arguments: (1) there is certainly evidence elsewhere that Paul applied early Jewish Wisdom ideas to Christ including ideas suggesting pre-existence (cf., e.g., 1 Cor. 1.30 and 10.4 and Col. 1 if it is Pauline);[121] (2) there is no evidence that Paul ever used the terms Son or Christ

---

116. It is very striking how close Josephus' portrayal of the Law is to Paul's in Gal. 3–4 at various points. For example at *Apion* 2.174 we find: "Beginning immediately from the earliest infancy and the appointment of everyone's diet, he [i.e., Moses] left nothing of the very smallest consequence to be done at the pleasure and disposal of the person himself . . . ; accordingly he made the Law the standard and rule that we might live *under* it as a father and master and be guilty of no sin through wilfulness or ignorance. For ignorance he left no pretext."

117. For a full-length treatment of this whole subject see A. J. Bandstra, *The Law and the Elements of World: an Exegetical Study in Aspects of Paul's Teaching* (Kampen: Kok, 1964).

118. See Lightfoot, *Galatians*, p. 168.

119. See E. Schweizer, "Zum religionsgeschichtlichen Hintergrund der 'Sendungs-formel' Gal. 4.4f., Rm. 8.3f., Joh. 3.16f., 1 Joh. 4.9," *ZNW* 57 (1966), pp. 199–210.

120. See Dunn *Christology in the Making* (Philadelphia: Westminster, 1980), pp. 39–43.

121. See my discussion of this material in *Jesus the Sage*, pp. 295ff. and in *Conflict and Community in Corinth*, ad loc.

in a less than personal way, and in Phil. 2.5–7 most scholars would agree Paul is referring to a pre-existent person; (3) Sonship language is not Adamic language; (4) Rom. 8.3 is a close parallel to Gal. 4.4–5 and most scholars would see pre-existence alluded to there; and (5) the order of Paul's verbs – 'sent . . . born . . . born' may suggest that the sending preceded the birth, or at the very least is coincident with it. Paul is not talking about a prophetic sending that comes after birth as in the case of an Amos or an Isaiah, and being set apart is not identical with being sent. The latter presupposes the former, and of course one must exist before one can be sent.[122] All in all, it seems likely that Paul is suggesting the pre-existence of the Son here, but the emphasis is clearly on what was the case with Jesus the human being.

Jesus was born of woman, which simply conveys the idea that he was a normal human being, coming into the world the normal way. Job 14.1 and Mt. 11.11/Lk. 7.28 and Josephus *Ant.* 7.21 (cf. 16.382) show that the phrase itself conveys nothing special about the person being referred to. Longenecker is right to say this phrase probably "provides no clue of itself whether . . . Paul believed in, or even knew of, Jesus's virginal conception. Rather, as a qualitative expression 'born of woman' speaks of Jesus' true humanity and representative quality . . ."[123] What the phrase emphasizes is that Jesus was truly human.

The phrase 'born under the Law' makes quite clear that Jesus was born a Jew, but it does not tell us in any full way what Jesus' relationship to the Law was. What we have heard earlier in Galatians,[124] is that Christ bore the Law's curse when he died (3.13). In Romans 10.4 Paul will say that Christ is the end of the Law, at least in so far as righteousness is concerned. Paul's thinking on this subject is clearly eschatologically conditioned. In Paul's view there was a specific and appropriate time for Christ to come on the human scene, just as there was an appropriate time for God's people to be under the Law. When the fullness of time came, the time to be under the Law was up and the time for new creation and to be in Christ had begun.

Verse 5 gives us two ἵνα clauses indicating the purpose of Christ's coming and being under the Law. He came to set Jews free who were confined under the Law. The verb ἐξαγοράσῃ refers to redemption, a term appropriate if one sees those under the Law as enduring some sort of slavery or confinement. Dunn rightly points to the parallels between 3.13–14 and 4.4–6. What needs to be stressed is that in both cases the 'us' who have been redeemed from the Law are Jewish Christians.[125] Paul also speaks here of 'we' who receive adoption as sons.

---

122. This is not an unimportant point. One can be chosen in advance. God can even intend to set someone apart in advance. But God cannot send someone in advance of their existing.

123. Longenecker, *Galatians*, p. 171.

124. See pp. 239ff. above.

125. Dunn, *Galatians*, p. 216.

The term υἱοθεσία is an important one for Paul; in fact it does not occur elsewhere in the NT outside the Pauline epistles nor does it appear in the LXX. Paul uses the term with a variety of nuances (cf. Rom. 8.15, 23; Ephes. 1.5), but perhaps most significant for our purposes is the use of the term in Rom. 9.4 of Israel. Paul says there that 'the adoption as sons' belongs first and foremost to Jews, but notice it is adoption he is speaking about. Inclusion in the 'remnant' is on the basis of grace, not natural inheritance or works (Rom. 10.5–6), and God has imprisoned all under disobedience so that he might have mercy on all, and that he might regraft in Jews into God's people on the basis of grace (Rom. 11.23, 31–32). It is important to bear in mind that the 'we' in 'we receive' must be taken in the same way it has been used since at least 2.11–14, namely it refers to 'we' Jews, or in this case 'we Jewish Christians'. Paul does not begin to speak of the condition of his Gentile converts until vs. 6.

Some scholars have suggested that the two ἵνα clauses are sequential in nature, reflecting Paul's concept of 'to the Jew first and also to the Greek'.[126] This suggestion arises because of the assumption that it would be unlikely for Paul to speak of the adoption of Jews as God's sons. However, this happens to be Paul's view. In the wake of the Christ event, all enter the new creation on the the basis of grace and faith, even Jews, and so even Jews can be spoken of as those who receive adoption, not least because the Christ is now seen as the only natural son or the only one born the Son of God.

In vs. **6,** but not before, Paul turns finally to a most pressing matter – what he wants to say to his Galatian Gentile converts. The δέ is meant to signal a mild contrast with what has been said before, or at least a distinction of audience, as the verb 'you are' (ἐστε) also makes clear. It is important at this juncture to deal with a textual problem. Is it 'our hearts' or 'your hearts' that Paul is referring to in this verse? On the one hand p46, ℵ, A, B, C, D*, G, P, a variety of other manuscripts as well as Tertullian have the reading 'our' here. The Textus Receptus and various later uncials (D, E, K, L) and most of the minuscules read 'your'.[127] Purely in terms of the weight of manuscript evidence the edge must be given to the reading 'our'; however, the question is whether this reading makes the best sense in this text. Both before and after the phrase 'your/our hearts' Paul is using second person verbs, second person plural before, and second person singular in vs. 7. The context thus favors the suggestion that 'your' is likely to be the original reading. I would suggest that in view of the care with which Paul has been building his argument, carefully distinguishing between 'we Jewish Christians' and 'you Gentile Christians', he

---

126. See Mussner, *Galaterbrief*, pp. 270–71; Betz, *Galatians*, p. 208.
127. See Metzger, *TC*, p. 595. 'Our' receives a B rating, indicating a certain measure of doubt about whether it was original or not.

probably continued that trend here,[128] though of course he believed that the Holy Spirit prompted both Jewish and Gentile Christians to cry out Abba, Father.

The question we must raise about vs. 6 is whether Paul is actually trying to speak of some chronology of Christian experience (first one becomes a son, then one receives the Spirit), or whether the two clauses are speaking of something that is coincident in time, the receiving of sonship and of the Spirit.[129] In view of 3.1–5 and 3.6ff. where Paul makes clear that hearing with faith, receiving the Spirit, and being justified were all part of the conversion experience of the Galatians it is unlikely that here at the end of the same argument Paul is saying anything different. Rather, he is rounding off his second major argument with the same sort of theological thrust that we saw at the beginning. Thus, the sense of vs. 6 is that it is precisely because they are now 'sons' that God sent the Spirit of his Son into their hearts,[130] a way of putting things which may be indebted to Wis. 9.17. The two things go together, the status and the condition and experience of sonship. The verb ἐξαπέστειλεν is aorist and refers to a definite event in the past, namely what happened at the conversion of the Galatians. Notice that it is the very same verb in the very same form as we find in vs. 4 in reference to the fact that God sent out his Son into the world. The sending of the Son and the sending of the Spirit were two parts of one purpose and salvific work of God, who in both cases is the sender.

This is the only place in the Pauline corpus that we find the phrase 'the Spirit of his Son', and it is worthwhile asking why we find this form here. Is the emphasis only on the fact that the Spirit is sent, or is there some importance in calling the Spirit, the Spirit of his Son? I think there is a fuller sense implied by this phrase. The emphasis surely cannot be on the notion that Christ sends the Spirit, since we are told quite explicitly here that God is the sender. Rather it is more likely that the focus is on the fact that the Holy Spirit is the one who forms Christ in the believer, conforming the believer to the image of the Son. In this regard we may compare the phrase here to the phrase 'Spirit of Christ' in Rom. 8.9 (cf. similarly Phil. 1.19), 'Spirit of the Lord' in 2 Cor. 3.17, and

---

128. It should be noted that the difference in the reading ἡμεῖς and ὑμεῖς is slight in the Greek, especially when writing in lower case letters, and when we are dealing with manuscripts where there is no separation between words the possibility of an accidental alteration or misreading of this one letter was all too common. We see this confusion between 'we' and 'you' quite regularly in the Pauline manuscripts; cf. Metzger's *Textual Commentary* on Rom. 13.11; 14.16, 15.7; 1 Cor. 7.15; 2 Cor. 1.11, 3.2, 6.16, 8.7, and Gal. 4.28.

129. So rightly Dunn, *Galatians*, p. 219.

130. See Longenecker, *Galatians*, p. 173: "Paul is not setting out the stages in the Christian life, whether logical or chronological. Rather his emphasis is on the reciprocal relation or correlational nature of sonship and the reception of the Spirit."

Spirit of sonship in Rom. 8.15. It is no use having the status of being God's son if one is not also being remolded to have the character of the Son. Paul then has spoken here of the objective and subjective dimensions of conversion, and in each case it has to do with being conformed to the image and status of the Son. What follows from this is that the believer is called upon to live a Christ-like life, a life following the pattern of the Son, or as Paul will put it later, following the Law of Christ. This is what it means to clothe oneself with Christ (cf. above on 3.27).

The confirmation that we are on the right track here comes in what we find the Spirit prompting the believer to do, which is to pray as Christ did, using the same intimate terms he used to address God, namely Abba. Because the believer is a son, like the Son he can pray to God as Father, Abba. I have argued elsewhere at some length for the distinctiveness and importance of this form of addressing God, as something we do not really find elsewhere in the prayer language of early Judaism.[131] We do not have evidence outside of the NT for any other early Jews praying to God as Abba. What is striking about this prayer language here is that the Aramaic is juxtaposed with the Greek, and even more striking is the fact that the one time we find this language on the lips of Jesus in Mk. 14.36 we find exactly the same form – literally 'abba, the Father' or 'abba, Father'.

What this suggests is that we have here not only a relic of the prayer life of the earliest Aramaic speaking Christians, but one which became common coin for non-Aramaic speaking Christians as well, hence the need to juxtapose the Greek equivalent with the Aramaic abba. For our purposes, what is critical to note is that Paul is suggesting that the Galatian Gentile converts also were prompted by the Spirit to cry out Abba, Father, just as Jesus and the earliest Jewish Christians had done before. What greater proof could there be that they already had, through the Spirit, all the benefits of an intimate and loving relationship with God they ever could need or ask for without having to submit to the Mosaic Law?[132]

The verb 'cry' here indicates a form of speaking that is intense in character. It may, as Dunn mentions, in fact refer to some sort of ecstatic utterance,[133] but in any case it indicates an expression from the depths of a person full of heartfelt joy. This is part of Paul's attempt to underpin his theological argument "by the appeal to the reality and vitality of their shared experience".[134]

131. See my *Christology of Jesus*, pp. 216–21.
132. Here as elsewhere in Pauline thought, the heart is seen as the seat of thought, will, feeling, and not just the locus of emotions. The Spirit renovates the whole person so that person may better pray and praise in a Christ-like fashion, renewing the mind, purifying the emotions, renovating the will.
133. Dunn, *Galatians*, p. 221.
134. Dunn, *Galatians*, p. 222.

Verse 7 brings this entire argument to closure by making clear what the Galatians have gained but also what they have left behind. Precisely because they have the Spirit they are sons and are no longer slaves. Paul personalizes these final remarks by using 'you' singular. He means 'therefore each one of you is no longer a slave but rather a son, and if a son, also a legal heir through God. Just as the first argument ended in 3.17–18 with Paul making his point about Gentiles already being heirs through Christ, so also in 4.1–7 Paul again makes his point by stressing this conclusion. They already have the inheritance from God that they now seek through the Law. Their actions or contemplated actions are not only pointless, they can in fact be harmful, as Paul will go on to say.

We have here in vs. 7b a first-class and real condition. Paul is quite convinced that the Galatians really are already sons and heirs.[135] This is why he is so exercised to head off their attempts to move in a nomistic direction. In order to accomplish this aim he knows it will not be enough to appeal to reason, and so in what follows in Gal. 4.8ff. Paul will rely more on *pathos* than on *logoi* so that his acts or persuasion will have their intended effect. It is interesting that even so Paul continues to follow the pattern we have already noted in the first two arguments of appealing first to experience, and then to Scripture to accomplish his aims. We shall see that 4.8–20 amounts to a large appeal to the experiences of the Galatians, while 4.21–5.1 amounts to another form of the appeal to a sacred text. There is a clear rhetorical and logical method to the way Paul arranges his arguments, placing those he deems likely to be seen as stronger by the Galatians first and then following them with other sorts of appeals. We must turn now to Paul's third major argument in 4.8–20, after some comments about the relevance of Paul's words for us today.

Bridging the Horizons

On the surface it might appear that Paul lived in such a different world from our own that it is virtually impossible to relate the one to the other. After all, where are the slave disciplinarians today? Where do we find adoption laws quite like the ones Paul is using in the analogy? Yet a moment's reflection will show that underlying this discussion are realities with which we are all too painfully familiar, namely broken relationships, single-parent families, children that need adopting, children being raised by someone other than their

135. Silva, *Explorations*, p. 189 n. 5 is quite right that all real conditions are first-class conditions, but that the converse does not always follow, as for instance in Gal. 2.21, 1 Cor. 12.19, 29–34 where we find unreal first-class conditional statements. Cf. M. Winger, "Unreal Conditions in the Letters of Paul," *JBL* 105 (1986), pp. 110–12.

parents, people oppressed by restrictive task masters, and people crying out to God in prayer, desperately in need of some sense of connectedness with God as caring parent in a world full of all sorts of alienation. This section of Galatians perhaps as much as any other shows that Paul is deeply concerned about the human need for community and family. He is well aware that there are numerous forces in the world working against such entities, and it is his personal belief that a lot of the social structures of the world that are so often taken for granted can be and must be deconstructed in the new community of Christ. Paul is not an advocate of the preservation of the status quo.

Paul knew, perhaps more than most, what submission to the Mosaic Law meant. It required a disciplinary commitment like that of an Olympic athlete, and more to the point, the way the Law was set up, it placed certain persons, especially healthy males, in privileged positions in Jewish community. Paul believed that this particular sort of patriarchal arrangement had had its day, and should not be imported into the new creation. He envisioned a community where Jew and Gentile, male and female, young and old, slave and free could all sit down together at table as equals, as brothers and sisters in Christ. It was this same vision that caused Martin Luther King Jr. to preach his famous 'I have a Dream' sermon in Washington D.C. some thirty years ago. It was this same vision that caused John Wesley in the eighteenth century to start orphanages, oppose slavery (calling it 'the most inexorable sum of all villainies'), and allow women exhorters and preachers in his movement. This vision of community is still compelling and it shows that the spiritual and social Gospel belong together. Paul believed there was no spiritual Gospel that did not have social implications, but equally that the social Gospel must be grounded in profound transforming experiences from God's Spirit.

The most extraordinary part of all this vision, is that Paul believes that even Jews must enter this community on the basis of grace through faith in Christ. They are not already, or automatically, in just because they believe in God and have observed the Law. Even Jews must give up their privileged status to be part of the 'one person', the one body of Christ, and Paul makes very clear in texts like Phil. 3 that he had indeed left all the prerogatives and privileges of his former Jewish life behind to start afresh in Christ. Those things were not bad things, but they simply no longer were of ultimate concern now that the new creation had appeared.

One of the things implied by Paul's discussion of the pedagogue is that when spiritual maturity arrives in a person's life, or in the lives of a group of people, it is time to leave elementary teachings behind and go on to deeper and more challenging teachings. Today, however, when we find that even longtime church members are Biblically illiterate, we find it necessary to revisit over and over the elementary teachings of the faith. Sometimes it seems the church at the end of the twentieth century is arrested in a state of spiritual infancy, and has become satisfied with being spoon-fed an infant's formula, and satisfied with having guardians, rather than assuming the privileges but also the spiritual and social duties of Christian maturity. To such a church Paul's word to the Galatians is directly relevant. He would be saying to us all, 'Wake up, grow up, stand up on your own feet and follow the example of Christ.'

This maturity of which he speaks is not a matter of outgrowing a sense of one's need for God. To the contrary, it is mature persons who know that they are created for relationship with God, and have put their rebellious period behind them, and can pray Abba Father as a liberating cry, not as a token of bondage. Paul believes that true freedom comes when the presence of God truly fills a person's life, not when they have finally wrenched themselves free from the grasp of the Almighty. Pascal once said that there is a God-shaped vacuum in every human soul, which only God can fill. To the extent that a person seeks to fill that void with anything less than God, even if it be a good thing, such as family, or performing honorable tasks, to that extent they will not find final or complete satisfaction.

Argument III: 4.8–20

But then on the one hand not knowing God you were in bondage to those gods who by nature are not gods. But now knowing God, or better said being known by God, how can you turn again to the weak and poor elementary principles? Do you wish to be enslaved again from the beginning? Do you observe closely days and months and seasons and years? I am afraid for you lest somehow I have toiled for you for nothing.

Become as I am, because I became as you, brothers, I beseech you. You did me no injustice, but you know that formerly through weakness of the flesh I preached the Gospel to you, and your trials in my flesh you thought nothing of, nor did you spit, but rather received me as an angel of God, as Christ Jesus. Where then is your blessedness? For I can bear you witness that if you were able you would have plucked out your eyes and given them to me. So I have become your enemy by speaking the truth to you! They are zealous for you, but it is not in a good way. They wish to shut you out in order that you might be zealous for them. But it is good to have been zealous in a good way at all times and not only in the time when I am present with you. My little children, with whom I am in birth pangs until Christ might have been formed in you, I could wish to be present to you now and change my tone, because I am at a loss about you.

Argument III, Division 1: 4.8–11

Déjà Vu

It will be remembered that at the beginning of his first argument, Paul appealed to the experience of the Galatians when they became Christians. It is obvious that Paul feels that this is rhetorically a strong move liable to persuade his audience and so he returns to it here in both divisions of argument three. In the first division of this argument Paul will focus on the experience of the Galatians before and after their conversions, and then in the second division in 4.12–20 in an emotion-laden move Paul will appeal to the experiences he shared with his Galatian converts when he visited them. Both portions of this argument will conclude with an appeal to the emotions as Paul conjures up feelings of fear, anxiety, pity, compassion and the other deeper emotions that come under the heading of *pathos* (cf. 4.11 to 4.19–20). In short, Paul has once again carefully crafted his argument so that it will have the maximum persuasive impact.

To understand what Paul is doing in this third argument it will be well to review briefly what Quintilian says about the appeal to emotions. Firstly, it was appropriate to appeal to the emotions in every portion of a speech, though it was especially appropriate to appeal to the deeper emotions in the peroration. Quintilian stresses that the deeper emotions "present great variety, and demand more than a cursory treatment, since it is in their handling that the power of oratory shows itself at its highest" (*Inst. Or.* 6.2.2). He goes on to add that while logical arguments may induce the audience to consider one's case believable or superior to the case being argued by others "the appeal to the emotions will do more for it will make them wish our case to be the better. And what they wish they will also believe. For as soon as they begin to be angry, to feel favorably disposed, to hate or to pity, they begin to take a personal interest in the case . . . For it is in its power over the emotions that the life and soul of oratory is to be found" (6.2.5–6).

It is no surprise that Paul's arguments in Galatians are so emotion laden. He believes that a matter of enormous consequence lies in the balance, namely whether or not the Galatians will commit apostasy from the one true Gospel, and so he is prepared to move heaven and earth rhetorically, and pull out all the emotional stops to get them not to pursue the course the agitators are urging them to adopt. He knows that the appeals to the emotions and to the Galatians' own experiences are more likely to move them than all the logic in the world. As an effective rhetor, then Paul adopts tactics he deems most likely to accomplish his rhetorical aims.

4.8 begins with a strongly adversative connector, ἀλλὰ, setting apart what follows from the previous argument just concluded. Verses 8–9 must be read together as a contrast (μὲν . . . δὲ, on the one hand . . . on the other), between what was true of the Galatians before their conversions and what is true now that they are Christians. It must be kept steadily in view that Paul is here addressing a largely Gentile audience, and he does so in typically Jewish terms, speaking of pagans as those who do not know God (cf. below). Paul's rhetorical strategy and approach here is revealed at the end of vs. 9 where it becomes clear that as in his earlier appeal to the Galatians' experience he will use the method of *interrogatio*, calling upon rhetorical questions to move the argument forward and press home his point.[1]

---

1. See rightly, Betz, *Galatians*, p. 213.

In vs. 8 Paul explains the benighted condition of a pagan. Not only do they not know the true God, but they are enslaved to τοῖς φύσει μὴ οὖσιν θεοῖς. There are two ways that this phrase could be read. If one takes οὖσιν substantively with 'gods' as the predicate then one can translate 'to those things that are not by nature gods'.[2] If on the other hand takes φύσει μὴ οὖσιν as an adjectival phrase limiting gods then one can translate 'to those gods who are not (by nature) gods at all'. It would appear that the latter translation makes better sense in this context.[3] Here we should compare what Paul says in 1 Cor. 8.5 which shows that Paul could use the term θεός of beings he did not consider gods, but did consider real. That Paul believed he was talking about real beings, though they are not gods, is shown in 1 Cor. 10.20 where he speaks of demons as the beings to whom pagans sacrifice. It is not surprising under these circumstances that Paul speaks of relationships with such beings as slavery, especially in view of the fact that it was believed that a person could become demon possessed and so totally enslaved to one or more demons.

It is appropriate to ask who these beings are who are not in reality gods. It must be first noted that Paul does not say that these beings are the στοιχεῖα, though many have drawn this conclusion because of the close connection between vss. 8 and 9. The question is whether the στοιχεῖα in vs. 9 refers back to these beings or refers forward to what is spoken of in vs. 10. I would suggest that it is the latter. Submitting to the στοιχεῖα is defined as submitting to religious rules and observances set on the basis of the calendar.[4] We can now return and ask again – who are these beings who are not gods that Paul alludes to here?

One suggestion which has not been given careful enough consideration is that Paul may be alluding to the cult of the Emperor in Asia Minor and the observances that are involved in that cult. We know for a fact that the cult of the Emperor was extremely popular in Asia Minor, and that various Asian cities sought to enhance and promote this cult, not least because it would help

---

2. See Matera, *Galatians*, p. 152.

3. See Burton, *Galatians*, pp. 228–29.

4. It is often assumed on a basis of an amalgamation of the ideas in vss. 8–10 that Paul is talking about matters astrological, the worship of star gods or the planets and stars as objects of worship, and that this is what στοιχεῖα means. It must be pointed out that astronomy and astrology were not necessarily one and the same in antiquity. Astrology certainly involved astronomical observances and calculations, but not all astronomical observances led to or entailed the worship of star gods, or the heavenly host and the like. This point has recently been forcefully made at the Nov. 1996 meeting of the SBL by the classics scholar K. M. Irwin, in a lecture entitled "The Use of Astronomical Imagery by Roman Religions of late Antiquity." The upshot of this is that it cannot simply be assumed that because Paul mentions calendrical observances in vs. 10 that he had in mind cosmic spirits or star gods and the like when he refers to the στοιχεῖα and the beings which are not really gods.

them gain greater favor with the Emperor. Not surprisingly Roman colony cities led the way in promoting the worship of the Emperor. "When Augustus made Galatia a province and established Roman colonies throughout the province, emperor worship became a prominent part of the religious life of the province . . . When Paul visited Pisidian Antioch, the most dominant building in that city was the Temple of Augustus in the centre of the city."[5] In addition one must also reckon with the fact that Iconium was a colony city, and it and another city nearby, Derbe, underwent a renaming process at the hands of the governor Annius Afrinus, because of 'progress' they had made on behalf of things Roman, of the Emperor, and of the Empire. They came to be called Claudicomium and Claudioderbe during the rule of Afrinus (A.D. 49–54) and under the emperorship of Claudius. This is the very time when Paul will have been writing this letter to the Galatians, and it must be kept very steadily in view that Paul will not have failed to notice that the life of the cities he visited often revolved around the celebrations connected with the Emperor's cult which included the observance of various special days (e.g., the Emperor's birthday) and seasons and the offering of various sacrifices, games, gladiatorial shows, and distributions of oil and grain. S. Mitchell reminds us the major "obstacle which stood in the way of the progress of Christianity, and the force which would have drawn new adherents back to conformity with the prevailing paganism, was the public worship of the Emperor. The packed calendar of the ruler cult dragooned the citizens . . . into observing days, months, seasons and years which it laid down for special recognition and celebration."[6]

Keeping this in mind vss. 8–10 become much clearer. Paul is drawing an analogy between going back to observing the calendrical feasts and days of the Emperor cult with going forward and accepting the calendrical observances enunciated in the Mosaic covenant. He wishes his Galatians converts to do neither, and so he throws odium on what the audience is contemplating doing by suggesting it would be similar to committing apostasy, it would be similar to going back to Emperor worship.[7] But the Emperor Claudius, while of course a real being, was most definitely not a real god, nor were his forebears in the Julio-Claudian clan including Julius Caesar, Augustus, Tiberius, and Caligula.[8]

5. Hansen, "Galatia," *AIIFCS 2*, p. 394.

6. S. Mitchell, *Anatolia: Land, Men and Gods in Asia Minor, Volume 2 The Rise of the Church* (Oxford: Clarendon Press, 1993), p. 10.

7. Notice the strong contrast in 1 Thess. 1.9 of worshipping the living and true God and committing idolatry coupled with the language of turning from one to the other.

8. D. L. Jones, "The Imperial Cult in Roman Pergamum," in his Nov. 1996 SBL lecture has rightly stressed the growing importance and dominance of the religious landscape in Asia Minor by the Imperial Cult. This was not just because the Emperor had his own cult, but also because rooms in other cults, such as the cult of Asclepius in

The most basic or elementary principles of religion, whether pagan or Jewish, involved the observance of certain sacred days, times and rites. Paul calls these elementary principles weak and poor in vs. 9 "for they have no power to rescue [a person] from condemnation [and] . . . they bring no rich endowment of spiritual treasures"[9] in spite of the promises of blessing by the Emperor and others. Paul also believes that observance of the Mosaic Law does not bring life nor convey right standing with God[10] and so in his view turning to the Mosaic Law will no more bring these sorts of benefits than following the rules and observances of the Emperor cult had when his converts were pagans. Paul is not the only one ever to have made a comparison between Jewish calendrical observances and those of pagans. Consider for example the similar remarks in Jub. 6.32ff. in particular the worry that some Jews might 'forget the feasts of the covenant and walk in the feasts of the Gentiles, after their errors and after their ignorance'.

This leads to a few remarks on what is said in vs. 10 about observing days, months, seasons, and years. Commentators have often tried to parallel this list with various Jewish sources, but in fact there is no Jewish list that actually matches up with this list. It is clear enough from texts like Col. 2.16 that if Paul wanted to present his audience with a specifically Jewish list of calendrical observances he could have done so and would have mentioned sabbaths and probably new moons as well. Betz is on the right track when he says that Paul is describing in vs. 10 "the *typical* behavior of religiously scrupulous people".[11] Paul has provided here a generic list that could apply equally well to Jewish as well as to pagan observances, including observances in the Emperor cult. The rhetorical effect of this is to maximize the similarities between the observances the Galatians have left behind and those they are, or are contemplating, taking up. "The cultic activities apply both to their pagan past and to their future life in Judaism, if they so choose."[12]

The question then becomes whether Paul actually thinks the Galatians are already practicing Jewish calendrical observances or are merely contemplating doing so. In the first place the rhetorical question 'Do you wish to serve them all over again?' seems to favor the view that they are not yet observing the Jewish calendar. In the second, we have a textual question about

---

Pergamum were being dedicated exclusively to the Emperor. Thus the worship of the Emperor was being integrated into already existing cults, hastening the spread of the practice of Emperor worship.

9. Lightfoot, *Galatians*, p. 171.
10. See the discussion on pp. 262ff. above.
11. Betz, *Galatians*, p. 217.
12. Betz, p. 218.

what the original reading of vs. 10 is, for what is probably our earliest manuscript containing Galatians, p46, has the reading 'by observing days . . .' Thus connecting vs. 10 with the rhetorical question in vs. 9. On this showing Paul is not suggesting in vs. 10 that they are already observing the Jewish calendar, but they are seriously considering it. I think this is likely to be the case,[13] though it cannot be ruled out that they had begun to gradually adopt Jewish practices but had not yet gone on to accept circumcision.[14] Finally, it is possible to take vs. 10 as a question, even if one separates it from vs. 9. In other words it is perfectly feasible to read here 'Are you actually observing days . . .?'[15] This is perhaps the best way to deal with the relationship of vs. 10 to vs. 9 without suggesting that Paul is contradicting himself in the span of two verses. We must now go back and consider some of the details of this argument.

The language of knowing and not knowing God in vss. 8–9 raises questions about other Pauline texts, for example Rom. 1.18–23 where Paul speaks of all human beings, including pagans, knowing God because God has revealed certain basic things about the divine nature to them. Did Paul change his mind on this issue between the time of writing Galatians and the writing of Romans? In all probability he did not, for the key to understanding vss. 8–9 has been rightly summed up by Longenecker: "'To know' [here] is not used in any mundane sense of either 'to perceive' or 'to acquire knowledge about', but in the biblical sense of 'to experience'. For in being sons of God (3.26) and having 'the Spirit of his Son' (4.6) Galatian Christians had come to experience God in the intimacy of a family relationship."[16] Paul then is referring here to the fact that before their conversion the Galatians had not experienced God or God's presence in the form of the Spirit.

Verse 9 then goes on to stress that the Galatians have come to know,[17] or better said are known by God. Μᾶλλον suggests that Paul is not merely supplementing what has just been said but rather correcting or at least putting things more correctly by what follows the words 'but rather'. What really is significant and what really amounts to knowledge is the knowledge God has and the acknowledgment by God of his children. Paul is emphasizing that God took the initiative with the Galatians bestowing on them the Spirit and reckoning them as righteous. "Relationship with God does not have its basis in [human] seeking (mysticism), or doing (legalism) or knowing

---

13. See Mussner, *Galaterbrief,* pp. 301–2 and Betz, *Galatians,* pp. 217–18.
14. See Dunn, *Galatians,* pp. 225ff.
15. See Bruce, *Galatians,* p. 205.
16. Longenecker, *Galatians,* p. 180.
17. The participle here is in the aorist and is probably to be seen as an inceptive aorist 'having come to know'.

(gnosticism), but it originates with God . . . and is carried on always by divine grace."[18]

The problem with not experiencing the true God is that the alternative is not nothing but rather being under the control of beings which are not real gods. That Paul associates these so-called gods with the στοιχεῖα is clear enough but he does not simply equate the two.[19] The στοιχεῖα are the elementary religious principles and rules which one follows in relating to these so-called gods, but they are not beings any more than Paul sees the Law as a being. Rather, the Law, like other forms of the στοιχεῖα, are means by which one relates to, worships, responds to, obeys God.

The second clause in vs. **9b** is a crucial one, and notice the emphasis on 'again', πάλιν being used twice here. The verb ἐπιστρέφετε is in the present tense and indicates something the Galatians are presently doing or more likely are seriously contemplating doing. Paul is asking them how they *can* do this, not how they *could* have already been doing this. The verb 'to turn around' is something of a technical term in a religious discussion referring either to conversion (cf. 1 Thess. 1.9; Lk. 1.16; Acts 3.19; 9.35; 11.21; 14.15; 15.19; 26.18, 20) or apostasy (cf. Num. 14.43; 1 Sam. 15.11; 1 Kngs. 9.6; Ps. 78.41; Jerm. 3.19; 2 Pet. 5.2–4). Paul is using the term in the manner it is most often used in the OT to refer to turning back to something that had been left behind. Notice the redundant and so emphatic way of putting things – 'do you wish to be enslaved to them again anew' (ἄνωθεν)? Alternatively, one could take ἄνωθεν to mean 'from the beginning', as if Paul were accusing the Galatians of going back to the ABCs of religion. Paul sees the Law, like the other forms of elementary religious principles, as 'weak' as it is unable to change human nature or provide it with the spiritual life and power it needs to obey God and 'poor' because it can not deliver the benefits that God promised to Abraham, it cannot provide the inheritance of eternal life or the presence of God's Spirit which is the means by which such life is given to the believer.

Verse **10** speaks not merely of observances of days, months, seasons and years, but the verb παρατηρεῖσθε suggests scrupulous observance of these calendrically based rites. This verb is not used elsewhere in the NT or in the LXX in a religious sense but we do find it used in Josephus to speak about observance of the Mosaic Law (cf. *Ant.* 3.91. 11.294, 14.264; *Ap.* 2.282). The point of this verse is to draw a close parallel between what the Galatians used to do in regard to religious observances and what they are now doing or at least contemplating doing by following the Mosaic Law. Without question, the agitators would never have agreed that following the Mosaic Law was anything like practicing pagan rituals or participating in the worship

18. Longenecker, *Galatians*, p. 180.
19. *Pace* Betz, *Galatians*, p. 214.

of the Emperor, but that is what Paul's analogy is meant to suggest, in so far as the effect on the worshipper is concerned.[20] What they are about to do is a case of *déjà vu*; they have already been there and done that before when they were pagans.[21]

Verse 11 concludes this subdivision of the argument with an appeal to emotions. Paul is indirectly accusing his converts of acting in a shameful fashion, in a manner that would invalidate all that their spiritual father had done for them previously.[22] Paul's concern, however, is not for himself but rather for his converts – he fears for them (cf. similarly 1 Thess. 3.5). We are meant to hear a note of despair here that is stronger than the tone of 3.4, for as this document progresses the appeals to the emotions become ever stronger. The phrase or idea of 'for nothing' or 'in vain' is meant to ring in the Galatians' ears (cf. 2.2; 3.4; 4.11; 5.2; 6.15). The verb κεκοπίακα (have worked) is in the perfect referring to Paul's past ministry and its ongoing effects. Paul is worried it won't have any lasting benefit for his converts. As Martin Luther once said, Paul is suggesting that the Galatians are contemplating giving up the substance for that which is but a foreshadowing of that substance or to put it in his terms, they are like "the dog who runs along a stream with a piece of meat in his mouth, and deceived by the reflection of the meat in the water, opens his mouth to snap at it, and so loses both the meat and the reflection".[23] It is Paul's task to make clear that the Galatians already have what they are looking for, long for, and need.

It must be stressed at this point that the appeal to advantage or benefit is the sort of appeal that characterizes deliberative, not forensic rhetoric, and furthermore exhortation (and especially exhortation to imitation which immediately follows this verse) is truly appropriate in deliberative rhetoric but is generally inappropriate in forensic rhetoric. We have noted in the

---

20. Belleville, "'Under Law'" p. 69 is quite right to stress that "Paul does not state in vv. 1–5 that the Jewish Christian prior to faith in Christ served that which is by nature 'not gods'. This is an indictment that Paul makes in vv. 8–11 specifically against Gentiles . . . Not that the Law and the 'rudimentary principles' are one and the same . . . [but] being 'under the Law' and being 'under the rudimentary principles of the world' are similar experiences with similar results." Cf. Ziesler, *Galatians*, p. 59: "if they accept the Law they will enter a slavery which is parallel to but not identical with their former bondage." So also Matera, *Galatians*, p. 155.

21. Dunn, *Galatians*, p. 226 seeks to avoid the force of Paul's argument by suggesting that what Paul is saying the Galatians would be enslaved to is a misrepresentation of the Law. But Paul is not arguing about a misrepresentation of the Law, but about the effect the Law actually has on human beings as opposed to the effect the Spirit has already had on his converts.

22. Chrysostom in his comment on 4.11 rightly saw that Paul was trying to shame his converts here.

23. In "The Freedom of the Christian" in *Luther's Works*, Vol. 31, p. 356.

introduction to this commentary that as a letter Galatians falls into the category of the 'rebuke-request' letter, not an apologetic letter.[24] Here we would stress that whether rebuke or request these are the activities of one who exhorts, in other words the activities of one who is engaging in deliberative rhetoric. Thus when we turn to the 'request' portion of the letter, which really begins in 4.12, this transition makes perfectly good sense within a piece of deliberative rhetoric that is moving towards a final exhortation in the *peroratio*. Both rebuke, as in 4.11, and request, as in 4.12 can be part of one deliberative argument, as is the case here. The point to be observed is that it is the rhetorical conventions, rather than the letter conventions, that are dominant here and are structuring the discourse, for 4.12–20 is meant to be seen as the second division of one appeal to the experience of the Galatians which began in 4.8. The parallel between 4.11 and 4.20 make this especially clear. We must now turn to the second division of this appeal to experience.

Argument III, Division 2: 4.12–20

PAUL'S LABOR PAINS

It has been argued by Longenecker, chiefly on the basis that we have our first request of the letter at 4.12, that we have a major division in the letter between 4.11 and 4.12.[25] This overlooks several important factors not the least of which is that rhetorical conventions are dictating the internal structure of Galatians far more than any epistolary conventions. In the first place, 4.12ff. simply continues the appeal to the Galatians' experience Paul began already at 4.8. Having spoken first of the before and after of the Galatians' experience, with conversion being the dividing point, now Paul speaks about the 'then' and 'now' of their Christian experience, including their former experiences with Paul and their present relationship to him. There is absolutely no grammatical marker in the text at 4.12 such as ἀλλά or even δὲ to indicate that we should set off 4.12 from 4.11 to any significant degree. Indeed, 4.12 builds on what is said in 4.10–11. The exhortation 'become as I am' is based on the fear that the Galatians are on the verge of becoming as he was (cf. Gal. 1), and as the agitators are, it is based on the fear that they are 'turning' in another direction rather than continuing to follow his example. The emotional thrust and tone

24. See pp. 36ff. above.
25. See Longenecker, *Galatians*, pp. 183–87.

of 4.11 is matched by the similar tone in 4.19–20, both bringing closure to the two halfs of this argument from experience. Furthermore, the middle of each of these parts of this argument is about the effect or potential effect of the agitators on the Galatians – they are about to become disciples of the agitators by taking on themselves the yoke of the Law (cf. 4.10 to 4.17). In short, we need to see 4.8–11 and 4.12–20 as two parts of a well integrated and rhetorically effective appeal to experience, drawing heavily on emotional language to persuade the audience.

Finally, it will not work to suggest that up to 4.11 we have judicial rhetoric, whereas beginning in 4.12 we have deliberative rhetoric. In both halves of this particular argument Paul is trying to dissuade the Galatians from Judaizing. Both 4.8–11 and 4.12–20 fit what Aristotle said about deliberative rhetoric: "the end of the deliberative speaker is the expedient or harmful; for he who exhorts recommends a course of action as better, and he who dissuades advises against it as worse" (*Rhetoric* 1.3.5). The 'better' here has to do with 'becoming as I am', the 'worse' with observing days, months and years and in general following the lead and advice of the agitators.[26]

Unfortunately, various commentators, due to lack of knowledge or lack of attention to rhetorical conventions about how to make an effective argument, have seen in 4.11–20 an example of irrational Paul being overcome by emotion and leaving logic behind; indeed he has been accused by Mussner of losing control of the argument.[27] Schlier says we find here an erratic train of thought.[28] It is clear from these sort of comments that there is lack of understanding of the rhetorical force and persuasive power of an emotional appeal to experience.[29] Accordingly, it is necessary at this point to say something about emotional appeals, the weight of experience, and the tone of this section from a rhetorical point of view. In addition, some remarks about friendship and enmity conventions are in order.

---

26. There are equally great problems with trying to start the 'exhortation' section of this argument at 4.21, 4.31, 5.1 or even later at 5.2 or 5.7 or 5.13. As Longenecker says, the first exhortation occurs at 4.12, and as we have argued it does not mark a new section in the letter. The reason for this is precisely because rhetorical considerations are dictating the structure of this document and also exhortation is a regular part of a deliberative speech and can occur at various points in the speech, though we would expect that since a deliberative argument develops in linear fashion that the punchline or bulk of the exhortation would come at or near the end of the speech, as is the case in Galatians. It must also be kept in mind that the exhortation 'become as I am' is dependent cn the autobiographical remarks set forth in Gal. 1–2 where Paul makes clear what Paul the exemplar gave up and what he became after conversion.

27. Mussner, *Galaterbrief*, pp. 304–5.

28. Schlier, *Galaterbrief*, p. 188.

29. Note Betz's proper complaint about the failure to recognize the rhetorical character of this argument; Betz, *Galatians*, p. 221.

The word *pathos*, as Quintilian reminds us, can properly be called 'emotion', in particular the deeper emotions, the ones that really motivate people to act in particular ways. Pathos "is almost entirely concerned with anger, dislike, fear, hatred, and pity" (*Inst. Or.* 6.2.20) to which one could also add love as another of the deeper emotions. Quintilian says very clearly that "the aim of appeals to emotion is not merely to show the bitter and grievous nature of ills that actually are so, but also to make ills which are usually regarded as tolerable seem unendurable, as for instance when we represent insulting words as inflicting more grievous injury than an actual blow or represent disgrace as being worse than death" (6.2.23). Quintilian gives the name of *deinosis* (literally 'making terrible') to the rhetorical tactic of using strong and emotional language to give added force to one's arguments.

Obviously, the appeal to emotions can be a two-edged sword, especially if there is any hint of mere play-acting or insincerity. It may as well turn off as win over an audience if they perceive it as a rhetorical trick or as something merely feigned and not real. This is why Quintilian warns the "prime essential for stirring the emotions of others is, in my opinion, first to feel those emotions oneself. It is something positively ridiculous to counterfeit grief, anger, and indignation . . . our eloquence must spring from the same feeling that we desire to produce in the mind of the listener" (6.2.26–27). In other words, the appeal to the deeper emotions must be grounded in experience, and all the more effective will be the appeal if the rhetor can refer not only to his own genuine feelings that the audience knows the speaker has but those the speaker knows the audience has had in the past. This is a recipe for an effective appeal to experience and emotion, and it is a recipe Paul follows perfectly here.

Sometimes it is possible in an appeal to emotions in a rhetorical speech to move convincingly into 'impersonation' where one engages in "portrayal of the emotions of children, women, nations and even of voiceless things, all of which require to be represented in character" (11.1.41). We find this as well in this section at 4.19, as Paul brings his argument to the highest emotional pitch by reminding his audience that he gave spiritual birth to them (i.e., they are his spiritual children). One of the keys to making this sort of emotional appeal effectively is the need for there to be a genuine tie or relationship between the speaker and the audience. The author of *Rhetoric to Alexander* says "all persons pity those whom they conceive to be closely related to them" to which he adds "everybody therefore feels kindly towards people from whom personally or from whose friends they think that they themselves . . . have received or are receiving or are going to receive some unmerited benefit" (33.1439b). Both of those conditions apply here and are appealed to by Paul.

In short, what we find in 4.12–20 is a pulling out of all the emotional stops: (1) Paul appeals to the Galatians own feelings of kindness and fairness toward him in the past, reminding them of the kind of relationship they used to have (vs. 12, 15); (2) he appeals to their feelings of pity for his physical condition (vss. 13–14); (3) he reminds them he is their spiritual parent (vs. 19) and is still in the process of painful labor until Christ is fully formed in them (i.e., he is still making strenuous efforts on their behalf and giving undeserved benefits for which the audience should be grateful – a shaming device); (4) as a parent he tells them he wishes he could change his tone with them, but he is in doubt and worrying over them, indicating his love for them but also instilling fear in them about their own condition (had they lost their former 'blessing'? vs. 15, 20); (5) finally he speaks of good and bad sorts of zeal or zealous courting (yet another strong emotion) which lead to either love or enmity (vss. 16–17). This is not an erratic argument, or miscellany of ideas, it is a touching of all the major emotional bases in a masterful way, by using all the rhetorically appropriate sort of key terms listed under *pathos* and the tactics listed in the literature on appeals to *pathos* or the deeper emotions.

Something must also be said at this point about friendship and enmity conventions. Betz has made an extended argument that Paul is drawing on a variety of *topoi* based on friendship conventions and ideas here.[30] Betz is on the right track that Paul is using language about intimate relationships in this passage, but it is not mere friendship language. The term friends never occurs, rather Paul is referring to an even more intimate relationship, a family relationship where Paul can speak of himself as either their brother, or even their mother in the faith. He contrasts this with the courting relationship that the agitators are pursuing with the Galatians at present. As is typical of such rivalry relationships (in this case between the Galatians' 'mother' and those who are now trying to woo them) we are talking about envy (an unhealthy sort of emotion being exhibited by the agitators), and even the casting of Paul into the role of the enemy for telling the truth. In a love relationship, love, if it goes sour can quickly turn into its opposite, and Paul is playing the role here of the wounded, and potentially rejected loved one, in this case a parent.

As P. Marshall has pointed out, in a crucial study of the way enmity relationships played out in antiquity, when one rejected a blessing or a gift given by someone "one then incurred the burden of enmity".[31] Rejection led to an enmity relationship that could degenerate into slurs on one's social background, attacks on one's personal appearance, speech, dress, accusations of immorality, greed, devious deeds and the like.[32] Paul is reminding his

---

30. Betz, *Galatians*, pp. 223ff.

31. This last phrase actually comes from Marshall's mentor, E. A. Judge, "The Social Identity of the First Christians," *Journal of Religious History* 11 (1980), pp. 201–17, here p. 214.

32. P. Marshall, *Enmity in Corinth: Social Conventions in Paul's Relations with the Corinthians* (Tübingen: Mohr, 1987), pp. 35–69.

audience that they had received joyfully the free gift he had offered them when he was present with them, indeed they had treated him as the one who sent him, Christ. None of the enmity conventions had come into play when Paul was with them, they had not spit, or seen Paul as one who had cast the evil eye on them – indeed quite the opposite had been the case. They had not objected to or disdained him even in spite of his appearance due to illness or weakness. There had been no casting of aspersions then.

Now Paul fears that under the influence of their new courters, the Galatians are in danger of treating Paul as an enemy, while previously they had treated him and what they received from him as a great blessing sent from God. All of this language makes quite good sense once one is aware of how enmity conventions worked and how Paul is trying to counter them by reminding his audience of the relationship of intimacy and love he had established with the audience when with them, a relationship which was mutual, not one-sided or based in selfish motives. Paul himself will go on to turn the tables on the agitators by accusing them of deceptive and selfish practices (they will exclude you in the end so they can make you their disciples; or, as at 6.12, they wish to make a good show in your flesh so *they* can boast and avoid persecution). We must conclude that the keys to understanding this crucial section of Galatians is being attuned to the rhetorical and social conventions Paul is drawing on here to make his appeal.

Verse **12** begins with a bold if elliptical appeal which reads literally 'become as I am, because I also . . . as you, brothers I beseech you.' The first thing to be said about this appeal is that it would be totally inappropriate if this was a piece of forensic rhetoric. One doesn't appeal to the judge to imitate the lawyer who is making his case. Such an appeal, based on the role that examples were meant to play in arguments about the future was, however, extremely apropos in deliberative rhetoric and Paul resorts to it in other deliberative arguments of his (cf. 1 Cor. 4.16; 11.1; 1 Thess. 2.14; Phil. 3.17). I have elsewhere dealt at some length with Paul's use of this deliberative device,[33] and the issue here clearly is whether the Galatians will follow Paul's good example, or the bad example of the agitators, by becoming their disciples (cf. Isocrates, *Against the Sophists* 17). Here as elsewhere in deliberative rhetoric, the function of the appeal to imitation is as B. Sanders has noted, the attempt to create unitive and unifying or non-factious behavior in one's audience.[34] The issue is what will be of future benefit and advantage for the group as a whole, and in this case what will facilitate the ongoing relationship between Paul and his converts. If the Galatians will imitate Paul in his rejection of the yoke of the Law which was part of his past and in his pursuit of walking in the

---

33. See my *Conflict and Community in Corinth*, pp. 144ff.
34. See B. Sanders, "Imitating Paul: 1 Cor. 4.16," *HTR* 74 (1981), pp. 353–63.

Spirit and according to the pattern of Christ and the freedom that provides, then there will be unity in the churches in Galatia as all will relate to God and each other on the same basis, and there will be unity between Paul and his converts. In 1 Cor. 9.21 he says of himself that when he relates to Gentiles he is outside the Mosaic Law, but yet not a lawless person having become in-law of Christ.[35] By appealing to his role as the Galatians' spiritual 'mother' Paul is not trying to pull rank on his converts but make clear his love for them, and the fact that he wants them to grow up to full maturity in Christ, or as he puts it here, he wants Christ to become fully formed in them, so they will be Christ-like persons living on the basis of the Christ pattern even as Paul is doing.

Scholars have debated which verb we should insert in the second half of this opening appeal. The two most likely candidates are 'as I am' (εἰμί) or 'as I became' (γέγονα). It is right to compare here 1 Cor. 9.20–21 where Paul speaks of being the Gentile to the Gentile. Paul is surely not suggesting that Paul became like the Galatians were when they were pagans, but rather that his previous lifestyle was like the one they adopted after they became Christians and had not yet contemplated submitting to the Mosaic Law.[36] The word 'brothers' adds emotion and affection to this appeal, and the appeal itself bears witness to the fact that Paul does not yet think the situation is past the point of no return. In other words, he believes there is still enough respect in the audience that an appeal to imitate the speaker might actually work. To further enforce this appeal, Paul reminds the Galatians that they had not in the past done Paul any wrong or injustice (with the implication that now is no time to start).[37] Were they to reject the appeal to imitate Paul or begin to treat him as an enemy or to succumb to the wooing of the agitators they would indeed be doing an injustice to Paul, especially in the light of how hard he had worked for them. Such an outcome would be especially out of character when one bore in mind how the Galatians had previously treated Paul, a fact of which Paul now reminds them.

Verse **13** states that the occasion or cause of Paul's preaching to the Galatians was a weakness or sickness of the flesh. The word ἀσθένεια can refer to a disease, but it can also refer to a condition caused by an injury. Commentators have often related this verse to what we find in 2 Cor. 12.7, but this latter text surely refers to an incident considerably prior to this occasion. The question is whether Paul is talking about some ongoing or congenital condition, or whether he is referring to a disease or condition he had only on one particular occasion. Certainly the way Paul puts the matter does not

35. We will say more about this matter in our Excursus on Paul's view of the Law, pp. 341ff. below. Here, is important to note that Paul is certainly not urging his converts to adopt a non-Gentile lifestyle in his exhortation 'become as I am'.

36. See rightly Betz, *Galatians*, p. 223.

37. See Betz, *Galatians*, p. 223.

suggest he is talking about a condition he had had for a long time which was with him every day of his life. Rather, he seems to be referring either to a recurring problem or a recent one, hence the 'because (or through) of a sickness/weakness'. Furthermore, it is difficult to see how Paul could say that some bodily weakness had been the occasion of his preaching to a variety of Galatian groups in a variety of places. If one is beaten in a particular location it is understandable how one could say that that caused one to stay in a particular place and led to addressing the local populace. It is more difficult to see how that could be the occasion of preaching in a variety of spots unless one envisions a condition which required regular but intermittent rest and rest stops. It is then on the whole more likely than not that Paul is referring to some disease. This possibility becomes all the more likely when Paul refers to the fact that the audience was not repulsed by his appearance and did not spit. Disease-bearing people were often thought to be carriers of bad luck. A wounded or bruised person would be less likely to produce such a reaction. Can we be more specific about the disease, realizing that certainty is not possible?

The following clues are ready to hand: (1) the disease affected Paul's *ethos*. It was readily seen and could have caused repulsion in and rejection to the audience when seen (this is likely what 'your temptation in my flesh' refers to). This means we are talking about a disease which has visible manifestations, and probably manifestations on the parts of the body which would be naturally visible, taking into account the normal apparel of a first-century person (i.e., a lengthy robe or toga). In short, we are talking about a disease that probably affected some part of the head, the neck, the hands, the lower legs, or the feet; (2) Paul says in vs. 15b that when he first visited them they would have 'plucked out their eyes and given them to him, if possible'. Even if we grant that this is a metaphor or that Paul is speaking hyperbolically or at least hypothetically, the question is why choose this way of putting it? Paul is certainly speaking of an act of supreme kindness as the eyes were often considered in antiquity the most valuable of all organs, being the windows on the world (cf. Deut. 32.10; Ps. 17.8; Zech. 2.8). As Dunn says "the purpose of such tearing out . . . would evidently have been to give the eyes thus removed to Paul, and presumably not merely as a gruesome gift or act of homage. Despite the majority, therefore, and given the train of thought (4.13–15) the most obvious implication is that Paul's ailment affected his eyes most of all, presumably leaving him with greatly restricted vision and in a painful(?) condition which excited the pity of the Galatians . . ."[38] (3) Paul says in Gal. 5.11 'See with what *large* letters I make when I am writing in my own hand'. If we ask what sort of person needs 'large print editions' and often writes with large characters the answer is a person

---

38. Dunn, *Galatians*, p. 236.

with a visual impairment. This may in part explain Paul's regular use of a scribe to write out most of his letters especially the lengthy ones (cf. Rom. 16.22; 1 Cor. 1.1; 1 Thess. 1.18; 2 Thess. 3.17); (4) Paul calls his problem a weakness of the 'flesh', not a fever or a demon, or some non-visible internal condition, and a weakness of the flesh that was obvious to the Galatians such that Paul could say they knew about it; (5) such an impairment might also explain various things said or suggested about Paul in Acts and elsewhere, namely that he always or almost always traveled with one or more companions, and at least part of the time with a physician named Luke, or that his *ethos* or bodily presence when he preached was deemed weak by some (2 Cor. 10.10), and one must not forget that according to the three accounts in Acts 9, 22, 26 Paul was at least initially blinded when he was converted. Could this have triggered periodic bouts with eye problems? (6) Finally is it an accident that when Paul recounts the 'vision' that he had and says he was caught up into the third heaven, he says he 'heard' things that he is not permitted to repeat, but extraordinarily he does not say he 'saw' things, which is what one would expect when the subject is visions or revelations (2 Cor. 12.1 cf. vs. 7). Notice too that he immediately goes on to refer to his weaknesses (vs. 5 – ἀσθενείαις). I must conclude that no view so suits all the evidence, taking into account all the clues, as the view that Paul had, at least periodically, eye problems of some sort, which hampered his travel, and as an orator damaged his *ethos*.[39] Paul was indeed an 'angel' in disguise when he came to Galatia, but more on this in a moment.

We have had occasion to discuss in the introduction to this commentary Paul's use of τὸ πρότερον in vs. 13, and the fact that it probably does not indicate the first of two visits.[40] Here we can add the additional supporting evidence that Paul is making a contrast between formerly and now in terms of the Galatians' reaction to Paul (see vss. 15–16), not between the first and second times he visited them. The second extended time of discussion Paul has with these converts is 'now' and through this

---

39. The only advantage of Ramsay's view, which my view may not have, is that if Paul contracted malaria soon after landing in Asia Minor, it might explain why Paul left the southern coastal plain area and went up into the mountains to Pisidian Antioch. See his *Historical Commentary on Galatians*, pp. 422ff. This might explain why he went to part of Galatia in the first place, but it would not necessarily explain why he went on to Iconium, Lystra, and Derbe (unless we are to envision periodic recurrence of the disease), whereas if Paul had a bout of problems with his eyes while in Galatia, this might explain why he had to make more periodic stops at several places along the way. Furthermore, oozing or red and encrusted eyes or even the side effects associated with opthalmia (squinting, rubbing of eyes etc.) were far more likely to create an immediate visual impact than malaria would have.

40. See the discussion pp. 12ff. above.

letter.[41] Note too that the position of the word πρότερον is emphatic, indicating its importance.[42] Paul is stressing what used to be the case with their relationship.

Verse **14** is awkward, and there is some textual uncertainty as to whether Paul is speaking of 'my trial' or the Galatians' trial over Paul's flesh, but the more difficult reading is the latter and it is also the better supported one.[43] The Galatians are said not to despise or disdain such a trial, nor did they spit. As we have discussed previously,[44] Paul is probably referring here to customs associated with warding off the evil eye. It was thought that looking at a sick person might make the observer sick, especially if he or she also looked at you. One way to ward off this harmful effect was by spitting. The verb ἐκπτύω does literally mean spit out, though it also has a more metaphorical sense of disdain. If it simply means the latter here it is redundant,[45] as the copier of p46 recognized, for he omitted the second verb altogether. It is more likely that we should see the verbs as having distinct meanings, for Paul is talking about reactions to something visually repulsive. It needs to be added that spitting was not simply a reaction to epilepsy or the kind of response to be expected when someone encountered a person they thought to be possessed by a demon. Rather spitting was a regular part of the social conventions associated with the ideas about the evil eye, regardless of the disease in question.[46] Theocritus as early as the third century B.C. said that one could ward off the evil eye by spitting three times (6.39).

Paul says in vs. **14b** that, to the contrary, far from seeing Paul as one who cast the evil eye, they saw him as an angel of God, indeed they welcomed him as Christ come in person! Here something must be said about the concepts pagans had about the appearance of gods on earth, and how they were likely to come incognito, sometimes so disguised that they would be quite unrecognizable.[47] They would come as a feeble old man, or as a sickly woman and so forth, in order to test those that they ruled to see what kind of persons they really were. Paul is speaking about hospitality conventions when he uses the word 'welcomed' and it is not out of place to point out that there was indeed a famous story (connected with the Phrygian hill country which was part of the province of the Galatian province at this time) about the consequences of failing to welcome or alternatively welcoming the gods when

41. See Longenecker, *Galatians*, p. 190.
42. Lightfoot, *Galatians*, p. 175.
43. See Metzger, *TC*, p. 596. 'Your trial/temptation' is supported by both good Alexandrian and Western texts. P46, however, has μου.
44. See pp. 201ff. above.
45. But see Joseph and Aseneth 2.1 for the two verbs together.
46. Pace Betz, *Galatians*, p. 225.
47. On this subject see Winter, *Seek the Welfare of the City*, pp. 130ff.

they came incognito for a visit. The story is recounted in Ovid's *Metamorphoses* 8.626ff. and I have dealt with it at some length elsewhere.[48]

There is also inscriptional evidence from the Lystran area of altars dedicated to the god Zeus, and to the messenger of the gods, Hermes.[49] If indeed when Paul and Barnabas went to Galatia Paul was the main spokesman as Acts suggests (cf. Acts 13–14), then it is understandable why pagans in the region, especially if there were dynamic works of the Spirit and healings happening, might assume that Paul was *the* messenger of the Gods – Hermes in disguise. Of course the word ἄγγελος here can be translated either angel or messenger, so Paul may be engaging in a bit of word-play since elsewhere in this letter the term clearly means angel (see Gal. 1.8 and 3.19), but it must be remembered that pagans believed that Hermes *was* a supernatural messenger of the gods, not just a mere mortal. The Galatians would have welcomed Paul on the basis of the social conventions they already knew, and especially on the basis of what they knew about how they should treat a messenger from God.[50] The connection between Paul saying he was welcomed as a messenger of God and the story in Acts 14 about such a welcome in Galatia should not be lightly dismissed. This may provide us with a further clue not only in regard to the north Galatia versus South Galatia debate, but also in regard to the dating of this letter to the Galatians.

More importantly for our discussion, Paul says they welcomed him as Jesus Christ. The concept of agency may be in mind here, in which a person's agent was to be treated as the one who sent him.[51] More to the fore perhaps is the fact that Paul has just exhorted them to become as he is, namely Christ-like, and now he is reminding them of how they treated him 'as Christ Jesus' when he first visited. In short, these remarks are meant to strengthen the appeal for imitation. Paul is saying if you saw me as the very agent of God when I came to you, indeed as the embodiment of Christ, there should be no problem imitating me now and becoming more Christ-like.

Verse **15** raises a pointed and rhetorical question 'where then is your blessedness?' and we may assume Paul means where has your graciousness and your willingness to be a blessing to me, and perhaps receive one from me gone now? What happened to the people who had welcomed him with such open arms before? That this is the right way to view this question is shown by

48. See my *The Acts of the Apostles*, pp. 395ff. on Acts 14.8–20. One must ask whether it is mere coincidence that Paul speaks as he does here, in view of the account in Acts 14 which tells us that Paul and Barnabas were received as messengers from the gods come incognito.

49. See Hansen, "Galatia", *AIIFCS 2*, p. 393.

50. Dunn, *Galatians*, pp. 234–35.

51. On Paul as Christ's apostle cf. pp. 69ff. above, and see my discussion in *Conflict and Community*, pp. 453ff.

what immediately follows when Paul cites an illustration of how gracious they were prepared to be, and how he is prepared to give public testimony to the fact of their blessedness in this regard. The conditional remark in this sentence is a second-class contrary-to-fact condition, and it is qualified with the phrase 'if possible' which makes the remark less hyperbolic.[52] In other words, they were quite willing to help Paul in any way they could during his time of affliction, a sign of their blessed condition.

Verse **16** begins somewhat surprisingly with the word ὥστε, which we would normally assume introduced a conclusion or result of what has been previously said. "Elsewhere in the NT ὥστε ('therefore', 'so') is always used at the beginning of an independent clause to draw an inference from what has just been stated (cf. Gal. 3.9, 24; 4.7 etc.)."[53] This leads to the conclusion that we should probably take this remark not as another rhetorical question but as an exclamation – [54] 'So [now] I have become your enemy telling you the truth!'[55] The point of this remark is to show the Galatians how contradictory this sort of outcome or result would be when one considers their former relationship and conduct towards Paul. Paul intends for the Galatians to see what an absurdity, what a *non sequitur* this would be by juxtaposing this conclusion which does not follow from the immediately preceding remark. In short, Paul is using an oxymoronic rhetorical technique to wake up his converts to what is really happening as a result of the agitators being in their midst.

Verse **17** makes clear enough that Paul thinks that the changed or changing attitude the Galatians have toward Paul is caused by the presence of the agitators whom Paul will not deign to name but only refers to as 'they' here. Paul here again uses the language of zeal, as he had of himself previously in Gal. 1.14, to refer to the persistent courting of the Galatians by the agitators. Like the zeal Paul himself had previously exhibited, this zeal also is not according to knowledge and not going in a proper direction, it is to no good end. Paul then goes on to say 'they wish to exclude you (or shut you out) in order that you will zealously court them'.

The language here is the language of courtship, but it could also be used for the relationship between a teacher and his students (see Plutarch *De Virtute Morali* 448E; Philo, *Legat.* 58; and Chrysostom on this verse). The question is: exclude the Galatians from what? Paul is using boundary language here and while it is possible that he means 'they wish to cut you off from having fellowship with me',[56] it seems more likely that this is Paul's polemical way of

---

52. See Longenecker, *Galatians*, p. 193.
53. Ibid.
54. See Burton, *Galatians*, pp. 244–45.
55. It is interesting that later the Ebionites called Paul 'the enemy' of their form of Jewish Christianity; cf. Pseud. Clem. *Hom. Ep. Pet.* 2.3; Pseud. Clem. *Recog.* 1.70).
56. See Bruce, *Galatians*, p. 211.

saying that the agitators want to exclude the Gentile Christians from the people of God unless and until they are prepared to be circumcised and follow the Mosaic Law. Dunn is right to point out that the Mosaic Law which protected God's people also shut out the aliens. "It is thus very well suited to describe the typical attitude of the Jewish zealot – that is, to draw the boundary line sharply and clearly between the people of the covenant so as to exclude those not belonging to Israel . . . , or, in particular, of the Jewish-Christian zealot, to exclude all Gentiles other than proselytes from Christ, the Jewish Messiah, and from the eschatological community of his people."[57] If the agitators succeeded in convincing the Galatians they needed to follow the Mosaic Law, then the natural next step would be for the Galatians to become the disciples of the agitators, courting them, rather than continuing to be disciples of Paul. The net effect in any case would be a serious damaging of the relationship between Paul and his converts.

In vs. **18** Paul may indeed be citing a familiar aphorism – 'but the good is to be zealously courted always in a good manner'.[58] This is the opposite of the sort of zealous courting referred to in vs. 17. To the maxim Paul adds 'and not only when I am present with you'. The true test of discipleship is how one behaves when the teacher is not present or watching. It has been noted that Galatians is unlike other Pauline epistles in that it does not have a travelogue (cf. Rom. 15.14–33; 1 Cor. 4.14–21; 2 Cor. 12.14–13.13; Phil. 2.19–24). This is passing strange since on other occasions when Paul has converts in distress or trouble he normally tells them that he is anxious to come to them and explains when and how he will try to do so. This strongly suggests that "Paul is not in a position to visit the Galatians even though the crisis is acute".[59] The Galatians will have to settle for an apostolic parousia in the form of this letter. Paul says quite plainly in vs. 20a that he would like to be present with them now, but apparently he cannot do so. This suggests that the crisis at his present location is equally acute, and if indeed he is in Antioch as we have suggested,[60] no time so well suits this set of circumstances than the time just *before* the apostolic council recorded in Acts 15 (cf. Gal. 2.11–14 to Acts 15.1–2).

In bringing this appeal to experience to a close in vss. **19–20** Paul resorts to rhetorical 'impersonation' presenting the Galatians as his children, and himself as the mother who gave them spiritual birth, and is having to go through the labor pains all over again until Christ is properly formed in them and guides their conduct and decision making. If the emotional tone of vss. 17–18 is vexation and anger, here Paul concludes on a more tender and compassionate note, but a note nonetheless meant to shame the Galatians into

57. Dunn, *Galatians*, p. 238.
58. See Burton, *Galatians*, p. 247.
59. Matera, *Galatians*, p. 162.
60. See pp. 17ff. above.

rejecting the overtures of the agitators. We have a textual problem here, as there is difficulty in deciding whether τέκνα (children) or τεκνία (little children) is the right reading here. On the one hand elsewhere Paul always uses the former term to refer to his relationship with his converts (cf. 4.28; 1 Cor. 4.14, 17; 2 Cor. 6.13, 12.14; 1 Thess. 2.7,11; Philem. vs. 10). The textual evidence is rather evenly balanced, and certainly because of its singularity 'little children' is the more difficult reading. Also supporting this rendering is the metaphor of childbearing here.

Commentators have often glossed over the significance of this metaphor here, but B. R. Gaventa has recently remedied this problem.[61] The metaphor is a complex one to say the least. "If we draw a picture corresponding to Paul's words in this verse, we would have Paul concentrating in labor. Inside his 'womb' we would find the Galatians and the object of the labor is Christ who is born among the Galatians"[62] or perhaps better said, Christ who is growing within the Galatians. The metaphor here has to do not with the act of insemination or the event of birth itself, but with the laboring which leads up to birth and follows the planting of the seed.[63] It is noteworthy that we find this selfsame metaphor, a woman in travail with child, in 1QH 3.7–10 used to describe the birth pangs of the new community. It is also right to point to Gal. 2.20 where Paul speaks of Christ living in him. Gaventa has presented a strong argument that there was a regular use of this sort of metaphorical language in early Christianity to refer to the apocalyptic events that transpire through God's intervention in human history, events which lead up to or involve the climax of history (cf. Mk. 13.8; Mt. 24.8; Rev. 12; 1 Thess. 5.3; Gal. 4.27 quoting Is. 54.1). She thus concludes for "Christ to be formed in the Galatians is not simply for them to develop spiritually or morally or christologically . . . It means that the eclipse of the old order occurs among them."[64] What is happening is not just a matter of creating new creatures in Christ, or even a new community in Christ, but a whole new creation is on the way to being born (cf. Gal. 6.15) of which creatures and community are but a part. This thought does not exclude the idea that Paul envisions the spiritual, moral and Christological formation of the Galatians as individuals and as a group, but it simply sets it in its proper larger eschatological context.

If we raise the question whether Paul is thinking more of community or of individual formation when he refers to Christ being formed in them, we may say that Paul certainly means both – he is looking for Christ-like

61. See her "The Maternity of Paul: an Exegetical Study of Galatians 4.19," in *Studies in John and Paul*, pp. 189–201.

62. Gaventa, p. 189.

63. Notice that Paul says 'again' about being in labor, suggesting it was arduous the first time around to convert the Galatians. See Matera, *Galatians*, p. 167.

64. Gaventa, p. 196.

individuals and a Christian community as well.[65] Nevertheless, the emphasis here may be on the individual's formation for three reasons: (1) this comports better with what Paul says of himself in Gal. 1.20, and it better comports with the call to imitation which requires an individual response; (2) the apostasy which Paul fears is also an individual matter; (3) Paul is addressing not one but several assemblies in Galatia, and so the audience would not assume he was talking about Christ being formed in the midst of one particular unified community.

There is some debate as to whether in vs. 20 the verb ἀλλάξαι should be translated 'change' or 'exchange'. The latter translation would suggest that Paul would like to exchange the voice heard in this letter for his own personal presence with them if he could. The former translation would suggest he would like to change his tone of voice in this letter (so NRSV, NEB, NIV) or the content of the letter (so JB), but his doubt or perplexity over their condition does not allow it. The translation 'exchange', however, has this drawback. Paul is talking about doing something with his voice, not with his letter. We would have expected him to say that he wished he could exchange this letter for his personal presence but he speaks of his voice here. I would suggest that in view of the emotive tone of this entire subsection the translation 'change my tone of voice' is more likely (cf. Artemidorus II, 20). The issue of tone was an important one rhetorically speaking especially in an emotional appeal to experience (cf. *Inst. Or.* 6.2.1ff.). Quintilian stresses that the tone must suit the character of the message and that it is disastrous if the tone is at odds with the message being conveyed.[66]

The verb ἀπορούμαι brings to light a final rhetorical device – that of *dubitatio* (cf. Acts 25.20). Paul expresses doubt or perplexity or being at a loss about the Galatians, and suggests in general he is at his wits' end over them. Of course had Paul been totally at a loss, he would not have been able to write as powerful and effective a piece of rhetoric as this document manifests. This is not to say that Paul is play-acting here, but that he is genuinely concerned about the status of the Galatians, and wishes for them likewise to be concerned about it. Luther in his 1535 commentary says aptly: "He does not miss anything; he scolds the Galatians, beseeches them, soothes them, commends their faith with wonderful words, and as a genuine orator presents his case

---

65. See Ziesler, *Galatians*, p. 65.

66. See *Inst. Or.* 9.1.3: "What use is it if we employ a lofty tone in cases of trivial import, a slight and refined style in cases of great moment, a cheerful tone when it demands vehemence, threatening language when supplication, and submissive when energy is required or fierceness and violence when our theme is one that asks for charm. Such incongruencies are as unbecoming as it is for men to wear necklaces and pearls . . ." The short clipped phrases here, often elliptical or asyndetic convey well Paul's agitation and perturbation.

with great care and faith – all in order to call them back to the truth of the Gospel . . ."[67] That Paul is not totally pessimistic about the Galatians is clear enough from Gal. 5.10. Thus, Paul ends on a note of concern. This concern becomes more evident in the allegory that follows. What we have found is that once again Paul is proceeding in an orderly manner as he did when he began his first argument in 3.1–5. First came the argument from experience, and then the argument from Scripture,[68] and Paul will duplicate that pattern here. We must turn to the further Scriptural argument now, after our discussion of the import of this material for today.

Bridging the Horizons

The temptation to go back to old patterns of behavior is often great, especially if they are long-established ones and there are strong personal and even financial incentives to do so. Such is the situation the Galatians found themselves in. Attending banquets in pagan temples was a means of socializing and making business contacts in the ancient world. If one was going to cut onself off from this sort of activity, then one would be looking for something comparable, and the Jewish community in a city in Asia Minor would be the nearest parallel. Paul does not simply equate submission to the Mosaic covenant with going back to the elementary practices and principles of pagan religion, but he sees them as analagous. The issue here is whether the Galatians could be adequately socialized into the Pauline form of Christianity so that they would not feel they needed to be a part of either of these other sorts of communities.

This sort of issue, of the socialization of converts, has direct relevance to the church today, not only in regard to new converts, but also in regard to persons who transfer from one denomination to another. To a large, extent a new member of a church stays or moves on on the basis of whether they feel well received and whether they feel their needs are being met in their new setting. The converse of this is the reason people often leave a church.

Paul in this passage is making an impassioned plea of a very personal nature in order to forestall the Galatians from making a false move. Paul sees this possible move as a violation of the relationship he already has with the Galatians, and a repudiation of the benefits they have already received from Christ. The sense of possible betrayal is not far beneath the surface of the argument here, and Paul is not above making an emotional appeal to prevent

---

67. Luther sees more clearly than Betz, *Galatians*, p. 221 that this section is emotionally loaded, not light.
68. See pp. 199ff. above.

his converts from doing something they would later regret. It would be wrong to see this as an example of emotional blackmail, not least because Paul really does believe his converts are in some spiritual danger and he feels he has an obligation to warn them about it.

The open appeal to imitation in this text may seem to us a bit egocentric in character, but this is because we fail to understand the difference between Paul's culture and our own. This was a normal pedagogical technique in antiquity, and was part of the teacher serving as role model for the pupils. Character was crucial to ancient pedagogy since learning to a great extent was a matter of imitating one's teacher. In his *Canterbury Tales* Chaucer has one character remark, 'If gold rusts, what then will iron do?' The point is, that the example of the teacher is crucial, and if he fails to model Christ-like behavior, one can hardly expect the pupils to do so. Scott McKnight has wisely suggested that to get a full-orbed view of what Paul is asking for when he speaks of imitating or following his example the following passages should be consulted: our passage, 1 Cor. 4.16; 11.1; Phil. 3.7, 4.9; 1 Thess. 1.6; 2 Thess. 3.7,9.[69] The end result of examining these passages is that Paul is calling for imitation only in so far as he himself is following the model and manner of Christ.

Paul's presentation of himself as a woman in labor is meant to indicate the degree of love he has for his converts, but it also indicates the pain and difficulty he is having in bringing them into a fully Christian lifestyle. It further suggests how closely he sees himself connected to them, and vice versa. We see Paul's deep pastoral commitment to his charges, a commitment we would do well to imitate if we are ministers. A helpful resource that speaks of this particular role of the minister is Richard Baxter's classic work *The Reformed Pastor*. Whatever else one makes of this labor metaphor, it makes quite clear that ministry was hard and indeed gut-wrenching work even for apostles.

There was a graciousness about the Galatians which Paul finds commendable. They did not reject Paul even though he had a repulsive illness. It is to be noted that he praises them where and when he can. Church members, like children need this sort of affirmation on a regular basis. It is fair also to say that you can tell a lot about a person by how they react to you when you are not well.

Even today we are very concerned with the outward appearance of our leaders, what they wear and how they look, how healthy they appear to be. In my own living memory I can say that one of the most powerful sermons I ever heard was from a very frail man who was confined to a wheelchair and could barely speak above a whisper. His own testimony about the grace of God in his life and how he had overcome many odds was powerful. Perhaps Paul's testimony was similar. Certainly he believed that God's power was made

---

69. McKnight, *Galatians*, p. 223.

perfect in his own weakness, in other words that God most shone through when it was evident that the message and eloquence could not be attributed to human skill or ability. This passage stands as an indictment against all those who judge mainly by appearances, and do not have the graciousness the Galatians had when Paul first was with them.

Argument IV: 4.21–5.1

THE ALLEGORY OF ANTIPATHY

Tell me, you wishing to be under the Law, do you not hear the Law? For it is written that 'Abraham had two sons, one from a slave girl and one from a free woman'. But on the one hand the one from the slave girl was begotten according to the flesh, but on the other hand the one of the free woman through the promise. These things are an allegory. For these two women are two covenants, one on the one hand from Mount Sinai born unto slavery, who is Hagar, but on the other hand the Mount Sinai Hagar is in Arabia, but it corresponds to the present Jerusalem. For she is in bondage with her children. But the Jerusalem above is free, who is our mother, for it is written 'Be glad barren one, you who do not give birth, break forth and cry out, you who do not suffer birth pangs because much more numerous the children of the desolate woman than those having a man'.

But you brothers are children of the promise according to Isaac, but just as then the one born according to the flesh persecuted the one born according to the Spirit, so also now. But what does the Scripture say 'Cast out the slave girl and her son', for the son of the slave girl will never inherit with the son of the free woman. Therefore brothers you are not the slave girl's children but the free one's. For freedom Christ has set you free; stand firm then and do not be entangled again in a yoke of slavery.

Paul's fourth major argument among the λόγοι takes the form of what Paul calls an ἀλληγορούμενα (vs. 24). The question to be raised is whether Paul is referring to an allegory or an allegorizing transformation of a story that is not in itself an allegory, or an allegorical interpretation. It becomes clear from vss. 24–25 that either the second or the third of these is actually in view here, in all likelihood the second, for Paul adds new elements to the story itself, he does not simply interpret the OT text allegorically. In view of the history of interpretation of this text it is important to stress that allegory, allegorizing, and allegorical interpretation were not the special provenance of early Jews, though certainly early Jews did do these things. In fact, there were specific discussions about allegories and allegorizing in the Greek and Roman rhetorical handbooks and it will be well to review some of this data here.[1]

---

1. A distinction must be made between Jewish modes of handling Scriptural texts, such as midrash pesher and the like, and creating allegories and allegorizing which were much more common and universal practices in the first century. Furthermore, it must be borne in mind that with allegorizers such as Philo, we are dealing with highly Hellenized Jews, who grew up in a largely Greco-Roman environment. In other words, Philo's

From a rhetorical point of view an allegory falls under the category of a trope. A trope is by definition an "artistic alteration of a word or phrase from its proper meaning to another" (*Inst. Or.* 8.6.1). Tropes can be used either for stylistic purposes or to help express the orator's meaning, and surely the latter is the case in Gal. 4.21–5.1. The Greek word which we transliterate as 'allegory' is translated in Latin as *inversio* and is taken to mean a form of speaking which "presents one thing in words and another in meaning, or else something absolutely opposed to the [literal] meaning of the words" (*Inst. Or.* 8.6.44). We may compare this to what is said in *Rhet. ad Her.* 4.34.46: "allegory is a manner of speech denoting one thing by the letter of the words, but another by their meaning."

Quintilian tells us that rhetoricians made very frequent use of allegory (8.6.47) and we must stress that Paul is addressing a largely Gentile audience in Galatia whose primary contact with this sort of literary device was likely to be through hearing rhetorical speeches or receiving rhetorical training. Historically speaking, we have little reason to think that Paul could have expected this audience to be familiar with specifically Jewish forms of handling texts, and since his goal was to persuade the Galatians to a particular course of action, it is reasonable to assume that he would by and large use methods likely to be familiar and plausible and convincing to this particular audience.[2] In addition, there is strong evidence that Pharisees like Paul and before him Jewish teachers like Hillel had received rhetorical training, even in Jerusalem. In a much overlooked essay D. Daube has made a strong case for the view that the early Jewish methods of interpreting Scripture are frequently "derived from Hellenistic rhetoric. Hellenistic rhetoric is at the bottom of the fundamental ideas, presuppositions, from which the Rabbis proceeded and of the major details of application, the manner in which these ideas were translated into practice."[3]

---

allegorizing probably tells us more about his indebtedness to his Alexandrian setting than to his Jewish heritage. The proof of this is shown when we consider the works of others such as Clement or Origen who grew up in or lived for a considerable period of time in this same sort of environment. I submit it is no accident that the closest parallel to Paul's handling of the story of Sarah and Hagar is the way Philo deals with the story (see below). The reason for this is that they are both heavily indebted to rhetorical conventions and notions about how to allegorize and use such a text.

2. Even if some of Paul's converts in Galatia were God-fearers, it is not at all clear that they would have been familiar with the intricacies of peculiarly Jewish ways of handling texts.

3. D. Daube, "Rabbinic Methods of Interpretation and Hellenistic Rhetoric," *HUCA* 22 (1949), pp. 239–64. Daube shows that even Hillel's famous seven norms of interpretation are deeply indebted to rhetorical ideas about how to approach and use texts to persuade.

Quintilian speaks of a variety of kinds of allegories used in rhetorical pieces, but he says the most common type is the 'mixed' allegory in which "the ornamental element is provided by the metaphorical words and the meaning is indicated by those which are used literally" (8.6.48). In this lattermost comment Quintilian is referring to the sort of brief explanations that we find for instance in Gal. 4.24. I would suggest that what we have in Gal. 4.21–5.1 is what Quintilian calls a mixed allegory.[4] Quintilian also reminds us that what makes an allegory effective is "not merely what is said, but about whom it is said, since what is said may in another context be literally true" (*Inst. Or.* 8.6.55). It is of the essence of an allegory that the interpretation offered is not literally true about the subjects *within* the story, but rather it is true of persons outside the story, either members of the audience or those the audience knows about. Quintilian also refers to the allegorical use or interpretation of non-allegorical stories, for instance he refers to a fable which can be understood allegorically (5.11.21). All the above must be kept in mind when we compare Paul's handling of this story to that of other Jewish interpreters such as the author of Jubilees or Philo.

The later rabbinic discussion of the Sarah and Hagar story has been aptly summed up by Longenecker, and there is no need to repeat that discussion here, especially in view of its meagre results and in view of the methodological question of whether any of this material or means of handling the story goes back to the pre-70 A.D. period.[5] Basically in the rabbinic discussion Ishmael and also Esau are seen as wicked anomalies, and Ishmael in particular is characterized as doing evil works including indulging in idolatry (especially in the Targums).[6] The basic contrasts between Sarah and Hagar and between Isaac and Ishmael are inherent in the story itself and so the fact that both Paul and later rabbinic discussions of this story highlight these points need not suggest any direct connection between the two streams of interpretation. Of more direct relevance is the way we see the text handled in Jubilees and especially the way we find it handled by Philo.

In Jubilees 16 the author of this document, which surely pre-dates Galatians, sees Ishmael as representing Abraham's Gentile progeny, while Isaac represents the Jewish progeny. Thus, in this discussion Abraham is seen as the father of all nations, and this way of reading the Genesis 21 text led to the

---

4. The other possibility is that we are dealing with an allegory where "the meaning is contrary to that which is suggested by the words, involving an element of irony, or as our rhetoricians call it, *illusio*" (8.6.54). In our story Paul's way of associating Hagar with Mount Sinai and the present Jerusalem is in fact counter-intuitive considering the rather straightforward meaning of the text, and also how it was normally understood in early Judaism.

5. Longenecker, *Galatians*, pp. 200–6.

6. See Longenecker, pp. 202–3.

anomaly of Abraham, since he was the father of Ishmael first, being the father of Gentiles *before* he was the father of Jews. Yet this fact was offset by the fact that the text clearly said of Ishmael "he shall not be heir" (Gen. 21.10). Jub. 16.17–18 reads "All the seed of [Abraham's] sons should be Gentiles, and be reckoned among the Gentiles. For he should become the portion of the Most High, and all his seed had fallen into the possession of God, that it should be unto the Lord a people for possession above all nations and that it should become a kingdom of priests and a holy nation." Now it is possible, though we cannot be sure, that the agitators in Galatia had used some such text as Gen. 21 to make their point with the Galatians, for as C. K. Barrett says, it is an unlikely text for Paul to have chosen at random to argue his *own* case for a Law-free Gospel and an inheritance by grace through faith for the Gentiles.[7] It is believable that they would have stressed that the Galatian Gentiles could not be heirs, they were in the position of Ishmael, unless of course they submitted to circumcision and the keeping of the Mosaic Law.[8] It is clear enough that Paul is not himself indebted to this approach to Gen. 21, and furthermore what we find in Jubilees is not an allegory or even really an allegorizing of the text unless we count the identification of Ishmael with the Gentiles as allegorizing.

It is frankly surprising that Barrett pays a good deal of attention to the latter rabbinic discussion and also some attention to Jubilees, but dismisses any comparison of Paul's use of the text with Philo's use with a mere wave of the hand.[9] Yet only Philo and Paul in all of this Jewish literature really engage in a contemporizing of the text by means of allegorizing, and this fact alone should have caused more attention to be paid to the parallels. This is especially so when we discover that for Philo Hagar symbolizes elementary learning or education, that is "grammar, geometry, astronomy, rhetoric, music, and all the other branches of [elementary] intellectual study" (*Congr.* 11). In short she symbolizes something very close to what Paul calls the στοιχεῖα τοῦ κόσμου.[10] Philo sees the child of Sarah as symbolizing higher knowledge or true wisdom, for Sarah herself is seen as Virtue.

The gist of Philo's argument about this text is that just "as Hagar conceived before Sarah, so the search for wisdom must begin with the 'lower branches of school lore'; but just as Hagar was expelled at the command of Sarah, so it is necessary to move beyond mere sophistry and mundane learning

---

7. C. K. Barrett, " The Allegory of Abraham, Sarah, and Hagar," in *Essays on Paul*, pp. 154–70.

8. See the fruitful discussion of Hays, *Echoes of Scripture in Paul*, pp. 111–21.

9. Barrett, p. 169 n. 24: "the very extensive allegories of Abraham, Sarah, and Hagar by Philo contribute little, in form or substance to this discussion, and are therefore . . . left out of account; they are interesting but not illuminating."

10. On the meaning of which see pp. 284ff. above.

if one wishes to attain wisdom and virtue"[11] Philo says very plainly in *Cher.* 9 that when true wisdom is attained "then will be cast forth those preliminary studies which bear the name of Hagar, and cast forth too will be their son the sophist, Ishmael." Longenecker's conclusion is for the most part apt: "Philo's Hagar–Sarah allegory bears several striking surface similarities to Paul's in Gal. 4.21–31. Both depend on similar elements in the story: the contrast between slave and free; the two sons; the banishment of Hagar and Ishmael in favor of Sarah and Isaac. In both, Hagar and Ishmael represent a preliminary and preparatory stage that is superseded by something greater, rather than a totally negative and wicked quantity as is the case in the rabbinic tradition."[12] I would disagree, however, that these similarities are only on the surface. For one thing, as Hays says, in the LXX version of this story while Hagar is certainly called a slave girl, nowhere is Sarah called ἐλευθέρα.[13] This contrast is something both Philo and Paul highlight in a way that the text itself does not explicitly do. For another thing, Paul's entire series of arguments from 3.1 up to 4.20 has been stressing that the Law is indeed among the στοιχεῖα, the elementary principles, which God's people have now outgrown, since Christ has come and his people have gone on to true Wisdom found in him. Philo of course would not agree with placing the Law among the 'elementary studies' but the developmental way of arguing using Gen. 21 is strikingly similar in both these sources. I would suggest this similarity is not accidental. Both Paul and Philo have learned a good deal about how to use as evidence documents in proofs and how to handle sacred texts in a persuasive way from their own studies in rhetoric.[14]

Perhaps here is the place to offer a further tentative suggestion. If Paul intimates that the slave woman and her progeny need to be cast out of the Galatian assemblies, it seems clear enough that he means the agitators and perhaps also their adherents. The question then might be: who does Sarah represent, or perhaps better who represents and stands with Sarah in this story? And surely the answer must be the 'woman' who bore the Galatians in freedom – namely Paul! Perhaps it is no accident that the verses immediately preceding the beginning of this allegory, 4.19–20, are about Paul being the mother who is in labor until Christ is formed in his converts. If the agitators are to be cast out, then the original spiritual mother of the Galatians is to be once more embraced. Notice that the crucial verse, vs. 30 is a quotation of what Sarah said in Gen. 21.10. The voice of Sarah is now also the voice of Paul. Furthermore, Paul had just also argued that the Galatians needed to emulate Paul, becoming

11. Longenecker, *Galatians*, p. 204.
12. Longenecker, p. 205.
13. Hays, p. 112.
14. A detailed study of the similar ways Paul and Philo reacted to sophistic rhetoric has now been provided by B. Winter, *Are Paul and Philo among the Sophists?* (Cambridge: Cambridge University Press, 1997).

as he is (not by implication as the agitators are). Now of course Paul in his own allegory speaks of the one who is mother of all true believers, namely the Jerusalem which is from above (vs. 26), and he also says that 'we' are all children of the free woman', which presumably would include Paul himself (vs. 31). Nevertheless, Paul may have meant to leave as a subliminal message the sort of thing we suggested at the outset of this paragraph.

Finally, something needs to be said about why I think we are dealing with an allegory here and not a typology, and also what sort of allegory we are dealing with in Gal. 4.21–5.1. Had Paul wanted us to see this text typologically, he could easily have used the appropriate terminology to signal this fact. For example, Paul very clearly in 1 Cor. 10.6 identifies what he is talking about as a τύπος, and the context makes clear that he is making a comparison between two historical groups, a type and an antitype. This is far from clear in Gal. 4.21–5.1. In fact Paul tells us he is comparing two covenants, under the labels Sarah and Hagar, and the comparison doesn't amount to looking at historical types and antitypes. It involves *contrasting* two sorts of covenants. This becomes especially clear if we set up two parallel columns that summarize the discussion here.

HAGAR	[SARAH][15]
The covenant from Mount Sinai in Arabia	The covenant of the promise
The current Jerusalem	The Jerusalem that is above
The children of the slave woman [like Ishmael]	The children of the free woman [like Isaac][16]
Not sharing the inheritance	Sharing the inheritance[17]

15. Notice that Sarah is not mentioned by name, which we would expect if this were a typological comparison between two persons or two groups of persons. What is important here for Paul is not who Sarah is as a person but the fact that she was a free woman and bore free children. In other words, what is going on here is a contrast between freedom and slavery, two conditions the Galatians must choose between. The allegory, being part of a piece of deliberative rhetoric, is attempting to aid the Galatians' decision-making process by emphasizing the enslaving results of submitting to the Law. Paul also here takes the further step of giving the concrete advice of Sarah to his Galatian converts – 'cast out the slave and her child'. In other words not only are they not to submit to the Law, but they are to remove the source of temptation to follow it.

16. Compare J. L. Martyn, "Apocalyptic Antinomies in Paul's Letter to the Galatians," *NTS* 31 (1985), pp. 410–24, here p. 419.

17. There is some merit in Cosgrove's comment in "The Law," pp. 226–27 that the emphasis in the allegory is in establishing the connection between Hagar, Sinai, and Jerusalem and so on the Hagar side of the allegory. Paul does not defend but simply asserts the idea that the heavenly Jerusalem is our mother, and so perhaps this was common ground.

Such a contrast works well as an ancient allegory handled in rhetorical fashion where there is an expectation of a contrast between the plain sense of a text and its contemporized significance, and perhaps other surprises as well. Sarah is certainly not an antitype of Gentile believers. There is not enough similarity between the two to make a type–antitype relationship viable. There is only the quality of freedom that they share. An ancient allegory was not like Bunyan's *Pilgrim's Progress* or Spenser's *Faerie Queene* where detailed point by point 'this is that' sort of referents were the norm. One suspects that the resistance of many modern scholars to see allegory or allegorizing interpretation in Gal. 4 comes from bringing to the reading of this text more modern and western notions about what an allegory must look like. Bearing these things in mind we must turn to the detailed discussion of the text itself.

It is unfortunate that so many scholars have seen the material in 4.21–5.1 as something of an afterthought,[18] and a not very convincing one at that. Perhaps partly this reaction is due to the fact that many NT scholars trained in the historical critical method have something of an allergic reaction whenever they encounter allegory or allegorizing. There is of course a long pedigree for this sort of reaction going back to the ancient Antiochean school and people like Chrysostom who says in commenting on vs. 24, "Contrary to usage he calls a type an allegory; his meaning is as follows: this history not only declares that which appears on the face of it, but announces somewhat further, whence it is called an allegory."[19] Even Hays, who provides a more sympathetic reading of what is happening here, accuses Paul of "invoking a hermeneutical miracle calculated to end the argument by leaving his audience agape, [executing] a counterreading that reverses the terms of the discussion, claiming the putative hostile evidence for his own case".[20] But against the afterthought idea this text is in fact an integral part of Paul's overall argument against the Galatians submitting to the Law, climaxing what has been said before and preparing for the contrasts Paul will set up in the more exhortative material which follows in Gal. 5–6, where the Law is still seen as the issue and the problem.[21]

Against the idea that Paul is simply engaging in exegetical sleight of hand here, it must be recognized that ancient allegory and allegorizing follows its own rhetorical conventions and should not be judged on the basis of whether or not the argument measures up to modern canons of historical critical interpretation. Paul was not attempting to provide a historically grounded

18. So Burton, *Galatians*, p. 199.
19. Chrysostom himself, however, cannot resist the urge to allegorize because in his subsequent discussion he says that the Jerusalem from above is the church and the barren woman is the church of the Gentiles in particular, while the woman who is married is the synagogue.
20. Hays, p. 112.
21. See rightly, Hansen, *Abraham in Galatians*, pp. 151–54.

interpretation of portions of the OT here. As a pastor he was using a widely recognized rhetorical manner of handling a text so as to contemporize it. This falls under the heading of a homiletical and rhetorical use of the text, *not* a historical interpretation of it. In short Paul should not be faulted for something he wasn't trying to do, and on the other hand must be judged in the light of the applicable ancient literary and rhetorical conventions (cf. above). Paul is perhaps engaging here in the time-honored rhetorical practice of stealing another's thunder by taking his best argument and using it to support one's own case.

Verse **21** begins in dialogical fashion, with direct address to those contemplating submitting to the Law. As Betz says, this is reminiscent of the Hellenistic diatribe style.[22] Like the approach in the first major argument in 3.1–5, Paul seeks to engage his audience directly, only here he does not rely on rhetorical questions. Lest we assume that Paul had actually moved on to another subject, this verse reminds us that the Galatians' relationship to the Mosaic Law, and Paul's desire that they not submit to it, is the main subject of all the arguments in this letter. The present participle θέλοντες supports our contention that Paul believes he is addressing those on the verge of submitting to the Law, but not having done so yet.[23] A question may be raised as to whether Paul thinks all of his audience is in the position of wishing to submit to the Law, or only a significant portion of it. In either case, Paul thinks the situation serious enough publicly to address everyone about it.

As has often been noted, Paul uses the word Law in this verse in two slightly different ways. In the phrase 'under the Law' Paul means the stipulations of the Mosaic covenant properly speaking; but when he goes on to say 'do you not listen to the Law?' and then paraphrases portions of the patriarchal narratives in Genesis, we see in an instant why it is so difficult to disentangle Paul's discussion of the Law in Galatians.[24] In the second instance of νόμος the word simply means Scripture. Notice also that Paul speaks of hearing or listening to the Law, reminding us that the Galatians, like most ancients including most Diaspora Jews, would not have read the Law since they did not have copies or easy access to copies of the Hebrew Scriptures, but rather will have only heard it read. Here Paul, in order to be persuasive, may be counting on the fact that he knows the Scriptures far better than they do, and that they will respect and perhaps even defer to his expertise in this matter.

Verse **22** begins with the technical formula 'it is written' which sets up an expectation of Scriptural quotation to follow, but in fact Paul is summing up his version of part of the Abraham saga including portions of Gen. 16.15 and

22. Betz, *Galatians*, p. 241.
23. See pp. 299ff. above on 4.10.
24. On which see the Excursus below.

21.2–9 (LXX). He refers to the (first) two sons of Abraham,[25] one born of a slave girl, and one from a free woman. The term παιδίσκης has as its literal meaning young woman, but clearly enough in later Greek usage, including often in the LXX (see Gen. 16.1 LXX) it means young slave woman (cf. Acts 12.13; 16.16). Now as Hays has noted, in the LXX of Genesis while Hagar is repeatedly called a slave girl, Sarah is never called ἐλευθέρα,which means that the "emphasis on her free status, crucial for Paul's reading, is brought to the story by Paul himself".[26] Paul is here setting up a contrast or antinomy between slave and free that is going to resound through much of the rest of the document in one form or another, such that what is said here prepares for the later discussion, for instance in 5.13ff.[27] But in another way "the concept of 'freedom' will provide the major topic in the following sections of the letter (see 4.31; 5.1, 13)."[28]

Paul emphasizes in vs. 23 that the son of the slave girl was born 'according to the flesh', but the son of the free woman through promise. Notice that this argument is in a sense like what we find in Rom. 9.6–18 in that Paul is making a second-generation argument here. In other words, this argument builds on what Paul has already said in Gal. 3 about Abraham being reckoned as righteous by grace through faith, and now Paul is going to establish that the chosen line in the case of the second generation was also on the basis of grace, not on the basis of heredity or 'flesh'. Ishmael was after all a first-born, and one born of the flesh in a natural way. But this is not what determined who would inherit. In this fashion Paul will undermine any appeals to heredity or 'natural' connections with Abraham. Paul's point will be that even Isaac came to Abraham and into his inheritance by way of promise, just as the Galatians had.

Notice that Paul is not really interested in the characters in the story itself. Sarah is never mentioned by name nor is Ishmael, and Isaac is not mentioned by name until vs. 28. It is what these characters represent (promise and freedom on the one hand or flesh and slavery on the other) and what their story tells us about the ways of God with his people that Paul is interested in. There may also be another reason why Paul does not mention Sarah's name here – he is playing her role and speaking with her voice, in particular at vs. 30.[29]

Verse 24 stresses that 'these things are ἀλληγορούμενα'. This last word is a participial form of ἀλληγορέω and is a *hapax legomenon* in the NT, indeed

---

25. He makes no mention of the later children of Abraham by second marriage referred to in Gen. 25.1–6.

26. Hays, *Echoes*, p. 113.

27. Notice the deliberate μὲν ... δὲ contrast in vs. 23. Though p46 and B omit the μὲν here, it is well supported by many early, good quality manuscripts with considerable geographical spread including ℵ, A, C, D, F, G and numerous minuscules.

28. Betz, *Galatians*, p. 243.

29. See pp. 326ff. above.

in all of the literature of the earliest period of Christian writing. The verb is a compound of ἄλλο and ἀγορεύω which literally means to say something else. As we have noticed above in our discussion of rhetoric and allegory, the idea is that the words say and mean one thing but now are used to *refer* to something else. This is not a concept of a deeper meaning but rather a concept of another referent. Allegorizing an historical text is a way of contemporizing it, giving it a secondary referent not a deeper meaning.[30] Paul is saying for instance in vs. 24 that Hagar in her story corresponds in certain respects with a certain covenant and so is analogous to or should be placed in the same column with Mount Sinai in Arabia. Both Hagar and that covenant give birth 'unto slavery'.

In the second half of vs. 24 the reference to the Mosaic covenant is made explicit by juxtaposing the word 'covenants' with a mention of Mount Sinai. It is in order to point out that 2 Cor. 3.4–18 shows that Paul quite naturally associates the giving of the ten commandments with Mount Sinai. This, in his mind, is the heart of the Law. There is nothing in this allegory to suggest that Paul is simply polemicizing about a misunderstanding or a misuse of the Law, or against its boundary defining rituals. Had Paul wanted to attack legalism he could have done so, but this is not his aim here. Paul's view is that for Christians to submit to the Law is tantamount to submitting to slavery and giving up the freedom one has in Christ. It is tantamount to going back to Sinai, not on to the promised land.

The reference to covenants (plural) is striking and certainly the interpretation of Sarah and Hagar as representing two different covenants has no direct parallel in Jewish exegesis. If we ask what Jewish exegete could talk in these terms the answer must be only "one convinced as Paul was, that the Law of Moses was an interim arrangement designed to keep the people of God in protective custody until the promised 'Seed' of Abraham should come".[31] Dunn has failed to grasp the radical character of Paul's argument when he says "what Paul describes as two covenants for the purposes of his exegesis are in effect two ways of understanding the one covenant purpose of God through Abraham and for his seed."[32] It is the argument of the agitators, not Paul, that the Mosaic covenant is an extension of the Abrahamic covenant.

Some emphasis is probably to be put on the verb γεννῶσα and its tense. In fact this is a feminine present participle indicating an ongoing process. This Sinai covenant is still bearing children unto slavery, and Paul is worried that the Galatians might be the next ones experiencing such a birth which would

30. Strangely, even Betz, *Galatians*, p. 243 falls into the trap of speaking about deeper meanings. Allegory, however, in a rhetorical context is a form of extended metaphor and·so of analogy.

31. Hays, *Echoes*, p. 114.

32. Dunn, *Galatians*, p. 249.

be a very different sort of birth from the one Paul has been laboring to bring forth. Martyn rightly points out that Paul chooses to use the verb γεννάω in this discussion rather than τέκειν which is consistently the term used in the LXX versions of the story of the births of Ishmael and Isaac. Only in the quotation from Is. 54.1 do we find the latter verb here. The question is why Paul makes such a choice.

The first point to note is that there is a consistent distinction in meaning between these two verbs having to do with producing offspring. Γεννάω is used in the LXX to refer to the male's role in 'begetting' while τέκειν refers to the female's role. Clearly enough, however, Paul is not really interested in Abraham's role, but he is interested in the role of other males – his own role, and that of the Judaizers. Paul is seeking to beget children unto freedom, where as the agitators are capable of begetting only slave children. In support of this interpretation note that in Philem. 10 Paul speaks specifically of his begetting (γεννάν) of Onesimus, and in 1 Cor. 4.14–15 he refers to his begetting of the Corinthian Christians.[33] In other words, Paul is here doing an allegorical interpretation contrasting the effect of his own ministry with that of the agitators. This is not a contrast between Judaism and Christianity, but between a focus or reliance on two different covenants by two different groups of Christians, covenants which produce two different effects on Christians.[34] Furthermore, these are two covenants that are being followed at the same time, hence the tension in Paul's view, because in his view, it is not appropriate for his audience to follow one of these covenants.[35]

This still does not resolve the question of what the other covenant is which Paul has in mind. Here context is crucial. It is probably a mistake to read Gal. 4 in the light of 2 Cor. 3 where there is a clear contrast between an old and a new covenant, and between two different ministries. One must ask what the Galatians are likely to have understood Paul to mean in the light of what he has already said to them, and the most natural way to read the Scriptural discussion in Gal. 4 is in the light of the one Paul offers in Gal. 3.6ff. Furthermore, there are clues in our own text that Paul has the Abrahamic covenant primarily in mind here. For instance, there is the reference to Sarah

33. Here I am simply following Martyn, "The Covenant of Hagar and Sarah," in *Faith and History: Essays in Honor of Paul W. Meyer* (Atlanta: Scholars Press, 1990), pp. 160–92, here pp. 174ff.

34. Against Betz, *Galatians*, pp. 241ff. H. Lietzmann, *An die Galater* (Tübingen: Mohr, 1910), pp. 229ff. See C. H. Cosgrove, "The Law has given Sarah no Children (Gal. 4.21–30)," *NovT* 19 (1987), pp. 219–35. On the history of the mis-interpretation of this passage, particularly in the identifying of Hagar with Judaism and the heavenly Jerusalem with the church see Martyn, "The Covenant", pp. 166ff.

35. See Martyn, "The Covenant," p. 188 n. 55: "Paul makes clear that the gospel is carrying the world beyond all forms of religion, creating a community of former Jews and former Gentiles (3.28)."

and Isaac in this allegory. The Galatians are said to be *like* Isaac, being children of promise and inheritance, but the point is that the story being allegorized and contemporized is that of Sarah and her miraculous child Isaac, and so of the Abrahamic covenant. One must add that Paul closely connects the Abrahamic and new covenants; indeed it is plausible that here Paul is thinking of the fulfillment of the Abrahamic covenant in the new one.[36] He may well see the matter as the promise and fulfillment of one covenant. In any case, what we do not find here is the contrast between non-Christian Judaism and Christianity. The argument here is an in-house one involving polemics against Judaizing Christians.[37]

Verse **25** presents us with a difficult textual as well as an exegetical problem. Is the name Hagar a part of the original text or not? If not, what is the point of an apparently geographical remark like 'Now Mount Sinai is in Arabia'?[38] The reading with Hagar is supported by A, B, D, K, L and a variety of other manuscripts while p46, ℵ, C, F, G and others support the text without Hagar. The problem with the shorter reading is that it is innocuous and does not help Paul's argument.[39] As Cosgrove points out, what Paul wishes to do here is to associate Hagar with the Mosaic covenant. He did not need to argue for the connection between the Torah and Jerusalem.[40] Nor does he need to argue for a connection between the Torah and Mount Sinai. He *did* need to make clear or at least assert the connection between Hagar, Mount Sinai, and Jerusalem. There is already a geographical reference to Mount Sinai in vs. 24, and it is likely that this is meant to prepare us for what follows in vs. 25. A second textual problem is whether vs. 25 begins with γάϱ or with δέ. The

36. See Hays, p. 114: "The 'two covenants' of Gal. 4.24 are *not* the old covenant at Sinai and the new covenant in Christ. Rather the contrast is drawn between the old covenant at Sinai and the older covenant with Abraham, which turns out, in Paul's rereading, to find its true meaning in Christ. In Paul's scheme, the freedom and inheritance rights of the Gentile Christian communities are not novelties but older truths that were always implicit in Isaac, in the promise to Abraham."

37. One could of course argue that Paul would say the same thing about non-Christian Jews as he says here about Judaizers, but the fact is that Paul does not make that case here, and when we look at his later argument in Rom. 9–11, there he argues that non-Christian Jews are like branches temporarily broken off from the family tree, but that they can be grafted back in, and in fact when the full number of Gentiles comes in and Christ returns, Paul expects some kind of eschatologial miracle. See my discussion in *Jesus, Paul, and the End of the World* (Downers Grove: InterVarsity Press, 1992), pp. 99ff.

38. Or you could translate it 'Sinai is a mountain in Arabia'.

39. See Barrett, "The Allegory," pp. 163–64.

40. See Cosgrove, pp. 226ff. There may be something to the suggestion of Longenecker, *Galatians*, p. 213 that Paul chooses to use the more Hebraic (and LXX) version of the word Jerusalem ('Ιεϱουσαλήμ) here, as opposed to the more profane spelling which we find at 1.17–18 and 2.1, because here Paul is stressing the religious significance of the city, whether the earthly or the heavenly one.

latter reading has superior attestation (p46, A, B et al.) and is probably to be preferred.[41]

Why then the mention that Mount Sinai is in Arabia and why connect Hagar with it? Various scholars have suggested that this idea came to mind because Arabia is the land of Hagar's descendants through Ishmael (see Ps. 83.6). A connection with the Arabic word *hajar* which means rock or cliff, seems more remote, even though in later times this word is associated with certain place names in that area of the Sinai peninsula.[42] Paul's point then would be that the Law came from Hagar's territory, from outside the promised land. It might be added that here, besides Gal. 1.17, is the only other reference to Arabia in the Pauline corpus, and it may be suggested that since Paul claims to have been to Arabia in Gal. 1, he would have first-hand knowledge about the region. In other words he can speak on this subject about Arabia being Hagar's territory with some degree of expertise.

The second half of vs. 25 begins with the interesting verb συστοιχεῖ. Originally this verb was a military term referring to soldiers standing in the same line or file. Notice, however, that in Aristotle *Metaphysics* 986a it refers to the setting up of a table of paired opposites as we have done above.[43] The verb here is a third person singular present tense suggesting that the subject of this verb is Hagar. Paul is saying that Hagar stands in the same line with the 'now Jerusalem'. It is perhaps possible to translate this word a little more loosely as 'corresponds to'.[44] Scholars have suggested that Paul means that Hagar stands in the same column or on the same side of the ledger as the present Jerusalem (cf. the schematic above). Now the question is, why drag Jerusalem into this discussion at all? The most widely accepted suggestion, and still the most plausible, is that the agitators in Galatia were making much of their intimate relationship with the Jerusalem church, and perhaps their connection to Jerusalem in general.

What does Paul mean that the present Jerusalem is enslaved with her children? Is this a comment on the fact that Judea is a land ruled by Roman overlords? This is not impossible, but since elsewhere in this letter Paul has only spoken of slavery in connection with the Mosaic Law, not the Roman rulers, such a social reference is unlikely. Especially revealing is the similar language in Gal. 2.4 contrasting freedom in Christ with slavery in the context of mentioning the false brothers in Jerusalem. But is Paul speaking about Jews and the heart of Judaism being enslaved by the Law, or is he speaking in

---

41. See Meztger, *TC*, p. 596.

42. Longenecker, *Galatians*, p. 211 rightly points out that the Arabic *h* does not in fact correspond to the Hebrew ה.

43. See Martyn, "Apocalyptic Antinomies," p. 418 and n. 22 who says that the term is a technical term in this case.

44. See Burton, *Galatians*, pp. 261–62; Longenecker, *Galatians*, p. 213.

particular about the Jerusalem church with its Jewish Christians? The previous discussion by Paul about the 'guardian' that Jews were under during their spiritual minority suggests a broader reference here to all Torah-true Jews in Judea, which would include Jewish Christians of this orientation. It must be remembered that it appears that the Judaizing Christians of Jerusalem did not see themselves as a separate entity from Judaism, but rather a movement within that religious group. Their allegiance was to the present Jerusalem and their Jewish heritage, not just to the Jerusalem church. Paul does not necessarily disagree with this assessment if the Judaizers continue down a covenantally nomistic path, but his point is that this is not a viable option. It is a failure to grasp the radical implications of the Gospel, in particular of Christ's death and resurrection, and the implications of the new eschatological situation of Christians.

In vs. 26 Paul makes this apocalyptic and eschatological situation quite clear. There is another Jerusalem to which Christians should be pledging allegiance, the Jerusalem above which is not only free but is 'our mother', i.e., that of the author and the audience.[45] Paul is here drawing on early Jewish apocalyptic ideas which he has reshaped for his own ends. It is clear enough from a text like Phil. 3.20 that Paul can speak of this entity in several ways. It is instructive to compare 4 Ezr. 10.53ff. and 13.35ff. which speaks of the new Jerusalem appearing from heaven which is visible at present only to the apocalyptic seer (4 Ezr. 8.52; 10.25–27). Especially interesting is the fourth vision in 4 Ezra where the earthly Jerusalem is depicted as a barren woman (cf. below) who is given a son only through divine intervention. Less compelling but worth mention is 2 Bar. 4.2–7 which speaks of the heavenly Jerusalem as pre-existing and also as the eternal home of the saints. Notice that this does not cause the writer to give up on the present Jerusalem. Rather he believes it will be transformed in the age to come (2 Bar. 6.9; 32.4).[46] Finally we may refer to the heavenly journey of Enoch as recorded in 2 En. 55.2 which speaks of him going up into the highest heaven, the highest Jerusalem.

There is some evidence that Is. 54 was seen in early Judaism to refer to the heavenly Jerusalem (cf. B. Baba Bathra 75b; Ps. 87.3), a text which Paul will quote in vs. 27, but perhaps even more important is the evidence that there

---

45. This is to be distinguished from Paul who is simply the mother of his converts. As Lincoln, *Paradise Now*, p. 24 says, what is notable about this statement is that it includes Jews and Gentiles as having been sired by the Jerusalem that is above. The heavenly Jerusalem is not the church, but it has given birth to it. Nor is the earthly church the mother of believers. Both of these ideas which cropped up in later interpretation of Paul, even in Chrysostom's work, are misreadings of this influential but complex text.

46. On all of this material one should consult A. T. Lincoln, *Paradise Now and Not Yet. Studies in the Role of the Heavenly Dimension in Paul's Thought with Special Reference to his Eschatology* (Cambridge: Cambridge University Press, 1981), pp. 16ff.

was a rather widespread tradition in early Christian circles about a heavenly and new Jerusalem (cf. Heb. 11.10, 14–16; 12.22; 13.14; Rev. 3.12; 21.2). Of importance for us is the difference between Paul's handling of this whole tradition and the sort of handling we find in the material in early Judaism. "Whereas in 2 Baruch and 4 Ezra the heavenly Jerusalem guaranteed that in principle the earthly Jerusalem, whatever its present condition, would eventually fulfill its role in eschatological expectations, here in Galatians 4 there is no such hope for the present Jerusalem, for it is now classed as part of the old age and subject to the forces of that age, the law, sin and death. For Paul the element of continuity with the history of salvation under the old covenant lies not through Jerusalem as such but through Christ and those who by faith in him are children of Sarah through the promise (cf. verses 23, 28, 31)."[47]

In vs. 27 Paul, using a typical introductory formula ('it is written'), quotes Is. 54.1 virtually verbatim from the LXX. Paul here is in fact continuing his allegorizing interpretation, by once again suggesting that a familiar OT text has another referent. In this case, what originally seems to have been said about the earthly Jerusalem is now being said of something or someone else.[48] The quotation here has often been seen as strange. Is something to be made of several elements in the quotation, or is it quoted just to convey some particular idea?[49] If Is. 54.1 is seen as directed to Jewish exiles, are they originally being personified as a barren woman, in particular as Sarah? Do they represent Israel as a whole? Hays rightly points out that it is helpful to read the discussion in the light of the earlier Isaianic material in Is. 51.3 where for the only time in the OT there is a reference back to Sarah's story in Genesis – 'look to Abraham your father and Sarah who bore you'. There Sarah is seen as the mother of Jerusalem, so Is. 54.1 in describing a desolate Jerusalem creates an echo of the Genesis story about Sarah. "Consequently, Paul's link between Sarah and a redeemed Jerusalem surely presupposes Isa. 51.2, even though the text is not quoted in Galatians 4. It is Isaiah's metaphorical linkage of Abraham and Sarah with an eschatologically restored Jerusalem that warrants Paul's use of Isa. 54.1."[50] What Hays does not see is the role Paul plays in this dramatic story. He is the one who by God's grace begat the Galatians and placed them into relationship with the Jerusalem that is above.

---

47. Lincoln, p. 22.

48. Notice how the earthly Jerusalem is called mother in 2 Bar. 3.1ff. and in 4 Ez. 10.7, 17 and more importantly in texts Paul will have known – Is. 50.1; Jerm. 50.12; Hos. 4.5; cf. Ps. 87.5.

49. The recent dissertation by K. Blessing at Duke Divinity School under R. B. Hays shows the complexity of the issues here. See the abstract of her 1996 SBL lecture "Yet without Sin: the Meaning of the Barren Woman at Galatians 4.27," in *SBL Abstracts 1996*, p. 245.

50. Hays, p. 120.

Paul's citation of this text may be an example of his following Hillel's second hermeneutical rule about interpreting a text by means of verbal analogy (*gezera sawa*).[51] I would suggest that to make sense of the quotation we note the following: (1) there is an allusion to Sarah here, but the barren one who is playing the role of miraculous mother or Sarah in the Galatians' situation is Paul;[52] (2) the children of Paul, the desolate (or desert?) woman who spent time in Arabia, are more numerous than the children of those who are wedded to the present Jerusalem (who by implication is not 'our mother'). That is, the Gentile converts of Paul are more numerous (in Galatia?) than those of the agitators; (3) not only does vs. 28 follow quite naturally on this reading of Paul's allegorizing use of Is. 54.1, making very good sense of the contrast between the children of promise and Spirit and the children of the flesh and Law but the quotation follows nicely from the eschatological remarks in vss. 25–26; (4) The conclusion then must be that Paul is exhorting himself, as the barren woman, to rejoice over what God has already done among the Galatians, and building on that by urging them to act on the advice of Sarah to drive out the slave woman and her child.

Verse **28** returns to direct address ('but you brothers')[53] probably indicating that the referent and the one addressed in the previous quotation of Isaiah is someone *other* than the Galatians.[54] The Galatians are reassured that they are not children of slavery but rather children of promise κατὰ Ἰσαάκ. Does this last phrase mean 'in the line of Isaac'[55] or 'after the manner of Isaac'[56] or 'like Isaac'? In all likelihood the translation should be the second of these, because Paul wishes to stress that the Galatians came to receive the promise and the inheritance in the same miraculous fashion as Isaac had – by divine intervention. They had not received it by submitting to the Law. It is in this way that they are really like Isaac, because of course otherwise they are not like him. Isaac, unlike the Galatians was a Semite and a 'natural' son of Abraham in the proper line and born of the proper mother. Notice too the emphatic

---

51. On the indebtedness of Hillel's rules to long-standing canons of Hellenistic rhetoric see Daube, "Rabbinic Methods," pp. 252ff.

52. On the miraculous or gracious character of the conception of Isaac see Gen. 17.16, 18.10, 14, 21.1–2; Rom. 4.17–21, 9.7–9; Philo *Cher.* 45–7 and the discussion by Dunn, *Galatians*, p. 247.

53. A few manuscripts (S, A, C, D2) read 'we are' co-ordinating this verse with vs. 26 and 31. This is not likely to be original. See Matera, *Galatians*, p. 171.

54. Once again we find the phenomenon of various manuscripts (in this case the Textus Receptus, ℵ, A, C, D, K and others) having 'we are' (ἡμεῖς . . . ἐσμέν) here instead of 'you', probably influenced by vs. 26 and vs. 31. The 'you' reading is, however, well supported by p46, B, D*, G, 33 and various other manuscripts. See Metzger, *TC*, p. 597.

55. Matera, *Galatians*, p. 171.

56. See Bligh, *Galatians in Greek*, p. 185.

position of the word 'promise'. Paul is stressing the importance of the fact that his audience has the benefits of this promise already.[57]

As vs. **29** reveals, there turns out to be, in Paul's mind, another way that the Galatians are like Isaac. Both endured 'persecution' from the child of the slave woman. The word ὥσπερ indicates that the comparison between the Galatians and Isaac continues. Here it could be argued that we have a brief sort of typology involving Isaac and the Galatians but if so it is not identified as such. Whether or not we have typology here we certainly have a comparison. Notice the antinomy between those born according to the flesh and those born according to the Spirit. The question is here – who does Paul have in mind as 'persecutors'? Is he referring to Jewish persecution of the Galatians? A certain kind of reading of Gal. 3.4 could point in this direction. Cosgrove argues that the verb 'persecute' is not used elsewhere in the NT in a metaphorical sense of internal strife within the church.[58] He points to Gal. 1.13, 23, 5.11, and 6.12 to demonstrate that persecution of Christians by Jews is in view here.[59] In none of these other texts is persecution of the *Galatians* spoken of and for what it is worth in Acts 13–14 nothing is said about the persecution or suffering of the Galatians, only the persecution and suffering of Paul and Barnabas.[60]

There are, however, problems with this line of reasoning. In the first place, Paul in this passage is using and will go on using in a metaphorical way all sorts of language which is normally meant literally. For example, when Paul speaks of the slave girl in vs. 30 he is not referring to a literal slave girl. The whole allegorical context of the discussion here leads one to expect a metaphorical use of verbs. In fact, Paul here is alluding to Gen. 21.8–14 which at most refers to Ishmael playing with Isaac, but we know that in early Judaism this verb was taken in a metaphorical sense to mean more than just 'to engage in recreation with', indeed it was seen to mean something hostile or malicious (cf. Josephus *Ant.* 1.215; Targ. Ps-J. Gen. 21.9–11; JT Sota 6.6). My point is that the exegetical handling of this Genesis story in early Judaism already

---

57. Cosgrove, "The Law," p. 223 is right that vs. 28 is not the end or conclusion to the allegory, but neither is vs. 27. The conclusion comes in vs. 31, with 5.1 being a transitional verse looking both backward and forward.

58. This overlooks that Paul does in 2 Cor. 11.26 refer to dangers from false brothers.

59. Cosgrove, "The Law," p. 229.

60. It may be worth adding at this point that while we have plenty of evidence for the existence of Jews in south Galatia, the evidence for Jews in north Galatia is scant if not non-existent. Even I. Levinskaya in her *Diaspora Setting* volume in the *AIIFCS* series (Grand Rapids: Eerdmans, 1996) provides us with no new data or reason to think that there were any Jewish colonies in Ancyra and that vicinity. Thus when we hear about the agitators fearing persecution in 6.11 we must assume that Paul is alluding to Jewish persecution either in Judea or even in Galatia, perhaps set off by the agitators trying to maintain contact with the synagogues in Galatia.

involved a metaphorical handling of the key verb. It would not be surprising if Paul followed in that line. Notice too that none of these other references to persecution is given in the context of an allegory.

In the second place, if we look carefully at the similar language contrasting Spirit and flesh in Gal. 3.2–4 it will be remembered that we concluded that Paul is speaking there of the potential effect of the agitators on the Galatians and that Paul is speaking of the Galatians as having experienced so much, not suffered so much.[61] There is in fact nothing in this letter to suggest that the Galatians themselves are being literally persecuted or are literally suffering,[62] but it is quite clear that they are under enormous pressure to submit to the Law, an act which Paul, using strongly pejorative language, equates with submitting to slavery. In this context it is easy to believe that Paul could portray the agitators both as slaves and as slave drivers who are persecuting and enslaving the Galatians. Paul is drawing an analogy between the situation of Isaac and the situation now, and of course it must be remembered that the agitators were indeed Jews (born according to the flesh), only they were Jewish Christians.[63]

Paul arrives finally in vs. **30** at the climax of this argument, the point to which it has been driving all along. Here Paul will quote Scripture assuming that his converts will recognize its authority. Notice that Paul has altered the quotation just slightly from what we find in the LXX which reads 'cast out this *slave* woman and her son, for the son of *this* slave woman will not inherit with *my son Isaac*.' The changing of the latter to 'the son of the free woman' allows Paul to actualize the story not only for the Galatians but also for his relationship with them.[64] Notice the changing of the reference to stress that Sarah is a free woman. Freedom as opposed to slavery is the issue here. In some ways Paul's argument here builds on his previous arguments about the Law. In particular it should be remembered that the 'guardian' was a slave, and so Paul here uses another slave metaphor to describe the effect of the Law.[65]

The language of casting out and expulsion makes perfectly good sense and is apt if Paul is talking about the agitators who have made themselves a part of the Galatian Christian communities, but it makes far less sense if Paul is referring to non-Christian Jews persecuting Christians. Paul is encouraging the exercise of church discipline as he does in another way at Gal. 5.9–10 where he uses the analogy of bad leaven in the lump that needs to be thrown out and

---

61. See pp. 210ff. above.
62. In contrast to what is said about Paul himself in 5.11, and in 6.12 about the agitators who themselves are trying to avoid Jewish persecution.
63. See Ziesler, *Galatians*, p. 66.
64. See Matera, *Galatians*, p. 178.
65. See Cosgrove, "The Law," p. 234 and n. 61.

as in 1 Cor. 5.[66] Sociologically Paul is in fact suggesting that 'the slave woman and her son'[67] are not true members of the covenant community and so must be expelled. Paul is going about the business of defining boundaries. He does not want the Galatians to cross the line in the wrong direction, having already got in by grace and through the work of the Spirit, but he believes the agitators are in fact already beyond the pale, already false brothers – in the community but not of the community and outside the circle of the saved who will inherit. The proof that this is the correct reading of Paul's understanding of the matter is shown by the fact that Paul goes on to quote further 'for the son of the slave woman *will not inherit* with the son of the free woman'.

To sum up, in a *tour de force* argument Paul has identified the agitators in Galatia with Hagar, and himself with Sarah. Each is on the way to producing children, the former for slavery, the latter for freedom. Paul takes the high ground of identifying himself and his Gentile converts as the true heirs of the promises to Abraham, and suggests that the agitators, even in spite of their Jewishness, are the real Ishmaelites giving birth to slaves. Paul believes that the story of Isaac is being revisited in the experience of the Galatians, 'his children', just as the story of Sarah has been revisited in the experience of Paul (cf. 4.18–20).[68] His exhortation to them in essence is to become what they already are, and this is precisely what he will go on to say as he draws the argument to a close in vs. 31.

Verse **31** simply makes a strong affirmation with Paul going so far as to identify his own condition with that of his converts – 'therefore brothers *we* are not children of a slave woman but of the free woman'.[69] The διό here signals a conclusion based not on the immediately preceding citation of Scripture, but on the basis of the whole previous argument. Paul is asserting that because this conclusion is so, it makes no sense to begin acting like slave children.

---

66. Ziesler, p. 70 suggests Paul has the final judgment by God in mind, perhaps executed by God's angels, but there is nothing in the context which favors this view, and the direct address in vs. 28a and 31 is surely against it.

67. Is the latter a reference to Jewish Christians in Galatia who are going along with the agitators' agendas?

68. In this interpretation I am basically following the lead of Martyn, "The Covenant of Hagar and Sarah," pp. 160ff. And Matera, *Galatians*, p. 173 ably sums up why we find this allegory just here: "Having lamented that he must once more suffer the pangs of childbirth for his children ... (4.19), Paul talks about the children of two different apostolates; his circumcision-free apostolate and the circumcision-apostolate of the agitators."

69. Burton, *Galatians*, p. 267 rightly notes the definite article before 'free woman' and the absence of one before 'slave girl'. Paul has someone specific in mind when he speaks of the free woman, namely himself, but since he is uncertain who it is who is bewitching the Galatians, he uses a more generic reference for them. See pp. 21ff. above on uncertainty about the agitator or agitators.

Quoting a familiar rite of passage formula used in the emancipating of slaves Paul offers a final exhortation at the end of this argument in 5.1 – 'For freedom Christ has set us free, stand then and do not submit again to a yoke of slavery'. Consider the inscription found at Delphi: 'For Freedom, Apollo the Pythian bought from Sosibus of Amphissa a female slave whose name is Nicaea . . . The purchase, however, Nicaea has committed unto Apollo for freedom.'[70] Notice how the phrase 'for freedom' appears at both the beginning and end of the inscription. Paul is drawing on the concept of sacral redemption of slaves, a process involving the slave paying money into the temple treasury, because the slave as a slave could not initiate or negotiate a legal contract. Through a legal fiction the god in question then purchased the slave out of bondage, and thereby the slave became the property of the god and had to serve him. As the editors of the *Hellenistic Commentary to the New Testament* say, the "appropriateness of this practice as a soteriological metaphor that could be adopted by Christians is apparent: the slave is powerless, but the deity does what the slave cannot do. After being redeemed, the slave belongs to the god 'whose service is perfect freedom'."[71] We must note the Christological implication here. Paul is suggesting that Christ is the God who redeems the slave, something only a god could do.

On this high note, Paul's fourth major argument comes to a resounding conclusion. The theme of freedom versus slavery has been well announced and introduced, but Paul must pursue it, he must flesh out what freedom amounts to in the Christian life and how it should be used. He must explain what forms of bondage the Christians must seek to avoid.[72] This he will do beginning at 5.2,[73] where in the span of three verses he makes abundantly clear that the yoke he wants the Galatians to avoid is the yoke of the Mosaic Law.[74] At this point we must discuss in some detail Paul's view of the Law.

70. See *Hellenistic Commentary to the New Testament*, p. 463, following the inscriptions assembled by A. Deissmann.

71. Ibid.

72. See Lincoln, *Paradise Now*, p. 26: "The *tour de force* of Paul's allegory is that he is able to show that it is the very Law which the Galatians are allowing to enslave them (4.21) which should in fact speak to them of the freedom of the heavenly Jerusalem and those who belong to it. To understand this would be to be liberated specifically from any necessity for circumcision but also from the claims of the whole Law, from which this one particular demand cannot be separated (cf. 5.2, 3)."

73. The 'stand then' here shows that Paul's exhortation is based on what has just been argued in 4.21–31, but it looks foward to the further discussion of the Spirit, freedom, the Law slavery and the like. See Martyn, "The Covenant," p. 164 n. 11.

74. See Hansen, *Abraham in Galatians*, p. 152.

Excursus: Laying down the Law —————————————————————

It is quite impossible to say all that needs to be said about Paul's view of the Law in one excursus; whole books continue to be devoted to this controversial subject,[75] and so we must settle for speaking here almost exclusively about Paul's view of the Law as it is revealed in Galatians. One cannot avoid all discussion of Paul's treatment of the Law in other letters, particularly Romans and 1 Corinthians, but methodologically I agree that we must study this issue in the context of the particular letters and their agendas and not in the abstract. Paul does not offer us a treatise on Law, only letters where the Law comes up as an important subject of discussion from time to time.[76] F. Thielmann is right to proceed carefully in his study, looking at the material letter by letter. There is no letter where the Law is a more crucial or central subject than Galatians, and most scholars would agree that Galatians is the earliest Pauline letter where Paul discusses the matter somewhat fully.[77]

No one would disagree with the assessment that Paul's views on this subject are complex, and they are related closely to his views on a host of other key subjects. To ask Paul's view of the Law is to ask his view of God, salvation, anthropology, and human relationships, to mention a few related topics. Some of the problems in the discussion of the Law have arisen because the subject has been isolated from other aspects of Paul's thought world. In my view one of the most crucial oversights is the failure to recognize the narrative character of Paul's thought world and the role Law plays in it. Paul asserts repeatedly in Galatians, using a variety of means and metaphors (e.g., the 'pedagogue'), that the Law had an important but temporary role to play in the ongoing story of God's people. That role will not be understood unless one grasps the larger story and the way Paul understands its development.

75. Just the bibliography on this subject takes up an enormous amount of space. See now J. D. G. Dunn ed., *Paul and the Mosaic Law* (Tübingen: Mohr, 1996) presenting the papers from the 1994 conference on the Law in Durham. Pages 335–41 have an excellent beginning bibliography on the discussion of the subject between 1980 and 1994. For a sampling of the discussion from a variety of positions one may wish to compare and contrast J. D. G. Dunn, *Jesus, Paul and the Law* (Louisville: Westminster/John Knox, 1990); H. Hübner, *Law in Paul's Thought* (Edinburgh: T. & T. Clark, 1984); H. Räisänen, *Paul and the Law* (Philadelphia: Fortress, 1983); E. P. Sanders, *Paul the Law and the Jewish People* (Minnesota: Fortress Press, 1983); F. Thielmann, *Paul and the Law* (Downers Grove: InterVarsity Press, 1994); S. Westerholm, *Israel's Law and the Church's Faith. Paul and his Recent Interpreters* (Grand Rapids: Eerdmans,1988).

76. Note that there are entire letters, such as 1 Thessalonians or Philippians, where the matter can hardly be said to be discussed at all. This reminds us that this subject was not constantly on Paul's mind, and that the Law comes up because the subject was prompted by something that was going on in Paul's churches.

77. The vast majority of scholars agree that Galatians precedes Romans, whatever chronology they may otherwise adopt. If, as I hold, it precedes all the other letters, then it becomes an even more key text, aiding our understanding of Paul's views early in his ministry while there was still fairly close contact and relationships with the Jerusalem church.

If we ask why it is that Paul argues in the fashion he does about the Law we are pushed back to Paul's own story, in particular to his conversion which he sees as a matter of pure grace, and to the Copernican revolution that happened in Paul's way of viewing the world as a result of that conversion.[78] I would point to three aspects of changed thinking which came out of his conversion that led to Paul's new view of the Law and its role in the life of God's people: (1) as a result of his conversion, Paul had a totally different estimate of Jesus of Nazareth than he had before, in particular he saw Jesus as not only the messiah of Jews but also as the redeemer of Gentiles; (2) since he believed messiah had come, he also believed that the eschatological situation was different than he had thought before Damascus Road. The age to come and the new creation had broken into the present evil age and changed a host of things. Christ rather than the Law was now the mediator and means of the ongoing relationship between God and God's people; (3) Paul now viewed the world, the life of the believer, the Scriptures through the eyes of Christ rather than through the lens of the Law.

The age of spiritual maturity had arrived for God's people and this meant they were no longer 'under the Law'; they were no longer obligated to keep it.[79] The issue here is not merely the means of salvation, though that is an important part of the issue at least by implication,[80] but the means by which saved persons should live so as to please God. It is not 'getting in', or 'staying in' which is really at issue in Galatians, but the means of 'going on' in Christ. By what rule or standard will the Christian community live and be shaped? Paul's answer is that the community is to be cruciform and Christological in shape. It is to follow his example and the pattern of Christ and walk in and by the Spirit. It is, in short, to follow the Law of Christ which is not identical with the Law of Moses (on which more in a moment).

In our exegesis of the major argument which begins at Gal. 3.19 we pointed out that Paul's assessment of the Law is certainly not negative. In fact it is not very helpful to try to divide Paul's statements about the Law into negative and positive categories. Paul does not think the Law is against God's promises, he just does not think that Law-keeping is the means through which those promises come to fulfillment. He does not see it as a negative thing that the Law points out our sin, or better said turns sin into transgression for those under it.[81] It is true that the effect of the Law on fallen people is not pleasant – it involves condemnation rather than commendation. But the effect and the purpose and intent of the Law are not one and the same.

78. On which see pp. 107ff. above.

79. That a Jewish Christian, indeed Paul himself, might choose to follow some of the Law for a variety of mostly prudential or missionary reasons, is clear enough from a text like 1 Cor. 9.19–23. It is also clear that in this same passage Paul says that he is no longer 'under the Law', that is, no longer obligated to keep it. I would suggest the reason Paul says this is because he believes that the Mosaic covenant is no longer the covenant God's people are under, no longer seen by Paul as the necessary *modus vivendi* or way of living for Jew or Gentile in Christ.

80. In fact Paul reverses the equation in Gal. 5–6 (cf. pp. 359ff. below). If the Galatians go so far as to keep the Law, it will prove to be their means of 'getting out', of committing apostasy.

81. See pp. 249ff. above.

It is true that Paul sometimes uses the term νόμος to mean the Pentateuch in general (cf., e.g., Gal. 4.21) or even the Hebrew Scriptures more broadly conceived (1 Cor. 14.21 – here citing Is. 28.11), but he is also capable of distinguishing between the Law of the Mosaic covenant which Jews are under, and the larger role of Scripture. Scripture assigned all, both Jew and Gentile under sin (Gal. 3.22), but for those under the Mosaic covenant and its Law there was the further problem that sin had been turned into transgression. It had been made clear that a Jew's sin was against God and was a willful violation of his revealed intentions for God's people, Israel (3.19). Much confusion would have been avoided in the interpretation of the Galatians passages dealing with Law if closer attention had been paid to Paul's careful use of pronouns ('we' Jews, as opposed to 'you' Gentile Galatians).

In Paul's view the problem with the Law as a means of Christian living is at least sixfold: (1) its actual effect is to imprison those who are under it in a form of slavery, the Law acting as a rather strict guardian (3.23–4.7); (2) the Law involves God's elementary principles which a believer, as he or she grows up in the faith needs to get beyond; (3) the Law is a temporary expedient given by God until he sent his Son. To go back to it is not only to be anachronistic, but it is tantamount to a denial of the efficacy of the work of Christ and the Spirit; (4) the Law is quite incapable of giving what Christ and the Spirit give – life, freedom, fruit, gifts and the like. The Law is not seen as a bad thing, it is simply seen as impotent, unable to give someone the power or ability to keep God's commandments and unable to deliver the eschatological blessings of salvation and inheritance. It then becomes a question of whether or not it is right to complain about the Law for not doing what it was never intended to do; (5) the Mosaic Law was intended for Jews, and quite specifically meant to separate them from the other nations not only in social practice (e.g., Sabbath observance, circumcision, food laws etc.), but also to make them stand apart in moral behavior and theological belief (standing against immorality and idolatry). It must be borne in mind that the Ten Commandments and the Shema were at the very heart of the Law, something of which Paul was well aware, and yet Paul was still willing to place the Law in the categories of a ministry of death and a form of fleeting and fading glory *while talking about those very ten commandments* (2 Cor. 3). Paul says in Gal. 3.4–5 that Christ was born under the Law in order to redeem Jews from under the Law and give them adoption as children. This suggests that they did not have such adoption because of the Law or because of being Jews, but rather because of grace coming through Christ. (6) Paul opposes the mandatory observation of the Law by any Christians whether Jews (cf. the Antioch incident and Paul's reaction to Peter's and Barnabas' withdrawal from table fellowship with Jews) or Gentiles. No doubt the main reason he does so is because if some choose to be consistently and permanently Torah true, this will divide the community (as it had already done in Antioch), into clean and unclean, sinner and holy one, first- and second-class citizens. If fellowship is defined by the Law, then it requires Law observance by all so all can eat and live together. But in the Christian community the basis of association is simply being in Christ in whom there is no Jew or Gentile (Gal. 3.28). There is a sense in which Christ came not to renew Jewish or Gentile religion (the στοιχεῖα τοῦ κόσμου), but to get beyond both and form a 'more perfect union' between all peoples, classes, and both genders. This is what Paul calls 'a new creation'. If both Jew and Gentile are children of Abraham through faith in the

Faithful One Jesus Christ, the Seed of Abraham, then the Israel of God or people of God has been reconfigured in a new fashion and with a new charter or covenant. This is sectarian thinking and involves a sectarian reappropriation of familiar terms in a new way.[82]

Something should be said about the difference in Paul's mind between being under the Law covenant, and listening to any and all parts of the Hebrew Scriptures as God's Word, which reveals God's will. Paul's covenantal theology allows him to affirm that the Law tells the truth about human nature and about God and about their interrelationship. It reveals various of the fundamental things God expects of his people. It does not cease to be the Word of God just because God's people cease to be under a particular covenant spoken of in part of God's Word and cease to be obligated to keep *that particular covenant's* various requirements and obey its various stipulations. Paul does not think there is only one continuous covenant, in various forms, between God and his people, as is made quite clear in Gal. 4.24. Paul's view is that God is quite capable of giving both situation specific advice and contractual arrangements as well as more permanent ones.

Paul is quite capable of talking about the whole Law and its essential requirements as being 'summed up' in a single commandment – to love neighbor as self (5.14). In his view the Mosaic Law can be boiled down to its bare essence and will and should be reflected in the life of the Christian believer not because Christians have placed themselves under the Law and committed themselves to obey it all, but because the Spirit produces the essential qualities the Law demanded in the life of the believer.[83] To put it another way, the eschatological age is the age of fulfillment and the essential requirements of the Mosaic Law are fulfilled in the life of the Christian "not because they continue to be obligated to it but because, by the power of the Spirit in their lives, their conduct coincidentally displays the behavior the Mosaic law prescribes. In this verse then, Paul is claiming that believers have no need of the Mosaic law because by their Spirit-inspired conduct they already fulfill its requirements"[84] In fact Paul will go on to suggest that when the Spirit shapes Christian character, giving it fruit, they are in fact going beyond what the Law requires in a positive direction (Gal. 5.23).[85] Not surprisingly there is considerable principial overlap between the Mosaic Law and the

82. On sects see pp. 272ff. above.

83. To put it a slightly different way, in Paul's view the fulfillment of the Law comes about because the Holy Spirit works in the believer the essential qualities God has always wanted in his people (love of God and neighbor etc.).

84. Thielmann, *Paul and the Law*, p. 140, although he goes on rightly to qualify this remark by saying that to obey the summary of the Law in the love commandment is to complete the requirements of the Mosaic Law in some ultimate and eschatological sense. Obviously, one cannot say that Christians who do not submit to circumcision, do not keep Kosher, probably do not observe the sabbath, do not in general observe rules about Levitical purity, do not pray the Jewish hours of prayer, do not follow the Law's teaching on oaths, do not observe the Law's stipulations about foreigners within the believing community, and do not do a host of other things, have kept the entire Law. There must then be some distinction in Paul's mind between fulfilling the ultimate and eschatological sense of the Mosaic Law and keeping it all.

85. See below pp. 410ff. on this text.

Law of Christ since God has given them both. But this does not mean that Paul sees the 'Law of Christ' as simply Christ's interpretation of the Law. Indeed not. The phrase the Law of Christ first and foremost refers to the cruciform and resurrection pattern of the life of Jesus, which is to be replicated in the lives of Christ's followers by the work of the Spirit and by imitation. They are to clothe themselves with Christ and immerse themselves in his life and lifestyle. This pattern of a crucified and risen Savior is not enunciated in the Mosaic Law and certainly not enunciated there as a pattern for believers to imitate. The Law of Christ also entails various of the teachings of Christ, both the portions of the OT he reaffirmed during his ministry (such as love of God and neighbor) and the new teachings he enunciated which Paul draws on and sometimes even quotes (cf. 1 Cor. 7; Rom. 14).

Thus, Paul's answer to the question 'How then should Christians live?' is not 'Adopt Christ's interpretation of the Mosaic Law and follow it', but rather 'Follow and be refashioned by the Law of Christ' or 'walk in the Spirit'. Paul's letter to the Galatians is neither antinomian in character nor is it an attack on legalism. It is a salvation historical argument about recognizing what time it is, and what covenant God's people are and are not now under. The Law of Christ is not the Mosaic Law intensified or in a new guise. It is the new eschatological dictums appropriate for those living as new creatures albeit in an already and not yet situation. The above constitutes my constructive proposal on how to read Paul's complex view of the Law, particularly as it is expressed in Galatians. It remains to critique some of the other major proposals in the rest of this excursus. As we have made some comments along the way already on the contributions of H. Hübner and H. Räisänen to the discussion,[86] we will focus here on the contributions of three other scholars – E. P. Sanders, F. Thielmann, and J. D. G. Dunn.

It is fair to say that the recent renewed interest in Paul's view of the Law has in large part been sparked by the watershed study of E. P. Sanders entitled *Paul and Palestinian Judaism* which appeared in 1977. The study challenged a great deal of what passed for common assumptions about early Jews and the way they viewed and related to the Mosaic Law. In particular it challenged the assumption that Jews were bogged down in legalism and thought they obtained or maintained right standing with God through punctiliar observance of the Law. Rather, as Sanders argued, covenantal nomism rather than works righteousness is a fairer description of how early Jews viewed and related to the Law. Covenantal nomism was a response to the gracious saving work of God for his people, not the cause of that work or the means of appropriating it in the first place. Sanders is reacting against the still ongoing effects of Luther's analysis of Galatians and Romans and the stereotypes of early Judaism that that analysis produced. It is ironic then that he himself is indebted to that same sort of soteriological analysis in that he chooses to frame the discussion in terms of 'getting in' and staying in'.[87] But this is not in the main what Galatians and the discussion of the Law in this letter is about.

Paul is concerned not with Jews but with Christians, in particular Paul's Gentile converts in Galatia, submitting to the Law as an addition to their already extant faith

86. See pp. 252ff. and pp. 262ff. above.
87. See Sanders, *Paul, the Law, and the Jewish People*, p. 6.

in Christ. Nor does it appear that Paul is countering the position that Law-keeping was the means of maintaining their salvation or staying in the Christian community. Paul is attacking the view that submitting to the Law is the the means of going on to maturity in Christ, indeed even 'finishing' or 'completing' one's Christian life and so showing oneself approved at the final judgment (cf. Gal. 3.3 and 5.4).[88] If covenantal nomism is the grateful response of God's people to what God has already done in their lives, it would not appear that this is what Paul is discussing or trying to oppose in Gal. 3.3 and 5.4. The Galatians were looking to future benefits that accrued for submitting to the Law, not looking for a way to properly thank God for what they had already received in Christ.

Another major pillar in Sanders' edifice is that it is wrong to assume that the Law was unkeepable and that if it was not all kept there was no forgiveness for sins. On the former point Sanders points to Philo (*Praem.* 80), but one might also want to point to Phil. 3.6.[89] On the latter point Sanders points to all the material in the Pentateuch which stresses that atonement could be made for sin. Two things need to be said about this sort of argument. Firstly, what Philo or other Jews may say about whether one could keep the Law or not is one thing. Whether the Law was actually keepable by fallen human beings is quite another. Secondly, it is not at all clear that the Mosaic Law indicates that atonement was possible for any and all sorts of sins. In particular it is not clear that 'sins with a high hand' could be atoned for. Compare for instance what is said about sin in Num. 15.22–31. Here there are specifications made for when a person unintentionally fails to observe *all* the commandments that the Lord spoke to Moses or when he or she transgresses unintentionally.[90] Sacrifices could be offered and forgiveness could be granted in such cases. But then the text goes on to say 'But whoever acts high-handedly, whether an

88. Gal. 5.4, especially in view of vs. 5 ('the hope of righteousness'), would seem to be about final not initial justification. See pp. 368ff. below.

89. There is, however, a clear difference between blamelessness (which involves no standing Law having been violated), and innocence before God. Paul says all have sinned and fallen short of God's glory and that includes himself. What he does not say is that all have transgressed the Law. In the first place this would not be true for various Gentiles who were not under the Mosaic covenant. They were sinners, not transgressors. In the second place, avoiding transgression is not the same as fulfilling or keeping all the positive commandments of the Law. 'Falling short' of positive requirements is not identical with violation of an existing statute. 'Works of the Law' has to do with doing the positive things the Law says must be done. Transgression is obviously not a work of the Law! The curse falls on all who do not observe or obey all that the Law requires (Gal. 3.10), and therefore in Paul's view the curse falls on all who are under the Law (cf. his modified quotation of Ps. 143.2 in Gal. 2.16). Paul is not saying in Phil. 3.6 that while a Pharisee he observed all the positive statutes of the Law to perfection; he is saying that no one could accuse him of transgression on the basis of the Law's standards of righteousness. The old distinction between legally blameless and morally blameless is one Paul affirms and understands. In Paul's theology, no one is morally blameless, all are sinners, but not all are legally blameworthy, if one is speaking of the violation of a known statute.

90. It is precisely texts such as this that Paul is likely thinking of when he says that whoever submits to the Mosaic covenant sign is obligated to keep all the Law (cf. Gal. 5.3).

Israelite or an alien, affronts the Lord, and shall be cut off from among the people. Because of having despised the word of the Lord and broken his commandment, such a person shall be utterly cut off and bear the guilt' (cf. Acts 13.39). There is certainly no thought of forgiving the intentional sinner in this text, so Sanders' failure to really deal with these sorts of exceptions to the possibility of atonement and forgiveness makes his case quite weak.

Sanders in general is able to provide us with abundant evidence about the views of early Jews about the Law, but what he cannot and does not do is show that early Jews had in general correctly understood the Law and its purpose. The issue is not whether early Jews *felt* or *believed* the Law was too onerous a burden to bear, or whether it was believed that all sins could be atoned for, or whether it was believed that God did or did not require perfect obedience to all the Law.[91] The issue is whether the Law actually said these things or made these sorts of claims. Paul says that those who get themselves circumcised commit themselves to keeping the whole Mosaic Law, a perfectly plausible conclusion based on a close reading of what the Pentateuch actually says about obedience (see, e.g., Num. 15.22). In Paul's view the Law is a corporate entity (cf. Gal. 5.3 and 3.10 and the continual use of νόμος, never the plural) and Deut. 27.26 is paraphrased to make clear that all the words of the Law must be kept. Paul seems to believe that the Law has not in general been kept by God's people and so they need to be redeemed from under the Law (Gal. 4.5).[92] The question is whether Paul is justified in his interpretation of the OT.

There are other flaws in Sanders' treatment of Paul's discussion of the Law, not the least of which is that he does not attend to the differences between what Paul says about 'we' and 'you' in Gal. 3–4. Paul does not think that everyone is under the Law automatically, the Law is seen as but one form of the στοιχεῖα. It must be stressed that Paul does not think that the Mosaic Law was given to the world, but rather to God's first chosen people as the rule of life for their community. This is why the 'we Jews' and 'you Gentiles' are such important distinctions in this letter when the Law is under discussion. Paul does not want his converts to submit to a condition which Paul himself has left behind or, as he says in Gal. 2.18, these are the very things, the very barriers, he tore down when he became a Christian.

It may also be said that while I agree with Sanders that one must take into account the difference between Paul's arguments about the Law and the reasons for his arguments and also the fact that he is speaking in a polemical mode, using various rhetorical tactics, it does not follow from any of this that Paul is not arguing on the basis of a well thought out position. A good deal hangs on the way we interpret small turns of phrase. For example, should we translate Gal. 3.11 'But it is obvious that no one is justified before God by the Law because "the just shall live by faith" as most do,

91. While Dunn, p. 312, may be right that most scholars think that Second Temple Judaism did not teach the need for perfect Law-keeping, there are dissenting voices; cf. T. R. Schreiner, *The Law and its Fulfilment: A Pauline Theology of the Law* (Grand Rapids: Eerdmans, 1993), here pp. 71 and 181. The issue, however, is not what Second Temple Judaism taught or believed on this subject, but what the OT in fact says or commands.

92. See pp. 286ff. above on these texts.

including Sanders.[93] But as Thielmann shows, it is perfectly possible to translate the sentence 'But because no one is justified before God by the Law, it is obvious that "The just shall live by faith".[94] In fact this translation is far more likely, in which case Paul is not using the OT quotation as a proof text at all, but rather vs. 11 as a whole indicates the solution to the plight described in vs. 10. In other words, the reasoning here is not from solution to plight, but rather the other way around, with the OT being allowed to state the major thesis that the 'just shall live by faith'. Sanders is, however, right that Paul's arguments are not merely socially motivated;[95] they have theological roots and theological as well as social aims.

Enough has been said to show that Sanders' views are not without their problems, though he has quite rightly challenged us all to recognize that obedience in response to God's redemption of Israel from bondage, an obedience that is a response and so a form of covenantal nomism, is not the same as attempts to earn right standing with God by performing works of the Law. He has also rightly countered various caricatures of the *views* of early Jews about the Law and of how they saw their own condition under the Law.[96] It must be said once more that Paul is countering neither legalism nor Jewish covenantal nomism in Galatians;[97] he is trying to forestall his Gentile converts from submitting to the Law as a means of going on in Christ, as a means of making themselves fit subjects for final justification.

Our next dialogue partner is F. Thielmann, who in many ways has provided the clearest and most exegetically careful exposition of Paul's view of the Law, including the views expressed in Galatians. I should like to focus on one aspect of his treatment that sheds fresh light on the discussion, namely his treatment of 'the Law of Christ' as not merely Christ's interpretation of the Mosaic Law, but rather the new eschatological Law meant for those who are new creatures entering the Kingdom of God. Thielmann rightly points out that the terms 'transgressor' and 'transgression' have a quite specific nuance in the NT. These terms do not refer to sin or wickedness in general, but rather to violation of a particular Law or command (cf. Rom. 2.23; 4.15; Gal. 3.19; Heb. 2.2; 9.15 and on transgressor Rom. 2.25, 27; Jam. 2.9, 11). This means that we must ask why Paul says withdrawing from table fellowship with Gentiles in Gal. 2.18 would make him a transgressor, that is, a violator of some law.

As Thielmann goes on to say "This cannot, however, be the law of Moses, since that law builds a boundary between Jews and Gentiles, the crossing of which is sin (2.17; compare 2.15). The law that Paul would transgress if he did not associate with believing Gentiles then is another law, and the 'law of Christ' of 6.2 that incorporates

93. See Sanders, *Paul, the Law*, p. 22 where he argues that Paul cites Hab. 2.4 to prove that no one can be 'righteoused' by the Law.

94. Thielmann, *Paul and the Law*, pp. 127–28.

95. Against Watson, *Paul, Judaism and the Gentiles*, pp. 61ff.

96. See Dunn, *Paul and the Law*, p. 311: "Although some elements of legalism in Second Temple Judaism cannot be denied, we also cannot conclude that Second Temple Judaism as a whole is to be branded as 'legalistic' (that is, that salvation or life in the world to come is earned by obedience to Torah)."

97. Despite the contentions of many commentators, most recently Longenecker, *Galatians*, passim.

the Mosaic injunction to love one's neighbor seems the most likely candidate."[98] Thielmann also rightly points out that One must compare the phrase 'the Law of Christ' in Gal. 6.2 to what we find in 1 Cor. 9.21 where the Law of Christ is both *distinguished* from the Mosaic Law and at the same time *identified* with the law of God in 1 Cor. 9.19–23.[99] Paul does not see himself as beyond all law since he became a Christian. He sees himself as no longer under the Mosaic Law, but at the same time 'in the Law of Christ'. Paul is no antinomian and freedom in his view does not amount to exchanging obedience to the Mosaic Law for a condition in which no objective restrictions or requirements are placed on one's life. Paul believes that freedom in Christ means freedom from slavery, but it is also means freedom for 'obeying the truth' of the Gospel,[100] which is but another way of saying freedom to keep the Law of Christ, and as Thielmann says "the Law of Christ is something new".[101] This new Law is more understandable if one looks carefully at Gal. 6.2.

Fulfilling this new Law amounts to 'bearing one another's burdens'. This is not a quotation of the Mosaic Law but rather a paraphrase of an idea found in the Jesus tradition. The idea is found in a specific commandment said by the Fourth Evangelist to have been given by Christ: 'This is my commandment that you love one another as I have loved you. No one has greater love than this, to lay down one's life for one's friends' (Jn. 15.12–13). One may also wish to point to Jn. 13.14 'you also ought to wash one another's feet', and perhaps also the specific exhortation about burden carrying in Mt. 5.41 'if anyone forces you to go one mile, go also the second mile'.[102] What is interesting about all this material is that it shows up in the context where Jesus is saying something about loving one's neighbor or even one's enemy. Mt. 5.41 is followed in vss. 43–44 with the discussion about loving neighbor and even enemy, and loving neighbor is defined in Jn. 15.13 as being willing to die for them and in their place, the ultimate form of bearing of another's burden. As we shall see,[103] the Law of Christ refers not just to the pattern of Christ's life which should be emulated but to the teachings of Christ which flesh out this pattern. Thielmann has helped us by pointing us in this direction.

Thielmann is also quite correct that in Galatians Paul is operating with a very different definition of what constitutes a sinner than is found in the Mosaic Law. Gal. 2.17–21 demonstrates this fact. Paul insists that Christ is no servant of sin and that Christ desires Jews and Gentiles to fellowship together without Gentile's being required to keep Kosher food laws. Paul realizes that by his eating unclean food with 'unclean' Gentiles he might be 'found to be a sinner' by other Jewish Christians but he rejects this definition of sinner. "The implication of . . . [2.17–21] . . . is that by eating with 'Gentile sinners' Paul does not become a sinner, although the Mosaic law might

---

98. Thielmann, *Paul and the Law*, p. 142.
99. Thielmann, p. 141.
100. On this important phrase see p. 371 below.
101. Thielmann, p. 141.
102. See Mk. 15.21 for Simon of Cyrene as an example of one impressed to be a burden bearer. The difference is that the Johannine Jesus is exhorting his disciples to take on such burdens freely and of their own choice, as is Paul in Gal. 6.2.
103. See pp. 420ff. below.

define his action as sinful."[104] This is not a mere modification of what the Mosaic Law says about boundary markers or identity badges. Paul is offering a new definition of what constitutes sin and what constitutes transgression. He also makes regular comments suggesting that Christians are free from the Mosaic Law, not just in its condemning function or its boundary defining function but in other ways as well. The Mosaic Law is seen as a pedagogue whose time of guardianship is over, the ministry of Moses, though glorious, has now been set aside because of the greater and more permanent glory that has come through the ministry of Christ (cf. Rom. 7.6; 2 Cor. 3.9–11).

Equally telling is Thielmann's treatment of the question of whether Paul regarded all Jews as legalists or Judaism in general as a legalistic religion. Paul's argument rather is that any Jew familiar with Scripture will know the record of Israel's unfaithfulness to the Mosaic covenant and will be aware that the Scriptures themselves say that no one can be justified before God on the basis of their deeds or, as Paul puts it by 'works of the Law' (cf. Gal. 2.15–16). Thus, "far from attributing to most Jews a notion of salvation by works, these passages assume that most Jews understand that works of the law do not justify. Paul hopes that once reminded of the standard Jewish position on the plight of Israel, Judaizing Christians and unbelieving Jews will realize that . . . the Mosaic covenant is obsolete and they should embrace the Gospel of God's redemptive work in Christ."[105]

Though I find myself in essential agreement with Thielmann's approach, the same cannot be said about the views of J. D. G. Dunn. It is my view that at the end of the day, Dunn makes Paul sound as if he were one of the agitators, though holding to a less rigorous application of the Mosaic Law than they did. In short, Dunn sees Paul as yet another reformer of Judaism, not one who takes a sectarian approach to the issue of the community of God's people. I would disagree. It is easy to be beguiled by Paul's use of the OT into thinking that Paul is simply offering one more revision of the argument for continuity between God's OT people and his people now. Some Scriptural continuity should not be confused, however, with what we may anachronistically call 'ecclesial' continuity between 'Israel' then and now. Paul's view is that the way to obtain the benefits of the promise to Abraham is through Abraham's true and ultimate seed Christ, not through continuing to keep the Mosaic Law. It is Jew and Gentile united in Christ that are viewed by Paul as the people of God. In short, Paul is arguing that the people of God were narrowed down to the elect one, Christ, the seed, after which those who are in the seed, the elect one are in the people of God. One must quickly add that Paul does not think that Israel according to the flesh is broken off from the people of God forever, as Rom. 9–11 makes clear. They have not stumbled so as to fall permanently, but Paul envisions their reintegration

---

104. Thielmann, p. 141.

105. Thielmann, p. 239. I would demur from his further statement that the period of the restoration of Israel has dawned already, if by Israel he means Israel after the flesh. Paul's argument in Rom. 9–11 is that the period of real restoration for that Israel will not come until the full number of the Gentiles come in. See my *Jesus, Paul and the End of the World*, pp. 99ff. Until then Paul expects only some Jews, a distinct minority, to be converted.

into the people of God on the same basis as Gentiles had entered, by grace through faith in God's messiah, Jesus.

None of what I have just said detracts from the fact that few scholars have given as much time and detailed attention to the thorny questions that are raised when considering Paul's view of the Law as Dunn, and he has done much to help us reflect particularly on the social functions of the Law and the importance of taking the social dimensions of the question seriously. We are in his debt at many points, even if in the end we must disagree with some of his basic theses. It is in order to deal with some of the problematic aspects of his proposal at this juncture.

Some of Dunn's basic views can be summed up as follows: (1) Paul was converted from Judaism not in the sense in which we now use the term, but in the narrower sense as it was defined in the Maccabean literature (2 Macc. 2.21; 8.1; 14.38; 4 Macc. 4.26) "as the label coined or used to identify the national religion trying to define and defend itself over against the influences of Hellenism";[106] (2) Paul was converted from zeal for these Jewish traditions, zeal like that of Phineas, which caused him to persecute the church; (3) Paul was converted from a belief in the role of the Law as properly hedging around Israel and protecting it from outsiders, to a less restrictive view of the Law; (4) Paul was converted to the recognition that the gospel of Jesus must be taken to the Gentiles; (5) the phrase 'works of the Law' in Paul refers to the deeds required by the Law and should be exegeted in light of 4QMMT; it has a limited sense; (6) the term 'sinner' in Gal. 2.15–17 is used in a limited and factional sense as a means of distinguishing Jews from non-Jews and from other Jews who are perceived to be not as observant of the Law; (7) In general one must assume that wherever one finds the term νόμος in Paul's letters it refers to the Mosaic Law, even in the case of the phrase 'the Law of Christ' or of phrases like 'the law of faith' (Rom. 3.27) or 'the law of the Spirit of life' (Rom. 8.2–4). In other words, Paul sees that the Mosaic Law has a variety of facets and functions and he believes that only some of these facets and functions are obsolete.[107]

It will be seen from all this that Dunn's basic approach has to do with limiting the scope of what Paul means by certain of the key terms in the debate. Paul has not converted to a new religion, he does not think that the Mosaic Law as a whole is obsolete, he does not distinguish radically between the Abrahamic and the Mosaic covenants, and in general Dunn wishes to stress that there is still much continuity between Paul's views and those that are held by other early Jews on a variety of important issues, though he does deny discontinuity as well. Paul is in essence protesting not against the Mosaic Law itself in Galatians but rather "against the ethnic divisiveness which Paul saw as a consequence of Jewish over-evaluation of the role of the Law".[108] The problem is with particular views of the Law and particular social uses or aspects of the Law and not with the Law itself *per se*.

---

106. Dunn ed., *Paul and the Mosaic Law*, p. 313.

107. One can find all of this in Dunn ed., *Paul and the Mosaic Law*, pp. 309–34, but one should also consult his *The Theology of Paul's Letter to the Galatians*, pp. 87–95; and his *Jesus, Paul, and the Law*, pp. 89ff.

108. Dunn, *The Theology*, p. 95.

Now on the one hand Dunn is probably right that Paul would have been opposed to a legalistic misuse of the Law, but in fact Paul knows very well that it is not a misuse of the Law to insist on God's people being set apart from the outside world both ritually and morally. Indeed this is the very essence of the Levitical code, and is at the heart of the larger Mosaic code as well. The aim of the Law is holiness which inherently requires a being set apart from all uncleanness and unholiness whether that involves unclean food, things, places, or persons. According to the Mosaic Law, acceptance of *goyim* within Israel's community requires that the latter abide by various parts of the Mosaic Law. This is precisely what Paul is denying repeatedly and vehemently in Galatians when he says that Gentiles do not need to keep the Mosaic Law in order to be members in good standing in, and an ongoing part of, the Christian fellowship. In the second place, as Thielmann points out, it is the Law itself, not its misuse, to which Paul is denying justifying power.[109] Only Christ justifies either those under the Law or those outside it. This is the very point of Paul's modification of Ps.143.2 which he cites in Gal. 2.16.

In regard to the phrase 'works of the Law' Dunn is right that Paul is not attacking in Gal. 2.15ff. works or works righteousness or human attempts to earn salvation in general.[110] Dunn is also right that Paul knows that his fellow Jewish Christians by and large understood the Law was not given as a means to obtain right standing with God but rather was seen a means of living rightly before God. Dunn is also quite right that Paul is concerned with the social consequences of keeping the Law, namely the separation of Jews and Gentiles. Dunn is helpful then in defining what the phrase probably does not mean for Paul.

The problem comes when Dunn tries to define the positive content of the phrase. For instance, it is more than doubtful that 'works of the Law' can be limited to mean some of the deeds required by the Law, or the social function of the Law focusing on particular ritual requirements. Nor is it adequate to say that this phrase sums up "the attitude against which Paul was protesting".[111] The focus of this phrase is surely on actions, not attitudes about actions. Furthermore, it was not just an 'attitude' of Jews about the Law that led to their maintaining separation from Gentiles. Not only does the Law insist on such separation or set-apartness from the nations (cf., e.g., Ex. 19.5–6ff.), but in the visions of the prophets about the restoration of Jerusalem and Israel we hear 'Put on your beautiful garments O Jerusalem, the holy city; for the uncircumcised and the unclean shall enter you no more . . . The Lord has bared his arm before the eyes of all the nations; and all the ends of the earth shall see the salvation of our God. Depart, depart, go out from there! Touch no unclean thing; go out from the midst of it, purify yourselves, you who carry the vessels of the Lord . . .' (Is. 52.1–12).[112]

---

109. Thielmann, *Paul and the Law*, p. 139.

110. See Dunn, *Jesus*, p. 238.

111. Dunn, *Theology*, p. 75. Cf. his *Jesus*, p. 238, "For what he is attacking is a particular *attitude* to the law as such, the *law as a whole* in its social function as distinguishing Jew from Gentile."

112. Note that Paul is well familiar with this tradition. Not only do we find it quoted in 2 Cor. 6.17, but notice Paul's quotation of the continuation of this same address to Jerusalem at Gal. 4.27 where Is. 54.1 is drawn on.

Similar pronouncements about the problems of mixing with Gentiles or adopting Gentile practices can be found in Ezekiel and other prophets as well.

Notice the very similar way Paul puts things in Gal. 2.16 and 5.3–4. In the former text Paul denies that one can be justified at all by works of the Law. In the latter text he speaks of those desiring to be justified by the Law as being required to obey all of it. Works of the Law surely means all of the works of the Law which one is obliged to keep if one submits to the sign of the Mosaic covenant – circumcision. For Paul the Law is a package deal, and one cannot separate out one portion of its commandments from another. All must be obeyed if one is under the Law.

What then of Dunn's strong stress on the new evidence about the phrase 'the works of the Law' from 4MMT? At first blush, this material looks quite promising to help us understand Paul's meaning.[113] Here we find a discussion of works of the Law by the sectarians at Qumran, and what they are discussing in this document is boundary-marker issues, issues of clean and unclean, issues of what is holy and what is profane, in other words issues about what amounts to a trespassing of the community's boundaries (e.g., rules about the cleansing of lepers, the admitting of the blind and deaf into the Temple, the permitting of intermarriage with Ammonites and Moabites, the transmission of impurity by a flow of water, the cooking of sacrificial meat in unclean vessels). The key phrase comes at the very beginning of the document as part of the title which probably should be read to mean 'pertinent (or important) works of the Law'.[114] M. Abegg then suggests that what Paul is rebutting in using the phrase 'works of the Law' is the sort of sectarian thinking such as we find at Qumran. Especially intriguing is the fact that the final remarks of 4QMMT involve an allusion to Ps. 106.30–31 (LXX) where being reckoned righteous is said to come about because someone has been zealous like Phineas in upholding the Law and protecting the boundaries of the community. Righteousness is reckoned on the basis of deeds or works of the Law.

Now as intriguing as this material is, there are some major question marks to be raised about it. Notice that the key introductory phrase is not simply 'the works of the Law' but rather 'pertinent or important works of the Law'. In other words, in this phrase the unit 'works of the Law' describes a larger entity, a subset of which is the important or pertinent works of the Law. This means that the phrase 'works of the Law' *simpliciter* is no more a technical phrase for some specific legal works in 4MMT than it is in Paul's Galatians. The second major flaw in this argument is that as is well known, the sectarians at Qumran had long since anathematized the present Jerusalem and its religious regime and had set themselves apart in the desert. This seems to be quite the opposite of the agenda of the agitators in Galatia whose aim is to get the Galatians better connected with Jerusalem, the Jerusalem church, and the form of Judaism which was centered in Jerusalem. There is nothing at all sectarian about their insistence that the Galatians be circumcised and submit to the Mosaic Law. This is precisely what mainstream Judaism expected proselytes to do. I see no evidence that

113. See M. Abegg, "Paul, 'Works of the Law', and MMT," *BAR* 20.6 (1994), pp. 52–55 and p. 82. Cf. this discussion to Dunn, "4QMMT and Galatians," *NTS* 43 (1997), pp. 147–53.

114. So Abegg, pp. 52–53.

the agitators were urging on the Galatians multiple water ablutions or other of the supererogatory works on which the Qumranites insisted. The Judaizers or false brothers or agitators were not sectarians, if by sectarian one means a group self-consciously separating itself from some larger religious group. On the contrary, they were trying to stress as much as possible the continuity or connectedness between Jewish Christianity and Judaism in general, not least because they wanted to avoid persecution for the beliefs that they held which were distinctive (e.g., Christ's death on the cross – Gal. 6.12). Thus, the comparison between Paul and 4MMT does not suggest that Paul is using the phrase in some limited or narrow or sectarian way. Paul provides us with no list of important 'works of the Law', unlike 4MMT, and when he does mention circumcision, he connects it with obedience to the whole Law (Gal. 5.3)! Thus while the boundary defining rituals and identity markers are certainly a part of what Paul means by the works of the Law, they are by no means all that he means by the phrase, nor need we think he is especially focusing on such things. As J. Barclay points out, since Paul talks about dying to the Law himself, and he does not qualify this remark in any way, it is hardly likely when he is talking about wanting his converts to avoid works of the Law that he means something less than all the deeds required by the Law, whether ritual or otherwise. He does not want them to raise up a way of living in the Christian community in Galatia that he himself has left for dead.[115]

Let us consider for a moment why Paul objects to the agitators' view of the Law. The problem Paul has with the Law lies not only in its effect on fallen human beings, or its social effect of separating Jews and Gentiles, or even in its inability to give life and power to those under it, though all of these things are part of the problem. Paul's most basic problem with the Law is that it is obsolete and therefore following it is no longer appropriate. It is not the rule of the eschatological age and it is not to be imposed in the new creation which is already coming to be. If Christ came even to redeem Jews out from under the yoke of the Law, if the Law was a pedagogue meant to function only until Christ came, if the Law was 'set aside' as 2 Cor. 3.11 says, then it is a mistake, indeed a serious mistake to go back to keeping it, or in the case of Gentiles to begin to submit to it in any form or fashion. The Law had an important function and role to play in the divine economy, but the rule of the Mosaic Law has had its day and ceased to be. But it is not just the anachronism that bothers Paul about insisting that Christians, whether Jews or Gentiles, must keep the Mosaic Law. What bothers him most is that keeping the Law implies in Paul's mind that Christ's death did not accomplish what in fact he believes it did accomplish. To submit to the Mosaic Law is to nullify the grace of God (Gal. 2.21) and to deny that justification or righteousness, whether initial or final, comes through the death of Christ.

A further problem with Dunn's approach is his attempt to subsume all the Pauline uses of νόμος (or at least all the ones crucial to the Law debate) under the one heading of the Mosaic Law, when in fact this is quite impossible to do. For example, in Rom. 7.22–23 Paul is able to distinguish between the Mosaic Law and *another* law or principle resident in a person's members. Or again in Rom. 8.2 Paul distinguishes between the Law of sin and death and the law or principle of the Spirit of life. Now this latter cannot be a reference to the Mosaic Law at all because Paul says quite clearly

115. See Barclay, *Obeying the Truth*, p. 82 n.18.

that the Mosaic Law cannot give life. Only God in Christ through the work of the Spirit can (cf. Rom. 8.3; Gal. 3.21). He is equally clear that those led by the Spirit are not subject to the Mosaic Law (Gal. 5.18), but rather to the Law of Christ (6.2), which most certainly does involve good works as 6.4–5 makes clear.[116]

Finally, it is doubtful that Dunn's account of Paul's conversion is adequate. Paul was not simply converted from Maccabean-type zeal for the Law to some other less exuberant or stringent view of the Law. Clearly enough zeal characterizes Paul's arguing about the Law and the faith in Galatians just as it had probably done before his conversion. We have dealt at some length with the Pauline account of his conversion earlier in this study,[117] so we shall not rehearse all that data here, but we must reiterate the major conclusion that it really was a conversion. Paul had left Judaism behind when he became a follower of Christ, which meant that in the eyes of any normal Torah-true Jew, Paul would have been seen as apostate, as one beyond the pale, one who was now to be classed with the Gentile sinners. Also, Paul saw himself as no longer obliged to keep the Mosaic Law (1 Cor. 9), something no observant Jew would agree with. Saul before and Paul after the conversion probably saw a fundamental antithesis between Jesus Christ and the Law being the basic means of defining the boundaries of God's people.[118] In other words Paul the convert took a radical or sectarian approach to his Jewish heritage. In particular his views of the role, function, purpose, and applicability of the Mosaic Law to God's people now that Christ has come have changed dramatically.

More could be said along these lines, and the question of the possibility of development or even changing of mind in Paul's thinking about the Law after he wrote Galatians must be left until another occasion.[119] In the exposition of Galatians, these questions need not arise, since it is widely agreed that this is the earliest significant discussion of the Law we have from Paul. We may sum up by saying that for the Christian Paul, the Mosaic Law was a good thing, something that came from God, but that it was limited – limited in what it was intended to and could accomplish, limited in the time-span for which it was meant to be applicable, and limited in the

116. I will not dwell here on the problems with Dunn's analysis of the episode at Antioch, but Sanders has raised some telling objections to his treatment and to P. Esler's treatment of the food law issue as it affected the relationship between Jewish and Gentile Christians in his "Jewish Association with Gentiles and Galatians 2.11–14," in *Studies in Paul and John*, pp. 170–88. As Sanders says, there was no barrier to social intercourse between Jews and Gentiles provided a Jew did not eat the meat or drink the wine of a Gentile, but this is precisely what was happening in Antioch prior to the coming of the men from James. This is why Paul can castigate Peter for living like a Gentile, as he himself was also doing. In other words, it was not a matter of the Antioch church keeping some food laws already, and the men from James simply wanting a stricter approach.

117. See pp. 107ff. above.

118. See pp. 114ff. above.

119. It must be noted that much of Räisänen's case is based on perceived inconsistencies between what Paul argues in Galatians and what he argues elsewhere, particularly in Romans. My response to his suggestion of internal inconsistencies within Galatians itself can be found in the other parts of this commentary where the Law is discussed.

group to which it was meant to be applied (namely Jews and converts or adherents to Judaism). It was but one form of the στοιχεῖα, and it was something Christ's coming had rendered no longer in effect. The people of God were no longer to be under the Guardian now that the eschatological age had broken in and those in Christ could be new creatures and walk in the Spirit. We will say more on this last subject in the discussion of the next argument.

Bridging the Horizons

It is often eye-opening when we discover that things we thought we understood, are in fact not as we thought. Imagine for a moment Copernicus or Galileo trying to rethink all of the implications of the earth not being the center of the solar system, but rather the sun being that center. If you can imagine that, then you can imagine a radical Jew like Paul trying to conceive of the life of God's people without them submitting to the Mosaic covenant. For Paul, the encounter on Damascus Road led to a drastic re-evaluation of the Mosaic Law. In particular his assumptions about its everlasting applicability to God's people changed. Suddenly, he came to the conclusion that the Law had a rather different and more limited function in the divine economy than he had previously assumed. Like the person in the first two decades of this century who thought that the horse would never be replaced by the car as the major mode of transportation, Saul had apparently assumed that the Law was meant to last until the end of time. Its possible obsolescence, especially its possible obsolescence for Jews, had never crossed his mind. To say the least, his encounter with Christ changed his world view drastically. Does this mean that Paul suddenly concluded that God had changed his mind about the Law? Was God capricious? It would appear that Paul's answer to these questions was no, but only because God had now given an even greater and more personal thing than the Law to form a people, namely he had given his Son. In other words, unless one accepts Paul's premises about the eschatological state of affairs he finds himself and God's people in, what he says about the Law will make very little sense from a Jewish point of view. His account of things will look like the ultimate example of revisionist history writing, unless of course he was right about Jesus and the dawning of the new age of salvation and the coming of the new creation.

There has of late also been something of a Copernican revolution in the thinking about what Galatians is really all about and what Paul is combating. The Lutheran focus on the issue of how one gets into the people of God or gains right standing with God (justification by grace through faith), has been shown not to be the central focus of the letter, but rather an important and foundational presupposition for his argument about how those who are already Christians should live. The arguments, however, are about going on not getting in. Nor is Paul combating either legalism (a particular attitude about law) or libertinism, and he is certainly not replacing either one of these with some sort of antinomian message of unbounded freedom or freedom without obligation. The old clichés about Paul's view of the Law will simply no longer suffice, any more than the old antithesis between Gospel and Law will. Paul too is capable of saying faith without works is dead, if by works one means following the example and teachings of Christ (loving one another, bearing one another's burdens) rather than following the dictates of the Mosaic Law.

There is a place for imperatives and commandments in the life of a Christian just as there was in the life of a Jew. Did we really think that God would expect less of the people of God under grace than was required when they were under Law, especially when God had not only provided salvation from sin in Christ but also the empowering Holy Spirit as a means of Christian living? The issue here is not salvation but faithfulness, like the faithfulness of Christ; and what new creation involves if God is calling the eschatological people of God to a higher, not lower, standard of faithfulness and fruitful living than had been expected in the past. To whom more is given, more is required.

Argument V: 5.2–15

THE UNKINDEST CUT OF ALL

Though the material in Gal. 5–6 has sometimes been seen as a miscellany of ethical remarks and exhortations with no clear connection to what has preceded them, this conclusion must be rejected. In the first place we have noted how there has already been exhortation by Paul in Gal. 4, in fact as early as 4.12 and again at 5.30. In the second place it needs to be seen that the Mosaic Law is still the central factor prompting Paul's thinking here.[1] Not only in the material in Gal. 5.2–15 but also in what follows, the subject of law comes up repeatedly (cf. 5.14, 18, 23, 6.2; 6.13).[2] Even in the *peroratio* in 6.12–17 the subject of circumcision and the Law is still to the fore. Furthermore, as we have noted previously there is a sense in which the whole of Galatians is one large deliberative exhortation to the Galatians not to submit to the Law. While imperatives do not begin to appear until 4.12, the thrust of all the arguments in this letter has been pushing toward these concluding exhortations and providing a basis for them. It is thus artificial to separate these later arguments which have more imperatives from the earlier ones. While it is possible, with Matera, to see the whole of 5.1–6.17 as the climax of Paul's argument,[3] Dunn is surely much nearer the mark in arguing that the climax of the previous arguments comes here at the beginning of Gal. 5,[4] with 5.13ff. beginning something of a denouement. There are two major themes in the material in Gal. 5–6, one is the continuation of the arguments against circumcision and the Law, and the other is a positive assessment of how Christians *should* live since they are not to submit to the Mosaic Law and they are presented in that order. Paul will stress that the Spirit and the pattern or Law of Christ, not the Mosaic Law and circumcision, will provide the guidance and empowerment necessary to live a life pleasing to God.

There are rhetorical reasons for coming to the conclusion that 5.2–12 is the climax of Paul's deliberative discourse. It was the function of the *exordium* to prepare for and in a sense give a preview of the chief subject of a speech, just

---

1. See the balanced assessment of Ziesler, *Galatians*, p. 71: "Yet exhortation has never been far from the surface in any part of the letter, and conversely this present part is scarcely lacking argument. All the same, there is now a perceptible change of emphasis and the application of the argument is now more dominant and more direct."

2. See Hansen, *Abraham in Galatia*, p. 154.

3. Matera, "The Culmination of Paul's Argument to the Galatians: Gal. v .1–vi. 17," *JSNT* 32 (1988), pp. 79–91.

4. Dunn, *Galatians*, p. 261.

as it was the function of the *peroratio* to summarize and recapitulate the main subject of the discourse. It is not an accident that commentators have found detailed correspondences between 5.2–12 and what we find in 1.6–10 and between 5.2–12 and 6.12–17, though they have usually not recognized why we have these correspondences.

Longenecker is an exception, noting the numerous parallels between the *exordium* in 1.6–10 and the remarks in 5.2–12. Firstly, there is the severity of tone in both the *exordium* and 5.2–12. Secondly, the reference to deserting the one who called the Galatians in 1.6 is paralleled in 5.8 by a very similar remark. Thirdly, the phrase 'the grace of Christ' in 1.6 matches up with the reference to falling away from that grace and being alienated from Christ in 5.4. Fourthly, πάλιν is used in both texts to introduce corroborating statements in 1.9 and 5.3, and perhaps most importantly the double anathema in 1.8–9 is clearly paralleled by the threat of divine judgment in 5.10b and the invective in 5.12.[5] In short, the subject intimated in the *exordium* comes into the clear and brings climax to all the arguments at 5.2–12. Confirmation of this conclusion comes from the *peroratio* which is meant to review or summarize the main subject of the previous discourse. As Matera points out in both 5.2–12 and 6.12–17 we hear about doing and keeping the Law (5.3; 6.13a), we hear that neither circumcision nor its lack is important (5.6; 6.15), and mention is made of the relationship between circumcision and persecution in both texts (5.11; 6.12).[6] In short the rhetorical signals, both before and after our passage, point to this passage giving us the heart of the argument, the pith of the matter.[7]

It has been sometimes urged on rhetorical grounds that while we certainly have paraenesis and exhortations in Gal. 5–6, we do not have arguments. This conclusion must be rejected on several grounds. Firstly, as G. D. Fee has shown at considerable length, the most basic contrast that underlies all of Paul's arguments in this discourse is not between faith and works of the Law, but between life in the Spirit lived out by faith and life lived on the basis of Torah observance. This is what makes the material in Gal. 5–6, including the material in 5.13ff. "a crucial part of the *argument* of Galatians, not simply a collection of paraenesis added at the end, after the theological argument is in place. The ethical result of the life of the Spirit is part of the

5. Longenecker, *Galatians*, pp. 221–22.
6. Matera, *Galatians*, p. 186.
7. Notice that none of these parallels has anything to do with either 5.1, which is transitional, or 5.13–15, which must also be seen as transitional, preparing for what follows in 5.14ff. This sets 5.2–12 apart as the actual concluding argument on the primary subject of the discourse, with the materials in 5.13ff. being meant to address the subsequent and ancilliary question of how a Christian is to live if the advice of the agitators to submit to the Law is rejected and that of Paul is taken. 5.13ff. are meant to clear up or make more concrete Paul's vision of what the Christian life is meant to look like.

essential argument of the letter, since this is the burning question, 'How do believers *live?*'[8]

Secondly, deliberative speeches would often have arguments that had a considerable portion of them focused on ethical matters and they would include exhortations (cf., e.g., various of the orations of Demosthenes). It is a mistake then to assume that what we have in Gal. 5–6 is nothing but exhortations without arguments and to assume we must assign this material to the epistolary portion of the document rather than the rhetorical part.

Finally, the structured nature of the material in Gal. 5–6 should become increasingly apparent as this discussion progresses. Like Paul's earlier arguments, there are divisions and proper signals of starting and stopping. We must also be careful not to assume that once Paul has reached the climax of his argument, as here in 5.2ff., that there are no further arguments in the denouement, when in fact there are.

Perhaps a word is in order here about the Galatians' social situation. What would have made Gentiles find an appeal to be circumcised and follow the Mosaic Law tempting? J. Barclay rightly points to the sense of social dislocation that surely must have affected the Galatians once they had abandoned the worship of pagan deities (4.8–11). "To dissociate oneself from the worship of family and community deities would entail a serious disruption in one's relationships with family, friends, fellow club members, business associates and civic authorities . . . Paul's presence in Galatia and his creation of Christian communities there had helped to establish a social identity for these Christians; the lavish attention they bestowed on Paul (4.12–15) is probably a measure of their dependence on him. His departure from Galatia must then have underlined their social insecurity."[9] The Galatians were caught betwixt and between, neither part of the synagogue nor of their former pagan religious circles.

It must be stressed, as I have already had occasion to say, that the Gentile mentality was such that the very essence of religion was ritual, processions, ceremonies and the like. Also, Temples, priests, and sacrifices were what one identified with religion. If Paul had not established the Lord's Supper in a significant way as part of a community meal (and it is nowhere mentioned in Galatians), then the only real ritual the Galatians will have been initiated into by Paul was baptism – a one-time rite. He certainly had not set up any sacrifices, temples, or ordained any priests while he was there. There is also very little evidence of any leadership structure in Galatia, in fact only one verse may mention such local leadership (Gal. 6.6 – but note he speaks of teacher,

8. Fee, *God's Empowering Presence*, p. 385.
9. Barclay, *Obeying the Truth*, p. 58.

not teachers). In this social situation it is understandable why the Galatians were finding the overtures of the agitators appealing.

In the leadership vacuum and with what A. D. Nock calls "the ever-present loss of social amenities, club life and festivals",[10] the Galatians were susceptible to the arguments of the agitators for they were in need of a more concrete manner to express their Christian identity, a way that involved ritual and perhaps also a specific way of living religiously. This would give them a sense of belonging. Barclay also rightly points out that by accepting circumcision and following the Mosaic Law they could regularize their position in Galatian society. They would be seen as Jews, a part of the Jewish subculture in the cities of Galatia, and would avoid the suspicion that they were part of a novelty or a *superstitio*.[11] There had been a long-standing curiosity on the part of many pagans about Judaism. Josephus, perhaps somewhat hyperbolically refers to the multitude of admirers who desire to adopt various Jewish religious observances such as sabbaths, feasts, lighting of lamps (*Apion* 2.282). It would appear that various of Paul's converts may have fallen into this category. In order to counter the agitators appeal, Paul proposes an alternative way to deal with what Betz calls human failure and misconduct.[12]

> *Behold, I Paul say to you that if you have yourself circumcised, Christ will be of no benefit to you. But I bear witness again to all persons being circumcised that they are under obligation to do the whole Law. You are cut off from Christ, all you seeking to be justified by Law, you have fallen away from grace. For we in the Spirit from faith hope, we await eagerly righteousness. For in Christ Jesus neither circumcision nor uncircumcision is able, but faith active through love.*
>
> *You were running well, who blocked you so you were not persuaded about the truth? That persuasion is not from your calling. A little leaven leavens the whole lump. For I am persuaded about you in the Lord that none of you will think otherwise. But the one troubling you will bear the judgment, whoever he may be. But I brothers, if I still preach circumcision, why am I still persecuted? Then the scandal of the cross has been abolished. Would that those upsetting you would castrate themselves!*
>
> *For you were called in freedom brothers, only don't let that freedom be used as a pretext for the flesh, but through love enslave yourself to one another. For all the Law has been fulfilled in one word, in this 'Love your neighbor as yourself'. But if you are biting and devouring one another, see that you are not consumed by one another.*

10. Nock, *Conversion*, p. 58.

11. Barclay, *Obeying the Truth*, p. 60.

12. Betz, *Galatians*, p. 273. Cf. The comment of W. Meeks, "Toward a Social Description of Pauline Christianity," in *Approaches to Ancient Judaism II*, ed. W. S. Green (Missoula: Scholars Press, 1980), pp. 27–42, here p. 33.

We have arrived at the portion of the letter where exhortation comes more to the fore, or as the Greek rhetoricians called it παραινετικόν from which we get the word paraenesis (cf. *Inst. Or.* 9.2.103). As Paul moves toward the conclusion of his *tour de force* argument, he is well aware that the adept rhetorician will stress the strong emotions, in order sufficiently to warn his converts against the perils of doing what the agitators were urging them to do.[13] It is not just that Paul will resort to dramatic hyperbole to frighten his converts back to their senses (5.4); he will also resort to invective against the agitators (5.12) relying on the enmity conventions of the day, and the concern for creating pathos in the audience can be seen in the remarks about being persecuted (5.11).[14] It must be understood that the rhetorical handbooks are quite clear that there is a place for vehemence and threatening language if the situation is grave and it is imperative that a certain action be taken (cf. Quintilian *Inst. Or.* 11.1.3ff.). The intent of this sort of arguing is to force the audience to make a choice – either to follow Paul's guidance or that of the agitators. In other words this is a thoroughly deliberative argument. It is also a deliberative argument because it will deal with one of the main subjects the handbooks say should be dealt with in deliberative rhetoric – religious rituals. For example in *Rhetoric to Alexander* 2.20ff. religous ritual is mentioned first among all subjects as that which should be discussed in a deliberative speech and then we are told that there are three approaches one can take to a deliberative argument on this subject: "either we shall say that we ought to maintain the established ritual as it is, or that we ought to alter it to a more splendid form, or that we ought to alter it to a more modest form." Most of the stress in these sorts of arguments is on maintaining the status quo, and in fact that is what Paul will argue here. The Galatians had been running well (5.7); now is no time to change religious practices.

The agitators of course on their part could have appealed to the antiquity of the practice of circumcision and the like. In this regard, Paul had on his side the general suspicion in the Greco-Roman world about changing religious practices or about novelty. It may also be that Paul is drawing on a rather widespread aversion among pagans in the Greco-Roman world to the idea of circumcision, and indeed on fears of emasculation when the rite was practiced on adults.[15]

13. Notice how Quintilian stresses that the 'hortative' is peculiar to deliberative rhetoric (*Inst. Or.* 3.6.47).

14. On this last point note what is said in *Rhetoric to Alexander* 34.25ff.: "all men pity those whom they conceive to be closely related to them, or think not deserving misfortune."

15. We will say more below on circumcision and its social stigma in the excursus below pp. 455ff.

Deliberative rhetoric focuses on a variety of related matters all of which fall under the heading of that which is possible. Some of these would be that which is beneficial or profitable, that which is advantageous, that which is expedient, that which really matters, that which is honorable, and that which is lawful. The opposites of these may also be appealed to (e.g., that which is disadvantageous). It will be seen that in this argument Paul will go out of his way to make the appeal to 'benefit' right at the very beginning of this argument (5.2), followed by the appeal to what really matters or counts in 5.6, then the appeal to disadvantage comes at the conclusion of the argument (5.15). The appeal to what is honorable or virtuous will follow in the argument which begins in 5.16 as will the appeal to what is lawful (5.23). All of this follows the advice in the handbooks about the sort of appeals to make, especially when concluding a deliberative argument (*Inst. Or.* 3.8.25ff.).

Last but not least it should be noted that Paul's rhetorical strategy has been to delay until now addressing the real bone of contention – the issue of circumcision and the Galatians' contemplation of submitting to it. All that has come before has been laying the foundation for what he will say here. Clear proof that this is indeed *the* issue generating all this rhetoric is that Paul revisits this very matter of circumcision in a prominent way in his *peroratio* in 6.12–17. In other words, Paul has followed the indirect strategy known as *insinuatio*, reserving his direct comments about the problem in Galatia until near the end of his arguments. Pursuing such a strategy in a deliberative piece of oratory may be necessary if one is in a position of some disadvantage and if one's audience had in fact been giving serious consideration to doing the very thing one wishes them to avoid. Paul could not simply dismiss such considerations or ridicule them, he had first to provide solid arguments for his own views before he could exhort the audience to forgo circumcision. Finally, it should also be noted that the language of persuasion comes bubbling up to the surface here in 5.2–15. Paul will state that the agitators' persuasion does not come from God, but by implication Paul's rhetoric is divinely inspired. This argument, like Paul's first argument at 3.1ff., falls once more into three subdivisions – vss. 2–6, vss. 7–12, and vss. 13–15 – and Paul uses some of the same sort of rhetorical devices here as well (e.g., rhetorical question at 5.11, citing of a sacred text as an authority to support one's own case at 5.14). We must analyze these sections at this juncture.

Argument V, Division 1: 5.2–6

TESTIMONY FROM THE TOP

Quintilian reminds us that while arguments should take precedence, that nonetheless the testimony of witnesses can be important when trying to convince or persuade someone about something. Paul here in his climactic argument resorts to personal testimony. This testimony in a normal forensic setting would be given under oath, and a witness would be called because they claimed to know the facts about the matter under dispute (see *Inst. Or.* 5.7.26–37). So why has Paul put himself on the witness stand at this crucial moment? Precisely because, as he will intimate indirectly at 5.11, he himself had once 'preached circumcision'. He knew the significance and implications of the rite, he himself had been circumcised on the most appropriate day for a Jew to be circumcised (Phil. 3.5), furthermore he himself had once been a strong advocate of the rite, presumably even for Gentile converts to Judaism, and so he was in a strong position to say what were or were not the benefits of submitting to the rite. The Galatians would not be able to dispute that Paul was something of an expert on this subject.

From the outset in vs. 2, the apostle makes evident that this is Paul speaking personally to his converts. The word Ἴδε (look!) the imperatival form of εἶδον, serves to emphasize the importance of the words that follow, much like the exhortation 'pay attention' or 'listen' or even 'mark my words' today.[16] Adding to the emphatic beginning is the word ἐγώ, coupled with Paul's personal name – 'I Paul, I myself say to you . . .'[17] At the crucial point in the discourse, Paul throws the full weight of his personal authority and experience behind what he says.

What follows in vs. 2 is a third-class conditional construction (ἐὰν plus the subjunctive in the protasis, any verbal form in the apodosis). This surely indicates that the circumcision of the Galatians is an event still pending. It had not happened yet, and so there was still time for Paul's arguments to avail and change the course they were contemplating. The present subjunctive verb probably suggests, however, that Paul is not thinking of a mere hypothetical possibility. The Galatians are actually contemplating circumcision in the

16. See Longenecker, *Galatians*, p. 225.
17. Notice the other places where Paul uses the 'I Paul' formula to add weight to the testimony that follows (cf. 1 Thess. 2.18; 2 Cor. 10.1; Ephes. 3.1; Col. 1.23). Notice that Paul does not here in Galatians invoke his apostolic office. His apostolic status is not at issue or in question in this letter. The issue here is the weight of his personal testimony behind which stands his personal experience in this matter of circumcision.

present, even as Paul is writing. Sanders may be right that the agitators had been pursuing a policy of gradualism. The question is, gradualism of what sort? Had they gradually been working their way up to demanding circumcision, starting perhaps first with less obviously unappealing (to adult male Gentiles) requirements of the Law? This is certainly possible since circumcision was generally seen as the last hurdle before one became a full convert to Judaism,[18] and some have pointed to 4.10 as evidence of this sort of gradualism. There are, however, problems with this exegesis of Gal. 4.10,[19] and Sanders suggests just the opposite sort of gradualism – "requiring first some of the major commandments (circumcision, food, days), a policy which was probably not unique among Jewish missionaries."[20] I agree with this conclusion, for this makes sense of Paul's argument, namely that if they submit to circumcision *then* they will be obliged to keep the whole Law.[21] It is worth pointing out that Jewish tradition agrees with Paul's conclusion at this point. JT Demai 2.5 is quite clear that the proselyte is expected to accept the whole Law.

What is not usually stressed is that Paul feels the way he does because circumcision is the sign of the covenant; it is not just another Jewish ritual. There may, however, be much more beneath the surface as well. A close examination of Ancient Near East covenanting procedures, including those followed by the Israelites, shows that the sign of a covenant was often connected with the oath curse that went with the covenant, in fact symbolized the curses that applied if one didn't obey the covenant stipulations. In the case of the Mosaic covenant, the cutting off of the flesh was a symbol that God would cut off a person and perhaps also his descendants[22] from the community of believers, indeed perhaps even cut them off from the land of the living, if the covenant wasn't kept. This is what it meant to experience the *anathema* or oath curse, the judgment of God on covenant breakers.

The connections between 5.2–6 and 1.6–10 in the light of this information begin to take on new meaning. Paul is telling his converts here that if they submit to circumcision and the Mosaic covenant then they have excluded themselves from the other covenant to which they were already party – the new covenant. These are mutally exclusive covenants with differing

18. See P. Fredricksen, "Judaism, the Circumcision of Gentiles, and Apocalyptic Hope: Another Look at Galatians 1 and 2," *JTS* 42 (1991), pp. 532–58.

19. See pp. 301ff. above.

20. *Paul and the Law*, p. 29.

21. Supporting this conclusion is the Jewish evidence that a policy of gradualism was encouraged with proselytes – see BT *Shabb.* 31a for Hillel's view and cf. BT *Yeb.* 47a.

22. Hence the symbolism was especially apt. The sign applied to the organ of generation symbolized the cutting off of one's life and one's descendants if one didn't keep the covenant. See M. Kline, *By Oath Consigned* (Grand Rapids: Eerdmans, 1968).

stipulations and benefits. The agitators are treated in 1.6–10 as covenant breakers, those who have violated the new covenant, and upon whom the oath curse of that covenant falls if they preach 'another Gospel', that is, a different explanation of the relation between God and the community of faith.

This line of thinking also illuminates what Paul says about Christ, who bore the curse of the Law covenant, so God's people would not have to (as 3.10–14 indicates). What then is the connection between Christ's death or the offense of the cross (5.11) and the keeping of the Mosaic covenant? Simply this: Christ by his death has endured the curse of the Law covenant so no one else would have to endure it, and by doing so rendered the covenant's sanctions fulfilled, finished, over and done with, and thereafter null and void. The last act of any covenant agreement was when the superior party who initiated the covenant executed the oath curse on the covenant breakers and so brought the agreement to an end. Thereafter the covenant was null and void. In Paul's view, God only has one covenant, one agreement about relationship between himself and his people, at a time. To submit to the Mosaic covenant is to imply clearly that the covenant inaugurated by Christ is null and void. It is also to suggest that Christ's death did not accomplish what Paul says it did accomplish – exhaust the oath curse of the Law covenant and so bring to an end the reign of the Law covenant over God's people. Thus, the Galatians are confronted with a choice between two covenants and thus two manners of living faithfully before God. They are already Christians, the question is which covenant and covenantal stipulations will they live by?

In this world of mutually exclusive options, vs. **2b** makes very good sense. If they choose to submit to circumcision, Christ and his finished work will no longer be of benefit to them; rather they will have to observe the entire Mosaic Law. Having submitted to circumcision, "the consequence would be that they would have to begin living their lives according to a new set of rules for daily living."[23] The future tense of ὠφελέω is probably to be taken seriously. Paul perhaps has in mind the future eschaton. The point is that Christ will not come to the rescue or be able to help the Galatians at the last judgment, if they submit to the Mosaic Law. Rather they will be held accountable for obeying it all.[24]

Paul's personal and direct testimony is given in vs. **3**. A good deal of controversy has been aroused over why Paul says 'again' here. Is he referring to having previously already taught the Galatians about circumcision? This has led some to think that Paul must have made more than one visit to Galatia already. But if Paul had already taught the Galatians about the invalidity of circumcision, why had the agitators made such inroads on this front? Far more

---

23. Sanders, *Paul, the Law*, p. 29.
24. Longenecker, *Galatians*, p. 226.

likely is the suggestion of Matera that what we have in 5.2–3 is very much like what we find in 1.9–10 where Paul repeats himself for emphasis, saying the same thing twice in two slightly different ways in the space of two verses.[25] It is possible that we should take the main verb here as deponent, in which case Paul would be not merely bearing witness but saying 'I call God to witness that . . .'.[26] Paul says that a person who allows himself to be circumcised becomes obligated, indebted to do the whole Law.[27] There is a play on words here in vss. 2 and 3 between the word for debt (ὀφειλέτης) and the word for benefit in the previous verse (ὠφελήσει).[28] Chrysostom commenting on 5.3 sees clearly what Paul has in mind: "Circumcision has sacrifice connected with it, and the observance of days [e.g., the eighth day]; sacrifice again has the observance both of day and place; place has the details of endless purifications . . . Thus the Law introduces many things even by the one commandment." The Galatians had not realized the interlocking nature of the Law and how one thing entails and leads to another, or as Sanders puts it, Paul's point is once one starts then all of the Law must be kept; one can't be selective.[29]

Lest we think Paul is saying something atypical, the following will help us see this is not the case. Besides the comments in M. Abot. 2.1 and 4.2 which stress that a person must be as heedful of light commandments as of heavy commandments of the Law, we have the remarks of Eliezar in 4 Macc. 5.20–21 that the transgression of the Law whether in small or large things is equally as heinous, because both show that one despises the Law. Sir. 7.8 suggests that any sin renders one guilty of violating the Law, not just a law. To this one may add the numerous places in the Qumran literature where there is a strong emphasis on the necessity of doing all the commandments (1QS 1.14 and passim in 1QS). Finally, one must compare the very similar remarks in Jam. 2.10 – 'for whoever keeps the whole Law, and yet stumbles at one point is guilty of breaking all of it'. The point all of these remarks have in common is that the Mosaic Law is seen as a cohesive whole – obedience to any part of it is part of obedience to the whole, and transgression of any part of it, is transgression of the whole.

Paul begins a play on words in vs. 4, saying that the persons wishing to be justified by or in the Law have *cut* themselves off from Christ, and fallen from grace. The sentence has an interesting structure. Being cut off from Christ is at

---

25. Matera, *Galatians*, p. 181. It is much like the Biblical exhortation 'rejoice, again I say rejoice'. Redundancy is a rhetorical device which indicates emphasis and importance.

26. See Bligh, *Galatians in Greek*, p. 188.

27. Ὀφειλέτης strictly speaking means 'he is a debtor . . .' and elsewhere Paul indicates the creditor to whom the debt is owed. Cf. Rom. 1.14, 8.12, 15.27. Here it is the Law to which one becomes indebted.

28. See Dunn, *Galatians*, p. 265.

29. Sanders, *Paul, the Law*, p. 27.

the beginning, and having fallen from grace at the end. Both of the main verbs here are in the aorist, and are surely proleptic in character or else Paul's exhortation is pointless. What "is enunciated as a consequence of the condition is expressed as if it had already come to pass, the condition being regarded as fulfilled."[30] Paul could hardly have made any clearer that a person who chooses to submit to the Law who seeks final justification by being 'in the Law' (or we can translate 'by means of the Law'), has in effect committed apostasy, has fallen from grace, has even severed themselves from relationship with Christ. For Paul there is no room for compromise on this issue. Paul probably has final justification in mind here. Barrett suggests "justification, then, is a beginning, and a process; and it leads to a consummation at the future judgement, when God's initial gracious verdict on the sinner is – or, it may be, is not – confirmed. The negative possibility is real . . . no one can justify himself by his works, but he can de-justify himself and secure his condemnation by his flouting of grace."[31] This lattermost possibility Paul emphasizes here, but he believes that the one who submits to the Law has already in this act cut themselves off from Christ. The ultimate issue here is the necessity of the keeping of the Law for salvation, not the efficacy of this or that ritual. Paul's rhetoric is not merely an example of polemics or just hyperbole. His point is that it is neither necessary nor beneficial to keep the Law if the goal is justification before God or at the final judgment.

At vss. **5–6** we are once again confronted with the issue of whether 'we' means 'all we Christians', or whether, as Paul is continuing to give his personal testimony, 'we' means 'we Jews' (or 'Jewish Christians'). In the light of the previous consistent use and in the light of the testimony setting of this remark, and in the light of the clear use of 'you' to refer to the Galatians in vss. 1–4 and 7–10, Longenecker is probably right that 'we' here refers to Paul and other Jewish Christians.[32] The point is that even 'we' Jewish Christians through the Spirit by faith eagerly await the hope of righteousness. If this is the case, how much less should the Gentile Galatians expect to receive such benefits through covenantal nomism, through obedience to the Mosaic Law. The verb ἀπεκδέχεσθαι is always used by Paul of eschatological expectation (cf. Rom. 8.19, 23, 25; 1 Cor. 1.7; Phil. 3.20), and this text is no different. The question is of course whether we should translate δικαιοσύνη as justification or justice or righteousness. Now here Paul must be talking about some future condition or state, for as Paul himself elsewhere says 'who hopes for what they already have'? Yet it is possible to translate here 'we eagerly await the hoped for reality that righteousness brings'.[33] Yet since Paul is speaking here as a representative

30. Bligh, *Galatians in Greek*, p. 190.
31. Barrett, *Freedom and Obligation*, p. 65.
32. Longenecker, *Galatians*, p. 229.
33. See Fung, *Galatians*, pp. 224–27.

of Jewish Christians, it is more likely that he is speaking as Jews would about the righteousness before, or right standing with, God that only God can grant at the last judgment.[34]

Verse 6 brings the reason why Paul is able to say what he does in vs. 5. The verse reads literally 'for in Christ neither circumcision is able nor uncircumcision, but faith energized through love'.[35] This way of putting things should be compared to Gal. 6.15 and 1 Cor. 7.19,[36] but the thought is close to what we find in Gal. 3.28.[37] The participle in the phrase about love is probably to be understood as passive. This is the first mention of love in this letter, and it is in order to stress that love is an action word for Paul, referring not primarily to feelings but rather loving activities. The word ἀγάπη is rare in the LXX and also in extra-Biblical Greek sources from the earlier period. Yet the word is ever present in the NT (116 times, 75 in Paul's letters) and used repeatedly to express "with exceptional fitness their sense of the wholly generous, sacrificial and actively outreaching concern on their behalf shown by God in Christ (2.20)"[38] and meant to be shown by Christians to others. Faith is energized, flesh is put on bare bones believing, by loving actions. The consummation of faith is not found in doing works of the Mosaic Law, but by doing loving works of piety and charity. On this high note, the first division of this climactic argument comes to an end.

34. See rightly, Betz, *Galatians*, p. 262.

35. The point is well made by Dunn, *Galatians*, p. 271 that Paul does not seek to argue for one ritual (baptism) over another but rather he contrasts the benefits of the ritual of circumcision with the benefits of Christian experience – what they receive from the Spirit and through faith. Cf. 3.1–5.

36. Silva, *Explorations*, p. 182 rightly sees this connection and stresses the connection between keeping the commandments of God in 1 Cor. 7.19 and the new creation. This is correct, but the question must be raised – which commandments of God? The answer is those that are part of the Law of Christ, not simply those found in the Mosaic Law.

37. Which suggests that 3.28 is no mere repetition of a formula for Paul, but a matter of principle that should have social and spiritual effects on the community of faith.

38. Dunn, *Galatians*, p. 271.

Argument V, Division 2: 5.7–12

WHAT CUTS AND WHAT COUNTS

Paul has given his testimony in vss. 2–6 of what is true of himself and other Jewish Christians like him, and now he turns to the condition of the Gentile Galatians. Employing one of his favorite metaphors from athletics (cf. Gal. 2.2; 1 Cor. 9.24–27; Phil. 3.14; 2 Tim. 4.7; Acts 20.24), Paul says his converts 'were running well'. The verb is in the imperfect tense, referring to the Galatians' past responses to the Gospel Paul preached. Continuing the metaphor he then asks 'Who cut in on you?' referring to the idea of another runner cutting in front of someone and so breaking their stride and impeding their progress.[39] There were rules against such activities and against tripping in running races at Greek festivals.[40] The verb 'cut in on' is in the aorist indicating an activity that has already transpired. We must take this question seriously. Paul is lacking specifics about who it is that is troubling his converts.[41] Many commentators have overlooked the linguistic contacts between vs. 7b and what follows. Paul is using the verb πείθω and its cognates three times in vss. 7–10. Paul is asking in vs. 7 who has so cut in on the Galatians' proper running in the right direction that they are no longer persuaded of the truth. This prepares for the use of the noun in vs. 8.

Verse **8** supports this reading of vs. 7, for Paul then says that *that* particular persuasion did not come from the one who called them.[42] The verbal noun πεισμονή means persuasion and occurs only here in the NT, and indeed for the first time we know of in all of Greek literature. Paul is referring to the rhetoric of the agitators. It is worth pointing out that those who knew how to read rhetorical signals knew very well what Paul was thinking of here. Chrysostom indicates that Paul is talking about rhetorical flattery when he uses this word,[43] and more importantly Epiphanius associates the term with empty rhetoric (*Adv. Haer.* 30.21.2). Paul is by implication suggesting that his form of persuasion comes from God, the one who called the Galatians through the words of Paul.

---

39. See C. E. De Vries, "Paul's 'Cutting Remarks' about a Race: Galatians 5.1–12," in *Current Issues in Biblical and Patristic Interpretation,* ed. G. F. Hawthorne (Grand Rapids: Eerdmans, 1975), pp. 115–20, here pp. 118–19.

40. See E. N. Gardiner, *Greek Athletic Sports and Festivals* (Oxford: Clarendon Press, 1955), p. 146.

41. See pp. 21ff. above.

42. Noting the definite article before the noun.

43. See the discussion in Betz, *Galatians,* p. 265 n. 117 and Longenecker, *Galatians,* p. 231.

In vs. **9** Paul quotes what is probably a proverbial saying, a conclusion that is supported by the fact that he uses the exact same words elsewhere in a different context (1 Cor. 5.6), and that he introduces the maxim with a quotation formula (ὅτι). Most often in the NT and elsewhere in Greek and and later Christian literature leaven has negative connotations referring to the spread of some kind of corruption or evil (cf. Mk. 8.15; Plutarch, *Quaest. Rom.* 109; 1 Clem. 5.6; Ignatius *Magn.* 10.2). Here it is appropriate to ask whether Paul really means that only a little corruption has thus far been injected into the Galatian communities, and thus that the agitators had, at the point this letter was written, only begun to have an effect on Paul's converts, or whether this is overpressing the traditional maxim. Even if the corruption had only just begun, Paul judges the situation to be critical because he believes the corruption could spread fast if he does not act with dispatch.

Paul, in a somewhat surprising affirmation, says in vs. **10** that he himself[44] is persuaded about his converts. Note the key qualifier – 'in the Lord'. It is not that Paul thinks the Galatians are really in no danger, but that he believes the Lord is greater than the agitators. He goes on to say that he is persuaded that they will not think otherwise. In other words, Paul is counting on his converts continuing to be persuaded to follow his rhetoric and to reject that of the agitators.

By contrast, in vs. **10b** Paul indicates that the one who is disturbing the Galatians will suffer the judgment, whoever he may be. Here again Paul indicates his ignorance about the specifics of the situation in Galatia, apparently relying on hearsay evidence and sketchy reports. The singular, however, suggests that Paul thinks there is a ringleader of the agitators, who will come under especially strong condemnation from God at the last judgment for his actions. Κρίμα here with the definite article surely refers to the final judgment, and we may harken back to the anathema in 1.8–9.[45]

Verse **11** is one of the most enigmatic and debated verses in the whole letter,[46] leading to a variety of theories, even including the view that Paul tried preaching circumcision after his conversion and then later changed his mind.[47] Several points need to be made about the grammar here. We do indeed have a first-class condition here, usually called a real condition here, but not all first-class or 'real' conditions refer to actual situations.[48] We cannot simply assume

---

44. Note the emphatic ἐγώ here.

45. The concluding phrase, 'whoever he may be' has sometimes been compared to the indirect phrases used in 2.1–10. The context, however, differs. Here Paul is not referring to what others say about a person of repute whom Paul knows very well, but to someone of whose identity Paul is uncertain. See pp. 128ff. above on 2.1–10.

46. Notice that Paul, seeking to establish rapport, calls his audience 'brothers' here.

47. See Watson, *Paul, Judaism and the Gentiles*, passim.

48. See the discussion pp. 110ff. above.

that the protasis states a fact here. Secondly, due attention must be paid to the twofold use of ἔτι in this sentence. The first probably indicates that this activity happened but only in the past, the second that this activity of being persecuted is continuing even now.[49] Preaching circumcision and being persecuted are seen as activities that would not be happening at the same time by or to the same person. The simplest, and most straightforward way to read this verse is that Paul at one point did preach circumcision, presumably to God-fearers and proselytes in the Judean synagogues and temple precincts, before his conversion to Christianity.

Paul's zeal, referred to in Gal. 1–2 should be taken very seriously. Paul was adamant about the Law being upheld. While advancing in Judaism he may even have been preaching circumcision to Jews who were debating whether Gentiles really needed to submit to it or not.[50] The point is that he does not do so now. Had somebody suggested that he did? Some through the mirror-reading of this text had urged that the agitators must have accused Paul of inconsistency. Of sometimes preaching circumcision and sometimes not, depending on the audience. This is possible, but uncertain. Some have thought we have an echo here of the story of Paul's circumcising of Timothy (Acts 16.1–3), but the problem with that conclusion is twofold. Firstly, Timothy was probably a Jew not a Gentile in Paul's view,[51] and Paul is speaking here about what it is appropriate for his Gentile converts to do. More importantly, if Paul had really already circumcised Timothy by the time he had written this letter, he would have had to do a lot more explaining than just this passing remark. Then he would indeed have had to defend himself against the charge of inconsistency. Here he can pass off the remark with a mere rhetorical question. He assumes his audience does not really believe he has been preaching circumcision. What has really been happening is that Paul has been persecuted for his *lack* of preaching of circumcision, and this persecution, whether it amounted to physical or verbal abuse, was still going on when he wrote this letter.

49. Paul may be using the term 'persecution' metaphorically here. Paul may be referring to verbal abuse from false brothers, or even literal persecution from non-Christian Jews, as indicated in Acts 13–14 (cf. 2 Cor. 11.24–26). See Matera, *Galatians*, p. 190.

50. Dunn's objection in *Galatians*, p. 278 should not stand. It is irrelevant that we have no evidence that Paul evangelized Gentiles before his conversion. We do not need to envision any such activity. Gentiles were already in the synagogues all over the Empire, and Paul could have come in contact with them there, and preached circumcision on those occasions, or on occasions when he perceived he was dealing with lax Jews who needed such an exhortation. We do not need to envision Paul as a missionary to find a social situation before his conversion in which he might have preached circumcision.

51. See my discussion in *The Acts of the Apostles*, pp. 485ff.

In Paul's view preaching circumcision nullifies the scandal of the cross for the reasons stated above. It suggests that Christ's death was not sufficient to reconcile persons to God or keep them reconciled to God, or to prepare them to face the judgment of God on the last day. The word σκάνδαλον was originally associated with the Greek word for trap (παγίς) and together meant something that turns out to be a trap (cf. Rom. 11.9 quoting Ps. 69.22; Josh. 23.13 LXX; Ps. 141.9). The former term, however, eventually was used on its own to refer to something that grossly offends, causes revulsion, or even incites opposition (cf. Sir. 7.6; 27.23; Judith 5.20). Paul speaks elsewhere about the cross in these same terms (1 Cor. 1.23). The verb κατήργηται is in the perfect passive tense and should be translated 'has been abolished'. This indicates "that the preaching of circumcision is antithetical to and entirely nullifies the preaching of Christ crucified."[52]

As if this remark were not a strong enough statement, this section of the argument ends with invective. As Barrett says, it is a mistake to take vs. **12** as a joke,[53] for Paul is in no mood for witticisms, and circumcision, much less castration, was no laughing matter for Paul or other Jews. Furthermore, Romans even saw circumcision as a form of castration. It was the obligation of any good rhetor to resort to pathos, or the appeal to the stronger emotions, as he drew his discourse to a close, and Paul's deliberative discourse here is no different. He could draw on irony, sarcasm, invective on the negative side to cast odium on the arguments of the agitators, and on the positive side appeal to empathy, pity, compassion and the deeper positive emotions to get his audience to bond with himself and accept his argument. It was appropriate to leave such appeals to the end of the discourse when they would leave the most lasting impression.

Paul's remarks are ironic because of course if the agitators did emasculate themselves this would disqualify them from full participation in the Jewish community of faith, because Lev. 21.20 says that a man who has his male member cut off "shall not enter the assembly of the Lord" (cf. Lev. 22.24). The rite of dedication would become a rite of exclusion.[54] What Paul is really referring to here is the agitators inflicting the oath, curse upon themselves, and so cutting themselves out of the covenant community rather that cutting off the Galatians from the Christian community.

There is also a possibility that Paul is alluding to a practice the Galatians may have been well familiar with, namely the rite of self-emasculation which was part of the cult of the Cybele, a cult native to Galatia. If this is alluded to here, then "Paul's wish in effect was for the other missionaries to lapse into a form of paganism which could not but be thoroughly despised by

52. Longenecker, *Galatians*, p. 233.
53. Barrett, *Freedom and Obligation*, p. 70.
54. See Dunn, *Galatians*, p. 283.

Jews."[55] Other forces at play here may be the general fear and disgust with which many pagans reacted to the suggestion of circumcision, much less castration, which in turn made eunuchs one of the more despised groups in antiquity (cf. Lucian *Eunuch* 6; Josephus, *Ant.* 4.290–91). Not impossible is an allusion to Jesus' teaching about cutting off the offending member of the body (Mk. 9.43, 45), especially since the concept of scandal or stumbling-block and being cut off comes up there as well.

Because Paul certainly doesn't expect the agitators to carry out this action,[56] the words must be seen for the rhetorical effect they are meant to have – namely they are meant to set up distance between the audience and the agitators by creating disgust for the latter by the former group. The words are literal, even though Paul does not expect a literal fulfillment of them.[57] They show how passionately Paul cared about his converts, and how much he despised the actions of those who, in his view, were trying to corrupt them with a non-Gospel (cf. the similar language in Phil. 3.2–3).[58] He knows that his audience has a choice whether to follow their advice or his, and the decision now hangs in the balance. Therefore all the rhetorical stops must be pulled out to try and persuade the Galatians to pursue a certain course.

Argument V, Division 3: 5.13–15

FREEDOM'S SERVICE, LOVE'S LAW

Verses **13–15** should not be disconnected from the immediately preceding verses, they continue the discussion of the Law and of freedom. As Bligh says, the reason why Paul in the previous discussion has exhorted the Galatians to stand firm against the appeals to submit to the Law and has invoked the oath-curse of the Law on the agitators is made clearer here – because (γὰρ) Paul's Gentile Galatian converts were called (by God through Paul) to

---

55. Ibid.

56. The verb is a third person future indicative middle.

57. Attempts to reduce the offensiveness of the language, such as the translation by J. B. Phillips 'I wish they would cut themselves off from you and leave you alone', should be resisted. The language should be allowed to have its intended shock value.

58. See Ziesler, *Galatians*, p. 73: "This is not an argument, but a cry of exasperation and desperation . . ." Jerome offered the translation 'Tell those who are disturbing you I would like to see the knife slip.'

freedom.[59] To submit to the Mosaic Law is to renounce their divine calling. Notice that vs. 13 begins with an emphatic 'you'. Whatever may be true of others, Paul insists that his Gentile converts in Galatia have been called to freedom.[60] The term of family relationship is used here (brothers) not merely as a term of affection, nor even just to appeal to the Galatians on the basis of their already existing Christian status because of the work of God's Spirit in their lives, but because Paul must combat factionalism in Galatia caused by the introduction of the agitators into the Galatian congregations, and this verse prepares for what follows. Paul's converts are only partially socialized Christians, at least some of whom are looking for a way to become more fully a part of the body of Christ. The agitators have suggested to them one way of accomplishing this aim, and Paul must suggest another.

There was always the danger that in appealing to the heady notion of freedom in a world empty of democracies and full of slavery and oppression, that this would be understood to mean not merely liberty but license, not merely freedom from sin, oppression, the elementary principles of the world, but freedom to do what one pleased. This is why in vs. **13b** Paul must immediately qualify what he has just said about freedom. The neuter adverb μόνον intimates a limitation to the action or condition of freedom just spoken of.[61] The second occurrence of the word freedom in this verse is preceded by the definite article to indicate a very specific sort of freedom, the sort previously referred to in 5.1 and again in 5.13a, namely freedom in Christ. The word ἀφορμή is in fact a military term, the original meaning of which was a base of operations or a starting point of an expedition. In Koine Greek it had come to have a less technical sense of occasion, opportunity, or pretext. Either of the last two meanings are possible here (cf. Rom. 7.8, 11; 2 Cor. 5.12; 11.12; 1 Tim. 5.14), but since the term 'flesh' is about to be used in a moral and negative sense, the translation 'pretext' is probably most appropriate here.

Paul of course is perfectly capable of using the term σάρξ in a morally neutral sense and in fact he does so with a variety of nuances in this very letter. For example, in 3.3 and 6.13 the term is used to refer to skin – that which covers human bones, or again in 4.13–14 it refers to the physical body without any pejorative connotations. The same may be said about Paul's combining the term with the word 'blood' in 1.16 and 2.16. Yet starting with Gal. 5.13 Paul begins to use the term in a moral and negative sense. The question is, what does the term 'flesh' refer to precisely beginning at 5.13? Note that the term is associated with the passions and desires in 5.16–21, and more

59. Bligh, *Galatians in Greek*, p. 197.
60. See Matera, *Galatians*, p. 192.
61. Longenecker, *Galatians*, p. 239.

specifically with passions and desires that even Christians are capable of having.[62] Notice too that the term is set over against the guidance or leading of the Holy Spirit in this same passage.

Various scholars have suggested that the background to the use of the term 'flesh' here is to be found in the Jewish discussion about the *yetzer hara* and the *yetzer tov*, the evil and good inclination which, according to some early Jewish thinking, resided in every human being. There is perhaps something to be said for this view. Note, however, that this tension is not between two parts of the human being, but between one aspect of human existence and the Spirit of God who dwells within the Christian. It is important to recognize that it is a mistake to try and read back into the discussion in Gal. 5 what we find in Rom. 7.[63] In the latter text Paul is presenting a Christian view of a pre-Christian condition, here the apostle is clearly referring to what is the case with a Christian person. The tension in the Christian life is not between old person and new person (for the old person has been crucified and is dead and buried), but rather between Spirit and flesh.

Some conceptual translations of the term σάρξ are more helpful than others. For example, the translation 'physical nature' is seriously misleading, for it suggests that Paul subscribes to a sort of anthropological dualism in which matter, or at least the human body, is inherently evil and spirit is inherently good. This is clearly not Paul's view, as any fair reading of his creation theology, and what he says, for example, about human sexual relationships in 1 Cor. 7, will show. Neither is the translation 'lower nature' (NEB) much better for it suggests that human beings also have a higher nature which is untainted. But the Holy Spirit is not to be equated with a person's 'higher nature'. The Spirit is not an inherent part of human nature and life.

In fact Paul's view is that all human beings are fallen creatures, and that fallenness affects every aspect of human existence – the mind, the heart, the will, the emotions, the body, human social relationships, and human insititutions. The effect is extensive but it is not as intensive as it might be. By this I mean that Paul does not think that fallen human beings have lost the image of God or are incapable of being redeemed. It is perhaps possible to translate σάρξ as corrupt or sinful nature,[64] but I would suggest that the close association of the term with passions and desires and the contrast of flesh with love in vs. 13 suggests another rendering – namely sinful inclination. In other words, I think Paul is talking about the prompting within human beings for

62. See Betz, *Galatians*, p. 272.
63. See rightly the warning of Betz, *Galatians*, p. 272 n. 16, and see my discussion of the matter in *Paul's Narrative Thought World*, pp. 21–28 and 294–96.
64. See Longenecker, *Galatians*, p. 240.

their sin (the inclination to do that which they ought not to do), not the resulting effect (a corrupt nature).[65] In Paul's view, sin remains, but does not reign in the Christian's life. By the power of the Holy Spirit a Christian can reject or stifle sinful inclinations before they blossom into sinful deeds.

Furthermore, it seems to be Paul's view that the human body is indeed the weak link in the Christian's armor, for the very good reason that it is the one aspect of human existence that has not yet experienced redemption, and will not do so until the resurrection. The mind is being renewed, the heart refilled with God's love, the bent will straightened, fallen emotions being replaced by holy affections, but the fallen body which generates sinful inclinations is not; or at least one can say it is the portion of human personality least affected by redemption thus far. It is a mistake to assume that the term 'flesh' ever entirely loses its connection with the human body in Paul's usage. It often means more than body or physical nature, but it never leaves out that aspect of the term, any more than the term σῶμα does in Paul's thought when he is talking about individual human beings. Thus it is that the Christian person lives in a state of already and not yet, of tension between flesh and Spirit, between sinful inclinations and the leading of the Spirit.

The connective term ἀλλὰ which begins the last portion of vs. 13 should be seen as adversative in nature. Instead of using freedom as a pretext to indulge sinful inclinations, it should be used to enslave oneself to others voluntarily out of love for them. Paul is of course deliberately engaging in paradox here. The shock in this exhortation would come from the fact that the Gentile Galatians would probably think in terms of the Greek notion that slavery of any kind was the absolute antithesis of freedom, not a way of exercising freedom.[66] Rather than a self-seeking and sinful use of freedom, he is urging a self-sacrificial and sanctified use of it. I agree with those who suggest the translation of δουλεύετε ἀλλήλοις as 'enslave yourselves to (or be slaves of) one another', rather than merely 'serve one another'. As Matera says, Paul is setting up a contrast between the sort of slavery referred to in 5.1, slavery to the Mosaic Law, and slavery to other Christians through loving actions of

---

65. I suspect that the use of the term 'nature' in translating 'flesh' arises for the most part because translators have been conditioned to read this passage in the light of Rom. 7.

66. See rightly, Dunn, Galatians, p. 288. Martin, Slavery as Salvation, pp. 50ff. has rightly drawn attention to how Paul uses slavery language to convey various positive things about his own life and the life of Christians in general. Here, however, Paul is not referring to any topos about enslaved leaders, or prominent slaves who have their prominence because of the master they work for. Here Paul is using the metaphor in a more general way to describe the appropriate behavior of all Christians towards each other. This is the language of reversal which we also find in the Jesus tradition (e.g., first shall be last and servant of all), and suggests an attempt to deconstruct some of the major ideas about social status and social condition that existed in the ancient world.

service.[67] This verse must be set in contrast to its opposite in vs. 15 – but if you are biting one another, and tearing at each other, look out lest you consume one another.

In short, what we see in vss. 13 and 15 is the classic deliberative exhortation to avoid factious behavior and to engage in unitive behavior. Hays helpfully puts the matter this way:

> Paul's concern for communal unity surfaces clearly in the concluding hortatory portion of the letter to the Galatians. Not only in his list of 'works of the flesh' (5.19–21) heavily weighted toward offenses against the unity of the community ('enmities, strife, jealousy, anger, quarrels, dissentions, factions, envy') but the virtue and vice lists of 5.16–24 are also bracketed by clear directives against conflict in the church (5.13–15; 5.25–6.5). The conformity of the Galatians to Christ is to be expressed in their communal practice of loving, mutual service.[68]

It is the failure to see the intended rhetorical and social function of this material that has led to a mistaken notion that Gal. 5–6 is simply a disconnected miscellany of ethical exhortations of a very general, rather than situation specific, nature. Much nearer the mark is Betz who sees Paul attempting to deal with specific Galatian problems here.[69] If we ask for the connection between this material and what we have found in the earlier part of this letter, the answer in part is that Paul is combating factious behavior brought on by the introduction of the Mosaic Law into the situation in Galatia. Paul fears that what happened at Antioch (Gal. 2.12) when the 'men from James' came to town, is in danger of happening in Galatia, if it has not already begun to happen. If some of the Galatians accept circumcision and become observers of Torah, it will split the congregations in Galatia. Perhaps at this point they are only at the stage of contentious debate (cf. below on vs. 15), but the point is that disunity is already rearing its ugly head in Galatia because another Gospel has been introduced into the social life there. Paul must combat the fragmentation of the Galatian communities at all costs.[70]

Verse 14 is connected to vs. 13 by the mention of 'the love', specifically Christ-like love, in each verse.[71] Verse 14 provides the rationale (γὰϱ) for the behavior Paul has exhorted the Galatians to practice in vs. 13. This verse must

---

67. Matera, *Galatians*, p. 193.

68. Hays, *Moral Vision*, p. 33.

69. Betz, *Galatians*, p. 273.

70. One of the major mistakes in handling the ethical material in Galatians 5–6 is to assume that this is primarily advice by Paul to individual Christians, rather than to communities about communal life. Paul is not inculcating private virtues here or the cultivation of a Christian's individual progress in sanctification. He is specifically referring to the social dimension of Christian existence in Galatia.

71. Noting the use of the definite article before the noun 'love' in vs. 13c, to refer to a specific sort of love.

be analyzed with extreme care, especially in view of the parallels between vss.
13c–14 and Gal. 6.2. About a few of the aspects of this verse, scholars are in
relative agreement. Firstly, no one disputes that Paul is quoting Lev. 19.18,
probably following the LXX, here. Secondly, the vast majority of scholars
recognize that in view of this quotation, and also in view of the parallel
between this verse and 5.3 (the entire Law, all the Law), and furthermore in
view of the close parallels with Rom. 13.8–10, and finally in view of the fact
that up to this point in the letter Law has referred to the Mosaic Law, in all
likelihood Law here also must be seen to refer to the Mosaic Law.[72]

The question then becomes – Has Paul vitiated the argument he has
been building up in this entire letter against his converts submitting to the
Mosaic Law by in the end urging them to fulfill that same Law? Has
Paul's argument suddenly become hopelessly riddled with inherent contradictions? My response to the latter suggestion is that the great care in the
choice of terms and arguments up to this point in the letter leads one to suspect
that if there is another conclusion which can be drawn, it is surely to be
preferred.

Firstly, it must be remembered whom Paul is addressing here. He is not
addressing the agitators, but rather his converts, and more to the point, though
he wants all of his audience to hear these remarks, he has told us quite
specifically in 5.2–3 that he is addressing those Galatians who particularly want
to be 'justified' by the Mosaic Law and are seriously contemplating being
circumcised. They are the ones interested in and concerned about fulfilling
God's demands on their lives, even if it includes submitting to the Mosaic Law.
Paul is then suggesting here that there is a way of accomplishing that larger
aim, *without* submitting to circumcision and the Mosaic Law. The question is
– How?

Secondly, the details of the grammar must be attended to carefully. The
phrase about the Law found in 5.3 is not exactly identical to what we find here.
In 5.3 there is reference to all the detailed prescriptions of the Law, and as
Bligh says Paul is consistent in his use of the term ὅλος to mean the whole in
every part (cf. Gal. 5.9; Rom. 1.8; 1 Cor. 12.27). The phrase we have here in vs.
14 is literally 'the all Law', and the odd attributive position of the word 'all'
must have some significance. It must signify something like 'the whole
substance of the Law'.[73] This is even more the case in view of the exceptional
position of the definite article in this phrase.[74] Paul is dealing with what he
sees as the basic substance or heart of the Law, or at least that which fulfills the
Law's basic intent and design.[75]

72. Against Hübner, *Das Gesetz*, p. 116. Cf. Sanders, *Paul, the Law*, p. 96.
73. Bligh, *Galatians*, p. 200.
74. See Lightfoot, *Galatians*, p. 208.
75. See Betz, *Galatians*, p. 275.

Furthermore, Paul is making a statement of fact, using the indicative here of the verb πληροῦν; he is not exhorting his converts to fulfill the Mosaic Law. It is also not insignificant that Paul uses the perfect passive form of this verb. He is speaking of how the Law is fulfilled in one word (ἐν ἑνὶ λόγῳ). Those who have made much of the fact that Paul speaks of fulfilling rather than doing the Law here are emphasizing a crucial point. Paul is here using eschatological language, indeed the very same sort of language used to describe the fulfillment of a particular age of history or period in Gal. 4.4 (there using the noun form πλήρωμα). I would suggest this is a considerable clue to what Paul is doing here. The time when obedience to the Mosaic Law was obligatory on God's people is over and done with, Christians are now living in the eschatological age in which God's promises, prophecies, designs, will, are all being fulfilled. The intent or basic aim of the Law was to produce a unified people of God, unified on the basis of love toward the one true God and toward each other. This is still the will of God for the people of God, even though they are no longer under the Mosaic Law covenant. Thus it is that Paul can speak of the basic substance of the Law being fulfilled in the community of Christ, not because the Law continued to be the rule for believers' behavior and not by their submitting to that Law. Rather this fulfillment is what happens quite naturally when Christians follow the example and teaching of Christ. If the Galatians will continue to walk in the Spirit, pay attention to the Law of Christ, and run as they had already been running, they will discover that a by-product of this effort is that the basic aim and substance of the Law has already been fulfilled in their midst. They thus need not worry about submitting to the Law, when its whole or basic aim is already fulfilled in their midst. "Believers fulfill the Law not because they continue to be obligated to it but because, by the power of the Spirit in their lives, their conduct coincidentally displays the behavior that Mosaic Law prescribes. In this verse, then Paul is claiming that believers have no need of the Mosaic Law because by their Spirit-inspired conduct they already fulfill its requirements."[76] In short, Paul is not building up here in one verse what he labored the whole letter to dismantle. He is arguing that if the Galatians continue to follow his advice and the leading of the Spirit, the essential aims of the Law will be already fulfilled paradoxically without submitting to circumcision and the Mosaic covenant.

It must be kept steadily in mind that the context of this discussion is Paul's emphatic assertion of eschatological freedom (5.1) brought about in the Christian's life by the Holy Spirit. This is part of what it means to have been rescued from this present evil age (Gal. 1.4). "The theme of freedom is thus associated with the new age of faith, and the point is highlighted in 5.13–14 . . . where ἐλευθερία is contrasted with σάρξ, anticipating the σάρξ/

---

76. Thielmann, *Paul and the Law*, p. 140.

πνεῦμα antitheses of 5.16–26. In other words, true freedom comes through the blessing of the eschatological Spirit (2 Cor. 3.17 . . .)."[77]

Support for this approach to the interpretation of 'the Law is fulfilled' is found not only in the above considerations about Christian freedom but can also be mustered when one examines the use of fulfillment language elsewhere in Paul and in the NT.[78] The fulfillment of the Law by Christians comes up only in three places in Paul's letters (here and in Rom. 8.4 and Rom. 13.8–10). In each case Paul is not prescribing obedience to the Law, but describing the correspondence between Christian behavior and what the Law demands or describing how what has happened in the lives of Christians by means of the Spirit's work amounts to a fulfillment of the Law in believers.[79] Paul consistently distinguishes between the doing of the Law, which is incumbent upon those under it, and the fulfilling of the Law by or in the lives of Christians. To fulfill the Law implies to satisfy completely its essential requirements, and such fulfillment can only transpire among fallen human beings in the eschatological age among those guided and empowered by the eschatological gift of the Spirit, if at all.

Notice too how careful Paul is with his choice of words. In Rom. 13.8 he does not say that the Christian is striving to fulfill the Law, but rather that love is the fulfillment of the Law. Or again in Gal. 5.14 he does not say the Christian is fulfilling the Law, but rather that all the Law is fulfilled in one word. In each case the fulfillment language is in the perfect tense referring to something already accomplished in the past but now continuing to have lasting effects into the present. For this reason Longenecker's suggestion that Paul in these two texts is referring to "what Jesus did in fulfilling the Law (cf. Mt. 5.17)"[80] is worthy of careful consideration. Christ is the one who has truly manifested love, the one who has truly taken on the form of a slave and served others, even to the point of dying for them (Phil. 2). He is the paradigm and the measuring rod of love.

Confirmation for this sort of approach can be found in the other reference in Paul to the fulfillment of the Law – Rom. 8.3–4. This is where we hear 'For God has done what the Law, weakened by the flesh, could not do: by sending his own Son in the likeness of sinful flesh . . . , so that the just requirement of the Law might be fulfilled in us, who walk not according to the flesh but according to the Spirit.' What is this text asserting? Firstly, that God in Christ has done what the Law could not. Secondly, that Christians do not

77. Silva, *Explorations*, p. 181.
78. See C. F. D. Moule, "Fulness and Fill in the New Testament," *SJT* 4 (1951), pp. 79–86 and his "Fulfilment Words in the New Testament: Use and Abuse," *NTS* 14 (1967–68), pp. 293–320.
79. See Westerholm, *Israel's Law*, pp. 201ff.
80. Longenecker, *Galatians*, p. 243.

strive to fulfill the Law but rather walk in the Spirit. Thirdly, that the just requirements of the Law are fulfilled in the life of the Christian precisely by walking in the Spirit, not by obeying the Law.

It is surely not an accident that the only place in the NT outside of Paul that we find any discussion of fulfilling the Mosaic Law is in Mt. 5.17, where Christ says he has not come to abolish the Law and the Prophets but to fulfill them. Notice the conjunction here of Law and Prophets. The language here reflects Matthean convictions about "the fulfillment of Scripture in general and prophecy in particular"[81] in the ministry of Christ. Nevertheless, it may well be that Paul knew some form of this saying, and that his discussion of fulfillment of the Law is dependent upon it. This suggestion becomes especially plausible when one recognizes the likelihood of Paul's dependency here on the Jesus tradition in another way.

In documents composed before the writing of Paul's letters, explicit quotations of Lev. 19.18 with or without discussion of the text are basically lacking in early Judaism (but cf. the Qumran citation below).[82] As Dunn says, by contrast the passage from the Pentateuch most cited in the NT is Lev. 19.18 (cf. Mk. 12.31 and par.; Mk. 12.33; Mt. 5.43; 19.19; Rom. 13.9; Jam. 2.8; and also Didache 1.2).[83] Some explanation must be given for this notable contrast in emphasis between early Jewish and early Christian literature, and I agree with Dunn that the best explanation is that Jesus himself stressed this text in his own teaching as the heart of the Law.[84] It is true enough that there was a Jewish tradition of summing up the Law in one commandment, even in one case we have a tradition about Hillel summing up the Law (BT Shab. 31a cf. also BT Mak. 24a, Tob. 4.15).[85] It is in order to point out, however, that the verb 'fulfill' is not a synonym for 'sum up' and that if there is a close parallel between Paul's words and anyone else's, it is the words of Christ and the way he used Lev. 19.18.[86]

81. Barclay, *Obeying the Truth*, pp. 139–40.

82. See O. Wischenmeyer, "Das Gebet der Nächstenliebe bei Paulus," *BZ* 30 (1986), pp. 161–87.

83. See Dunn, *Galatians*, p. 291.

84. See in general V. P. Furnish, *The Love Commandment in the New Testament* (Nashville: Abingdon, 1972), passim.

85. Note that in the original Hillel tradition there is no direct connection to Lev. 19.18, only in the later Targum Pseudo-Jon. on Lev. 19.18, and furthermore the Hillel tradition is about the negative golden rule, not the positive formulation we find here and in Lev. 19.18. Paul surely did not get this material from a Hillelite source. See Longenecker, *Galatians*, pp. 243–44. The later traditions that Akiba in the early second century called Lev. 19.18 the greatest general principle in Torah (*Gen. Rab.* 24.7; *Sifra* on Lev. 19.18), may suggest that Paul and Jesus were not the only early Jews that thought along these lines.

86. As Barclay, *Obeying the Truth*, pp. 137–38 says no parallels can be adduced for translating πληροῦν as sum up. The discussion here is not about boiling down the law to one command, but about the eschatological fulfillment of its essence.

Before we deal with the meaning of the quotation itself, a preliminary conclusion is in order. What we see here is that both the life and teaching of Christ is the ground of Paul's teaching at this juncture. Christ fulfilled the Law, and made it possible for his followers to see the fulfillment of the Law and its requirements in their own lives simply by following his example of loving neighbor as self, simply by walking in the Spirit and following the example and teaching of Christ, the 'Law of Christ'.

As for the quotation itself, it cannot be denied that in its original context in Leviticus 19, 'neighbor' refers to fellow Israelite, not to all and sundry. Furthermore, an even more restrictive use of the term neighbor and the text of Lev. 19.17–18 is found at Qumran (CD 9. 2–8). It is thus quite possible, and in this context probable, that the focus for Paul here is on the Christian's duty to his fellow Christians. Paul is speaking about behavior within the Christian community, behavior that should characterize how Christians treat each other, in contrast to the sort of behavior he mentions in vs. 15. As we shall see, Paul will not treat love as just another human virtue, but rather as a fruit of the Spirit – something produced by God in the life of the believer, not something conjured up by the believer through his or her own efforts. This is precisely the focus of other similar Pauline texts such as 1 Thess. 3.12, though love of all is also mentioned there. Thus, while this quotation certainly does not exclude the need for Christians to love those who are not Christians, this is probably not the focus of the quotation here. Almost nothing in this letter is about how Christians should relate to outsiders, though the very conclusion of Paul's arguments in Gal. 6.10 briefly mentions the Christian obligation to this larger group. Paul is exhorting the Galatians to exhibit non-factious behavior toward each other, and the quotation of Leviticus is part and parcel of that exhortation here, as the connection between vs. 13, 14 and 15 suggests.

Verse 15 provides the conclusion of this particular argument meant to unify the Galatians in which Paul will sketch out what beastly as opposed to truly human behavior looks like. As Betz says comparisons of bad conduct with the behavior of wild animals was commonplace in certain kinds of Greek literature, particularly diatribe literature.[87] Paul occasionally uses this kind of language to describe sub-human behavior (cf. Gal. 3.15 with Phil. 3.2 and 1 Cor. 15.32). This verse describes a clear progression – first the animal bites the prey, then it tears at the flesh of the victim, then finally it consumes its prey. "The comparison describes mad beasts fighting each other so ferociously that they end up killing each other."[88] The present tenses used here in the protasis with the initial εἰ probably suggest that Paul believes that factious bickering and disputes are already probably happening in the Galatian

---

87. Betz, *Galatians*, p. 277.
88. Ibid.

congregations. The translation should be 'if you are biting . . .' not 'if you bite . . .'. The latter would suggest a future possibility and should have been introduced by ἐάν if that is what Paul meant.[89] Finally, it is important to note that Plutarch uses this very sort of language to describe the sort of behavior blood-brothers should avoid, as it brings shame to the family (*Peri Phil.* 486B). Paul is saying much the same, only in regard to the family of faith.

It is possible, as Brinsmead has suggested, that by the time we get to 5.13–15 we have arrived at Paul's rhetorical *refutatio*, a section meant to repudiate the complaint against his Gospel that it encouraged libertinism.[90] It is of course also true that the good rhetorician would not merely rebut existing objections to his argument, but forestall such objections before they arose. I would suggest that it is probably excessive mirror-reading to suggest that Paul is here rebutting existing charges against his Gospel by his opponents.[91] It is more likely that he is forestalling possible objections by answering the question – if Christians are not called upon to submit to the Mosaic Law, how then should they live out their Christian lives, what paradigms and guidelines must they follow?[92] Paul has begun to answer this question in the transitional section 5.13–15 which concludes one argument and prepares for the next. In his last major argument, Paul will 'flesh' out his case for Christian living beyond the Mosaic Law, but within the bounds of the Law of Christ. The real problem for the Galatians was not too much freedom, but the continuing beckoning call of the 'flesh'.[93] Chrysostom in commenting on 5.13 saw clearly where Paul's argument was heading:

> Lest anyone should suspect . . . that his object in enjoining an abandonment of the Law, was that one might live lawlessly, he corrects this notion, and states his object to be, not that our course of life might be lawless, but that our philosophy might surpass the [Mosaic] Law. For the bonds of Law are broken . . . not that our standard may be lowered, but that it may be exalted. For both he who commits fornication and he who leads a virgin life pass the bounds of the Law, but not in the same direction; the one is led away to the worse, the other is elevated to the better; the one transgresses the Law, the other transcends it.

---

89. See Bligh, *Galatians in Greek*, p. 200.
90. Brinsmead, *Dialogical Response*, p. 190.
91. Against Howard, *Crisis in Galatia*, p. 12.
92. See Dunn, *Galatians*, p. 285: It "was now incumbent on him to explain how the Spirit functioned to provide a viable pattern of living. A theology of freedom, particularly freedom from the Law, which did not explain how that theology translated into daily living would have been a theology of irresponsibility."
93. See rightly, Barrett, *Freedom*, p. 71; Matera, *Galatians*, p. 196.

Bridging the Horizons

Surveys have shown that perhaps no value is more highly prized by those who live in the West than freedom. Usually what is meant by freedom is something very different from what Paul has in mind here. In the modern world freedom usually means freedom to do as one pleases, freedom to live as one pleases, freedom to be left alone, freedom to be an individual without having to worry about encumbering laws or requirements or stipulations. In other words, freedom is defined in very individualistic, indeed egocentric, ways in our culture. What underlies this is the fundamental assumption that individual identity is more primary and important than community identity, an assumption grounded in the pervasive myth of the rugged individual who accomplishes great things by sheer willpower and ingenuity.

Paul, however, paints a very different picture of freedom. In his view the only true freedom to be had is freedom in Christ, freedom that comes with the presence of the Holy Spirit in one's life. Freedom from sin, not for sin, is what Paul has in mind. Freedom to serve others, not freedom from others, is his point. Paul is suggesting that what the world calls freedom is just another form of slavery. Even submitting to the disciplined rigor of God's good Mosaic Law doesn't bring freedom. Perhaps the Galatians had assumed that if they could submit to the Mosaic Law, then they would not have to worry about what sort of moral choices they would need to make; they could simply follow the instructions in the Book. This sort of absence of the process of moral decision-making is what Paul says characterizes spiritual infancy. Instead of exhorting his converts 'when all else fails follow the written instructions', Paul is urging them to grow up in Christ and act in Christian character, following Christ's pattern. Persuasion by means of arguments about a proper course to follow, not simply offering a series of imperatives, is the way Paul tries to guide his converts. His means of moral discourse entails treating his audience as adults, those who hopefully will listen to and heed reason and persuasion.

Maturity in Paul's view means understanding whose you are, not just who you are; which is to say, understanding that true identity is established in relationship with God, not through radical individualism. McKnight in discussing psychological freedom is right in saying that this sort of freedom is the result of God's grace working in relationship with a believer, not human effort.

> I am not opposed to becoming psychologically independent of our parents, our addictions, or our pasts so that we can become . . . personally responsible adults. But for many, the process of becoming a free-thinking individual, the process of growing up, or the process of working through one's past . . . is the essence of freedom and the goal of life. It is fundamentally important for every individual to be able to look in the mirror, admit who he or she is, and embrace that person . . . But

self-knowledge is not biblical freedom. Knowing ourselves is only a step in learning to know who we are before God and learning what we can be through Christ and in the Spirit . . . The Bible sees psychological health as a product of learning who we are (sinners), surrendering our egos to Jesus (conversion), and becoming what God wants (obedient Christians).[94]

None of what I have just said, however, is meant to deny that an essential part of freedom is being free from the things that enslave us. The Gospel is indeed about freedom from sin and evil, and this in turn means freedom from oppressive situations and structures and customs in society. Again McKnight speaks eloquently:

My contention here is that whatever cuts into freedom of God's Spirit needs to be cut out. We need to have services whose times are not determined by social convention, we need to have fellowships that are not segregrated by . . . race, we need to have churches that are not restricted by cultural background, and we need to have ministries that are not hedged by sexual identity.[95]

This is precisely what Paul has in mind when he speaks as he does in Gal. 3.28, or in Gal. 5.1. There is a social and communal dimension to Christian freedom which, if not realized, makes mere individual freedom in Christ inadequate and insufficient for any and all. When Martin Luther King Jr. ended his famous 'I Have a Dream' sermon with 'free at last, free at last, thank God Almighty, I'm free at last', he was not merely speaking about individual liberation from sin, but the liberation of a whole people from the larger evil of a fallen society with its prejudicial structures. Individual freedom that does not result in a free people of God, free to be the community in which there is neither Jew nor Greek, slave nor free, no male and female, is a truncated sort of freedom that does not fully describe what Paul has in mind. This vision of freedom in Christ still challenges us today to learn more fully that true freedom comes in the perfect service of love to one another, a sort of love that is not narcissistic but creates the true community of God.

94. McKnight, *Galatians*, p. 257.
95. McKnight, *Galatians*, p. 261.

Argument VI: 5.16–26

ANTISOCIAL BEHAVIOR AND ESCHATOLOGICAL FRUIT

In a striking argument, Paul contrasts the unitive effects of the work of God in the life of the various Christian communities with the divisive effects of following another course of living. In this argument the effects of following the guidance of the Spirit on the Christian community are pitted against acting on the basis of sinful inclinations which destroys community. In other words, we have here a deliberative argument for unity and concord, not merely an adaptation of a typical virtue and vice catalog. The argument builds on what Paul has just said about freedom and love on the one hand and about flesh and anti-social behavior on the other, but the argument is clearly distinguishable from what precedes. Like the beginning of the previous argument in which Paul makes a dramatic personal appeal, based on his own authority (5.2), this argument also starts with Paul's own personal but nonetheless authoritative assertion about the nature of the Christian life (5.16 – λέγω δέ). The argument has two parts: (1) vss. 16–21 which begins with the exhortation to walk according to the Spirit and then goes on to concentrate on activities that can destroy the community and keep persons out of the Kingdom of God; (2) vss. 22–26 which begins with mention of the fruit of the Spirit and concludes with an exhortation to stay in line with the Spirit and not engage in divisive behavior. Verse 16 should especially be compared to vss. 25–26, which reveals that the argument ends on the same note with which it began.

> *But I say walk by the Spirit and you will certainly not complete the desires of the flesh. For the flesh desires against the Spirit, but the Spirit against the flesh. For these are in opposition to one another, in order that you might not do what you might wish. But if you allow yourselves to be led by the Spirit, you are not under the Law. But it is obvious that the works of the flesh are sexual sin, sexual impurity, indecency, idol worship, sorcery, enmities, rivalry, jealousy, rage, selfish ambition, dissension, factions, envy, drinking bouts, orgies and things like this about which I forewarn you, just as I said before that those doing such things will not inherit the Dominion of God.*
>
> *But the fruit of the Spirit is love, joy, peace, long temper, kindness, faithfulness, gentleness, self-control. Against these sort of things there is no Law. But those of Christ Jesus have crucified the flesh with its passions and desires. Since we live by the Spirit, let us keep in line with the Spirit. Let us not become conceited, provoking one another, envying one another.*

Argument VI, Division 1: 5.16–21

FOILING THE FULFILLMENT OF THE FLESH

The question of the ethos of a community, its general character-traits and personality was an important question for those trained in the rhetorical tradition. Going all the way back to Aristotle's discussions of rhetoric and ethics, it was maintained that one can discern the ethos of a society or community (just as you can with an individual) by examining its "deliberative acts of choice".[1] In other words, you will know the tree by the fruit that it bears. If we examine what Aristotle says about how to persuade a group of people in regard to ethical matters, he says that one must take a rhetorical approach to convince through arguments using the empirical evidence of how the community actually is living or how they are inclined to think and act about a particular matter (cf. *Nic. Eth.* 7.1145B2–7). You must start where the community is, if you wish them to be persuaded to pursue a particular course of action. Thus the rhetorician's job is to search for aspects of the ethos of the society he is addressing, concrete data that reflect actual conditions or at least tendencies and work that into his argument. In fact, Aristotle suggests that it is by rhetoric, the art of persuasion, and in particular by deliberative rhetoric that one establishes in a society its proper ethos. "The ethos of a society is as it is because speakers using rhetoric persuade members of the society in a certain way about questions of good and evil, of virtue and vice. If the speakers were to convince differently, then the ethos would be different."[2]

Aristotle is quite clear that everyone who wishes to argue about ethics and persuade must make recourse to rhetoric, in particular deliberative rhetoric, to accomplish his or her aims (see *Rhet.* I 1354a3–6). Aristotle insists on this approach for several key reasons: (1) firstly, in ethical matters people will usually not listen to long philosophical discourses or elaborate syllogisms. Rather one must appeal to their actual experiences and inclinations and build on that reality to make a persuasive ethical argument; (2) deliberative rhetoric is the rhetoric of both exhortation and dissuasion about future courses of action and thus is ideally suited for an ethical discourse in which one will argue for a group either to maintain or change its course of behavior; (3) skill in rhetoric is necessary to be convincing on ethical matters because one needs

---

1. This is the phrase of E. E. Ryan, "Aristotle's *Rhetoric* and *Ethics* and the Ethos of Society," *Greek, Roman, and Byzantine Studies* 13 (1972), pp. 296–302, to whom I am indebted in the discussion in the next couple of paragraphs.

2. Ryan, p. 295.

a well-honed "faculty of observing about each matter what is possibly persuasive" (*Rhet.* 1355b25–26) in order meaningfully to address an audience about their conduct. Persuasion about ideas is one thing, persuasion about behavior is another, because now one is meddling in a person's or group's day-to-day *modus vivendi*; (4) especially crucial in a rhetorical argument about ethics is the ethical behavior and ethos of the speaker himself – "his own moral character is one of the most effective means to win the trust and agreement of the group he is addressing" (cf. 1377b28–1378a19).[3] It is important to stress that the place where vice and virtue lists show up in Aristotle is in the midst of his discussion of deliberative and epideictic rhetoric and the need to use such forms of rhetoric to persuade an audience on matters ethical (see *Rhet.* I, Chap. 9, and especially 1366a23–1367a33).

In Aristotle's account of things, what would a deviant society look like? Aristotle addresses this matter in his *Politics* (3, Chapter 6 and 5, Chapter 6). He says that deviant societies are malformed because of the efforts of tyrants or demagogues seeking their own private gain at the expense of the society. These societies are societies in name only because they do not have the unity and coherence and justice necessary to form a true society (see *Pol.* 1332b27–29). What makes virtue, virtue is that it promotes these qualities in society, and what makes vice, vice at the community level is that it tears apart a community, causes anarchy or chaos and reduces human beings to animal-like behavior.[4] Notice that Paul, in criticizing the agitators, accuses them of self-seeking behavior. While it may protect them, it is nonetheless dividing and destroying the Galatian Christian communities (6.12–13). They are in short demagogues out for their own gain, in contrast to Paul who has suffered and makes sacrifices and is nurturing his converts into being whole and healed people (cf. 4.12–20, 6.17).

How does all of this help us to understand the remainder of Gal. 5–6? Firstly, it helps to explain why Paul seems to have chosen rather typical (from a Jewish point of view) Gentile vices to contrast with the fruit of the Spirit. Paul must appeal to traits endemic to Galatian society or at least very familiar to the Galatian Gentiles. On closer inspection we shall discover that Paul will cluster together the sort of behavior thought to characterize pagan life, in particular when it met at the heart of its community for meals in pagan temples, ate too much, drank too much, engaged in idolatry and sexual dalliance, and during the symposium fell into debating, disputing, quarrelling,

---

3. See Ryan, p. 297. It is not an accident that at the end of Paul's ethical exhortations, after the concluding *peroratio*, he reminds his audience once more about his own ethos (6.17). Paul is simply following good rhetorical procedure in order to persuade his audience to act as he insists they should.

4. See Ryan, p. 305.

with party spirit and social pecking orders and societal divisions coming to the fore once all restraints and decorum had fallen away due to too much drink. Paul will contrast this sort of deviant behavior and society with the Christian one, characterized by love, joy, peace and the like. In short, the discussion here is primarily about two contrasting communities and their basic ethos, not two sorts of individuals.

Secondly, what Aristotle says helps us to understand why Paul does not offer lengthy arguments about these ethical matters but simply appeals to common experience, both Christian and pagan. Thirdly, we now understand better the relationship between Paul's deliberative rhetorical strategies and the content of these chapters. The material is not a miscellany of general ethical advice, but rather carefully selected and arranged material that the audience would be expected to be familiar with and could identify with, both formerly as pagans and now as Christians. Paul's basic strategy is to encourage his audience to continue on the Christian path they had already set out on when he was with them, not make the mid-course change suggested by the agitators.

The emotive side of the argument comes in when Paul implies that if the Galatians follow the agitators' advice it will amount to apostasy from Christ, and they will go back to a form of divided society little different from what they experienced as pagans. This manner of arguing was necessary because the Galatians had not yet experienced what it would be like to live in a Christian community in which many were Torah-true and others were not. What had happened in Antioch had apparently not yet really happened in Galatia, and so in order to appeal to the Galatians' own experience Paul must draw an analogy with their pagan past and what their future would look like if they listened to the agitators. We must bear in mind that for Paul, being under the στοιχεῖα was a benighted condition, whether it amounted to being under the Mosaic Law or under the elementary principles of pagan society.[5] In Paul's mind, the ethos of these two conditions was so similar and analogous that both could fall under the rubric of the στοιχεῖα. Neither could be called truly Christian, for neither was 'walking according to the Spirit', the Spirit who produces the qualities that bring harmony and unity to a community.

Lastly, it no longer needs to be a puzzle as to why Paul in this argument in Galatians seems to make a direct quotation of a key phrase from Aristotle (i.e., in 5.23 – 'against which there is no Law' – *Pol.* 3.13.12B4a). This quotation comes right in the middle of the discussion by Aristotle about what makes for an ethical society (cf. above) and the phrase in particular is used of persons who surpass their fellow human beings in virtue. In other words, Paul throughout this whole argument, in both parts is drawing on the familiar

---

5. See the discussion pp. 285ff. above.

discussions in Aristotle about ethics, ethos and rhetoric, a discussion his audience would probably be well familiar with, in order to persuade them to do what he wanted them to do.[6]

Verse **16** begins with the words 'but I say' which draw attention to the words that follow this remark (cf. Gal. 3.17; 4.1; 1 Cor. 10.29). A comparison with Gal. 3.17, 4.1 and 5.2 shows that λέγω δέ marks a new section in the discussion.[7] The expression 'walk by (or according to) the Spirit'[8] is a Jewish way of describing a manner of living, and is a deliberate echo of the OT phrase 'walk according to the statutes of the Law' (Ex. 16.4; Lev. 18.4; Jerm. 44.23; Ezek. 5.6–7). As Dunn says by "speaking . . . of a 'walk by the Spirit' Paul is deliberately posing an alternative understanding of how the people of God should conduct themselves".[9] Life in the Spirit, not life lived under the Mosaic Law should mark the Christian life.

In this same remark Paul goes on to explain a key benefit to living life according to the guidance and on the basis of the power of the Spirit, namely 'you will not complete the desires of the flesh'. The verbal form used here τελέσητε is deliberately chosen and it probably should be seen as an indicative rather than an imperative (cf. Lk. 6.37).[10] In the three examples in Paul, besides this one, where we have οὐ μὴ followed by the aorist subjunctive verb in something other than a quotation, this construction clearly is used to offer a negative assertion, not a command.[11] Notice the double negative which makes the statement emphatic and so may be translated 'certainly not'.[12] This way of putting things emphasizes that living life in the Spirit does not prevent one from having fleshly desires, but it does give one the power to avoid acting on these desires and so bringing them to completion. Once again we may say

6. In an important, and to my knowledge as yet unpublished, essay P. Esler has rightly stressed that at the heart of Paul's argument throughout Galatians, and perhaps especially in the climactic material in 5.13–6.10 is the attempt to maintain the Galatian *ekklesiai* as originally constituted by him in the face of pressure by the agitators aimed at integrating his converts into the Jewish people and a society with a rather different and more exclusive ethos. At stake are opposing views of community. Paul's argument is that the basic principle of the Law is fulfilled in the life of Christians by their simply being who they already are and walking in the Spirit, not by their submitting to the Mosaic Law and joining what in Paul's view is a different community. See Esler's 1994 lecture given at the annual SBL meeting – "Group Boundaries and Intergroup Conflict in Galatians: A New Reading of Galatians 5.13–6.10".

7. See Matera, *Galatians*, p. 199.

8. The dative case of Spirit probably is dative of formal cause. See Bligh, *Galatians in Greek*, p. 200.

9. See Dunn, *Galatians*, p. 295.

10. See the discussion by Bligh, *Galatians*, p. 201, but cf. Did. 4.13.

11. See R. Lutjens, "You do not do what you want': What does Galatians 5.17 really mean?" *Presbyterion* 16.2 (1990), pp. 103–17, here p. 111.

12. See Dunn, *Galatians*, p. 297 who suggests 'assuredly not'; cf. BDF sec. 365.

while sin remains in the Christian life, Paul is reassuring his converts that due to the presence of the Spirit within and among them sin need not reign. As Dunn puts it, the command to walk in or by the Spirit indicates that effort and resolve is required on the part of the Christian to proceed on the right course. It doesn't happen by accident or chance. At the same time the discussion about allowing one's self to be led by the Spirit makes equally clear that the Spirit must take the lead and must provide the power for 'walking'.[13]

Verse 17 involves a graphic way of speaking of the opposition between the leading of the Spirit and the desires of the flesh. Literally the text speaks of the flesh desiring against the Spirit.[14] The Christian lives in a tension between the urgings of the eschatological Spirit and inherent fallen desires and sinful inclinations. The second half of the verse has been much debated. It is simple enough to conclude that 'these' refers to Spirit and flesh which are sources of influence in the Christian life that stand in opposition to one another.

The real question is what to do with the ἵνα clause. Does it signal the purpose or the result of this opposition? One must also ask about the referent or identity of the 'wants'. The options may be narrowed down as follows[15]: (1) 'what you want' refers to *both* evil desires and holy desires; (2) 'what you want' refers only to Spirit prompted desires; (3) 'what you want' refers only to fleshly desires. It is important to stress that the context here is positive, especially in view of the second half of vs. 16, and furthermore Paul certainly does not think that the Spirit and the flesh are equal powers in the Christian's life, or in the life of the Christian community. It must be remembered that in Paul's own earlier argument he stressed that the Galatians had already started in the Spirit, and he was warning them against finishing or bringing the Christian life to a conclusion in the flesh (3.3). Gal. 5.16ff. is a further development of this earlier idea introduced by way of rhetorical question. The context therefore suggests it is unlikely that Paul is here speaking of the flesh frustrating the following of the Spirit's lead or of a stalemate of flesh and Spirit.[16]

Barclay has suggested that Paul means that the Galatians don't have to worry about unfettered freedom and incipient libertinism because they are too caught up in the war between flesh and Spirit.[17] This, however, assumes the Galatians were really in danger of being libertines, when in fact the whole

13. See Dunn, *Galatians*, pp. 299–300.
14. Notice, however, that there is no repetition of the verb 'desire' in the second half of the sentence – it simply reads 'but the Spirit against the flesh'.
15. See the discussion in Barclay, *Obeying the Truth*, pp. 112ff. and by R. Lutjens, "You do not do what you want': What does Galatians 5.17 really mean?" *Presbyterion* 16 (1990), pp. 103–17.
16. See rightly Matera, *Galatians*, p. 207.
17. Barclay, *Obeying the Truth*, p. 115.

letter suggests just the opposite. Paul feared they were in danger of submitting to the Mosaic Law, which is hardly the act of a libertine! Matera suggests that we translate the key phrase 'do *whatever* you want' with the idea that Paul is suggesting that it is impossible for the Galatians to have it both ways – "flesh and Spirit represent two different ways of living. The Galatians must choose one or the other; they cannot choose both."[18] This may well be correct, but how should we see the final clause – as purpose or result? Is Paul really saying that the purpose of the opposition between flesh and Spirit is so that the Galatians will not do what they want? This would suggest that what they want is something wicked, which is forestalled by the Spirit putting the brakes on runaway desire.

To take the clause as result leads to the conclusion that what they wanted was good, but the good was frustrated by the struggle between flesh and Spirit. Yet as Barclay says, this interpretation often relies too strongly on a supposed correspondence between this argument and the one in Rom. 7.14–25. "In most important respects . . . this verse is quite different from Rom. 7, and this interpretation would not only put 5.17 in sharp contrast to the confidence of 5.16 but it would also wholly undermine Paul's purpose in this passage; if he is admitting here that the flesh continually defeats the Spirit's wishes, Paul is hardly providing a good reason to 'walk in the Spirit'!"[19] Furthermore, in the classical writers ἵνα clauses of this sort always indicate purpose, and it is certainly more natural to take the combination of ἵνα μή with the subjunctive as a purpose clause. I thus conclude, especially in view of the warnings to the Galatians in this very context about avoiding acting on the desires of the flesh which lead to various works of the flesh, that 'what you want' refers to these sinful desires or inclinations and that Paul is saying in essence that the purpose of the conflict or tension in the Christian life, the purpose of the eschatological warfare between flesh and Spirit in their midst in which they must be active participants, is so that they will not act out their sinful desires.[20] This is precisely what the assurance in vs. 16 was about and vs. 17 just reinforces the point.

There is perhaps a larger issue below the surface here. Paul clearly enough associates works of the flesh with being under the Law in some way. The question is – In what way? Note that the phrase 'works of the flesh', found only

18. Matera, *Galatians*, p. 201.

19. Barclay, *Obeying the Truth*, p. 113.

20. For a full discussion of the relationship between what Paul is talking about here and the Jewish concept of the *yetzer hara*, see Davies, *Paul and Rabbinic Judaism*, pp. 20ff. I agree with Davies that Paul is probably drawing on this Jewish idea, but in regard to the positive influence of the Spirit, this should not be identified with the *yetzer hatov*, as if Paul were talking about something inherent in human personality. Notice that the earliest reference to the *yetzer hatov* is in Test. Asher 1.6, and thus it was not a long-standing idea in Paul's day in any case.

in vs. 19 in all of Paul's letters (cf. below) is surely reminiscent of the phrase 'works of the Law', which we have had occasion to discuss at length before.[21] Now if we ask which work of the Law could most aptly be called a work of the flesh, surely the act of circumcision is the one. Here is where what Philo says (*Migr.* 92) about circumcision becomes relevant – circumcision, says Philo, symbolizes 'the excision of pleasure and all passions'. In fact it would be quite natural for a Gentile to assume or fear that circumcision of an adult male would do more than just symbolize the quenching of passion, they would assume it would in some measure actually effect it!

We know for a fact that the agitators were urging the Gentile converts in Galatia to be circumcised. It is quite plausible that they may have preyed on the fears of the Gentiles that unless they did something definite and even drastic they were in danger of falling back into their old pagan ways. They were only partially socialized converts and the agitators were urging them to go the whole way, making a full break with their pagan past by becoming fully integrated with the Jewish community. The way to do this was to take the first, but also the definitive, step – be circumcised. By contrast, Paul is arguing that walking in the Spirit is the way to quench the old pagan desires. It is this which he will go on to argue in vss. 18ff. In other words, here we have no random paraenesis but yet one more clearly planned argument to suggest once more that the Galatians already have the resources and benefits in the Spirit that they were hoping to get in the flesh by submitting to circumcision and the Law. Do they fear a return to their old pagan ways and a reintegration into pagan society and community life? Fair enough, but the remedy is to walk in and by the Spirit, not to Judaize.

Thus the mentioning of the Mosaic Law in vs. **18** does not appear abrupt or offered up out of the blue. Here we have a first-class or real condition with the verb in the indicative, and I quite agree with those who suggest that it is no accident that Paul uses the verbal form of the word παιδαγωγός here. If the Galatians allow themselves to be led by the Spirit,[22] they are not being led by the pedagogue, namely the Law.[23] Christians are no longer under the Law, not even under the moral law, as this context makes very clear. It is precisely in the middle of speaking of illicit desires, or passions, and immoral acts that Paul says they are no longer under the Law! While it is saying too much to argue that the Spirit provides *all* the necessary guidance in the fight against the flesh[24] (otherwise this letter is pointless, as is the later discussion of the Law of Christ),

21. See pp. 175ff. above.
22. The verb is probably a reflexive middle: 'If you allow yourselves to be led by the Spirit . . .' See Bligh, *Galatians*, p. 203.
23. The phrase 'under the Law' is a certain echo of the discussion of 3.23–4.5; see especially 3.23–25.
24. Barclay, *Obeying the Truth*, p. 116.

nevertheless Paul is saying that they "do not need the [Mosaic] Law to marshall their behaviour; in the Spirit-led battle against the flesh they have all the direction they need".[25]

Verse **19a** provides us with an introduction to the list of nineteen sinful desires or acts that follow. It is perhaps because, as vs. 21b will indicate, Paul has spoken previously to the Galatians about such sins, presumably when he was with them, that he can now say even to Gentile Christians that it is perfectly obvious or open to public observation (φανερὰ) what the works of the flesh are.[26] Paul will draw here not just on his own previous teaching but also on the common pre-conversion experiences of his converts to drive his point home.

It has been seen, at least since Lightfoot, that there is a certain ordering of the so-called vices in this list. The first three refer to sexual sins, the next two to spiritual sins, the next eight to social sins against the community of faith, and the final two to social sins in the larger society of which the audience was a part.[27] It will be seen that by sheer weight of numbers the emphasis in this list is on social sins against the community of faith.[28] I would like now to suggest that there is even more method to Paul's arrangement of these sins – the first and last ones listed have to do with sins associated with the sort of κοινωνία that went on in pagan temples (at least was believed to go on by Jews like Paul), while those in the middle refer to sins that went on within the very different fellowship of the community of faith. There was danger from without and from within for the Galatians. Without there was the lure of the pagan environment, within there was the divisive teaching of the agitators urging the Judaizing of these Gentiles. Both extremes must be combated, and countered with: (1) being led by the Spirit, which provides the primary answer to the pagan past; and (2) the Law of Christ which provides the primary alternative to the exhortation to follow the Mosaic Law. Paul will focus on the former in this argument, and turn to the latter in his final argument beginning at 6.1.

There is an extremely interesting discussion of the vice list by Ramsay. He argues that Paul is speaking directly about familiar social aspects of

25. Ibid.
26. Ramsay, *Paul's Epistle*, pp. 446ff.
27. On the fourfold division see Lightfoot, *Galatians*, p. 210.
28. Several textual variants need to be dealt with at this point. At the beginning of the list several manuscripts add 'adultery' (μοιχεία) – א², D, ψ and several others, probably on the basis of the assumption that Paul was providing a general list of a variety of sexual sins and to conform this list to what we find in Mk. 7.21–22 (cf. Mt. 15.19, Rom. 1.29). At the other end of the list A, C, D, G and a variety of other manuscripts add φόνοι (murders), perhaps again to conform the list to Mk. 7.21–22. In addition, various scribes, seeking more uniformity in the list have turned plurals into singulars in the list of social sins against the community (in particular with discords and jealousies). See Metzger, *TC*, p. 597 and Longenecker, *Galatians*, p. 248.

Galatian and Greco-Roman society: (1) first he lists vices connected with the national Anatolian religion; (2) vices associated with municipal life; (3) vices associated with customs of society in Hellenistic cities.[29] For our purposes it is sufficient to note that Paul deliberately does not specify some one form of idolatry or pagan festival to attack. He critiques them all. It is true enough, however, that the Galatians would be well familiar with the effects of social rivalries and of quarrels that led to factions, because of the rivalries between the cities in the region and between social groups within each of the cities themselves, though Ramsay also is careful to mention that Paul is likely to have in mind the effects of Judaizing on the Christian community in his list of eight social sins.

Paul does not seek to give an exhaustive list of these sins as the word καὶ τὰ ὅμοια τούτοις (and these sort of things) in vs. 21 make clear; rather it is meant to be a representative list. The issue of venue is important in the way Paul arranges his material. For example, the first three items on the list, which begins at vs. **19b**, refer to sexual sins, headed with the word πορνεία. This word can refer to sexual sin in general, but its basic and original sense is prostitution, including temple prostitution associated with some pagan temples. On the close relationship of idolatry and cult prostitution in the Jewish mind one may compare Wis. 14.12–27. The second term in the list refers to sexual uncleanness, and the third to extreme and public debauchery of a kind that would be shocking even to a pagan.

These three sins are followed immediately at vs. **20a** by εἰδωλολατρία and φαρμακεία. The former refers to idol worship or idolatry, while the latter in conjunction with 'idolatry' surely refers to aberrant religion and so sorcery or witchcraft are possible translations. More literally it may refer to the use of drugs in pagan religion to enchant or induce an altered state of consciousness. In view of the various places where we find the conjunction of idolatry and sexual immorality elsewhere in the NT, including in the Pauline letters (cf. Acts 15.20, 29; 21.25; 1 Cor. 10.1–22 [this latter text also refers to drunken carousing as well] and Rev. 2.14), it is quite possible that Paul means for his audience to reflect on the social setting in which one would find all of these sins happening at once – namely at banquets in pagan temples.[30] This is especially likely if one takes seriously the literal meaning of the first term – idol worship, which strongly suggests a temple venue. This conclusion can be reinforced if we now turn to the two social sins mentioned at the end of the list in vs. **21a**.

The term μέθαι, as most commentators have rightly noted, is plural and suggests not just drinking or drunkenness but regular bouts of drinking, the sort that took place at symposiums both in homes but also especially at major

---

29. Ramsay, pp. 446ff.
30. See my discussion of 1 Cor. 10 in *Conflict and Community in Corinth*, pp. 217ff.

feasts in pagan temples. This last connection is firmed up by the last term κῶμοι which regularly refers not just to drunken revelry but to "carousing or orgies such as accompany bouts of drinking and the festivals honoring the gods, particularly the god Dionysius (or Bacchus)".[31] In fact, as Ramsay reminds us, Komos, the revel, was in fact made a Greek God and his rites were carried on quite regularly in Asia Minor. In short, all of these terms have associations in Jewish propaganda against paganism with what was believed to go on in pagan temples in the Diaspora. Paul then would be telling his converts that through the Holy Spirit, they could resist the lure to return again to the social milieu they left behind when they converted and especially the social location where one regularly found these sorts of things happening. It is clear enough from a text like 1 Thess. 1.9 that one of the most fundamental things that Paul must have preached to his pagan audiences when he first addressed them is the turning from idolatry and immorality to the true God and to a chaste lifestyle (cf. also Acts 15.19–20 on this basic appeal to Gentiles).

I am suggesting then that we have a list that has an A, B, A pattern and the A has to do with sins associated with the audience's pagan past.[32] The B list, however, found in vss. **20–21**, has to do with sins against the community of faith and here the main emphasis lies, to judge from the number of sins listed.[33] These are the sins Paul envisions happening when the Law and its observance is introduced into the mix of the Christian community, and so these sins reflect most directly a 'fleshing out' of the argument put forth in vs. 18. What needs to be understood about this string of negative social characteristics is that Paul is drawing here a picture of what happens when first-century people take sides and the enmity conventions are set in motion. Social divisions and distinctions of social status are reinforced when such conventions are followed – the very opposite of what Paul expected to happen in the Christian community which followed the blueprint enunciated in texts like Gal. 3.28. While the A list focuses on sins of the past, the B list focuses on sins of the present or potentially the future if the agitators' agendas are followed. Paul wishes his community of converts to be like neither the community centered on the pagan temple nor

31. Longenecker, *Galatians*, p. 257.

32. It is possible to say at this point that if I am right about the social categories that these three groups of sins fall into, then there is another reason to reject the variants which wish to add, for instance, murder, near the end of the list. Whoever added this sin did not understand that Paul was typifying the kinds of sins thought to happen at community events in pagan temples and during festivals and convivial gatherings. Likewise adultery, if by this one means sexual sharing between married persons who are not married to each other, does not fit this venue either. The normal procedure at a Greco-Roman banquet was for the wives and children, if they came to the meal at all, not to stay for the drinking party that followed, at which event sexual dalliance was apparently not infrequent. See my discussion in *Conflict and Community in Corinth*, pp. 191–95.

33. See the remark cited above by Hays, p. 379.

the community centered upon the Mosaic Law. Rather they are to be a community centered on Christ and in the Spirit.

One of the clues to the importance and immediate focus on these social sins comes in vss. 22–23 where we find the list of the fruit of the Spirit. These clearly are the qualities that are supposed to characterize and generate a Christian ethos in Galatian Christian assemblies. This being so, it becomes clear that the opposite of these qualities would be the attributes Paul most hoped his communities would avoid. In other words the nine words called fruit are to be contrasted with and seen to overcome the eight words beginning with 'hostilities'. This makes clear that the B list in vss. 20–21 is Paul's central concern as a live option for what could and was already happening in Galatia.

Basically the B list which starts in the middle of **vs. 20** proceeds from feelings (e.g., hostilities) to actions (quarrels) to results (factions). The first term in the list, ἔχθραι is exceedingly common in Greek classical writings. In the singular the word refers to enmity or hatred but it is possible that in the plural abstract nouns like this refer to repeated demonstrations or manifestations of this quality.[34] Abstract nouns could be made concrete by using them in the plural, called the *pluralis poeticus*.[35] Since the focus here is on social sins, or sins against one's fellow community members we may compare a text like Lk. 23.12 as opposed to the examples where the term is used to refer to hostility toward God (Rom. 8.7; Ephes. 2.14; Jam. 4.4). The opposite of this term was φιλία in the older Greek discussions but it may be 'love' here. I would suggest that if the list of eight social sins here are meant to be seen as the mirror opposites of those qualities or actions listed as the fruit of the Spirit in vss. 22–23, then hatred is contrasted with love in this discussion.

The second social sin listed in vs. 20 is ἔρις which means strife or discord, not only here but elsewhere in the Pauline corpus (cf. Rom. 1.29; 13.13; 1 Cor. 1.11; 3.3; 2 Cor. 12.20; Phil. 1.15; 1 Tim. 6.4; Tit. 3.9). It is a natural mirror opposite to the third fruit listed in vs. 22, namely 'peace'. The third item listed is ζῆλος and in a list of this sort certainly does not have the positive sense of passionate devotion to something or someone. Rather here it must mean a quick temper or anger (cf. Acts 5.17; 13.45; Heb. 10.27; cf Josephus *Ant.* 15.82). As such it may be contrasted to the fourth item listed in vs. 22 – μακροθυμία which in its adjectival form most "commonly . . . occurs in the NT in the sense of a patient endurance of wrong without anger"[36] (cf. 2 Cor. 6.6; Ephes. 4.2; Col. 1.11; 3.12 cf. the verbal form in 1 Thess. 5.14).

34. See Longenecker, *Galatians*, p. 253.
35. See Bligh, *Galatians in Greek*, p. 203. In Didache 5.1 we have eleven poetic plurals in a vice catalog followed by eleven unpoetic singulars. Notice that there is a certain parallel to Gal. 5.21 in the way Did. 3.1 refers to fleeing the listed sins, and 'those of the same species'.
36. Longenecker, *Galatians*, p. 262.

The fourth social sin, θυμοί, again in the plural, must be taken here in its negative sense of fits of rage, or repeated outbursts of anger (cf. 2 Cor. 12.20; Ephes. 4.31; Col. 3.8 cf. Rom. 2.8 where it is coupled with wrath).[37] Such selfish and self-centered acts against others may be contrasted with 'kindness' (χρηστότης cf. Rom. 2.4; 11.22; 2 Cor. 6.6), the fifth item listed as part of the fruit. Kindness is by definition a beneficent disposition toward others, which according to Lightfoot did not necessarily take a practical form.[38]

The fifth social sin, ἐριθεῖαι, again in the plural, refers in the NT to repeated acts of selfish ambition (cf. Rom. 2.8; 2 Cor. 12.20; Phil. 1.17; 2.3). In its classic origins the term originally referred to someone who was a seeker of offices (Aristotle *Pol.* 5.2.9). The term in the plural is the virtual antithesis to the sixth part of the fruit – generosity or goodness toward others (ἀγαθωσύνη). The latter is a term found in the NT only in Paul's writings (Rom. 15.14; Ephes. 5.9; 2 Thess. 1.11). As Lightfoot says, this latter Greek word refers to an energetic principle which does lead to practical acts generosity.[39]

Διχοστασίαι again in the plural refers to dissensions or seditions. It is basically a political term even in Jewish writings (cf. 1 Macc. 3.29). Such a term is not surprising in a piece of political or deliberative rhetoric such as we find in Galatians, and in fact several of the terms Paul uses here come straight out of the political arena, though now applied to the disagreements and divisions that are beginning to happen within the Galatian assemblies. It is noteworthy that this term's only other occurrence in Paul's writings is found at Rom. 16.17 where he is warning the Romans to watch out for those who cause dissensions or divisions among them. The next term naturally follows after 'dissensions' for αἱρέσεις refers to parties or factional groups (cf. Acts 5.17; 15.5; 24.4; 26.5). Factions are created by dissensions within an assembly or community. Αἱρέσεις can be used in a positive sense, but here as is often the case it is meant negatively and may be compared to the usage in 1 Cor. 11.19 and 2 Pet. 2.1. These two terms taken together may be contrasted with 'faithfulness' which is the attribute of those who are dedicated to others, those who serve rather than sever the body of Christ, those who overlook differences, rather than use differences as an excuse to create factions.

The final item in the list of sins against the community of faith is φθόνοι, again in the plural, referring to acts of ill will, malice or envy (cf. Mt. 27.18; Mk. 15.10; Rom. 1.29; Phil. 1.15; 1 Tim. 6.4; 1 Pet. 2.10). This term is perhaps reserved for last in this particular part of the list because Paul was fearful it could become a besetting sin of the Galatians and the root cause of divisions and factions as is shown by its recurrence at the climax of this argument in

37. See Burton, *Galatians*, pp. 307–8.
38. Lightfoot, *Galatians*, p. 213.
39. Lightfoot, *Galatians*, p. 213 "ἀγαθωσύνη is energizing χρηστότης".

5.26. The verse 5.26 also supports our conclusion that these eight social sins lie at the heart of the matter and problem in Galatia, in Paul's view. This term is in various respects the opposite of πραΰτης which in the NT almost invariably means considerateness or gentleness toward others (1 Cor. 4.21; 2 Cor. 10.1; Gal. 6.1; Ephes. 4.2). The person who envies or is malicious considers only himself and his desires. The focus is on what others have that he or she wants. By contrast is the considerate person who manifests a concern for others' well being, considerateness being "the opposite of an arrogant and self-assertive spirit".[40]

We may sum up this portion of our discussion by suggesting that Paul holds up three mirrors to the Galatians in 5.19–23 – the mirror of the pagan past, the mirror of the present and possible future if dissensions and factions grow under the malign influence of the agitators, and finally the mirror of the true Christian community. The first two stand as contrasts to the third, but there is an especial effort on Paul's part to contrast the social sins which are beginning to plague the Galatians with the fruit of the Spirit, as we can see now from the following chart:

> Acts of hatred *versus* Love (and joy)
> Discord *versus* Peace
> Anger (quick temper) *versus* Patience
> Fits of rage *versus* Acts of kindness
> Acts of selfish ambition *versus* Acts of generosity
> Dissensions leading to factions *versus* Faithfulness to others
> Acts of envy *versus* Acts of considerateness.

The first column characterizes persons or groups who are selfish, mean-spirited and generally out of control. The second column describes persons or groups that are other-directed, community-spirited and have self-control. I would suggest that this is why Paul chooses to end his list of fruit with one of the paradigmatic Hellenistic virtues – self-control (cf. below). The point is that the Christian community, the community that models the character of Christ, just by being itself, not only manifests the character that was at the heart of the Mosaic Law (love) but also the best of the Greek virtues (including 'self-control'). One need not join either pagan or Jewish communities to see these traits properly manifested; the Spirit produces such things in and among Christians. We may also note that if we are right about the contrast between the fruit and the social sins at the center of the vice list, then Paul has indeed filled out in a very clear way what he meant when he spoke of the antagonism between flesh and Spirit, what he meant by 'the flesh desires against the Spirit,

---

40. Longenecker, *Galatians*, p. 263.

and the Spirit against the flesh'. This was the heading for the contrasting lists that follow. At this juncture we must look in more detail at some of the major ways the vice list has been understood in NT scholarship.

Excursus: The Virtue of Vice Lists ────────────────────────

There has been a great deal of discussion among NT scholars about the so-called Lasterkatalogs, but not many detailed treatments of late.[41] Though much is the subject of debate, two conclusions have been rather universally received: (1) that catalogs of virtues and vices are basically not to be found in the OT,[42] and so in the quest for the origins of this material one must look elsewhere; (2) that both early Jewish and pagan Hellenistic literature is of relevance in looking for parallels. As we have already suggested above, the Greek tradition goes back at least to Aristotle and here we should quote at length a passage from *Rhetoric* 1.9.4ff. (1366b):

> The components of virtue are justice, courage, self-control, magnificence, magnanimity, liberality, gentleness, practical and speculative wisdom . . . Justice is a virtue which assigns to each one his due in conformity with the law; injustice claims what belongs to others, in opposition to the law. Courage makes persons perform noble acts in the midst of dangers according to the dictates of the law and in submission to it; the contrary is cowardice. Self-control is a virtue . . . the contrary is licentiousness. Liberality is a virtue . . . the contrary is avarice. Magnanimity is a virtue . . . The contrary is little mindness . . .

What is notable about this passage is the setting up of lists of paired opposites. It of course differs from what Paul is doing in Gal. 5 in that Aristotle is talking about 'natural' human qualities, traits, and actions, while Paul is referring, when he speaks of positive traits, to qualities produced in the life of Christians and the Christian community by God's Holy Spirit. Nevertheless, the reference in this list to gentleness, generosity, and self-control all find their counterparts in Paul's list in Gal. 5.

Now it must be stressed that in Greek literature such lists began to appear before the Stoics popularized the practice, and existed in non-Stoic sources as well as Stoic ones well into the NT era. Thus, the older study by B. S. Easton,[43] while still useful is, however, misleading in suggesting that the numerous vice and virtue lists in the NT

41. The two major studies are now somewhat dated. Cf. A. Vögtle, *Die Tugend und Lasterkataloge im Neuen Testament* (Munster: Aschendorff, 1936), and S. Wibbing, *Die Tugend- und Lasterkataloge im Neuen Testament und ihre Traditionsgeschichte unter besonderer Berücksichtigung der Qumran Texte* (Berlin: Topelmann, 1959). Helpful summaries and updates can be found in Betz, *Galatians*, pp. 281–83 and Longenecker, *Galatians*, pp. 249–50.

42. Though of course there are more discursive treatments of such matters especially in the Wisdom literature cf. Prov. 6.16–19; 8.13–14; Ps. 15.1–5; see also Ezek. 18.5–17; Jerm. 7.5–9; Hos. 4.1–2.

43. B. S. Easton, "New Testament Ethical Lists," *JBL* 51 (1932), pp. 1–12.

derived ultimately from Stoic ethical teaching. This may be a source of influence and a resource drawn upon, but it is not the resource. One can make as good a case for indebtedness to Aristotle and the rhetorical discussions of such matters (cf. above). One can also point to a wide variety of possible influences from Judaism, for example, consider the vice list in Wis. 14.25–26, or the even more extensive list (150 vices!) in Philo *Sacrif.* 15–33 (cf. the numerous others in *Post. Cain* 52; *Deus* 164; *Leg. Alleg.* 86–87; *Cher.* 71.92; *Spec. Leg.* 4.84, 87–90 et al.). There are also such lists to be found in 4 Macc. 1.18–28, in the Sibylline Oracles 2.254–63; 3.36–41, and in the Testaments of the Twelve Patriarchs (cf. Test. Reub. 3.3–8; Test. Iss. 7.2–5).

None of this is to dispute that these sorts of lists were enormously popular in literature influenced by Stoicism (cf. Seneca *De brevitate vitae* 10.2–4; 22.11; Epictetus *Diss.* 2.8.23; 14.8; 16.14; Plutarch *De liberis educandis* 12B; *De tranquillitate animi* 465D; 468B), but it should be stressed that such lists were popular not just in philosophical discussion but also were a part of the stock and trade of orators offering deliberative and epideictic discourses (cf. Dio Chrysostom *Or.* 2.75; 3.39–41; 8.8; 49.9; 66.1; 69.6, 9). Diogenes Laertius *Lives* (Zeno 7) has various virtue lists and he lists as the primary virtues wisdom, justice, courage and temperance. It is striking that none of these overlaps with Paul's list of the fruit, unless one counts self-control. My point would be that it is reasonable to expect that Paul, and other NT authors, who lived in a multi-cultural environment, were influenced by a variety of sources when they composed these catalogs, but notably none of them is the OT itself and Paul is not simply taking over any particular Greek list.[44] The emphasis on things like love, joy and peace sets Paul's discussion apart from most Greek discussions of virtue.[45]

One fairly recent trend in NT scholarship has been the attempt to suggest that Paul is indebted to the Jewish Two Ways tradition which does in fact go back ultimately to the OT, but has expression in Paul's day at Qumran – 1QS 3.25–4.11.[46] This passage speaks of two spirits, the spirit of truth and the spirit of perversity which are set by God in every person and then a list of vices and virtues is offered. Also in Test. Ash. 2.5–8 the indebtedness to the Two Ways traditions, coupled with a vice and virtue list, seems evident. These sorts of combinations of ideas (Two Ways tradition plus vice/virtue catalog) can be seen in somewhat later Christian literature (Did. 1–5; Barn. 18–20; Hermas *Mand.* 6.2.1–7), but the question is whether we see

44. Though not our immediate concern here, notice the frequency with which such lists appear in the NT: Mk. 7.21–22/Mt. 15.19; Jam. 3.13–18; and most especially in Paul: Rom. 1.29–31; 13.13; 1 Cor 5.9–11; 6.9–10; 2 Cor. 12.20–21; Ephes. 4.31–32; 5.3–5; Col. 3.5–8; 1 Tim. 1.9–10; 2 Tim. 3.2–5; Tit. 3.3.

45. One suspects that one reason for the differences is that in the Greek tradition and also in the Jewish tradition (particularly in early Judaism in the wake of the Maccabean legacy), virtue is associated with courage and is seen as compatible with fighting and waging war. In the Christian tradition, however, love, peace and turning the other cheek, even love of enemy, led to a very different view of virtue and what counted as true humanness and real virtue.

46. See M. J. Suggs, "The Christian Two Ways Tradition: Its Antiquity, Form and Function," in *Studies in the New Testament and Early Christian Literature*, ed. D. E. Aune (Leiden: Brill, 1972), pp. 60–74 and the discussion in Boring et al. ed., *Hellenistic Commentary*, pp. 473–74.

this influence in Galatians (or elsewhere in Paul) or not. As Longenecker says, against the idea that Paul is dependent on this sort of combined tradition is the fact that the idea of Two Ways never specifically comes up in Gal. 5, and in fact none of the catalogs elsewhere in Paul or the rest of the NT manifests the Two Ways language. "It seems best, therefore, to view 5.19–23 as modeled after the Hellenistic catalogue genre and not a Jewish Two Ways tradition . . . The duality of Paul's catalog in 5.19–23 results, it appears not from a Jewish Two Ways tradition but from the apostle's own ethical dualism of 'the flesh' versus 'the Spirit'."[47] I would add that Paul's indebtedness to the Aristotelean discussion of rhetoric and virtue in various parts of this argument should not be overlooked and provides a significant key to understanding this material.

If we ask about the social location of this material, two answers may have to be given in regard to the material we have designated as list A and list B. The list A material may well have been part of the original Christian and even catechetical teaching that Paul offered to the Galatians when he was first with them. The material in list B is more likely to derive from Paul's knowledge of the rhetorical discussions about factionalism and is perhaps emphasized, if not introduced into the discussion here for the first time in view of the developing situation in Galatia. It is easy to see how, if one skips directly from 'sorcery' to drinking bouts and the carousing associated with pagan festivals and meals in temples, this material may well have been part of Paul's original instructions to pagans in various places (cf., e.g., 1 Thess. 1.9–10; 1 Cor. 10).

While some of the material in these lists, both the vices and the 'virtues' is perhaps conventional, what is certainly not merely conventional is Paul's association of the vices with the future Kingdom of God and the association of the virtues with the present work of the eschatological Spirit. In other words, Paul has made this material his own, and especially in his list of the fruit of the Spirit, Paul goes beyond Greek conventions. I cannot agree therefore with Betz's conclusion that "the primary function was to make clear that Christian ethical life should roughly conform to the moral convention of the time" especially since he himself has to qualify this remark by adding "Christian life went beyond common morality, and it certainly included a critique and even a replacement of conventional morals".[48] In Betz's discussion there is too much indebtedness to the older notion of Dibelius that this material is just general paraenesis inserted into place here. On the contrary, understanding the rhetorical background and the social location in the foreground shows that this is not the case.

Paul has a rather specific vision of life in Christian community characterized by love, the presence of the Spirit, the example of Christ which distinguishes it in large measure from pagan community and to a significant degree from the ethos of Jewish community. Furthermore, Easton was right to conclude "the remaining eight terms – 'enmities, strifes, jealousies, wraths, factions, divisions, parties, envyings' – fit perfectly into the plan of Galatians. They form the counterpart of the nine virtues that follow . . . every one of which reinforces the lesson that Paul was endeavoring to teach. This catalog of nine [*sic* eight] sins, consequently is Paul's own composition, which he has

47. Longenecker, *Galatians*, p. 252.
48. Betz, *Galatians*, p. 282.

inserted into a conventional citation. In support of this we may note in addition that in Greek these eight terms . . . have little discoverable assonance, while in the terms which remain when these are deleted – πορνεία, ἀκαθαρσία, ἀσέλγεια, εἰδωλολατρία, φαρμακεία, μέθαι, κῶμοι – the euphony is well marked. Unlike Romans 1.29–31 Paul has chosen terms that as a whole describe sins of act rather than of disposition and so is Jewish rather than Stoic."[49] Support for the non-conventionality of this list of eight social sins also comes from realizing that terms such as dissensions, factions, enmities are not found in the vice lists of popular philosophers,[50] only the general ideas are part of the essential subject matter of deliberative or political oratory. As Matera says this suggests "Paul is addressing a specific problem in the Galatian congregation . . . even if Paul is drawing upon traditional material at this point, he has chosen and introduced material which focuses upon the situation at Galatia."[51]

One final point should be stressed. "Paul's vice lists, unlike those of the Hellenistic world in general which emphasized 'personal' vices, are particularly formed for the life of the community. Paul was not a wandering street preacher, but an apostle and a leader of congregations, and his ethical lists reflect this function."[52] This is why Paul's lists are so heavily freighted with 'social' sins.[53]

At the conclusion of the vice list, at vs. **21b** Paul offers a stern warning – those doing the sort of things mentioned in the vice list will not inherit the Dominion of God. This sort of eschatological language is reminiscent of the teaching of Jesus, perhaps deliberately so (cf. Mk. 10.17 and par.) and is relatively rare in Paul's letters.[54] Paul makes very similar remarks in 1 Cor. 6.9–10 and also refers to the Dominion as something future in 1 Cor. 15.50. Yet Paul can also speak about the Dominion as a condition in the present which believers alone experience (cf. Rom. 14.17; 1 Cor. 4. 20; 6.9–10; Col. 4.10–11; 1 Thess. 2.11–12; 2 Thess. 1.5–12). In general, as I have argued elsewhere, when Paul speaks about the Dominion as something future he speaks of it as a realm that one enters or inherits or obtains. When he speaks of it as something present he speaks of it as a condition experienced by believers.[55] In other words the Dominion is in an already and not yet state of affairs, as is true of other

49. Easton, "New Testament," pp. 6–7. In this way Easton vitiates his own earlier conclusion about the indebtedness to Stoic lists.

50. See Wibbing, *Die Tugend*, p. 97.

51. Matera, *Galatians*, p. 210.

52. Cf. V. P. Furnish, *Theology and Ethics in Paul* (Nashville: Abingdon, 1968), p. 84 and Wibbing, *Die Tugend*, pp. 95ff.

53. It is perhaps worth stressing that these vice and virtue catalogs must be distinguished from the various tribulation catalogs which we also find in Paul (cf., e.g., 2 Cor. 11.23–27) and the discussion in R. Hodgson, "Paul the Apostle and First Century Tribulation Lists," *ZNW* 74 (1983), pp. 59–80 and J. T. Fitzgerald, *Cracks in an Earthen Vessel* (Atlanta: Scholars Press, 1988).

54. See Dunn, *Galatians*, p. 306.

55. See my *Jesus, Paul and the End of the World*, pp. 52ff.

eschatological realities such as salvation or conformity to the image of Christ. The warning here must be taken quite seriously. Paul is telling his Galatian Christian converts that if they behave in these sorts of ways they will find themselves on the outside looking in, without inheritance when the Dominion comes in fullness to earth. This comports with what he has already said earlier in 5.4 – if they allow themselves to be circumcised they will have cut themselves off from Christ (and so the inheritance that comes in Christ).

Argument VI, Division 2: 5.22–26

THE SPIRIT'S FRUIT

Clearly enough, we are meant to see the items listed in vss. 22–23 as standing in direct contrast to what has been said before, and we have already had occasion to remark on the nature of that opposition. Here we must concentrate on the positive traits that Paul says should and does characterize the Christian life. There are of course numerous lists of virtues that one could compare this list to (cf. 1QS 4.2–8; Philo *Sac.* 27; *Virt.* 182; Josephus *Apion* 2.146; cf. above on Aristotle), but in fact few of them comment on love at all (the exception being 1QS 4.5) or have an arrangement of nine traits anything like we find here. What we can say is that the last three items in our list were characteristic Greek virtues (cf. below) which Aristotle and many others commented on, but that the first six listed here are closely paralleled only by material elsewhere in the NT, and mostly in the Pauline corpus or in a document influenced by the Pauline corpus (cf. 2 Cor. 6.6; 1 Tim. 4.12; 6.11; 2 Tim. 2.22; 2 Pet. 1.5–7). Most important is the conclusion of Dunn about this material:

> In view of the clear echo of Jesus' characteristic teaching on the theme (see . . . 5.14), and the immediately following description of those who bear this fruit as 'those of Christ Jesus' who have patterned themselves on Christ's passion (5.24) and who are to 'fulfil the Law of Christ' (6.2), the suggestion is also very inviting that Paul had in mind here a kind of 'character-sketch' of Christ. This would certainly tie in with his characteristic understanding, and indeed definition of the Spirit as the Spirit of Christ, who reproduces the prayer and status of Christ in the believer (see . . . 4.6) and who transforms the believer into the image of Christ (see . . . 4.19).[56]

56. Dunn, *Galatians*, p. 310.

If this remark is anywhere near correct, it shows that Paul was indeed trying to inculcate a rather distinctive ethos for his Christian community, an ethos that could be distinguished from that of pagan or Jewish community, though obviously there was some overlap in the ethical qualities inculcated. W. Meeks puts the matter thusly: "*Theologically* it is correct to say that the scriptures and traditions of Judaism are a central and ineffaceable part of the Pauline Christian's identity. *Socially*, however, the Pauline groups were *never a sect of Judaism*. They organized their lives independently from the Jewish associations of the cities where they were founded . . ."[57]

The first observation of import about vs. 22 is that Paul says fruit, not fruits. Various commentators have suggested that the singular fruit should be contrasted with the multiplicity of the works of the flesh just listed.[58] Others have suggested that the emphasis should be on the fact that Paul calls these qualities fruit rather than works, suggesting that they are something the indwelling presence of the Spirit produces in the believer and the community, rather than something the believer acquires, achieves or develops. If this is the case, it would be better not to speak of virtues, but rather of character traits. The warning of Longenecker at this point is, however, apt: "though indeed the virtues listed are given as gifts by God through the Spirit, one must not unpack the metaphor of 'fruit' in such a manner as to stress only the given quality of the virtues listed, implying an ethical passivity on the Christian's part."[59] I would suggest that the singular here suggests the unity and unifying nature of these qualities as opposed to the divisive effects of the traits listed in the vice list.[60] The singular also suggests that Paul expects all of these traits to be manifested not only in any Christian community but in any Christian life, not love in one person, peace in another and so on. Whatever else one can say, it appears certain that Paul is not talking about natural traits or abilities or talents here, but rather qualities produced in the life of the community by the Spirit.

It is not surprising that the first part of the fruit listed is love, for this in Paul's view should be the signature quality of Christian community. As a text like Rom. 5.5 shows, Paul is talking about the love poured into the hearts of believers by the Spirit, not natural love. This is perhaps why Paul chooses the

---

57. Meeks, "Breaking Away: Three New Testament Pictures of Christianity's Separation from Jewish Communities," in *To See Ourselves as Others See Us: Christians, Jews, "Others" in Late Antiquity*, ed. J. Neusner and E. S. Frerichs (Chico: Scholars Press, 1985), pp. 93–155, here p. 106, the emphasis at the end of the quotation is my addition. Meeks is using the term sect in a different way than I have in this study (see pp. 272ff. above). He means a party or movement within Judaism, rather than a breakaway group by the term.

58. See, e.g., Matera, *Galatians*, p. 202.

59. Longenecker, *Galatians*, p. 259.

60. See Betz, *Galatians*, p. 286.

noun ἀγάπη to signal what he means. This noun is not found in classical Greek writings nor in Josephus, yet it dominates the discussion in the NT of the personal relationships, both those between the believer and God, and those between believers. Notice how Paul has already illustrated what he means by this term in Gal. 5.6 (faith working through love) 5.13 (through love serve one another) and 5.14 (love your neighbor as yourself). We know from 1 Cor. 13 how Paul saw this as the most important of all Christian qualities of life and so it is no surprise it is listed first here.

The term χαρά is a term we do find frequently in Greek literature. It seems to have meant something like contentment, the ability to find the golden mean between extremes and so be happy, or it could be used to indicate the sort of feeling of exhilaration one got at an exciting religious festival.[61] The term has a somewhat different nuance for Paul. Joy for Paul is not something produced by circumstances, nor ephemeral pleasures, but rather is generated by the indwelling Spirit and so can be manifested often in spite of one's circumstances or health. Eschatological joy involves a future-looking attitude that is hopeful (cf. Rom. 5.2, 11; 14.17; 15.11), and is of the essence of the Dominion of God.

It must be kept steadily in view that Paul is here describing social traits, not primarily inner qualities of individuals. This is especially to be emphasized with the word εἰρήνη which is surely grounded in the Hebrew concept of *shalom* rather than in the Greek and particularly in the Stoic idea of serenity, a quiet mind, or the absence of activity and especially the absence of pain and other disturbances. The Jewish concept by contrast has to do with personal wholeness, with healthy relationships, in other words with positive relational concepts rather than the absence of opposition or pain or trouble. Once again, in Paul's view this sort of peace comes from being placed in right relationship with God who is a God of peace (cf. Rom. 15.33; 16.20; 2 Cor. 13.11; Phil. 4.29; 1 Thess. 5.23), which then affects the way Christians relate to each other and to outsiders (Rom. 14.19).[62] To wish someone *shalom* was to wish them not merely good health or fortune but peace with God and the best of human relationships as well.

Μακροθυμία is a term which appears regularly in Greek literature and means having a long temper, or as we might say having a slow fuse (cf. Plutarch, *Lucull.* 32.3; 33.1; Menander, *Fgm.* 19). The term is also found in Jewish literature (cf. Test. Jos. 2.7; 17.2; 18.3). Usually in the NT it refers to patient endurance of some wrong or suffering without responding in anger or without taking revenge (cf. 2 Cor. 6.6; Ephes. 4.2; Col. 1.11; 3.12). Once again

---

61. See Dunn, *Galatians*, p. 310.
62. There is a possibility that the triad, love, joy, peace goes back to the teaching of Jesus on these matters – see Jn. 14.27, 15.9–11.

we have a quality of God and God in Christ, which is now to be mirrored in the believer (cf. Rom. 2.4).

The terms we translate 'kindness' and 'goodness' are also relational terms, with perhaps more emphasis in the former on attitude and in the latter on actions on behalf of others. It is interesting that in the classical Greek writers χρηστότης normally means excellence when referring to things but goodness or even honesty when referring to persons. Ἀγαθωσύνη by contrast is not found in classical writings nor even in Josephus, but in the NT it is found only in Paul as a near synonym to 'kindness' (cf. Rom. 15.14; Ephes. 5.9; 2 Thess. 1.11).[63]

In a list such as this πίστις in all likelihood does not refer to faith, but rather to faithfulness, and so it is once again an attribute of God (Rom. 3.3) now predicated of the believer. More importantly for our discussion, Paul sees it as the paradigmatic term to describe the self-giving action of Christ, in particular referring to his voluntary surrender to death on the cross in obedience to God's will and plan. The faithfulness of Christ is to be likewise mirrored by Christians.[64] This term in Greek literature refers to trust-worthiness, a person who acts in good faith, and it is perhaps likely that the Gentile Galatians would hear some of these sorts of overtones here, especially in view of the two terms which follow this one and conclude the list.

As Betz says, faithfulness, gentleness or mildness, and self-control were three famous virtues in Hellenistic ethics.[65] The term πραΰτης which begins vs. 23 is one we find regularly in Aristotle's discussion of ethics. In *Nic. Eth.* 2.1108A he defines this term as the golden mean between excessive anger and the inability to be angry. In other words it refers to a person who is in control of his or her emotions and can choose to act with gentleness or mildness in dealing with others. In Paul's writing the term refers to considerateness in actions toward others, and so is the mirror opposite of a person who is arrogant and self-assertive (cf. 1 Cor. 4.21; 2 Cor. 10.1; Gal. 6.1; Ephes. 4.2; Col. 3.12).

The final term in our list, ἐγκράτεια, likewise had a long history in Greek discussions of ethics. Xenophon says Socrates introduced the term into ethical discussion (*Mem.* 1.5.4). Plato uses it to refer to the opposite of gluttony and also of the over-indulgence in sex (*Republic* 390B, 430E). Aristotle's discussion, however, was paradigmatic for much of what followed in Greek literature and he stresses that the term refers to the control of the passions in general and the ability to resist temptations. Besides here, the term only rarely occurs in Christian discussions in the NT (cf., however, Acts 24.25; 2 Pet. 1.6 and the

---

63. See Longenecker, *Galatians*, p. 262.
64. See above pp. 260ff. on Gal. 3.22.
65. Betz, *Galatians*, p. 288.

adjectival form in Tit. 1.8 and later Clem. 38.2 where it is seen as God's gift).[66] That this term had become a central term in Hellenistic ethics, and Aristotle was usually referred to in this discussion, prepares us quite well for the Aristotelean phrase which immediately follows this list. It is hard to doubt the Galatians would have heard the phrase in that light in view of the Greek triad of qualities that conclude our list.[67]

The phrase κατὰ τῶν τοιούτων οὐκ ἔστιν νόμος is nearly identical to the one we find in Aristotle's *Pol.* 3.13.1284a κατὰ δέ τῶν τοιούτων οὐκ ἔστι νόμος. These two texts are frankly too similar for there not to be some relationship, and I would suggest that here in these last three traits and this quotation we have an example of Paul's attempt to relate to ethical discussions his audience would most likely know. The question about both of these phrases is whether we should take τοιούτων as masculine (such persons) or neuter (such things). Either is possible in either one of these texts. The parallel with the end of the vice list (τὰ ὅμοια τούτοις) is usually thought to favor the translation 'such things' as is the fact that in both lists Paul is describing traits or actions, not persons. The parallel with the end of the vice list, however, is not precise. There the reference is to other similar traits not mentioned, here the reference is to these positive traits just mentioned and those like them. Not only the parallel with the phrase in Aristotle but also the usual use of κατὰ favors translating this particular word as 'against', and what is probably decisive on this point is that κατὰ with the genitive used to mean 'against' is precisely the construction used twice in Gal. 5.17.[68] The proper translation seems to be then 'against such things there is no law'.

Now in Aristotle's discussion what he means by this self-same phrase is that there are persons who surpass their fellow human beings in virtue, and so live like gods among humans. These sorts of persons do not need to have their conduct regulated by law, indeed they constitute a law or standard by which others can measure themselves.[69] This discussion is of direct relevance to the Galatian situation. Paul is not merely making the innocuous remark that there is no law that proscribes or legislates against love, joy and the like. He is also not saying that no law prescribes such things since in fact he has just said that the Mosaic Law does prescribe love.[70] In line with Aristotle's discussion he is

66. Not surprisingly, various manuscripts (D* F G goth and various of the church fathers including Cyprian, Irenaeus, and Origen) supplement Paul's list here with the word ἀγνεία, chastity, reflecting the later Christian stress on this virtue. See Metzger, *TC*, p. 598.

67. Furnish, *Theology and Ethics*, p. 88 is surely right that this list of virtues is Paul's own composition, drawing on a variety of ideas and sources. He may also be right that the nine virtues are grouped in three triads.

68. Thus we must reject the suggestion of Ziesler, *Galatians*, pp. 91–92 to translate κατὰ as 'in relation to'.

69. See the helpful discussion by Bruce, *Galatians*, p. 255.

70. See the discussion of Barclay, *Obeying the Truth*, pp. 122–25.

asserting that persons who manifest these traits are exceedingly virtuous and have no need of Law, in this case the Mosaic Law. Indeed they constitute a law or standard by which others should be measured.

Christ is the Christian's standard, and to the extent they manifest Christ-like qualities they too become a standard for others, indeed they appear as Christ among others (cf. 4.14; 6.17). "Where God's Spirit is at work, Paul contends, the result will be peace and holiness, not moral anarchy."[71] In other words, this is one more argument against submitting to the Mosaic Law, this time with the help of Aristotle and the Galatians' own Greek ethical heritage. This remark is especially appropriate here because it prepares, as do vss. 24–26, for Paul's final argument about the Law or Standard of Christ which begins at 6.1.

Verse **24** begins by referring to 'those of Christ', usually interpreted to mean those who belong to Christ, but in view of the parallel use of the genitive in Gal. 3.29 it probably also implies those who are in Christ Jesus. As Matera says, it refers to participation in the life of Christ, or better said the recapitulation of Christ's story in the life of the believer.[72] Paul is saying something different in this verse than what we find in 2.19 and 6.14 where we hear about being crucified with Christ. Here "Christians are described not as the objects but as the agents of this crucifixion".[73] The verb crucified is in the aorist, referring to an event in the past. It would appear that Paul is referring both to the experience of conversion and to the decision to become a Christian and the ethical commitments that went along with it. Bligh has suggested we see this verb as an inceptive aorist signifying the commencement of an action (in the past) which continues on in the present, and this is probably correct.[74] Those in Christ must continue to crucify the flesh when ever it comes to life again, for the Christian in this life always stands in the battle zone between flesh and Spirit and has a decisive role to play in his or her own moral progress. Notice the emphasis on the flesh having passions and desires. Lightfoot says that these two terms can be distinguished as the passive and active sides respectively of this vice.[75] This favors our suggestion above that the term flesh here refers to sinful inclinations resident in human beings, including in Christians. The point is that now the Spirit gives the believer the power to overcome the desires of the flesh, not merely capitulate to them.

Verse **25** presents us with a first-class and real condition and thus it is possible to translate 'since' rather than just 'if' here. Since all believers (notice

71. Hays, *Moral Vision*, p. 37.
72. See Matera, *Galatians*, p. 204 and my discussion in *Paul's Narrative Thought World*, pp. 245ff.
73. Barclay, *Obeying the Truth*, p. 117.
74. Bligh, *Galatians*, p. 205.
75. Lightfoot, *Galatians*, p. 213.

the 'we' here which for the first time in Galatians refers to both the author and the audience, not merely the author and his fellow Jewish Christians) live in and by the Spirit, they must also walk in step with the Spirit. The verb στοιχῶμεν is not chosen by accident in view of the previous discussions about the στοιχεῖα.[76] Paul is suggesting that the Galatians do not need to place themselves under any elementary principles of the universe, either pagan or Jewish ones precisely because they already live in and by the Spirit of God and should follow the Spirit's lead, staying in line or step with the Spirit, not the Law. The verb here probably has the same sense as in Rom. 4.12 of follow or keep in step with, and it is also an apt choice since Paul began this argument at vs. 16 by speaking of walking in the Spirit and being led by the Spirit (vs. 18). The term was originally a military term referring to standing in a row or line of soldiers. The overtones then are that if the Galatians want to place themselves under a sort of martial law, all they really need do is stay in step with the Spirit and they will receive all the guidance and discipline they need.[77] Barrett puts the matter eloquently: 'The Spirit which affects this disregard of self is in no sense legal, still less legalistic; yet in its effect it is entirely moral.'[78]

Verse **26** stands as the mirror opposite of vs. 25. Having told them what they ought to do, Paul now concludes this argument by telling them what they must not do. Paul once again refers to divisive behavior. Notice that Paul here refers to a future possibility, although one which Paul sees as likely if the Galatians listen to the agitators. He says 'let us not become (γινώμεθα) conceited or boastful'. This idea will arise again when Paul characterizes the agitators in 6.13 as those who wish to boast about things. He may well have them in mind already here. The term κενόδοξοι occurs only here in the NT,[79] but it would be a term well familiar to anyone raised in a Greek-speaking environment. The two participles that follow help us to see what in particular Paul has in mind, namely provoking one another and being envious of one another. These participles may well describe the agitators (the provokers who are unsettling the Galatians) and those Galatians who wish to be under the Law, and so are envious of the agitators' full Jewish status, as Chrysostom suggests in his comment on this verse. Paul sees both provoking and envy as falling under the heading of false pride and misplaced values. The Galatians must concentrate on becoming what they already are in the Spirit (as Bultmann once suggested), not trying to emulate the agitators. Verse 26 then confirms our suspicions that the eight social sins which stood at the heart of the vice list are uppermost in Paul's mind as the primary problem in Galatia.

76. See pp. 284ff. above.
77. See the discussion on στοιχεῖα pp. 286ff. above.
78. Barrett, *Freedom and Obligation*, p. 77.
79. For the cognate see Phil. 2.3, cf. 4 Macc. 2.15.

The Galatians are called upon to bear the image of Christ, and so reflect the new ethos of the Christian community not the old ethos of either Jewish or pagan society. As Betz says, Paul's virtue list reminds us that he thinks that Christian ethics not only fulfills the essential demand of the Torah but also the central demands of Greek ethics as well.[80] Beliefs of course affect social cohesion within a group and Paul is convinced that certain beliefs about Christ and the Spirit should shape the way Christians will approach the ethical task. "A group of people who strongly hold a set of beliefs about what is real and valuable, different in some salient aspects from beliefs held in the general society, and who also share emotionally effective symbols for those beliefs, naturally find communication with one another easier and more satisfying than communication with those who do not share their way of seeing."[81] Paul is here trying to create a certain way of seeing Christian community as a community not essentially defined by Torah or pagan norms, but consonant with the highest aspirations of both Jewish and Greek society.

It is notable that in this argument and the next one Paul has once again chosen to appeal first to the Galatians' own experience and then to other 'authorities' to convince them to take a particular course of action. In the first argument the second line of argument came from the Scriptures. As we will see in 6.1ff., the second line of argument now comes from the Law of Christ. To this final argument we must now turn, after considering the implications of this section for us today.

Bridging the Horizons

Certainly one of the key observations about ethics is that ethical behavior must be enforced and reinforced by a community in its day to day life. With the breakdown of basic social units of community such as the family and even the church which normally would provide the moral glue to society, we live in an age when Paul's exhortations in this chapter take on an especial urgency. The answer to the decaying morals of modern society is not merely to try and rebuild some of the major building blocks of society such as the family (à la 'Promise Keepers'), but to do a better job of creating a Christian church family in which all such sub-units of society can be nurtured and if they are broken, healed.

---

80. Betz, *Galatians*, p. 288.
81. Meeks, "The Social Context of Pauline Theology," *Int* 36 (1982), pp. 266–77, here p. 271.

Paul's exhortations here are not to private individual Christians, but to the Galatian assemblies as communities of Christ. Paul does not assume that individual Christians can win the battle against the flesh and against factors that divide us from others merely by individuals doing a better job of relying on the resources of the Spirit. The Spirit indwells the community as well as the individuals, and more to the point, as Paul says in Philippians 'you all must work out your salvation with fear and trembling, for God is at work in the midst of you all to will and to do'. In other words, a corporate and communal effort is required to win these sorts of battles against the flesh. That is why we have all the discussion here about burden bearing and loving neighbor. These are the bases of forming a resilient and enduring community.

Paul is also under no illusions about there being any quick fixes to moral dilemmas by means of the Galatians joining a community grounded in the Mosaic covenant. His view is that the Law cannot provide the power or life needed to enable the Christian to be who he or she ought to be. Information without transformation is inadequate, but at the same time Paul understands that he must give some concrete shape to his exhortations to the Galatians. It is not enough to simply say 'rely on the leading and power of the Spirit'. This is why Paul will go on to speak about the Law of Christ. In Paul's view, the Christian and the Christian community has both internal (the Spirit) and external resources (the Law of Christ and the pattern of other Christ-like lives) to guide it in its course of behavior. Furthermore, there is nothing wrong with drawing on the best insights of pagan and Jewish thinking about ethics, so long as these ideas are placed in a Kingdom or Spirit or eschatological context.

The community Paul wishes to form is not like a sect which simply withdraws from the world in hopes of creating a utopian society on a small scale. He wishes his converts to continue to live in, but not of the world. The Christian community is to be a city set on a hill where all can see it, not a light hiding in the wilderness or desert. This is one of the main reasons why establishing Christian community is so hard. There are so many competing other communities right in the neighborhood. In practice this means that Paul must allow a certain amount of porousness to the boundaries of the community, so more can enter and so interaction with the world is possible and ongoing. But porous boundaries also means it is not all that difficult to exit, hence the exhortations about apostasy.

If I were to sum up Paul's thoughts on apostasy, the following can be said: (1) in Paul's view falling from grace is a possibility for believers, though it would perhaps be better to speak of wrenching oneself free from the grasp of God and God's community rather than falling, for the word falling suggests it could happen by accident; (2) apostasy involves defection in the area of both belief and behavior. Theology and ethics are intermingled in Paul's thought. One cannot simply submit to circumcision and observing the Jewish calendar and assume this has no theological implications for one's views about the sufficiency of Christ's death to provide the believer with the resources needed for Christian life; (3) Paul believes that a person is eternally secure only when he or she is securely in eternity. Short of that, Christians live in need of exhortations like we find in Gal. 5–6, and live in hope, fighting to deal with the tension in the Christian life between Spirit's leading and the flesh's urging.

Oscar Wilde once said that he could resist anything but temptation. Paul does not believe that fighting the flesh is a losing battle. While sin remains, it need not reign. Christians can have victory over sin and sins, and they can on the other hand manifest in their lives the fruit of the Spirit. A person who is living a Christ-like life does not need to be constantly reminded of how they ought to act. They will have gone beyond society's basic requirements. Virtue then is not summed up in the adage 'to do what is required', or even 'to obey the Law' but rather Christian virtue is summed up in the phrase to do what Christ would and does do. This is what it means to follow the Law of Christ, as we shall see.

Argument VII: 6.1–10

BEARABLE BURDENS
AND THE YOKE OF CHRIST

Paul's final argument is set off from what precedes it by the apostle's return to addressing his audience as brothers, a signal for a new division in the argument (cf. 3.15; 4.12, 28; 5.13). This final section has been seen by Betz as a collection of rather loosely connected aphorisms or *sententiae*;[1] however, there is a theme that runs throughout this argument, namely doing good rather than evil, and in particular doing good that helps others, especially the household of faith (cf. 6.1, 2, 8, 9, 10 on doing good; 6.1, 3, 4, 7, 8 on avoiding evil or helping others out of it). What Paul intends to do in this section is spell out what characterizes Christian inter-personal behavior, and so make clearer what walking in the Spirit and what the Law of Christ are. Paul will gradually work his way from how to relate to a Christian who has sinned, to how to evaluate one's own life including one's temptations and actions, to how to relate to one's teacher, and finally to how we may expect to be evaluated by God 'at harvest time'. In other words, Paul's ethics are given an eschatological sanction as is also true in 1 Cor. 15. What stand in the background are God's past actions in Christ which set a pattern for believers; what stands in the foreground is God's future action which will bring the divine plan for God's people to completion. Between this already and that not yet stands the believer who is called upon to emulate the behavior of Christ, the ultimate burden bearer, who came to restore not condemn the sinner.

> *Brothers, even if a person is caught in the act of some transgression, you who are spiritual should restore such a one to a proper condition, in the spirit of gentleness, looking to oneself lest even you might be tempted. Bear the weight of one another and thus you will fulfill the Law of Christ. For if someone thinks himself to be someone when he is no one, he deludes himself. But each one must put to the test the work of each, and then each one alone has the reason for boasting, and not unto the other. For each must carry his own burden.*
>
> *But those teaching the word should share with those taught in all good things. Make no mistake, God is not mocked, for whatever a person sows, this also will he reap, so that the one sowing unto his own flesh will reap corruption from the flesh, but those sowing unto the Spirit will reap from the Spirit eternal life. But do not become weary in doing the good,*

---

1. Betz, *Galatians*, pp. 291ff.

for in due time we will reap the same, if we are not slackening. So then while we have time, we do the good to all, but most of all to those of the household of faith.

There is a reasonably clear structure to Paul's final argument, and like the last one it falls into two subdivisions – 6.1–5 and 6.6–10; the former portion focuses mainly on the Law of Christ, the latter portion on the aphorism about sowing and reaping. Barclay has suggested that we see in this material an alternating between words about corporate responsibilities to one another, and words concerning individual accountability as follows:

> 6.1a – corporate responsibility to correct a sinning Christian
> 6.1b – individual accountability – 'look to yourself' (you singular)
> 6.2 – corporate responsibility to bear the burdens of one another
> 6.3–5 – individual accountability – test your own works, bear your own load
> 6.6 – corporate responsibility to support those who teach
> 6.7–8 – individual accountability – how one sows will be how one reaps
> 6.9–10 – corporate responsibility – everyone should do good to all, especially to Christians.[2]

Throughout this argument Paul is seeking to give some specificity to his exhortations in the previous argument, making clearer what the Christian life should look like.

Argument VII, Division 1: 6.1–5

THE LAW OF CHRIST

The question that affects how we interpret all of this advice in Paul's seventh argument is how specific is this advice really? Is Paul simply collecting and arranging some general maxims here that he sees as reasonably apt for his converts' situation, or is this advice more pointed? Without neglecting the spiritual dimension of what is said here, I would suggest that this argument has a social dimension usually overlooked by modern commentators, but it was not always thus. Chrysostom in commenting on this very material not

---

2. Barclay, *Obeying the Truth*, pp. 149–50; cf. also Matera, *Galatians*, p. 218.

only sees 6.6 as an explicit reference to the financial support of Christian teachers, but sees vss. 7–10 as an expansion of the same idea of giving material aid to others, including especially the household of faith. In the course of his exposition of 6.1 he also says "for as rich men convey contributions to the indigent, that in case they should be themselves involved in poverty they may receive the same bounty, so ought we also to do."[3] In a detailed study, J. G. Strelan has argued at length that the primary subject of discussion in this whole passage is matters financial.[4] In support of this conclusion he argues that if one looks to the Greek papyri and other Greek resources the following comes to light: (1) Προλαμβάνειν in 6.1 can refer to money received previously or in advance or money given as a retainer, and παράπτωμα can refer to an error in the amount of payments;[5] (2) In 6.2 βάρος is used at least half the time in Paul's letters to refer to financial burdens, βαστάζειν can mean carry, as in assume someone else's indebtedness,[6] and ἀναπληροῦν often in the papyri means to pay in full, fulfill a contract, make up a debt;[7] (3) in 6.4 δοκιμάζειν refers regularly to the testing of the genuineness of metals and coins (cf. Prov. 8.10; 17.3) while ἔργον is often used of trade or commerce (cf. Rev. 18.17); (4) in 6.5 φορτίον regularly refers to freight, cargo, wares, merchandise;[8] (5) in 6.6 κοινωνεῖν can of course refer to sharing a financial burden or material resources in common (cf. Acts 2.42ff.; 4.32) while λόγος can refer to an account or account of expenses (cf. Phil. 4.14–15);[9] (6) in 6.7–8 we have the language of sowing and reaping, and the only other places in Paul that we have this language, the context indicates that money matters are at issue (cf. 1 Cor. 9.10–11; 2 Cor. 9.6); (7) in 6.9–10 the term καιρός can refer to the time when a payment is due; (8) to this we may add the argument of J. Bligh that the 'household of faith' in 6.10 refers to the Jerusalem Christians,[10] to which L. W. Hurtado has added the suggestion that 6.10 is about the collection for the Jerusalem church.[11] This last suggestion can perhaps build on Gal. 2.10 and it would seem strange that Paul simply drops the matter with the passing reference in 2.10. Another example of the fruitfulness of Strelan's argument can be seen when one pays attention to the fact that 6.3 is connected

3. Though here it is less clear that he understands the word 'burden' as referring to finances.

4. J. G. Strelan, "Burden-Bearing and the Law of Christ: a Re-Examination of Galatians 6.2," *JBL* 94 (1975), pp. 266–76.

5. See Moulton and Milligan, *Vocabulary of the Greek Testament*, p. 489.

6. Ibid., p. 106.

7. Ibid., p. 37.

8. Ibid., pp. 674–75.

9. Ibid., p. 379.

10. See J. Bligh, *Galatians* (London: St Paul, 1969), p. 486.

11. L. W. Hurtado, "The Jerusalem Collection and the Book of Galatians," *JSNT* 5 (1979), pp. 46–62.

to 6.2 by means of a γάϱ. Unless the term is purely superfluous, then one must posit some connection between 'bear one another's burdens' and 'if anyone thinks he is something . . .'. Strelan plausibly suggests that Paul has in mind a person who balks at the thought of having to share a common financial burden with persons of lower social status, because of that person's sense of self-importance. "No matter how important a man is or thinks he is, he is not relieved of the obligation to take a responsible share of the work in and for the Lord."[12]

Or again there can be seen to be a connection between 6.5 and 6.6, with the latter being a qualification of the former. Christians should carry their own weight financially, but when someone gives a great deal of their own time to the task of teaching fellow Christians, there is an obligation to support such a person. This builds on the notion that Paul has in mind a saying of Jesus in 6.6 (cf. below). Not all of this evidence is of equal weight, but taken as a whole the case is impressive. One must, however, bear in mind that Paul is quite capable of using 'material' language in transferred and spiritual senses, for instance when he uses the various terms and ideas associated with slavery to speak of salvation and of service in the Christian community. Yet Strelan's explanation makes good sense of various aspects of the text, and we shall in part be following his suggestions. This means, that far from offering merely general maxims here, Paul in his concluding argument provides us with some very specific examples of what it means to bear burdens and follow the Law of Christ.

6.1 begins the discussion of this subsection with a conditional statement. The protasis is a third-class future more probable condition (ἐάν with a future subjunctive verb), indicating a condition that is deemed likely to happen. The apodosis gives clear directions of what to do if and when such a thing happens, but there is an added statement, by way of concession, to guide how the response should be carried out. The main verb πϱολαμβάνω can mean to forestall or anticipate in the active, and in the passive is usually thought to mean taken by surprise or overtaken or even entrapped (cf. on the meaning of the passive, e.g., Josephus *Ant.* 5.79 cf. Wis. 17.17). The verb never appears elsewhere in the NT in the passive. The verb suggests an unanticipated interruption of an action in progress, not a dealing with an action already completed. Paul uses the term ἄνθϱωπος to indicate the general applicability of this statement – no one is exempt. The phrase 'in some transgression' (ἔν τινι παϱαπτώματι) also indicates that we are dealing with a procedure that should be applicable in a variety of cases, not just when dealing with one specific sort of transgression. This means that the case for Paul having a specific financial kind of transgression here in mind is weak. It is interesting that the

12. Strelan, p. 271.

key term here means literally to make a false step, an apt way of putting it right after Paul has spoken of walking and staying in line with the Spirit.[13]

Paul is, however, talking about a violation of an existing law of some sort.[14] Now it is most unlikely that Paul would be offering up hypothetical remarks about the Galatians violating in the future a law code that he has been urging them not to submit to, especially not in this kind of conditional statement that assumes they will indeed be under this law and likely to violate it. Rhetorically that would be to concede the case Paul has been arguing against throughout the letter which is no way to make one's concluding arguments if one wishes to persuade. We must be dealing here with some sort of law that Paul does see his converts as already under, and in the future, in some danger of violating. There are, it would appear, only two options. Paul is speaking of a transgression against some secular law code or against a code he will mention in this very context – namely the Law of Christ. Strongly in favor of this last suggestion are the parallels in substance between Gal. 6.1 and the teaching of Jesus found in Mt. 18.15, 'If your brother sins [against you], go and point out the fault when the two of you are alone. If the brother listens to you, you have regained that one.' The words 'against you' are very doubtful in this text. They are not included in two very important early witnesses ℵ and B, as well as a significant number of other manuscripts, and their addition is explicable because of the phrase 'sins *against me*' in vs. 21 and copyists' tendencies to make the text have more uniformity and usefulness for church life.[15] Both in Mt. 18.15 and in Gal. 6.1 then, we hear about what to do when a follower of Christ is found to be sinning.[16] In both texts the concern is with restoration of the believer, not disciplinary treatment of him or her. What we are going to discover is that Paul in his final argument will begin each division of his argument (vss. 1 and 6) with his own restatement of two of the 'words' of

13. Matera, *Galatians*, p. 213.

14. On the meaning of 'transgression' in Paul's letters, see pp. 187ff. above.

15. See Metzger, *TC*, p. 45.

16. The family language of 'brother' is common to both these texts, and as P. Esler has stressed, Paul is trying to create in his converts the sense that they are family, and that therefore they should treat each other as family, with the sort of rules in regard to honor and shame being applied that suited the family, not just any sort of relationship. It was widely believed and urged in antiquity that families needed to live in harmony due to the damage done to family honor if this was not the case (cf. Plutarch, *Peri Phil.* 478C). But Paul is not just drawing on conventional notions of family and honor, he is transforming such notions in various ways, such that the family of faith looks not just like a model first-century family, but like the kin of Jesus, who follow his example and imitate his profile. But see Esler, "Family Imagery and Christian Identity in Gal. 5.13–6.10," forthcoming. That Christians met in homes does not necessarily mean that the assemblies simply incorporated the values of the home they met in, though undoubtedly there was some social influence, presumably in both directions (from family to family of faith and vice versa).

Jesus. This, in part, must be considered part of what Paul means by the Law of Christ.

There has been considerable debate about what Paul means by 'you, the spiritual ones'. Is Paul referring to a particular group of Christians in Galatia? This is unlikely on at least two counts. Firstly, whenever we have had the address 'you' previously in this letter, it has always referred to all Paul's Gentile converts in Galatia who are the recipients of this letter. Secondly, Paul in this letter has repeatedly spoken of all Christians as having the Spirit (3.2–5, 14; 4.6, 29; 5.5, 16–18, 22–23, 25; 6.8) and has emphasized that the Galatians received the Spirit when they were converted, indeed this is what distinguished them or set them apart as and to be Christians (cf. 3.1–5). There may be, however, a contrast between the 'transgressor' and the 'spiritual ones', namely all those in the Galatian assemblies not involved in this sinful matter.[17]

The verb καταρτίζετε means to restore or put in order. The goal here is not punishment or expulsion of the transgressor but restoration to the person's former state of rectitude. It may be, in view of the phrase 'such a one' here, that we are meant to think back to 5.21 and the reference to the 'such ones' who will not inherit the Dominion if they continue on that sinful course.[18] This allusion is perhaps even more likely in view of the reference to the spirit of gentleness which seems to be a rather clear echo of the reference to gentleness in the list of fruit of the Spirit at 5.23 (πραΰτης in both cases). In other words, here we have a clear practical example of how the fruit of the Spirit ought to affect one's behavior.

The concessive clause in 6.1c is made more personal and direct by the use of 'you' singular at the end of the clause. Paul is saying 'though you must watch out, lest any one of you (singular) be tempted.' Paul is reminding the correctors that they too are morally vulnerable and so they must take care lest they get caught up in the same transgression. Gentiles correcting Gentiles in regard to sins that they were both vulnerable to in view of their shared pagan past left no room for any attitude of moral superiority on the part of the correctors.

6.2 should probably not be seen as connected to 6.1 as there are no connecting particles here. Notice that the word 'one another' (ἀλλήλων) is in the emphatic position, stressing the placing of others first. The words τὰ βάρη

17. Notice that as in 1 Cor. 5 the whole congregation and not just the leaders are involved in this process, if spiritual means Christians in general. See Barrett, Freedom, p. 79. It is perhaps possible to distinguish the situation here with someone just caught in a transgression, and the situation in 1 Cor. 5, where action is taken after the fact in the case of an ongoing flagrant sin. This may explain the difference in action proposed here as opposed to what we find in 1 Cor. 5.

18. Longenecker, Galatians, p. 273.

refer to some sort of burden or load. It was not uncommon for it to be a reference to a financial burden (see Sir. 13.2, cf. Neh. 5.18). About half the time in the Pauline corpus the term and its cognates refers to some financial burden (cf., e.g., 1 Thess. 2.5–9; 2 Thess. 3.8; 2 Cor. 12.16), and this is quite possible here as well. It will be remembered that there is the exhortation in the Jesus tradition to 'give to everyone who begs from you, and do not refuse anyone who wants to borrow from you' (Mt. 5.42), to which one may add the probable allusions to the Jesus tradition in Jam. 2.15–16. We know for a fact Paul was concerned about the burdens of the poor Christians, as Gal. 2.10 shows. It is thus possible that Strelan is right about this verse and also its connection with 6.3. On the other hand, it appears to me a stronger case can be made that Paul has a broader reference in mind here, which would *include* helping fellow Christians financially (see on vs. 6 below), but is not limited to that sort of aid in this verse.[19]

A strong case has been made by R. B. Hays that Paul has in mind here the example of Christ as the ultimate burden bearer. Even if one limits oneself to what Paul says in Galatians about Christ we hear of 'Christ who gave himself for our sins, so he might deliver us out of this present evil age' (1.3–4), or in 2.20 about 'the Son of God who loved me and gave himself for me', or in 3.13–14 about Christ who 'redeemed us out of the curse of the Law by becoming a curse for us' probably alluding to the notion of the burden-bearing scapegoat.[20] To this we may add the phrase 'the faithfulness of Jesus Christ' a shorthand way of speaking of his obedience even unto death on the cross in conformity with God's plan that he bear the burden of the punishment for human sin. Furthermore, account must be taken of the language in Galatians about both Paul and other Christians bearing the image of Christ, even the image of his passion. "Paul understands his own life as a recapitulation of the life-pattern shown forth in Christ. The most important text here, of course, is Gal. 2.19b–20: 'I have been crucified with Christ. No longer do I live but Christ lives in me.'"[21] In other words, this pattern of burden bearing and self-giving is

19. It is not impossible that Paul is drawing on a well-known maxim here to which he gives a Christian interpretation, as Betz, *Galatians*, pp. 298–99 has suggested. For example, one can point to Menander no. 370 'accept the misfortunes of your friends as your own' or the words attributed by Xenophon to Socrates (*Mem.* 2.7.1–14), 'one must share one's burden with one's friends, for possibly we may do something to ease you'. Even if Paul is drawing on a well-known maxim, by the second half of the verse he has given it an entirely new context and new overtones.

20. Is it accidental that in Jn. 19.17 Christ is said to bear his cross, using the same verb as here?

21. R. B. Hays, "Christology and Ethics in Galatians: The Law of Christ," *CBQ* 49 (1987), pp. 268–90, here p. 280. He rightly points to the similar sort of discussion in Rom. 15.1–9. Another helpful study along these lines is J. B. Webster, "Christology, Imitability and Ethics," *SJT* 39 (1986), pp. 309–26. Also to be consulted is G. M. Styler, "The Basis of

seen as the essence of what Christ was about and so rightly at the heart of what Paul means when he speaks of the Law (or main principle) of Christ. This exemplary pattern is filled out from time to time with the judicious use by Paul of the Jesus tradition as is the case in this very passage. In other words by 'the Law of Christ', Paul does not mean Christ's interpretation of the still binding Mosaic Law,[22] nor even the Torah of the Messiah in some general sense not based in the actual experience of Jesus, including his death on the cross. The apostle who is capable of speaking of two covenants in Galatians, and of a new covenant in 2 Cor. 3 is also perfectly capable of speaking of two different Laws.[23]

The decisive considerations in my mind against other views than the one taken here are: (1) the similarity between what Paul says here and what he says in 1 Cor. 9.19–23 must not be minimized. There Paul distinguishes between the Law of Christ and the Law of Moses and says that the Law of Christ is the same as the Law of God. "In 1 Cor. 9.21, then, the law of Christ has become God's law in place of the law of Moses."[24] In other words C. H. Dodd was at least partly correct when he said "the Torah is not conceived as being identical, or equivalent, or at any rate co-extensive, with the law of God . . . The law of God, which at one stage and on one level finds expression in the Torah, may at another stage and on a different level find expression in the 'law of Christ'".[25] Paul's argument is based on being at a different stage in salvation history since the coming of Christ, and his views of the Mosaic Law are affected by this perspective;[26] (2) as Thielmann points out, in Gal. 2.17–21 Paul speaks about transgressing some Law that is not the Mosaic Law, by withdrawing from association with Gentile Christians. Gal. 6.1 also probably speaks of transgression against some non-Mosaic Law (cf. above). Paul speaks about

---

Obligation in Paul's Christology and Ethics," in *Christ and the Spirit in the New Testament. Studies in Honour of C. F. D. Moule*, ed. B. Lindars and S. S. Smalley (Cambridge: Cambridge University Press, 1973), pp. 175–87.

22. *Pace* Barclay, *Obeying the Truth*, pp. 132–34.

23. The confusion comes from the fact that there is overlap. Christ endorsed a certain amount of the principles within the Mosaic Law as part of his own teaching, in particular the love commandment, but he also declared void other parts, and intensified yet other parts of the Mosaic Law. In other words, he was not engaging in an act of mere covenant renewal, but offering a new covenant between God and his people, which required a new Law.

24. Thielmann, *Paul and the Law*, p. 141.

25. C. H. Dodd, "Ἔννομος Χριστοῦ," in *More New Testament Studies* (Manchester: Manchester Univiersity Press, 1968), pp. 134–48, here pp. 135–37.

26. See Thielmann, *Paul and the Law*, p. 142: "Aspects of Moses' law such as the famous summary in Leviticus 19.18 are absorbed into this new law, but the covenant made with Moses at Mount Sinai is considered obsolete, and in its place Paul has substituted 'the law of Christ'."

being a transgressor if he rebuilds or reaffirms the Mosaic Law (2.18);[27] (3) there is insufficient evidence for a prevalent or clearly defined notion of a New Torah of the Messiah and messianic age in the early Judaism,[28] that is, apart from the NT evidence itself. I would suggest then that Paul is not reflecting ideas from his Jewish heritage here, but drawing out nuances from the way he understood the Christ event and the teaching of Christ; (4) the arguments that Paul always means the Mosaic Law when he uses the term νόμος are frankly unconvincing. For example, Paul is perfectly capable of using this term to mean simply a principle or rule. For example, in Rom. 7.21 it is clear enough that Paul is not quoting or alluding to the Mosaic Law, he is simply saying 'I find it to be a rule that when I want to do the good . . .' Or again in Rom. 7.22–23 he can contrast the Law of God (also called the Law of mind) with another law, and does so even more explicitly in 7.25 with law meaning rule ('the rule of sin') in the second half of the lattermost verse but meaning the Mosaic Law in the first half of the verse. Or again in Rom. 8.2–3 Paul is surely not referring to the same Law from two different perspectives, but to two different laws. The Law of the Spirit of Life in Christ Jesus (Rom. 8.2)[29] has just the opposite effect of the Law of sin and death. The two cannot be equated.[30] Finally, a careful reading of Rom. 3.25–27 shows that Paul contrasts the Law of works, clearly the Mosaic Law, with some other Law, the Law of faith. This latter law has to do with Christ's death (vss. 21–26).

It is over mirror-reading to suggest that the agitators had come up with the phrase the Law of Christ and that Paul has taken it captive and is using it polemically here. Nothing in the immediate context here or in 1 Cor. 9 suggests a polemical edge to the phrase, and what Paul has told us suggests that the only Law the agitators were touting was the Mosaic Law. It is not possible here to sort out all the intricacies of Paul's complex arguments about law and the Law in Rom. 1–8,[31] but at the very least one can say that Paul's use of the term νόμος is far from univocal, and therefore one cannot assume that the Law of Christ refers to the Mosaic Law, especially in view of what Paul has said about the Mosaic Law earlier in Galatians. Finally, if we ask what image Gal. 6.2 would have conjured up in the minds of the Galatians it would have been the story of Christ's life, death, and teaching that Paul had told the Galatians when he was with them. To bear one another's burdens was a fulfillment of the Law

27. Thielmann, *Paul and the Law*, p. 141.

28. See P. Schafer, "Die Torah der Messianic Zeit," *ZNW* 65 (1974). pp. 27–41; *Räisänen, Paul and the Law*, pp. 77–80; Furnish, *Theology and Ethics*, pp. 59–65.

29. I consider this a possible third reference to the Law of Christ beyond the ones in Gal. 6.2 and 1 Cor. 9, though this is uncertain.

30. See rightly Thielmann, *Paul and the Law*, pp. 201ff. against Dunn, *Galatians*, pp. 323ff.

31. I hope to return to this issue before too long in a commentary on Romans.

of Christ because it amounted to taking up one's cross and following the pattern of Christ's life and also heeding his teaching about self-sacrificial behavior.[32]

Christians live in the age of fufillment of prophecies and of covenants, and in general of all God's plans for humankind. There is some debate as to whether in 6.2 the original reading is the aorist imperative ἀναπληρώσατε which is strongly supported by ℵ, A, C, D, K, P and a host of other manuscripts, or the future tense which also has early and impressive support from p46, B, G and most ancient versions. Metzger's committee gives a slight preference to the future reading in view of a possibility that scribes might tend to conform the tense and mood of this verb to that of the main verb in vs. 1.[33] Lightfoot suggests that we should take seriously the prepositional prefix on this verb and so translate 'you will rigorously or completely fulfill' the Law of Christ.[34] He may well be correct, as Paul is still especially addressing those concerned about and contemplating keeping the Mosaic Law and trying to offer them a satisfactory alternative.

Verse 3 may not begin a new subject, but rather may be a further development of what has just been said. Paul is here chastising those who think they are something, but in fact are nothing. This could be a chastisement of those who think they are too good or important for burden bearing. This stands in stark contrast to the pattern of Christ who while he was certainly something and somebody special in Paul's view, emptied himself and made himself as nothing, taking on the form of the servant (Phil. 2). In other words, Paul is probably here making a not too veiled reference to those who are not following the pattern of Christ in the way they live and behave, those who are basing their estimate of self on the basis of false criteria. I would suggest that it may well be that in this verse Paul begins to allude to the agitators. This is plausible if we are meant to take vss. 3–5 together, especially when we peek ahead and see what Paul says about boasting and about circumcision being nothing in 6.11–16.[35] The word φρεναπατᾷ is a hapax legomenon, not only in the Pauline corpus but in all the NT, nor does it appear in the LXX or any other Jewish writing. It refers to deception, in this case self-deception, and presumably the conceit involved leads a person to be unwilling to bear other

---

32. Notice the early interpretation of this key phrase in *Barnabas* 2.6: 'These things then he abolished in order that the new Law of our Lord Jesus Christ, which is without the yoke of necessity might have its oblation not made by human beings.'

33. Metzger, *TC*, p. 598.

34. Lightfoot, *Galatians*, p. 216.

35. The *peroratio* was supposed to sum up matters, not introduce any completely new arguments, which in turn suggests that we should look for what Paul says there in some other form earlier in the discourse.

people's burdens, or perhaps being unwilling to shoulder the burden of the shame of the cross (cf. 6.14–15).

It is important to keep in mind both how natural boasting and self-promotion was in an ancient honor and shame culture, and at the same time how counter-intuitive it was to suggest that some one of higher status should actually step down and become a servant of those less well off and more burdened. The pattern of Christ and the message of the cross went against many of the major social assumptions of Greco-Roman culture. Few pagans were eager to take on the jobs of a slave, which of course included various forms of burden bearing.

Verse **4** shows that Paul indeed operates within a world that had conventions about when and what sort of boasting or self-praise was appropriate and what sort was inappropriate.[36] Notice that Paul does not say that no boasting is appropriate, but that one may consider one's own work a cause for pride, not that of a neighbor. The verb δοκιμάζω appears elsewhere in the Pauline corpus with the meaning of test or approve (1 Cor. 3.13; 11.28; 2 Cor. 13.5; 1 Thess. 5.21; 1 Tim. 3.10) as it appears to mean here, but the word can also mean to accept as proven or approve (Rom. 2.18; 14.22; 1 Thess. 2.4; 2 Cor. 8.22), and finally to think best or even to choose (1 Cor. 16.3). I submit that there may well be a veiled allusion here to what Paul will say more clearly in 6.12–13. There Paul complains about the agitators trying to make a good showing in the Galatians' flesh, and boasting about the Galatians' circumcision (not their own). This is very good illustration of someone judging another, in this case the Galatians, to be in a deficient position, and then wishing to boast in what the Galatians will do in regard to circumcision. Yet the agitators had not been self-critical enough. In Paul's view they thought themselves to be something when in fact they were not, and more to the point, they thought circumcision to be something crucial, when in Paul's view it was an indifferent matter – ἀδιάφορα.

Notice that in vs. 4 Paul is not talking about the eschatological testing of one's works, but rather of critical self-appraisal. The noun καύχημα appears

---

36. I have addressed the issue of what was called in antiquity inoffensive self-praise and how Paul deals with these conventions in *Conflict and Community in Corinth*, pp. 432–37. The key points for this discussion are: (1) self-praise was a primary characteristic of popular teachers of the day, both rhetors and philosophers; (2) it was acceptable to refer to one's own real accomplishments, but it was arrogant to claim more than was the case (see Cicero, *De Inven.* 1.16.22); (3) the extent to which these conventions were followed and considered important throughout the Empire is shown by the treatise of Paul's near contemporary, Plutarch, entitled *On Inoffensive Self-Praise*; (4) Paul tends to use these conventions but in a highly ironic way, as is shown in 2 Cor. 10–13. See the discussion in E. A. Judge, "Paul's Boasting in Relation to Contemporary Professional Practice," *Australian Biblical Review* 16 (1968), pp. 37–48 and in C. Forbes, "Comparison, Self-Praise and Irony," *NTS* 32 (1986), pp. 1–30.

some ten times in Paul's writings (Rom. 4.2; 1 Cor. 5.6; 9.15, 16; 2 Cor. 1.14; 5.12; 9.3; Phil. 1.26; 2.16). Burton stresses that the word does not have as strongly negative a sense as the English word boast, but can refer to exultation that is warranted and not excessive.[37] Here the noun with the definite article probably points to the ground or basis for boasting or exulting.[38] I would suggest it is a mistake, however, to translate the end of this verse as 'in comparison to another'.[39] The point here is not comparison, and the end of the verse should be translated 'and then in himself alone and not in the other he will have a basis for boasting'.[40]

The question then becomes how vs. 5 fits into this scenario of veiled references to the agitators and their malign influence.[41] What is Paul referring to when he says that each person must carry their own loads? Does this not contradict what he has just said in vs. 2? Is there some reason why Paul uses a different word for 'burden' here than in vs. 2? First of all, it is not likely Paul would flatly contradict himself in the span of three or four verses. It is even possible to conclude that φορτίον is a synonym for the word for burden in vs. 2 and still find an explanation for the apparent contradiction between these two verses. One could argue that here Paul is saying that a person who can be self-supporting should not expect others to take care of them, but at the same time if one is able to help bear someone else's burden who really needs the help, this one should do. In other words the two verses are about the difference between an egocentric imposition on other people's good will (vs. 5), and the Christian duty, self-sacrificial in character, for Christians to help each other with life's burdens (vs. 2). It is possible, however, that Paul intends a slightly different nuance to 'burden' here than in 6.2. The term here seems to have been used less frequently in a metaphorical or non-material sense. For instance, in Xenophon *Mem.* 3.13.6 the word φορτίον refers to a soldier's pack, and it is commonly used in this sense. It is most unlikely that Paul is promoting the Greek philosophical notion of self-sufficiency here in vs. 5.[42] Paul doesn't believe in that idea; he believes in the sufficiency of depending on God. Nearer to the mark about this verse is Dunn when he says that the

37. Burton, *Galatians*, p. 333.
38. See Longenecker, *Galatians*, p. 277.
39. Against Longenecker, *Galatians*, p. 277.
40. In other words there is no reason to read this verse in the light of vs. 1. Nothing is said here about comparing oneself with a wrong doer and thereby feeling better about oneself. The issue here is the all too common practice of boasting about (and taking credit for) someone else's accomplishments or actions.
41. If we ask how vss. 1–2 fit in with vss. 3ff. if the latter allude to the agitators, the answer is that Paul is offering positive and negative examples of Christian behavior, behavior that follows Christ's pattern in vss. 1–2, and another sort of behavior that requires rebuke in vss. 3–5.
42. Against Betz, *Galatians*, p. 304, with Dunn, *Galatians*, p. 326.

"mature spiritual community . . . is the one which is able to distinguish those loads which individuals must bear for themselves, and those burdens where help is needed."[43] It is possible, in view of the future tense of the verb 'bear', that Paul has an eschatological scenario in view here – each person will bear responsibility for their own sins or actions (cf. 4 Ezr. 7.104–5). More likely in view of vs. 2, the verb here is gnomic rather than a true future.[44] Had Paul, meant something eschatological here, he probably would have phrased matters a bit differently (cf. Rom. 2.1–10).

If we are meant to see a connection between vss. 5 and 6, with the latter qualifying the former,[45] then another view is possible. I suggest the following hypothesis: (1) the relationship between the word work (ἔργον) and 'burden' in vss. 4–5 must be considered. Paul is talking about a person's own work or gainful employment and how one assesses it; (2) the burden in vs. 5 is indeed a financial one – each person should carry their own financial weight if at all possible and not be an unnecessary burden on another's patronage or charity (cf. above); (3) the exception to this rule is the one offered in vs. 6 which alludes to the teaching of Jesus when he says 'a worker is worthy of his hire', a saying which Paul draws on in several places to affirm that he, and other evangelists and missionaries, had the right to financial support from the congregations they were or had been serving. These proclaimers could refuse such aid if they wished, but they had a right to it, so they could be freed up to concentrate on sharing the Gospel; (4) 'all good things' in vs. 6 refers to material support for the teacher given by their disciples (5) the agitators and whoever followed their lead in and teaching about circumcision, however, were mocking God, sowing unto the flesh and were going to reap the whirlwind in due course; (6) the warning is given to the Galatians lest they follow in the footsteps of the agitators; (7) the Galatians should not weary of doing good of the sort specified in vss. 1–2 and 6 as there will in due course be reward for such and (8) this meritorious doing should concentrate on the household of God, but should also include everyone within its scope. If I am right about the above, there is more of a flow of thought to the argument, especially its second part, than is usually supposed. At this point, however, we must consider some more of the details of the second half of the argument.

43. Dunn, *Galatians*, p. 326.
44. Cf. Betz, *Galatians*, p. 304; Barclay, *Obeying the Truth*, p. 162.
45. Noting the δὲ ('but') in vs. 6.

Argument VII, Division 2: 6.6–10

DOING GOOD TO TEACHERS AND OTHERS

The second half of the argument, which is connected to the first half by δὲ making vs. 6 a qualification of vs. 5, focuses primarily on matters financial. As with the first half of the argument, Paul will begin with his own paraphrasing of a teaching of Jesus, now applied to his Galatian converts' situation. He says 'but the one being taught the word should share in common with the one teaching in all good things'. This exhortation is based on the dominical saying found in Lk. 10.7 and expounded by Paul at some length in 1 Cor. 9.3–14. In that latter text we also have the discussion about being scrutinized or examined by others (9.3), about the right to be supported as teachers of the word (9.6, 13–14),[46] and about teachers sowing spiritual good and reaping material benefits (9.11). These parallels must be allowed to have their full weight, and they make it likely that throughout vss. 6–10, Paul is talking about pertinent financial (and spiritual) matters. It is, however, difficult to know whether Paul here is making a veiled reference to himself, and the Galatians' obligation to support him. This is certainly a topic which comes up regularly in Paul's letters (cf. 2 Cor. 11.7–11; 1 Thess. 2.9; 2 Thess. 3.7–10; Rom. 15.24; Phil. 1.5, 4.15). Then too, the phrase 'the good things' comes up elsewhere in the NT with reference to material support or aid or food (cf. Lk. 1.53; 12.18–19).

Is the singular 'the one teaching' to be taken literally? If so, then a reference to Paul may be meant. The alternative, however, which is perhaps more likely, is to suggest that Paul has in mind some local Christian teacher or teachers in Galatia that are deemed worthy of the Galatians' support. Completely unlikely is a positive reference to the agitators who are on the local scene as worthy of support. The reference to 'good things' here may well prepare us for the concluding exhortation in vs. 10, in which case 'the good' there is not some vague reference, but alludes back to the 'all good things' here, which would include material and financial aid.

There is some debate about whether in vs. 7a we should take the verb πλανᾶσθε as a present indicative ('you are deceived') without the negative qualifier (omitted by Marcion and Tertullian), or as a present imperative 'do not be deceived', but the overwhelming weight of the manuscripts supports

---

46. Notice that it is 'the word' which the teachers teach, here referring to the Christian message, presumably the message of salvation focusing on the story of Jesus Christ.

the latter reading. It was a common interjection before some serious warning (cf. 1 Cor. 6.9; 15.33; Jam. 1.16; Lk. 21.8). Paul is talking about an all too common problem, even among Christians. People assume that they can get away with certain things without God paying attention or without God finally holding them accountable. This is why Paul goes on to say literally 'you can't turn up (or thumb) your nose at God'. The verb μυκτηρίζω refers to turning up the nose or treating with contempt or mocking someone. In a culture where face and honor and shame was very important, to turn up one's nose at someone was to shame them, it was to treat them as someone weak, as someone beneath one's own dignity, and as unworthy of one's respect. Mockery was however a regular practice of rhetoricians and was seen as a species of irony (see Quintilian *Inst. Or.* 8.6.59). God, however, could not be duped by rhetorical sleight of hand or human rationaliziations.

The verb μυκτηρίζω is a NT hapax legomenon, but it and its cognates are found quite commonly in the LXX especially in the Wisdom literature and the Psalms (cf. Job 22.19; Ps. 44.13; 80.6; Prov. 1.30 of mocking God [cf. Ezek. 8.17]; Prov. 11.12; 12.8; 15.5, 20; 23.9). The idea here is that one cannot act with impunity and not expect God to take notice or hold one accountable, even as a Christian. Judgment of all human actions is certain.

Paul then quotes in vs. 7b what was probably a proverbial saying found in both Greek and Jewish literature (cf. Aristotle, *Rhet.* 3.3.4; Plato *Phaedrus* 260D; Job 4.8; Prov. 22.8; Jerm. 12.13; Sir. 7.3; Test. Levi 13.6), in order to provide backing or basis for the warning just given. For our purposes what is important to stress is that the only other two places where Paul draws on this metaphor, in 1 Cor. 9.10–11 and in 2 Cor. 9.6, financial matters are at issue. This sort of use probably goes back to the discussion in Prov. 22.7–9: 'The rich man lords it over the poor, the borrower is the lender's slave. He who sows injustice reaps disaster and the rod of anger falls on himself.' Notice too that the exhortation not to grow weary in doing good also shows up in 2 Thess. 3.13 at the end of an exhortation about earning one's own living and not being idle.[47] If we put all this together the meaning of vss. 7–8 becomes clearer.

Verse **7b** gives us a statement about anyone, including Christians (ἄνθρωπος), which Paul then applies in vs. **8** using his flesh-Spirit antithesis. I would suggest that the sowing unto the Spirit which Paul has in mind is the supporting of proper teachers, materially and otherwise. Verses 6–8 must be read together. The sowing unto one's *own* flesh (εἰς τὴν σάρκα ἑαυτοῦ) could refer merely to selfish and self-centered behavior or even to sexually immoral behavior. In view of the overarching argument and purpose of this entire letter, however, it is quite believable that we have here a reference to circumcision, especially since Paul says not merely 'unto the flesh' but 'unto one's *own* flesh'.

47. See Strelan, p. 272.

The result of following the latter course is corruption which can be contrasted with eternal life in the former case. Corruption here means not merely death, but probably eternal death which is seen as the opposite of resurrection (cf. 1 Cor. 15.42, 50).[48] Paul here, as in Gal. 5.21, is indeed suggesting that the behavior of Christians affects their eternal status and reward. One must compare the strong words in Gal. 5.3–4 about those who let themselves be circumcised, cutting themselves off from Christ, having fallen from grace. It is interesting that Paul here suggests that it is the Spirit who is the dispenser of eternal life in the future.[49] Paul does not often use the term 'eternal life'. In the undisputed Paulines there is only this verse and Rom. 2.7; 5.21, and 6.22–23.

Despite Ziesler's confident assertion that by the phrase 'eternal life' Paul means life with God in heaven,[50] if one looks closely at each of these Pauline texts it seems far more likely that he means the life which will be dispensed to believers when the Lord returns, when judgment has been rendered, when resurrection has happened and death has been overcome. For example, Rom. 2.1–8 has various parallels to our text and needs to be cited in part here for comparison's sake: 'Therefore you have no excuse . . . when you judge others; for in passing judgment on another you condemn yourself . . . But by your hard and impenitent heart you are storing up wrath for yourself on the day of wrath, when God's righteous judgment will be revealed. For he will repay according to each one's deeds; to those who by patiently doing good seek for glory and honor and immortality, he will give eternal life; while for those who are self-seeking and who do not obey the truth but wickedness there will be wrath and fury.' The context shows that Paul has a historical conclusion to matters in mind, not an other-wordly one. In Rom. 5.21 Paul speaks of sin exercising dominion in death and grace exercising dominion through justification leading to eternal life. Once again, eternal life is seen as something the believer gets in the future, nothing is said of heaven. Similarly in Rom. 6.21–23 while sanctification is said to be now, eternal life (like death) is said to be in the audience's future, but nothing is said about receiving it at death or in heaven. Paul simply says that the τέλος, the end or aim or goal, is eternal life. Elsewhere, the τέλος is associated with what happens when Christ returns to earth and the dead are raised, not what happens in heaven at the believer's death (cf. 1 Cor. 15.24). In the later Paulines as well, eternal life is seen as in the

48. See Matera, *Galatians*, p. 216.
49. The future tense of the verb θερίσει is probably to be taken seriously. If so, then Paul is not talking about present salvation here, any more than he is talking about present judgment in vss. 8–9. Eternal life then is seen as a future state here, to be equated with entering the Dominion of God. One becomes eternally secure when one is securely in eternity.
50. Ziesler, *Galatians*, p. 97.

future (cf. Tit. 1.2; 3.7; 1 Tim. 1.16; 6.12). Finally, in the Jewish discussion of eternal life, which arises only after most of the canonical OT books were already written (cf. Dan. 12.2; 2 Macc. 7.9; Ps. Sol. 3.12; 1QS 4.7; Philo, *Fuga.* 78; 4 Macc. 15.3), "the language emerged in Jewish theology in connection with the hope of resurrection"[51] not the hope of life everlasting in heaven.

In vs. 8 then Paul has contrasted an essentially self-directed act, getting oneself circumcised, with concern for and actions on behalf of others. The former is of the flesh, the latter is of the Spirit. This comports with the overall theme of this section stressing others regarding actions and warning against selfish ones. It also comports with the same sort of discussion of the relationship of present deeds and future destiny in Rom. 2 as we have seen above.

Verse **9** warns against weariness in doing good (here καλόν rather than ἀγαθόν, but they are basically synonyms; cf. 2 Thess. 3.13), and promises that at the appropriate time in the future a harvest will be reaped by these doers, if they do not give up. Since this verse is connected to vs. 8 by a δέ we should probably see a qualification here of the preceding remark. This verse like the last suggests the pay off is in the future. The eschatological note in the phrase καιρῷ . . . ἰδίῳ should not be missed and it refers to the appropriate or proper time, or one might translate 'in due season' in view of the sowing and reaping metaphor. The implication is that this time is set by God (cf. especially 1 Tim. 6.15 and also 1 Tim. 2.6). It is worth pointing out that Paul is implying that the end may not be imminent – worrying about weariness, perseverance and not giving up are not apposite if one is convinced the Lord's return is *necessarily*, not merely possibly, imminent.[52]

The final adverbial participle ἐκλυόμενοι sets a condition on reaping. It will not happen for individuals, even for Christian individuals, automatically. They must not grow weary of well doing and also they must not give up. Here as elsewhere Paul conjures with the possibility that those currently in Christ might commit apostasy or give up the faith, and so miss out on eternal life and the rest of the eschatological benefits (see 5.3–4). Paul is not saying a person is saved *by* good works, but he is saying that where there is time and opportunity for doing such things, one will not be saved without them. They are not optional extras in the Christian life. "For Paul, the fruit of a spiritual harvest comes through the concurring actions of both God and the believer, with the believer's perseverance being generally in response to the Spirit's work in his or her life and specifically an expression of the virtue 'patience.'"[53]

51. Dunn, *Galatians*, p. 331.

52. On this whole subject, and the misreading of Paul's eschatology by A. Schweitzer and his offspring, see my *Jesus, Paul, and the End of the World*, passim and see Dunn, *Galatians*, p. 332.

53. Longenecker, *Galatians*, p. 282.

In vs. 10 Paul will conclude his argument by making a little clearer what he means by sowing unto the Spirit, a little clearer what vs. 9 was meant to imply. Ἄρα οὖν 'therefore then', here as elsewhere in Paul signals the conclusion and or a main point of an argument (cf. Rom. 5.18; 7.3, 25; 8.12; 9.16, 18; 14.12, 19; Ephes. 2.19; 1 Thess. 5.6; 2 Thess. 2.15). Its presence here makes quite clear that it is inadequate to see this section as simply individual maxims with little or no connection to one another or with the larger argument of the letter. The qualifier for what follows is 'as time allows' or 'as we have time (and opportunity)'. Paul says that we Christians (both the author and the audience here as in vs. 9) should 'work the good to all'. Paul has absolutely nothing against working, or good works, his earlier critique had to do with very specific sort of works – the works of the Law. Indeed, Paul throughout this whole argument in vss. 1–10 has argued for the necessity of good works by his converts, as well as the necessity of avoiding bad ones. Doing good to all would surely at the very least include charitable works toward the needy and poor. The phrase 'the good' is not a philosophical term here but must be seen in light of the reference to all good things in vs. 6 and the good in vs. 9. Paul qualifies his final positive exhortation by urging that especial efforts should be made on behalf of the household of faith.

The phrase 'household of faith' is a significant, and probably a sectarian phrase referring to those who are bound together in a spiritual family by their shared Christian faith and life. "The phrase is presumably constructed in conscious contrast to the typical OT 'house of Israel' (e.g., Num. 20.29; 2 Sam. 1.12; Ezek. 3.4; Judith 4.15; Ps. Sol. 17.42), or some such sectarian variant as we find in the DSS – 'the house of truth in Israel' (1QS 5.6), 'the house of holiness for Israel' (1QS 8.5) . . . and 'the house of the Law' (CD 20.10, 13). In which case it will be significant once again that the bonding characteristic of this household is faith, and not membership of ethnic Israel, and not the Torah."[54] This specific phrase is only found elsewhere at Ephes. 2.19, and in neither case does the context suggest either that there is a particular focus on the fact that the church met in houses at this stage of their existence[55] or a particular focus on some specific group of Christians in a particular location, such as the Jerusalem church.[56] Thus, while it is not impossible that Paul is

---

54. Dunn, *Galatians*, p. 333. This remark, which is right on target, makes various of Dunn's other remarks about Torah and continuity with Judaism very difficult to comprehend. Paul is using sectarian language here.

55. The term οἰκεῖοι means literally those persons of the same household, but it could also mean in a wider sense kindred or even friends; cf. Philo *Cher.* 20.

56. Esler, "Family Imagery," p. 15 of mss. forthcoming suggests that "the congregations were actually swept up into the social realities, the roles, values, institutions, of particular families in the cities in which they were located." I would suggest there was influence in this direction as 1 Cor. 11 shows in regard to family meals, but that Paul is

alluding to the need to contribute to the poor in Jerusalem, I think this is unlikely especially in view of the rather universal way the matter is put. The Galatians are to do good to everyone (Christian and non-Christian alike), and the particular subset of that larger group on which they must devote especial attention consists of Christians, not just the Jerusalem church. Had Paul said do good to all Christians, and especially to the household of faith, then Hurtado's suggestion might have more plausibility.[57]

We have now come to the end of Paul's formal arguments, and we have seen that Paul ended with some practical exhortations about what the Galatians ought and ought not to be doing. Far from being vague and purely general, Matera is probably right that we have here "a moral exhortation that is precise, concrete, and practical."[58] They are to restore erring Christians, bear one another's burdens, support their teachers, and indeed do good to all, especially to Christians. In all of this they are following the pattern of life and teaching of Jesus, which Paul calls the Law of Christ.

In contrast to self-indulgent behavior the Galatians are to evaluate themselves critically, not to over-estimate themselves, nor boast about what others have done. The example of Christ, not the example of the agitators was to be followed, especially in the matter of sowing unto their own flesh (i.e., circumcision) as opposed to doing self-sacrificial works that benefit others. Such good works would not go unrewarded, just as bad works would not go unnoticed by God at the appropriate eschatological time for judgment. Thus the Galatians find themselves with the example of Christ (and Paul) behind them and the eschaton before them and their behavior as Christians is to be shaped in light of this already and not yet. They must not turn back to the Law of Moses, but go forward following the Law of Christ, a Law which requires an other-directed orientation in life, not one that focuses on self, and one's anxieties about one's own condition. Notice that in this passage as a whole,

---

also trying to Christianize 'family values' not simply baptize existing ones. The influence goes in both directions, and to a real degree Paul is deconstructing some of the concepts of family honor and shame in his letters, not least by offering servant models of leadership and behavior.

57. See Hurtado, "The Jerusalem Collection," pp. 54–56. It is no mystery that the collection is not stressed in this letter, if this is the first Pauline letter we have. We could say, however, that the exhortation in 6.1–10 could be seen as a priming of the pump in regard to financial responsibilities within the body of Christ, which would prepare the way for a later exhortation about the Collection. Notice that there is nothing in this letter even remotely comparable to the remark affecting both Paul's advice to Galatia and to Corinth which we find in 1 Cor. 16.1–3. This strongly suggests to me that 1 Corinthians must be seen as a letter written after Galatians. Had it come before Galatians, the absence of any clear discussion of the Collection in Galatians is very hard to account for.

58. Matera, *Galatians*, p. 217.

Paul has been illustrating in practical fashion how the fruit of the Spirit, such as love, gentleness, goodness, self-control, patience, acts of kindness can be manifested in the community's life.[59]

As we have tried to demonstrate there is a cohesiveness to all Paul's arguments in Galatians, the more paraenetic and social ones still have theological grounding, and the more theological ones still have ethical implications. While a bit of an overstatement, Hays is basically right when he says there "is no meaningful distinction between theology and ethics in Paul's thought, because Paul's theology is fundamentally an account of God's work of transforming his people into the image of Christ."[60] Sometimes there is more focus on God's part in this process, sometimes more on the Christian's response but the overarching goal of conformity to the image of Christ is the same in either case. Thus in a very real sense the story of Christ is to be recapitulated in the life not merely of Paul but of all Christians. If one does not recognize the narrative framework of Paul's teaching, one will not understand the 'plot' of his arguments here in Galatians. Failure to see the narrative framework especially leads to a misunderstanding of Paul's view of the Mosaic Law. We have sought to avoid that pitfall by making the mistake of trying to pigeonhole Paul as either a legalist or a libertine. In Paul's view the Law of Christ and the work of the Spirit were the outer and inner aspects of Christian life that guide and guard, prod and protect Christians as they move forward toward the due season of eschatological harvest. Christians do not stand between Sinai and the promised land, but rather between Golgotha and glory. Understanding this salvation historical perspective is the key to understanding Paul's narrative thought-world.

Bridging the Horizons

Obviously, in a general way much of this advice is easily transferrable to our own day. What is often lacking when such a transfer is made is the eschatological framework and Christological focus of the advice. To take the advice outside of the eschatological framework is not only to forget the source of the sanction for the exhortation but also to forget that Christians are a pilgrim people – they live in hope, with one eye on the horizon, looking for and believing in God's final resolution of the human dilemma. To ignore the Christological paradigm and story out of which this advice comes is to reduce

59. Longenecker, *Galatians*, p. 271.
60. Hays, *Moral Vision*, p. 46.

this material to mere good advice. But Paul does not believe such advice can be followed except by means of the power of the Spirit of Christ and then too he assumes his audience have a rather full mental picture of what following Christ's example must entail. His narrative thought-world, and the fact that he lived in a time when there were still many who had a living memory of Jesus must be recognized.

In a very real sense we live in the most litigious age in human history. Very few people wish to take responsibility for their own actions, if they are not laudable, never mind taking responsibility for others. The cry 'take personal responsibility' often heard in our time is not enough. It is not enough to own up to one's own actions and duties, Christ also calls the believer to have a plan of deliberately undertaking self-sacrificial and charitable works. The Christian is to be pro-active not just reactive to the misery index in society.

We may well ask why Paul says 'especially to the household of faith'. I would suggest the reason is because the Christian community is not an insular community but rather a community of witness. If the community cannot and does not take care of its own, why should any onlooker believe Christians are sincere when they speak of doing good to all or of Christ's concern for all? One must remember that the Galatians were probably in the early stages of their Christian life, and it was especially crucial that they establish a pattern of behavior that would be a good witness in their largely pagan environment.

The sort of advice we find here has been taken and fruitfully applied in numerous different settings. One excellent example of how the material can be transferred to a modern setting can be seen in Dietrich Bonhoeffer's classic works *Life Together* and *The Cost of Discipleship*. Bonhoeffer himself, of course, paid the last full measure for his belief in following the example of Christ, for he was executed by Hitler as one of the last acts of hate undertaken by the Nazis at the end of World War II. His was not merely an armchair faith or a mere notional assent to the following of the sort of advice we find in Gal. 6.[61]

The ultimate moral sanction which Paul mentions in this section is of course the final judgment by God. In a moral universe, even a moral universe gone wrong, it must be the case that there is some sort of final reckoning or else God is indeed an absentee landlord about whom no one ever need worry. What Paul affirms in his sowing and reaping metaphor, however, is also that sin, however pleasurable in the undertaking, always has consequences, bad consequences even in this lifetime. We see this fact again and again when we have to deal with the problems arising from sexually transmitted disease spread by means of sexual promiscuity. Paul believes in a moral world not primarily because he believes that the universe is programmed in some fatalistic sense so that 'what goes around comes around' but because he believes the one who

---

61. See McKnight, *Galatians*, pp. 293ff.

came around before will come around again demanding accountability and that also God has made human beings so that moral living is a key to happiness, good health, and longevity. In other words, there is not only a sanction but also an inherent incentive underlying Paul's exhortations.

In the end Paul believes it is possible, by the grace of God, to follow the Law of Christ, and actually be a concrete help to others who are in need. At the same time he believes that all those who are able to take care of themselves should not seek to become a burden to others. Paul is not looking for disciples who are hoping for fellow burden sharers to lighten their own load, he is looking for disciples who are prepared to be burden bearers, with a willingness to make sacrifices to help others in need. The Law of Christ is seen as both practical and practicable as the believer lives between already and not yet.

Paul's Autograph: 6.11

Gal. 6.11 reminds us that Paul is not simply offering a speech or a discourse, but rather doing these things within an epistolary framework. As we shall see shortly, Paul is far more concerned with following rhetorical rather than epistolary conventions as he concludes Galatians, but nonetheless he does not fail to give at least a nod in the direction of the rules of first-century letter writing, as is evident here in this verse.

> *See with what large letters I write to you in my own hand.*

There are a variety of imponderables about this verse. Should we take the Greek to mean that Paul has been writing this letter all along in his own hand, but only now reminds his audience of the fact? This was in fact the view of Chrysostom who took the aorist verb here to be a real rather than an epistolary aorist (see with what large letters I wrote to you . . .),[1] and argued that Paul, because of the urgency of the matter in Galatia, had taken the trouble to offer a full length testimony, written personally and with great labor. Against this suggestion is the fact that we know from Rom. 16.22 that Paul did use scribes to compose his letters, and we have numerous examples where Paul closes his letters or refers to the one he is now writing using an epistolary aorist (see Rom. 15.15; 1 Cor. 5.11; 9.15; Philem. vss. 19, 21 and Phil. 2.28; Col. 4.8 and Philem. vs. 12).[2] The evidence is considerable that it was a very regular

---

1. Chrysostom also has another interesting suggestion, namely that the word translated 'large' really means crude or clumsy, but this is unlikely; see below.
2. An epistolary aorist is a verb tense which reflects the time when the letter is read rather than when it was written. In other words, when the Galatians read this letter Paul's writing of it was of course a past event.

procedure for the author to take up the pen at the end of the letter and add anything from a signature, to a final farewell, to a closing personal note, to a final exhortation and benediction, as here.[3] There is even clear evidence of a different handwriting style in the concluding part of a letter or subscription from the one in the bulk of the letter (see P. Oxy. 265, 499, 513 for records with this trait, and P. Lond. 897 and 1173 for letters with this trait). In other words, when one finds two different hands, the author's is alway the one that adds the conclusion, not the one that wrote the bulk of the letter, for no one would employ or use an amanuensis just to write subscripts! Occasionally, though it is rare, we find in the papyrus letters the attempt to summarize or at least mention the main concern of the letter once again in a clear way in the subscript, to emphasize the point (P. Oxy. 264), but more often we find appended an extra personal note, not related to the body of the letter.[4] In other words, it is much more likely that Paul is following rhetorical than epistolary conventions in what follows 6.11.

It is perhaps possible that one could translate Gal. 6.11 'see what long letters I write to you . . .'. The problem with this conjecture is that while γράμμα in the singular and the plural can certainly refer to a letter (cf. Herodotus 5.14; P. Grenf. 1.30.5; 1 Macc. 5.10; Acts 28.21), as Lightfoot says we would have expected not γράμμασιν γράφειν here, but rather γράμματα γράφειν. The former surely means to write *with* letters,[5] and furthermore when Paul wants to speak of epistles rather than characters of the alphabet (cf. 2 Cor. 3.7 on the latter) he regularly uses the word ἐπιστολή in either the singular or plural (Rom. 16.22; 1 Cor. 5.9; 16.3; 2 Cor. 3.1; 7.8; 10.9–11; Col. 4.16; 1 Thess. 5.27; 2 Thess. 2.2, 15; 3.14, 17). The above means that the usual translation of this verse is probably the correct one.

There is something of a textual problem in regard to the word πηλίκοις. Some manuscripts have the classical form of this same word ἡλίκος, in particular p46 and B. In either case the meaning is the same.[6]

The question becomes *why* Paul is writing these words, and presumably the remainder of the letter with such large letters. Notice that Paul says 'see with what large letters . . .' implying that he expects his audience actually to

---

3. See G. J. Bahr, "The Subscriptions in the Pauline Letters," *JBL* 87 (1968), pp. 27–41; J. A. Fitzmyer, "Some Notes on Aramaic Epistolography," *JBL* 93 (1974), pp. 201–25; and R. N. Longenecker, "Ancient Amanuenses and the Pauline Epistles," in *New Dimensions in New Testament Study*, ed. Longenecker and M. C. Tenney (Grand Rapids: Zondervan, 1974), pp. 281–97.

4. See Bahr, pp. 32–33.

5. See Lightfoot, *Galatians*, pp. 220–21.

6. In fact πηλίκος is the interrogative pronoun which NT authors tend to prefer in such a case, unlike the classical writers (cf. Mk. 2.24; 15.4). See Bligh, *Galatians in Greek*, p. 216.

examine this document, perhaps with the reader of the document holding up the last portion so the congregation could view it. Whatever else this imperative signifies, Ziesler is probably right that it implies that there was originally only one copy of this letter with Paul's handwriting which circulated through the Galatian congregations, being carried from place to place by Paul's messenger.[7]

Some have concluded that the large letters signify emphasis, as if Paul were offering us the ancient version of bold print, and this may well be correct. Yet in other Pauline epistolary conclusions, Paul refers to taking up the pen but says *nothing* about large letters and there were points he wanted to stress in those letters too (cf. Philem. vs. 19; 1 Cor. 16.21; Col. 4.18a; 2 Thess. 3.17).[8] In each of these other cases, Paul refers to writing a greeting in his own hand, except in Philemon where Paul takes the pen to offer a sort of promissory note. In other words, Gal. 6.11 is distinct from these other references in its reference to large letters, but they at least confirm the thesis that Paul regularly used amanuenses. I would suggest that it is wrong to dismiss the suggestion that Paul writes with large letters at least in part because of his own eye difficulties,[9] difficulties that seem to have plagued him while he was in Galatia (cf. 4.15) and continued to bother him when he wrote this letter.[10] This is not an unimportant point as it would help explain why some complained about Paul's weak ethos. The visual impression his appearance left would have been considered rhetorically bad form (see 2 Cor. 10.10).[11] Paul's concern and his belief in the urgency of the situation in Galatia helps to explain why Paul writes a good deal more than a closing greeting here compared to other letters. He writes his own *peroratio* as he wants to make sure the audience understands his main points.

That Paul used scribes is beyond dispute, but how, and how much did he use them? Much would depend on the caliber of the scribe and of how much he was trusted by Paul. It would appear from Rom. 16.22 (cf. 1 Cor. 1.1, the mention of Sosthenes; Col. 1.1, the mention of Timothy) that Paul used his

---

7. Ziesler, *Galatians*, p. 98.

8. Longenecker, "Ancient," p. 290 suggests Paul's letters were large in comparison to the scribes smaller regular hand.

9. See pp. 36ff. above.

10. Barrett, *Freedom*, p. 84 makes light of this view: "The suggestion that his sight was defective and that he was obliged to write [with] a large and flowing hand is one of the unintentional jokes of New Testament criticism." This simple dismissal is a mistake; cf. J. S. Clemens, "St. Paul's Handwriting," *ET* 24 (1912–13), p. 380. Another conjecture, originally by A. Deissmann, is that the large letters reflect an artisan's handwriting, caused by too many years toiling with one's hands. But cf. W. K. L. Clarke, "St. Paul's Large Letters," *ET* 24 (1912–13), p. 285.

11. See my discussion of this verse in my *Conflict and Community in Corinth*, ad loc.

own Christian co-workers as scribes. The trust factor therefore was probably strong. The question is how much facility these persons had. Could they take word-for-word dictation? This was not impossible, as there were forms of short hand in the first century that scribes could use (cf. Plutarch, *Lives* Cato the Younger 23; Seneca, *Ad Lucilius Epist. Mor* 15.25). It is also possible, however, that Paul delineated the main lines of discussion and left the composition to his trusted co-worker. Least likely, in the case of Galatians, is that Paul simply left the composition to the scribe, and then added a few concluding remarks. "In the case of Galatians, however, given the severity of the crisis, it seems unlikely that Paul would have commissioned anyone to write in his name without first defining the content of the letter to be written. Moreover, given the highly theological nature of the argument, and the emotional tone of this letter, it seems most probable that Paul took an active role in the composition of Galatians, perhaps dictating it word-for-word."[12] Paul's own Gospel and the Christian life of his converts were believed to be hanging in the balance. It is hardly likely Paul would have left the composition of this letter to another.

As Betz says, the autographic postscript serves to authenticate the letter, and it also strongly suggests care in the composition of the document for "the very employment of an amanuensis rules out a haphazard writing of the letter and suggests the existence of Paul's draft and the copy by an amanuensis, or a sequence of draft, composition, and copy. The highly skillful composition of the letter leaves us the choice of attributing this high degree of epistolographic expertise to Paul, to the amanuensis, or to both."[13] I quite agree with Betz that the creativity we find in the composition of this document, which involves a flexible use and combination of the epistolary and rhetorical conventions, strongly suggests that more than just a scribe stands behind this document, whoever's hand may have done the actual writing.[14]

12. Matera, *Galatians*, p. 229.
13. Betz, *Galatians*, p. 312.
14. Ibid.

Peroratio: 6.12–17   The Sum of the Matter

Those who have done epistolary analysis of Galatians have often puzzled over the end of this document. A typical Hellenistic letter concludes with a brief health wish and a farewell, for example 'I pray for your health continually together with that of your children. Farewell'.[1] We find nothing like this at the end of Galatians, unless one counts the final benediction as a health wish, which is stretching things.[2] In fact we do not find a whole host of elements normally associated with the end of a letter: (1) there is no mention of travel plans; (2) there are no final greetings; (3) there are no prayer requests; (4) there is no expression of joy; (5) there is no doxology; (6) the final peace benediction is conditional.[3] In other words, the ending of this letter is in some respects not even typical of Paul's own letter writing habits. It does not follow from this, however, that Paul is haphazard in the way he concludes this document. The tone is extremely serious, not light-hearted or friendly, and this prepares admirably for a *peroratio* which is full of sound and fury and pathos. In fact, in 6.12–17 we find a carefully crafted *peroratio*, the proper conclusion to a rhetorical composition.

As regards to whether a *peroratio* was necessary in a deliberative speech such as we find in Galatians,[4] it must be remembered that the *peroratio* had

1. See S. Stowers, *Letter Writing in Greco-Roman Christianity*, (Philadelphia: Westminster, 1986), p. 61.

2. However, there is evidence from Aramaic letters written by Jews of opening greetings that are like benedictions, e.g., A.P. 30.1–3: 'May the God of Heaven be much concerned for the well being of our lord' (Bagohi), and at the end concluding mentions of *shalom* (5/6 Hev. 4.5 and 11.3). See Fitzmyer, pp. 214–17 here.

3. See Longenecker, *Galatians*, p. 289.

4. Longenecker, *Galatians*, p. 287 seems to assume this was only a feature of forensic rhetoric, which is incorrect.

two major functions: to sum up the most essential parts or points of the previous act of persuasion *and* to arouse the emotions, to which one might also add amplification on major points. It will be seen shortly that Gal. 6.12–17 does both of the first two of these and amplification is not absent either. Notice here what Quintilian says about the appeal to the emotions: "these are especially necessary in deliberative oratory. Anger has frequently to be excited or assuaged and the minds of the audience have to be swayed to fear, ambition, hatred, reconciliation. At times again it is necessary to awaken pity . . ." (*Inst. Or.* 3.8.12). Even more to the point, various examples of a *peroratio*, or as the Greeks called it an ἐπιλόγος which focuses on summing up, can be cited from deliberative speeches (cf. Demosthenes *Or.* 3.36; 2.31; Isocrates *Or.* 5.154; Aristides *Or.* 23.80). It was thus quite appropriate for Paul to end a deliberative discourse in this fashion.[5] Furthermore, it is stressed in *Rhetorica ad Alexandrum* 33.1439b.12ff. that the recapitulation within the deliberative 'epilogue' could take five different forms – argument, enumeration, proposal of policy, interrogation, or irony. Here we have basically a summary of argument with an implied proposal of policy (do not be circumcised) and a strong attempt to arouse rejection of the agitators (vvs. 12–13) and empathy with Paul (vss. 14, 17).

Betz's analysis is basically right that here Paul first offers the *recapitulatio* or summation of the major argument, coupled with the *indignatio* or arousal of anger against the agitators,[6] followed by the *conquestio*,[7] a final remark which stimulates pity for the speaker and his cause (6.17). He is also right that there needed to be some correspondence between the *peroratio* and either the *exordium* and/or the *propositio*, in this case both of these two parts of the speech.[8] The conclusion makes clear what the other Gospel being advocated was, and how the Gospel of circumcision was not to be followed, as it was not the true Gospel. Instead the Galatians must stay faithful to the Gospel Paul had preached when he was there, a Gospel summed up in the *propositio* in 2.15–21.

In an excellent study, J. A. D. Weima has shown the logical connection between the various elements in this *peroratio*.[9] This section is built upon a series of antitheses between the views of Paul and those offering 'another

5. It is to be noted that most ancient rhetorical experts saw recapitulation, emotional appeal, and amplification as the three parts of the 'epilogue' (Aristotle, *Rhet.* 3.19.1; *Rhet. ad Her.* 2.30; Cicero, *De Invent.* 1.52.98–99) But Quintilian (*Inst. Or.* 6.1.1–2) speaks of these as different types of conclusion. Paul is here following what was largely the Greek tradition in this matter.

6. See Cicero, *De Invent.* 1.55.106.

7. Cicero, *De Invent.* 1.55.106.

8. See Betz, *Galatians*, p. 313.

9. See J. A. D. Weima, "Gal. 6.11–18: A Hermeneutical Key to the Galatian Letter," *CalvTheoJourn* 28 (1993), pp. 90–107.

Gospel': (1) boasting in circumcision versus boasting in the cross; (2) seeking to avoid persecution for the cross versus willingly accepting such persecution and bearing the marks of the crucified one; (3) compelling someone to be circumcised versus seeing circumcision or uncircumcision as an indifferent matter; (4) living under the influence of the old age versus living under the influence of new creation. As Weima goes on to show, the thing that really upsets Paul about the agitators' message and efforts is that the offense and the importance and the sufficiency of the cross is in his view removed by their message and efforts. Notice the close connection between persecution, circumcision and the cross in Gal. 5.11, as here in 6.12–17. Even vs. 17 is seen to be a logical part of this final argument for what Paul is talking about is that he has been persecuted for the message of the cross he preached.[10]

It must be stressed that what the *peroratio* tells us is that the *most* fundamental thing Paul wants his audience to understand and embrace is not the experience of the Spirit or even justification but rather the cross. Justification is only possible, and the Spirit can only be experienced, because of the prior reality of the cross. For the agitators to neglect or downplay or vitiate the message of the cross is to cut off the very foundation of the faith, the very essence of the Gospel, the very means of salvation. Ultimately, neither circumcision nor uncircumcision matters to Paul, unless of course an emphasis on its necessity undercuts the heart of the Gospel. Then, the Holy Grail has been touched and Paul must respond with his whole arsenal. This, explains the tone, the polemics, the urgency we sense throughout this letter. It is because, in Paul's view, so much is at stake, that he must respond as he does. The message of the cross and the cruciform pattern of Christian life are non-negotiables for this apostle.

Thus, understanding that we have a *peroratio* in 6.12–17 means understanding that we have here the essential clarification and summing up of the real issue prompting this letter and of Paul's advice that we have needed all along. As Betz rightly stresses: "It contains the interpretive clues to the understanding of Paul's major concerns in the letter as a whole and should be employed as the hermeneutical key to the intentions of the apostle."[11] Indeed it provides a key to understanding much that is at the heart of Paul's theological and ethical and social vision of the world and the Christian life in general. It will thus repay us to examine these concluding verses especially closely.

> Those who wish to make a good showing in the flesh, they try to force you to be circumcised, only in order not to be persecuted for the cross of Christ. For not even the circumcised themselves observe the Law, but they wish

10. See Weima, pp. 98–101.
11. Ibid.

you to be circumcised in order to boast in your flesh. But God forbid I should boast except in the cross of our Lord Jesus Christ through whom the world is crucified to me and I to the world. For neither is circumcision nor uncircumcision anything, but a new creation. And to those who will keep in line with this rule, peace upon them and mercy and upon the Israel of God. From now on let no one provide me any more trouble for I bear the marks of Jesus in my flesh.

In order to understand vs. **12** it is important once again to emphasize the importance of the concept of face and honor in Paul's world. The verb εὐπροσωπέω, found only here in the NT, means literally to present a good face, hence the translation to make a good showing or a good outward appearance. The people in question are concerned about their honor rating with someone or some group. As Bligh says, the phrase to make a good showing in the flesh means much the same as to boast in the flesh.[12] In neither case is the term flesh used in the moral sense we found at the end of Gal. 5. The boasting in this case is about circumcision, and not their own circumcision but rather that of the Galatians. If with Bligh we ask what sort of person boasts in what is done to someone else's private parts, the answer must surely be Jews, and in this case Jewish Christians.[13] Here we have nearly conclusive proof, if any were needed, that the agitators were not Gentiles.[14] When Gentiles became Jewish proselytes in the first-century A.D., they endured circumcision, they did not boast about it, as its social cost to a non-Jew was evident even to Jews (cf. Josephus *Ant.* 20.38–42 on King Izates to Martial 7.82).[15] In fact, various Romans closely associated circumcision with castration, seeing both as abhorrent.[16]

It is difficult to know how much weight to put on the verb ἀναγκάζουσιν. Some would translate it 'they try to force you', or even 'they force you'. While this may be a correct translation, it appears nearly certain that since Paul is busy trying to dissuade the Galatians from submitting to the rite what he means is 'they bring moral pressure or acts of persuasion to bear on you'. Here it surely has the same sense as in 2.3 and 14 of moral not physical compulsion. One must not forget that in the *peroratio* it was normal to use emotionally charged and polemical language in the last-ditch effort to persuade one's audience to follow one's advice.

12. Bligh, *Galatians in Greek*, p. 217.
13. Bligh, p. 217 makes the interesting suggestion that Paul is insinuating a comparison between the agitators and David, who won his bride by collecting 100 Philistine foreskins (1 Sam. 18.27)!
14. Against J. Munck, *Paul and the Salvation of Mankind* (Richmond: John Knox, 1959), pp. 87–90.
15. See the Excursus below pp. 455ff.
16. See J. P. V. D. Balsdon, *Romans and Aliens* (London: Duckworth, 1979), pp. 216, 231.

In the second half of vs. 12 Paul tells us clearly why they are under-taking this activity – 'only in order that they not be persecuted because of the cross of Christ'. Since Paul will go on to give other reasons why the agitators are acting in this way, we may take the μόνον as rhetorical, added to emphasize what Paul saw as the main underlying reason. The connection of persecution and circumcision was also found in 5.11, only there in reference to Paul. It has been debated how seriously we may take Paul's psychological analysis here. Is Paul just using the old rhetorical ploy of accusing his adversaries of cowardice, of acting out of fear rather than on the basis of principles? Is this just an example of *indignatio*, the casting of odium on one's opponents in order to remove the audience's admiration of and inclination in their direction?[17] Presumably, the agitators would have seen the matter differently. Furthermore, we may ask, who is doing the persecuting and where?

The theory of Jewett was of course that there was a Zealotic persecution going on in the late 40s in Judea, and I think he is probably right.[18] After all, since Saul had engaged in such activities in less trying times in the early 30s, why should we be surprised about such activities in the late 40s after the rule of the virulently anti-Semitic Caligula with his oppressive policies, and during the reign of Claudius who alternated between oppression and limited tolerance of Jews?[19] If this persecution in Jerusalem and Judea of the Jewish Christians is what the agitators are concerned about, then their motives may have involved more than just self-preservation.

Paul says, however, that they are motivated by their desire personally to avoid persecution for the cross. If the agitators are still in Galatia this would presumably at least involve a reference to fear of being persecuted by Galatian Jews, a not unreasonable fear if one takes Acts 13–14 to be anything like an accurate historical account.

B. W. Winter has suggested that the problem being dealt with here has to do with Gentile Christians being caught out because they no longer observed the rites of the Emperor cult. "Becoming Jewish was the solution that would protect all the Jewish Diaspora Christians from persecution. In the eyes of the authorities of Galatia they would all be Jewish and not a mixed association. Those Gentiles who joined them and observed the Jewish law in daily life would, as Jewish converts, be exempt from the imperial cult."[20] Winter suggests that the sort of 'face' that is at issue here is Jewish Christians having good legal

17. See Betz, *Galatians*, pp. 313–14 and cf. Cicero, *De Invent*. 1.55.106.
18. On which see pp. 21ff. above.
19. See my discussion of Claudius in *The Acts of the Apostles*, pp. 507ff.
20. B. W. Winter, *Seek the Welfare of the City* (Grand Rapids: Eerdmans, 1994), p. 136. Winter also thinks the Judaizing pressure is coming from Jewish Christians who are part of the Galatian communities. If this were the case, we would expect Paul to know who is bringing this pressure to bear, but in fact he does not seem to know.

face in the community with both Jewish and Gentile officials, and also these Jewish Christians securing a good legal face for Gentile converts who were caught out since they no longer participated in the Emperor cult. Circumcision and keeping the Mosaic Law would secure this good legal face for they would then be associated with a 'licit' religion, since it would exempt them from having to be participants in the Emperor cult.

This argument is plausible, but there are several potential problems with it: (1) Paul is basically silent on the Emperor cult in this letter. The issues he raises and problems he deals with are Jewish in character, though it is possible he alludes to the cult very indirectly earlier in the letter.[21] Whether this is so or not, the Emperor cult is surely not uppermost in Paul's mind in this letter; (2) when in the earlier part of the letter we hear about persecution connected with Christ, it had to do with Jews like Saul persecuting Christians and this persecution had nothing to do with the Emperor cult. Here too persecution is said to be for the cross of Christ, not for non-observance of the Emperor's rites. In fact it appears Paul says nothing about the Galatian Gentiles themselves being persecuted;[22] (3) we would have thought that it would be the Gentiles among the Galatian Christians who would be under the heavy pressure if observance of the Emperor's rite lay in the background here; (4) nothing is said about civic officials providing the impetus for persecution or pressure being brought to bear.[23]

I thus must conclude that while I think Jewett is right about what was going on in Judea, and this explains the action of the men who came from James in Antioch (Gal. 2), it probably does not fully account for this text about the agitators in Galatia. We must presume, I think, that the agitators were concerned about their honor rating and relationship with local Jews in Galatia, and wished to be able to report to them that they were proselytizing Gentiles and that in due course they would come around to accepting the Mosaic Law including circumcision in addition to what they believed about Jesus. Gradualism was after all a widely accepted approach in early Judaism to the acceptance of Gentiles within the people of God, as the existence of God-fearers in the synagogues shows.[24] In this way the agitators could maintain friendly contact in and with the local synagogues as well as with the Christian community in Galatia, and furthermore could report to Jerusalem that an

21. See pp. 298ff. above.

22. See above pp. 214ff. on Gal. 3.4.

23. Winter, *Seek the Welfare*, pp. 125ff. is, however, certainly right about the presence and importance of the Emperor's cult in various places in Galatia (we are certain about Pisidian Antioch and Iconium). I would suggest that this cult and its stipulations may be part of what Paul means when he speaks of the στοιχεῖα which Gentiles were under before conversion.

24. On which see my *The Acts of the Apostles*, pp. 350ff.

approach satisfactory to the most conservative Jewish Christians, and presumably various Jews as well, was being pursued on the mission field. The above scenario best accounts for all the data in Galatia.

In vs. 13 we probably find the phrase οἱ περιτεμνόμενοι (supported by א, A, C, K, P and others, and note the present tense in 5.2–3),[25] so here we have a clear characterisation of the agitators as the circumcision party. Paul says they do not themselves keep the Law. Again one must ask how seriously to take this. Is this just polemics, or is it perhaps a reflection of Paul's own past (and present) rigorist view of keeping Torah? Bear in mind that Paul says in this letter that the one who submits to circumcision is bound to keep every last jot and tittle of it (Gal. 5.3).

What we know of Saul the Pharisee from Gal. 1, Acts, and Phil. 3.4–6 all leads to the conclusion that Paul is judging the agitators on the basis of his own (former) high legal standards. He would be saying, I know personally what it takes to keep the Law, and the agitators themselves fall far short. Thus, this may not be mere polemics, but Paul's genuine assessment.

We learn more clearly than before in vs. 13c that the agitators 'wish you to be circumcised' which tells us that Paul does not think the deed has transpired quite yet. There is still time for dissuasion. At the end of this verse, Paul provides us with a second rationale for why the agitators are insisting on circumcision. So they can boast about their accomplishments among the Gentile Galatians to Jews. Here again the term 'flesh' must be taken literally, not as a moral term.

You can tell a lot about a person by what they boast of. In vs. 14 Paul makes clear that he would rather be cursed than boast in anything other than the cross of 'our Lord Jesus Christ'. The δὲ which introduces this remark is clearly adversative, as Paul sets up a contrast between himself and the agitators, punctuated by the use of μὴ γένοιτο.[26] Notice too the emphatic position of 'to me'. Paul has personalized the struggle here in the *peroratio*. The audience is forced to make a choice between their loyalty to Paul and his Gospel or to the agitators and theirs.

---

25. The perfect, περιτετμημένοι, is, however, supported by good witnesses (p46, B, ψ, 614 and others), which make the agitators those who 'had been circumcised' and so possibly Gentiles, or it could even refer to the Galatian Christians who had already been circumcised but were not yet keeping the entire Law. As Longenecker, *Galatians*, p. 292 rightly suggests, however, had Paul meant Galatian Christians who had been circumcised he would surely have been likely to use the aorist passive substantival participle, not the present. Furthermore, Paul consistently speaks of his Galatian audience in the second person and the agitators in the third person as distinguishable from his converts. When Paul says 'Who has cast the evil eye on you Galatians' (see pp. 201ff. above), he is surely not referring to some of his own converts. The rest of the argument in Galatians stands against the Gentile theory of Munck.

26. See pp. 186ff. above.

The last portion of vs. 14 is especially important as it shows us once more Paul's apocalyptic perspective on things. When he was converted to Christ, through[27] the cross of Christ he was crucified to the world and the world to him. It is possible to read the Greek here to mean that through the *person* of Christ, Paul was crucified to the world.[28] This, however, is less likely in view of the emphatic position of the word cross, and the focus on the cross in this concluding section of the discourse.[29] In any case it does not matter greatly since as Betz says for Paul Christ was always the crucified One – the two things went together.[30]

Paul is saying his conversion to a belief in a crucified messiah entailed an enormous transvaluation of values, and an adoption of a new paradigm of what God was really doing in the world, how he was doing it, and therefore what the believer's life meant. But notice Paul is not simply talking about an experience that happened to him. He also says that the world was crucified to him, by which he means that he believes that the death of Christ on the cross changed the world, it had cosmic effects. Paul has partially addressed this subject when he spoke about what the Galatians had been freed from – the elementary principles of the universe which enslave fallen human beings,[31] and it is attended to even more fully in the later Paulines (cf. especially Col. 2.15 to Ephes. 4.7–10). Here Martyn is quite right to stress the importance of this phrase and the mention of the new creation and connect them both with Gal. 1.4.[32]

In Paul's view the present evil age exists, but has been dealt a death blow by the crucifixion of Jesus. All of the world's basic values and assumptions and operating procedures have been put on notice that they are passing away (cf. 1 Cor. 7.31). What really matters are the new eschatological realities brought about because of the death of Christ. In Paul's view, even the Law, as well as other good things about the material world, are part of the things that are passing away or are fading in glory (cf. 2 Cor. 3). Having lost their controlling grip on a human life when Christ came and died, one must not submit to such forces again, but rather live on the basis of the new eschatological realities. The new age has already dawned and Christians should live by its light and follow the path it illuminates.

Thus Paul is able to say quite frankly in vs. **15** that 'neither circumcision nor uncircumcision *is anything*, but a new creation'. That which has real

---

27. Διά not ἐν here.
28. The genitive relative pronoun οὗ could be either masculine referring to Christ or neuter referring to the cross.
29. See rightly, Bligh, *Galatians*, p. 219.
30. See Betz, *Galatians*, p. 318.
31. See the discussion pp. 284ff. above.
32. See Martyn, "Apocalyptic Antinomies," pp. 410ff.

existence, that which has reality and meaning is that which has begun and will last forever, that which has the power to recreate human life, not that which has had its day and is ceasing to be. The phrase καινὴ κτίσις is an important one, and it reappears in 2 Cor. 5.17. Κτίσις is a verbal noun which can mean either the act of creating or the result of that act, and if one chooses the latter option it can be taken either collectively referring to the creation, or individually to the creature. Rom. 8.19–22 suggests the former of these two options (cf. 8.39), but the fuller parallel in 2 Cor. 5.17 suggests that Paul means new creature, though even there one could translate 'if anyone is in Christ, there is a whole new act of creation'.[33] Perhaps the contrast here with the 'cosmos' gives a slight edge to the translation 'new creation', and it may be that Paul is drawing on Is. 65.17–25.[34] It is difficult, however, not to hear in the background the language used in Judaism about proselytes being as newborn children, especially since the agitators wanted to treat the Galatians like proselytes.[35] Paul is then saying, as he has all along in this letter, you already have in Christ what they are offering you through the Law.

Verse **16** offers a conditional benediction on whoever is prepared to keep in step with this rule. The word κανών here of course does not mean canon in the later sense of the term but rather is closer to its root meaning of a rule or means of measuring the straightness of something. Paul is saying that the new creation, not circumcision or uncircumcision, is the measuring rod by which persons should evaluate their lives. Dunn puts it this way:" By 'rule' . . . Paul means clearly the norm by which he lives and judges the 'other gospel' . . ."[36] If they are part of the new creation, neither circumcision nor uncircumcision really matters. The former will add nothing to their status or condition and the latter will take nothing away. If the Galatians are part of the new creation, they are already part of God's eschatological people. The verb στοιχέω here is used in much the same manner as at Gal. 5.25 and refers to living in line with or keeping in step with something, here with 'the rule' just given.[37] The 'them' referred to in vs. 16b must surely be the 'whoever' of vs. 16a, and equally certainly must refer to those in Paul's audience who will follow Paul's dicta.

The end of vs. 16 is, however, quite awkward, for Paul adds '. . . and mercy and upon the Israel of God'. Now it is of course possible to translate the second καὶ here as 'also' so that Paul would be saying '. . . and mercy also upon the

33. See Bligh, *Galatians*, p. 220.
34. See Hays, *Echoes*, pp. 156–59.
35. See my *Conflict and Community in Corinth*, p. 395.
36. Dunn, *Galatians*, p. 343.
37. It is worth pointing out that this verse shows that Paul has nothing against laying down certain rules or ruling principles which he expects his converts to follow. This is part of the Law of Christ, which involves more than just the pattern of Christ's life being experienced and lived out in the Christian.

Israel of God', in which case Paul would apparently be pronouncing peace on one group and mercy upon another. The possibilities of who this other group would include: (1) non-Christian Jews, in which case the usage here would foreshadow some of what we find in Rom. 9–11 where Paul foresees a future, apparently by means of eschatological miracle, for the nation of Israel; (2) Christian Jews, and perhaps in particular those that he is upset with in Jerusalem, Antioch, and Galatia. If the latter is meant then this could be something of a last-minute olive branch offered in direction of the adversary, or if stress is placed on the word mercy Paul might be saying 'and may the Lord have mercy on the circumcision party (because they will face God's judgment for this)'. This latter interpretation dovetails nicely with the curse invocations on the agitators in Gal. 1.8–9, so Paul would be ending where he began with them.

Many interpreters, however, have understood the final καί here to mean 'that is' in which case the text reads 'peace upon them and mercy, that is upon the Israel of God'. In other words, Israel here refers to all Christians, both Jews and Gentiles united in Christ, both the author and his audience, and others. Now it is important, as Longenecker points out, that the phrase 'the Israel of God' occurs nowhere else in Paul, nor can it be found in the extant writings of second temple Judaism or even in later rabbinic writings.[38] It is possible this is a phrase used by the agitators, which Paul has taken over and given a different sense, but there is no way of knowing if this is the case. We must interpret the phrase in the context of this letter, and secondarily in the larger context of Paul's thought, and perhaps we may consider for a moment the suggestion that Paul is modifying or editing the Nineteenth Benediction used in synagogue worship which reads 'bestow peace, happiness, and blessing, grace and loving-kindness and mercy upon us and upon all Israel, your people'. Notice not only the similar reference to peace and mercy but also the partial distinction between us and all Israel. The problem is, however, that we do not know the date of this benediction. It may or may not have existed in Paul's day, though certainly a text like Ps. 125.5 was known.[39]

In my view one of two possibilities is the more likely. Paul may be referring to Jewish Christians here that he has been arguing against in this letter and saying 'may God have mercy on them'. The distinction between two different groups of Christians is in fact possible in the Pauline corpus, and I would suggest we find it in the later Pauline material in Ephes. 1–2 (see especially 2.11–3.6, but also 1.1) where the saints are Jewish Christians to be distinguished from the Gentiles who have now become co-heirs of the promises with them (cf. Rom. 15.25). It seems clear, however, that in Ephes.

---

38. Longenecker, *Galatians*, p. 299.
39. See Barclay, *Obeying the Truth*, p. 98 and notes 53 and 54.

2.12 the commonwealth of Israel refers to Jew and Gentiles united in Christ, even though the author can still distinguish between the saints and the Gentile believers. In other words, this text does suggest distinctions were possible, but the term Israel is used there of the church. If it favors any view, it favors the view that Israel here also means the church. This brings me to the second, and I think, far more likely view.

N. A. Dahl in a crucial essay has pointed out the following: (1) Paul has been arguing throughout Galatians for a sectarian understanding of the people of God, and in particular he has been arguing that the promise to Abraham is for those who are in Christ – both Jews and Gentiles. Paul transfers a variety of ideas and terms in this letter formerly used only of Jews and converts to Judaism and now uses them of Christians;[40] (2) elsewhere Paul is perfectly capable of distinguishing between a true and false Israel, or an Israel according to the Spirit as opposed to an Israel according to the flesh. He says quite explicitly that not all Israel is true Israel (cf. Rom. 2.29; 9.6; Phil. 3.2–3; 1 Cor. 10.18; Gal. 4.21–31), and when he refers to true Israel he means those who believe in Jesus as the crucified messiah.[41] To this may be added the fact that Paul frequently uses the 'other' name for God's people, namely 'the assembly (*qahal*) of God' to refer to the church, indeed he does so in this very letter (Gal. 1.13; 1 Cor. 1.2; 10.32 et al.).[42]

Finally, if I am right that Paul distinguishes between the Mosaic Law and the Law of God now expressed in and as the Law of Christ, we must expect a transfer of the term Israel to Jew and Gentile united in Christ. As Weima says it "is difficult to believe . . . that in a letter where Paul has been breaking down the distinctions that separate Jewish and Gentile Christians and stressing the equality of both groups, that he in the closing would give a peace benediction addressed to believing Jews as a separate group within the church"[43] much less to non-Christian Jews whom he nowhere really discusses in this letter.[44] Paul will wrestle with the fate of non-Christian Jews in Rom. 9–11, but they are not in view here.

Verse 17 is a bit anti-climactic. Τοῦ λοιποῦ probably means 'finally' here, rather than 'from now on' though either is possible (cf. 1 Cor. 1.16; 4.2; 2 Cor. 13.11; Ephes. 6.10; Phil. 4.8; 1 Thess. 4.1; 2 Thess. 3.1 for the meaning 'finally'; 1 Cor. 7.29; 2 Tim. 4.8 and possibly Phil. 3.1 for the meaning 'henceforth'). Paul is concluding his *peroratio*. Paul warns the agitators indirectly and those of the Galatians who side with them directly. The warning is 'let no one

40. See, e.g., pp. 272ff. above.
41. See N. A. Dahl, "Der Name Israel: Zur Auslegung von Gal. 6.16," *Judaica* 6 (1950), pp. 161–70.
42. See Barclay, *Obeying the Truth*, p. 98.
43. Weima, "Gal. 6.11–18," p. 105.
44. Against Dunn, *Galatians*, pp. 346–48.

continue to cause me work' or more likely κόπος means 'trouble' here (cf. Sir. 22.13; 29.4; 1 Macc. 10.15; Lk. 11.7; 18.5). Paul gives as his reason for this warning that he bears the marks of Christ. The term στίγματα does not refer in all likelihood to the later phenomenon of people miraculously manifesting the wounds of Christ on their own body, nor should the word be translated brand, since it is in the plural. Paul is surely referring to the fact that he is indeed being crucified to the world in the sense that he is suffering for his message of the cross, and it may well be that he is referring literally to his wounds and scars incurred when he was persecuted for his preaching (2 Cor. 11.23–27; cf. Rom. 8.17; 2 Cor. 1.5; 4.8–10; Phil. 3.10; Col. 1.24). Rhetorically speaking it was considered somewhat risky and gruesome to display graphic evidence such as wounds to create an emotional response at the end of a speech, but the practice was certainly not unknown (see Quintilian *Inst. Or.* 6.1.32). It was more likely to be used in Asiatic-style rhetoric which was more given to display and hyperbolic language than Attic rhetoric, and Asiatic would appear to be the style that Paul uses.

There may be, however, something else lying in the background here, especially since this verse involves a warning. It was a well-known practice for a person to dedicate themselves or be dedicated to a particular god in order to come under the god's protection (see, e.g., already Herodotus 2.113 and Lucian, *De Dea Syr.* 59; and on the use of the word 'stigma' in this fashion Pseudo. Phocy. 212).[45] Like the mark of Cain (Gen. 4.15; cf. Ezek. 9.4; 3 Macc. 2.29–30; Rev. 7.2–4), Paul may be saying that the marks of Christ are on him, and those who trouble Paul also trouble Christ, indeed those who mess with Paul's Gospel may find themselves under a curse. In this case, Paul would be drawing on the ancient idea of a talisman, and suggesting that the marks of Christ on him should have warned people off from troubling Christ's agent or apostle. In a world where the evil eye notion was very much alive, a warning about talismans from a deity would be readily accepted as a very serious one indeed. Paul was a marked man.

Notice, as Chrysostom points out that Paul says here 'I bear' not 'I have', echoing the description of Christ and Christians in general being those who bear burdens. Chrysostom adds "these wounds utter a voice louder than a trumpet against those who say I play the hypocrite in my teaching, and speak what may please men. For no one who saw a soldier retired from the battle bathed in blood and with a thousand wounds would dare accuse him of cowardice . . ." Rhetorically it might be very effective to say 'see my wounds' if the goal is to create pathos,[46] but whether effective or not, it still echoed the

---

45. The religion of the Cybele in Galatia is relevant at this point as well. See Lightfoot, *Galatians*, p. 225.

46. See pp. 443ff. above.

Christ who himself is said to have made such a gesture on one occasion (Jn. 20). At this point it will be in order to say a few things in some detail about circumcision.

Excursus: Circumcision and Decision ——————————————————

It is of first importance to recognize that circumcision, while not widely practiced in the western end of the Roman Empire, was in fact a regular practice in the Ancient Near East and as a result in the eastern part of the Empire.[47] Certain groups of Egyptian men, in particular priests, at least slit the foreskin, and there is evidence that various western Semitic groups, not just in Palestine but also in Syria, removed the foreskin entirely.[48] There is evidence of the rite being practiced in Syria as early as the third millennium B.C.[49] Our interest, however, is not so much in the origins of the rite, which, wherever and whenever the rite began, Jews had been practicing for a long time before the NT period, but with its practice just before and during the NT era.

It is important that Greek sensibilities were to accept public nudity but to reject the notion of circumcision. Indeed so repugnant was this idea to Greeks that various sources indicate that even those simply born with a short foreskin would sometimes submit to epispasm, surgery designed to lengthen and so restore the foreskin to its proper size and shape (cf. Celsus, *Med.* 7.25; Soranus, *Gynecology* 2.34; Discorides 4.153). Some Greeks were so concerned about not revealing the penis head that they had the foreskin held in place with a string or even a pin (*fibula* – hence the name of the practice, infibulation; Celsus *Med.* 7.25.2; cf. Martial 7.82). This attitude about a visible penis head continued among Greeks right through the Hellenistic era and was later shared by the Romans. The great satirist Martial represented the attitude of many Greeks and Romans when he made circumcision the object of ridicule and various course jokes (see his *Epigrams* 7.35, 82). The degree of repulsion can be gauged by the fact that at least two rulers, one from just before and one from just after the NT era, prohibited circumcision on pain of death – Antiochus Epiphanes (around 160 B.C.; cf. 1 Macc. 1.48, 60–61; 2 Macc. 6.10) and of course the Emperor Hadrian in the early second century A.D. Even during the NT era, after the Jewish war (A.D. 66–72) a tax was levied on circumcised Jewish males, with the funds going to support the worship of Jupiter Capitolinus. This was no doubt in retaliation for the rebellion itself. Suetonius tells us that this practice was even enforced on an elderly Jewish man who had not been a practicing Jew for a long time (*Dom.* 12.2). In other words, one could not avoid the stigma of Jewishness if one was a circumcised male by ceasing to be a Torah-observant Jew.

47. See J. M. Sasson, "Circumcision in the Ancient Near East," *JBL* 85 (1966), pp. 473–76.

48. See R. G. Hall, "Circumcision," *ABD* I, pp. 1025–34. This excursus is indebted throughout to the seminal work of Hall; see also his "Epispasm and the Dating of Ancient Jewish Writings," *Journal for the Study of Pseudepigrapha* 2 (1988), pp. 71–86.

49. See the text that was on a stele in *ANET*, p. 326.

One may be surprised to learn that despite all of this there were various pagans who were in fact not only attracted to Judaism, and prepared even, if need be, to submit to circumcision (see Juvenal *Sat.* 14.96–106) and that various Jews encouraged them to do so (Horace *Sat.* 1.4.14–43). It is important to recognize that these last references occur, as in the case of the material in Martial in the context of satire, so it is not always easy to know how much to trust what is said. One must assume that conversion to Judaism was a familiar enough topic and a frequent enough occurrence, even though involving only a tiny minority of pagans, that satirists could assume the audience would not only understand the satire, but agree with the repugnance that such things actually happen to Greeks and Romans.

Hellenised Jews, which is to say almost all if not all Jews in the NT era, felt both the effects and burden of these attitudes when Greco-Roman culture became the dominant culture throughout the Mediterranean crescent. Jews who wanted to use the public baths or even share in Greek athletics faced ridicule from Greeks and Romans if they were circumcised, and ostracism from many of their fellow Jews if they tried to have the evidence of circumcision removed. This problem was especially severe for lower class Jews. As Hall says "Greek athletics offered lower class boys of ability one of the readiest avenues for social and economic advancement, but since athletes competed naked, those who were circumcised could not compete".[50] Furthermore, in Greek cities in the Empire, such as Alexandria, sometimes citizenship depended on completion of training to be an ephebe, which training involved exercising in the gymnasia. Winter rightly stresses that the reason for reversing circumcision related primarily to social standing and career opportunities and only secondarily to concerns about ridicule.[51]

The response of Jews to the attitudes of the dominant culture varied. Some became overly Hellenized and sought to have the marks of circumcision covered up (see Martial *Epig.* 7.35, 82 by infibulation; and by epispasm, see 1 Macc. 1.15; Josephus *Ant.* 12.241; cf. 1 Cor. 7.18). Others simply tried to explain the fact in a way Greeks and Romans might accept, still others had an allergic reaction to various aspects of Hellenization and then Romanization, and so emphasized circumcision more than ever as a necessity for God's people. The book of Jubilees, written some time in the 170s B.C., is extremely helpful in revealing this attitude of reaction to Hellenization. The most telling passage is Jub. 15.25–34. Here Moses learns that circumcision is necessary because evil spirits or demons rule the nations. Circumcision removes a person from the evil sphere and into the realm of God and God's presence. "Circumcision determines the sphere in which one lives: the uncircumcised are dominated by evil, the circumcised, being ruled by God, experience his blessing."[52] Even more intriguing is the way that the Qumran community further developed the theology of circumcision by suggesting that circumcision freed one from the angel of enmity (CD 16.4–6), and to go further afield, Test. Levi 6.3 implies that circumcision exempts a person or group from experiencing the coming wrath of God against the heathen and apostates. We also find in books like Judith a stress on

50. Hall, "Circumcision," p. 1027.
51. Winter, *Seek the Welfare*, p. 152.
52. Hall, p. 1028.

the need for proselytes to be circumcised (Judith 14.10 – already mentioned in Esther 8.17). The relevance of these passages to the study of Galatians should be immediately apparent. While the agitators may have been urging that the Galatians needed to be circumcised to make a full and clean break with the present evil age, Paul by contrast was urging that this break happened by means of grace through faith in the crucified Christ who dispensed the Spirit to the believer and thereby conveyed God's very presence to the person in question.[53] Christ's being cut off by God made unnecessary submission to the sign of the oath curse by Christ's followers.[54]

It is interesting that some early Jewish sources suggest that circumcision might not be required of proselytes, though in some cases baptism was required instead (see Sib. Or. 4.163–70; Philo, *Quaest. Ex.* 2.2; cf. *Spec. Leg.* 1.52–54), and Ignatius seems to know of those who teach Judaism but themselves are not circumcised (*Phil.* 6.1).[55] The agitators in Galatia clearly enough do not fall into this camp. They are what one might call hardliners on this issue, as Saul no doubt was prior to his conversion.[56] It is worth stressing, however, that there is a salient difference between Paul and the agitators. Paul as a missionary seeks to convert to the Christian faith those who are simply pagans as well as Jews. The agitators seem to be dealing only with those already in the Christian community. Their target audience is different, and they would seem to reflect the larger general picture that Judaism was not by and large engaged in proselytism of Gentiles in the first century.[57] Fredricksen is, however, surely right that like the agitators, Paul spent time in synagogues (as 2 Cor. 11.24 proves) and evangelized there. Perhaps one reason his congregations were subject to the agitators' appeals is that there were at least some Jews and some former Gentile God-fearers in the Galatian churches who would support their arguments. According to Josephus and also Philo, God-fearers could be found in any urban location in the Empire where there were also Jewish communities, as certainly was the case in south Galatia (cf., e.g., *War* 7.3.3; *Ant.* 14.7.2).

We have spoken previously of why pagans would find the appeal to rituals and sacred times cogent.[58] It is also plausible that the agitators also understood that if the Galatians submitted to circumcision at their hands, it would be a tacit admission of the agitators' authority over them.[59] Here we can simply add that there may have been a concern on the part of various pagans that it was needful to be associated with a recognized ancient religion, not an unsanctioned *superstitio*. However much many educated Greeks and Romans may have despised Judaism, there was even greater

53. See Hall, p. 1030.
54. On this point see pp. 239ff. above.
55. On the issue of Jewish ideas about proselytism and salvation see my *The Acts of the Apostles*, pp. 397ff.
56. See J. J. Collins, "A Symbol of Otherness: Circumcision and Salvation in the First Century," in *To See Ourselves as Others See Us*, pp. 163–86.
57. On this point see S. McKnight, *A Light among the Gentiles* (Minnesota: Fortress, 1991) and P. Fredricksen, "Judaism and Circumcision of Gentiles, and the Apocalyptic Hope: Another Look at Galatians 1 and 2," *JTS* 42 (1991), pp. 532–64.
58. See pp. 301ff. above.
59. See Barrett, *Freedom*, p. 84.

opprobrium associated with being part of a new and unrecognized religion. Thus we see that part of Paul's strategy in Galatians is to suggest that his Gospel goes back to Abraham, and that the people he is referring to are Abraham's descendants, indeed are the true Israel of God. This appeal was necessary in a world where in matters religious, older was often thought to be superior and more reliable.

The last verse of Galatians, vs. **18**, provides us with a simple but meaningful benediction. Paul prays or wishes for God's grace to be with the turbulent spirits and troubled congregations in Galatia. It is more than a perfunctory wish, for this is what Paul wanted them not merely to experience but to focus on and believe in. Notice that the final two words are 'brothers' and 'amen'. Thus, Paul ends reaffirming one last time his family ties with his converts, however, upset with them he has been, and he leaves the entire matter in God's hands, saying 'may it be so'.[60] The letter thus ends where it began, with the invocation of God and God's will.

Bridging the Horizons

The issue of cultural imperialism is an important one. There is a sense, as McKnight says, that the agitators could be called the cultural imperialists of their day.[61] They believed that everyone needed to become a Jew to be a true follower of Christ and a true descendant of Abraham. Their understanding of the Gospel was ethnically narrow, and Gal. 1 and Gal. 3.28 shows that Paul's answer to such a message was μὴ γένοιτο, no way! Before we feel too superior, however, it is well to remember the sort of cultural imperialism that has gone along with the spread of the Gospel even in the twentieth century. Often missionaries have carried not just Christ but the message and values of Western capitalism with them to Africa, Asia and elsewhere, often with devastating effects. The assumption that all cultures are or ought to be just like American or European culture makes the sharing of the Good News exceedingly difficult.

Consider for example the plight of the young missionaries from the Midwest of America who went to evangelize an African tribe untouched by the Gospel. Without cultural training about those they would minister to, they shared the story of Christ's betrayal by one of his own disciples, his death and his resurrection. They discovered to their amazement that the tribe they were trying to reach viewed treachery and trickery as admirable, and so they assumed that Judas was the hero of the story! It took a long time for them to

---

60. A few manuscripts add at this point that Paul was writing from Rome, a guess, and a bad one at that. See Metzger, *TC*, p. 599.

61. McKnight, *Galatians*, p. 305.

discern a way to reach such a people. Finally, they noticed that the tribe they were dealing with, while engaged in tribal warfare with their neighbors, had a ritual of peacemaking. The tribal elder who wished to stop the hostilities offered the elder of the neighboring tribe his own newborn child in exchange for peace. In fact the child was called a peace child. Suddenly the light dawned and the missionaries realized they could tell the story of the heavenly father who sent his son as a peace child, to bring reconciliation between God and humankind. This would be, and indeed proved to be, a point of entry for sharing the Good News with this African tribe. Even well meaning and self-sacrificial Christians can be guilty of cultural imperialism, and Paul wishes to make clear that such attitudes should not be mixed together with the Gospel. God does not give face to any particular race or ethnic group, now that Christ has come.

Sometimes we may wonder why in the world Paul suffered all that he suffered and did what he did. It is because he truly believed in the new creation God was bringing about, and he was convinced that the old one was passing away. What happened to his body really did not matter in the long run. Jim Elliott, another missionary, once said 'He is no fool who gives up what he cannot keep to gain what he cannot lose'. Paul certainly believed this, and he was prepared to give his very life for the sake of the Gospel, knowing that eternal life and the new creation were already available. His final appeal to the marks of Christ on his body must surely have been moving. The Galatians could never accuse Paul of lacking the courage of his convictions.

It would appear that this emotional and polemical appeal we call Galatians did not go unheeded, if the later reference to the Galatians in 1 Cor. 16 is any clue. Paul's persuasive message about one God, one Gospel, one people, one new creation must in the end have not fallen on deaf ears. It is still a message that moves and challenges us all.

Index of Authors

Index of References

APOCRYPHA AND PSEUDEPIGRAPHA

Printed in the United States
38480LVS00003B/61-102

9 780802 844330